Multidimensional Poverty Measurement and Analysis

Multidimensional Poverty Measurement and Analysis

Sabina Alkire,

James Foster,

Suman Seth,

Maria Emma Santos,

José Manuel Roche,

and Paola Ballón

OXFORD
UNIVERSITY PRESS

OXFORD
UNIVERSITY PRESS

Great Clarendon Street, Oxford, OX2 6DP,
United Kingdom

Oxford University Press is a department of the University of Oxford.
It furthers the University's objective of excellence in research, scholarship,
and education by publishing worldwide. Oxford is a registered trade mark of
Oxford University Press in the UK and in certain other countries

Published in the United States of America by Oxford University Press
198 Madison Avenue, New York, NY 10016, United States of America

British Library Cataloguing in Publication Data
Data available

Library of Congress Control Number: 2015931637

ISBN 978-0-19-968949-1

Printed and bound by
CPI Group (UK) Ltd, Croydon, CR0 4YY

■ ACKNOWLEDGEMENTS

As authors and contributors to this book, we have worked as an intellectual team among ourselves and with colleagues and students. Many techniques arose in conversation, and were developed by being passed around, critiqued, commented upon, improved, and reassessed iteratively, in theory and in practice, before they were written down systematically. A sense of adventure and spirit of precision continued to the very end. Among us, Ballón's precise and clear contributions covered multivariate statistical methods, associations across indicators, standard errors, bootstrapping, and regression. As the leader of the global MPI calculations 2011–13, Roche's practical wisdom seeped into many parts; he contributed in particular to fuzzy set methods, poverty dynamics, standard errors, and data analysis. Foster's intellectual contributions are evident throughout the book as well as via less visible channels, given that Seth and Santos were his students. Seth, Santos, and Alkire worked as a close-knit team across dozens of versions, covering very new ground in some cases, as well as revisiting and trying to distil for readers the key issues. Each contributed deeply to this process of ongoing development of a public good, perhaps in the hope that our joint work might be of some practical use.

Many others also contributed definitive insights to this creative process.

The materials for this book developed greatly over a series of two-week intensive summer schools that we held in Delhi (2008), Lima (2009), Santiago and Amman (2010), Delft (2011), Jakarta (2012), Washington DC and Managua (2013), and Oxford (2014). We are grateful to our students, and to our other colleagues, for the learning that occurred together on those occasions. We also presented materials from this book in our lunchtime seminar series, and in conferences and workshops, and benefited tremendously from the exchanges that ensued.

We received very helpful comments, corrections, improvements, and suggestions from many across the years, and are especially indebted to Tony Atkinson who read the full manuscript. We are also grateful for direct comments from the following: Khalid Abu-Ismail, Sudhir Anand, Gordon Anderson, Roberto Angulo, Kaushik Basu, Francois Bourguignon, Cesar Calvo, Satya Chakravarty, Mihika Chatterjee, Adriana Conconi, Conchita D'Ambrosio, Jorge Davalos, Koen Decancq, Séverine Deneulin, Jean Drèze, Jean-Yves Duclos, Indranil Dutta, Marc Fleurbaey, Betti Gianni, Lu Gram, John Hammock, Bouba Housseini, Stephan Klasen, Jeni Klugman, Jaya Krishnakumar, Guy Lacroix, Achille Lemmi, Xavier Mancero, Enrica Chiappero Martinetti, Adib Nehmeh, Brian Nolan, Prasanta Pattanaik, Natalie Quinn, Amartya Sen, Jacques Silber, Frances Stewart, Joanne Tomkinson, Nicolas Van de Sijpe, Ana Vaz, Christopher Whelan, Gaston Yalonetzky, and Asad Zaman.

We have deeply appreciated the attentive and gentle support of Ann Barham, who corrected English and other matters throughout the whole text, and of Maarit Kivilo, who assembled the bibliography with exquisite precision and good humour. Research assistants included Garima Sahai, who expertly processed dozens of literature searches and organized the pdf files at the start of this project, and Alejandro Olayo-Méndez SJ, who steered the project calmly to its conclusion. Elizaveta Fouksman provided substantive and thoughtful pieces of analysis on a regular basis. Timely, insightful, and very pertinent inputs came from research assistants, including Aparna John, Arif Naveed, Esther Kwan, Felipe Roa-Clavijo, Laurance Eschamps-Laporte, Maria Mancilla Garcia, Putu Natih, Saite Lu, and Franziska Mager.

A book is a team effort within a research centre such as the Oxford Poverty and Human Development Initiative (OPHI). So we are more than usually grateful for the diligent backstopping by our colleagues as we addressed this book project and they took leadership in other areas. Heartfelt thanks to Mauricio Apablaza, Mihika Chatterjee, Adriana Conconi, Paddy Coulter, Emma Feeny, Lara Fleischer, Heidi Fletcher, Natasha Francis, John Hammock, Bouba Housseini, Usha Kanagaratnam, Thomas Morgan, Laura O'Mahony, Christian Oldiges, Kim Samuel, Moizza Sarwar, Tery van Taack, Joanne Tomkinson, Ana Vaz, and Diego Zavaleta.

The authors warmly acknowledge and thank ESRC-DFID RES-167-25 ES/1032827/1 for research support, and Santos thanks ANPCyT-PICT 1888 for research support. Finally, we thank our families and friends for their enduring patience and kind support throughout this process. The usual disclaimers apply.

CONTENTS

LIST OF FIGURES

■ LIST OF TABLES

LIST OF BOXES

1 Introduction

'I live under the roof of falling tiles.' This self-description of poverty, tucked away in Victor Hugo's *Les Misérables*, is by a character called Bossuet, who was, it seems, both merry and unlucky. Yet 'he accepted ill-luck serenely, and smiled at the pin-pricks of destiny like a man who is listening to a good joke. He was poor, but his wallet of good-temper was inexhaustible … When adversity entered his room he bowed to his old acquaintance cordially; he tickled catastrophes in the ribs, and was so familiar with fatality as to call it by a nick-name. These persecutions of fate had rendered him inventive …' (Hugo 2007: ii.136–7).

Hugo's delicate portraits render the 'multidimensionality' of poverty with rather greater colour than economists and statisticians tend to indulge. Yet many of these are converging on a similar assessment. Their characteristically parsimonious description stretches to a mere three words: 'poverty is multidimensional'. Nonetheless this recognition has far-reaching implications for diverse fields of study that intersect with poverty reduction, including our focal area: poverty measurement.

Poverty is a condition in which people are exposed to multiple disadvantages—actual and potential. In Bossuet's case, the disadvantages encompassed homelessness, landlessness, joblessness, and health catastrophes as well as low income. In other cases violence, humiliation, and poor education contribute. Across many developing countries, the pioneering *Voices of the Poor* study, completed shortly before the Millennium, conveyed poor people's own vision of their condition, forcefully delineating its multidimensionality:

Poverty consists of many interlocked dimensions. [First,] although poverty is rarely about the lack of one thing, the bottom line is lack of food. Second, poverty has important psychological dimensions such as powerlessness, voicelessness, dependency, shame, and humiliation … Third, poor people lack access to basic infrastructure—roads … transportation, and clean water. Fourth … poor people realize that education offers an escape from poverty. … Fifth, poor health and illness are dreaded almost everywhere as a source of destitution. Finally, the poor people rarely speak of income, but focus instead on managing assets—physical, human, social, and environmental—as a way to cope with their vulnerability. In many areas this vulnerability has a gender dimension. (Narayan et al. 2000: 4–5)

One great merit of the Millennium Declaration and specifically the Millennium Development Goals has been to flag the multidimensionality of poverty, so as to incentivize concrete action. A broader view of poverty is also held in Europe, where Nolan and Whelan observed that, 'It can be argued with some force that the underlying notion of poverty that evokes social concern itself is (and has always been) intrinsically multidimensional' (2011: 17). Philosophically, Amartya Sen (2000) observes that 'human lives are battered and diminished in all kinds of different ways'—a situation Wolff and De-Shalit (2007) call 'clustered disadvantage'. Bossuet's phrase about living 'under the roof of falling tiles' thus aptly describes multidimensional poverty, whose protagonists know that, in their condition, multiple disadvantages are going to keep striking, although they may not know which problems will strike when, or how.

In consequence, multidimensional poverty measurement and analysis are evolving rapidly. The field is being carried forward by activists and advocates, by political leaders, firms, and international assemblies, and by work across many disciplines, including quantitative social scientists working in both research and policy. As a contribution to this polycephalous endeavour, this book provides a systematic conceptual, theoretical, and methodological introduction to quantitative multidimensional poverty measurement and analysis.

Our focal methodology, the Alkire–Foster (AF) counting approach, is a straightforward multidimensional extension of the 1984 Foster–Greer–Thorbecke (FGT) approach, which has had a significant and lasting impact on income poverty measurement. Although quite recent, this particular methodology for measuring multidimensional poverty has generated some practical interest. For example, estimates of a Multidimensional Poverty Index (MPI) are published and analysed for over 100 developing countries in the United Nations Development Programme's (UNDP) *Human Development Reports*.[1] Governments of countries that include Mexico, Colombia, Bhutan, and the Philippines use official national multidimensional poverty measures that rely on this methodology,[2] and other regional, national, and subnational measures are in progress.[3] Adaptations of the methodology include the Gross National Happiness Index of the Royal Government of Bhutan (Ura et al. 2012) and the Women's Empowerment in Agriculture Index (Alkire et al. 2013). Academic articles engage, apply, and develop further this methodology as we document in Chapter 5. Thus the book aims to articulate the techniques of multidimensional poverty measurement using the AF methodological approach, and situate these within the wider field of multidimensional poverty analyses, thereby also crystallizing the value-added of an array of alternative approaches.

---

[1] UNDP (2010a); Alkire and Santos (2010, 2014); Alkire, Roche, Santos, and Seth (2011); Alkire, Conconi, and Roche (2013); Alkire, Conconi, and Seth (2014a).

[2] See, for example, *Social Indicators*, special issue, 112 (2013); *Journal of Economic Inequality*, 9 (2011); Arndt et al. (2012); Duclos et al. (2013); Ferreira (2011); Ferreira and Lugo (2013); Foster et al. (2010); Ravallion (2011b); Batana (2013); Battison et al. (2013); Betti et al. (2012); Callander et al. (2012a–d, 2013a,b); Cardenas and Carpenter (2013); Castro et al. (2012); Gradín (2013); Larochelle et al. (2014); Mishra and Ray (2013); Nicholas and Ray (2012); Siani Tchouametieu (2013); Siegel and Waidler (2012); Notten and Roelen (2012); Roche (2013); Trani and Cannings (2013); Trani, Biggeri, and Mauro (2013); Alkire and Seth (2013a, 2013b); Azevedo and Robles (2013); Alkire, Meinzen-Dick, et al. (2013); Beja and Yap (2013); Berenger et al. (2013); Foster, Horowitz, and Méndez (2012); Tonmoy (2014); Mitra, Posarac, et al. (2013); Mitra, Jones, et al. (2013); Nussbaumer et al. (2012); Peichl and Pestel (2013a, 2013b); Siminski and Yerokhin (2012); Smith (2012); Wagle (2014).

[3] CONEVAL (2009, 2010); Angulo et al. (2013); National Statistics Bureau, Royal Government of Bhutan (2014); and Balisacan (2011), respectively.

While subsequent chapters are mainly concerned with quite technical matters, the book keeps a window open to policy. For example, it assesses properties of measures alongside their feasibility (given data constraints), communicability, and policy relevance. Indeed it was Atkinson's (2003) call for policy-relevant, analytically specified multidimensional poverty measures that motivate our own and many other works. And this brings us back to *Les Miserables* one last time.

Hugo's perceptive character sketches did not always step so lightly over poverty's grim despair as the opening quotes suggest. Taken together, his characters were intended to unveil the intricacy of lives affected by misery, to elicit and educate disquiet, and to spur political action. Similarly, while the proximate objective of poverty measurement is rigour and accuracy, an underlying objective must also be to use well-crafted measures to give a different kind of voice to concerns with injustice—to document raw disadvantage, to order complexity, monitor and evaluate advances, and mark routes for tangible policy responses. So without sacrificing rigour, our underlying hope is that as the field of multidimensional poverty measurement advances, both methodologically and practically, it may contribute more effectively to the reduction or eradication of multidimensional poverty.

This chapter presents the motivation for focusing on multidimensional poverty measurement and analysis. Our motivation essentially comes from three sources: normative arguments, empirical evidence, and a policy perspective. We end this chapter by presenting how this book can be used.

1.1 Normative Motivation

One key motivation for measuring multidimensional poverty is ethical, and that is to improve the fit between the measure and the phenomenon it is supposed to approximate. Poverty measures, to merit the name, must reflect the multifaceted nature of poverty itself. The characteristics poor people associate with poverty have been well documented (Narayan et al. 2000; Leavy and Howard, et al. 2013; see also Table 6.1 in Chapter 6), as have the hopes of millions for a fairer world (UNDP 2013a). Such insights must affect tools to study poverty. Amartya Sen's quote continues, 'Human lives are battered and diminished in all kinds of different ways, and the first task … is to acknowledge that deprivations of very different kinds have to be accommodated within a general overarching framework' (2000).

Conceptually, many frameworks for multidimensional poverty have been advanced, from Ubuntu (Metz and Gaie 2010) to human rights (CONEVAL 2010), livelihoods (Bowley and Burnett-Hurst 1915) to social inclusion (Atkinson and Marlier 2010), *Buen Vivir* (Hidalgo-Capitán et al. 2014) to basic needs (Hicks and Streeten 1979; Stewart 1985), from the Catholic social teaching (Curran 2002) to social protection (UNRISD 2010; Barrientos 2013) to capabilities (Sen 1993; Wolff and De-Shalit 2007), among others. If poverty is understood to be a shortfall from well-being, then it cannot be conceptualized or measured in isolation from some concept of well-being.[4] This is not to say that a fully specified concept of welfare is required to measure poverty, only that these endeavours are inherently connected. Box 1.1 explores options for linking these two concepts.

BOX 1.1 POVERTY, WELFARE, AND POLICY

How are poverty and welfare measures linked? Poverty measures could be explicitly linked to particular **functions** of welfare in order to facilitate interpretation.[5] This approach is quite demanding, because a welfare function must be able to make meaningful evaluations at all levels of achievements across all persons, and this requires strong assumptions about the measurement scales of data[6] as well as the functional form. Additionally, there will likely be a plurality of plausible welfare functions. Even if a unique welfare function could be agreed upon, there may be no unique transformation from welfare function to poverty measure.

An alternative way of linking poverty and welfare is to follow a more conceptual approach and consider whether the various trade-offs implied by a poverty measure are broadly consistent with some underlying notion of social welfare. This is indeed a reasonable route, but one whose conclusions are often ignored in practice. For example, the so-called headcount ratio, which is simply the proportion of people considered poor in a population, is the most commonly used measure in traditional poverty measurement exercises (the income approach) as well as in the basic needs tradition (the direct approach). However, such a measure has the interesting property that a decrease of any size in the income (or unmet basic needs) of a poor person paired with a corresponding increase for a non-poor person will leave poverty unchanged. This, of course, is rather untenable from many welfare perspectives. Likewise, a decrease in the income of a poor person (no matter how large the decrease) paired with an increase in the income of another poor person sufficient to lift that person to the income poverty line (no matter how small the increase) will decrease poverty. Again, this would appear to be inconsistent with any reasonable welfare function censored at the poverty line.

Note, though, that the fact that these trade-offs are not justified in welfare terms has not forced the removal of the headcount ratio income poverty measure from consideration. This brings us to the third consideration of policy. For in fact other considerations also apply—such as comprehensibility, which a measure needs in order to advance welfare in practice. The level and composition of poverty must be communicated relatively accurately to journalists, non-specialist decision-makers, activists, and disadvantaged communities to motivate action. The headcount ratio is a remarkably intuitive, if somewhat crude, measure that takes the identification process very seriously and reports a meaningful number: the incidence of poverty. The fact that it is at odds with notions of welfare appears to be of second-order importance, because users have not found a comparably meaningful number with better welfare properties to highlight as the 'headline' statistic. So the welfare implications of poverty measures need to be considered *alongside* political economy and operational considerations of such measures, such as their communicability. We adopt this wider approach—which

---

[4] Note that when referring to welfare here (and throughout the book) we do not refer to any particular so-called welfare programme, but rather to the concept of well-being. We do so because a body of economic literature developed in the twentieth century, namely 'welfare economics', is a conversation partner for multidimensional poverty measurement (Atkinson 2003).

[5] For example, the Watts unidimensional poverty measure is related to the geometric mean—one of Atkinson's social welfare functions. See Alkire and Foster (2011b); cf. Foster, Seth, et al. (2013).

[6] See section 6.3.7 and section 2.3.

BOX 1.1 *(cont.)*

considers properties of measures alongside their accuracy, ease of understanding, and policy salience—and understand such a wider set of considerations to be consistent with Sen's capability approach which we discuss subsequently.[7]

Multiple concepts of poverty will continue to be used to inform multidimensional poverty design.[8] The remainder of this section as well as parts of Chapter 6 illustrate how such concepts inform measurement, by drawing upon one particular approach: Amartya Sen's *capability approach*. The capability approach has been key in prompting a 'fundamental reconsideration of the concepts of poverty' (Jenkins and Micklewright 2007: 9), particularly in economics broadly conceived. Building upon a line of reflection advanced by Aristotle, Adam Smith, Karl Marx, John Stuart Mill, and John Hicks, the capability approach sees human progress, ultimately, as 'the progress of human freedom and capability to lead the kind of lives that people have reason to value' (Drèze and Sen 2013: 43).

Sen argues that well-being should be defined and assessed in terms of the *functionings* and *capabilities* people enjoy. Functionings are beings and doings that people value and have reason to value, and capabilities represent 'the various combinations of functionings ... that the person can achieve' (Sen 1992: 40). In *The Idea of Justice*, Sen describes them thus: 'The various attainments in human functioning that we may value are very diverse, varying from being well nourished or avoiding premature mortality to taking part in the life of the community and developing the skill to pursue one's work-related plans and ambitions. The capability that we are concerned with is our ability to achieve various combinations of functionings that we can compare and judge against each other in terms of what we have reason to value' (Sen 2009: 233).

Assessing progress in terms of valuable freedoms and capabilities has implications for measurement. All multidimensional measures need to define the focal space of measurement. Whereas economics assessed well-being in the space of utility, or resources, the capability perspective—in line with human rights approaches—defines and in some cases measures well-being in capability space. Capabilities are defined to have *intrinsic* value as well as *instrumental* value—to be ends rather than merely means. Hence, the capability approach 'proposes a serious departure from concentrating on the *means* of living to the *actual opportunities* of living' (Sen 2009: 233).

Moving now to poverty, Sen argues that poverty should be seen as capability deprivation (Sen 1992, 1997, 1999, 2009—Box 1.2 presents a succinct overview of related considerations). Defining poverty in the space of capabilities (as Sen does) has multiple implications for measurement. The first is *multidimensionality*: 'the capability approach is concerned with a plurality of different features of our lives and concerns' (2009: 233).

---

[7] These considerations also pertain to measures of welfare and inequality (section 6.2).
[8] Ruggeri-Laderchi, Saith, and Stewart (2003), Deutsch and Silber (2005, 2008).

This plurality applies also to poverty measurement: 'The need for a multidimensional view of poverty and deprivation guides the search for an adequate indicator of human poverty' (Anand and Sen 1997).

BOX 1.2 CAPABILITIES, RESOURCES, AND UTILITY

Sen's capability approach comprises opportunity freedoms, evaluated in the space of capabilities and functionings, as defined just above, and process freedoms, ranging from individual agency to democratic and systemic freedoms. This box reviews the value-added of capabilities in comparison with a focus on resources or utility.[9]

Sen proposes that poverty should be considered in the space of capability and functionings (they are the same space), rather than in the space of income or resources, Rawlsian primary goods, utility, or happiness. Sen has persuasively set out the advantages of doing so—rather than measuring poverty in the space of resources or utility—along the following lines.[10]

The traditional approach to measuring poverty focuses on the **resources** people command. The most common measures of resources by far are monetary indicators of income or consumption. In some approaches resources are extended to include social primary goods.[11]

While resources are clearly vital and essential instruments for moving out of poverty, Sen's and others' arguments against measuring resources alone continue to be relevant.[12] First, many resources are not intrinsically valuable; they are instrumental to other objectives. Yet, '[t]he value of the living standard lies in the living, and not in the possessing of commodities, which has derivative and varying relevance' (Sen 1987). This would not be problematic if resources were a perfect proxy for intrinsically valuable activities or states. But people's ability to convert resources into a valuable functioning (personally and within different societies) actually varies in important ways. Two people might each enjoy the same quality and quantity of food every day. But if one is sedentary and the other a labourer, or one is elderly and one is pregnant, their nutritional status from the same food basket is likely to diverge significantly. Functionings such as nutritional status provide direct information on well-being. This remains particularly relevant in cases of disability. Also, while resources appear to refrain from value judgements or a 'comprehensive moral doctrine' (Rawls 1999a), the choice of a precise set of resources is not value-free.

Although resources may not be sufficient to assess poverty, *indicators* of resources—of time, of money, or of particular resources such as drinking water, electricity, and housing—remain important and are often used to proxy functionings (at times adjusted for some interpersonal variations in the conversion of resources into functionings) and to investigate capability constraints (Kuklys 2005; Zaidi and Burchardt 2005). Thus a conceptual focus on capability poverty may still employ information on resources, alongside other information.

Utility, happiness, and subjective well-being form another and increasingly visible source of data and discussion on many topics, including poverty.[13] The welfare economics advanced by Bentham, Mill, Edgeworth, Sidgwick, Marshall, and Pigou relied on a utilitarian approach. Sen criticized the regnant version of utilitarianism in economics for relying solely upon utility information (rather than seeing well-being more fully), for focusing on average utility (ignoring its distribution) and for ignoring process freedoms. These criticisms were powerful

---

[9] For introductions to Sen's capability approach see Sen (1999), Atkinson (1999), Alkire (2002), Anand (2008), Alkire and Deneulin (2009), Basu and López-Calva (2010), and Nussbaum (2011) among many others.

[10] A recent treatment is in Sen (2009: chs 11–13).

[11] Rawls (1971, 1993); Rawls and Kelly (2001). For a very useful update of the capability approach vs social primary goods, see Brighouse and Robeyns (2010).

[12] These arguments appear, for example, in Sen (1984, 1985, 1987, 1992, 1993, 1999).

[13] The literature is vast: see Layard (2005); Fleurbaey (2006b).

BOX 1.2 *(cont.)*

because, as Sen observed, 'utilitarianism was for a very long time the "official" theory of welfare economics in a thoroughly unique way' (2008).

Taking psychic utility as a sufficient measure of well-being (and its absence to measure poverty) has practical problems for poverty measurement. Sen observed that happiness could reflect poor people's ability to adapt their preferences to long-term hardships. Adaptive preferences may affect 'oppressed minorities in intolerant communities, sweated workers in exploitative industrial arrangements, precarious share-croppers living in a world of uncertainty, or subdued housewives in deeply sexist cultures'. The measurement issue is that these people may (rather impressively) 'train themselves to take pleasure in small mercies'. This could mean that their happiness metrics would not proxy capabilities and functionings: 'In terms of pleasure or desire-fulfilment, the disadvantages of the hopeless underdog may thus appear to be much smaller than what would emerge on the basis of a more objective analysis of the extent of their deprivation and unfreedom' (2009: 283).[14]

Recent empirical research on happiness has enriched the field of measurement, and Sen's work has developed accordingly. Put simply, he argues that happiness is clearly 'a momentous achievement in itself'—but not the only one.

Happiness, important as it is, can hardly be the only thing that we have reason to value, nor the only metric for measuring other things that we value. But when being happy is not given such an imperialist role, it can, with good reason, be seen as a very important human functioning, among others. The capability to be happy is, similarly, a major aspect of the freedom that we have good reason to value. (2009: 276)

This discussion is of direct relevance to measures of well-being, perhaps more so than poverty measurement. For example, the Stiglitz–Sen–Fitoussi Commission Report (2009) included subjective well-being as one of the eight dimensions of quality of life proposed for consideration.

While a complete analysis of poverty and well-being requires insights on people's resources and psychological states as well as their functionings and capabilities, the oversights that purely resource-based or purely subjective measures have for such analyses remain salient, and will be further discussed in Chapter 6.

A second implication of viewing multidimensional poverty as deprivations in valuable capabilities is that value judgements are required—for example, in order to select which dimensions and indicators of poverty to use, how much weight to place on each one, and what constitutes a deprivation. By facing ethical value judgements squarely, rather than confining attention to technical matters, the capability approach has at times created consternation among quantitative social scientists. Sen reassures readers that addressing such value judgements is not an insurmountable task: 'the presence of non-commensurable results only indicates that the choice-decisions will not be trivial (reducible just to counting what is "more" and what is "less"), but it does not at all indicate that it is impossible—or even that it must always be particularly difficult' (2009: 241). Chapter 6 points out some practical ways forward.

These value judgements are to reflect capabilities that people value and have reason to value. This has implications for the processes of measurement design. In order to reflect people's values, such judgements might be made through participatory or deliberative processes, perhaps supplemented by other inputs to guard against distortions (Wolff and De-Shalit 2007). At a minimum, Sen has argued, the final decisions should

---

[14] On adaptation, see also Burchardt (2009) and Clark (2012).

be transparent and informed by public debate and reasoning: 'The connection between public reasoning and the choice and weighting of capabilities in social assessment is important to emphasise' (2009: 242).

Another critical issue is how to reflect the *freedom* aspect of capabilities. For example, in selecting the indicators of capability poverty it is normally more possible to measure or proxy achieved functionings than capabilities (opportunity freedoms). While initially this was considered a severe shortcoming there are also well-developed arguments for doing so. For example, Fleurbaey (2006b) observes that group differences in functionings may suggest inequalities in capabilities (cf. Drèze and Sen 2013). Also, functionings may be particularly relevant for some people such as small children and those with intellectual disabilities. Measuring capabilities could require counterfactual information on 'roads not chosen', and may depend in part on families and social forces, both of which complicate the empirical task.[15] However, Chapter 6 suggests conditions under which a multidimensional poverty measure using functionings data may be interpreted as a measure of capability deprivation or unfreedom (Alkire and Foster 2007). So, multiple empirical routes to considering freedom may be explored.

Using the capability approach to motivate poverty measurement also draws attention to aspects beyond capability deprivations such as agency and process freedoms, and plural principles (Sen 1985, 2002). For example, the capability approach sees poor people as actors, so poverty measurement must be compatible with, if not actively facilitate, their agency in their own lives as well as in the struggle against poverty. An example of plural principles is how Sen urges a reformulation of *sustainable development*, so that the environment is not only valued as a means to human survival (although it is that) but also as a location of beauty, of commitment, and of responsibility to future generations and to other life forms (2009: 251–2).

In sum, as we stated earlier, multidimensional poverty measurement engages, fundamentally, a normative motivation that is shared across a wide range of conceptual frameworks. The capability approach is a prominent framework among them. Considering multidimensional poverty to be capability deprivation has a number of implications for measurement, which we have sketched here.

1.2 Empirical Motivations

We now turn to consider various empirical arguments why poverty measurement should be multidimensional. Nolan and Whelan (2011), observing the rise of multidimensional approaches in Europe, identify three reasons that non-monetary as well as monetary indicators have come to be used: meaning, identification, and multidimensionality. The first notes that non-monetary deprivations 'play a central role in capturing and conveying

---

[15] See Fleurbaey (2006a) and Robeyns and van der Veen (2007).

the realities of the experience of poverty, bringing out concretely and graphically what it *means* to be poor' (2011: 16). Non-monetary indicators may also improve identification in two ways. They may help 'in arriving at [and justifying] the most appropriate income threshold'. Also, empirical studies motivated a critique that low income, surprisingly, 'fails in practice to identify those unable to participate in their societies due to lack of resources' (2011: 16), and that non-monetary deprivation indicators were more reliable tools for identification. This may be due to differences in people's abilities to convert income into resource-based outcomes, or due to challenges such as equivalence scales. The third reason poverty is measured directly using multiple indicators is that poverty itself is defined as being intrinsically multidimensional.

Nolan and Whelan very helpfully observe that in all three of these situations, and particularly the last, 'The need for a multidimensional measurement approach in identifying the poor/excluded is an *empirical* matter, rather than something one can simply read off from the multidimensional nature of the concepts themselves'. If, for example, poverty were defined as multidimensional but any single indicator, including household income, were sufficient to identify the poor and measure the level and trends of poverty in a society (including 'those other dimensions of deprivation and exclusion', p. 19), a multidimensional methodology would not be required for poverty measurement.

We explore whether various unidimensional measures accurately reflect the level and trend of multidimensional poverty and related questions. We first probe whether monetary poverty measures can be assumed to be a sufficient proxy to identify who is poor and monitor the level and trends of other dimensions of poverty. As evidence indicates this is not the case, we then ask whether some non-monetary indicator can play that role but again find large mismatches. So we enquire whether a single policy lever, such as GDP growth, has been shown to be sufficient to reduce poverty in its many dimensions, and again find a negative answer. Finally, we observe that a dashboard of single indicators overlooks clustered disadvantages, and that monetary measures do not necessarily identify the same group of people as poor in comparison with multidimensional measures. These reasons thus also point out the need for multidimensional poverty measures that reflect the joint distribution of disadvantages.

1.2.1 MONETARY VS NON-MONETARY HOUSEHOLD DEPRIVATIONS

The prominent focus on income poverty reduction is built on the implicit assumption that monetary poverty measures adequately identify who is poor. Yet an increasing empirical literature documents a mismatch between monetary and non-monetary deprivations. This leads to analysts to ask, 'What is the relationship between deprivation indicators and household income, how is that to be interpreted, and what conclusions can be drawn?' (Nolan and Whelan 2011: 31).

As we survey extensively in Chapter 4, in both Europe and developing countries, studies since the early 1980s have repeatedly documented the fact that income or consumption poverty measures identify different people as poor than other deprivation indicators.[16] Kaztman (1989) found that 13% of households in Montevideo, Uruguay, were income poor but did not experience unsatisfied basic needs, whereas 7.5% were in the opposite case. Ruggeri Laderchi (1997) concluded on the basis of Chilean data that 'income in itself is not … conveying all of the information of interest if the aim is to provide a comprehensive picture of poverty'. Stewart, Saith, and Harriss-White (2007) found that 53% of malnourished Indian children in that study did not live in income-poor households and 53% of the children living in income-poor households were not malnourished. Bradshaw and Finch (2003) find that while 17–20% of people are income poor, and subjective poor, and materially deprived, only 5.7% of the population experience all three dimensions, leading them to conclude that 'it is not safe to rely on one measure of poverty—the results obtained are just not reliable enough'. Across nine European countries, Whelan, Layte, and Maître (2004) used panel data to compare the persistently income poor and the persistently materially deprived, and found that roughly 20% of people were persistently poor by each measure but only 9.7% were poor according to both measures. These and many other empirical studies show that in many cases there are large mismatches between income poverty and deprivations in other indicators: income does not accurately proxy non-monetary deprivations in identifying the poor.

1.2.2 TRENDS IN MONETARY POVERTY VS TRENDS IN NON-MONETARY DEPRIVATIONS

But it may be that while the details differ, a decrease in income poverty heralds a decrease in other indicators also—that the trends will be similar. Yet using all presently available data across developing countries, there does not appear to be a high association across levels of *progress* shown in different indicators.

Motivated by Bourguignon et al. (2010), we performed a very similar exercise using national aggregate data from 1990–2012.[17] Figure 1.1 depicts the association between the change in $1.25/day income poverty and the change in some non-income Millennium Development Goal (MDG) indicators, namely, the prevalence of underweight children, primary school completion rate, the ratio of female to male primary school enrolment, and under-5 mortality during this period. The size of the bubble represents the

---

[16] See Ruggeri Laderchi (1997); Klasen (2008); Whelan, Layte, and Maître (2004); Bradshaw and Finch (2003); Wolff and De-Shalit (2007); Nolan and Whelan (2011).
[17] These results were completed by the authors with Mihika Chatterjee.

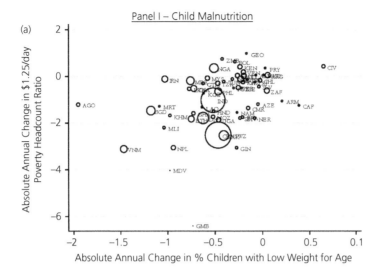

Figure 1.1. Scatter plots comparing cross-country reductions in income poverty to progress in other Millennium Development Goal

Source: Authors' elaboration using World Development Indicators (World Bank) 1990–2012

population size in the year 2000 (UNDESA 2013).[18] Progress in these four indicators is not strongly associated with progress in $1.25/day income poverty reduction.[19]

To cross-check this finding, we investigate a raft of recent studies considering country trajectories in meeting the MDGs.[20] Figure 1.2 presents the share of countries that have met different MDG targets at the national level, where it is evident that although a number of countries have met the goal of extreme poverty reduction in terms of $1.25/day, these countries have largely failed to meet the goals in many non-income indicators.

---

[18] Given a variable y, observed in two time periods t^1 and t^2, the annual absolute growth rate is computed as $(y^2 - y^1)/(t^2 - t^1)$. In each case we consider countries satisfying the following requirements: (a) their initial observation was between 1990 and 2000, and there was a period of at least five years to the latest observation available; and (b) the distance between the initial observation in the considered non-income MDG indicator and the initial observation in $1.25/day poverty was not more than five years apart, and the same for the final observation. This allowed us to use sixty-three countries for underweight children, sixty for primary school completion rate, sixty-eight for female to male ratio in primary school enrolment, and sixty-three for under-5 mortality rate.

[19] In order to show the strength of the association, we compute the Pearson's correlation coefficients between the changes in $1.25/day poverty and the changes of each non-monetary deprivation presented in Panels I–IV. The Pearson's correlation coefficients are only 0.40, −0.15, −0.46, and 0.37 for Panels I–IV, respectively. Given the non-linear relationships in the scatter plots, we also compute the Spearman and Kendall's rank correlation coefficients. The Spearman's coefficient relaxes the non-normality assumption and Kendall's coefficient is a non-parametric estimate of correlation. The Spearman's coefficients for the four plots are 0.44, −0.16, −0.25, and 0.35, respectively; whereas Kendall's coefficients for the four plots are 0.30, −0.10, −0.17, and 0.26, respectively. For mathematical construction of Spearman's and Kendall's coefficients, see the discussions in section 8.1.2.

[20] World Bank (2013).

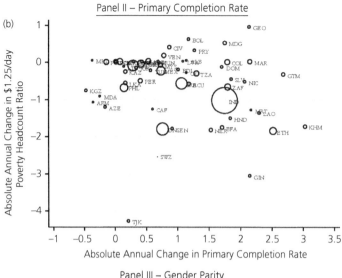

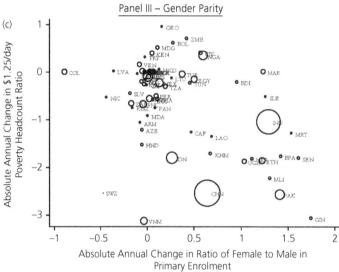

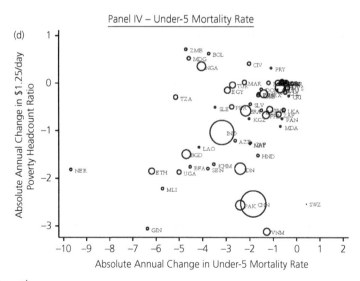

Figure 1.1. (*cont.*)

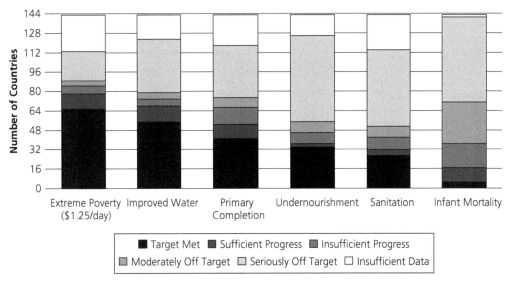

Figure 1.2. Progress in different MDGs across countries

Source: Global Monitoring Report 2013 (World Bank 2013). The data were downloaded from http://data.worldbank.org/mdgs/progress-status-across-groups-number-of-countries accessed on April 1, 2014.

The emerging conclusion is that meeting the goal of income poverty reduction does not ensure reducing deprivations in non-income indicators.[21]

These two examples clearly suggest, as Bourguignon et al. (2010) concluded, that income poverty trends do not proxy trends in the reduction of non-income deprivations. The evidence and literature reviewed in this and the previous section suggest that whether information on multidimensional poverty levels or trends is required, or policy impacts on poverty are to be measured, income poverty measures must be complemented by measures reflecting other dimensions of poverty.

1.2.3 ASSOCIATIONS ACROSS NON-MONETARY DEPRIVATIONS

If consumption and income do not map multidimensional poverty, perhaps another indicator could be identified that was highly associated in level and trend with deprivations in other non-monetary dimensions. Such a headline indicator could summarize progress in non-income spheres. Indicators like girls' education or malnutrition are often heralded as general-purpose measures. Yet to date, systematic cross-tabulations of deprivations or assessments of redundancy, which will be introduced in section 7.3, have not identified a bellwether indicator.

---

[21] Unfortunately as Figure 1.2 implies, MDG monitoring reports tend to count countries, not people. This convention implicitly considers the life of one person in a small country like Maldives to be thousands of times more important than the life of a person in India. From a human rights perspective this could hardly be acceptable.

Table 1.1 Cross-tabulation of deprivations in two indicators

		All members completed five years of schooling		
		Yes (%)	No (%)	Total (%)
All Children	Yes	68.4	13.6	**82**
Attending School	No	10.6	7.4	**18**
	Total	**79**	**21**	**100**

To give one example of one variable pair for one country, data from the National Family Health Survey 2005–6 of India shows that around 21% of the population live in a household in which no member has completed five years of schooling and, in 18% of the population, a child is not attending school up to the age at which he or she would complete class 10. With these two educational indicators, one might expect a high association, as educated families should send their children to school. But only 7.4% of households experience both deprivations whereas 13.6% and 10.6% are deprived in one indicator but not in the other. This situation can be summarized by a simple cross-tabulation presented in Table 1.1 (section 2.2.3 discusses such tables containing the joint distribution of deprivations).

This type of mismatch is repeated throughout many countries. In fact, we did a simple exercise using a sample of seventy-five developing countries and using the six of the ten indicators that form the Global Multidimensional Poverty Index (MPI).[22] We computed the proportion of people in these seventy-five countries who are deprived in each of the six indicators and report these in the second column and the second row of Table 1.2. The remaining entries show the proportion of the population who are simultaneously deprived in each pair of these indicators.[23] For example, 17.7% of the population live in households deprived in years of schooling and 19.3% of the population live in households where at least one school-aged child does not attend school. However, only 7.3% of the population live in households that are deprived in both indicators. This information thus summarizes the cross-tabulation between these two indicators as in Table 1.1 (but now using the population of all seventy-five countries).

Overall, we find that the proportion of people in households with deprivation in these six indicators ranges from 17.7% to 35.2%, and deprivations in *both* indicators in each pair ranges from 6% to 16.2%. The size of the mismatch (i.e. the proportion of people in households with one deprivation but not the other) can be large. The highest match in this pair is between asset ownership and undernutrition – which match in just over half of the people; otherwise the matches are lower. Thus it is clearly not possible to

---

[22] We use countries for which information on all indicators is available for the global MPI 2014 (Alkire et al. 2014a).

[23] We use population-weighted country averages while computing the overall deprivation in each indicator as well as simultaneous deprivations in each pair of indicators.

Table 1.2 Average deprivation in pairwise indicators across seventy-five developing countries

	Years of schooling (%)	School attendance (%)	Child mortality (%)	Under-nutrition (%)	Improved drinking water (%)
Population deprived in indicator	**17.70**	**19.30**	**25.10**	**31.80**	**22.00**
		Percentage of population simultaneously deprived in the column and row indicators			
School Attendance	**19.30**	7.30				
Child Mortality	**25.10**	6.20	8.20			
Undernutrition	**31.80**	7.80	9.60	11.40		
Improved Drinking Water	**22.00**	6.50	6.50	7.70	8.10	
Asset Ownership	**35.20**	12.50	10.70	11.40	16.20	11.80

infer deprivation in one indicator by observing deprivation in another.[24] If, as it seems, no single non-income deprivation reflects all others, multidimensional measures and analyses are required to make visible the highly differentiated profiles of interconnected deprivations that poor people experience.

1.2.4 ECONOMIC GROWTH AND SOCIAL INDICATORS

Perhaps then we should move back from single indicators of human lives to more general-purpose indicators like economic growth, and ask whether growth in Gross National Income catalyzes reductions in various deprivations. This question coheres with a sentiment that growth clearly matters greatly—but growth *of what?*[25] Is it growth of average income or growth of incomes of the bottom 40%—or is it inclusive growth that reduces non-income dimensions? Despite differing ideological perspectives on this question, the question of how growth is associated with trends in non-income deprivations is fundamentally an empirical question, and one on which more data are available now than previously.

Drèze and Sen's *Uncertain Glory* (2013) provides a meticulous yet rousing document-ation of the empirical disjunction between growth and progress in social indicators in India. After noting the environmental damage that accompanied India's growth, Drèze and Sen argue that 'the achievement of high growth—even high levels of *sustainable* growth—must ultimately be judged in terms of the impact of that economic growth on the lives and freedoms of the people' (2013: vii). And it is no mystery that this impact de-pends on public action: 'It is not only that the new income generated by economic growth has been very unequally shared, but also that the resources newly created have not been utilized adequately to relieve the gigantic deprivations of the underdogs of society' (p. 9).

As a concrete example, they compare India's advances in growth and social indicators 1990–2011 with those of Bangladesh and find that India's per capita GDP growth was much larger than that of Bangladesh between 1990 and 2011, and by 2011 its per capita GDP was about double that of Bangladesh. Yet Bangladesh, during the same period, has overtaken India in terms of a wide range of basic social indicators. In Table 1.3, we present India's performance, as well Bangladesh's and Nepal's, in GDP and certain non-income indicators. It is clear that India's GDP per capita was already much higher in 1990 and, because of a much higher growth rate, India became richer. However, India's improvements in some of the crucial selected non-income indicators have been much slower for the same period than both Bangladesh and Nepal.[26]

Looking internationally, other studies also did not find a strong association between economic growth and progress in non-income social indicators. For example, analysing

---

[24] Chapter 7 presents measures of association and overlap between deprivations, and proposes a redundancy measure that is related to this table.

[25] Drèze and Sen (2013), Foster and Székely (2008), and Ravallion (2001).

[26] Nepal's strong reduction of multidimensional poverty is analysed in section 9.2.

Table 1.3 Comparison of India's performance with Bangladesh and Nepal

	Year	India	Bangladesh	Nepal
GDP per capita (PPP, constant	1990	1,193	741	716
2005 international $)	2011	3,203	1,569	1,106
	Growth (p.a.)	*4.8%*	*3.6%*	*2.1%*
Under-5 Mortality Rate	1990	114	139	135
(per 1,000)	2011	61	46	48
	Change	*−53*	*−93*	*−87*
Maternal Mortality Ratio	1990	600	800	770
(per 100,000)	2010	200	240	170
	Change	*−400*	*−560*	*−600*
Infant Immunization	1990	59	64	44
(DPT) (%)	2011	72	96	92
	Change	*13%*	*32%*	*48%*
Female Literacy Rate,	1990	49	38	33
Age 15–24 Years (%)	2010	74	78	78
	Change	*25%*	*40%*	*45%*

Source: Drèze and Sen (2013) and World Bank Data Online accessed at <http://data.worldbank.org/indicator>

the cross-country data from 1990–2008, Bourguignon et al. (2008, 2010) found a strong relation between economic growth and income poverty reduction. They found, however, 'little or no correlation' between growth and the non-income MDGs:

The correlation between growth in GDP per capita and improvements in non-income MDGs is practically zero … [thereby confirming] the lack of a relationship between those indicators and poverty reduction … This interesting finding suggests that economic growth is not sufficient per se to generate progress in non-income MDGs. Sectoral policies and other factors or circumstances presumably matter as much as growth (2010: 28).

1.2.5 THE VALUE-ADDED OF THE JOINT DISTRIBUTION OF DEPRIVATIONS: CLUSTERING AND IDENTIFICATION

If income poverty measures, and indeed any single non-income indicator, fail to predict the levels and trends of other deprivations, wouldn't a dashboard of indicators be sufficient? We address this question precisely in section 3.1 and observe that while dashboards will always be used, they fall short in key ways. Leaving aside other disadvantages, the fundamental reason is that they ignore what we call the 'joint distribution of deprivations', namely, that there are people who experience simultaneous deprivations.

To clarify the point, consider the case of Brazil between 1995 and 2006 (Figure 1.3). The left panel presents the percentage of the population deprived in six indicators in 1995 and 2006. The indicators were typically considered in the unsatisfied basic needs approach in Latin America. Note that all deprivation rates decreased over this period. For example, the percentage of the population living in households with incomes less than $2/day was reduced from 29% in 1995 to 13% in 2006. The right panel presents

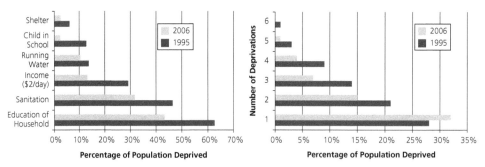

Figure 1.3. The importance of understanding joint distribution of deprivations in Brazil

Source: Battiston et al. (2013)

distinctive and important information that is *not possible* to infer from the left panel. Specifically, we see that in 1995, 28% of the population lived in households with just one deprivation, 21% in households with two deprivations, and so on. In 2006, the joint distribution of deprivations had improved. In fact, joint deprivations in two or more indicators went down, and the proportion of the population in households with just one deprivation increased to 32%. Tellingly, if we were only to make a conclusion based on a dashboard of indicators, we would have missed this information on the *multiplicity* of deprivations experienced. Thus, the consideration of joint distribution is crucial. But should it affect the *identification* of who is poor also?

We have already discussed evidence that income poverty is not necessarily associated with deprivations in other dimensions. Does this disjunction vanish when income or consumption poverty is compared to multidimensional poverty measures accounting for simultaneous deprivations? Or do both identify the same people as poor? Surprisingly, mismatches remain high. Klasen (2000: table 10) found large mismatches between income and multiple deprivations in South Africa. For example, when 20.3% of the population (7.7 million people) were identified as severely income poor, and 20.3% identified (7.7 million) as severely multiply deprived, only 2.9% of the population—1.1 million people—were *both* severely income poor and severely deprived. Moving to Bhutan, its official MPI and income poverty measure are both drawn from the same 2012 Bhutan Living Standards Survey dataset. About 12% of the population were income poor, and 12.7% of people were multidimensionally poor. Yet merely 3.2% of Bhutanese experienced both income and multidimensional poverty (National Statistics Bureau, Royal Government of Bhutan 2014; see also chapter 5).[27] Similarly high mismatches were found in studies using thirteen databases in eleven countries (Alkire and Klasen 2013).

And likewise in Europe—Nolan and Whelan list twenty-six European countries, and in none of them were more than half of the income-poor or materially deprived populations poor by both indicators, and in twelve countries less than one-third of the

---

[27] As we discuss in Chapter 7, this disjunction requires further research to ascertain the extent to which it might be influenced by survey issues such as the short recall period for consumption data.

income poor also experienced multiple material deprivations (2011: table 6.2). Hence monetary measures do not necessarily identify the same group of people to be poor as multidimensional measures do.

1.2.6 DATA AND COMPUTATIONAL TECHNOLOGIES

The measurement of multidimensional poverty reflecting the joint distribution of deprivations requires data to be available for the same unit of analysis in all dimensions. However, data on poverty are severely limited in coverage and frequency. While stock market data are available hourly, labour force surveys may be quarterly, and GNI data are annual; poverty data are often only available every three to ten years. The High-Level Panel (2013) rightly demanded a 'data revolution'. Given a data deluge in many domains, the lack of up-to-date information on—and across—key dimensions of poverty like health, nutrition, work, wealth, and skills (as well as violence, decent work, and empowerment) has been rightly recognized as a travesty.[28] Such data is needed to design high-impact interventions and evaluate policy success.

What is less recognized is that data on multidimensional poverty are already on the upswing (Alkire 2014). Much of the increase is occurring in national surveys; Alkire (2014) also summarizes increases in poverty-related internationally comparable survey data availability. For example, non-income MDG indicators are often drawn from four international household surveys: the Demographic and Health Survey (DHS), the Multiple Indicator Cluster Survey (MICS), the Living Standard Measurement Survey (LSMS), and the Core Welfare Indicators Questionnaire (CWIQ). Figure 1.4 shows that the number of countries which have fielded at least one of these surveys increased from five in 1985—the first year in which any was fielded—to 127 countries in 2010. By 2011, around ninety countries had completed at least three surveys. In Europe, a similar increase in household and registry data, and in harmonized data, has occurred. For example, the EU-SILC survey, which began in the mid-2000s, now releases data annually across over thirty countries.

While the quality, periodicity, and range of data have increased dramatically there is still no one survey that collects all key dimensions of poverty in an internationally harmonized way and with sufficient frequency and quality (Alkire and Samman 2014). Nor indeed is there agreement on key poverty dimensions and periodicity. Despite these shortcomings, the quality, frequency, and range of data and of data sources have increased. Further increases in data availability, accompanied by powerful technologies of data processing and visualization, permit computations and analyses of multidimensional poverty measures that were not possible even twenty years ago. Box 7.1 discusses

---

[28] For example, the splendid Demographic and Health Surveys (DHS) have been updated every 5.88 years across all countries that have ever updated them (across a total of 155 'gaps' between DHS surveys). If we drop all instances where ten or more years have passed between DHS surveys, the average falls only to 5.31 years (Alkire 2013).

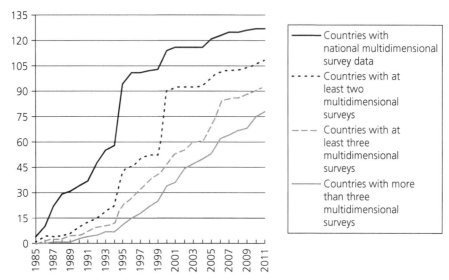

Figure 1.4. Availability of developing country surveys: DHS, MICS, LSMS, and CWIQ

in more detail the different fronts on which data collection can be improved in the near future.

1.3 **Policy Motivation**

Numbers, as Székely (2005) observed, can move the world. Thus, the third and equally central motivation for multidimensional poverty measurement is to inform policy, and thereby join the struggle to confront and overcome the pressing hazards and disadvantages that blight so many lives. While a good poverty measure alone cannot manufacture potent policy, it can be designed with that goal in mind. Naturally, some deprivations are intangible and others incomparable, so even good poverty measures are incomplete in many ways. Also, measures must be analysed with imagination and determination—and be complemented by strategic actions that go well beyond measurement.

Thus far we have discussed the ethical or normative reasons to consider the many faces of poverty. These are echoed in the policy fields. Scouring many empirical studies, we have concluded that it does not seem possible to proxy multidimensional poverty levels or trends using a single indicator. Many important and informative measurement methodologies have been developed, and will continue to be used and advanced in appropriate contexts, and Chapters 3 and 4 discuss these in depth. Further, this area of study is advancing rapidly. Still, in this last section, we mention why the AF methodology may add value empirically and theoretically, and in so doing open a window onto policy.

The building blocks of counting measures, including the AF class, are individual deprivation profiles. These show what deprivations one particular person or household experiences. For example, we might find that someone called Miriam is deprived in nutrition, in housing, in sanitation, and clean fuel, and literacy. This is called Miriam's joint distribution of deprivations—the deprivations she experiences at that particular point in time. These are summed, with weights, to create Miriam's deprivation score. The AF class of measures is constructed from the deprivation scores of poor people. This basis for measurement has an ethical appeal, as mentioned above, but also a policy one. As articulated by the Stiglitz, Sen, and Fitoussi Commission, 'the consequences for quality of life of having *multiple disadvantages* far exceed the sum of their individual effects' (2009)—a point also underlined by Wolff and De-Shalit (2007). The Commission called for '[d]eveloping measures of these cumulative effects [using] information on the "*joint distribution*" of the most salient features'.

But would any measure do? A salient feature of the AF methodology is its properties—as described in Chapters 2, 3, and 5—which make it an attractive option for informing policy transparently. Among AF measures, the so-called Adjusted Headcount Ratio or M_0 measure is particularly suitable due to three properties: (a) its ability to use ordinal or binary data rigorously, given that poverty indicators regularly have such data; (b) its ability to be decomposed by population subgroups like states or ethnic groups, to understand disparities and address the poorest; and (c) its ability to be broken down by dimensions and indicators, to show the composition of poverty on aggregate and for each subgroup. To this we might add a non-formal feature, which is the intuition of the measure and its partial and consistent sub-indices, which include a familiar headcount ratio, and also a novel feature reflecting the intensity or average share of deprivations poor people experience.

Because of these properties an M_0 measure has been described as a high-resolution lens. The single index value gives an overview of poverty levels and how these rise or fall over time. But it can (and should) be unfolded in different ways—by groups and by dimensions; at a single point in time or across time—to inform various policy purposes. It can therefore been used:

- to produce the official measures of multidimensional poverty;
- to identify overall patterns of deprivation;
- to compare subnational groups, such as regions, urban/rural, or ethnic groups;
- to compare the composition of poverty in different regions or social groups;
- to report poverty trends over time, both on aggregate and by population subgroups;
- to monitor the changes in particular indicators;
- to evaluate the impact of programmes on multiple outcomes;
- to target geographical regions or households for particular purposes;
- to communicate poverty analyses broadly.

Initial applications of multidimensional measurement methods used individual- or household-level data. More recently, the methodology is being applied to different units of analysis and with respect to different focal areas such as women's empowerment, targeting, child poverty, governance, fair trade, energy, and gender, with other applications, including using mixed methods and participatory work, in progress. The policy avenues for these alternative applications are a bit different from those outlined above, but continue to draw on the policy-salient features of the methodology.

1.4 **Content and Structure**

This book aims (a) to introduce the AF methodology as one approach among a wider set of multidimensional techniques; (b) to provide a clear and systematic introduction to multidimensional poverty measurement in the counting and axiomatic tradition, with a specific focus on the AF Adjusted Headcount Ratio (M_0); and (c) to address empirical and normative issues, as well as recent methodological extensions in distribution and dynamics.

The book may be divided into four parts, each containing two or three chapters. The first part introduces the framework for multidimensional measurement and systematically presents and critically evaluates different multidimensional methods that are frequently used for assessment of multidimensional poverty. The second part presents the counting-based measures that have been widely used in policy, and the Alkire–Foster methodology which joins together the axiomatic and counting approaches. The third part addresses pre-estimation issues in poverty measurement—the normative and empirical aspects of constructing a poverty measure. The fourth and final part of the book deals with the post-estimation issues—analysis after the poverty measure is constructed.

In the first part, Chapter 2 presents the framework for the whole book, outlining the basics of unidimensional and multidimensional poverty measurement, introducing the terminology and notation to be used throughout the book, discussing the scales of measurement of indicators and comparability across dimensions, and describing with illustrations the properties of multidimensional poverty measures. Chapter 3 then provides an overview of a range of methods used for assessing and evaluating multidimensional poverty and considers the scope as well as limitations of each. We cover the dashboard approach, composite indices, Venn diagrams, the dominance approach, various commonly used statistical approaches, the fuzzy sets approach, and axiomatic measures (which include measures from information theory).

In the second part, Chapter 4 reviews the counting approaches to multidimensional poverty measurement that have been widely applied and used for policy. Then Chapter 5 provides an in-depth account of one particular axiomatic and counting-type multidimensional poverty measurement methodology: the AF counting methodology. Specifically, the chapter presents the AF methodology of identification and presents the Adjusted Headcount Ratio or M_0 measure and its partial and consistent sub-indices.

In the third part, Chapter 6 clarifies and outlines the normative choices in measurement design, drawing on Sen's capability approach and related applied literature; and Chapter 7 provides a synthetic overview of distinctive practical issues in multidimensional poverty measurement design and analysis. In the final part, Chapter 8 presents avenues for performing robustness analysis and statistical inference, and Chapter 9 discusses different methodologies for conducting distributional and dynamic analysis. Chapter 10 presents some relevant regression techniques for analysing the M_0 measures.

1.5 **How to Use this Book**

This book was written with academic researchers, technical staff in governments and international agencies, and graduate students in quantitative social sciences in mind. Readers are likely to have a quantitative interest or training and come from different disciplines, ranging from economics to statistics, sociology, social policy, gender studies, education, public health, development studies, and area studies.

Naturally, some sections will be of more relevance to each reader than others. Those who are interested in the practicalities of constructing poverty measures will want to learn the formulae and selection of parameters for immediate implementation; those who are working in axiomatic traditions may wish to elaborate additional tools; and those in applied microeconomics or in sectoral or area studies may wish to adapt the methodologies to their own problems and contexts.

Also, readers will come to this book with varying degrees of familiarity with terms and operations. Some will have a deep familiarity with axiomatic approaches to poverty measurement; others with empirical operations such as bootstrapping, regression analysis, and robustness checks; whereas others might have greater familiarity with the choice of indicators and cutoffs. Still other readers will have knowledge of tests of indicator validity and reliability or may focus more on categorical and ordinal data analysis or on the link between measurement and policy processes. We have sought to explain key operations or to point researchers to background reading. Some content may seem rather basic but is included in order to be intelligible to others from different backgrounds. In addition, a substantial body of more intuitive and less technical materials that could not fit in the book are available on our associated website, <www.multidimensionalpoverty.org>. These online resources also include relevant software codes, training videos, and problem sets. The book, together with the online resources, thus provides a systematic introduction to the field for those learning these techniques and a set of reference materials for those implementing multidimensional measures.

2 The Framework

This chapter introduces the notation and basic concepts that will be used throughout the book. The chapter is organized into four sections. Section 2.1 starts with a review of unidimensional poverty measurement with particular attention to the well-known Foster–Greer–Thorbecke (FGT) measures (Foster, Greer, and Thorbecke 1984) because many methods presented in Chapter 3, as well as the Alkire and Foster (2007, 2011a) measures presented in Chapter 5, are based on FGT indices. Section 2.2 introduces the notation and basic concepts for multidimensional poverty measurement that will be used in subsequent chapters. Section 2.3 delves into the issue of indicators' scales of measurement, an aspect often overlooked when discussing methods for multidimensional analysis and which is central to this book. Section 2.4 addresses comparability across people and dimensions. Finally, section 2.5 presents in a detailed form the different properties that have been proposed in axiomatic approaches to multidimensional poverty measurement. Such properties enable the analyst to understand the ethical principles embodied in a measure and to be aware of the direction of change they will exhibit under certain transformations.

2.1 Review of Unidimensional Measurement and FGT Measures

The measurement of multidimensional poverty builds upon a long tradition of unidimensional poverty measurement. Because both approaches are technically closely linked, the measurement of poverty in a unidimensional way can be seen as a special case of multidimensional poverty measurement. This section introduces the basic concepts of unidimensional poverty measurement using the lens of the multidimensional framework, so serves as a springboard for the later work.

The measurement of poverty requires a reference population, such as all people in a country. We refer to the reference population under study as a *society*. We assume that any society consists of at least one observation or unit of analysis. This unit varies depending on the measurement exercise. For example, the unit of analysis is a child if one is measuring child poverty, it is an elderly person if one is measuring poverty among the elderly, and it is a person or—sometimes due to data constraints—the household for measures covering the whole population. For simplicity, unless otherwise indicated, we refer to the unit of analysis within a society as a *person* (Chapter 6 and Chapter 7). We denote the number of person(s) within a society by n, such that n is in $\mathbb{N}$ or $n \in \mathbb{N}$, where

$\mathbb{N}$ is the set of positive integers. Note that unless otherwise specified, n refers to the total population of a society and not a sample of it.

Assume that poverty is to be assessed using d number of dimensions, such that $d \in \mathbb{N}$. We refer to the performance of a person in a dimension as an achievement in a very general way, and we assume that achievements in each dimension can be represented by a non-negative real valued indicator. We denote the achievement of person i in dimension j by $x_{ij} \in \mathbb{R}_+$ for all $i = 1, \ldots, n$ and $j = 1, \ldots, d$, where $\mathbb{R}_+$ is the set of non-negative real numbers, which is a proper subset of the set of real numbers $\mathbb{R}$.[1] Subsequently, we denote the set of strictly positive real numbers by $\mathbb{R}_{++}$.

Throughout this book, we allow the population size of a society to vary, which allows comparisons of societies with different populations. When we seek to permit comparability of poverty estimates across different populations, we assume d to denote a fixed set (and number) of dimensions.[2] The achievements of all persons within a society are denoted by an $n \times d$-dimensional achievement matrix X which looks as follows:

$$
\begin{array}{c}
\textbf{Dimensions} \\
X = \begin{bmatrix} x_{11} & \cdots & x_{1d} \\ \vdots & \ddots & \vdots \\ x_{n1} & \cdots & x_{nd} \end{bmatrix} \text{People}
\end{array} .
$$

We denote the set of all possible matrices of size $n \times d$ by $\mathcal{X}_n \in \mathbb{R}_+^{n \times d}$ and the set of all possible achievement matrices by $\mathcal{X}$, such that $\mathcal{X} = \cup_n \mathcal{X}_n$. If $X \in \mathcal{X}_n$, then matrix X contains achievements for n persons in d dimensions. Unless specified otherwise, whenever we refer to matrix X, we assume $X \in \mathcal{X}$. The achievements of any person i in all d dimensions, which is row i of matrix X, are represented by the d-dimensional vector x_i. for all $i = 1, \ldots, n$. The achievements in any dimension j for all n persons, which is column j of matrix X, are represented by the n-dimensional vector $x_{\cdot j}$ for all $j = 1, \ldots, d$.

In the unidimensional context, the d dimensions considered in matrix $X \in \mathcal{X}$—which are typically assumed to be cardinal—can be meaningfully combined into a well-defined overall achievement or resource variable for each person i, which is denoted by x_i. One possibility, from a welfarist approach, would be to construct each person's welfare from her vector of achievements using a utility function $x_i = u(x_{i1}, \ldots, x_{id})$.[3] Another

---

[1] Empirical applications may encounter negative or zero income values, which require special treatment for certain poverty measures to be implemented.

[2] In practical implementations of the unidimensional method, a fixed set and number of dimensions is rarely obtained. Survey-based consumption items or income sources often differ in number and content.

[3] A utility function is a (mathematical) instrument that intends to measure the level of satisfaction of a person with all possible sets of achievements (usually consumption baskets). Utility functions represent consumer preferences. The use of the utility framework for distributional analysis faces two well-known problems. First, in principle, utility functions are merely ordinal, that is, they indicate that a certain consumption basket (or achievement vector) is preferred to some other, without providing the magnitudes of the difference between two utility values. Second, in principle, the utility framework does not allow interpersonal comparability, in the sense that one cannot decide whether some utility loss of a given person

possibility is that each dimension j refers to a different source of income (labour income, rents, family allowances, etc.). Then, one can construct the total income level for each person i as the sum of the income level obtained from each source, that is $x_i = \sum_{j=1}^{d} x_{ij}$. Alternatively, each dimension j can be measured in the quantity of a good or service that can be acquired in a market. Then, one can construct the total consumption expenditure level for each person i as the sum of the quantities acquired at market price, that is $x_i = \sum_{j=1}^{d} p_j x_{ij}$, where p_j, the price of commodity j, is used as its weight. In any of these three cases, the achievement matrix X is reduced to a vector $x = (x_1, \ldots, x_n)$ containing the welfare level or the resource variables of all n persons. In other words, the distinctive feature of the unidimensional approach is not that it necessarily considers only one dimension, but rather that it maps *multiple* dimensions of poverty assessment into a *single* dimension using a common unit of account.[4]

2.1.1 IDENTIFICATION OF THE INCOME POOR

Since Sen (1976), the measurement of poverty has been conceptualized as following two main steps: **identification** of who the poor are and **aggregation** of the information about poverty across society. In unidimensional space, the identification of who is poor is relatively straightforward: the poor are those whose overall achievement or resource variable falls below the poverty line z_U, where the subscript U simply signals that this is a poverty line used in the unidimensional space. Analogous to the construction of the resource variable, the poverty line can be obtained aggregating the minimum quantities or achievements z_j considered necessary in each dimension. It is assumed that such quantities or levels are positive values, that is $z_j \in \mathbb{R}^d_{++}$.[5] These minimum levels are collected in the d-dimensional vector $z = (z_1, \ldots, z_d)$.

If the overall achievement is the level of utility, a utility poverty line needs to be set as $z_U = u(z_1, \ldots, z_d)$.[6] On the other hand, when the overall achievement is total income or

(say a rich one) is less important than some utility gain of another person (say a poor one). As Sen observed, '...the attempt to handle social choice without using interpersonal comparability or cardinality had the natural consequence of the social welfare function being defined on the set of individual orderings. And this is precisely what makes this framework so unsuited to the analysis of distributional questions' (Sen 1973: 12–13). In order to make this framework applicable to distributional analysis, one needs to broaden individual preferences to include interpersonally comparable cardinal welfare functions (Sen 1973: 15). One particular way in which this has been implemented is through the so-called utilitarianism approach, which defines the measure of social welfare as the sum of individual utilities; moreover, it is frequently assumed—as in the framework described above—that everyone has the same utility function.

⁴ Alkire and Foster (2011b) provide further discussion on uni- vs multidimensional approaches.

⁵ The concept of the poverty line dates to the late 1800s. Booth (1894, 1903), Rowntree (1901), and Bowley and Burnett-Hurst (1915) wrote seminal studies based on surveys in some UK cities. As Rowntree writes, the poverty line represented the 'minimum necessaries for the maintenance of merely physical efficiency' (i.e. nutritional requirements) in monetary terms, plus certain minimum sums for clothing, fuel, and household sundries according to the family size (Townsend 1954: 131).

⁶ Axiomatic measures described in section 3.6.2 take this approach.

total consumption expenditure, the poverty line is given by the estimated cost of the basic consumption basket $z_U = \sum_{j=1}^{d} p_j z_j$—or some increment thereof.[7]

Then, given the person's overall resource value or utility value and the poverty line, we can define the identification function as follows: $\rho_U(x_i; z_U) = 1$ identifies person i as poor if $x_i < z_U$, that is, whenever the resource or utility variable is below the poverty line, and $\rho_U(x_i; z_U) = 0$ identifies person i as non-poor if $x_i \geq z_U$. We denote the number of unidimensionally poor persons in a society by q_U and the set of poor persons in a society by Z_U, such that $Z_U = \{i | \rho_U(x_i; z_U) = 1\}$.

2.1.2 AGGREGATION OF THE INCOME POOR

In terms of aggregation, a variety of indices have been proposed.[8] Among them, the FGT (1984) family of indices has been the most widely used measures of poverty by international organizations such as the World Bank and UN agencies, national governments, researchers, and practitioners.[9]

For simplicity, we assume the unidimensional variable x_i to be income. Building on previous poverty indices including Sen (1976) and Thon (1979), the FGT family of indices is based on the normalized income gap—called the 'poverty gap' in the unidimensional poverty literature—which is defined as follows: given the income distribution x, one can obtain a *censored* income distribution $\tilde{x}$ by replacing the values above the poverty line z_U by the poverty line value z_U itself and leaving the other values unchanged. Formally, $\tilde{x}_i = x_i$ if $x_i < z_U$ and $\tilde{x}_i = z_U$ if $x_i \geq z_U$. Then, the normalized income gap is given by

$$g_i = \frac{z_U - \tilde{x}_i}{z_U}. \tag{2.1}$$

The normalized income gap of person i is her income shortfall expressed as a share of the poverty line. The income gap of those who are non-poor is equal to 0.[10] The individual income gaps can be collected in an n-dimensional vector $g^\alpha = (g_1^\alpha, g_2^\alpha, \ldots, g_n^\alpha)$. Each g_i^α element is the normalized poverty gap raised to the power $\alpha \geq 0$ and it can be interpreted as a measure of *individual poverty* where α is a 'poverty aversion' parameter. The class of

---

[7] The interpretation of the variable is different if total income or total expenditure is used, with the former reflecting 'what could be' and the latter reflecting 'what is' (Atkinson 1989 cited in Alkire and Foster 2011b: 292).

[8] See Foster and Sen (1997), Zheng (1997), and Foster (2006) for a review of unidimensional poverty indices and Foster, Seth, et al. (2013) for pedagogic coverage of poverty and other unidimensional measures, with tools for practical implementation.

[9] Ravallion (1992) offers an early guidebook on the wide range of possible uses of the FGT measures, and Foster, Greer, and Thorbecke (2010) provide a detailed retrospective of the use and extensions of this class of measures.

[10] An alternative way to define the normalized income deprivation gap not using the censored distribution is that $g_i = (z_U - x_i)/z_U$ for $x_i < z_U$, and $g_i = 0$ for $x_i \geq z_U$.

FGT measures is defined as $P_\alpha = \sum_{i=1}^{n} g_i^\alpha / n$, thus P_α can be interpreted as the average poverty in the population. The FGT measures can also be expressed in a more synthetic way as $P_\alpha = \mu(g^\alpha)$, where μ is the mean operator and thus $\mu(g^\alpha)$ denotes the average or mean of the elements of vector g^α. This presentation of the FGT indices is useful in understanding the Alkire–Foster (AF) class (Alkire and Foster 2011a).

Within the FGT measures, three measures, associated with three different values of the parameter α, have been used most frequently. The deprivation vector g^0, for $\alpha = 0$, replaces each income below the poverty line with 1 and replaces non-poor incomes with 0. Its associated poverty measure $P_0 = \mu(g^0)$ is called the headcount ratio, or the mean of the deprivation vector. It indicates the proportion of people who are poor, also frequently called the incidence of poverty.[11] The normalized gap vector g^1, for $\alpha = 1$, replaces each poor person's income with the normalized income gap and assigns 0 to the rest. Its associated measure $P_1 = \mu(g^1)$, the poverty gap measure, reflects the average depth of poverty across the society. The squared gap vector, g^2 for $\alpha = 2$, replaces each poor person's income with the squared normalized income gap and assigns 0 to the rest. Its associated measure—the squared gap or distribution-sensitive FGT—is $P_2 = \mu(g^2)$; it emphasizes the conditions of the poorest of the poor as Box 2.1 explains.

The FGT measures satisfy a number of properties, including a subgroup decomposability property that views overall poverty as a population-share weighted average of poverty levels in the different population subgroups.[12] As noted by Sen (1976), the headcount ratio violates two intuitive principles: (1) monotonicity: if a poor person's resource level falls, poverty should rise and yet the headcount ratio remains unchanged; (2) transfer: poverty should fall if two poor persons' resource levels are brought closer together by a progressive transfer between them, and yet the headcount ratio may either remain unchanged or it can even go down. The poverty gap measure satisfies monotonicity, but not the transfer principle; the P_2 measure satisfies both monotonicity and the transfer principle.[13]

---

[11] In the epidemiological literature there is a clear distinction between the terms 'incidence' and 'prevalence'. Incidence refers to the number or rate of people becoming ill *during a period* of time in a specified population, whereas prevalence refers to the number or proportion of people experiencing an illness at a *particular point* in time (regardless of the moment at which they became ill). In general usage, this distinction is usually ignored and the expression 'poverty incidence' or 'incidence of poverty' frequently refers to the proportion of poor people in a certain population at a certain point in time (which strictly speaking in epidemiological terms would be poverty prevalence), and not to the proportion of people who became poor over a certain time period (which strictly speaking in epidemiological terms would be incidence). The expression 'poverty prevalence' or 'prevalence of poverty' is also sometimes, although much less frequently, found but refers to the same concept as when incidence is used. In this book we follow the poverty literature and refer to poverty incidence as the poverty rate at a particular point in time.

[12] Note that the population subgroups are mutually exclusive and collectively exhaustive.

[13] Although we address the issue of scales of measurement later on in this chapter, it is worth anticipating that while all three mentioned members of the FGT family (P_0, P_1, and P_2) can be applied to cardinal variables (where distances between categories are meaningful) only the headcount ratio can be used with an ordinal variable (where distances between categories are meaningless).

BOX 2.1 A NUMERICAL EXAMPLE OF THE FGT MEASURES

A simple example[14] can clarify the method and these axioms, and will also prove useful in linking the Alkire and Foster methodology (fully described in Chapter 5) to its roots in the FGT class of poverty measures. Consider four persons whose incomes are summarized by vector $x = (7, 2, 4, 8)$ and the poverty line is $z_U = 5$.

The headcount ratio P_0: Consider first the case of $\alpha = 0$. Each gap is replaced by a value of 1 if the person is poor and by a value of 0 if non-poor. The deprivation vector is given by: $g^0 = (0, 1, 1, 0)$, indicating that the second and third persons in this distribution are poor. The mean of this vector—the P_0 measure—is one half: $P_0(x, z_U) = \mu(g^0) = 2/4 = 0.5$, indicating that 50% of the population in this distribution is poor. Undoubtedly, it provides very useful information. However, as noted by Watts (1968) and Sen (1976), the headcount ratio does not provide information on the depth of poverty nor on its distribution among the poor. For example, if the third person became poorer, experiencing a decrease in her income so that the income distribution became $x' = (7, 2, 3, 8)$, the P_0 measure would still be one half; that is, it violates monotonicity. Also, if there was a progressive transfer between the two poor persons, so that the distribution was $x'' = (7, 3, 3, 8)$, the P_0 measure would not change, violating the transfer principle. This has policy implications. If this was the official poverty measure, a government interested in maximizing the impact of resources on poverty reduction would have an incentive to allocate resources to the least poor, that is, those who were closest to the poverty line, leaving the lives of the poorest of the poor unchanged.

The poverty gap P_1 (or FGT-1): Here $\alpha = 1$. Each gap is raised to the power $\alpha = 1$, giving the proportion in which each poor person falls short of the poverty line and 0 if the person is non-poor. The normalized gap vector is given by $g^1 = (0, 3/5, 1/5, 0)$. The P_1 measure is the mean of this vector. $P_1(x; z_U) = \mu(g^1) = 4/20$ indicates that the society would require an average of 20% of the poverty line for each person in the society to remove poverty. In fact, \$4 is the overall amount needed in this case to lift both poor persons above the poverty line. Unlike the headcount ratio P_0, the P_1 measure *is* sensitive to the depth of poverty and satisfies monotonicity. If the income of the third person decreased so we had $x' = (7, 2, 3, 8)$ the corresponding normalized gap vector would be $g^{1'} = (0, 3/5, 2/5, 0)$, so $P_1(x'; z_U) = 5/20$. Clearly, $P_1(x'; z_U) > P_1(x; z_U)$. Indeed, all measures with $\alpha > 0$ satisfy monotonicity. However, a transfer to an extremely destitute person from a less poor person would not change P_1, since the decrease in one gap would be exactly compensated by the increase in the other. By being sensitive to the depth of poverty (i.e. satisfying monotonicity), the P_1 measure does make policymakers want to decrease the average depth of poverty as well as reduce the headcount. But because of its insensitivity to the distribution among the poor, P_1 does not provide incentives to target the very poorest, whereas the FGT-2 measure does.

The squared poverty gap P_2 (or FGT-2): When we set $\alpha = 2$, each normalized gap is squared or raised to the power $\alpha = 2$. The squared gap vector in this case is given by $g^2 = (0, 9/25, 1/25, 0)$. By squaring the gaps, bigger gaps receive higher weight. Note, for example, that while the gap of the second person (3/5) is three times bigger than the gap of the third person (1/5), the squared gap of the second person (9/25) is nine times bigger than the gap of the third person (1/25). The mean of the g^2 vector—the P_2 measure—is $P_2(x; z_U) = \mu(g^2) = 10/100$. The P_2 measure is sensitive to the depth of poverty: if the income of the third person decreases one unit such that $x' = (7, 2, 3, 8)$, the squared gap vector becomes $g^2 = (0, 9/25, 4/25, 0)$, increasing the aggregate poverty level to $P_2(x'; z_U) = 13/100$). It is also sensitive to the distribution among the poor: if there is a transfer of \$1 from the third person to the second one, so $x = (7, 2, 4, 8)$ becomes $x'' = (7, 3, 3, 8)$, the squared gap vector becomes $g^2 = (0, 4/25, 4/25, 0)$, decreasing the aggregate poverty level to $P_2(x''; z_U) = 8/100$. Squaring the gaps has the effect of emphasizing the poorest poor and providing incentives to policymakers to address their situation urgently. All measures with $\alpha > 1$ satisfy the transfer property.

---

[14] Alkire and Santos (2009).

2.2 **Notation and Preliminaries for Multidimensional Poverty Measurement**

We now extend the notation to the multidimensional context. We represent achievements as $n \times d$ dimensional achievement matrix X, as in the unidimensional framework described in section 2.1. We make two practical assumptions for convenience. We assume that the achievement of person i in dimension j can be represented by a non-negative real number, such that $x_{ij} \in \mathbb{R}_+$ for all $i = 1, \ldots, n$ and $j = 1, \ldots, d$. Also, we assume that higher achievements are preferred to lower ones.[15] In a multidimensional setting, in contrast to a unidimensional context, the considered *achievements* may not be combinable in a meaningful way into some overall variable. In fact, each dimension can be of a different nature. For example, one may consider a person's income, level of schooling, health status, and occupation, which do not have any common unit of account. As in the unidimensional case, we allow the population size of a society to vary, and we assume d to denote a fixed set (and number) of dimensions.[16]

We denote the set of all possible matrices of size $n \times d$ by $\mathcal{X}_n \in \mathbb{R}_+^{n \times d}$ and the set of all possible achievement matrices by $\mathcal{X}$, such that $\mathcal{X} = \cup_n \mathcal{X}_n$. If $X \in \mathcal{X}_n$, then matrix X contains achievements for n persons and a fixed set of d dimensions. Unless specified otherwise, whenever we refer to matrix X, we assume $X \in \mathcal{X}$. The achievements of any person i in all d dimensions, which is row i of matrix X, are represented by the d-dimensional vector $x_{i\cdot}$ for all $i = 1, \ldots, n$. The achievements in any dimension j for all n persons, which is column j of matrix X, are represented by the n-dimensional vector $x_{\cdot j}$ for all $j = 1, \ldots, d$.

In multidimensional analysis, each dimension may be assigned a weight or deprivation value based on its relative importance or priority. We denote the relative weight attached to dimension j by w_j, such that $w_j > 0$ for all $j = 1, \ldots, d$. The weights attached to all d dimensions are collected in a vector $w = (w_1, \ldots, w_d)$. For convenience we may restrict the weights such that they sum to the total number of considered dimensions, that is, $\sum_j w_j = d$. Alternatively, weights may be normalized; in other words, the weights sum to one: $\sum_j w_j = 1$.[17]

---

[15] In empirical applications some indicators may not be restricted to the non-negative range, or be scored such that *larger values are worse*, or that the lowest attainable value is strictly positive. For example, the z-scores of children's nutritional indicators may take negative values; in a people-per-room indicator, larger values are worse. And the lowest possible Body Mass Index for human survival is strictly positive. Such indicators may require rescaling.

[16] For simplicity of presentation, in theoretical sections, we use the term 'dimension' to refer to each variable; in empirical presentations often we use the term 'indicator' for the variables, while 'dimension' refers to groupings of indicators.

[17] Note that the prices used in the unidimensional case provide a particular weighting structure, where the weights do not necessarily sum to d or 1.

2.2.1 IDENTIFYING DEPRIVATIONS

A common first step in multidimensional poverty assessment in several of the methodologies reviewed in Chapter 3, as well as in the Alkire and Foster (2007, 2011a) methodology, requires defining a threshold in *each* dimension. Such a threshold is the minimum level someone needs to achieve in that dimension in order to be non-deprived. It is called the dimensional **deprivation cutoff**. When a person's achievement is strictly below the cutoff, she is considered deprived. We denote the deprivation cutoff in dimension j by z_j; the deprivation cutoffs for all dimensions are collected in the d-dimensional vector $z = (z_1, \ldots, z_d)$. We denote all possible d-dimensional deprivation cutoff vectors by $z \in \mathbb{R}^d_{++}$. Any person i is considered deprived in dimension j if and only if $x_{ij} < z_j$.

For several measures reviewed in Chapter 3, and for the AF method, it will prove useful to express the data in terms of deprivations rather than achievements. From the achievement matrix X and the vector of deprivation cutoffs z, we obtain a deprivation matrix g^0 (analogous to the deprivation vector in the unidimensional context) whose typical element $g^0_{ij} = 1$ whenever $x_{ij} < z_j$ and $g^0_{ij} = 0$, otherwise, for all $j = 1, \ldots, d$ and for all $i = 1, \ldots, n$. In other words, if person i is deprived in dimension j, then the person is assigned a deprivation status of 1, and 0 otherwise. Thus, matrix $g^0(X)$ represents the deprivation status of all n persons in all d dimensions in matrix X. Vector $g^0_{i\cdot}$ represents the deprivation status of person i in all dimensions and vector $g^0_{\cdot j}$ represents the deprivation status of all persons in dimension j. From the matrix g^0 one can construct a deprivation score c_i for each person i such that $c_i = \sum_{j=1}^{d} w_j g^0_{ij}$. In words, c_i denotes the sum of *weighted* deprivations suffered by person i.[18] In the particular case in which weights are equal and sum to the number of dimensions, the score is simply the number of deprivations or deprivation counts that the person experiences. Whenever weights are unequal but sum to the number of dimensions, person i's **deprivation score** is defined as the sum of her weighted deprivation counts. The deprivation scores are collected in an n-dimensional column vector c.

On certain occasions, it will be useful to use the deprivation-cutoff **censored achievement matrix** $\tilde{X}$ which is obtained from the corresponding achievement matrix X in $\mathfrak{X}$, replacing the non-deprived achievements by the corresponding deprivation cutoff and leaving the rest unchanged. We denote the ij^{th} element of $\tilde{X}$ by $\tilde{x}_{ij}$. Then, formally, $\tilde{x}_{ij} = x_{ij}$ if $x_{ij} < z_j$, and $\tilde{x}_{ij} = z_j$ otherwise. In this way, all achievements greater than or equal to the deprivation cutoffs are ignored in the censored achievement matrix.

When data are cardinally meaningful for all $i = 1, \ldots, n$ and all $j = 1, \ldots, d$, and $z_j \in \mathbb{R}_{++}$, in other words, when all the achievements take non-negative values and the deprivation cutoffs take strictly positive values, one can construct dimensional gaps or shortfalls from the censored achievement matrix $\tilde{X}$ as[19]

---

[18] Alternative notations for the AF methodology are presented and elaborated in Chapter 5.

[19] This is an analogous construct to the income gaps in the FGT measures. An alternative way to define the deprivation gaps not using the censored distribution is that $g_{ij} = (z_j - x_{ij})/z_j$ when $x_{ij} < z_j$ and $g_{ij} = 0$ when $x_{ij} \geq z_j$.

$$g_{ij} = \frac{z_j - \tilde{x}_{ij}}{z_j}.$$ (2.2)

Each g_{ij}, or normalized gap, expresses the shortfall of person i in dimension j as a share of its deprivation cutoff. Naturally, the gaps of those whose achievement x_{ij} is above the corresponding dimensional deprivation cutoff z_j are equal to 0. Generalizing the above, the individual normalized gaps can be collected in an $n \times d$ dimensional matrix g^α where each g_{ij}^α element is the normalized gap defined in (2.2) raised to the power α; such normalized gaps can be interpreted as a measure of *individual deprivation* in dimension j. When $\alpha = 0$, we have the g^0 deprivation matrix already defined. When $\alpha = 1$, we have the g^1 matrix of normalized gaps, and when $\alpha = 2$, we have the g^2 matrix of squared gaps. Analogous to the FGT measures, $\alpha \geq 0$ is a deprivation aversion parameter.

2.2.2 IDENTIFICATION AND AGGREGATION IN THE MULTIDIMENSIONAL CASE

Sen's (1976) steps of **identification** of the poor and **aggregation** also apply to the multidimensional case. It is clear that the identification of who is poor in the unidimensional case is relatively straightforward. The poverty line dichotomizes the population into the sets of poor and non-poor. In other words, in the unidimensional case, a person is poor if she is deprived. However, in the multidimensional context, the identification of the poor is more complex: the terms 'deprived' and 'poor' are no longer synonymous. A person who is deprived in any particular dimension may not necessarily be considered poor. An identification method, with an associated identification function, is used to define who is poor.

We denote the identification function by ρ, such that $\rho(\cdot) = 1$ identifies person i as poor and $\rho(\cdot) = 0$ identifies person i as non-poor. Analogous to the unidimensional case, we denote the number of multidimensionally poor people in a society by q and the set of poor persons in a society by Z, such that $Z = \{i | \rho(\cdot) = 1\}$. It could be the case that the identification method is based on some 'exogenous' variable, in that it is a variable not included in achievement matrix X. For example, the exogenous variable could be being the beneficiary of some government programme or living in a specific geographic area. One may also define an identification method based on one particular dimension j of matrix X. One may consider the corresponding normative cutoff z_j to identify the person as poor, in which case the function is $\rho(x_{ij}; z_j)$, or one may consider a relative cutoff identifying as poor anyone who is below the median or mean value of the distribution, in which case the function is $\rho(x_{\cdot j})$. Alternatively, identification may be based on the whole set of achievements, not necessarily considering dimensional deprivation cutoffs but rather the relative position of each person on the aggregate distribution $\rho(X)$.

There are many different ways of identifying the poor in the multidimensional context. A particularly prevalent set of methods consider the person's vector of achievements and corresponding deprivation cutoffs, such that $\rho(x_{i\cdot};z) = 1$ identifies person i as poor and $\rho(x_{i\cdot};z) = 0$ identifies person i as non-poor.[20] Within this specification of the identification function, at least two approaches can be followed. An approach closely approximating unidimensional poverty is the 'aggregate achievement approach', which consists of applying an aggregation function to the achievements across dimensions for each person to obtain an overall achievement value. The same aggregation function is also applied to the dimensional deprivation cutoffs to obtain an aggregate poverty line. As in the unidimensional case, a person is identified as poor when her overall achievement is below the aggregate poverty line. Another method, which we refer to as the 'censored achievement approach', first applies deprivation cutoffs to identify whether a person is deprived or not in each dimension and then identifies a person by considering only the deprived achievements. The 'counting approach' is one possible censored achievement approach, which identifies the poor according to the number (count) of deprivations they experience. Note that 'number' here has a broad meaning as dimensions may be weighted differently. Chapter 4 and the AF method (Chs 5–10) use a counting approach. When the scale of the variables allows, other identification methods could be developed using the information on the deprivation gaps.

In counting identification methods, the criterion for identifying the poor can range from 'union' to the 'intersection'. The union criterion identifies a person as poor if the person is deprived in *any* dimension, whereas the intersection criterion identifies a person as poor only if she is deprived in *all* considered dimensions. In between these two extreme criteria there is room for intermediate criteria. Many counting-based measurement exercises since the mid-1970s have used an intermediate criterion (see Chapter 4). The AF methodology formally incorporated it into an axiomatic framework.[21]

Once the identification method has been selected, the aggregation step requires selecting a poverty index, which summarizes the information about poverty across society. A poverty index is a function $P : \mathcal{X} \times z \to \mathbb{R}$ that converts the information contained in the achievement matrix $X \in \mathcal{X}$ and the deprivation cutoff vector $z \in z$ into a real number. We denote a poverty index as $P(X;z)$. An identification and an aggregation method that are used together constitute what we call a multidimensional poverty methodology, and we denote it as $\mathcal{M} = (\rho, P)$.

It will prove useful to introduce notation for two consistent sub-indices related to the overall poverty index $P(X;z)$. Each of them offers information on different 'slices' of the achievement matrix X as analysed by the corresponding multidimensional poverty

---

[20] Note that this identification function differs from the one introduced in the unidimensional case in that it depends on the vector of achievements $x_{i\cdot}$ and the vector of dimensional deprivation cutoffs z. In the unidimensional case, identification depends on the already-aggregated overall achievement or resource variable x_i and the aggregate poverty line z_U, which of course may depend upon the prices of certain commodities.

[21] Within the aggregate achievement approach, the intermediate criterion is operationalized by using the so-called 'poverty frontier', defined as the different combinations of the d achievements that provide the same overall achievement as the aggregate poverty line. Duclos, Sahn, and Younger (2006a) further elaborate the poverty frontier; cf. Atkinson (2003) and Bourguignon and Chakravarty (2003).

methodology $\mathcal{M} = (\rho, P)$; that is, the consistent sub-indices are dependent on the selected identification and aggregation methods. One of these consistent sub-indices is the poverty level of a particular subgroup within the total population, denoted as $P(X^\ell; z)$, where X^ℓ is the achievement matrix of this particular subgroup ℓ (which could be people of a particular ethnicity, for example) contained in matrix X. Visually, this consistent sub-index is based on a horizontal slice of the achievement matrix X (i.e. a set of rows).

The other consistent sub-index is a function of the **post-identification dimensional deprivations**, denoted as $P_j(x_{\cdot j}; z)$, where, as stated above, vector $x_{\cdot j}$ represents the achievements in dimension j for all n persons and z is the deprivation cutoff vector.[22] This is precisely why the full vector of deprivation cutoffs z is an argument of the index and not just the particular deprivation cutoff z_j. Recall that under some identification methods, it is possible to have some people who experience deprivations but are not identified as poor (for example, when a counting approach is used with an identification strategy that it is not union). In such cases, their deprivations will not be considered in the poverty measure and therefore will not be considered in this consistent sub-index either. In a visual way, this consistent sub-index is based on a vertical slice of the achievement matrix X (i.e. a column). These two consistent sub-indices will be used when introducing the different principles of multidimensional poverty measures in section 2.5.3.

As we shall see, although identification and aggregation have, since Sen (1976), usually been recognized as key steps in poverty measurement, some methods in the multidimensional context do not follow these steps. We will clarify this in Chapter 3.

2.2.3 THE JOINT DISTRIBUTION

Throughout this book we will frequently refer to the **joint distribution** in contrast to the **marginal distribution** and we will also use the expression **joint deprivations**. The concept of a joint distribution comes from statistics where it can be represented using a joint cumulative distribution function.[23] The relevance of the joint distribution in multidimensional analysis was articulated by Atkinson and Bourguignon (1982), who observed that multidimensional analysis was *intrinsically different* because there could be identical dimensional marginal distributions but differing degrees of interdependence between dimensions.[24]

---

[22] In one of the measures in the AF class, the Adjusted Headcount Ratio, this consistent sub-index is called the censored headcount ratio. See section 5.5.3 for a detailed presentation.

[23] Given two random variables, y_1 and y_2, the joint distribution can be described with the bivariate cumulative distribution function $F(b_1, b_2) = Prob\left(y_1 \le b_1, y_2 \le b_2\right)$. In words, the joint distribution gives the proportion of the population with values of y_1 and y_2 lower than b_1 and b_2 correspondingly and simultaneously.

[24] The authors analyse inequality in the two-dimensional case. They introduce the transformation in which there is an increase in the correlation of the achievements, leaving the marginal distributions unchanged—something we discuss in section 2.5.2. They extend the conditions for second-order stochastic dominance, noting that such conditions depend on the joint distribution.

Table 2.1 Joint distribution of deprivation in two dimensions

		Dimension 2		
		Non-deprived	Deprived	Total
Dimension 1	**Non-deprived**	n_{00}	n_{01}	n_{0+}
	Deprived	n_{10}	n_{11}	n_{1+}
	Total	n_{+0}	n_{+1}	n

In this book we treat the achievement matrix X as a representation of the joint distribution of achievements. Each row contains the (vector of) achievements of a given person in the different dimensions, and each column contains the (vector of) achievements in a given dimension across the population. From that matrix, considered with deprivation cutoffs, it is possible to obtain the proportion of the population who are simultaneously deprived in different subsets of d dimensions. In other words, it is possible to obtain the proportion of people who experience each possible profile of deprivations. This is visually clear in the deprivation matrix g^0, which represents the joint distribution of deprivations. The higher-order matrices g^1 and g^2 obviously offer further information regarding the joint distribution of the depths of deprivations.

The importance of considering the joint distribution of achievements, which in turn enables us to look at joint deprivations, is best understood in contrast with the alternative of looking at the **marginal distribution** of achievements, and thus, the **marginal deprivations**. The marginal distribution is the distribution in one specific dimension without reference to any other dimension.[25] The marginal distribution of dimension j is represented by the column vector $x_{.j}$. From the marginal distribution of each dimension, it is possible to obtain the proportion of the population deprived with respect to a particular deprivation cutoff. However, by looking at only the marginal distribution, one does not know who is simultaneously deprived in other dimensions.[26]

Table 2.1 illustrates the relevance of the joint distribution in the basic case of n persons and two dimensions using a contingency table.

We denote the number of people deprived and non-deprived in the first dimension by n_{1+} and n_{0+}, respectively; whereas, the number of people deprived and non-deprived in the second dimension are denoted by n_{+1} and n_{+0}, respectively. These values correspond to the marginal distributions of both dimensions as depicted in the final row and final column of the table. They could equivalently be expressed as proportions of the total, in which case, for example, (n_{1+}/n) would represent the proportion of people deprived (or the headcount ratio) in Dimension 1.

---

[25] Given any random variable y_j, the marginal distribution can be described with the cumulative distribution function $F_j(b_j) = Prob(y_j \leq b_j)$.

[26] Only in the very particular case in which the two variables are statistically independent, can one obtain the joint distribution from the marginal ones. In such a case, the proportion of people deprived simultaneously in a number of variables can be obtained as the product of the proportions of people deprived in each variable. Although this is a topic for further empirical research, *a priori*, it seems unlikely that the independence condition will be satisfied, especially as the number of considered dimensions increases.

Table 2.2 Comparison of two joint distributions of deprivations in four dimensions

$$g^0(X) = \begin{bmatrix} 0 & 0 & 0 & 0 \\ 0 & 0 & 0 & 0 \\ 0 & 0 & 0 & 0 \\ 1 & 1 & 1 & 1 \end{bmatrix} \qquad g^0(X') = \begin{bmatrix} 1 & 0 & 0 & 0 \\ 0 & 1 & 0 & 0 \\ 0 & 0 & 1 & 0 \\ 0 & 0 & 0 & 1 \end{bmatrix}$$

Dimensional P_0: [0.25 0.25 0.25 0.25]   [0.25 0.25 0.25 0.25]

The marginal distributions, however, do not provide information about the joint distribution of deprivations, which is described in the four internal cells of the table. In particular, the number of people deprived in both dimensions is denoted by n_{11}, the number of people deprived in the first but not the second dimension is denoted by n_{10}, and the number of people deprived in the second and not in the first dimension is denoted by n_{01}. We know that n_{11} people are deprived in both dimensions and the sum of $n_{11} + n_{01} + n_{10}$ is the number of people deprived in at least one dimension. These values correspond to the joint distribution of deprivations.

Consider now the case of four dimensions and four people, to see how valuable information can be added by the joint distribution. Table 2.2[27] presents the deprivation matrix g^0 of two hypothetical distributions, X and X'. Such a matrix presents joint distributions of deprivations in a compact way and is used regularly throughout this book.

In the table, the marginal distributions of each dimension's P_0 are identical in deprivation matrices $g^0(X)$ and $g^0(X')$. Thus, the proportions of people deprived in each dimension are the same in the two distributions (25%). Yet, while, in distribution X, one person is deprived in all dimensions and three people experience zero deprivations, in distribution X', each of the four persons is deprived in exactly one dimension. In other words, although the marginal distributions are identical, the two joint distributions X and X' are very different. We understand that multiple deprivations that are *simultaneously* experienced are at the core of the concept of multidimensional poverty, and this is the reason why the consideration of the joint distribution is important. However, as we shall see, not all methodologies consider the joint distribution. In the next section, we introduce the notation for two methodologies of this type.

2.2.4 MARGINAL METHODS

Some of the methods for multidimensional poverty assessment introduced in Chapter 3 can be called **marginal methods** because they do not use information contained in the joint distribution of achievements. In other words, they ignore all information on links across dimensions. Following Alkire and Foster (2011b), a marginal method assigns the

---

[27] Alkire and Foster (2011b). Similar examples on the relevance of considering the joint distribution in the measurement of multidimensional welfare and poverty can be found in Tsui (2002), Pattanaik, Reddy, and Xu (2012), and Seth (2009).

same level of poverty to any two matrices that generate the same marginal distributions. In Table 2.2, a marginal method would assign the same poverty level to distribution X (four deprivations are experienced by one person) and distribution X' (each person experiences exactly one deprivation). That is, it would not be able to show whether the deprivations are spread evenly across the population or whether they are concentrated in an underclass of multiply deprived persons. Such marginal methods can also be linked to the order of aggregation while constructing poverty indices (Pattanaik et al. 2012). Specifically, a measure can be obtained by first aggregating achievements or deprivations across people (column-first) within each dimension and then aggregating across dimensions, or it can be obtained by first aggregating achievements or deprivations for each person (row-first) and then aggregating across people. Only measures that follow the second order of aggregation (i.e. first across dimensions for each person and then across persons) reflect the joint distribution of deprivations (Alkire 2011: 61, figure 7). Measures that follow the first order of aggregation fall under marginal methods of poverty measurement.

Marginal methods also include cases where achievements for different dimensions are drawn from *different* data sources and/or from *different* reference groups within a population—as occurred, for example, in many indicators associated with the Millennium Development Goals. In this case, rather than having an $n \times d$ dimensional matrix X of achievements, one may have a 'collection' of vectors $x^j \in \mathbb{R}_+^{n_j}$, representing the achievements of n_j people in dimension j for all $j = 1, \ldots d$. Note that each x^j vector may refer to *different* sets of people such as children, adults, workers, or females, to mention a few.

Suppose, as before, that a deprivation cutoff $z_j \in \mathbb{R}_{++}$ is defined. Then, we define a **dimensional deprivation index** $P_j(x^j; z_j)$ for dimension j by $P_j : \mathbb{R}_+^{n_j} \times \mathbb{R}_{++} \to \mathbb{R}$, which assesses the deprivation profile of n_j people in dimension j. The deprivation index might be simply the percentage of people who are deprived in this indicator or some other statistic such as child mortality rates. Note that deprivations are clearly identified in each dimension; however, because the underlying columns of dimensional achievements are not linked, no decision on who is to be considered multidimensionally poor can be made. This is a key difference between the dimensional deprivation index $P_j(x^j; z_j)$ and the post-identification dimensional deprivation index $P_j(x_{\cdot j}; z)$, which depends on the entire deprivation cutoff vector z (and not just z_j) and thus captures the joint distribution of deprivations (see section 2.2.2). Different dimensional deprivation indices $P_j(x^j, z_j)$ can be considered in a set, constituting the 'dashboard approach', or combined by some aggregation function, which is often called a 'composite index' (Chapter 3).

2.2.5 USEFUL MATRIX AND VECTOR OPERATIONS

Throughout the book, we use specific vector and matrix operations. This section introduces the technical notation covering vectors and matrices.

We denote the transpose of any matrix X by X^{tr} where X^{tr} has the rows of matrix X converted into columns. Formally, if $X \in \mathbb{R}^{n \times d}$ and the ij^{th} element of X is written x_{ij}, then $X^{\text{tr}} \in \mathbb{R}^{d \times n}$, where $x_{ji}^{\text{tr}} = x_{ij}$ is the ij^{th} element of X^{tr} for all $j = 1, \ldots, d$ and $i = 1, \ldots n$. The same notation applies to a vector, with x^{tr} being the transpose of x. Thus, if x is a row vector, x^{tr} is a column vector containing the same elements.

As stated in section 2.1 the average or mean of the elements of any vector x is denoted by $\mu(x)$, where $\mu(x) = \sum_{i=1}^{n} x_i / n$. Similarly, the average or mean of the elements of any matrix X is denoted by $\mu(X)$, where $\mu(X) = \sum_{i=1}^{n} \sum_{j=1}^{d} x_{ij} / (nd)$.

Later in the book we use a related expression, the so-called 'generalized mean of order' $\beta \in \mathbb{R}$. Given any vector of achievements $y = (y_1, \ldots, y_d)$, where $y_j \in \mathbb{R}_{++}^{d}$, the expression of the weighted generalized mean of order β is given by

$$
\mu_\beta(y; w) = \begin{cases} \left(\displaystyle\sum_{j=1}^{d} w_j y_j^\beta \right)^{\frac{1}{\beta}} & \text{for } \beta \neq 0 \\[3mm] \displaystyle\prod_{j=1}^{d} (y_j)^{w_j} & \text{for } \beta = 0 \end{cases}, \tag{2.3}
$$

where $w_j > 0$ and $\sum_j w_j = 1$. When weights are equal, $w_j = 1/d$ for all j. Each generalized mean summarizes distribution y into a single number and can be interpreted as a 'summary' measure of well- or ill-being, depending on the meaning of the arguments y_j. When $w_j = 1/d$ for all j, we write $\mu_\beta(y; w)$ simply as $\mu_\beta(y)$. When $\beta = 1$, $\mu_\beta(y)$ reduces to the arithmetic mean and is simply denoted by $\mu(y)$. When $\beta > 1$, more weight is placed on higher entries and $\mu_\beta(y)$ is higher than the arithmetic mean, approaching the maximum entry as β tends to ∞. For $\beta < 1$ more weight is placed on lower entries, and $\mu_\beta(y)$ is lower than the arithmetic mean, approaching the minimum entry as β tends to $-\infty$. The case of $\beta = 0$ is known as the geometric mean and $\beta = -1$ as the harmonic mean. Expression (2.3) is also known as a constant elasticity of substitution function, frequently used as a utility function in economics. When generalized means are computed over achievements, it is natural to restrict the parameter to the range of $\beta < 1$, giving a higher weight to lower achievements and penalizing for inequality (Atkinson 1970). Likewise when generalized means are computed over deprivations, it is natural to restrict the parameter to the range of $\beta > 1$, giving a higher weight to higher deprivations and also penalizing for inequality. Box 2.2 contains an example of generalized means.

BOX 2.2 EXAMPLE OF GENERALIZED MEANS

Consider[28] two distributions y and y' with the following distribution of achievements in a particular dimension: $y = (2, 6, 7)$ and $y' = (1, 5, 9)$. We first show how to calculate $\mu_\beta(y)$ for certain values of β and then compare two distributions with a graph where β ranges from -2 to 2. In this example, we assume that all dimensions are equally weighted: $w_1 = w_2 = w_3 = 1/3$.

Arithmetic Mean: The arithmetic mean $(\beta = 1)$ of distribution y is $\mu_1(y) = (2 + 6 + 7)/3 = 5$.

---

[28] Alkire and Santos (2009).

BOX 2.2 *(cont.)*

Geometric Mean: If $\beta = 0$, then μ_β is the 'geometric mean' and by the formula presented in (2.3) can be calculated as $\mu_0(y) = (2)^{1/3} \times (6)^{1/3} \times (7)^{1/3} = 4.38$.

Harmonic Mean: If $\beta = -1$, then μ_β is the harmonic mean and can be calculated as $\mu_{-1}(y) = \left[\frac{(2)^{-1} + (6)^{-1} + (7)^{-1}}{3}\right]^{-1} = 3.71$.

The following graph depicts the values of the μ_β of y and y' for different values of β. Note that $\mu_\beta(y) = \mu_\beta(y')$ when $\beta = 1$, given that the two distributions have the same arithmetic mean. In both cases, when $\beta < 1$, the generalized means are strictly lower than the arithmetic mean, because the incomes are unequally distributed. Note moreover that for this range, $\mu_\beta(y') < \mu_\beta(y)$, because y' has a more unequal distribution. On the other hand, for $\beta > 1$, $\mu_\beta(y') > \mu_\beta(y)$, as the higher incomes receive a higher weight.

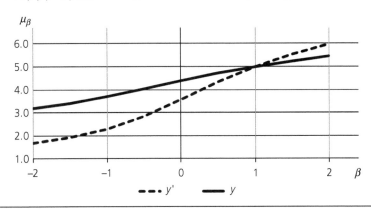

Another matrix transformation that we use is **replication**. A matrix is a replication of another matrix if it can be obtained by duplicating the rows of the original matrix a finite number of times. Suppose the rows of matrix Y are replicated γ number of times, where $\gamma \in \mathbb{N}\setminus\{1\}$. Then the corresponding replication matrix is denoted by $rep(Y; \gamma)$. This notation may be used for replication of any vector y: $rep(y; \gamma)$. We do not consider column replication, as we consider a fixed set of dimensions.

We also use three types of matrices associated with particular operations: a **permutation matrix**, a **diagonal matrix**, and a **bistochastic matrix**. A permutation matrix, denoted by Π, is a square matrix with one element in each row and each column equal to 1 and the rest of the elements equal to 0. Thus the elements in every row and every column sum to one. We eliminate the special case when a permutation matrix is an 'identity matrix' with the diagonal elements equal to 1 and the rest equal to 0. What does a permutation matrix do? If any matrix Y is pre-multiplied by a permutation matrix, then the rows of matrix Y are shuffled without their elements being altered. Similarly, if any matrix Y is post-multiplied by a permutation matrix, then the columns of Y are shuffled without their elements being altered.

Example of Permutation Matrix: Let $Y = \begin{bmatrix} 6 & 4 & 2 \\ 8 & 6 & 4 \end{bmatrix}$. Consider $\Pi = \begin{bmatrix} 0 & 1 \\ 1 & 0 \end{bmatrix}$. Then $\Pi Y = \begin{bmatrix} 8 & 6 & 4 \\ 6 & 4 & 2 \end{bmatrix}$. Thus, the rows of Y are merely swapped. Similarly, consider

$\Pi' = \begin{bmatrix} 1 & 0 & 0 \\ 0 & 0 & 1 \\ 0 & 1 & 0 \end{bmatrix}$. Then $Y\Pi' = \begin{bmatrix} 6 & 2 & 4 \\ 8 & 4 & 6 \end{bmatrix}$. Note that the second and the third columns have swapped their positions. The first column did not change its position because the first diagonal element in Π is equal to one.

A diagonal matrix, denoted by Λ, is a square matrix whose diagonal elements are not necessarily equal to 0 but all off-diagonal elements are equal to 0. Let us denote the ij^{th} element of Λ by Λ_{ij}. Then, $\Lambda_{ij} = 0$ for all $i \neq j$. For our purposes, we require the diagonal elements of a diagonal matrix to be strictly positive or $\Lambda_{ii} > 0$. What is the use of a diagonal matrix? If any matrix Y is post-multiplied by a diagonal matrix, then the elements in each column are changed in the same proportion. Note that different columns may be multiplied by different factors.

Example of Diagonal Matrix: Let $Y = \begin{bmatrix} 6 & 4 & 2 \\ 8 & 6 & 4 \end{bmatrix}$. Consider $\Lambda = \begin{bmatrix} 0.5 & 0 & 0 \\ 0 & 1 & 0 \\ 0 & 0 & 2 \end{bmatrix}$. Then $Y\Lambda = \begin{bmatrix} 3 & 4 & 4 \\ 4 & 6 & 8 \end{bmatrix}$. Each element in the first column has been halved and each element in the third column has been doubled. However, the second column did not change because the corresponding element of Λ is equal to one.

A bistochastic matrix, denoted by B, is a square matrix in which the elements in each row and each column sum to one. If the ij^{th} element of B is denoted by B_{ij}, then $\sum_i B_{ij} = 1$ for all j and $\sum_j B_{ij} = 1$ for all i. Why do we require a bistochastic matrix? If a matrix is pre-multiplied by a bistochastic matrix, then the variability across the elements of each column is reduced while their average or mean is preserved. Note that if a diagonal element in a bistochastic matrix is equal to one, the achievement vector of the corresponding person remains unaffected. If the bistochastic matrix is a permutation matrix or an identity matrix, then the variability remains unchanged.

Example of Bistochastic Matrix: Let $Y = \begin{bmatrix} 6 & 4 & 2 \\ 8 & 6 & 4 \end{bmatrix}$. Consider $B = \begin{bmatrix} 0.5 & 0.5 \\ 0.5 & 0.5 \end{bmatrix}$. Then $BY = \begin{bmatrix} 7 & 5 & 6 \\ 7 & 5 & 6 \end{bmatrix}$. The bistochastic matrix equalizes the achievements across its elements.

2.3 Scales of Measurement: Ordinal and Cardinal Data

An important element of the framework in multidimensional poverty measurement relates to the scales of measurement of the indicators used. Scales of measurement are key because they affect the kind of *meaningful* operations that can be performed with indicators. In fact, as we will observe, certain types of indicators may not allow a number of operations and thus cannot be used to generate certain poverty measures.

What does **scale of measurement** refer to exactly? Following Roberts (1979) and Sarle (1995), we define a scale of measurement to be a particular way of assigning numbers or symbols to assess certain aspects of the empirical world, such that the relationships of these numbers or symbols replicate or represent certain observed relations between the aspects being measured. There are different classifications of scales of measurement. In this book, we follow the classification introduced by Stevens (1946) and discussed in Roberts (1979). Stevens' classification is consistent with Sen (1970, 1973), which analysed the implications of scales of measurement for welfare economics, distributional analysis, and poverty measurement, and it has largely stood the test of time.[29]

Stevens' (1946) classification relies on four key concepts: assignment rules, admissible transformations, permissible statistics, and meaningful statements. First, the defining feature of a scale is the **rule** or basic empirical operation that is followed for assigning numerals, as elaborated below. Second, each scale has an associated set of **admissible mathematical transformations** such that the scale is preserved. That is, if a scale is obtained from another under an admissible transformation, the rule under the transformed scale is the same as under the original one. Third, a **permissible statistic** refers to a statistical operation that when applied to a scale, produces the same result as when it is applied to the (admissibly) transformed scale. While the word 'permissible' may sound rather strong, it is justifiable under the premise that 'one should only make assertions that are invariant under admissible transformations of scale' (Marcus-Roberts and Roberts 1987: 384).[30] Fourth, a statement is called **meaningful** if it remains unchanged when all scales in the statement are transformed by admissible transformations (Marcus-Roberts and Roberts 1987: 384).[31]

Stevens (1946) considered four basic empirical operations or rules that define four types of scales: equality, rank order, equality of intervals, and equality of ratios. Following them, he defined four main types of scales: nominal, ordinal, interval, and ratio. Stevens' classification is not exhaustive. For example, it only applies to scales that take real values and which are regular.[32] Also, note that alternative terms are sometimes used for some of Stevens' types. For example, nominal scales are sometimes referred to as categorical scales.

Table 2.3 lists the scale types mentioned above from 'weakest' to 'strongest' in the sense that interval and ratio scales contain much more information than ordinal or nominal scales. The column that presents the rule defining each scale type is cumulative in the sense that a rule listed for a particular scale must be applicable to the scales in rows preceding it. The column that lists the permissible statistics is also cumulative in the

---

[29] Stevens' work belongs to a branch of applied mathematics called measurement theory, which is useful in measurement and data analysis.

[30] 'The criterion for the appropriateness of a statistic is invariance under the [admissible] transformations' (Stevens 1946: 678).

[31] The notion of meaningfulness is alluded to in Stevens (1946) and used in Roberts (1979).

[32] An irregular scale does not always generate an acceptable scale from an admissible transformation (see Roberts and Franke 1976, cited in Marcus-Roberts and Roberts 1987: 384).

Table 2.3 Stevens' classification of scales of measurement

Type of variable (scales)		Rule for creating the scale	Admissible transformations	Admissible mathematical operations	Admissible statistics	Particular cases	Examples relevant for poverty measurement
Qualitative	Nominal or categorical	Determination of equality	Permutation group* $x'_{ij} = f(x_{ij})$ where f is any one-to-one substitution	None	Frequency distribution, mode, contingency correlation		Gender, caste, civil status, ethnicity
	Ordinal	Determination of greater or less	Isotonic group** $x'_{ij} = f(x_{ij})$ where f is any monotonic increasing function	None	Median percentiles	Ordered categorical or weak ordinal	Type of source of drinking water, sanitation facility, cooking fuel, floor. Levels of schooling
Quantitative or cardinal	Interval scale	Determination of equality of intervals or differences	General linear group*** $x'_{ij} = ax_{ij} + b$, with $a > 0$	Add, subtract	Mean, standard deviation, rank-order correlation, product-moment correlation.	Dichotomous variables	z-scores of nutritional indicators (ex. weight for age) Body Mass Index
	Ratio scale	Determination of equality of ratios	Similarity group**** $x'_{ij} = ax_{ij}$, with $a > 0$	Divide, multiply	Coefficient of variation	Count variables, Dichotomous variables	Income, consumption expenditure, number of deaths a mother experienced, years of schooling,‡ numbers of Jersey milk cows owned

Source: Stevens (1946). The columns on 'Particular cases' and 'Examples' have been added by the authors.
* A permutation group here refers to the composition of permutations that can be performed with elements of a group.
** An isotonic group here refers to the set of transformations which preserve order.
*** A general linear group here refers to the set of linear transformations (with the specifications stated above).
**** A similarity group here refers to the set of ratio transformations (with the specifications stated above).
‡ Note that years of schooling may also be interpreted in an ordinal sense, depending on the meaning attached.

same sense. In contrast, the column that lists the admissible transformations goes from general to particular: the particular operation listed in a row is included in the operation listed above.

We now introduce each scale 'type'. The scale pertains to an indicator used to measure dimension j. The term 'indicator j' denotes the indicator of dimension j. Achievements in indicator j across the population are represented by vector $x_{ij} \in \mathbb{R}^n_+$, where x_{ij} is the achievement of person i in the jth indicator.

Indicator j is said to be **nominal** or **categorical** if the scale is based on mutually exclusive categories, which are not necessarily ordered. Nominal variables are frequently called **categorical** variables. The rule or basic empirical operation behind this type of scale is the determination of equality among observations. A nominal scale is 'the most unrestricted assignment of numerals. The numerals are used only as labels or type numbers, and words or letters would serve as well' (Stevens 1946: 678). That is, numbers assigned to the various achievement levels in this domain are simply placeholders.

Stevens introduces two common types of nominal variables. One uses 'numbering' for identification, such as the identification number of each household in a survey or the line number of individuals living within a household. The other uses numbering for a classification, such that all members of a social group (ethnic, caste, religion, gender, or age) or geographical region (rural/urban areas, states, or provinces) are assigned the same number. The first type of nominal variable is simply a particular case of the second. There is a wide range of admissible transformations for this type of scale. In fact, any transformation that substitutes or permutes values between groups, that is, any one-to-one substitution function f such that $x'_{ij} = f(x_{ij})$ for all i, will leave the scale form invariant.

Given that in a nominal variable the different categories do not have an order, neither arithmetic operations nor logical operations (aside from equality) are applicable. In terms of relevant statistics, if the nominal variable is simply an identifier, then only the number of categories is a relevant statistic; if the nominal variable contains several cases in each category, then the mode and contingency methods can be implemented, as can hypotheses tests regarding the distribution of cases among the classes (Stevens 1946: 678–9).

Indicator j is said to be **ordinal** if the order matters but not the differences between values. The rule or basic empirical operation behind this type of scale is the determination of a rank order. Categories can be ordered in terms of 'greater', 'less', or 'equal' (or 'better', 'worse', 'preferred', 'not preferred'). Admissible transformations consist of any order-preserving transformation, that is, any strictly monotonic increasing function f such that $x'_{ij} = f(x_{ij})$ for all i, as these will leave the scale form invariant. Thus, admissible transformations include logarithmic operation, square root of the values (non-negative), linear transformations, and adding a constant or multiplying by another (positive) constant. Examples of ordinal scales are preference orderings over various categories, or subjective rankings. Given that the true intervals between the scale points are unknown, arithmetic operations are meaningless (because results will change with a change of scale), but logical operations are possible. For example, we can assert that someone reporting a health level of four feels 'better' than someone reporting a health level of 'three', who in turn feels better than a 'two', but we cannot assert whether the difference between level three and four is the same as the difference between level two and three. Nevertheless, some statistics are applicable to ordinal variables, namely, the number of cases, contingency tables, the mode, median, and percentiles.[33] Statistics such as mean and standard deviation cannot be used. Clearly, an ordinal variable is a nominal variable but the converse is not true. Ordinal and nominal (or categorical) variables are also sometimes referred to as qualitative variables.

Unordered categorical variables—such as eye colour—are not relevant for the construction of poverty measures. Relevant categorical variables are those that can be exhaustively and non-trivially partitioned into at least two sets according to some exogenous condition, and in which those sets can be arranged in a complete ordering. There will be fewer sets than there are categorical responses, or else the original variable would already have been ordinal. If a set contains multiple elements, it may not be possible to rank those elements against one another. Hence the resulting construction would be a 'semi-order' (Luce 1956) or 'quasi-order' (Sen 1973). Additionally, it may be possible to distinguish set(s) that are considered to be adequate achievements from those that are inadequate, forming a 'weak order' that is, some pairs of responses can be ranked as 'preferred to' and some others cannot be ranked.[34] For example, because it is difficult to assess whether it is better to have access to a public tap than to a borehole or a protected well as sources of drinkable water, the Millennium Development Goal indicator considers all three of them to be adequate sources of drinkable water (unrankable). Similarly, while one cannot rank access to an unprotected spring versus access to rainwater, both sources are considered inadequate by MDG standards. A variable thus constructed is often called an 'ordered categorical'; we might also call the variables obtained as a weak order of categories in a nominal variable, a 'weak-ordinal' variable. Admissible transformations of weak ordinal variables include any transformations that partition the categorical variables into the relevant sets (safe water sources) in the same order; any apparent ordering of elements within the relevant sets can vary freely.

Indicator j is said to be of **interval scale** if the rule or basic empirical operation behind its scale is the determination of the equality of intervals or differences. Importantly, interval scales do not have a predefined zero point. The admissible transformations of interval scale consist of the linear transformation $x'_{ij} = ax_{ij} + b$ (with $a > 0$), as this preserves the differences between categories. While the *difference* between two values of an interval-scale variable is meaningful, the ratios are not. The most cited example in

---

[33] Although Stevens (1946) considers these statistics as 'permissible' with these variables, he warns: 'although percentiles measures may be applied to rank-ordered data …the customary procedure of assigning a value to a percentile by interpolating linearly within a class interval is, in all strictness, wholly out of bounds. Likewise, it is not strictly proper to determine the mid-point of a class interval by linear interpolation, because the linearity of an ordinal scale is precisely the property which is open to question' (Stevens 1946: 679).

[34] Relatedly, Luce (1956) distinguished a weak order from a semi-order over the same set of elements. In a weak order the indifference relation is transitive, but in a semi-order it is not.

this literature refers to two temperature scales: Celsius (°C) and Fahrenheit (°F). While the difference between 15°C and 20°C is the same as the difference between 20°C and 25°C, one cannot say that 20°C is twice as hot as 10°C because 0°C does not mean 'no temperature'. That is, the Celsius scale (and Fahrenheit scale) lack a natural zero. Also, the difference between 15°C and 20°C and between 20°C and 25°C is also precisely the same if measured in Fahrenheit (59°F and 68°F vs 68°F and 77°F) although the value of the difference is nine rather than five degrees. An interval scale allows addition and subtraction and the computation of most statistics, namely, number of cases, mode, contingency correlations, median, percentiles, mean, standard deviation, rank-order correlation, and product-moment correlation, but it is not meaningful to compute the coefficient of variation or any other 'relative' measure.

In multidimensional poverty measurement, one indicator that is usually of interest is the z-score of under 5-year-old children's nutritional achievement. We consider a nutritional z-score to be of interval-scale type. Box 2.3 provides a more detailed explanation of how to compute z-scores. Z-scores range from negative to positive values, spaced in (the reference population's) standard deviation units, and the zero value means that the child's nutritional achievement is at the median of what is considered a healthy population.

Indicator j is said to be of *ratio scale* if the rule or basic empirical operation behind its scale is the determination of equality of ratios. Such a rule requires the scale to have a 'natural zero': namely the value 0 means 'no quantity' of that indicator. In other words, the value 0 is the absolute lowest value of the variable. Admissible transformations of interval-scale variables consist of functions such as $x'_j = ax_j$ (with $a > 0$), as this preserves the ratio differences. Examples of ratio-scale variables are age, height, weight, and temperature in Kelvin, as 0° Kelvin means 'no temperature', 200 pounds is twice as much as 100 pounds, sixty years as thirty years, and so on. Ratio-scale variables allow statements such as 'a value is twice as large as another', and they allow any type of mathematical operation, as well as the computation of any statistic (number of cases, mode, contingency correlations, median, percentiles, mean, standard deviation, rank-order correlation, product-moment correlation, and coefficient of variation). Interval- and ratio-scale variables constitute what are commonly referred to as **cardinal** variables.

It is interesting to observe that in the order presented, from nominal to ratio scales, the admissible transformations become more restricted but the meaningful statistics become more unrestricted, 'suggesting that in some sense the data values carry more information' (Velleman and Wilkinson 1993: 66). Stevens (1959: 24) provided an insightful example of how measurement can progress from weaker to stronger scales. Early humans probably could only distinguish between cold and warm and thus used a nominal scale. Later, degrees of warmer and colder had been introduced and so the use of an ordinal scale gained prominence. The introduction of thermometers led to the use of an interval scale. Finally, the development of thermodynamics led to the ratio scale of temperature by introducing the Kelvin scale.

BOX 2.3 CHILDREN'S NUTRITIONAL Z-SCORES

The nutritional status of children under 5 years old is assessed with three anthropometric indicators: weight-for-age, also called 'underweight'; weight-for-height, also called 'wasting'; and height-for-age, also called 'stunting'. The indicators are constructed as follows. The World Health Organization has measured the height and weight of a reference population of children from different ethnicities, which is considered to constitute a standard of well nourishment (WHO Multicentre Growth Reference Study Group 2006). From that population, a distribution of weights according to each age, a distribution of heights according to each age, and a distribution of height according to each weight are obtained. Each of these is classified by gender.

How is a child's nutrition assessed? Let us consider the case of the weight-for-age (w/a) indicator. Once the weight and age of the child have been documented, this information can be expressed in her weight-for-age z-score. This is computed as the child's observed weight minus the median weight of children of the same sex and age in the reference population, divided by the standard deviation of the reference population. That is

$$zs_{w/a} = \frac{(y_{i,w/a} - \bar{Y}_{w/a})}{\sigma_{w/a}},$$

where $zs_{w/a}$ is the z-score of weight-for-age, $y_{i,w/a}$ is the observed weight of child i, $\bar{Y}_{w/a}$ is the median weight of children of the same sex and age as child i in the reference population (healthy children), and $\sigma_{w/a}$ is the standard deviation of the weight of children of that age in the reference population. The z-scores for weight-for-height (w/h) and height-for-age (h/a) are computed in an analogous way. Thus, $zs_{i,j} = (y_{i,j} - \bar{Y}_j)/\sigma_j$ for all i and all $j = w/a$, w/h, and h/a.

Thus, for example, suppose 14-month-old Anna weighs 8.3 kilograms. The median weight in the reference population of children of that age is 9.4 and the standard deviation is 1.* Thus, the z-score of Anna is -1.1, meaning that Anna is about one standard deviation below the median weight of healthy children.

It is considered that children with z-scores that are more than two standard deviations below the median of the reference population suffer moderate undernutrition, and if their z-score is more than three standard deviations below, they suffer severe undernutrition (underweight, wasting, or stunting, correspondingly). Children with a z-score of weight-for-height above $+2$ standard deviations above the median are considered to be overweight (WHO 1997).

An alternative way to assess the nutritional status of children is to use percentiles rather than z-scores, but z-scores present a number of advantages. Most importantly, they can be used to compute summary statistics such as a mean and standard deviation, which cannot be meaningfully done with percentiles (O'Donnell et al. 2008).

Note that if we take a linear transformation of the z-score for weight-for-age such that $zs'_{i,w/a} = a \times zs_{i,w/a} + b$, where $a = 1/\sigma_{w/a}$ and $b = \bar{Y}_{w/a}/\sigma_{w/a}$, then $zs'_{w/a} = y_{i,w/a}$. Note that the difference $y_{i,w/a} - y_{i',w/a}$ (or $zs'_{i,w/a} - zs'_{i',w/a}$) has the same implication as the difference $zs_{i,w/a} - zs_{i',w/a}$. This equivalence would hold for any linear transformation, exhibiting the characteristics of an interval-scale indicator.

* These values were taken from WHO's reference tables: http://www.who.int/childgrowth/standards/sft_wfa_girls_z_0_5.pdf

---

Having introduced the scales of measurement, it is worth making a few clarifications regarding other frequently mentioned types of indicators. First, Stevens' classification makes no reference to **continuous** versus **discrete** variables, for example. Continuous variables can take any value on the real line within a range. Discrete variables, in contrast, can only take a finite or countably infinite number of values.[35] Ordinal variables are discrete variables, but cardinal ones (interval and ratio scale) can be either discrete or continuous.[36] Second, note that **count** variables such as counts of publications, number of children in a household, or number of chickens, are particular cases of ratio-scale variables (Stevens 1946), such that the only admissible transformation is the identity function, i.e. $a = 1$. Roberts (1979) refers to the counting scale type as an **absolute scale.**

Third, **dichotomous** (also called binary) variables can be of different scales, depending on the meaning of their categories. When the two values simply refer to unordered, mutually exclusive categories, such as being male or female, the variable is of nominal scale. When there is an order between the categories, such as being deprived or not in a specific dimension, the variable is **cardinal**. If the two values refer to having or lacking the same thing, such as a fully functional method for wood smoke ventilation, the variable may be interpreted as of **ratio scale**.[37]

Fourth, the reader may wonder where do **Likert scales**—introduced by Likert (1932) and often used in social sciences—fit? Likert scales are obtained from responses to a set of (carefully phrased) statements to which each respondent expresses her level of agreement on a scale such as one to five: strongly disagree, disagree, neutral, agree, or strongly agree. Each statement and its responses are known as a Likert item. A Likert scale is obtained by summing or averaging the responses to each item so that a score is acquired for each person. Likert scales are frequently treated as interval scales, under the assumption (at times empirically verified) that there is an equal distance between categories (Brown 2011; Norman 2010). Thus, descriptive statistics (like means and standard deviations) and inferential statistics (like correlation coefficients, factor analysis, and analysis of variance) are regularly implemented with Likert scales. However, this has been criticized as being 'illegitimate to infer that the intensity of feeling between "strongly disagree" and "disagree" is equivalent to the intensity of feeling between other consecutive categories on the Likert scale' (Cohen et al. 2000, cited in Jamieson 2004: 1217). Thus, there is ongoing disagreement about whether Likert scales should be treated as ordinal scales (Pett 1997; Hansen 2003; Jamieson 2004). Often empirical psychometric tests are performed to 'verify' whether the assumption that the scale can be treated as cardinal holds for a particular dataset.

Stevens' (1946) landmark work sparked a body of literature on measurement theory, which raised strong warnings regarding the applicability of statistics to different scales, including Stevens (1951, 1959), Luce (1959), and Andrews et al. (1981). This engendered

---

[35] Countably infinite means that the values of the discrete variable have one-to-one correspondence with the natural numbers.

[36] Note that other authors equate the distinction between qualitative/ordinal vs quantitative/cardinal with the distinction between discrete vs continuous variables (e.g. Bossert, Chakravarty, and D'Ambrosio 2013). In our definitions, cardinal variables can be either continuous or discrete, so the two pairs are not equivalent.

[37] Dichotomous variables can also be obtained from nominal ones. For example, given a nominal variable on age intervals, a dummy variable can be created for each age interval ('belongs' or 'does not belong' to that particular age range). More commonly, one can dichotomize variables with categorical responses into deprived and non-deprived states; for example, classifying 'sources of water' into two exhaustive groups reflecting 'safe' and 'unsafe' water.

an extensive and ongoing debate across literatures from psychology to statistics. Some social scientists and statisticians consider that although, in theory, certain statistics such as the mean and standard deviations are inappropriate for ordinal data, they can still be 'fruitfully' applied if the problem in question and data structure (and comparability, if relevant) have been tested and seem to warrant assumptions that they can be treated as interval scale. The arguments in favour of this position are interestingly articulated by Velleman and Wilkinson (1993). For example, it is stated that 'the meaningfulness of a statistical analysis depends on the questions it is designed to answer' (Lord 1953; Guttman 1977), that in the end 'every knowledge is based on some approximation' (Tukey 1961), and that '…if science was restricted to probably meaningful statements it could not proceed' (Velleman and Wilkinson 1993). Another argument is that parametric methods are highly robust to violation of assumptions and thus can be implemented with ordinal data (Norman 2010). Although we acknowledge this ongoing debate, in what follows we do endorse the requirement of **meaningfulness**—as defined above—in order to compute statistics or mathematical measures in each scale type; hence, we limit the operations with ordinal data to those that cohere with its definition and point out deviations from this.

As this section suggests, the indicators' scale and the analysts' considered response to scales of measurement must be articulated before selecting a methodology to measure and assess multidimensional poverty. In Chapter 3, we clarify whether each method surveyed can be used with ordinal data. In general, when an indicator is of ratio scale, such as income, consumption, or expenditure (all expressed in monetary units), arithmetic operations with elements of the scale are permissible. Thus, it is meaningful to compute the normalized deprivation gaps as defined in Expression (2.2). When all considered indicators are of ratio scale, multidimensional poverty measures based on normalized deprivation gaps can be used. If the indicator is of interval scale, gaps may be redefined appropriately. When indicators are ordinal, measures based on normalized deprivation gaps are meaningless because results would vary under different admissible transformations of the indicators' scales. The Adjusted Headcount Ratio presented in Chapters 5–10 can be meaningfully implemented using ordinal indicators, provided that issues of comparability are addressed, as we will now clarify.

2.4 **Comparability across People and Dimensions**

The last section established the scales of measurement by which we can rigorously compare achievement levels in one variable, and the mathematical and statistical operations that can be performed on that variable. The discussion enabled us to identify the scale of measurement of each single indicator. Yet multidimensional measures seek to compare people's achievements or deprivations *across* indicators, in ways that respect the scale of measurement of each indicator. This is by no means elementary. As Sen (1970) pointed out, cardinally meaningful variables may not necessarily be cardinally comparable—across people or, in multidimensional measurement, across dimensions. This section scrutinizes how these comparisons can legitimately proceed. That is, it takes a step back from the material presented thus far to make explicit assumptions that have usually been implicit in work on multidimensional poverty measurement.

The issue of comparability across dimensions raised in this section has potentially significant empirical implications for quantitative methods beyond measurement. For example, as Chapter 3 will show, dichotomous data are regularly used in techniques that implicitly attribute cardinal meaning *and* comparability to the 0–1 deprivation status from several dimensions. If the values associated with deprivation statuses differ, results based on techniques that treat each 0–1 variable as cardinally equivalent may be affected, because they implicitly impose equal weights. Such exercises should, strictly, employ the $0-w_j$ variables because it is their relative weights or deprivation values (w_j for all $j = 1, \ldots, d$) that create cardinal comparability across dimensions. Hence the issues raised in this section, in a preliminary and intuitive way at this stage, have far-reaching implications for multidimensional analyses.

The properties we will present in section 2.5 define certain characteristics that a poverty measure may fulfill. Underlying many properties is an assumption that the poverty measure itself is cardinally meaningful. Based on this assumption, a change in the underlying $n \times d$ achievement matrix will change the poverty measure in desired and predictable ways according to the properties. In order to generate a cardinally meaningful multidimensional poverty index, it is necessary to treat indicators correctly according to their scale of measurement, as we have seen already. But it is also necessary to compare and aggregate a set of indicators (i) across people and (ii) across dimensions. Neither of these steps is trivial.[38]

It must be recalled that variables used to construct unidimensional poverty measures, as defined in section 2.1, already entail comparisons across themselves as component dimensions and across people and households. In terms of interpersonal comparisons, the same household income level is normally assumed to be associated with the same level of individual welfare or poverty.[39] Components of such measures (sources of income, or consumption/expenditure on different goods) are usually assumed to be additive as cardinal variables having a common unit (usually, a currency like pounds or rupees), hence prices (adjusted where necessary) are used as weights. Equivalence scales may be used to augment comparability across households.

Multidimensional poverty measures, like income poverty measures, entail a basic assumption that the indicators are interpersonally comparable. Additionally, counting-based measures further assume that the same deprivation score is associated with the same level of poverty for different people. This assumption implies that deprivations have been made comparable. Comparability across dimensions must be obtained in order to generate cardinally meaningful deprivation scores and associated

[38] There is a very large literature on interpersonal comparisons and partial comparisons, stemming from Sen (1970). Basu (1980) raises comparability across dimensions in the context of government preferences and helpfully distinguishes comparability and measurability (ch. 6, 74–5).

[39] Sen (1980, 1985, 1992, 1997) has powerfully observed how the same level of resources may in fact be associated with different levels of well-being because of differences in people's ability to convert resources into well-being.

multidimensional poverty measures. But how? Multidimensional poverty measures may contain fundamentally distinct components that are not measured in the same units and may have no natural means of conversion into a common variable.

Empirically, the mechanics by which apparent comparability has been created in counting-based measures are clear (Chapter 4). When data are dichotomous and interpersonally comparable, the application of *deprivation values* is understood to create cardinal comparability across dimensions. When data are ordinal or ordered categorical, deprivation cutoffs are used to dichotomize the data; and those cutoffs, together with *deprivation values*, establish cardinal comparability across deprivations. In the case of appropriately scaled cardinal data, comparability across deprivations is created by the *weights* and the *deprivation cutoffs*.

Let us start with the most straightforward case: the deprivation matrix. This presents dichotomous values either because the original indicator is dichotomous (access to electricity), or because a cardinal, ordinal, or ordered categorical variable has been dichotomized by the application of a deprivation cutoff into two categories: deprived and non-deprived.

As mentioned above, we can consider dichotomous deprivations to be (trivially) cardinal.[40] More precisely, the deprivation cutoff establishes a 'natural zero' in the sense that any person whose achievement meets or exceeds the natural zero is non-deprived, and anyone who does not, is deprived. We require the natural zeros to be comparable states across dimensions for the purposes of poverty measurement. But how are the 'one' values, reflecting deprived states, comparable? The vector of relative weights create an explicit *deprivation value* for each of the deprived states across the set of possible finite dimensional comparisons. After the deprivation values have been applied, deprivations may be cardinally compared across dimensions.

The reason we draw the reader's attention at this stage to the assumptions underlying cardinal comparisons across people and across dimensions is in order that they might observe how differently multidimensional poverty measurement techniques, such as those surveyed in Chapter 3, undertake and justify such comparisons, and also so that some readers might be encouraged to explore these important issues further—both theoretically and empirically.

2.5 **Properties for Multidimensional Poverty Measures**

In selecting one poverty measurement methodology from a set of options, a policymaker thinks through how a poverty measure should behave in different situations in order to

---

[40] Earlier we defined a cardinal variable to be interval-scale type if the rule or basic empirical operation behind its scale is the determination of equality of intervals or differences. Consider a variable having exactly two points, neither of which is a natural zero. In this case, they can be understood to be equally spaced along any scale, hence trivially satisfy this definition. If either of the points occurs at a natural zero then the dichotomous variable is 'trivially ratio scale'.

be a 'good' measure of poverty and support policy goals. Then she asks which measure meets these requirements. For example, should the poverty measure increase or decrease if the achievement of a poor person rises while the achievements of other people remain unchanged? Should poverty comparisons change when achievements are expressed in different units of measurement? Should the measure of poverty in a more populous country with a larger number of poor people be higher than the poverty measure in a small country with a smaller number of, but proportionally more, poor people?

A policymaker seeking to ameliorate poverty should have a good understanding of the various normative principles that her chosen poverty measure embodies, just as a pilot of a plane must have a sound understanding of how a particular plane responds to different operations. If the policymaker has a good understanding of the principles embodied by alternative measures then she will be able to choose the measure most closely reflecting publicly desirable ethical principles and most appropriate for the application—just as a pilot will choose the best way to fly the plane for a particular journey.

The normative judgements embodied by a poverty measure are reflected in its mathematical properties, including its structure and its response to changes in its argument. The axiomatic method, formally introduced to this field by Sen (1976),[41] refers to measures that have been designed based on principles that are taken by the researcher as **axioms**, i.e. as statements that are accepted as true without proof.[42] In this section, we define and discuss the various properties proposed in the literature on multidimensional poverty measures. A consensus may emerge around some properties, thus they may be considered as axioms, while others may remain optional. In what follows, we use the words 'principles' and 'properties' interchangeably.

The set of properties for multidimensional measurement has been built upon its unidimensional counterpart. However, as noted by Alkire and Foster (2011a), there is one vitally important difference: in the multidimensional context, the identification step is no longer elementary and properties must be viewed as restrictions on the overall poverty methodology $M = (\rho, P)$, that is, as **joint restrictions** on the identification and the aggregation method. For simplicity, in what follows, we state the properties

---

[41] Watts (1968) offered an early intuitive (non-formal) justification for selecting the functional form of a poverty measure according to the properties it should satisfy.

[42] Within the poverty measurement literatures, there are essentially two procedures for constructing measures in the axiomatic framework. In the first, known as **characterization**, a number of principles that are considered desirable are introduced and then the *entire* class of measures (one or many) that embody these principles is determined. This procedure entails a sufficiency condition, which shows that the measure satisfies these principles, and, simultaneously, a necessity condition, which shows that this is the *only* measure (or the family of measures) that satisfies the set of desirable principles. Studies that follow this procedure include Sen (1976), Tsui (2002), Chakravarty, Mukherjee, and Ranade (1998), Bossert, Chakravarty, and D'Ambrosio (2013), Chakravarty and Silber (2008), Bossert, Chakravarty, and D'Ambrosio (2013), Hoy and Zheng (2011), and Porter and Quinn (2013). Second, studies may introduce a number of properties that are considered desirable and then propose a measure or family of measures satisfying these properties, without claiming it to be the only measure or family of measures to do so. Studies following this procedure include Bourguignon and Chakravarty (2003), Calvo and Dercon (2009), Foster (2009), Alkire and Foster (2011a), and Foster and Santos (2013).

in terms of the poverty index $P(X;z)$, which entails two assumptions. First, that any multidimensional poverty index is associated with an identification function. Second, that the identification function relies on a functional form of the type $\rho\,(x_{i\cdot};z)$.[43]

We classify the properties into four categories.[44] The first set of properties requires that a poverty measure should not change under certain transformations of the achievement matrix. We refer to these as **invariance properties**, which are **symmetry**, **replication invariance**, **scale invariance** and two alternative focus properties, **poverty focus** and **deprivation focus**. The second set requires poverty to either increase or decrease with certain changes in the achievement matrix. We refer to these as **dominance properties**, which are **monotonicity**, **transfer**, **rearrangement**, and **dimensional transfer** properties. The third set of principles relates overall poverty to either groups of people or groups of dimensions and thus is called **subgroup properties**. Other properties that guarantee that the measure behaves within certain usual, convenient parameters, we refer to as **technical properties**. Each of the four following sections provides a formal outline and intuitive interpretations of each set of properties.

2.5.1 INVARIANCE PROPERTIES

The first invariance principle is **symmetry**. Symmetry requires that each person in a society is treated anonymously so that only deprivations matter and not the identity of the person who is deprived. Hence this property is also often referred to as **anonymity**. As long as the deprivation profile of the entire society remains unchanged, swapping achievement vectors across people should not change overall poverty.[45] This type of rearrangement can be obtained by pre-multiplying the achievement matrix by a permutation matrix of appropriate order.

Symmetry: If an achievement matrix X' is obtained from achievement matrix X as $X' = \Pi X$, where Π is a permutation matrix of appropriate order, then $P(X';z) = P(X;z)$.

---

[43] Other possible identification methods may violate some of the properties stated in this section. Future research may develop a set of properties for the identification function in the multidimensional context.

[44] This classification follows Foster (2006).

[45] The principle of anonymity should not be misunderstood as making poverty measurement blind to subgroup inequalities or identities. Often disadvantaged groups are discriminated against because of their religion, ethnicity, gender, age, or some other characteristic. In such cases, two people, one from the disadvantaged group and the other from a non-disadvantaged group, may have exactly the same deprivation profile in the d considered dimensions. Yet one person from the disadvantaged group may experience an *effectively* higher deprivation than another. Such situations can be addressed in different ways. One way is analysing poverty by subgroup (this is where the subgroup consistency and decomposability properties addressed below become useful). Another is to incorporate another dimension that reflects the disadvantage of this group such that the deprivation profiles of the two people are no longer equal.

Example: Suppose the initial achievement matrix is $X = \begin{bmatrix} 4 & 4 & 2 \\ 3 & 5 & 4 \\ 8 & 6 & 4 \end{bmatrix}$ and the permutation

matrix is $\Pi = \begin{bmatrix} 0 & 1 & 0 \\ 1 & 0 & 0 \\ 0 & 0 & 1 \end{bmatrix}$. Then $X' = \Pi X = \begin{bmatrix} 0 & 1 & 0 \\ 1 & 0 & 0 \\ 0 & 0 & 1 \end{bmatrix} \begin{bmatrix} 4 & 4 & 2 \\ 3 & 5 & 4 \\ 8 & 6 & 4 \end{bmatrix} = \begin{bmatrix} 3 & 5 & 4 \\ 4 & 4 & 2 \\ 8 & 6 & 4 \end{bmatrix}$. Note

that the first and the second person (rows) in matrix X have swapped their positions. However, as long as the deprivation cutoffs remain unchanged, there is no reason for the level of poverty to be different for these two societies. Hence, $P(X';z) = P(X;z)$.

The second invariance principle, **replication invariance**, requires that if the population of a society is replicated or cloned with the same achievement vectors a finite number of times, then poverty should not change.[46] In other words, the replication invariance property requires the level of poverty in a society to be standardized by its population size so that societies with different population sizes are comparable to each other, as are societies whose populations change over time. Thus, this property is also known as the **principle of population**.[47]

Replication Invariance: If an achievement matrix X' is obtained from another achievement matrix X by replicating X a finite number of times, then $P(X';z) = P(X;z)$.

Example: Suppose we are required to compare the level of poverty in two societies with the

initial achievement matrices $X = \begin{bmatrix} 4 & 4 & 2 \\ 3 & 5 & 4 \\ 8 & 6 & 4 \end{bmatrix}$ and $Y = \begin{bmatrix} 8 & 8 & 8 \\ 9 & 9 & 9 \end{bmatrix}$. Note that the population

sizes in these societies are different. In order to make them comparable, we replicate X twice to obtain

$X' = \begin{bmatrix} 4 & 3 & 8 & 4 & 3 & 8 \\ 4 & 5 & 6 & 4 & 5 & 6 \\ 2 & 4 & 4 & 2 & 4 & 4 \end{bmatrix}^{\text{tr}}$ and Y thrice to obtain $Y' = \begin{bmatrix} 8 & 9 & 8 & 9 & 8 & 9 \\ 8 & 9 & 8 & 9 & 8 & 9 \\ 8 & 9 & 8 & 9 & 8 & 9 \end{bmatrix}^{\text{tr}}$. By replication

invariance, we know that $P(X;z) = P(X';z)$ and $P(Y;z) = P(Y';z)$. Thus, it is equivalent comparing X to Y and X' to Y'.

---

[46] This principle was first suggested by Dalton (1920) in the context of inequality measurement.

[47] In the context of welfare measurement, Foster and Sen (1997) referred to this as the 'symmetry for population'. Chakravarty, Mukherjee, and Ranade (1998), Bourguignon and Chakravarty (2003), and Deutsch and Silber (2005) call it the 'principle of population'. Bossert, Chakravarty, and D'Ambrosio (2013) introduce a separate principle called the 'poverty Wicksell population principle' to compare societies with different population sizes. This property requires that if a person is added to the society with the same level of poverty as the aggregate poverty of the society, overall poverty should not change.

The third invariance principle, **scale invariance**,[48] requires that the evaluation of poverty should not be affected by merely changing the scale of the indicators. For example, if the duration of completed schooling is an indicator, then deprivation in education, thus overall poverty, should be the same regardless of whether duration is measured in years or in months, provided the deprivation cutoff is correspondingly adjusted.

The scale of any indicator in an achievement matrix can be altered by post-multiplying the achievement matrix by a diagonal matrix Λ of appropriate order (d, the number of dimensions). If a diagonal element is equal to one, then the scale of the respective indicator does not change. The diagonal elements of Λ need not be the same because different indicators may have different scales and units of measurement. A weaker version of the scale invariance principle, referred to as 'unit consistency', has been proposed by Zheng (2007) in the context of unidimensional poverty measurement and extended to the multidimensional context by Chakravarty and D'Ambrosio (2013). This principle requires that poverty comparisons, but not necessarily poverty values, should not change if the scales of the dimensions are altered.[49] The scale invariance property implies the unit consistency property, but the converse does not hold.

Scale Invariance: If an achievement matrix X' is obtained by post-multiplying the achievement matrix X by a diagonal matrix Λ such that $X' = X\Lambda$, and the deprivation cutoff vector z' is obtained from z such that $z' = z\Lambda$, then $P(X';z') = P(X;z)$.

Unit Consistency: For two achievement matrices X and X'' and two deprivation cutoff vectors z and z'', if $P(X'';z'') < P(X;z)$, then $P(X''\Lambda;z''\Lambda) < P(X\Lambda;z\Lambda)$.

Example: Suppose the initial achievement matrix is $X = \begin{bmatrix} 4 & 4 & 2 \\ 3 & 5 & 4 \\ 8 & 6 & 4 \end{bmatrix}$ and the deprivation cutoff vector is $z = [5, 6, 4]$. Matrix X is post-multiplied by the diagonal matrix $\Lambda = \begin{bmatrix} 1 & 0 & 0 \\ 0 & 12 & 0 \\ 0 & 0 & 2.2 \end{bmatrix}$ to obtain $X' = X\Lambda = \begin{bmatrix} 4 & 4 & 2 \\ 3 & 5 & 4 \\ 8 & 6 & 4 \end{bmatrix} \begin{bmatrix} 1 & 0 & 0 \\ 0 & 12 & 0 \\ 0 & 0 & 2.2 \end{bmatrix} = \begin{bmatrix} 4 & 48 & 4.4 \\ 3 & 60 & 8.8 \\ 8 & 72 & 8.8 \end{bmatrix}$.

---

[48] Most of the studies, such as Chakravarty, Mukherjee, and Ranade (1998), Bourguignon and Chakravarty (2003), and Deutsch and Silber (2005), have used the term 'scale invariance', whereas Tsui (2002) uses the term 'ratio-scale invariance'.

[49] Both the scale invariance and the unit consistency principles refer to cases in which achievements are changed in a certain proportion (which may differ or not across achievements). A different principle known as 'translation invariance', popularized by Kolm (1976a,b), requires the poverty level to remain the same if each achievement and its corresponding deprivation cutoff are changed by adding the same constant for every person (although the constant added can differ across dimensions). Technically, if an achievement matrix X' is obtained from another achievement matrix X so that $X' = X + \Gamma$, where $\Gamma \in \mathbb{R}_+^{n \times d}$ and $\Gamma_{i \cdot} = \Gamma_{i' \cdot}$ for all $i \neq i'$, and $z' = z + \Gamma_{i \cdot}$, then $P(X';z') = P(X;z)$.

Similarly, vector z is post-multiplied by Λ to obtain $z' = [5, 72, 8.8]$. Note that the first indicator and its deprivation cutoff did not change at all because the first diagonal element in Λ is 1. The second diagonal element in Λ is 12, as in 1 year $= 12$ months, and the third diagonal element in Λ is 2.2, as in 1 kilogram $= 2.2$ pounds. Scale invariance requires that this transformation does not change overall poverty. Hence, $P(X'; z') = P(X; z)$.

Now suppose that there exists a hypothetical achievement matrix X'' such that $P(X''; z) < P(X; z)$. Then, the unit consistency property requires that the comparison does not change if both matrices and the vector z of deprivation cutoffs are multiplied by a diagonal matrix. Hence, $P(X'' \Lambda; z'' \Lambda) < P(X \Lambda; z \Lambda)$.

The fourth invariance principle is **focus**. The primary difference between the measurement of welfare and inequality and the measurement of poverty is that the latter is concerned with the base or bottom of the distribution whereas welfare and inequality are concerned with the entire distribution. The focus principle is crucial because it requires the poverty measure to respond only to the achievements of the poor. The **poverty focus** principle requires that poverty should not change if there is an improvement in any achievement of a non-poor person. This principle is a natural extension of the focus principle in the single dimensional context, which requires that overall poverty remains unchanged with an increase in the income of the non-poor.

Poverty Focus: If an achievement matrix X' is obtained from another achievement matrix X such that $x'_{ij} > x_{ij}$ for some pair $(i, j) = (i', j')$ where $i' \notin Z$, and $x'_{ij} = x_{ij}$ for every other pair $(i, j) \neq (i', j')$, then $P(X'; z) = P(X; z)$.

However, in the multidimensional framework, the terms 'deprived' and 'poor' are not synonymous. Someone can be poor yet not deprived in every single indicator. The poverty focus principle does not cover the situation where a poor person's achievement increases in a dimension in which that person is not deprived. If poverty were to change in this case, the non-deprived attainments would compensate deprived attainments, creating a form of substitutability across dimensions. Practically, this could encourage a policymaker who is enthusiastically interested in reducing the poverty figures to assist the poor in their non-deprived dimensions, instead of addressing the dimensions in which they are deprived. Thus, a second focus principle might be relevant. The **deprivation focus** principle requires that overall poverty not change if there is an increase in achievement in a non-deprived dimension, regardless of whether it belongs to a poor or a non-poor person. This property prevents poverty from falling when a poor person's achievements increase in non-deprived dimensions. Note that focus properties motivate the construction of a censored achievement matrix $\tilde{X}$, as described in section 2.2.1.[50]

---

[50] Bourguignon and Chakravarty (2003) refer to the deprivation focus as 'strong focus' and the poverty focus as 'weak focus'. Chakravarty, Mukherjee, and Ranade (1998) and Tsui (2002) only used the deprivation focus and did not consider the poverty focus.

Deprivation Focus: If an achievement matrix X' is obtained from another achievement matrix X such that $x'_{ij} > x_{ij}$ for some pair $(i,j) = (i',j')$ where $x_{ij} \geq z_{j'}$ (whether or not i' happens to be poor), and $x'_{ij} = x_{ij}$ for every other pair $(i,j) \neq (i',j')$, then $P(X';z) = P(X;z)$.

Example: Suppose the initial achievement matrix is $X = \begin{bmatrix} 4 & 4 & 2 \\ 3 & 5 & 4 \\ 8 & 6 & 4 \end{bmatrix}$ and the deprivation cutoff vector is $z = [5,6,4]$. Clearly, the third person is not deprived in any dimension, thus cannot be considered poor. If matrix X' is obtained from X such that $X' = \begin{bmatrix} 4 & 4 & 2 \\ 3 & 5 & 4 \\ 8 & 6 & 5 \end{bmatrix}$, then by poverty focus, $P(X';z) = P(X;z)$. The second person is deprived in two out of three dimensions. If the second person is considered poor and X'' is obtained from X by increasing the person's achievement in the non-deprived dimension (third dimension) such that $X'' = \begin{bmatrix} 4 & 4 & 2 \\ 3 & 5 & 5 \\ 8 & 6 & 4 \end{bmatrix}$, then by the deprivation focus principle, $P(X'';z) = P(X;z)$.

The focus principle is one example in which it can be verified that the properties of multidimensional poverty measures are, as stated at the beginning of this section, joint restrictions on the identification and the aggregation methods. For example, for the deprivation focus principle to be satisfied, the identification method cannot follow the aggregate achievement approach. Also, as Alkire and Foster note (2011a: 481), the relevance of the two focus principles is connected to the criterion used to identify the poor (within a counting approach to identification). When a union criterion is used to identify the poor, the deprivation focus principle implies the poverty focus principle, whereas when an intersection criterion is used to identify the poor, the poverty focus principle implies the deprivation focus principle. When intermediate criterions are used, neither of the two principles implies the other.

The last invariance property '**ordinality**' relates to the type of scale of the particular indicator used for measuring each dimension. As we explained in section 2.3, the scale of an indicator affects the type of operations and statistics that can be meaningfully applied, in the sense that statements remain unchanged when all scales in the statement are transformed by admissible transformations. Building on this notion of meaningfulness, ordinality requires the poverty estimate not to change under admissible transformations of the scales of the indicators that compose the poverty measure.[51]

More formally, we say that $(X';z')$ is obtained from $(X;z)$ as an *equivalent representation* if there exist appropriate admissible transformations $f_j : R_+ \to R_+$ for $j = 1, \ldots, d$ such that $x'_{ij} = f_j(x_{ij})$ and $z'_j = f_j(z_j)$ for all $i = 1, \ldots, n$. In other words, an equivalent representation

---

[51] A nice theorem would be to prove that the only poverty measure invariant to admissible transformations of the nominal or ordinal variables is one based on dichotomous variables.

can comprise a set of admissible transformations, each of which is appropriate for each scale type, and which assigns a different set of numbers to the same underlying basic data. For example, an equivalent representation can include monotonic increasing transformations for ordinal variables, linear transformations for interval-scale variables, and proportional changes for ratio-scale variables. We now state the ordinality axiom as follows:

Ordinality: Suppose that $(X';z')$ is obtained from $(X;z)$ as an equivalent representation, then $P(X';z') = P(X;z)$.

Example: Suppose the initial achievement matrix is $X = \begin{bmatrix} 4,100 & 2 & 0 \\ 3,500 & 3 & 0 \\ 8,200 & 4 & 1 \end{bmatrix}$ and the deprivation cutoff vector is $z = [5,000,4,1]$, where the first dimension is measured with a ratio-scale indicator, say income in dollars; the second dimension is measured with an ordinal-scale indicator, say self-rated health on a scale of one to five; and the third indicator is measured with a dichotomous 0–1 variable, say access to electricity. Suppose that income is now expressed in some other currency Å, such that Å $= \$0.5$ (note that $x'_{ij} = 0.5x_{ij}$ in this case), self-rated health is now expressed with the scale $(1,4,9,16,$ and $25)$ (note that $x'_{ij} = (x_{ij})^2$), and access to electricity is now coded as 1 for no access and 2 for access (i.e. $x_{ij} = x_{ij} + 1$). Thus matrix X' obtained from X is such that $X' = \begin{bmatrix} 2,050 & 4 & 1 \\ 1,750 & 9 & 1 \\ 4,100 & 16 & 2 \end{bmatrix}$, and $z = [2,500,16,2]$, then the ordinality property requires that $P(X';z') = (X;z)$.

2.5.2 DOMINANCE PROPERTIES

This section covers six principles, each of which has a stronger version and a weaker version. The stronger version requires that a poverty measure strictly moves in a particular direction, given certain transformations in the achievements of the poor. The weaker version does not *require* a poverty measure to move in a particular direction but ensures that the poverty measure does not move in the opposite (wrong) direction under certain transformations of the achievements.[52] The first dominance principle, **monotonicity**, requires that if the achievement of a poor person in a deprived dimension increases while other achievements remain unchanged, then overall poverty should decrease. Normatively, this principle considers that improvements in deprived

---

[52] In the unidimensional case, Chakravarty (1983a) defined the weak version of the transfer principle differently (as requiring poverty to change in a particular dimension under the relevant transformation of the achievement but such that the number of poor people did not change). In this book the weak version of a principle differs from the strong one in stating a weak inequality as opposed to a strict one.

achievements of the poor are good and should be reflected by producing a reduction in poverty. Its weaker version, referred to as weak monotonicity, ensures that poverty should not increase if there is an increase in any person's achievement in the society.[53]

Monotonicity: If an achievement matrix X' is obtained from another achievement matrix X such that $x_{ij} < \min\{x'_{ij}, z_j\}$ for some pair $(i,j) = (i',j')$ where $i' \in Z$, and $x'_{ij} = x_{ij}$ for every other pair $(i,j) \neq (i',j')$, then $P(X';z) < P(X;z)$.

Weak Monotonicity: If an achievement matrix X' is obtained from another achievement matrix X such that $x'_{ij} > x_{ij}$ for some pair $(i,j) = (i',j')$ and $x'_{ij} = x_{ij}$ for every other pair $(i,j) \neq (i',j')$, then $P(X';z) \leq P(X;z)$.

Example: Suppose the initial achievement matrix is $X = \begin{bmatrix} 4 & 4 & 2 \\ 3 & 5 & 4 \\ 8 & 6 & 4 \end{bmatrix}$ and the deprivation cutoff vector is $z = [5,6,4]$. Clearly, the first person is deprived in all three dimensions and is considered poor. If matrix X' is obtained from X such that $X' = \begin{bmatrix} 4 & 4 & 3 \\ 3 & 5 & 4 \\ 8 & 6 & 4 \end{bmatrix}$, then by the monotonicity principle, $P(X';z) < P(X;z)$. On the other hand, weak monotonicity requires that $P(X';z) \leq P(X;z)$; it ensures that poverty does not increase due to the increase in achievement.

The monotonicity and weak monotonicity principles are natural extensions of the analogous concepts in the unidimensional poverty analysis. However, the next principle in this category, referred to as **dimensional monotonicity**, is specific to the multidimensional context. This principle was introduced by Alkire and Foster (2011a). Dimensional monotonicity requires that if a poor person who is not deprived in all dimensions, becomes deprived in an additional dimension then poverty should increase. This principle ensures that we are not only concerned with the number of poor in a society but also with the extent to which the poor are deprived in multiple dimensions—what we call the intensity of their deprivation. A measure that satisfies monotonicity also satisfies dimensional monotonicity.

Dimensional Monotonicity: If an achievement matrix X' is obtained from another achievement matrix X such that $x'_{ij} < z_j \leq x_{ij}$ for some pair $(i,j) = (i',j')$ where $i' \in Z$ and $x'_{ij} = x_{ij}$ for every other pair $(i,j) \neq (i',j')$, then $P(X';z) > P(X;z)$.

---

[53] Alkire and Foster (2011a) distinguished the monotonicity principle from the weak monotonicity principle. Others, including Chakravarty, Mukherjee, and Ranade (1998), Tsui (2002), Bourguignon and Chakravarty (2003), and Deutsch and Silber (2005) imply weak monotonicity by their monotonicity principle. Bossert, Chakravarty, and D'Ambrosio (2013) did not introduce a weak monotonicity principle.

Weak Dimensional Monotonicity: If an achievement matrix X' is obtained from another achievement matrix X such that $x'_{ij} < z_j \leq x_{ij}$ for some pair $(i,j) = (i',j')$ where $i' \in Z$ and $x'_{ij} = x_{ij}$ for every other pair $(i,j) \neq (i',j')$, then $P(X';z) \geq P(X;z)$.

Example: Suppose the initial achievement matrix is $X = \begin{bmatrix} 4 & 4 & 2 \\ 3 & 5 & 4 \\ 8 & 6 & 4 \end{bmatrix}$ and the deprivation cutoff vector is $z = [5,6,4]$. Suppose the second person is identified as poor by some criterion but is not deprived in all dimensions. If matrix X' is obtained from X by the second person becoming deprived in a principle additional dimension such that $X' = \begin{bmatrix} 4 & 4 & 2 \\ 3 & 5 & 3 \\ 8 & 6 & 4 \end{bmatrix}$, then by dimensional monotonicity, $P(X';z) > P(X;z)$.

The third principle in the category of dominance principles, **transfer**, is concerned with inequality among the poor. This property has been borrowed from the multidimensional inequality measurement literature and governs how a poverty measure should behave when the distribution of achievements among the poor becomes more or less equal while their average achievements remain the same. There are different ways of reducing inequality within a multidimensional distribution (see Marshall and Olkin 1979). We follow the approach known as **uniform majorization** introduced by Kolm 1977). A uniform majorization among the poor is a transformation in which the achievements among the poor are averaged across them or, equivalently, the original bundles of achievements of poor individuals are replaced by a convex combination of them. It is worth noting that the 'averaging' occurs within dimensions, across people.[54] Mathematically, this transformation is obtained by pre-multiplying the achievement matrix by a bistochastic matrix. The transfer principle requires that if an achievement matrix is obtained from another achievement matrix by reducing inequality among the poor, while the average achievement among the poor remains the same, then poverty decreases.[55] The **weak transfer** principle ensures that poverty does not increase when achievements among the poor become more equal.

---

[54] See Fleurbaey (2006a) and Duclos et al. (2011) for discussion on axioms based on uniform majorization.

[55] Note that it is not possible for a multidimensional poverty measure to satisfy the deprivation focus principle and the transfer principle simultaneously (Tsui 2002). For example, suppose the initial achievement matrix is $X = \begin{bmatrix} 2 & 3 & 8 \\ 2 & 3 & 10 \end{bmatrix}$ and the deprivation cutoff vector is $z = [5,6,4]$ and both of them are identified as poor by some criteria. Consider the bistochastic matrix $B = \begin{bmatrix} 0.5 & 0.5 \\ 0.5 & 0.5 \end{bmatrix}$. Then, $X' = BX = \begin{bmatrix} 2 & 3 & 9 \\ 2 & 3 & 9 \end{bmatrix}$. The transfer principle now requires that $P(X';z) < P(X;z)$, but by the deprivation focus principle, we should have $P(X';z) = P(X;z)$.

Transfer: If an achievement matrix X' is obtained from another achievement matrix X such that $X' = BX$ where B is a bistochastic matrix which is not a permutation or an identity matrix and $B_{ii} = 1$ for all $i \notin Z$, then $P(X';z) < P(X;z)$.

Weak Transfer: If an achievement matrix X' is obtained from another achievement matrix X such that $X' = BX$ where B is a bistochastic matrix which is not a permutation or an identity matrix and $B_{ii} = 1$ for all $i \notin Z$, or $P(X';z) \le P(X;z)$.

Example: Suppose the initial achievement matrix is $X = \begin{bmatrix} 4 & 4 & 2 \\ 3 & 5 & 4 \\ 8 & 6 & 4 \end{bmatrix}$ and the deprivation cutoff vector is $z = [5,6,4]$. The first person is indeed poor—being deprived in all three dimensions. Suppose the second person is also identified as poor by some criterion. Consider the bistochastic matrix $B = \begin{bmatrix} 0.5 & 0.5 & 0 \\ 0.5 & 0.5 & 0 \\ 0 & 0 & 1 \end{bmatrix}$, where the achievements are distributed equally across the two poor persons so that $X' = \begin{bmatrix} 3.5 & 4.5 & 3 \\ 3.5 & 4.5 & 3 \\ 8 & 6 & 4 \end{bmatrix}$. The transfer principle requires that $P(X';z) < P(X;z)$, whereas the weak transfer principle requires that $P(X';z) \le P(X;z)$.

The transfer principle in the multidimensional context is similar to its unidimensional counterpart, which is also concerned with the spread of the distribution. There is a second form of inequality among the poor that is only relevant in the multidimensional context and depends on how dimensional achievements are associated across the population. This second form of inequality corresponds to the joint distribution of achievements and was introduced by Atkinson and Bourguignon (1982): 'in the study of multiple deprivation, investigators have been concerned with the ways in which different forms of deprivation (…) tend to be associated …' (p. 183). Authors working on this issue have used both the term 'correlation' and the term 'association'. Correlation refers to the degree of linear association between two variables, whereas association is a broader term that includes linear association and also encompasses other forms of association such as quadratic or simply rank association.[56] Given a monotonic transformation of a variable, it is possible that while some form of association, such as rank association, remains invariant, the degree of correlation changes. Thus, here we prefer to use the broader concept of association to define the related properties.

The principles that require a measure to be sensitive to the association between dimensions refer to a specific type of rearrangement of the achievements across the

---

[56] Rank association refers to the degree of agreement between two rankings. In the context of the properties discussed here, perfect rank association would occur if person i', having higher achievement than person i in dimension j', also has higher achievements in all the other dimensions $j \ne j'$. That is: $x_{i'j} \ge x_{ij}$ for all $j = 1, \ldots d$.

population that we call 'association-decreasing rearrangement'.[57] The intuition is as follows. Imagine that originally person i' is at least as well off in all dimensions as person i. Then, there is a switch in the achievement of one or more dimensions, but not in all dimensions, between the two persons such that, after the switch, person i' no longer has achievements equal to or higher than person i in *all* dimensions but only in some. Suppose also that the achievements of everyone else remain unchanged. Such a transformation constitutes an association-decreasing rearrangement. Formally, given two persons i and i' in $Y \in \mathcal{X}_n$ such that $y_{i'j} \leq y_{ij}$ for all j, if matrix X is obtained from Y such that $x_{ij} = y_{i'j}$ and $x_{i'j} = y_{ij}$ for some dimension j and $x_{i''j'} = y_{i''j'}$ for all $i'' \neq i, i'$ and all $j' \neq j$, and X is not a permutation of Y, then X is stated to be obtained from Y by an association-decreasing rearrangement. The requirement that X is not a permutation of Y prevents the switch from taking place in dimensions where both people have equal achievements.

Example: Suppose the initial achievement matrix is $Y = \begin{bmatrix} 3 & 4 & 2 \\ 4 & 5 & 4 \\ 8 & 6 & 4 \end{bmatrix}$. Suppose X is obtained from Y so that $X = \begin{bmatrix} 4 & 4 & 2 \\ 3 & 5 & 4 \\ 8 & 6 & 4 \end{bmatrix}$. Note that the persons in the first two rows have switched their achievements in the first dimension so that the person in the first row no longer has a lower achievement than the next person in all three dimensions. Thus, X is obtained from Y by an association-decreasing rearrangement. In fact, note that the achievement vectors of the first and the second person are comparable by vector dominance in Y (each element in one vector is equal to or greater than the same element in the other vector) but not in X. Hence, the overall association between dimensions in X is lower.

To be relevant to the analysis of poverty, there is one further qualification: the transformation must take place among two poor persons. Thus, in the example above, both the first and the second person must have been identified as poor in order for this transformation to affect the poverty measure. For example, if the deprivation cutoff vector $z = [5, 6, 4]$, then initially in Y the first person is deprived in three dimensions, the second person is deprived only in the first two dimensions, and the third person is non-deprived in all three dimensions. Suppose that the identification function identifies the first two persons as poor. When X is obtained from Y, the first and the second person have switched their achievements in the first dimension so that now the first person is no longer more deprived than the second person in all three dimensions. Thus, in this case, X is said to be obtained from Y by an association-decreasing rearrangement *among the poor*.[58]

---

[57] This transformation was motivated by Boland and Proschan (1988).

[58] Note that if Y, on the contrary, is obtained from X, then it is called 'basic rearrangement' by Boland and Proschan (1988). In multidimensional poverty measurement, it is referred to as 'basic

Should poverty increase or decrease due to an association-decreasing rearrangement among the poor? One possible intuitive view is that poverty should go down or at least not increase because the association-decreasing rearrangement seems to reduce inequality among the poor. In the numerical example above, the first person was originally more deprived in all dimensions than the second person, and after the rearrangement, she is less deprived in one dimension. This was the argument provided by Tsui (2002). However, in line with Atkinson and Bourguignon (1982), Bourguignon and Chakravarty (2003) argued that the change in overall poverty should be contingent on the relation between dimensions, namely, whether they are substitutes or complements. When dimensions are thought to be substitutes for one another, poverty should not increase under the association-decreasing rearrangement. The intuition is that if dimensions are substitutes, an association-decreasing rearrangement helps both people compensate for their meagre achievements in some dimensions with higher achievements in other, a capacity that was limited for one of them before the rearrangement. When indicators are thought to be complements, poverty should not decrease under the described transfer. The intuition is that the association-decreasing rearrangement has reduced the ability of one of the persons to combine achievements and reach a certain level of well-being.[59] Based on the arguments above, the following properties can be defined. As with the case of monotonicity and transfer, we may define a strong and a weak version of each of the properties.

Weak Rearrangement (Substitutes): If an achievement matrix X' is obtained from another achievement matrix X by an association-decreasing rearrangement among the poor, then $P(X';z) \leq P(X;z)$.

Converse Weak Rearrangement (Complements): If an achievement matrix X' is obtained from another achievement matrix X by an association-decreasing rearrangement among the poor, then $P(X';z) \geq P(X;z)$.

rearrangement-increasing transfer' by Tsui (2002), 'correlation increasing switch' by Bourguignon and Chakravarty (2003), and 'correlation increasing arrangement' by Deutsch and Silber (2008). In multidimensional welfare analysis, an analogous concept has been called 'association increasing transfer' (Seth 2013), and in multidimensional inequality analysis it has been called 'correlation increasing transfer' by Tsui (1999) and 'unfair rearrangement principle' by Decancq and Lugo (2012).

[59] In the multidimensional measurement literature the substitutability and complementarity relationship between indicators is defined in terms of the second cross-partial derivative of the poverty measure with respect to any two dimensions being positive or negative. This obviously requires the dimensions to be cardinal and the poverty measure to be twice differentiable. Practically, given two dimensions j and j', substitutability implies that poverty decreases less with an increase in achievement in dimension j for people with higher achievements in dimension j' (Bourguignon and Chakravarty 2003: 35). Conversely, complementarity implies that poverty decreases more with an increase in achievement in dimension j for people with higher achievements in dimension j'. If the dimensions are independent, the second cross-partial derivative is zero and poverty should not change under the described transformation. This corresponds to the Auspitz–Lieben–Edgeworth–Pareto (ALEP) definition and differs from Hick's definition, traditionally used in demand theory (which relates to the properties of the indifference contours) (Atkinson 2003: 55). See Kannai (1980) for critiques of the ALEP definition. For a critique of Bourguignon and Charkavarty's (2003) association axiom, see Decancq (2012).

Strong Rearrangement (Substitutes): If an achievement matrix X' is obtained from another achievement matrix X by an association-decreasing rearrangement among the poor, then $P(X';z) < P(X;z)$.

Converse Strong Rearrangement (Complements): If an achievement matrix X' is obtained from another achievement matrix X by an association-decreasing rearrangement among the poor, then $P(X';z) > P(X;z)$.

The weak versions of these properties have been previously defined; the strict versions have not.[60] Note that the properties above are applicable when the identification function uses the deprived as well as the non-deprived dimensions to identify poor people. In other words, a poor person's identification status is allowed to change even when their achievements in non-deprived dimensions change while their achievements in the deprived dimensions remain unchanged.

The rearrangement set of properties could be made more precise when the identification of the poor respects the deprivation-focus property as well as the poverty-focus property. Identification that respects deprivation focus occurs when identification is solely based on dimensions in which poor persons are deprived, not on dimensions in which poor persons are not deprived. For example, these properties cannot distinguish situations when a poverty measure satisfying the deprivation-focus property should be strictly or weakly sensitive to the joint distribution of achievements among the poor. Let us consider the following two examples where the deprivation cutoff vector is $z = [5, 6, 4]$.

In the first example, suppose the achievement matrix $X = \begin{bmatrix} 3 & 4 & 5 \\ 4 & 5 & 4 \\ 8 & 6 & 4 \end{bmatrix}$ is obtained from

$Y = \begin{bmatrix} 3 & 4 & 4 \\ 4 & 5 & 5 \\ 8 & 6 & 4 \end{bmatrix}$ by switching the achievements between the two poor persons in the third

dimension. Clearly, an association-decreasing rearrangement has taken place between the two poor persons in X, but this switch should not affect overall poverty as none of these two persons is deprived in the third dimension.

In the second example, suppose $X = \begin{bmatrix} 3 & 4 & 5 \\ 4 & 4 & 4 \\ 8 & 6 & 4 \end{bmatrix}$ is obtained from $Y = \begin{bmatrix} 4 & 4 & 5 \\ 3 & 4 & 4 \\ 8 & 6 & 4 \end{bmatrix}$

by switching the achievements between the two poor persons in the first dimension. Again, certainly an association-increasing rearrangement has taken place, but if we look at the achievements in the deprived dimensions of the two poor persons, they

---

[60] For various weak versions of the sensitivity to rearrangement properties in poverty measurement literature, see Tsui (2002), Chakravarty (2009) (which contains a modified version of the properties in Bourguignon and Chakravarty (2003)), and Alkire and Foster (2011a). For different statements of the stronger versions of the property in the measurement of welfare and inequality, see Tsui (1995), Gajdos and Weymark (2005), Decancq and Lugo (2012), and Seth (2013).

appear to be permutations of each other and thus overall poverty should not change. In order to make the transformations relevant in this situation, we need to ensure that the association-decreasing rearrangements occur only among the deprived dimensions of the poor. Thus, there is a need to define a new set of properties that is compatible with the deprivation-focus property, which can be done by defining the properties in terms of the censored achievement matrices.

In this book, we define an additional set of new rearrangement properties by defining a transformation called **association-decreasing deprivation rearrangement among the poor**. Let $\tilde{Y}$ and $\tilde{X}$ denote the censored achievement matrices for Y and X, respectively (defined in section 2.2.5). Consider two poor persons i and i' in $Y \in \mathcal{X}_n$ such that $y_{i'j} \leq y_{ij}$ for all j. If matrix X is obtained from Y such that $x_{ij} = y_{i'j}$ and $x_{i'j} = y_{ij}$ for some dimension j, and $x_{i''j'} = y_{i''j'}$ for all $i'' \neq i,i'$ and all $j' \neq j$, and $\tilde{X}$ is not a permutation of $\tilde{Y}$, then X is stated to be obtained from Y by an association-decreasing deprivation rearrangement among the poor. The requirement of $\tilde{X}$ not being a permutation of $\tilde{Y}$ has two analogous implications as in case of the association-decreasing rearrangement. It prevents the two cases presented in the previous paragraph. Thus, it does not consider the cases where the switch of achievements between the two (poor) persons takes place in their non-deprived dimensions instead of the deprived dimension. Also, it prevents the censored deprivation vectors from being permutations of each other due to an association-decreasing rearrangement. The following example illustrates the transformation.

Example: Suppose the initial achievement matrix is $Y = \begin{bmatrix} 3 & 4 & 2 \\ 4 & 5 & 4 \\ 8 & 6 & 4 \end{bmatrix}$ and the deprivation cutoff vector is $z = [5,6,4]$. Thus, the first person is deprived in three dimensions, the second person is deprived only in the two first dimensions, and the third person is non-deprived in all three dimensions. Moreover, the first person is more deprived than the second one in every dimension. The corresponding censored achievement matrix is given by $\tilde{Y} = \begin{bmatrix} 3 & 4 & 2 \\ 4 & 5 & 4 \\ 5 & 6 & 4 \end{bmatrix}$. Now, suppose X is obtained from Y such that $X = \begin{bmatrix} 4 & 4 & 2 \\ 3 & 5 & 4 \\ 8 & 6 & 4 \end{bmatrix}$. Note that the first and the second person have switched their achievements in the first dimension so that now the first person is no longer more deprived than the second person in all three dimensions. The corresponding censored achievement matrix is given by $\tilde{X} = \begin{bmatrix} 4 & 4 & 2 \\ 3 & 5 & 4 \\ 5 & 6 & 4 \end{bmatrix}$ which is clearly not a permutation of $\tilde{Y}$. In this case, X is said to be obtained from Y by an association-decreasing deprivation rearrangement among the poor.

We define the following four additional properties using the same concept of substitutability and complementarity between dimensions discussed previously, but require the association-decreasing rearrangement to take place between the deprived dimensions of the poor. Note that, due to the transformation, the set of poor remains unchanged.

Weak Deprivation Rearrangement (Substitutes): If an achievement matrix X' is obtained from another achievement matrix X by an association-decreasing deprivation rearrangement among the poor, then $P(X';z) \leq P(X;z)$.

Converse Weak Deprivation Rearrangement (Complements): If an achievement matrix X' is obtained from another achievement matrix X by an association-decreasing deprivation rearrangement among the poor, then $P(X';z) \geq P(X;z)$.

Strong Deprivation Rearrangement (Substitutes): If an achievement matrix X' is obtained from another achievement matrix X by an association-decreasing deprivation rearrangement among the poor, then $P(X';z) < P(X;z)$.

Converse Strong Deprivation Rearrangement (Complements): If an achievement matrix X' is obtained from another achievement matrix X by an association-decreasing deprivation rearrangement among the poor, then $P(X';z) > P(X;z)$.

How are deprivation rearrangement properties related to or different from the rearrangement properties? First, if a poverty measure satisfies the (converse) weak deprivation rearrangement property, then the poverty measure will satisfy the (converse) weak rearrangement property, and the converse is true as well. Also, a poverty measure that satisfies the (converse) strong deprivation rearrangement property automatically satisfies the (converse) strong rearrangement property. But a poverty measure that satisfies the (converse) strong rearrangement property does not necessarily satisfy the (converse) strong deprivation rearrangement property. Therefore, the main difference between these two set of properties lies in their strong versions.

Although the rearrangement properties show technically how the change in poverty is related to association between dimensions, further research is required to understand the practicalities of rearrangement properties. Importantly, note that these properties require a uniform assumption across dimensions: either they are *all* substitutes or they are *all* complements, which may be highly constraining. On the empirical side, there does not seem to be a standard procedure for determining the extent of substitutability and complementarity across dimensions of poverty. Moreover, it is not entirely clear that any interrelationships across variables must be incorporated into the overarching methodology for evaluating multidimensional poverty. Instead, the interconnections might plausibly be the subject of separate empirical investigations that supplement, but do not constitute, the underlying poverty measure.

A related property, which is consistent with the ordinality property discussed in section 2.5.1, is dimensional transfer. The association-decreasing rearrangement, as well as the association-decreasing deprivation rearrangement among poor people, requires the achievements of poor people to be rearranged. However, some rearrangements, even when achievement matrices are not permutations of each other, may not alter the deprivation status of the poor, and thus the corresponding deprivation matrices may either be identical or a permutation of each other. Therefore, the rearrangement properties discussed above are not useful for judging whether an ordinal poverty measure (as we discuss in section 3.6.1) is strictly or weakly sensitive to data transformations when deprivations are transferred between poor persons. Let us show with an example how an association-decreasing rearrangement among the poor may cause no change in the deprivation matrices. Suppose two achievement matrices $Y = \begin{bmatrix} 3 & 4 & 2 \\ 4 & 5 & 4 \\ 8 & 6 & 4 \end{bmatrix}$ and $X = \begin{bmatrix} 4 & 4 & 2 \\ 3 & 5 & 4 \\ 8 & 6 & 4 \end{bmatrix}$ with deprivation cutoff vector $z = [5, 6, 4]$, where X is obtained from Y by an association-decreasing rearrangement among the poor. These two achievement matrices have identical corresponding deprivation matrices, such that $g^0(Y) = g^0(X) = \begin{bmatrix} 1 & 1 & 1 \\ 1 & 1 & 0 \\ 0 & 0 & 0 \end{bmatrix}$.

A **dimensional rearrangement among the poor** is an association-decreasing rearrangement among the poor (in achievements) that is simultaneously an association-decreasing rearrangement in deprivations. In other words, the initial deprivation vectors (and achievement vectors) are ranked by vector dominance, while the final deprivation vectors (and achievement vectors) are not. The extra condition ensures that the person with a lower level of achievements is actually deprived in some dimensions in which the other person is not and that, through the rearrangement, one or more of these deprivations (but not all) are traded for non-deprived levels. More formally, let $g^0(Y)$ and $g^0(X)$ denote the deprivation matrices for Y and X, respectively (defined in section 2.2.1). Consider two poor persons $i \in Z$ and $i' \in Z$ (according to some identification method ρ) in $Y \in \mathcal{X}_n$ such that $g^0_{i'j}(Y) \leq g^0_{ij}(Y)$ for all j. If matrix X is obtained from Y such that $g^0_{ij}(X) = g^0_{i'j}(Y)$ and $g^0_{i'j}(X) = g^0_{ij}(Y)$ for some dimension j, and $g^0_{i''j'}(X) = g^0_{i''j'}(Y)$ for all $i'' \neq i, i'$ and all $j' \neq j$, and $g^0(X)$ is not a permutation of $g^0(Y)$, then we define X to be obtained from Y by a dimensional rearrangement among the poor. A dimensional rearrangement among the poor does not affect the number of poor persons, and neither does a dimensional increment among the poor. This transformation can be interpreted as a progressive transfer in that it transforms an initial 'spread' in joint deprivations between two poor persons into a moderated situation where neither person has unambiguously more than the other. The overall achievement levels in society are unchanged, but the correlation between dimensions (and hence inequality) has been reduced. The following property requires poverty to decrease when there is a dimensional rearrangement among the poor.

Dimensional rearrangement among the poor, as defined above, covers only switches of achievements and deprivations in deprived dimensions among people who are and remain poor, and excludes permutations of corresponding deprivation matrices.

Dimensional Transfer: If an achievement matrix X' is obtained from another achievement matrix X by a dimensional rearrangement among the poor, then $P(X';z) < P(X;z)$.[61]

2.5.3 SUBGROUP PROPERTIES

The next set of principles is concerned with the link between overall poverty and poverty in different subgroups of the population, and the link between overall poverty and dimensional deprivations.

The first principle—**subgroup consistency**—ensures that the change in overall poverty is consistent with the change in subgroup poverty.[62] For example, suppose the entire society is divided into two population subgroups: Group 1 and Group 2. Poverty in Group 1 remains unchanged while poverty in Group 2 decreases. One would expect overall poverty to decrease. If overall poverty did not reflect subgroup poverty, there would be an inconsistency, which would be conceptually and politically problematic. As a result, national poverty estimates would not reflect regional successes in poverty reduction. A related principle with a stronger requirement is **population subgroup decomposability**. This principle requires overall poverty to be equal to a weighted sum of subgroups' poverty, noted as $P(X^\ell;z)$ in section 2.2.2, where the weight attached to each subgroup's poverty is the population share of that subgroup.

Suppose an achievement matrix X is divided into $m \geq 2$ subgroups, such that X^ℓ and n^ℓ denote, correspondingly, the achievement matrix and the population size of subgroup ℓ, for all $\ell = 1, \ldots, m$, and the subgroups are mutually exclusive and collectively exhaustive: $\sum_{\ell=1}^{m} n^\ell = n$.

Subgroup Consistency: If an achievement matrix X' is obtained from the achievement matrix X such that $P(X'^{\ell'};z) < P(X^{\ell'};z)$ but $P(X'^\ell;z) = P(X^\ell;z)$ for all $\ell \neq \ell'$, and total population, as well as subgroup population, remains unchanged, then $P(X';z) < P(X;z)$.

Population Subgroup Decomposability: $P(X;z) = \sum_{\ell=1}^{m} (n^\ell/n) P(X^\ell;z)$

Example: Suppose the initial achievement matrix is $X = \begin{bmatrix} 4 & 4 & 2 \\ 3 & 5 & 4 \\ 8 & 6 & 4 \end{bmatrix}$. Let us divide X into two subgroups $X^1 = \begin{bmatrix} 4 & 4 & 2 \end{bmatrix}$ with population size $n^1 = 1$ and $X^2 = \begin{bmatrix} 3 & 5 & 4 \\ 8 & 6 & 4 \end{bmatrix}$ with population

---

[61] For a different statement of the strong dimensional transfer property using an association-increasing rearrangement, see Seth and Alkire (2014a,b).

[62] The concept of subgroup consistency in poverty measurement has been motivated by Foster and Shorrocks (1991).

size $n^2 = 2$. Now, suppose X^1 changes to $X'^1 = \begin{bmatrix} 4 & 4 & 3 \end{bmatrix}$ and $X'^2 = X^2$. We know that by the monotonicity principle, $P(X'^1; z) < P(X^1; z)$. Then the subgroup consistency principle requires that $P(X'; z) < P(X; z)$.

The additive decomposability principle requires that overall poverty can be expressed as $P(X; z) = \frac{1}{3} P(X^1; z) + \frac{2}{3} P(X^2; z)$.

The population subgroup decomposability property has been one of the most attractive properties for policy analysis as it can be particularly useful for targeting and monitoring progress in different subgroups. It is worth noting that a poverty measure that satisfies population subgroup decomposability necessarily satisfies subgroup consistency. However, the converse is not true, which means subgroup consistency does not necessarily imply population subgroup decomposability.

The other form of decomposition that is of tremendous relevance in the policy analysis of multidimensional poverty refers to the possibility of breaking down poverty by deprivations across dimensions among the poor. This property, called **dimensional breakdown**, requires overall poverty to be equal to a weighted sum of the dimensional deprivations *after identification* $P_j(x_{\cdot j}; z)$ introduced in section 2.2.2. It creates a consistency between the post-identification dimensional deprivations and overall poverty.

In the particular case in which a counting approach using a union criterion is followed for identification, then $P_j(x_{\cdot j}; z) = P_j(x_{\cdot j}; z_j)$, provided the base population $n_j = n$ for all j. In other words, the dimensional deprivation of any dimension j after identification coincides with the dimensional deprivation level before identification. In this special case, the property of dimensional breakdown coincides with the property of 'factor decomposability' introduced by Chakravarty, Mukherjee, and Ranade (1998) and referred to by Bossert, Chakravarty, and D'Ambrosio (2013) as 'additive decomposability in attributes'. In other cases, dimensional breakdown is done after the identification of the poor and shows only the deprivations faced by the poor.

Dimensional Breakdown: For an $n \times d$ dimensional achievement matrix X, $P(X; z) = \sum_{j=1}^{d} w_j P_j(x_{\cdot j}; z)$, where w_j is the weight attached to dimension j and $P_j(x_{\cdot j}; z)$ is the dimensional deprivation index after identification in dimension j.

Given that the dimensional breakdown property requires additivity in the deprivations, it is not consistent with the properties of association sensitivity in their strict form—that is, with requiring decreasing or increasing poverty under an association-decreasing rearrangement.[63]

---

[63] For a formal discussion of this inconsistency, see Alkire and Foster (2013).

2.5.4 TECHNICAL PROPERTIES

Finally, we introduce certain technical principles, which ensure that the poverty measure is meaningful. These principles are **non-triviality**, **normalization**, and **continuity**.

The **non-triviality** principle requires that a poverty measure takes at least two different values. This property may appear to be trivial by its name, but it is important: unless a measure takes two different values, it is not possible to distinguish a society with poverty from a society with no poverty. Note that when a measure satisfies the strong version of at least one of the dominance principles, this property is automatically satisfied (by definition, poverty will take at least two different values). However, when a measure only satisfies the weak version of all dominance principles, this property becomes necessary.

The **normalization** principle requires that the values of a poverty measure lie within the 0–1 range. It takes a minimum value of 0 when there is no poverty in a society, and it takes a maximum value of 1 when poverty is at its maximum. The **continuity** property prevents a poverty measure from changing abruptly, given marginal changes in achievements.

> **Non-triviality:** A poverty measure should take at least two distinct values.
>
> **Normalization:** A poverty measure should take a minimum value of 0 and a maximum value of 1.
>
> **Continuity:** A poverty measure should be continuous over the achievements.

It is worth noting that not all properties defined above are applicable across all scales of measurement, just as not all mathematical operations are admissible for all scales of measurement. Thus, some of these properties may need to be adapted according to the requirements of different scales. The next chapter outlines various poverty measurement methodologies based on the framework introduced in this chapter and discusses which scales of measurement they use and which properties they satisfy.

3 Overview of Methods for Multidimensional Poverty Assessment

Since the early twentieth century, poverty measurement has predominantly used an income approach.[1] Yet the recognition of poverty as a multidimensional phenomenon is not new. From the mid-1970s at least, empirical analyses have considered various non-monetary deprivations that the poor experience, complementing monetary measures. Conceptually, many analyses were motivated by the basic needs approach, the capability approach, and the social inclusion approach, among others. A number of methodologies have emerged to assess poverty from a multidimensional perspective. This chapter presents a constructive survey of the major existing methods. Each section describes a methodology; identifies the data requirements, assumptions, and choices made during measurement design; and lists the types of problems it best analyses—as well as its challenges. A reader, upon reading this chapter and the next, should have a clear overview of existing methodologies as well as the Alkire–Foster measures, their applicability, and insights. The AF methodology, which we focus on from Chapter 5 onwards, draws together the axiomatic and counting approaches explicitly, yet builds upon insights from other methodologies too. So a further motivation for this chapter is to acknowledge intellectual debts to many others in this fast-moving field.

This chapter reviews the dashboard approach, the composite indices approach, Venn diagrams, the dominance approach, statistical approaches, fuzzy sets, and the axiomatic approach. Some techniques within each approach can be used with ordinal as well as cardinal data. These methods can be grouped into two broad categories. One category encompasses methods that are implemented using aggregate data from different sources. These thus ignore the joint distribution of deprivations and are 'marginal measures' as defined in Chapter 2. The second category encompasses methods that reflect the joint distribution and thus are implemented using data in which information on each dimension is available for each unit of analysis.

Among marginal methods, dashboards assess each and every dimension separately but *a priori* impose no hierarchy across these dimensions. Also dashboards do not identify who is to be considered multidimensionally poor. Thus the dashboard method does

---

[1] This is evidenced in the seminal surveys of Booth (1894, 1903), Rowntree (1901), and Bowley and Burnett-Hurst (1915) conducted in specific cities in the UK.

not indicate the direction and extent of changes in overall poverty. Composite indices have 'the powerful attraction of a single headline figure' (Stiglitz et al. 2009) but like the dashboard approach, have the disadvantage of missing a key aspect of multidimensional poverty assessment: the joint distribution of deprivations. Dashboards and composite indexes are discussed in section 3.1.

Within the second group of methods, Venn diagrams, outlined in section 3.2, graphically represent the joint distribution of individuals' deprivations in multiple dimensions. Yet they become difficult to read when more than four dimensions are used and do not per se contain a definition of the poor. The dominance approach, covered in section 3.3, enables us to state whether a country or region is or is not unambiguously less poor than another with respect to various parameters and functional forms, but it becomes empirically difficult to implement beyond two or more dimensions. It also shares with the Venn diagrams the disadvantage of not offering a summary measure. Moreover, the dominance approach only ranks regions or poverty levels from different periods ordinally; it does not permit a cardinally meaningful assessment of the extent of the differences in poverty levels.

Statistical approaches (section 3.4) comprise a wide range of techniques. Techniques such as principal component analysis and multiple correspondence analysis extract information on the correlation or association between dimensions to reduce the number of dimensions; other techniques, such as cluster analysis, identify groups of people who are similar in terms of their joint deprivations. These and other methods, such as factor analysis and structural equation models, can be used to construct overall indices of poverty. It should be noted that even when overall indices of poverty can be obtained, because statistical techniques rely on the particular dataset used, it may be difficult to make intertemporal and cross-country comparisons.

The fuzzy set approach, outlined in section 3.5, also falls within the second category of techniques and builds on the idea that there is ambiguity in the identification of who is deprived or poor. Thus, instead of using a unique set of deprivation cutoffs for identification, it uses a band of deprivation cutoffs for each dimension. A person falling above the band is identified as unambiguously non-deprived, whereas a person falling below the band is identified as unambiguously deprived. Within the band of ambiguity, a membership function is chosen to assign the degree to which the person is deprived. Fuzzy sets are used to construct a summary measure, and they may address joint deprivations. The challenge lies in selecting and justifying the membership function, as well as in communicating results.

It is worth noting that the measurement methods just mentioned are not regularly scrutinized according to the set of properties stated in Chapter 2. Finally, the measures developed within the axiomatic approach, discussed in section 3.6, articulate precisely some of the properties for multidimensional poverty measurement they satisfy. Measures that clearly specify the axioms or properties they satisfy enable the analyst to understand the ethical principles they embody and to be aware of the direction of change they will exhibit under certain transformations. Note that the appropriateness of axiomatic measures critically depends on whether their properties are essential or useful given the purpose of measurement.

3.1 **Dashboard of Indicators and Composite Indices**

A starting point for measuring the multidimensionality of poverty is to assess the level of deprivation in dimensions separately, in other words, to apply a 'standard unidimensional measure to *each* dimension' (Alkire, Foster, and Santos 2011). This is the so-called dashboard approach, which consists of considering a set of dimensional deprivation indices $P_j(x^j; z_j)$, defined in section 2.2.2. The dashboard of indicators, denoted by DI, is a d-dimensional vector containing the deprivation indices of all d dimensions: $DI = (P_1(x^1; z_1), \ldots, P_d(x^d; z_d.))$.

Writing from within a basic needs approach framework, Hicks and Streeten proposed the use of dashboards: 'as a first step, it might be useful to define the best indicator for each basic need …. A limited set of core indicators covering these areas would be a useful device for concentrating efforts' (1979: 577).[2] A prominent implementation of a dashboard approach has been the Millennium Development Goals: a dashboard of 49 indicators was initially defined to monitor the eighteen targets to achieve the eight goals. Improvements in different aspects of poverty are evaluated with independent indicators, such as the proportion of people living below $1.25 a day, the fraction of children under 5 years of age who are underweight, the child mortality rate, the share of seats held by women in single or lower houses of national parliaments, and so on. This provides a rich and variegated profile of a population's achievements across a spectrum of dimensions and their changes over time. Furthermore, in many cases the indicators can be decomposed to illuminate disparities.

Observe that the different indicators in a dashboard are not necessarily based on the same reference population (section 2.2.4). In our notation, the n_j population may be different for each j dimension. For example, the indicator of the proportion of people living below the $1.25-a-day poverty line reflects the entire population, whereas the indicator of the fraction of children under 5 years of age who are underweight is based only on children under 5 years old. In turn, the share of seats held by women in single or lower houses of national parliaments reflects only the men and women in the single or lower houses of national parliaments. The different reference populations shown in the indicators of a dashboard may be 'disjoint' (that is, they have no people in common) or overlapping (they have people in common).

An example of disjoint indicators is child malnutrition (computed using information for children under 5 years of age) and share of seats held by women in parliament (computed using information for men and women in the single or lower houses of national

---

[2] See also Ravallion (1996, 2011b).

parliaments). If the indicators pertain to disjoint populations, there seems to be no need to consider joint deprivations. However, even in this case, joint deprivations could be relevant if the disjoint populations have something in common—such as belonging to the same household. Under such circumstances, the deprivation experienced by one individual (for example, a child who is malnourished) can affect others (like her mother). This is known as an intra-household negative externality. Thus, ignoring the joint distribution of a composite unit of analysis (households in the example) may obscure important aspects of poverty. An example of indicators with overlapping populations is the proportion of people living on less than $1.25 a day and the percentage of people without adequate sanitation. In this case, because both deprivations can be experienced by both groups of people, the information on the extent to which those living on less than $1.25 a day are also deprived in sanitation and vice versa may be relevant.

Dashboards have the advantage of broadening the set of considered dimensions, offering a rich amount of information, and potentially allowing the use of the best data source for each particular indicator and for assessing the impact of specific policies (such as nutritional or educational interventions). However, they have some significant disadvantages. First of all, dashboards do not reflect the joint distribution of deprivations across the population and precisely because of that they are marginal methods. Recall the example presented in Table 2.2 in section 2.2.3, which used two deprivation matrices with equal marginal distributions but different joint distributions, one in which each of the four persons in the distribution is deprived in exactly one dimension and another distribution in which one person is deprived in all dimensions and three persons experience zero deprivations. A dashboard of dimensional deprivation indices for these four dimensions would indicate that the level of deprivation in each of the four dimensions is the same in both distributions.

Technically, a dashboard could also include a measure of correlation or association between every pair of dimensions, which may account for the joint distribution in some restricted sense. However, a large number of indicators in dashboards require an even larger number of pairwise correlations to be reported, which is definitely expected to increase complexity. Perhaps that is why such kinds of correlation indicators are not in practice included in dashboards. Even if bivariate associations/correlations are reported, they still do not account for the underlying multivariate joint distribution, and thus remain silent in identifying who the poor are. Secondly and relatedly, '... dashboards suffer because of their heterogeneity, at least in the case of very large and eclectic ones, and most lack indications about ... hierarchies among the indicators used. Furthermore, as communications instruments, one frequent criticism is that they lack what has made GDP a success: the powerful attraction of a single headline figure that allows simple comparisons of socio-economic performance over time or across countries' (Stiglitz et al. 2009: 63).

One way to overcome this heterogeneity and communications challenge is through composite indices. A composite index (*CI*) is a function $CI : P_1(x^1; z_1) \times P_2(x^2; z_2) \times \ldots \times P_d(x^d; z_d) \rightarrow \mathbb{R}$ that converts d deprivation indices (which one may consider in a dashboard) into a real number. An example of an aggregation function used in composite indices is the family of generalized means of appropriate order β, introduced in section 2.2.5.

There is a burgeoning literature on composite indices of poverty or well-being.[3] Well-known indices include the Physical Quality of Life Index (Morris 1978), the Human Development Index (HDI) (Anand and Sen 1994), the Gender Empowerment Index (GEM) (UNDP 1995), and, within poverty measurement, the Human Poverty Index (HPI) (Anand and Sen 1997). These indices have been published in the global *Human Development Reports* for several years.[4] A prominent policy index is the official EU-2020 measure of poverty and social exclusion, which uses a union counting approach across three dimensions: income poverty, joblessness, and material deprivation (Hametner et al. 2013).

Composite indices, like dashboards, can capture deprivations of different population subgroups and can combine distinct data sources. In contrast to dashboards, they impose relative weights on indicators, which govern trade-offs across aggregate dimensional dimensions. Such normative judgements are very demanding (Chapter 6) and have been challenged (Ravallion 2011b). In practice, they have catalysed expert, political, or public scrutiny of and debate about these trade-offs, facilitating a process of public reasoning as recommended by Sen (2009).

Like dashboards, composite indices do not reflect the joint distribution of deprivations. In fact, a composite index of the four dimensional deprivations presented in Table 2.2 would combine these indices with some aggregation formula, but would show the level of overall deprivation in the two distributions as being identical. In other words, both the dashboard and composite indices are insensitive to the degree of simultaneous deprivations.

Moreover, composite indices like dashboards remain silent to one of the basic steps of poverty measurement: identification of the poor. Even when a composite index is constructed by considering all deprivations within a society in the selected dimensions, it fails to identify the set of the poor Z within the society. It may appear that, when the base population is the same for all considered dimensions, such composite indices follow the union criterion to identification as they consider all deprivations, but this notion is not correct because the identification of all deprivations does not ensure the identification of the set of poor. In fact as long as there is at least one person experiencing more than one deprivation, counting the deprived in each dimension would lead to a

---

[3] For further discussions on composite indices see Nardo et al. (2008), Bandura (2008), Alkire and Sarwar (2009), Maggino (2009), Fattore, Maggino, and Colombo (2012), Fleurbaey and Blanchet (2013), and Santos and Santos (2013).

[4] The HDI has been published since the first *Human Development Report* in 1990. The GEM was published between 1995 and 2009; in 2010, it was replaced by the Gender Inequality Index (GII), which is based on the methodology proposed by Seth (2009). The HPI was published between 1997 and 2009; in 2010, it was replaced by the Multidimensional Poverty Index (Alkire and Santos 2010), when the IHDI or Inequality Adjusted HDI was added (Alkire and Foster 2010).

double counting of the number of the 'union poor' (see Bourguignon and Chakravarty 2003: 28–9). Thus neither dashboards nor composite indices can answer the questions: Who is poor? How many poor people are there? How poor are they? (Alkire, Foster, and Santos 2011). In sum, the dashboard approach and composite indices represent important tools for understanding poverty based on multiple dimensions, and can be used with multiple data sources covering different reference populations. However, their inability to capture the joint distribution of multiple dimensions and to identify what proportion of the population are poor make them limited tools for multidimensional poverty measurement and analysis.[5] In the following sections, we introduce approaches that address the joint distribution of deprivations.

3.2 **Venn Diagrams**

Venn diagrams are a diagrammatic representation that shows all possible logical relations between a finite collection of sets. The name of Venn diagrams refers to John Venn who formally introduced the tool (Venn 1880), although the tool pre-dates this and was known—as Venn himself mentions—as Eulerian circles (in fact, although Euler used them, there were uses of similar representations even before Euler).[6] Venn diagrams consist of a collection of closed figures, such as circles and ellipses, that include, exclude, or intersect one another such that each compartment is associated with a class.[7]

3.2.1 THE METHODOLOGY AND APPLICATIONS

Applied to the analysis of multidimensional poverty measurement, the interior of each closed figure in a Venn diagram can be used with a set of indicators and associated deprivation cutoffs to represent the number of people who are deprived in a certain dimension. Naturally, the exterior of each closed figure can be used to represent the number of people who are non-deprived in the same dimension. Note that these two groups—deprived and non-deprived—within each dimension are mutually exclusive and collectively exhaustive with respect to the considered population. The intersections between the closed figures show the extent to which deprivations in different dimensions overlap, that is, the number of people who are jointly deprived in certain dimensions in a particular society.

[5] Seth (2010) pointed out the key difference between composite indices and multidimensional indices, which is that the former do not capture the joint distribution of achievements.
[6] Venn (1880) does not refer to the diagrams as 'Venn diagrams'. Lewis (1918) first named the tool as a Venn diagram.
[7] '... any closed figure will do as well ... all that we demand of it ... is that it shall have an inside and an outside, so as to indicate what does and what does not belong to the class' (Venn 1880: 6).

Table 3.1 Joint distribution of deprivations in two dimensions

		Dimension 2		
		Non-deprived	Deprived	Total
Dimension 1	**Non-deprived**	n_{00}	n_{01}	n_{0+}
	Deprived	n_{10}	n_{11}	n_{1+}
	Total	n_{+0}	n_{+1}	n

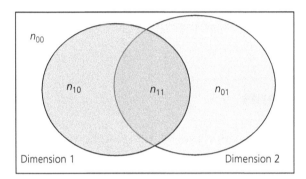

Figure 3.1. Venn diagram of joint distribution of deprivations in two dimensions

When there are only two dimensions, a Venn diagram provides a diagrammatic representation of a 2×2 contingency table, introduced in section 2.2.3. Here we reproduce Table 2.1 as Table 3.1 in order to visually link it to Figure 3.1 below. Figure 3.1 contains the same pattern of joint distribution as Table 3.1, but in a Venn diagram. The circle with a darker shade to the left denotes the number of people who are deprived in Dimension 1, whereas the circle with a lighter shade denotes those who are deprived in Dimension 2. In this example, without a loss of generality, we assume that more people are deprived in Dimension 2 than in Dimension 1; hence, the circle corresponding to Dimension 2 is larger than that of Dimension 1. The intersection of the two circles represents the number of people who experience deprivations in both dimensions, n_{11}, and is larger or smaller according to the extent of overlap. The diagram also represents the number of people deprived in the first but not in the second dimension, n_{10}, and those deprived in the second but not the first dimension, n_{01}. If some people are deprived in each dimension but no one is jointly deprived, the two circles do not intersect.

The Venn diagram is particularly useful when two to four dimensions are involved, because the visual representation is easy to interpret. A three-dimension Venn diagram is shown in Figure 3.2. The diagram depicts the frequencies for all the possible combinations of deprivations using the notation $n_{j_1 j_2 j_3}$, such that $j_i = 1$ signals deprivation in dimension j_i and $j_i = 0$ signals non-deprivation in dimension j_i for all $i = 1, 2, 3$. Thus, for example, n_{111} in the intersection of the three circles denotes the number of people who are deprived in all three dimensions, n_{010} denotes the number of people who are deprived in the second dimension only, and so on for other combinations.

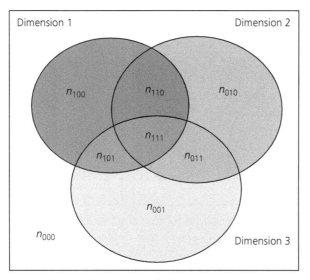

Figure 3.2. Venn diagram of joint distribution of deprivations in three dimensions

In empirical work, the Venn diagram has been used as an exploratory tool to understand the overlapping deprivations in various dimensions and to draw attention to mismatches between them (Ferreira and Lugo 2013). For example, Atkinson et al. (2010) use a three-dimension Venn diagram to depict joint deprivations in income poverty, severe material deprivation, and joblessness. Naga and Bolzani (2006) employ a three-dimension Venn diagram to show how there are disagreements on which households are identified as poor when three different definitions based on income, consumption, and predicted permanent income are used. Venn diagrams have also been selected to capture how different poverty measures or multidimensional targeting instruments agree with each other. For example, Roelen, Gassman, and de Neubourg (2009) created a two-dimension Venn diagram to present the mismatch between the monetary poor and the multidimensionally poor; Alkire and Seth (2013a) used Venn diagrams to portray the mismatches and overlaps between multidimensional poverty targeting instruments; and Decancq, Fleurbaey, and Maniquet (2014) evaluated the degree of overlap between measures of poverty based on expenditures, counting, and preference sensitivity.[8]

3.2.2 A CRITICAL EVALUATION

Venn diagrams are simple and intuitive, yet powerful and information-rich visual graphics. They depict the level of deprivation by dimension (the relative size of the circles) as well as the matches and mismatches across deprivations. By presenting the

[8] Decanq and Neumann (2014) do so for measures of individual well-being.

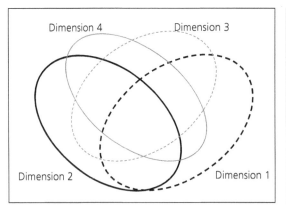
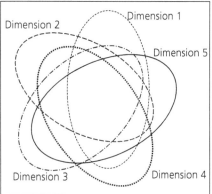

Figure 3.3. Venn diagrams of deprivations for four and five dimensions

joint distribution, Venn diagrams provide more information than dashboard measures or composite indices. Additionally, although Venn diagrams do not identify who is poor, they organize the information on the joint distribution in such a way that one could graphically outline an equally weighted identification function of the poor. In terms of limitations, Venn diagrams are intuitively interpretable when there are up to four dimensions. As can be seen from Figure 3.3, the rudimentary diagrammatic interpretation becomes highly complicated when there are five or more dimensions involved, a weakness Venn (1880) highlighted: 'it must be admitted that such a diagram is not quite so simple to draw as one might wish it to be' (p. 7) and 'beyond five terms it hardly seems as if diagrams offered much substantial help' (p. 8). Furthermore, this tool does not generate a summary measure, so it is not necessarily possible to conclude if one society has higher/lower poverty than another society, unless, in addition, an identification criterion of the poor has been implemented with the diagram. Finally, the tool does not reflect (when an indicator has a cardinal scale) the depth of deprivation in each dimension. Regardless of the scale, every dimension is converted into the binary states of deprived and non-deprived.

3.3 **The Dominance Approach**

The dominance approach provides a framework to ascertain whether unambiguous poverty comparisons can be made across a whole class or range of poverty measures and parameter values. If an unambiguous comparison is claimed to have been made, either across two societies at a given time or across two time periods of a certain society, then such an ordering will hold for a wide range of poverty measures within a certain class and for a range of parameter values. This is an important claim to establish: if poverty comparisons differ depending upon the choice of parameter values and poverty measures, then their credibility may be contested. On the contrary, if the conclusions are the same regardless of those choices, this can soften disagreements about measurement design. This section focuses on dominance approaches across any choice of parameter values and across poverty measures that use various functional forms.

The dominance approach has been widely used in the measurement and analysis of poverty and also of inequality within a unidimensional framework (Atkinson 1970, 1987; Foster and Shorrocks 1988a,b; Jenkins and Lambert 1998). It was extended to the multidimensional framework for inequality measurement by Atkinson and Bourguignon (1982, 1987) and Bourguignon (1989), then to the context of multidimensional poverty measurement by Duclos, Sahn, and Younger (2006a) and Bourguignon and Chakravarty (2009). We first elaborate the dominance approach in the unidimensional context and then show how it has been extended to the multidimensional context.

3.3.1 POVERTY DOMINANCE IN UNIDIMENSIONAL FRAMEWORK

In the unidimensional context, a society is judged to 'poverty dominate' another society with respect to a particular poverty measure if the former has equal or lower poverty than the other society for all poverty lines and strictly lower poverty for at least some poverty lines. On the contrary, if poverty in the former society is lower for some poverty lines and higher for other poverty lines, we cannot claim that either of the two societies poverty dominates the other. We formally define the concept by drawing on Foster and Shorrocks (1988a,b).[9] Suppose there are two societies with achievement vectors x, $y \in \mathbb{R}_+^n$. The society with achievement vector x poverty dominates the society with achievement vector y for poverty measure P, which we denote as xPy, if and only if $P(x; z_U) \leq P(y; z_U)$ for all poverty lines $z_U \in \mathbb{R}_{++}$ and $P(x; z_U) < P(y; z_U)$ for some poverty lines $z_U \in \mathbb{R}_{++}$.

In poverty measurement, the tool most frequently used for dominance analysis is **stochastic dominance**. Stochastic dominance has different orders: first, second, and higher, which can be presented in terms of univariate cumulative distribution functions (CDF). The two achievement vectors x and y presented in the previous paragraph may also be represented by using CDFs F_x and F_y, respectively. Thus, vectors x and y can also be referred to as distribution x and y, respectively. The value of CDF F_x at any achievement level $b \in \mathbb{R}_+$, denoted by $F_x(b)$, is the share of population in distribution x with achievement levels less than b. Similarly, $F_y(b)$ denotes the share of the population in distribution y with achievement levels less than b.

We first introduce the concept of first-order stochastic dominance for a unidimensional distribution.[10] Distribution x first-order stochastically dominates distribution y, which

---

[9] Fields (2001: ch. 4) helpfully introduces unidimensional dominance in poverty measurement.

[10] Here we present the dominance conditions in terms of the cumulative distribution function. It could be presented in terms of the quantile function by exchanging the vertical and the horizontal axes (Foster, Seth, et al. 2013: 71).

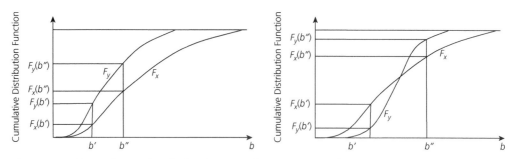

Figure 3.4. First-order stochastic dominance using cumulative distribution functions

is written x *FSD* y, if and only if $F_x(b) \leq F_y(b)$ for all b and $F_x(b) < F_y(b)$ for some b.[11] In other words, the CDF of x lies to the right of the CDF of y. This is shown in Panel I of Figure 3.4. The horizontal axis denotes the achievements and the vertical axis denotes the values of the CDFs for the corresponding achievement level. For example, $F_x(b')$ and $F_y(b')$ denote the values of CDF F_x and F_y corresponding to achievement level b'. Note that $F_x(b') < F_y(b')$ and also $F_x(b'') < F_y(b'')$. In fact, there is no value of b, for which $F_x(b') > F_y(b')$.

The value of a CDF corresponding to a certain level of achievement is the proportion of the population with achievements below that level. Interestingly, if a particular level of achievement is set as a unidimensional poverty line ($b' = z_U$), then the value of the CDF at z_U is the headcount ratio P_0 (see section 2.1). Thus, $F_x(z_U)$ and $F_y(z_U)$ are the headcount ratios for distributions x and y for poverty line z_U, respectively. Then, x FSD y if and only if $P_0(x; z_U) < P_0(y; z_U)$. In other words, first-order stochastic dominance is equivalent to the condition when the headcount ratio in distribution x is either equal to or lower than that in distribution y for all poverty cutoffs. Equivalently, y has no lower headcount ratio than x for all poverty cutoffs. Moreover, first-order stochastic dominance provides results beyond the headcount ratio. As Atkinson (1987) shows, if one distribution first-order stochastically dominates another distribution, then poverty is equal or lower in the former distribution for all poverty measures (and any monotonic transformation of these measures) satisfying population subgroup decomposability and weak monotonicity. The result, as Atkinson discusses, can be extended to measures that are not necessarily subgroup decomposable.

Unlike Panel I, Panel II shows a situation where the CDFs cross each other. For all b to the left of the crossing, $F_x(b) > F_y(b)$, whereas for all b to the right of the crossing, $F_x(b) < F_y(b)$. Thus, in this case, no distribution first-order stochastically dominates the other. When a pair of distributions cannot be ranked by first-order stochastic dominance, one should look at second- or higher-order stochastic dominance. The second-order

---

[11] Note that in empirical applications, some statistical tests cannot discern between weak and strong dominance and thus assume x first-order stochastically dominates distribution y, if $F_x(b) < F_y(b)$ for all b. See, for example, Davidson and Duclos (2012: 88–9).

stochastic dominance is equivalent to comparing the area underneath the CDFs for every achievement level. In this section, our objective is to provide a brief overview of the dominance approach, and so we mainly focus on the first-order stochastic dominance and its extension to the multidimensional context. Foster and Shorrocks (1988a,b) show how higher orders of stochastic dominance are linked to poverty dominance for different poverty measures in the Foster–Greer–Thorbecke (FGT) class (see Box 2.1 for a numerical example of the FGT measures).[12] Atkinson (1987) provides a condition when poverty measures satisfying certain properties agree with the second-order stochastic dominance condition.

3.3.2 POVERTY DOMINANCE IN THE MULTIDIMENSIONAL FRAMEWORK

This approach has been extended to the multidimensional context by Duclos, Sahn, and Younger (2006a) and Bourguignon and Chakravarty (2009). Poverty dominance in the multidimensional framework is slightly different in that it needs to consider the identification method as well as the assumed relationship between achievements, namely, whether they are considered substitutes, complements, or independent. As discussed in Chapter 2, the identification of those who are multidimensionally poor is not as straightforward as in the unidimensional framework. In a multidimensional dominance approach, a poverty frontier based on an overall achievement value of well-being for each individual is used for identification, and the overall achievement is required to be non-decreasing in each dimensional achievement. The poverty frontier belongs to the so-called aggregate achievement approach (section 2.2.2) and it is defined as the different combinations of the d achievements that provide the same overall achievement as an aggregate poverty line or subsistence level of well-being. If a person's set of d achievements produces a lower level of well-being than the subsistence level of well-being, then that person is identified as poor.

The poverty frontier method—like other identification methods such as counting—encompasses the two extreme criteria for identification, namely, union and intersection, as well as intermediate cases. The poverty frontier method for identification is presented in Figure 3.5 using two dimensions. The horizontal axis of the diagram represents achievements in dimension 1, and the vertical axis denotes achievements in dimension 2. The deprivation cutoffs of both dimensions are denoted by z_1 and z_2, respectively. The intersection frontier is given by the bold black line, and any person with achievement combinations to the left of and below this line is identified as poor. Similarly, the union frontier is given by the dotted line, and any person with achievement combinations to the left of or below the dotted line is considered poor.

---

[12] For graphical depictions of higher-order stochastic dominance conditions in terms of different dominance curves, see Ravallion (1994) and Foster, Seth, et al. (2013).

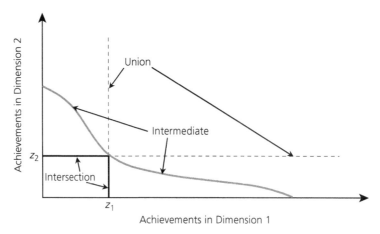

Figure 3.5. Identification using poverty frontiers

Finally, an example of an intermediate criterion is given by the bold grey line, and any person with an achievement combination falling below this frontier is identified as poor.

Poverty dominance is defined by Duclos, Sahn, and Younger (2006a) in the multidimensional context as follows. Once a poverty frontier is selected for identifying the poor, for any two societies with achievement matrices $X, Y \in \mathcal{X}$, the society with achievement matrix X poverty dominates the society with achievement matrix Y for poverty measure P, which we refer to as XPY, if and only if $P(X;z) \leq P(Y;z)$ for all $z \in z$ and $P(X;z) < P(Y;z)$ for some $z \in z$.

As in the unidimensional framework, the achievement matrices presented in the previous paragraph may also be represented using joint CDFs F_X and F_Y, respectively.[13] Each column of an achievement matrix can be represented by a univariate marginal distribution. In a multidimensional framework, in order to have poverty dominance between X and Y, it is not sufficient to check for deprivation dominance in each of the marginal distributions. It is, in fact, possible to have two different joint CDFs that have the same set of marginal distributions. For example, while comparing child poverty in two dimensions between Madagascar and Cameroon, Duclos, Sahn, and Younger (2006a) found that although statistically significant dominance held for each of the marginal distributions, dominance did not hold for the joint distribution. Hence, although it was apparent that deprivation was unambiguously higher in one country when examining both dimensions separately, the same could not be concluded when looking at two dimensions together. It is thus imperative to consider the joint distribution or the association between dimensions.

How overall multidimensional poverty is sensitive to association between dimensions depends on the relation between dimensions as discussed in section 2.5.2. If dimensions

---

[13] See Chapter 2 (section 2.2.3) for a definition of joint CDF in the two-dimension case.

are seen as substitutes, then an increase in association between dimensions, with the same set of marginal distributions, should not reduce overall poverty. On the contrary, if dimensions are complements, then an increase in association between dimensions, with the same set of marginal distributions, should not increase poverty. Duclos, Sahn, and Younger (2006a) present the stochastic dominance results for two dimensions, assuming the dimensions are substitutes. Thus, they show under the assumption of substitutability that if the joint cumulative distribution function Y lies above the joint cumulative distribution X or $F_Y(b_1, b_2) > F_X(b_1, b_2)$ for all $b_1 b_2 \in R_+$, then XPY for all poverty measures that satisfy weak monotonicity and subgroup decomposability and use either union, intersection, or any intermediate poverty frontier method for identification. Note that the condition $F_Y(b_1, b_2) > F_X(b_1, b_2)$ for all $b_1 b_2 \in R_+$ is an intersection-like condition because $F_Y(b_1, b_2)$ and $F_X(b_1, b_2)$ denote the shares of population with achievements less than b_1 in dimension 1 and at the same time achievements less than b_2 in dimension 2. This is analogous to the rectangular area bounded by the black bold lines in Figure 3.5. Thus, the novelty of this finding is that one should only check the intersection-like condition. For higher-order stochastic dominance conditions, readers are referred to Duclos, Sahn, and Younger (2006a).[14]

Bourguignon and Chakravarty (2009) develop related first-order dominance conditions for multidimensional poverty measurement in the two-dimension case. Unlike Duclos, Sahn, and Younger, they use a counting approach for identification. They show that for poverty measures that satisfy deprivation focus, symmetry, replication invariance, population subgroup decomposability, weak monotonicity, and weak deprivation rearrangement (substitutes), poverty dominance is required with respect to each marginal distribution and with respect to the joint distribution in the intersection area (the rectangular area bounded by solid bold lines in Figure 3.5). This result is consistent with Duclos, Sahn, and Younger (2006a). Additionally, Bourguignon and Chakravarty (2009) show that for poverty measures that satisfy the same previously mentioned properties but also converse weak deprivation rearrangement (complements), poverty dominance is required with respect to each marginal distribution and with respect to the joint distribution in the union area (L-shaped area bounded by the dotted lines in Figure 3.5). For a detailed discussion, see Atkinson (2003).

[14] Note that when using a sample rather than the whole population, there is a difference between the mathematical conditions for poverty dominance and the statistical tests that determine when such conditions hold in a statistically significant way. In other words, it is possible to find cases in which although mathematically the dominance condition holds, the difference between the two joint distributions is not statistically significant, thus dominance cannot be concluded. Statistical tests for the dominance conditions in the multidimensional case have been developed by Duclos, Sahn, and Younger (2006a) and Batana and Duclos (2010), among others. Issues of statistical significance in poverty comparisons when using samples should also be considered when implementing other methodologies presented in this chapter. Chapter 8 and Chapter 9 present statistical tools to be used alongside the AF methodology.

3.3.3 APPLICATIONS OF THE MULTIDIMENSIONAL DOMINANCE APPROACH

The Duclos, Sahn, and Younger (2006a) framework has been applied in several empirical studies. Batana and Duclos (2010) used the technique with two dimensions to compare multidimensional poverty across six members of the West African Economic and Monetary Union: Benin, Burkina Faso, Côte d'Ivoire, Mali, Niger, and Togo. The comparison of these six countries involved fifteen pairwise comparisons, and identified a statistically significant dominance relation for twelve of the pairwise comparisons. Anaka and Kobus (2012) employed the technique, also using two dimensions, to compare multidimensional poverty across Polish *gminas* or municipalities. Labar and Bresson (2011) used this approach to study the change in multidimensional poverty in China between 1991 and 2006 and showed that the change in multidimensional poverty was not unambiguous. Gräb and Grimm (2011) extended this multidimensional dominance framework to the multi-period context and illustrated their approach using data for Indonesia and Peru.

Other applications of dominance analysis have also been undertaken recently. For example, Duclos and Échevin (2011) used a dominance approach to find that welfare in both Canada and the United States did not unambiguously change in terms of the joint distribution of income and health. In fact, although dominance in terms of income was prominent across the entire population, dominance across incomes did not hold across each health status. Extending the Atkinson and Bourguignon (1982) framework using four dimensions in the Indian context, Gravel and Mukhopadhyay (2010) found a robust reduction in multidimensional poverty between 1987 and 2002. The study used municipality-level information for three dimensions, not household-level information.

The above studies assume that the dimensions are continuous. In practice, most relevant indicators are discrete. Duclos, Sahn, and Younger (2006b) extend their multidimensional robustness approach to situations where one dimension is continuous but the rest of the dimensions may be discrete (Batana and Duclos 2011). For an alternative approach to discrete variables extending the Atkinson and Bourguignon (1982) framework, see Yalonetzky (2009, 2013).

3.3.4 A CRITICAL EVALUATION

The strength of the dominance approach is that when poverty dominance holds between a pair, then the comparison is unambiguous. No alternative specifications can alter the direction of comparison. Thus, it offers a tool to produce strong empirical assertions about poverty comparisons—assertions that hold across a range of poverty measures and in spite of any 'controversial' decisions on parameter values. Even if distributions cross, and thus it is not possible to have a rank, it is possible to check where the crossing has taken place and identify limited areas of dominance, which can provide important information. In addition, the dominance approach takes into account the joint distribution of achievements when identifying the poor and making poverty comparisons. The dominance approach has been used with both discrete and continuous data.

Despite its strengths, this approach has certain limitations that prevent it from being more widely used for empirical analysis. First, when dominance holds, conclusions about comparisons can be made, but when there is no dominance, no unambiguous comparisons can be made. In other words, the dominance approach can only provide a partial ordering—similar to Lorenz dominance in inequality measurement. Second, even in situations in which dominance comparisons are empirically possible and generate ordinal rankings of regions or societies across time, it is not possible to compare the extent of differences in poverty across two populations in any cardinally meaningful way. In other words, it is not possible to say how poor a region is compared to another or how much poverty has fallen or gone up over a certain period of time. The complete orderings and meaningful cardinal comparisons achieved using other methods, such as axiomatic measures, can be criticized as imposing arbitrariness or 'creating artificial problems' (Sen 1997: 5). However, it must also be recognized that the inability to offer a complete ranking in certain cases can make this tool of limited use from a policy perspective.

A third limitation of this approach (although not exclusive to it) is that the dominance conditions depend on assumptions regarding the relationship between achievements (either substitutes or complements). In practice, all empirical applications so far have assumed substitutability between achievements because conditions and their statistical tests in this case are more fully developed. As Duclos, Sahn, and Younger (2006a) point out, one of the reasons for not pursuing the case of complementarity further is that it would drastically limit the scope of robust orderings across alternative poverty frontiers. Furthermore, the test developed by Duclos, Sahn, and Younger (2006a) is more suitable for measures that use the aggregate achievement approach (poverty frontier) to identification than for measures that use a counting approach.

Fourth, although in this section we present the results in terms of population, it may be empirically challenging to compute dominance using more than two or three dimensions due to the 'curse of dimensionality'—the need for the sample size to increase exponentially with the number of dimensions. As Duclos, Sahn, and Younger (2006a) put it, 'in theory, extending our results to more than two dimensions is straightforward. In practice, though, most existing datasets in developing countries are probably not large enough to support tests on more than a few dimensions of wellbeing. This is because [of] the curse of dimensionality ...' (p. 944). In such cases of higher dimensionality, other tests or procedures may be required.[15] Another relevant point for the empirical implementation of the dominance approach is that there is often noise at the extremes of the distribution that one may wish to ignore, because otherwise results may be artificially

---

[15] This is well discussed in Anderson (2008), and several empirical routes have been designed due to this problem, as well as the problem of correlated samples. Of course all measures must assess how many indicators are enough (Chs 6, 8).

biased. For this reason, one may want to base the dominance criteria on a range that starts, for example, at certain percentage of the median of the distribution of each variable.

Finally, in the multidimensional context, dominance results beyond first order require more stringent conditions on the individual poverty function, such as those on signs of third order, fourth order, derivatives, and cross-derivatives, which are less intuitive (see Duclos, Sahn, and Younger 2006a and Atkinson 2003).

The remaining three sections present methodologies that create indices of multidimensional poverty reflecting the joint distribution across dimensions. As in the case of Venn diagrams and the dominance approach, each approach requires that information be available for the same unit of analysis so that the joint distribution among dimensions can be captured. We first outline some of the widely applied multivariate statistical techniques used in the analysis and measurement of multidimensional poverty and well-being.

3.4 **Statistical Approaches**

Statistical techniques are widely used in the design of poverty measures as well as in measures of well-being (Nardo et al. 2008; Maggino and Zumbo 2012). Key techniques include principle component analysis, multiple correspondence analysis, cluster analysis, latent class analysis, and factor analysis. These techniques use information from the joint distribution of indicators to inform different aspects of poverty measurement such as identifying who is poor, setting indicator weights, constructing individual deprivation scores, and aggregating information into poverty indices representing the level of poverty in a society. The techniques are often used because they are well-documented in the statistical literature. However, they also entail normative judgments that are often ignored in practical applications. This section first provides a synthetic overview of the various contributions of statistical techniques to poverty measurement design and their applicability to cardinal and ordinal data. It then introduces the most commonly implemented techniques of principle component analysis, multiple correspondence analysis, factor analysis, and structural equation modelling. The section concludes with an assessment of the insights and oversights that can occur in measures based on statistical approaches.

We divide the statistical techniques into two categories. Figure 3.6 sketches this classification. The two categories are: **descriptive methods**, whose primary aim is to describe a multivariate dataset, and **model-based methods**, which additionally attempt to make inferences about the population (Bartholomew et al. 2008). One of the challenges in surveying statistical approaches is that applied methodologies vary widely, but our classification does summarize the methods most frequently used.[16]

---

[16] For discussions and applications of further statistical methods, see Mardia, Kent, and Bibby (1979) and Bartholomew et al. (2008); for poverty in particular, see Kakwani and Silber (2008).

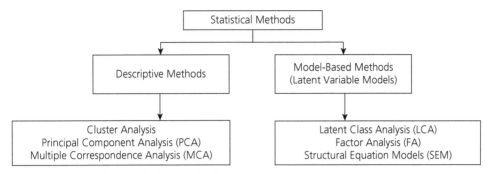

Figure 3.6. Multivariate statistical methods

As depicted in Figure 3.6, descriptive methods comprise cluster analysis, principal component analysis (PCA), and multiple correspondence analysis (MCA). The main difference between PCA and MCA is the scale of variables used. PCA is used when variables are of cardinal scale, while MCA is appropriate when variables are categorical or binary.[17] The model-based methods are latent variable models and cover latent class analysis (LCA), factor analysis (FA), and, more generally, structural equation models (SEM).[18] This section illustrates the use of PCA, MCA, and FA for aggregating dimensional achievements or deprivations for each person. These aggregated values may subsequently be used to identify the poor and to create poverty indices. We also illustrate cluster analysis and LCA as methods for grouping similar individuals or households together, which can be understood as a form of identification of the poor.

3.4.1 SUB-STEPS IN AGGREGATION WITHIN MULTIVARIATE STATISTICAL METHODS

The process of constructing a poverty index for a population has different sub-stages. Often these sub-stages of aggregation do not receive enough attention in the literature covering composite indices built using statistical methods, as the primary goal is to obtain a final aggregate number. In contrast, this section follows and makes explicit every single step followed in each of these techniques and itemizes the decisions made at each step. For different decisions taken, at each stage, different conclusions may arise. This novel

---

[17] Greenacre (1984) and Jolliffe (2002); see also section 2.3. It must be noted that, as stated in section 2.3, categorical variables need to be ordered when being used in poverty measurement. In fact, Asselin (2009: 32) explicitly makes this assumption. In this section, when we refer to categorical variables, we implicitly mean categorically ordered variables.

[18] Sometimes descriptive methods such as PCA or MCA are misunderstood as modelling a latent variable. While descriptive methods are linked to a latent *concept*, they do not explicitly model a latent *variable*. Also, note that factor models for binary data are occasionally referred to as Item Response models. For an application of such an approach to poverty analysis, see Deutsch et al. (2014).

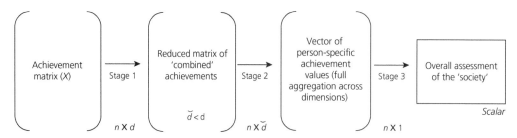

Figure 3.7. Aggregation sub-steps within multivariate statistical methods

presentation will enable readers to transparently compare poverty measures built using statistical methods with other approaches such as counting-based methods.

For example, when PCA or MCA is used, one needs to determine the number of components or axes to retain. There are several rules for choosing among these 'new' variables, which are essentially transformations of the original indicator variables. The users of PCA or MCA are often unaware of these various rules and their consequences in the construction of the individual achievement/deprivation values or the final poverty index (Coste et al. 2005). Moreover, if more than one component or axis is retained, the user also needs to decide how to combine them. In this regard, Asselin (2009) discusses the consistency requirements (axioms) that, in his view, a multidimensional poverty index obtained through MCA should satisfy and suggests using more than the first factorial axis. Whether or not one agrees with these particular axioms and requirements, it shows that when constructing measures through multivariate techniques one needs to be aware of the intermediate processes of aggregation, as the decisions made at each stage are likely to lead to varying results.

To provide an overview of statistical methods, we distinguish three sub-stages that may be used when generating summary measures of poverty (Figure 3.7). While these techniques are used for both well-being and deprivation analyses, here they are presented for deprivation analysis.

The aggregation sequence begins with a multivariate achievement matrix (X) as defined in Chapter 2, where the joint distribution of n persons across d indicators is often represented by second-order moments such as the correlation/covariance matrix (in the case of cardinal variables) or the multi-way contingency table (in the case of categorical variables) across the d indicators.[19] Using these second-order moments of the joint distribution in the first stage of aggregation, one applies a multivariate method (say, PCA, MCA, or FA) that combines the d indicators into a smaller number of $\breve{d}$ ($< d$) new variables.

In PCA and MCA, one seeks to replace the original set of d indicators with a smaller number of $\breve{d}$ variables that account for *most* of the information in the original set, which

---

[19] When variables' scales are of mixed nature (i.e. both cardinal and categorical), the correlation matrix adjusts for this difference in the scale of measurement. See section 3.4.3.

in PCA are uncorrelated or orthogonal. The new sets of variables are transformations of the original ones and are referred to as 'components' in PCA and 'axes' in MCA. In FA, one retains $\check{d}$ number of common factors that explain the common variance among the d original indicators. Note that FA focuses on explaining the *common variance* across indicators, whereas PCA seeks to account for *total variance*. FA assumes that a set of indicators vary according to some underlying statistical model, which partitions the total variance across indicators into common and unique variances. The common variance is represented by the factors and is the basis for interpreting the underlying structure of the data. Clearly, this first stage reduces the dimensionality of the $n \times d$ achievement matrix to a matrix of size $n \times \check{d}$ with $\check{d}$ ($< d$) new variables.

The second stage of aggregation uses the reduced achievement matrix of size $n \times \check{d}$ and combines the $\check{d}$ variables, either by applying a multivariate method or an ad hoc procedure, to create a vector of size $n \times 1$ that represents the aggregate achievement values for each of the n persons. As a special case, if there is only one $\check{d}$ and if there is no further aggregation, then $\check{d}$ itself gives an overall measure of achievement for each person. An example of the two aggregation steps described above is followed by Ballon and Krishnakumar (2011). They first implement a so-called first-order factor model, where the d indicators are assumed to be manifestations of $\check{d}$ latent or unobserved variables using confirmatory factor analysis in the form of a structural equation model.[20] Then, they suggest using a so-called second-order factor model that combines these $\check{d}$ variables into an 'overall' factor, assuming that these $\check{d}$ variables are also manifestations of a latent variable.[21] The overall factor score for each person in this case is analogous to the aggregate achievement value in the aggregate achievement approach to identification described in section 2.2.2.

Alternatively, rather than using a multivariate method, one may use an ad hoc procedure—a common one being to combine the $\check{d}$ variables using some form of weighted average. For example, in their study of quality of life among forty-three countries, Rahman et al. (2011) use the proportion of the total variance accounted for each component as its weight. Krishnakumar and Ballon (2008), in their estimation of children's capabilities in Bolivia, use the inverse of the factor's variance as its weight. However, other functional forms of weights could be envisaged. Note that the choice of weights may affect the cardinal interpretation of the results but not the ordinal one if the chosen weights preserve the order of the distribution of the factor scores as in the case of Krishnakumar and Ballon (2008).

---

[20] Exploratory factor models make no assumptions regarding the relationships among the observed indicators and the latent factors. One chooses the number of factors to retain, much like PCA or MCA. Confirmatory factor models (CFA), on the other hand, do assume pre-specified patterns of these relationships.

[21] Second-order factor models are applied when the hypothesis is that several related factors can be accounted for by one or more common underlying higher-order factors. In multidimensional poverty, a first-order model hypothesizes that each dimension is a factor measured by multiple indicators. As each of these dimensions is a partial representation of the multidimensional phenomenon of poverty, one can further hypothesize that each dimension can be accounted for by a single and common factor (see Ballon and Krishnakumar 2011).

The third stage aggregates the person-specific aggregate achievement values of all persons into an index that reflects the overall poverty of the population. Clearly, to achieve such a poverty index, identification of the poor needs to take place, comparing the person-specific aggregate achievement value against some poverty cutoff. This cutoff may be absolute but typically is relative in these methods. Thus, in this third stage, the $n \times 1$ vector, containing person-specific achievements, is compressed into a scalar measure to assess poverty in the society. Section 3.4.2 presents a brief overview of implementations of the various statistical approaches.

3.4.2 APPLICATIONS OF STATISTICAL APPROACHES IN POVERTY AGGREGATION

Filmer and Pritchett (1999, 2001) applied PCA to a set of asset variables found in the Demographic and Health Surveys and retained the first principal component in order to construct a household asset index. The asset index scores were standardized in relation to a standard normal distribution with a mean of 0 and a standard deviation of 1. All individuals in each household were assigned the household's standardized asset index score, and all individuals in the sample population were ranked according to that score. The sample population was then divided into quintiles of individuals, with all individuals in a single household being assigned to the same quintile. In this case, the third sub-step was not completed and no scalar societal measure was generated. Filmer and Pritchett's approach has since been used for the analysis of health inequalities (Bollen, Glanville, and Stecklov 2002; Gwatkin et al. 2000; Schellenberg et al. 2003), child nutrition (Sahn and Stifel 2003), and child mortality (Fay et al. 2005; Sastry 2004) among other purposes. In the field of poverty and inequality, PCA and FA have been applied by Sahn and Stifel (2000), Stifel and Christiaensen (2007), McKenzie (2005), Lelli (2001), and Roche (2008), among others.

Within the correspondence analysis literature, we find applications by Asselin and Anh (2008), Booysen et al. (2008), Deutsch, Silber, and Verme (2012), Batana and Duclos (2010), and Ballon and Duclos (2014). Asselin and Anh (2008) built an MCA composite index of human and physical assets to study poverty dynamics in Vietnam between 1999 and 2002. Booysen et al. (2008) applied MCA to obtain an asset index for comparing poverty over time and across seven West African countries. Deutsch, Silber, and Verme (2012) use correspondence analysis to analyse social exclusion in Macedonia. Batana and Duclos (2010) calculated a multidimensional index of wealth (ownership of durable goods and access to services) using MCA for a series of sub-Saharan African countries. This index was used to compare cross-country multidimensional poverty via sequential stochastic dominance analysis. Ballon and Duclos (2014) applied MCA to obtain two sets of values reflecting households' access to 'public' assets (basic services) and 'private' assets (durable goods) in Sudan and South Sudan. These two sets of MCA values were further used for measuring multidimensional poverty according to the Alkire and Foster (2011a) methodology.

Interesting applications of statistical techniques up to the last stage of aggregation (i.e. obtaining an overall well-being or deprivation index for the society) include those used by Kuklys (2005), Klasen (2000), and Ballon and Krishnakumar (2011). Kuklys used the factor scores obtained from a structural equation model as the input distributions in FGT poverty-type measures (Foster, Greer, and Thorbecke 1984). Ballon and Krishnakumar (2011) proposed an index of capability deprivation, where the input variables were the factor scores of a structural equation model that estimated children's capabilities. Klasen (2000) derived a material deprivation index for households in South Africa. Other interesting applications of structural equation models in development studies, although not focused on aggregation into a scalar measure, are the ones proposed by Di Tommaso (2007) for India, Wagle (2008) for Nepal and the United States, and Ballon (2011) for Cambodia.

3.4.3 A BRIEF AND FORMAL OUTLINE OF DIFFERENT STATISTICAL APPROACHES

This section presents in greater detail the three methods most commonly implemented for both identification and aggregation, namely, PCA, MCA, and FA. Additional methodological variations are also implemented; this section covers the more standard approaches.

3.4.3.1 Principal Component Analysis

Principal component analysis was first proposed by Pearson (1901) and was further developed by Hotelling (1933). Hotelling derived principal components using mathematical arguments, leading to the standard algebraic derivation that optimizes the variance of the original dataset (known as an 'eigen decomposition'), while Pearson approached PCA geometrically.[22]

The main aim of PCA is parsimony.[23] Basically, in PCA the d indicator variables are transformed into linear combinations called principal components. In this search for parsimony, one seeks to find fewer principal components (PCs) that retain most of the information in the original set of observed indicators. The information retained by the

---

[22] Pearson's geometric derivation defines principal components as 'optimal' lines and planes. The first principal component is the line that best fits a set of n points in a reduced $\check{d}$ dimensional space. The first two principal components define a plane that best fits a cloud of n points in the $\check{d}$ dimensional space, and likewise for other principal components. Jolliffe (2002) and Basilevsky (1994) provide historical surveys of the development of PCA.

[23] Other aims of PCA include addressing multicollinearity issues in regression analysis, the detection of outliers, or the interpretation of the underlying structure of a set of observed indicators (Jolliffe 2002). The latter is similar to factor analysis, which is discussed later on in this section, but there are important differences between these two techniques.

PCs is measured by the proportion of the total (sample) variance that is accounted for in each of the PCs. There is usually a trade-off between a gain in parsimony and a loss of information. If the original indicators are correlated, and especially if they are highly correlated, then one can replace them by a relatively small set of PCs—say, $\check{d}$, where $\check{d}$ is smaller than d. If the original indicators are only slightly correlated, the resulting PCs will largely reflect the original set without much gain in parsimony. Clearly, the full set of PCs will fully account for the total variance of the original indicators and will be the case where no reduction in dimensionality is achieved. A particular feature of PCs is that these are uncorrelated (orthogonal).

Let us denote each PC by f^{PC}. In order to retain comparability with notation in other sections and chapters of this book, we denote the $n \times d$-dimensional achievement matrix by X, where d is the number of observed indicators, n is the number of persons, and x_{ij} is the achievement of person i in dimension j for all $i = 1,\ldots,n$ and $j = 1,\ldots,d$. We denote the jth observed indicator by $\check{x}_j$.[24] For a given person i, the full set of PCs is a system of d linear combinations of these observed indicators.

This is written as

$$
\begin{aligned}
f_{1i}^{PC} &= w_1^1 \check{x}_{i1} + w_2^1 \check{x}_{i2} + \cdots + w_d^1 \check{x}_{id} \\
&\ \ \vdots \\
f_{li}^{PC} &= w_1^l \check{x}_{i1} + w_2^l \check{x}_{i2} + \cdots + w_d^l \check{x}_{id} \ . \\
&\ \ \vdots \\
f_{di}^{PC} &= w_1^d \check{x}_{i1} + w_2^d \check{x}_{i2} + \cdots + w_d^d \check{x}_{id}
\end{aligned}
\tag{3.1}
$$

The system of equations in (3.1) shows that each principal component is a weighted sum of the observed indicators, where w_j^l is the weight or coefficient assigned to indicator j for the lth principal component. Thus, for the lth PC, $w_1^l, w_2^l, \ldots, w_d^l$ are the weights of the d indicators, respectively, in the lth linear combination. In order to preserve parity of notation with other sections and chapters, the subscript j of each coefficient w_j^l denotes the indicator or variable and the superscript l denotes the component.

Our aim in poverty analysis is to replace the set of d observed indicators with a much smaller number of 'transformed variables', here the PCs, that retain most of the information in the indicators, which is measured by the proportion of the total variance accounted for by each PC (Bartholomew et al. 2008: ch. 5). To obtain each PC, one requires an estimate of the weights (w_j^l) and of the variance of the PCs. These are obtained using the maximum variance properties. For a given sample, the maximum variance property of PCA defines the first principal component as the linear combination with maximal sample variance among all linear combinations of the indicators, so that it accounts for the largest proportion of the total sample variance (Rencher 2002). To achieve a maximum, one needs to add some normalization constraints on the coefficients

---

[24] Note that in section 3.4.3 we formalize the use of statisitcal approaches using sample moments instead of population moments. For this reason, we use $\check{x}_{ij}$ instead of x_{ij}, to denote the observed achievement of person i in dimension j.

w_j^l, which usually require that the sum of squares of these coefficients is equal to one.[25] This leads to an optimization problem, where one maximizes the variance of the first linear combination subject to the sum of squares of the weights being equal to one to find the coefficients w_j^1 for all $j = 1, \ldots, d$, and the variance of the first PC. If we write the first principal component (f_1^{PC}) as

$$f_1^{PC} = \sum_{j=1}^{d} w_j^1 \check{x}_j, \tag{3.2}$$

its sample variance

$$Var\left[f_1^{PC}\right] = Var\left[\sum_{j=1}^{d} w_j^1 \check{x}_j\right] = \sum_{j=1}^{d} \left(w_j^1\right)^2 s_j^2 + \sum_{j \neq j'}^{d} w_j^1 w_{j'}^1 s_{jj'} \tag{3.3}$$

is given by the variance of the linear combination of the indicators, which takes into account the sample variances s_j^2 of the indicators and also the sample covariances $s_{jj'}$ across indicators. Thus to obtain the first PC, one will maximize $Var\left[f_1^{PC}\right]$ given by equation (3.3) subject to $\sum_{j=1}^{d} \left(w_j^1\right)^2 = 1$. This will provide an estimate of the weight vector w_j^1 for all $j = 1, \ldots, d$ and of the variance of f_1^{PC}.

The second principal component is the linear combination that accounts for the second largest proportion of total variance among indicators that is orthogonal (uncorrelated) to the first PC. To find the second PC one will maximize $Var\left[f_2^{PC}\right]$ subject to $\sum_{j=1}^{d} \left(w_j^2\right)^2 = 1$ and the orthogonality constraint between the first and second PC, given by $\sum_{j=1}^{d} w_j^1 w_j^2 = 0$. This optimization will give estimates of the weight vector w_j^2 for all $j = 1, \ldots, d$ and of the variance of f_2^{PC}. In a similar manner, one can define the third PC as the weight vector that maximizes the third linear combination, given that the sum of squares of the coefficients is equal to one and that the third PC is orthogonal to the first two PCs, and so on and so forth for the fourth, fifth, and d^{th} PC.

It turns out that the maximization problem is equivalent to finding the eigenvalues and eigenvectors of the sample covariance matrix.[26] The eigenvalues usually denoted by $\lambda_1, \lambda_2, \ldots, \lambda_d$ are listed from largest to smallest $\lambda_1 \geq \lambda_2 \ldots \geq \lambda_d$ and determine the variances of each PC. The eigenvector associated with each eigenvalue determines the weights or coefficients of the indicators on the corresponding component. Thus the variance of component l, $Var\left[f_l^{PC}\right]$, is the eigenvalue λ_l, and the eigenvector $w^l = (w_1^l, w_2^l, \ldots, w_d^l)$ associated with this eigenvalue λ_l gives the coefficients or weights of each indicator on the lth PC. The percentage of variance accounted for by f_l^{PC} is therefore $\lambda_l / (\lambda_1 + \lambda_2 + \cdots + \lambda_d)$.

[25] This restriction ensures that weights are non-negative and each weight is bounded above by one.
[26] For definitions of eigenvalues, eigenvectors, and singular value decomposition, see the statistical appendix A.6 of Mardia, Kent, and Bibby (1979).

When the units of measurements across (cardinal) indicators vary or when the variances[27] across them differ widely, one may wish to use the sample correlation matrix $\mathbf{R}$ instead of the sample covariance matrix $\mathbf{S}$. This is equivalent to standardizing each of the d indicators to have a mean of 0 and variance of 1, then finding the PCs of the standardized covariance matrix $\mathbf{R}$. The principal components obtained from $\mathbf{R}$ will contribute evenly to total variation and thus be more interpretable. However, the components extracted from $\mathbf{S}$, the unstandardized covariance matrix, will differ from those extracted from the correlation matrix[28] $\mathbf{R}$, and so the percentage of variance accounted for by the components of each of the matrices will be different. Thus the decision to use either $\mathbf{R}$ or $\mathbf{S}$ may affect the final results.

Once one has computed the PCs and obtained an estimate of the weights and the variances of each PC, one needs to decide the number of components to retain. This is especially important in studies of deprivation that use PCA as the basis for obtaining either a person-specific or a society measure of poverty, as the results may vary depending on the number of PCs retained. This aspect has been thoroughly examined by Coste et al. (2005) while obtaining synthetic measures of deprivation in health.

There is a multiplicity of rules for determining the number of components to retain (Jolliffe 2002). The main guidelines for selecting components in PCA are based on a combination of the percentage of variance accounted for as in (3.3), the scree plot,[29] and the useful interpretation that the retained components may provide for analysis (Rencher 2002; Bartholomew et al. 2008). Following the first criterion, one will retain the first l components which account for a large proportion of total variation, say 70–80%. If the correlation matrix is used, this 'rule of thumb' suggests retaining those components whose eigenvalue is greater than one. The second criterion suggests viewing a scree graph, which plots the eigenvalues, to find a visual break (or 'elbow') between 'large' and 'small' eigenvalues and discarding the smallest ones. The accuracy of the scree plot method for discarding components is between 65–75% and depends on the sample size and degree of correlation of the indicators (Rencher 2002). According to the third criterion, one shall retain those components that provide a useful and coherent interpretation for the analysis. Coste et al. (2005) suggest more robust rules for the selection of components, which basically involve repeating the analysis across samples, assessing the selection through quality-of-fit indices, and considering complementary methods to PCA, especially confirmatory factor analysis.

Having selected the number of components to retain, the next step is to obtain a person-specific measure of deprivation by computing the component scores for each individual in the sample as given in (3.1). These scores, if further aggregated, may

---

[27] In PCA, by meaningful variances, we mean the variances of cardinal indicators having a meaningful scale of measurement. For binary or categorical indicators, MCA should be used instead of PCA.

[28] Note that for $\mathbf{R}$ the sum of the eigenvalues will be equal to the number of indicators, d in our context, and hence the proportion of variance due to the lth PC is $\tilde{\lambda}_l/d$, where $\tilde{\lambda}_l$ is the lth eigenvalue of $\mathbf{R}$.

[29] A scree plot is a line graph that shows the fraction of total variance in the data that each principal component accounts for.

create societal measures. To ease the interpretation of the components, the weights are often rescaled so that those related to the components accounting for a greater proportion of the total variance are larger. The rescaled weights are referred to as component 'loadings' and may be interpreted as the correlation coefficient(s) between indicator j and component l when the correlation matrix or the standardized covariance matrix is used. In a similar manner, to facilitate the comparison across components, it is often convenient to rescale the components. This is equivalent to standardizing them to have unit variance. This leads to a standardized representation of the lth PC of person i as

$$\tilde{f}_{li}^{PC} = \tilde{w}_1^l \check{x}_{i1} + \tilde{w}_2^l \check{x}_{i2} + \cdots + \tilde{w}_d^l \check{x}_{id}, \tag{3.4}$$

where $\tilde{f}_l^{PC} = f_l^{PC}/\sqrt{Var[f_l^{PC}]} = f_l^{PC}/\sqrt{\lambda_l}$ is the standardized l-th component and $\tilde{w}_j^l = w_j^l/\sqrt{\lambda_l}$ is the standardized component score weight or coefficient for component l and indicator j, for all l and all j. Note that the number of retained components and the standardization procedure may affect the cardinal interpretation of results in empirical studies of poverty.

As in section 3.4.2, the dimensional components may be combined into an individual score using a multivariate or an ad hoc procedure, and individual component scores may be aggregated, for example, by using a simple average.

3.4.3.2 Multiple Correspondence Analysis

When the indicators are ordinal, binary, or categorical, a more suitable multivariate technique for a lower-dimensional description of the data is correspondence analysis (CA). The use of correspondence analysis in social sciences increased significantly in the late 1980s, inspired mainly by the work of Bourdieu (1986, 1987). The history of CA can be traced back to the mid-1930s during which various authors defined correspondence analysis in different but mathematically equivalent ways.[30] An intuitive and widely used definition in the multivariate statistical literature is the geometrical approach suggested in Greenacre (1984) and Greenacre and Blasius (2006) who follow the ideas of the French mathematician and linguist Jean-Paul Benzécri (Benzécri and Bellier 1973). This geometric approach sees CA as an adaptation of PCA to categorical data.

Like PCA, CA is based on a geometric decomposition.[31] Simple correspondence analysis explores the association between two categorical indicators, $\check{x}_j$ and $\check{x}_{j'}$ having categories l and l', respectively, using a two-way contingency table or cross-tab of relative

---

[30] Greenacre (1984) and Gifi (1990) provide an overview of the historical development of CA dating back to Hirschfeld (1935), Fisher (1940), and Guttman (1941). Louis Guttman was the first to extend the ideas behind simple CA to the general case of more than two variables, leading to what today is known as MCA.

[31] In PCA this involves the eigen decomposition of the correlation matrix, while in CA this involves the singular value decomposition of the standardized residual matrix.

frequencies denoted by P, which is also referred to as the correspondence matrix. The elements of P are the set of relative frequencies across pairs of categories of the two indicators, denoted by $\mathbb{p}_{ll'}$, for all $l = 1, \ldots, \mathbb{L}; l' = 1, \ldots \mathbb{L}'$, where $\mathbb{L}$ and $\mathbb{L}'$ denote the number of response categories of each of the two indicators, respectively.

The basic MCA algorithm analyses the association using the singular value decomposition (SVD) of the matrix of standardized residuals Z with the ll'^{th} element being $\mathbb{z}_{ll'} = (\mathbb{p}_{ll'} - \mathbb{p}_{l+}\mathbb{p}_{+l'})/\sqrt{\mathbb{p}_{l+}\mathbb{p}_{+l'}}$, where $\mathbb{p}_{l+} = \sum_{l=1}^{\mathbb{L}} \mathbb{p}_{ll'}$ and $\mathbb{p}_{+l'} = \sum_{l'=1}^{\mathbb{L}'} \mathbb{p}_{ll'}$ are the row and column margins. These margins are the marginal frequencies also known as masses in the CA literature (see section 2.2.3 for an explanation of a 2×2 contingency table). The standardized residuals $\mathbb{z}_{ll'}$ are similar to those used in the calculation of the Pearson chi-square statistic (χ^2), which measures dissimilarity between the row and column profiles of a two-way contingency table. For this reason, in CA the total variance in the cross-tab, called 'total inertia', is equal to χ^2 divided by the sample size. Similar to PCA, in CA one also needs estimates of the total inertia ('variance') and of the component weights or coefficients to obtain person-specific achievement values. These are obtained from the SVD of Z where the eigenvalues,[32] called 'principal inertias', quantify the variance in the cross-tab and the singular vectors give the axes' coordinates for the low-dimensional representation and play a similar role as weights or coefficients in PCA. When the reduction in dimensionality involves two axes, one can plot the axes' coordinates, providing a visual representation (bi-plot) of the association across categories of the indicators.

In the general case of a set of categorical indicators, CA extends the analysis to a multiway table of all associations amongst pairs of variables. This is an MCA, which performs a CA on a Burt or indicator matrix. The indicator matrix I is an individuals-by-categories matrix. The elements of this matrix are 0s and 1s with columns for all categories of all indicators and rows corresponding to individuals. A value of 1 indicates that a category is observed; a 0 indicates that it is not. The Burt matrix is a matrix of all two-way cross-tabulations of the categorical variables. MCA on either the Burt or indicator matrix gives equivalent standard coordinates, but the total principal inertias obtained from each of the two approaches differ.

As with simple correspondence analysis, the principal inertias and the singular vectors are used to obtain person-specific achievement or deprivation values. Thus, the person's deprivation score will vary depending on whether the Burt or indicator matrix is used. The Burt matrix is the most commonly used.[33]

---

[32] Or squared singular values.

[33] A slight inconvenience of MCA is that it artificially inflates the chi-squared distances between profiles and the total inertia. This can be partially remedied after CA of the Burt matrix by scale readjustments of the MCA solution. Additionally, in MCA the notion of accounted inertia has less justification because the χ^2 statistic involves distances not only between categories of two different variables but also between two categories of the same variable. These within-variable distances depend only on the marginal frequencies of each indicator and do not contribute to the analysis of association with other indicators (cf. Greenacre and Blasius 2006).

3.4.3.3 Factor Analysis and Structural Equation Modelling

Factor Analysis (FA) and structural equation models fit within the broad class of Latent Variable Models (LVM). LVMs are regression models that make assumptions and express relationships between observed and unobserved (or latent) variables. The development of the single-factor model was initiated by Spearman (1904) to measure overall intelligence. This was further generalized by Garnett (1919) and Thurstone (1931), among others. In an FA model, the main assumption is that several observed indicators depend on the same latent variable or variables. This dependence is reflected in the correlation matrix across indicators. Thus FA is a model-based technique that assumes an underlying statistical model regarding the variation in a set of indicators. As discussed earlier, the common variance is represented by a factor. Like PCA, FA is also used as a data reduction method; however, there is a fundamental difference between the two methods. PCA is a descriptive method that attempts to interpret the underlying (latent) structure of a set of indicators on the basis of their total variation, while FA is a model-based method that focuses on explaining the common variance across indicators instead of total variance.

Factor models could be either exploratory or confirmatory. Exploratory factor analysis (EFA) models make no prior assumptions regarding the pattern of relationships among the observed indicators and the latent factors. Confirmatory factor analysis (CFA) models do assume a pre-specified pattern of relationships.

In the general linear (exploratory) factor model with observed cardinal indicators, the d indicators are expressed as linear combinations of a few unobserved factors $f_1^{FA}, f_2^{FA}, \ldots, f_{\check{d}}^{FA} (\check{d} < d)$. For a given individual i, this takes the form of a measurement equation:

$$\check{x}_{ij} = \check{\gamma}_0 + \check{\gamma}_j^1 f_{1i}^{FA} + \check{\gamma}_j^2 f_{2i}^{FA} + \cdots + \check{\gamma}_j^{\check{d}} f_{\check{d}i}^{FA} + \epsilon_{ij}; \quad j = 1, \ldots, d, \tag{3.5}$$

where $f_1^{FA}, f_2^{FA}, \ldots, f_{\check{d}}^{FA}$ are the common factors, ϵ_{ij} are residuals, and $\check{\gamma}_j^l$ is the lth regression parameter for the jth indicator—referred to as 'factor loading'.

The general linear factor model assumes that the factors have a mean of 0, a variance of 1, and are uncorrelated with each other. It also assumes that the residuals have a mean of 0, are heteroscedastic, and that they are uncorrelated with the factors. The general linear factor model may lead to the normal linear factor model if, additionally, it is assumed that the observed indicators and the residuals follow a multivariate normal distribution.

The essence of factor models is the correlation structure of the model's indicators. This is reflected by the correlation matrix predicted by the model. To fit factor models, one looks for values of the parameters such that the observed correlation matrix is as close as possible to the one predicted by the model. The estimation could be done through a variety of methods comprising generalized least squares and maximum likelihood (cf. Joreskog 1970; Bollen 1989; Joreskog and Sorbom 1999; Muthén 1984; Muthén and Muthén 1998–2012). The adequacy of the model and the selection of the number of factors to retain are checked through goodness-of-fit statistics (Bartholomew and Tzamourani 1999). When the observed indicators comprise categorical variables it is possible to construct a meaningful correlation matrix. This 'adjusted' correlation matrix will include standard Pearson correlations for pairs of cardinal indicators, tetrachoric (polychoric) correlations for pairs of binary (categorical) indicators, and bi-serial (polyserial) correlations for pairs of cardinal and dichotomous (categorical) variables. For such purposes, one can assume that a latent continuous variable, normally distributed, underlies every categorical variable. This is referred to as the underlying variable approach (cf. Joreskog and Moustaki 2001).

Following the estimation, and to ease interpretation, the factors are transformed into a 'new' set of factors. This process is called 'rotation' and involves orthogonal and oblique rotations, among others. The latter requires relaxing the assumption of absence of correlation among factors.

Once the factors have a meaningful interpretation, it is possible to obtain person-specific achievement values on the latent variable. The prediction of the achievement/deprivation values could be achieved through several methods that lead to highly correlated but different cardinal values of the factor (Bollen 1989). In the presence of only cardinal variables, factor scores often come from regression analysis (see, for example, Lawley and Maxwell 1971). In the presence of binary or categorical variables, factor scores may be computed through Bayesian estimation.

CFA models differ from EFA models as they pre-specify patterns of relationships between the observed indicators and the latent variables. These models extend to structural equation models, which, in addition to the measurement equation, specify relationships across factors and between factors and other explanatory variables. The second type of relationship is referred to as the structural part of the model. Hence in this case the statistical model is composed of two parts: a measurement part and a structural part (Bollen 1989).

Among these models we find the so-called multiple-indicator multiple-causes models (MIMIC), which are characterized by a latent endogenous variable but no measurement error in the explanatory variables. The full structural equation model corresponds to a regression model where both dependent and explanatory variables are measured with error (cf. Bollen 1989; Browne and Arminger 1995; Joreskog and Sorbom 1979). As with EFA, with CFA models one needs to estimate the model, assess its quality of fit, and predict factor scores. Further, one could also be interested in performing statistical inference with the predicted scores. For a discussion of the exact statistical properties of scores resulting from factorial methods, see Krishnakumar and Nagar (2008).

3.4.4 A CRITICAL EVALUATION

The strengths of statistical methods that we have presented in this section are several. First, descriptive techniques such as PCA and MCA aim to reduce dimensionality and can be used in an appropriate normative setting to create an aggregate achievement value that can be further used for identification of the poor and for constructing poverty indices. In addition to the reduction of dimensionality, model-based techniques are appropriate when poverty is considered to be an unobserved or latent phenomenon, and the measurement purpose is to specify relationships between the unobserved variables and some observed indicators that are assumed to partially and indirectly measure this abstract concept. Furthermore, statistical techniques are easy to apply, and certain methods can be used with ordinal as well as cardinal data. Also, statistical methods can be used in conjunction with other approaches. For example, PCA, MCA, or FA could be helpful for the selection and categorization of indicators when constructing a multidimensional poverty measure. Thus, statistical methods can complement other methods presented in this chapter.

Despite their strengths, statistical methods have certain limitations when constructing poverty measures. First, it remains unclear which of the axiomatic properties outlined in Chapter 2 these indices do and do not satisfy. As explained in Chapter 2, an understanding of the embedded properties is important in order to follow how a poverty index behaves, given various changes in the joint distribution of achievements or deprivations. As it may not be intuitively easy to understand various properties that indices based on statistical methods may satisfy, further research is required. For example, recall that all statistical methods, in practice, use sample moments. For second-order sample moments, in order to obtain an unbiased estimate of the variance and covariance, we lose one degree of freedom, i.e. instead of dividing by the sample size, we divide by the sample size minus one. This may cause the overall poverty index based on these methods to violate the replication invariance property (section 2.5.1), which would make the comparison of countries with different population sizes very difficult. Measures based on certain statistical applications may violate other axioms such as deprivation focus or monotonicity.

Second, comparisons across different datasets require considerable care when statistical methods are used to create individual achievement values or an overall poverty index. For example, when comparing two countries or time periods using the standardized component score or weights in equation (3.4), one should bear in mind that the comparisons are relative. That is, they depend on the eigen decomposition of the corresponding datasets. Even if datasets are pooled in order to improve comparability, the resulting weights are still relative. For example, suppose that to compare the weights in equation (3.4) across two time periods, one pools two national datasets. Now suppose a third period is added and must be compared with the previous two periods. In order to preserve comparability of weights across all three periods, one now needs to pool all three datasets. But the conclusions for the first two datasets in the three-way pooling may not remain the same as the conclusions when only two datasets were pooled. Hence, the conclusions remain relative even when datasets are pooled.

The assumptions underlying statistical methods also require scrutiny. For example, some descriptive methods capture the associations between dimensions using Pearson's correlation, which is only a linear measure of association and may not always be successful in capturing the more complex association structure between dimensions. In the case of model-based methods, one should bear in mind the underlying statistical assumptions, specifically bivariate normality used for computing the tetrachoric correlations. This correlation applies to binary indicators and is used for fitting purposes in the model. But the assumption of bivariate normality may not be an appropriate assumption when indicators are binary (Mardia, Kent, and Bibby 1979).

Another challenge is that it may be difficult to provide an intuitive interpretation of the person-specific achievement/deprivation values or the overall poverty index constructed through PCA or EFA. For example, the well-known person-specific asset index scores that are often used to rank the population may not have an intuitive interpretation, nor may components such as the weights. Thus, in the analysis of poverty using the asset index scores, it is often not possible to set an absolute poverty cutoff to identify the poor. The usual practice is to follow a relative approach, dividing the entire population into percentiles and then identifying the population in the bottom percentiles as 'poor'.

Finally, as this section has specified perhaps more clearly than in standard expositions of these techniques, the precise applications of statistical methods can vary a great deal, and seemingly minor or incidental methodological choices may affect results. Relevant decisions include the selection of the statistical method, the number of components to retain, the method for combining components (multivariate or ad hoc), the selection of weights to combine factors (e.g. proportion of variance, inverse of variance, or some other approach), and the functional form used to aggregate across individuals. Other choices that may affect results include the selection of the unstandardized or standardized covariance matrix in PCA, the choice of the Burt or indicator matrix in MCA, and the choice of CFA rather than EFA, as well as methods used to rescale weights or generate factor scores, if relevant. The normative basis of such a multidimensional poverty measure could be difficult to ascertain. The reach of statistical approaches could be greatly strengthened if the axiomatic properties were clarified, methodological choices were justified normatively, and the robustness of results to alternative justifiable implementation methods were routinely and transparently assessed.

3.5 **Fuzzy Set Approaches**

One challenge of poverty measurement is that it requires *identifying* who is poor. As presented in Chapter 2, such identification is traditionally accomplished using poverty lines in the unidimensional framework. In a multidimensional counting framework, deprivation cutoffs enable us to identify who is deprived and a cross-dimensional poverty cutoff identifies who is poor. In each of these cases, a 'crisp' threshold dichotomizes the population into two groups that are understood to be qualitatively different, with an implicit presumption of certainty about such a distinction. Yet, intuition suggests that there might actually be considerable ambiguity in such an exercise. In fact, for example, in the unidimensional space, one might argue that being one cent above or below the income poverty line of US$1.25/day does not make any substantive difference in the person's actual situation. Similarly with ordinal data, there may be some uncertainty about the cutoffs distinguishing 'safe' from 'unsafe' water. Amartya Sen has warned about the risks of merrily ignoring such ambiguity:

If an underlying idea has an essential ambiguity a precise formulation of that idea must try to capture that ambiguity rather than attempt to lose it. Even when precisely capturing an ambiguity proves to be a difficult exercise, that is not an argument for forgetting the complex nature of the concept and seeking a spuriously narrow exactness. In social investigation and measurement, it is undoubtedly more important to be vaguely right than to be precisely wrong.[34]

3.5.1 FUZZY SET POVERTY APPROACH

It is precisely with the aim of dealing with such ambiguity that the fuzzy set theory—a technique extensively used in computer science and mathematics literature—was adapted for poverty measurement. The concept of fuzzy sets was first articulated by Zadeh (1965) and then developed by a large academic community, including Dubois and Prade (1980). Beginning with the seminal work of Cerioli and Zani (1990), fuzzy sets began to be used for multidimensional as well as unidimensional poverty analysis.[35] The use of this technique in poverty analysis expanded considerably, following Chiappero-Martinetti (1994, 1996, 2000) and Cheli and Lemmi (1995), during a period of fast-emerging research on the capability approach.[36]

A significant academic literature now applies the fuzzy set approach to poverty measurement. The theoretical contributions include Betti and Verma (2008), Cerioli and Zani (1990), Chakravarty (2006), Cheli and Lemmi (1995), Chiappero-Martinetti (1994, 1996, 2000), Clark and Hulme (2010), and Qizilbash (2006). Papers with comparative empirical analysis across methodologies include Amarante et al. (2010), Belhadj (2011), Belhadj and Matoussi (2010), Belhadj and Limam (2012), D'Ambrosio et al. (2011), Deutsch and Silber (2005), Lelli (2001), and Roche (2008). The context of analysis varies from countries in Europe to developing countries. Most analyses use household survey data; others employ macro data in which the country is the unit of analysis (see Baliamoune-Lutz and McGillivray 2006; Berenger and Verdier-Chouchane 2007). While most published materials are academic papers, there are also policy applications—such as a targeting method implemented for the ministry of planning in Colombia by Flórez et al. (2008, 2011) and a proposal for fuzzy targeting applied to Chile by Makdissi and Wodon

[34] Sen 1992: 48–9.
[35] See Ragin (2000) for an extensive application and Smithson and Verkuilen (2006) for a review of applications in the social sciences.
[36] Chiappero-Martinetti and Roche (2009) review empirical work in the late 1990s and early 2000s.

(2004). The book edited by Lemmi and Betti (2006) presents a valuable compilation of conceptual and empirical papers on the fuzzy set approach.

Fuzzy sets extend classical set theory, on which the Venn diagrams introduced in section 3.2 are based. While in classical set theory elements either belong to a set or not, fuzzy sets allow elements to have different *degrees of membership* to a set. Applied to poverty measurement, a key innovation is that rather than defining a person as either belonging to the set of the poor or not (i.e. identifying in a crisp way), the approach allows for degrees of membership to the set of the poor or deprived. Fuzzy set theorists believe that poverty is conceptually a 'vague predicate' and that the fuzzy set approach deals systematically with the vagueness and complexity of multidimensional poverty (Chiappero-Martinetti 2008; Qizilbash 2006).[37] At the time of its first implementation, the fuzzy set approach was one of the techniques aiming to deal with various dimensions and level of measures systematically. Chiappero-Martinetti (2008) argued that the fuzzy set approach offered a way to deal systematically with the *complexity in the measurement of multidimensional poverty* that emerges because of the need to make various choices (dimensions, weights, cutoffs, and so on).

Identification of poverty status is typically clear in cases of the undeniably rich or the absolutely destitute. But there are many intermediate cases where it is not completely clear if people are poor or not.[38] This is typical of vague predicates.[39] The predicate 'being poor' is subject to what is known as the Sorites paradox. Suppose that we take one dollar away from someone who we consider undeniably rich, say a billionaire. We would be prepared to accept that this act would not change the fact that the person is rich. Taking another dollar away would not make any difference either. If we continue repeating this act and asking the same question every time, we would always need to accept that taking one dollar away does not make the wealth level of the billionaire significantly different. However, the paradox is that if one continues repeating this action long enough, at some point we would have to accept that the billionaire is no longer a rich person and may have even become poor. Although it would be a paradox if the billionaire were rich and poor at the same time, there remains a vagueness about the exact point at which the billionaire became poor.

The fuzzy set approach addresses the intrinsic vagueness of the 'being poor' predicate by using so-called 'membership functions' at the identification step. Instead of setting a crisp deprivation or poverty cutoff, it defines a 'band' where the predicate is neither true nor false. Within the poverty band, a membership function is chosen to establish the

---

[37] In addition to applying to the predicates of being poor or deprived, the fuzzy set approach applies to other similar predicates such as 'being ultra poor' or 'being in chronic poverty' (Chiappero-Martinetti 2008; Qizilbash 2006).

[38] Chiappero-Martinetti (2008) distinguishes intrinsic vagueness and vagueness in measurement. The former is a theoretical conception; the latter is a methodological response.

[39] Qizilbash (2006) identifies three interrelated characteristics of vague predicates: (1) there are borderlines where it is not possible to establish with complete certainty if the person is poor; (2) there is not a sharp limit from which the predicate is undeniably true; and (3) the predicate is susceptible to the Sorites paradox.

degree of certainty of the predicates 'this person is poor' or 'this person is deprived' in a particular dimension. A fuzzy set approach may aggregate across dimensions using fuzzy logic operators and across individuals using an aggregation function. As we will see, the fuzzy set approach has been applied with cardinal or ordinal variables.

Fuzzy set approaches have been applied mainly to deprivation cutoffs and to an overall poverty cutoff used to identify who is poor. These are sketched in the next two sections.

3.5.2 MEMBERSHIP FUNCTIONS

In a traditional **crisp set**, a person i is deprived in a given dimension j (among all d dimensions) by comparing her achievement in that dimension, x_{ij}, with the deprivation cutoff z_j. If the achievement is below the deprivation cutoff, the individual is considered unambiguously deprived and otherwise she is considered unambiguously non-deprived. Let $\mathrm{m}_j(x_{ij})$ denote the membership function of individual i to the set of those deprived in dimension j, which is a function of the level of achievement of an individual i in a dimension j. In a crisp set, the membership function is given by

$$\mathrm{m}_j^C\left(x_{ij}\right) = \begin{cases} 1 & \text{if } x_{ij} < z_j \\ 0 & \text{if } x_{ij} \geq z_j \end{cases} . \tag{3.6}$$

Thus each individual is either a member of the set of the deprived, in which case she is assigned a value of 1, or not a member of the set of the deprived, in which case she is assigned a value of 0.[40] In the unidimensional case, such as for income or consumption poverty measurement, the individual is considered unambiguously poor or non-poor correspondingly.

In contrast, fuzzy sets allow for partial membership in the set of the deprived by considering a more general function, which can take different values ranging from 0 to 1; that is $\mathrm{m}_j : \mathbb{R}_+ \to [0,1]$ for all j. When the result is 0 or 1, we have complete certainty that the individual is non-deprived or deprived (or non-poor and poor), respectively. However, any value between 0 and 1 indicates a partial degree of certainty in the predicates 'being deprived' or 'being poor'.[41]

Naturally, as Cerioli and Zani (1990) explain, the main challenge of this approach is selecting and justifying a particular membership function from various alternatives.[42] The appropriate membership function will depend on the purpose of the study and the nature of the variable (Cerioli and Zani 1990; Chiappero-Martinetti 1994, 1996, 2000; Cheli and Lemmi 1995). The simplest membership function for cardinal variables is a simple linear form in which the lower bound is the minimum achievement value and the upper bound

---

[40] We refer to 'deprived' and 'deprivation cutoff' following the notation and terminology from Chapter 2. The fuzzy set literature often describes these as 'poor in dimension j' and 'poverty line'.

[41] Note that the interpretation is different from the depth or severity of poverty in FGT measures.

[42] For a summary of common membership functions, see Chiappero-Martinetti (2000).

is the maximum, and a linear function is used for all intermediate values (Cerioli and Zani 1990). Instead of using a linear function in (3.7), it is also possible to use a non-linear function such as a trapezoidal function in (3.8) or a sigmoid function in (3.10).

Other common membership functions include normalized deprivation gaps below an upper bound with the lower bound being the minimum achievement value (Chakravarty 2006).[43] A particularly interesting approach is Cheli and Lemmi's (1995) Totally Fuzzy and Relative (TFR) method, in which the degree of membership is defined by the cumulative frequency distribution function. It is argued by the proponents of this approach that relative membership functions like this can be used uncontroversially with ordinal data because the distance between categories is defined directly from the relative frequency of the event. Recently, a series of membership functions based on the notion of inequality have also been proposed (Betti et al. 2006; Betti and Verma 1999, 2008; Cheli and Betti 1999).

We do not provide a comprehensive list of membership functions but present four illustrations.[44]

Linear function (Cerioli and Zani 1990)

$$
\mathrm{m}_j^L\left(x_{ij}\right) = \begin{cases} 1 & \text{if } x_{ij} = \min(x_{\cdot j}) \\ \frac{\max(x_{\cdot j}) - x_{ij}}{\max(x_{\cdot j}) - \min(x_{\cdot j})} & \text{if } \min(x_{\cdot j}) < x_{ij} < \max(x_{\cdot j}) . \\ 0 & \text{if } x_{ij} = \max(x_{\cdot j}) \end{cases} \tag{3.7}
$$

Trapezoidal function

$$
\mathrm{m}_j^T\left(x_{ij}\right) = \begin{cases} 1 & \text{if } x_{ij} \leq z_j^l \\ \frac{x_{ij} - z_j^h}{z_j^h - z_j^l} & \text{if } z_j^l < x_{ij} < z_j^h , \\ 0 & \text{if } z_j^h \leq x_{ij} \end{cases} \tag{3.8}
$$

where z_j^l and z_j^h denote the lower and upper cutoffs. Any value or category between z_j^l and z_j^h has an associated degree of uncertainty with respect to the predicates 'being poor' or 'being deprived'.

Normalized gap membership function (Chakravarty 2006)

$$
\mathrm{m}_j^C\left(x_{ij}\right) = \begin{cases} 1 & \text{if } x_{ij} = 0 \\ \left(\frac{z_j - x_{ij}}{z_j}\right)^{\alpha_j} & \text{if } 0 < x_{ij} < z_j , \\ 0 & \text{if } x_{ij} \geq z_j \end{cases} \tag{3.9}
$$

where $\alpha_j \geq 1$ is a parameter for dimension j.

---

[43] This function is similar to the FGT normalized deprivation gap.
[44] We refer the reader to the following works for further study of alternative membership functions: Chiappero-Martinetti (2000), Deutsch and Silber (2005), Verkuilen (2005), Belhadj (2011), Betti et al. (2006), and Betti and Verma (2008).

Sigmoid function

$$
m_j^S(x_{ij}) = \begin{cases} 1 & \text{if } x_{ij} < z_j^l \\ 1 - \frac{1}{2}\left[\frac{z_j^l - x_{ij}}{z_j^l - z_j^s}\right]^2 & \text{if } z_j^l \leq x_{ij} < z_j^s \\ \frac{1}{2}\left[\frac{z_j^h - x_{ij}}{z_j^s - z_j^h}\right]^2 & \text{if } z_j^s \leq x_{ij} \leq z_j^h \\ 0 & \text{if } z_j^h < x_{ij} \end{cases} \tag{3.10}
$$

Totally Fuzzy and Relative (TFR) function

$$
m_j^{TFR}(x_{ij}) = \begin{cases} 1 & \text{if } x_{ij} = \min(x_{\cdot j}) \\ 1 - F_j(x_{ij}) & \text{if } \min(x_{\cdot j}) < x_{ij} < \max(x_{\cdot j}) \\ 0 & \text{if } x_{ij} = \max(x_{\cdot j}) \end{cases} \tag{3.11}
$$

A key challenge of the fuzzy set approach is choosing and justifying the appropriate membership function, because measurement estimations are sensitive to the choice of membership function.[45] It would be necessary to run a series of robustness tests to check the sensitivity of various membership functions. A further challenge is that the choice of membership function and even the results are less intuitive than other approaches and therefore difficult to assess normatively or to communicate. Fuzzy aggregation across dimensions or across individuals presents additional challenges, and each requires similar robustness tests across membership functions.

3.5.3 AGGREGATION ACROSS DIMENSIONS

Once the degree of deprivation in each dimension has been determined for each person, the next step involves aggregating across dimensions to obtain a synthetic individual measure indicating the degree to which someone is considered poor.[46] This step is equivalent to constructing the deprivation score in the counting approach described in Chapter 2.

The aggregation function for dimensional deprivation membership values that has been most frequently used was suggested by Cerioli and Zani (1990) and Cheli and Lemmi (1995). It is the weighted arithmetic mean across the degree of membership in each dimension, where the weights represent the importance attributed to each dimension. Let $\mathbb{M}_i$ denote the aggregated degree of membership for individual i. Using the arithmetic

---

[45] Note that, depending on interpretation, the membership function can also be seen as a welfare function, which is certainly the case in equation (3.7) or even (3.9). Theorists of the fuzzy set approach prefer to interpret the membership function strictly as the area of uncertainty with respect to the predicates 'being deprived' or 'being poor'. This is more evident when bounded functions are used as in equations (3.8) or (3.10).

[46] Again our terminology follows the framework outlined in Chapter 2.

mean expression, this is given by

$$\mathbb{M}_i = \frac{\sum_{j=1}^{d} \mathrm{m}_j\left(x_{ij}\right) w_j}{\sum_{j=1}^{d} w_j}, \tag{3.12}$$

where w_j denotes the weight attributed to dimension j. Note that, like the degrees of membership to each deprivation, the overall degree of membership $\mathbb{M}_i$ also ranges from 0 to 1, and it denotes the degree of membership to the set of the multidimensionally poor people. Naturally, as stated by Chiappero-Martinetti (1996, 2000), the aggregation function in (3.12) can be generalized to the weighted generalized means family (see section 2.2.5). In terms of the dimensional weights, different alternatives have been proposed, including those by Cerioli and Zani (1990) and Cheli and Lemmi (1995).

Chiappero-Martinetti (1996, 2000) summarizes other possible aggregation functions that use fuzzy logic operators based on Zadeh (1965), including the intersection approach, which are listed in Box 3.1. Further aggregation functions are presented in Betti and Verma (2004) and summarized in Betti et al. (2006). Most commonly, when the $\mathbb{M}_i$ function has been used in the fuzzy set literature, the implicit identification function has been $\rho\left(\mathbb{M}_i\right) = 1$ if $\mathbb{M}_i > 0$ and $\rho\left(\mathbb{M}_i\right) = 0$ otherwise. In other words, a union criterion as been used implicitly to identify the multidimensionally poor.

BOX 3.1 DIFFERENT IDENTIFICATION FUNCTIONS BASED ON FUZZY LOGIC OPERATORS

For person i and dimensions j and j', the different fuzzy logic operators can be defined as follows.[47]

Strong union

$$\mathbb{M}_i^{SU} = \mathrm{m}_{j \cup j'}\left(x_{ij}, x_{ij'}\right) = \max\left[\mathrm{m}_j\left(x_{ij}\right), \mathrm{m}_{j'}\left(x_{ij'}\right)\right]. \tag{3.13}$$

Weak union (probabilistic sum)

$$\mathbb{M}_i^{WU} = \mathrm{m}_{j+j'}\left(x_{ij}, x_{ij'}\right) = \mathrm{m}_j\left(x_{ij}\right) + \mathrm{m}_{j'}\left(x_{ij'}\right) - \mathrm{m}_j\left(x_{ij}\right) \times \mathrm{m}_{j'}\left(x_{ij'}\right). \tag{3.14}$$

Bounded sum

$$\mathbb{M}_i^{BS} = \mathrm{m}_{j \bar{\cup} j'}\left(x_{ij}, x_{ij'}\right) = \min\left[1, \mathrm{m}_j\left(x_{ij}\right) + \mathrm{m}_{j'}\left(x_{ij'}\right)\right]. \tag{3.15}$$

$$\mathrm{m}_{j \cup j'}\left(x_{ij}, x_{ij'}\right) \leq \mathrm{m}_{j+j'}\left(x_{ij}, x_{ij'}\right) \leq \mathrm{m}_{j \bar{\cup} j'}\left(x_{ij}, x_{ij'}\right) \tag{3.16}$$

Strong intersection

$$\mathbb{M}_i^{SI} = \mathrm{m}_{j \cap j'}\left(x_{ij}, x_{ij'}\right) = \min\left[\mathrm{m}_j\left(x_{ij}\right), \mathrm{m}_{j'}\left(x_{ij'}\right)\right]. \tag{3.17}$$

---

[47] This box is a summary of the operators in Chiappero-Martinetti (1996) which are based on Zadeh (1965).

BOX 3.1 *(cont.)*

Weak intersection (algebraic product)

$$\mathbb{M}_i^{WI} = \mathbb{m}_{j*j'}\left(x_{ij}, x_{ij'}\right) = \mathbb{m}_j\left(x_{ij}\right) \times \mathbb{m}_{j'}\left(x_{ij'}\right) \tag{3.18}$$

Bounded difference

$$\mathbb{M}_i^{BI} = \mathbb{m}_{j\cap j'}\left(x_{ij}, x_{ij'}\right) = \max\left[0, \mathbb{m}_j\left(x_{ij}\right) + \mathbb{m}_{j'}\left(x_{ij'}\right) - 1\right] \tag{3.19}$$

$$\mathbb{m}_{j\cap j'}\left(x_{ij}, x_{ij'}\right) \geq \mathbb{m}_{j*j'}\left(x_{i.}\right) \geq \mathbb{m}_{j\cap j'}\left(x_{i.}\right) \tag{3.20}$$

3.5.4 AGGREGATION ACROSS PEOPLE

The final step consists of aggregating across individuals to obtain an overall indicator that quantifies the total extent of poverty.[48] Cerioli and Zani (1990) propose a fuzzy poverty measure that is the arithmetic average of the individual grade of membership to the set of the poor, given by

$$P_{CZ} = \frac{\sum_{i=1}^{n}\mathbb{M}_i}{n}. \tag{3.21}$$

Inserting (3.12) in (3.21), the poverty measure is given by

$$P_{CZ} = \frac{\sum_{i=1}^{n}\sum_{j=1}^{d}\mathbb{m}_{ij}\left(x_{ij}\right)w_j}{n\sum_{j=1}^{d}w_j}. \tag{3.22}$$

As in other methods of multidimensional poverty measurement, the researcher or analyst implementing a fuzzy set approach needs to make a number of decisions in each of the measurement steps: selecting a membership function to identify deprivations, choosing a function and a weighting structure to aggregate deprivations, then selecting an aggregation function across individuals.

3.5.5 A CRITICAL EVALUATION

The novel conceptual contribution of the fuzzy set approach lies at the identification stage of poverty measurement. The notable merit of the approach is that it tries to systematize

---

[48] In addition to these commonly used functions, Vero (2006) proposed an approach to deal with issues of collinearity between indicators that Deutsch and Silber (2005) implemented. Betti et al. (2006) and Betti and Verma (2008) address redundancy using Betti and Verma's (1999) relative weighting system that places less importance on dimensions displaying lower deprivations.

into measurement the ambiguity frequently faced when defining the poor using crisp cutoffs.

Using fuzzy set methods, analysts can construct empirical poverty indices that can reflect the joint distribution of deprivations when certain fuzzy logic operators are used. Some of the proposed measures within this approach can be meaningfully implemented with ordinal data, such as those based on relative membership functions. Others require value judgements that may be contested. Additionally, the measures are described normatively with reference to some of the basic properties of multidimensional poverty measurement discussed in Chapter 2. Specifically, certain measures have been shown to satisfy symmetry, replication invariance, scale invariance, weak monotonicity, population subgroup consistency, and dimensional breakdown. Using the arithmetic mean aggregation formula stated in (3.21) with membership functions that are not of the relative type, the measures also satisfy population subgroup decomposability.

However, fuzzy set measures have some important challenges. Depending on the type of membership function used, fuzzy set measures may not satisfy other properties usually considered key: focus, weak transfer, and, in some cases, subgroup decomposability. For example, any measure based on an unbounded membership function, such as (3.7), (3.10), and (3.11), violates the focus axiom: poverty will change when the achievement of an arguably rich person—i.e. someone at the upper end of the distribution—changes.

As Chakravarty (2006) shows, a measure using the membership function in (3.9) and an aggregation such as (3.21) satisfies a number of desirable properties, including focus, monotonicity, and transfer. Indeed, such a gap-based measure is actually a generalized FGT measure, which coincides with the non-fuzzy approach to poverty measurement traditionally used not only in FGT measures but in other poverty measures as well (Sen 1976, for example). The only difference is a matter of interpretation of the gap as a degree of membership to the set of the deprived. In contrast, in the standard version of Cerioli and Zani (1990) and Cheli and Lemmi (1995), which use relative membership functions such as the one in (3.11), the measures are not decomposable across population subgroups because they depend on the rank order across categories and are relative to the frequency distributions.

In terms of measures based on membership functions that use a lower and an upper bound, there are two fundamental concerns. First, reductions in achievements among those who are certainly poor are not reflected in the overall measure unless the achievement value falls lower than the lower bound, i.e. in this range they only satisfy weak monotonicity. Second, a measure using such a membership function will definitely violate the transfer axiom. If there is a progressive transfer between a person whose achievement is above the lower bound z_j^l but below the upper bound z_j^h and a person whose achievement is below the lower bound z_j^l so that the latter does not surpass it, the measure will reflect an increase in poverty rather than registering the expected decrease. Conversely, a regressive transfer between the same two persons will create a decrease in the overall poverty measure rather than the expected increase.

A second challenge with the fuzzy set approach is the grounds on which membership functions are selected and justified, and how robust results are to the selection of a particular membership function. In this case, one needs to justify the choices, and perform sensitivity analyses or robustness tests on the alternative membership functions used at different steps of poverty measurement. This raises the question as to how value is added by performing essential robustness tests across membership and aggregation functions, rather than performing these directly on a set of crisp deprivation and poverty cutoffs. One might argue that in a crisp set, the method is easier to communicate and so are the underlying normative choices.

A third challenge relates to the use of ordinal data. Some fuzzy set approaches in effect cardinalize ordinal data through assumptions such as equidistance between points. In this book, we adopt a rather more cautious approach to ordinal data as a starting point. Assumptions regarding the value of ordinal data must themselves be subject to a further series of evaluations as to whether the same policy-relevant results hold for alternative plausible cardinalizations of the same ordinal data.

In sum, the fuzzy set approach has contributed greatly to the literature by bringing attention to the importance of the identification of the poor, which is very often—paradoxically—overlooked in poverty measurement methodologies. However, in the current state of the literature, measures that propose incorporating fuzziness at the identification step violate some basic properties of poverty measurement such as focus and transfer, and may require quite an array of sensitivity and robustness analyses. There is thus room for further developments in a fuzzy set measure that can incorporate the ambiguity in identification while respecting key properties. At the moment, non-fuzzy approaches to measurement typically deal with ambiguity in the identification of the poor by testing a measure's robustness to changes in the cutoffs used, as is recommended when using the AF methodology and addressed in detail in Chapter 5. The following section discusses in more detail the measures based on axiomatic approaches.

3.6 Axiomatic Measures

The axiomatic approach to multidimensional poverty measurement refers to measures that, given their mathematical structure, satisfy principles or axioms—in other words, behave in predictable ways. Chapter 2 introduced and discussed the various properties proposed in the literature on multidimensional poverty measurement and their normative justification. We observed that no measure can satisfy all axioms because some of them formally conflict. This section briefly surveys key multidimensional poverty measures that have been proposed and the different subsets of those properties each satisfies. The decision of which measure to choose often distils into a discussion of which axiom sets are more desirable. To blend this assessment with feasibility considerations, we follow Alkire and Foster (2013) in introducing indicator scales of measurement into the axiomatic assessment using the property of ordinality.[49] It is worth noting that all measures in the axiomatic approach comply with the two steps of poverty measurement: identification and aggregation (Sen 1976).

In the axiomatic approach literature, two broad identification methods have been used: the **aggregate achievement approach** and the **censored achievement approach**, both described in Chapter 2. Within the censored achievement approach, a prominent method used is the **counting approach**. The counting approach entails defining a deprivation cutoff z_j for each dimension j, so that each person is defined as deprived or not in each dimension by comparing her dimensional achievement with the corresponding deprivation cutoff. Formally, if $x_{ij} < z_j$, person i is considered deprived in dimension j and assigned $g_{ij}^0 = 1$; otherwise, person i is considered non-deprived and assigned $g_{ij}^0 = 0$. Subsequently, a weight for each dimension w_j is defined, and a deprivation score c_i is computed such that $c_i = \sum_{j=1}^d w_j g_{ij}^0$; in other words c_i is the weighted sum of deprivations. When dimensions are equally weighted, the deprivation score is equal to the number of deprivations. The deprivation score is compared to the poverty cutoff denoted by k (Alkire and Foster 2011a), which is the minimum score a person must have to be considered poor. A person is considered poor if $c_i \geq k$. The poverty cutoff k can range from the union to the intersection criterion. The union criterion requires $k \in (0, \min_j(w)]$ and identifies a person as poor if the person is deprived in *any* dimension. The intersection criterion requires $k = \sum_{j=1}^d w_j$ and identifies a person as poor only if she is deprived in *all* considered dimensions. In-between these two extreme criteria there is room for intermediate criteria. Note that unless the union criterion is used, someone may experience some deprivations and yet not be identified as poor. The deprivations of those who have been identified as poor are then aggregated to obtain a poverty measure.

In turn, the aggregate achievement approach consists of applying some aggregation function f_s to the achievements across dimensions for each person to obtain an overall or aggregate achievement value $f_s(x_i; w)$. The same function is also applied to the dimensional deprivation cutoffs to obtain an aggregate poverty line $f_s(z; w)$. A person is identified as poor when her aggregate achievement is below the aggregate poverty line. This resembles the unidimensional case. Formally, a person i is identified as poor if $f_s(x_i; w) < f_s(z; w)$ and non-poor otherwise. The summary well-being measures of the poor are then aggregated to obtain a poverty measure.

The main difference between these two identification approaches is that the counting approach gives independent importance to each deprivation. This is appropriate normatively if not being deprived has intrinsic value—for example, one could not compensate the violation of a human right of freedom from torture by offering someone more of another right like more job opportunities within the right to work. In poverty, a severely malnourished child's future is impaired and nutritional deficiencies matter directly—they cannot be compensated, for example, by giving the child better clothes. In line with

---

[49] Even if axiomatic measures satisfy relevant properties, other empirical, normative, and policy issues must be addressed during their implementation and analysis, as Chapters 6–8 clarify.

these requirements a counting approach does not allow a non-deprived dimension to compensate for a deprived dimension, whereas the aggregate achievement approach allows such compensation. Thus, the aggregate achievement approach can violate the deprivation-focus property.

Before we present the different measures proposed within each identification method, let us introduce the most basic measure that has been used in the multidimensional context: the multidimensional headcount ratio.[50] This measure can be used with different identification methods. Recall that q is the number of people who have been identified as poor, regardless of the identification method used—that is, all people i such that $i \in Z$. The multidimensional headcount ratio is given by

$$P_H = \frac{q}{n}.$$ (3.23)

In other words, the headcount ratio, or incidence of poverty, is the proportion of the population who have been identified as poor. The headcount ratio applies to indicators of any scale type. It satisfies symmetry, replication invariance, scale invariance, poverty focus, and, depending on the identification method used, may also satisfy deprivation focus. In addition, it satisfies weak dimensional monotonicity, weak monotonicity, weak transfer, and weak rearrangement. However, it does not satisfy any of the strong versions of the previous properties. It is fully subgroup decomposable, but, importantly, it does not satisfy dimensional breakdown and continuity.

3.6.1 MEASURES BASED ON A COUNTING APPROACH

Most of the multidimensional poverty measures introduced in the axiomatic approach use a counting approach to identifying the poor. Among those, most use the union criterion; that is, anyone deprived in any one or more dimensions is considered multidimensionally poor. The measures presented in this section can be computed from the censored achievement matrix $\widetilde{X}$, introduced in Chapter 2, such that $\tilde{x}_{ij} = x_{ij}$ if $x_{ij} < z_j$ and $\tilde{x}_{ij} = z_j$ otherwise. Alternatively, they can be computed from the normalized gap matrices of different orders introduced in Chapter 2. Specifically, measures that apply to dimensions of either ordinal or cardinal scale use the deprivation matrix g^0.[51] Measures that apply only to dimensions that are cardinal in nature can use any normalized gap matrix of order α corresponding to $\widetilde{X}$ as g^α, where its typical ij^{th} element is $g_{ij}^\alpha = (g_{ij})^\alpha$ such that $g_{ij} = (z_j - \tilde{x}_{ij})/z_j$ and $\alpha > 0$, as defined in section 2.2.1. In other words, the typical element is the normalized gap with respect to the deprivation cutoff z_j for all $j = 1, \ldots, d$ dimensions and for all $i = 1, \ldots, n$ people. Clearly, normalized gaps are greater

---

[50] See Chapter 4 for examples of uses of the headcount ratio alongside counting approaches to identify the poor in the multidimensional context.

[51] See section 2.3 for a discussion on scales of measurement.

the further the deprived achievements are beneath the deprivation cutoff. Note that for any non-deprived achievement, $\tilde{x}_{ij} = z_j$, and naturally $g_{ij} = 0$. The value taken by α depends on the kind of dominance properties—monotonicity or transfer—that must be satisfied.

In what follows, we classify the measures that use a counting approach for identifying the poor according to the property of ordinality, beginning with those which can only be implemented when all indicators are cardinal, then turning to those which permit indicators of an ordinal nature.

3.6.1.1 Measures Applicable to Cardinal Variables

Let us first present key multidimensional poverty measures that employ a counting approach to identification, use the union criterion, and assume the underlying variables to be cardinal. The earliest axiomatic multidimensional measures were proposed by Chakravarty, Mukherjee, and Ranade (1998) and are defined in a general way as

$$P_{CMR}(X;z) = \frac{1}{n}\sum_{i=1}^{n}\sum_{j=1}^{d} w_j f\left(\frac{\tilde{x}_{ij}}{z_j}\right), \tag{3.24}$$

where f is continuous, non-increasing, and convex such that $f(0) = 1$ and $f(1) = 0$. Note that $f(1)$ is obtained when $\tilde{x}_{ij} = z_j$, which means that person i is not deprived in dimension j. On the other hand, $f(0)$ is obtained when $\tilde{x}_{ij} = 0$. The measure satisfies many of the properties introduced in section 2.5. In particular, P_{CMR} satisfies symmetry, replication invariance, scale invariance, poverty focus, deprivation focus, weak monotonicity, dimensional monotonicity, weak transfer, weak deprivation rearrangement, population subgroup decomposability, dimensional breakdown, normalization, non-triviality, and continuity. However, the measure does not satisfy the strong deprivation rearrangement property.

Chakravarty, Mukherjee, and Ranade (1998) offer several formulations of f as examples. Two of them are as follows: (i) $f(\cdot) = 1 - (\tilde{x}_{ij}/z_j)^\alpha$ for $0 \leq \alpha \leq 1$ and (ii) $f(\cdot) = g_{ij}^\alpha$ for $\alpha \geq 1$. The functional form of $f(\cdot)$ in (i) is inspired by Chakravarty's (1983b) unidimensional poverty measure, and thus the index is as follows:

$$P_{CMR1}(X;z) = \frac{1}{n}\sum_{i=1}^{n}\sum_{j=1}^{d} w_j\left[1 - \left(\frac{\tilde{x}_{ij}}{z_j}\right)^\alpha\right]. \tag{3.25}$$

P_{CMR1} increases as α increases; as $\alpha \to 0$, $P_{CMR1} \to 0$; and for $\alpha = 1$, $P_{CMR1} = \frac{1}{n}\sum_{i=1}^{n}\sum_{j=1}^{d} w_j g_{ij}$. The functional form in (ii) is inspired by Foster, Greer, and Thorbecke's (1984) unidimensional poverty measure, thus the index is as follows:

$$P_{CMR2}(X;z) = \frac{1}{n}\sum_{i=1}^{n}\sum_{j=1}^{d} w_j g_{ij}^\alpha. \tag{3.26}$$

Note that for $\alpha = 1$, $P_{CMR1} = P_{CMR2}$, being the average normalized deprivation gap across dimensions and across people.

The class of indices P_{CMR} was designed to satisfy the dimensional breakdown property. As discussed in section 2.5, this property is incompatible with strong versions of rearrangement properties (Alkire and Foster 2013). Other measures have been designed to be sensitive to associations between dimensions. For example, Tsui (2002) proposed two different classes of multidimensional indices of poverty. One is based on the unidimensional measure proposed by Chakravarty (1983b). The other is based on the unidimensional index proposed by Watts (1968).[52] The first class of indices is defined as

$$P_{T1}(X;z) = \frac{1}{n} \sum_{i=1}^{n} \left[\prod_{j=1}^{d} \left(\frac{\tilde{x}_{ij}}{z_j} \right)^{-\alpha_j} - 1 \right], \tag{3.27}$$

where $\alpha_j \geq 0$ for all j and the α_js have to be chosen so that $\prod_{j=1}^{d} (\tilde{x}_{ij}/z_j)^{-\alpha_j}$ is convex in its arguments. The requirement of convexity is to guarantee that the measure satisfies the transfer principle stated in section 2.5.2. P_{T1} satisfies symmetry, replication invariance, scale invariance, poverty focus, deprivation focus, weak monotonicity, dimensional monotonicity, weak transfer, weak deprivation rearrangement (assuming achievements to be substitutes), population subgroup decomposability, and continuity. It does not satisfy dimensional breakdown and normalization because the maximum value is not bounded by 1; however, the measure is bounded at 0, i.e. $P_{T1} = 0$ whenever there is no one who is poor in the society. P_{T1} satisfies non-triviality when at least one $\alpha_j > 0$ and strong deprivation rearrangement when $\alpha_j > 0$ for all j.

The second family of indices proposed by Tsui (2002) is given by

$$P_{T2}(X;z) = \frac{1}{n} \sum_{i=1}^{n} \sum_{j=1}^{d} \alpha_j \ln \left(\frac{z_j}{\tilde{x}_{ij}} \right), \tag{3.28}$$

where $\alpha_j > 0$, but need not necessarily sum up to one. However, $\alpha_j / \sum_{j=1}^{d} \alpha_j$ can be understood as the relative weight assigned to dimension j. It is worth noting that P_{T2} is in fact a member of the P_{CMR} general class. P_{T2} satisfies symmetry, replication invariance, scale invariance, poverty focus, deprivation focus, weak monotonicity, dimensional monotonicity, weak transfer, weak deprivation rearrangement, population subgroup decomposability, dimensional breakdown, and continuity. However, the measure does not satisfy the property of strong deprivation rearrangement. The property of normalization is not satisfied because its upper bound is not equal to one.

---

[52] Tsui (2002) introduced three other multidimensional indices of poverty. One of these was developed to consider dimensions with non-positive values, and the other two indices were developed to satisfy the translation invariance property discussed in section 2.5.1. For further discussion on the measure proposed by Tsui (2002) and also by Chakravarty, Mukherjee, and Ranade (1998), see Chakravarty (2009).

The next two classes of multidimensional poverty indices were proposed by Bourguignon and Chakravarty (2003). The first class of indices is a straightforward extension of the unidimensional family of indices by Foster, Greer, and Thorbecke (1984). The class of measures is defined as follows:

$$P_{BC1}(X;z) = \frac{1}{n}\sum_{i=1}^{n}\sum_{j=1}^{d} w_j g_{ij}^{\alpha_j}; \quad \text{with } \alpha_j \geq 1. \tag{3.29}$$

By design, the class of indices in (3.29) is identical to the class of indices in (3.26) and so satisfies identical properties. Bourguignon and Chakravarty (2003) extended Tsui (2002), in terms of the sensitivity of a poverty index to association between dimensions, to the case in which achievements can be considered complements. The second class of measures proposed by Bourguignon and Chakravarty is

$$P_{BC2}(X;z) = \frac{1}{n}\sum_{i=1}^{n}\left[\sum_{j=1}^{d} w_j g_{ij}^{\beta}\right]^{\alpha/\beta}, \tag{3.30}$$

where $\beta > 1$ and $\alpha \geq 0$. Note that the class of indices in (3.30) has two parameters α and β. The relationship between these two parameters determines whether poverty should increase or decrease due to an association-decreasing rearrangement. When dimensions are substitutes, $\alpha > \beta$ and P_{BC2} satisfy weak rearrangement. On the other hand, when dimensions are complements, $\alpha < \beta$ and P_{BC2} satisfy converse weak rearrangement.[53]

The Bourguignon and Chakravarty (2003) measure in (3.30) was used by Maasoumi and Lugo (2008) as one of their measures within an **information theory approach** (see Box 3.2 for the intuition of this approach). Breaking down expression (3.30) one can note that in the first place normalized deprivation gaps are aggregated across dimensions for each person using the so-called 'generalized mean of order β', introduced in section 2.2.5 (see also Box 2.2).

Maasoumi and Lugo (2008) also proposed another measure within an information theory approach. The measure can be computed over the censored matrix of achievements $\tilde{X}$ as

$$P_{ML1}(X;z) = \frac{1}{n}\sum_{i=1}^{n}\left[\frac{\mu_{\beta}(z;w) - \mu_{\beta}(\tilde{x}_{i\cdot};w)}{\mu_{\beta}(z;w)}\right]^{\alpha}, \tag{3.31}$$

where μ_{β} is the generalized means operator defined in section 2.2.5 and the value of the parameter in the range is $\beta < 1$, $\alpha \geq 1$ and $\sum_{j=1}^{d} w_j = 1$. A generalized mean is computed using different dimensional deprivation cutoffs, such that, for $\beta \neq 0$:

[53] Note that Bourguignon and Chakravarty (2003) did not explore the deprivation rearrangement properties. Whether their measures satisfy the deprivation rearrangement properties weakly or strictly is a subject for further research.

$\mu_\beta(z; w) = \left(\sum_{j=1}^{d} w_j(z_j)^\beta \right)^{1/\beta}$, and using different censored dimensional achievements,

such that $\mu_\beta(\tilde{x}_i; w) = \left(\sum_{j=1}^{d} w_j(\tilde{x}_{ij})^\beta \right)^{1/\beta}$. For $\beta = 0$, $\mu_\beta(z; w) = \prod_{j=1}^{d} z_j^{w_j}$ and $\mu_\beta(\tilde{x}_i; w) = \prod_{j=1}^{d} (\tilde{x}_{ij})^{w_j}$. The measure is analogous to an FGT unidimensional measure outlined in section 2.1. This measure satisfies symmetry, replication and scale invariance, deprivation focus, poverty focus, monotonicity, and weak transfer. Interestingly, when $\beta = 0$ and $w_j = -\alpha_j$, measure P_{ML1} is a monotonic transformation of Tsui's P_{T1} measure in (3.27).

All measures presented thus far satisfy the scale invariance property, which means that they automatically satisfy the unit consistency property presented in section 2.5.1. Recently, Chakravarty and D'Ambrosio (2013) have proposed a class of indices that satisfies the unit consistency property and, only for a particular restriction on a parameter, satisfies the scale invariance property. The measure can be expressed as

$$P_{CDU}(X; z) = \frac{\alpha \prod_{j=1}^{d} z_j^\beta}{n} \sum_{i=1}^{n} \left[1 - \prod_{j=1}^{d} \left(\frac{\tilde{x}_{ij}}{z_j} \right)^{\alpha_j} \right], \tag{3.32}$$

where β is a real number and parameters α and α_j should be chosen in such a way that $\alpha \alpha_j > 0$ for all $j = 1, \ldots, d$. The measure satisfies symmetry, replication invariance, unit consistency, poverty focus, deprivation focus, monotonicity, dimensional monotonicity, population subgroup decomposability, and continuity. It also satisfies other properties based on different restrictions on the set of parameters. First, P_{CDU} satisfies scale invariance when $\beta = 0$. Second, it satisfies strong deprivation rearrangement when $\alpha \alpha_j \alpha_{j'} > 0$ for all $j \neq j' = 1, \ldots, d$ and satisfies converse strong deprivation rearrangement when $\alpha \alpha_j \alpha_{j'} < 0$ for all $j \neq j' = 1, \ldots, d$. Third, when there are two dimensions ($d = 2$), the authors show that the necessary and sufficient condition for the weak transfer property to be satisfied is $\alpha \alpha_1(\alpha_1 - 1)$ and $\alpha_1 \alpha_2(1 - \alpha_1 - \alpha_2) < 0$. For a higher number of dimensions, the parametric conditions are not derived, as they become quite complicated.

Finally, Alkire and Foster (2007, 2011a) proposed a family of measures, some of which are only applicable when variables are cardinal and one of which can be implemented with both cardinal and ordinal variables. The AF family of measures is explained in greater detail in Chapter 5. Here we introduce the expression synthetically. It must be noted that the AF methodology, as the other measures presented in this section, uses a counting approach for identifying the poor. However, it departs from considering only the union criterion and actually allows for a range of different possible identification cutoffs, from union to intersection, i.e. $0 < k \leq \sum_{j=1}^{d} w_j$. A person is identified as poor if $c_i \geq k$. Note that when an intermediate criterion (neither union nor intersection) is used to identify the poor, the weights assigned to each dimension start playing an important role in identification and not just in aggregation, as in the axiomatic measures presented thus far. Subsequently, a censored matrix of α-deprivation gaps $g^\alpha(k)$ is obtained such that the typical element $g_{ij}^\alpha(k) = g_{ij}^\alpha$ if $c_i \geq k$, and $g_{ij}^\alpha(k) = 0$ if $\sum_{j=1}^{d} w_j g_{ij}^0 < k$. In other words, the deprivations of those who are not identified as poor are replaced by zero, whereas the deprivations of those who are identified as poor are left unchanged. The family of measures proposed by Alkire and Foster (2007, 2011a) can be expressed as

$$P_{AF}(X;z) = \frac{1}{n}\sum_{i=1}^{n}\sum_{j=1}^{d} w_j g_{ij}^{\alpha}(k); \alpha \geq 0.^{54} \tag{3.33}$$

All measures in the P_{AF} family satisfy symmetry, replication invariance, scale invariance, poverty focus, deprivation focus, dimensional monotonicity, population subgroup decomposability, dimensional breakdown, and weak deprivation rearrangement. For $\alpha = 0$, the measure in the AF family is named as the 'Adjusted Headcount Ratio', further discussed in the next section because it is suitable when there are ordinal variables among the considered indicators. For $\alpha > 0$, the measures require all indicators to be cardinal. When $\alpha = 1$, the measure is referred to as the 'Adjusted Poverty Gap'. This and any member with $\alpha > 0$ satisfy monotonicity. When $\alpha = 2$, the measure is referred to as the 'Adjusted Squared Poverty Gap', which satisfies weak transfer, as well as any member with $\alpha \geq 1$. When the union criterion is used for identification and $\alpha > 0$, the measures satisfy continuity.

Finally, comparing the different formulas one can find coincidences across the measures. For example, when $\alpha = 1$, and the union criterion is used, $P_{CMR1} = P_{CMR2} = P_{AF}$. Also, if all $\alpha_j = \alpha \geq 1$ for all j and the union criterion is used for identification, then $P_{BC1} = P_{CMR2} = P_{AF}$.

3.6.1.2 Measures Applicable to Ordinal Variables

The measures in (3.24) to (3.33) assume the indicators under consideration to be cardinal. However, the indicators in which achievements in many dimensions are expressed are very often ordinal in nature. Thus, the following measures have been designed in order to be suitable when variables are ordinal. Specifically, achievements are dichotomized into deprived and non-deprived, that is, the elements of the deprivation matrix g^0 are used (where $g_{ij}^0 = 1$ when $x_{ij} < z_j$ and $g_{ij}^0 = 0$ otherwise).

One measure of multidimensional poverty that can handle ordinal indicators has recently been proposed by Aaberge and Peluso (2012). For simplicity's sake, we assume that all dimensions are equally weighted, i.e. $w_j = 1$ for all j and thus $c_i = \sum_{j=1}^{d} w_j g_{ij}^0$ is the deprivation count of person i. Let us denote the proportion of people with exactly j number of deprivations by $\bar{\pi}_j$. For example, $\bar{\pi}_d$ denotes the proportion of people deprived in all d dimensions simultaneously, where $\bar{\pi}_0$ is the proportion of people not deprived in any dimension. The measure proposed by Aaberge and Peluso (2012) is

$$P_{AP}(X;z) = d - \sum_{j'=0}^{d-1} \bar{\Gamma}\left(\sum_{\bar{j}=0}^{j'} \bar{\pi}_{\bar{j}}\right), \tag{3.34}$$

---

[54] Alkire and Foster (2011a) use the notation 'M_α' to denote the family of measures, which is used from Chapter 5. In order to preserve uniformity in the use of notation across this chapter, we use the notation onwards P_{AF}.

where $\bar{\Gamma}$ is increasing in its argument with $\bar{\Gamma}(0) = 0$ and $\bar{\Gamma}(1) = 1$. When there is no poor person in the society, then $\bar{\pi}_0 = 1$ and $\bar{\pi}_j = 0$ for all $j = 1,\ldots,d$. Therefore, $\bar{\Gamma}(\cdot) = 1$ for all $j' = 0,\ldots,d$ and so $P_{AP} = 0$. On the other hand, if everybody is poor in the society, then $\bar{\pi}_d = 1$ and $\bar{\pi}_{j'} = 0$ for all $j' = 0,\ldots,d - 1$. Thus, $\bar{\Gamma}(\cdot) = 0$ for all j' and so $P_{AP} = d$. The measure P_{AP} satisfies symmetry, replication invariance, scale invariance, poverty focus, deprivation focus, ordinality, dimensional monotonicity, weak deprivation rearrangement, and normalization (if the measure is divided by d).[55] However, this class of measures does not satisfy additive decomposability and subgroup consistency unless $\bar{\Gamma}$ is an affine transformation. No measure in this class satisfies the dimensional breakdown property.

Another measure suitable for ordinal variables has been proposed by Chakravarty and D'Ambrosio (2006) as an index of social exclusion:

$$P_{CD}(X;z) = \frac{1}{n}\sum_{i=1}^{n} f\left[\sum_{j=1}^{d} w_j g_{ij}^0\right], \qquad (3.35)$$

where $f(0) = 0$ and f is increasing and convex in its argument. In the empirical application of their measure, they use the following particular functional formulation of f:

$$P_{CD1}(X;z) = \frac{1}{n}\sum_{i=1}^{n}\left[\sum_{j=1}^{d} w_j g_{ij}^0\right]^{\beta}, \qquad (3.36)$$

where $\beta \geq 1$. The measure P_{CD1} has been used by Jayaraj and Subramanian (2009) to analyse multidimensional poverty in India. P_{CD1} satisfies symmetry, replication invariance, scale invariance, poverty focus, deprivation focus, ordinality, dimensional monotonicity, dimensional transfer, weak deprivation rearrangement, normalization, and population subgroup decomposability. It does not satisfy the dimensional breakdown property.

A third measure in this group is Bossert, Chakravarty, and D'Ambrosio's (2013) family of multidimensional measures

$$P_{BCD}(X;z) = \left(\frac{1}{n}\sum_{i=1}^{n}\left[\sum_{j=1}^{d} w_j g_{ij}^0\right]^{\beta}\right)^{1/\beta}, \qquad (3.37)$$

where $\beta \geq 1$. Note that this family also makes use of the generalized means expression for aggregating deprivations across people, and in fact P_{BCD} is a monotonic transformation of P_{CD1}. The measure P_{BCD} satisfies symmetry, replication invariance, scale invariance,

---

[55] Silber and Yalonetzky (2013) have presented the Aaberge and Peluso measure by dividing by the total number of dimensions d so that the measure lies between 0 and 1.

poverty focus, deprivation focus, ordinality, dimensional monotonicity, weak depriva-tion rearrangement, normalization, and subgroup consistency. It does not satisfy the axioms of population subgroup decomposability and dimensional breakdown.

Finally, it should be emphasized that one of the measures of the AF family introduced in the previous section is suitable for ordinal variables—the Adjusted Headcount Ratio. Following (3.33), the measure can be expressed as

$$P_{AF0}(X;z) = \frac{1}{n} \sum_{i=1}^{n} \sum_{j=1}^{d} w_j g_{ij}^0(k).\text{[56]}$$ (3.38)

This measure satisfies symmetry, replication invariance, scale invariance, poverty focus, deprivation focus, ordinality, dimensional monotonicity, weak monotonicity, normaliz-ation, non-triviality, weak rearrangement, population subgroup decomposability, and dimensional breakdown. However, it does not satisfy monotonicity, weak transfer and strong rearrangement. Note that the P_{AF0} measure coincides with both P_{CD1} and P_{BCD} for $\beta = 1$, when a union criterion is used for identifying the poor (see Chapter 5).

It is worth noting that, like the multidimensional headcount ratio in (3.23), the measures (3.34) to (3.38) are suitable for ordinal variables, but they are also superior to measure (3.23) because they satisfy dimensional monotonicity. Additionally, the Adjusted Headcount Ratio in (3.38) satisfies the dimensional breakdown property.

3.6.2 MEASURES USING AN AGGREGATE ACHIEVEMENT APPROACH

In the aggregate achievement line approach, we find one measure developed by Maasoumi and Lugo (2008) within the so-called information theory approach (see Box 3.2).[57] It is should be observed that these measures require indicators to be cardinal. The measure is defined as follows:

$$P_{ML2}(X;z) = \frac{1}{n} \sum_{i=1}^{n} \left[\max\left\{ \frac{\mu_\beta(z;w) - \mu_\beta(x_{i\cdot};w)}{\mu_\beta(z;w)}, 0 \right\} \right]^\alpha,$$ (3.39)

where μ_β is the generalized means operator defined in section 2.2.5 and the values of the parameters in the range are $\beta < 1$, $\alpha \geq 1$, and $\sum_{i=1}^{d} w_j = 1$. A generalized mean is computed using the different dimensional deprivation cutoffs, such that, for $\beta \neq 0$: $\mu_\beta(z;w) = \left(\sum_{j=1}^{d} w_j(z_j)^\beta \right)^{1/\beta}$, and using the different dimensional achievements, such that $\mu_\beta(x_{i\cdot};w) = \left(\sum_{j=1}^{d} w_j(x_{ij})^\beta \right)^{1/\beta}$. For $\beta = 0$, $\mu_\beta(z;w) = \prod_{j=1}^{d} z_j^{w_j}$ and $\mu_\beta(x_i) =$

---

[56] Alkire and Foster (2011a) use the notation 'M_0' to denote the Adjusted Headcount Ratio, which is used from Chapter 5 onwards. In order to preserve uniformity in the use of notation across this chapter, we use the notation P_{AF0}.

[57] They build upon Maasoumi's (1986) multidimensional measure of inequality.

$\prod_{j=1}^{d}(x_{ij})^{w_j}$. The max function implies that the normalized gap between the overall achievement value $\mu_\beta(x_i; w)$ and the aggregate poverty line $\mu_\beta(z; w)$ is positive for everyone with an overall achievement value below the aggregate poverty line, and zero otherwise. This measure is also analogous to an FGT unidimensional measure.

It should be noted that measure P_{ML2} in (3.39) allows achievements below the poverty line to be compensated for by achievements above the poverty line. The degree of compensation or substitution is determined by the parameter β, with $1/(1-\beta)$ being the standard's elasticity of substitution. In other words, P_{ML2} satisfies the poverty focus property, but it does not satisfy the deprivation focus property (because changes in the achievements above the corresponding deprivation cutoff of poor people can reduce the poverty measure). The measure also satisfies symmetry, replication and scale invariance, monotonicity, and transfer. The measure may satisfy rearrangement properties depending on the parameter values. P_{ML2} can be decomposed by population subgroups, but it does not satisfy dimensional breakdown.

BOX 3.2 INFORMATION THEORY MEASURES

Maasoumi and Lugo's (2008) multidimensional poverty measures emerged from the so-called **information theory approach**. The approach is called 'information theory' because it borrows from measures of information related to event occurrences in the context of engineering (Shannon 1948). The approach is built around three main concepts: (1) information content, (2) measurement of entropy, and (3) measurement of entropy divergence or relative entropy between two probability distributions.

(1) **Information content**: Suppose one has a set of possible events, each of which has an associated probability of occurrence. The information content that a certain event has occurred is greater the lower its probability of occurrence is. In other words, the information content of the occurrence of an event is inversely related to its probability of occurrence. If the event was very likely to occur, then the information that it has occurred is not very interesting, as this was highly expected. On the contrary, if the event was unlikely, the information that it has occurred is indeed very interesting.

(2) **Measure of entropy**: Given an experiment with n possible outcomes, entropy is defined as the expected information content—that is, the sum of the information content of each event weighted by its probability. Entropy can be understood as a measure of uncertainty, disorder, or volatility associated with a distribution (Maasoumi 1993: 141). The more concentrated the probability of occurrence around one event is, the lower entropy will be: that is, the lower will be the expected information content from those possible outcomes as one particular outcome is highly predicted. On the other hand, when all events are equally likely to occur, entropy is higher: that is, the expected information content from those possible outcomes will be higher as no particular outcome is highly predicted; thus, there is a lot of uncertainty.

(3) **Measure of entropy divergence or relative entropy**: Given two probability distributions, a measure of entropy divergence or relative entropy between them assesses how the two distributions differ from each other (Kullback and Leibler 1951).

The concepts of information theory were first used in distributional analysis in order to measure income inequality by Theil (1967). Consider an income (achievement) distribution x with n incomes. Here each particular income value is an 'event'. The distribution of income shares, where each share is given by $\frac{x_i}{\sum_{i=1}^{n} x_i}$, can be interpreted as a probability distribution. If all incomes are obtained by only one person (i.e. one share equals 1 and the rest equal 0), this is the situation of lowest entropy. Undoubtedly, it is also the situation

BOX 3.2 (*cont.*)

of highest inequality. On the other hand, if every person receives the same share of income (1/n), this is the situation of highest entropy. Undoubtedly, it is also the situation of lowest inequality. Thus, inequality can be seen as the complement of entropy. Equivalently, a measure of inequality can be constructed using a measure of entropy divergence, where inequality is given by the distance between the probability distribution of a perfectly equal distribution (each probability being 1/n) and the actual observed income distribution (each probability being the actual income share of each person). Theil proposed two measures of income inequality which are essentially the minimum possible distance between an 'ideal' distribution (perfectly equal) and the one observed (Maasoumi and Lugo 2008).

Although not easily interpretable, Theil indices became attractive measures of inequality because they satisfy four properties considered to be essential to inequality measurement (Atkinson 1970; Foster 1985; Foster and Sen 1997) and are also additively decomposable, meaning that they can be expressed as a weighted sum of the inequality values calculated for population subgroups (within-group inequality) plus the contribution arising from differences between subgroup means (Shorrocks 1980: 613). Given their attractive characteristics, these measures were extended by Shorrocks (1980), Cowell (1980), and Cowell and Kuga (1981) into a parametric family named 'generalized entropy (GE) measures'.

It is worth emphasizing that the expressions of the generalized means (as described in section 2.2.5) are closely linked to information theory measures. In fact, it is found that the expression of the generalized means is such that it minimizes the entropy divergence or relative entropy between two distributions (Maasoumi 1986; Maasoumi and Lugo 2008).

3.6.3 A CRITICAL EVALUATION

Axiomatic measures present a number of convenient features. First, they comply with the two necessary steps of poverty measurement: identifying the poor and aggregating the information into a single headline figure. Second, the portfolio of axiomatic measures includes measures that only apply when indicators are cardinal but also includes measures that apply when indicators are ordinal. Third, the axiomatic measures described in this section, unlike dashboards and composite indices, can use the joint distribution of achievements both at the identification and at the aggregation step. Measures that use a counting approach with the union criterion to identify the poor do not incorporate joint deprivations at the identification step. However, such measures could be implemented with a different criterion requiring joint deprivations as a restriction. In terms of aggregation, only the headcount ratio of multidimensional poverty is insensitive to the joint distribution; the other measures satisfy dimensional monotonicity, and some of them also satisfy the strict versions of rearrangement properties.

A fourth advantage of axiomatic measures is that it is possible to know exactly how they behave under different transformations of the data. Thus, policymakers and researchers can select a particular measure based on the properties it satisfies as well as on its data requirements, namely, whether it requires variables to be cardinal. As mentioned when introducing the properties in section 2.5, some properties are incompatible: a measure can satisfy one or the other but not both, i.e. there is a trade-off. The key decision among feasible axiomatic measures is which properties are to be privileged.

For example, in the presence of cardinal variables, one may want to privilege dimensional breakdown and thus select a measure from the Alkire and Foster (2011a) family of measures. Alternatively, one may want to privilege sensitivity to associations among dimensions (strong rearrangement), foregoing dimensional breakdown, and thus select the P_{BC2} measure of the Bourguignon and Chakravarty (2003) family or the P_{T1} measure proposed by Tsui (2002). At the same time, it is also clear that as long as one of the considered dimensions is measured with an ordinal indicator, the set of applicable measures is substantially reduced but the practicality is greatly expanded, so again decisions need to be made. If one is not concerned about capturing the intensity of deprivations (dimensional monotonicity), the headcount ratio of multidimensional poverty will work. On the contrary, if one wants a measure that is sensitive to intensity and provides policy incentives to address those with high deprivation scores, one can select the P_{AF0} measure of the Alkire and Foster (2011a) family, the P_{BCD} measure proposed by Bossert, Chakravarty, and D'Ambrosio (2013), or the P_{CD1} measure proposed by Chakravarty and D'Ambrosio (2006). However, if one would like the measure to satisfy dimensional breakdown as well, then neither the P_{BCD} measure nor the P_{CD1} measure are suitable—although P_{AF0} is. Note that these types of decisions regarding the trade-offs between certain properties are not minor issues as they have direct implications for policy design and assessment. Ultimately, these decisions reflect the properties that the researcher or policymaker holds to be so important that they should be axioms—that is, undisputable attributes a measure must exhibit.

Constructing measures based on axiomatic properties has several merits. First, for any poverty index, it is important to understand how the measure behaves with respect to various data transformations. A measure that does not satisfy certain properties understood to be fundamental—say, weak monotonicity—may lead to dire policy consequences. Despite the advantages of axiomatic poverty measures, they also have limitations—as is true for any measurement methodology. First, for the reasons already stated, no single measure can satisfy all the properties presented in Chapter 2 at the same time. Thus, the selection of one measure over others always involves normative trade-offs. Yet, as long as such action is explicit and justifications are provided, by no means should this discourage the use of axiomatic measures. Second, the measures presented in this section require data to be available from the same source for each unit of identification. This may reduce the applicability of these measures when it is not possible to obtain such data. Yet, as data collection continues to improve, this difficulty will be progressively eased. Third, as mentioned at the end of the dominance approach section, axiomatic measures might be criticized for providing a complete ordering and cardinally meaningful distances between poverty values at the cost of imposing an arbitrary structure. However, not only are these properties desirable from a policy and practical perspective, but axiomatic measures are transparent about the structure they impose.

Despite these limitations, we take the view that axiomatic measures offer a strong tool for measuring multidimensional poverty, with the advantages outweighing the potential

Table 3.2 Summary of the multidimensional poverty measurement methodologies

Method	Able to capture joint distribution of deprivations: require microdata	Identification of the poor	Provide a single cardinal index to assess poverty
Dashboards	No	No	No
Composite Indices	No	No	Yes
Venn Diagrams	Yes	May	No
Dominance Approach	Yes	Yes	No
Statistical Approaches	Yes	May	May
Fuzzy Sets	Yes	Yes	Yes
Axiomatic Approaches	Yes	Yes	Yes

Note: 'May' means that the compliance with that criterion depends on the particular technique used within that approach.

drawbacks. Yet many of the other methodologies for poverty measurement addressed throughout this chapter can work as invaluable complementary tools, as we shall see.

This chapter provides an overview of methodologies that are used for multidimensional poverty measurement or analysis other than the counting approach, to which we shall shortly turn. The chapter has described the main characteristics, scopes, and limitations of these methodologies. Table 3.2 presents a schematic summary of the reviewed methodologies in terms of three essential characteristics, namely: whether the methodology is able to capture the joint distribution of deprivations, whether it identifies the poor (i.e. dichotomizing the population into poor and non-poor, creating the set of the poor), and whether it provides a single cardinal figure to assess poverty.

Many methodologies outlined in this chapter rely on the assumption that data for all dimensions are cardinal. Others are applied to ordinal data, but make strong assumptions that the ordinal information can be treated as cardinal equivalent. Poverty measures based on the counting approach, however, do not make such assumptions and satisfy the ordinality property. Chapters 5–10 focus on a particular poverty measurement methodology proposed by Alkire and Foster (2011), that is based on a counting approach. Before introducing this particular poverty measurement methodology, we step back in Chapter 4 to present a historical review of applications of the counting approach to identify the poor and the ways it has been used in different parts of the world.

4 Counting Approaches: Definitions, Origins, and Implementations

An assessment of measurement methodologies based on their properties and normative characteristics is illuminating and draws our attention to many interesting distinctions among measures, as we saw in Chapter 3. Yet, as Tony Atkinson observed in the landmark 2003 paper that catalysed many responses, including this book, 'Empirical studies of multiple deprivation to date have not typically adopted a social welfare function approach. Rather they have tended to concentrate on counting the number of dimensions in which people suffer deprivation'. To catalyse policy-relevant measurement methodologies, it may be useful to analyse some measures which have served to guide policy, to see why they were implemented and how they have been used, as well as the criticisms and difficulties they faced. Our task in this chapter is to begin such an exploration of counting-based measures.

4.1 Definition and Origins

The measurement of multidimensional poverty, as discussed in Chapter 1, involves three fundamental steps: selecting the space, deciding who is poor, and aggregating the information of the poor. The fundamental step of deciding who is poor is **identification** (Sen 1976). A 'counting approach' is one way to identify the poor in multidimensional poverty measurement. It entails, as Atkinson (2003: 51) notes, 'counting the number of dimensions in which people suffer deprivation, (...) the number of dimensions in which they fall below the threshold'.[1]

As mentioned in section 2.2.2 and section 3.6.1, a counting approach to identifying the poor can be broken down into the following steps:

1. defining a set of relevant indicators;
2. defining a threshold of satisfaction (deprivation cutoff) for each indicator such that if the person does not reach it, she is considered deprived;

---

[1] Note that a counting approach to identifying the poor can be implemented only with multidimensional poverty measures that use unit-level data to consider the joint distribution of achievements across dimensions.

3. creating binary deprivation status for each person in each indicator, where 1 is deprived and 0 is non-deprived;
4. assigning a weight or deprivation value to each considered indicator;
5. producing a deprivation score by taking the weighted sum of deprivations (or counting the number of deprivations, if they are equally weighted);
6. setting a threshold score of poverty (or poverty cutoff) such that if the person has a deprivation score at or above the threshold, she is considered poor.

Most steps involve normative judgements, which are largely discussed in Chapter 6. Step (4) entails deciding whether all deprivations should be given the same weight. Step (6) specifies the extent of deprivations which must be experienced by a person in order to be considered poor which, as outlined in section 2.2.2, can range from experiencing at least one deprivation (union) to experiencing all deprivations (intersection). In practice, either the union or intermediate criteria have been most commonly used; the intersection criterion has rarely been used. The need to define a 'poverty cutoff' in step (6) is what led Alkire and Foster to name their identification methodology as 'dual cutoff', as it involves defining a set of indicator cutoffs in step (2) and the poverty cutoff in step (6). The dual-cutoff strategy is clearly applicable to any approach following a counting method to identify the poor.

Counting approaches have been widely used in empirical studies, with one developed and one developing region being particularly pioneering in this work: Europe and Latin America. Interestingly, applications of the counting approach have been inspired and motivated by different conceptual approaches, and have developed relatively independently of each other.

One such influential approach was the basic needs approach, which emerged in the mid-1970s as a reaction to the prevailing economic growth-centred approach to development of the time.[2] The Cocoyoc Declaration, adopted in 1974 by participants in the UNEP/UNCTAD symposium on 'Patterns of Resource Use, Environment and Development Strategies', articulated this approach as follows: 'Human beings have basic needs: food, shelter, clothing, health, education … We are still in a stage where the most important concern of development is the level of satisfaction of basic needs for the poorest sections in each society … Development should not be limited to the satisfaction of basic needs … Development includes freedom of expression and impression, the right to give and to receive ideas and stimulus … , the right to work' (UNEP/UNCTAD 1975: 896–7). The Cocoyoc Declaration was echoed by several subsequent studies and reports released in 1976.[3,4]

---

[2] The study of how economic growth occurs and how it advances basic needs has evolved significantly. See Commission on Growth and Development (2008); Stiglitz, Sen, and Fitoussi (2009); Drèze and Sen (2013).

[3] Dag Hammarskjöld Foundation (1976); Herrera et al. (1976); ILO (1976).

[4] Philosophically, the basic needs approach seeks to elaborate some minimal material requirements of human well-being and justice. See Rawls (1971), Stewart (1985), Braybrooke (1987), Hamilton (2003), and Reader (2006).

The basic needs approach had a policy focus, but in practice it influenced poverty measurement, especially in Latin America. Until the 1970s, the prevailing approach to measuring poverty used an income poverty line for identifying the poor, which Sen (1981) called the **income method**.[5] The first European use of an (implicit) poverty line was by the London School Board during the 1880s in order to exempt destitute families from paying school fees (Gillie 1996).[6] The poverty line was then used in the seminal surveys of Booth (1894, 1903), Rowntree (1901), and Bowley and Burnett-Hurst (1915), which were conducted in specific cities in the UK. As expressed by Rowntree, the poverty line represented the 'minimum necessaries for the maintenance of merely physical efficiency' (i.e. nutritional requirements, clothing, fuel, and household sundries) in monetary terms (Townsend 1954: 131).[7] The poor were those whose household income was below the poverty line corresponding to their family size. In the 1950s, the income method of poverty measurement appeared to be consistent with the growth emphasis of development (Sen 1960). Clearly, a commodity-focused concept of basic needs underlay the income method of poverty measurement, as the poverty line indicated the minimum amount of resources to cover such needs. Subsequently the basic needs approach, alongside other approaches, such as social exclusion, drew attention to the importance of looking at the *actual* satisfaction of basic needs (or at least access to key commodities), thus fostering the so-called **direct method** of poverty measurement (Sen 1981). A list of needs considered to be basic alongside minimum levels of satisfaction (cutoffs) would be specified. It is in such a context that counting the number of deprivations naturally emerged as a method of identifying the poor and of monitoring progress towards meeting basic needs.

As the Cocoyoc Declaration quote shows, the basic needs approach was originally quite comprehensive in the goals it regarded as intrinsically important, including, for example, freedom of expression and the right to have decent work. Later, as the approach was intended to have a direct policy impact, empirical studies were conducted in order to determine which goods and services, incomes, and resources were needed for everyone to enjoy a 'full life' (Streeten et al. 1981). Resources were understood to be of secondary importance and merely as means to ends by most basic needs advocates (Stewart 1985). Unfortunately, when the idea caught on, some operational programmes designed by the International Labour Organization (ILO) and the World Bank, under Robert MacNamara, were 'focused on commodity inputs to health, education, clothing, shelter, sanitation and hygiene .... The problem was that the overemphasis on commodities

---

[5] Alkire and Santos (2014) further elaborate the income method vs direct methods of poverty measurement.

[6] Earlier the Poor Laws in England and Wales provided a nascent welfare system. They started in the mid-1350s in response to the Black Death in England and an increase in the number of beggars and people looking for better pay as feudalism started to decay. The goal was to induce every able-bodied person to work (Townsend 1786; Quigley 1998; Hollen Lees 1998). Targeting was accomplished using a mix of 'visual' verification and 'self-targeting' rather than income poverty or counting-based measures.

[7] Cf. Tout (1938), Pagani (1960), Dubois (1899), and Townsend (1952).

misinterpreted the basic needs approach, and in so doing redefined and subverted it' (Alkire 2002a: 116, cf. 2006). The policy urgency was defended as being appropriate and necessary, but in fact it implemented only a subset of priorities of the basic human needs approach (Stewart 1985).

Some years before the emergence of the basic needs approach, Europe started to develop social indicators, which enabled empirical studies of non-monetary aspects of social welfare (Delors 1971). Erikson (1993) describes how criticisms of GNP per capita as a measure of welfare in the 1950s led to a 1954 UN expert group, which proposed to measure well-being using 'level of living'. In the late 1960s, interest was renewed in constructing 'a parsimonious set of specific indices covering a broad range of social concerns' (Vogel 1997: 105). In 1968 Sweden implemented a Level of Living Survey that was repeated and spread in other Scandinavian countries, and this, together with parallel work on social indicators such as Delors (1971), catalysed discussions of poverty measurement: 'Johansson [(1973)], in his first discussion of the level of living concept, suggested a concentration on "bad conditions"' (Erikson 1993: 80).[8]

While basic needs was one concept informing measures of deprivation in Europe (Galtung 1980), this was supplemented by other conceptual motivations.[9] Atkinson and Marlier (2010) observe that the multidimensional concept of 'social exclusion' (Lenoir 1974) has most widely motivated European approaches to measurement for public policy. In 1974, the Council of the European Union adopted a 'resolution concerning a social action programme' which prompted responses to poverty and social exclusion (Atkinson et al. 2005: 29). The Council defined the poor (in 1975) as 'individuals or families whose resources are so small as to exclude them from the minimum acceptable way of life of the Member State in which they live', with 'resources' being defined as 'goods, cash income plus services from public and private sources' (Atkinson et al. 2005: 18).[10] Social exclusion became seen as going 'beyond the elimination of poverty' to focus on 'the mechanisms whereby individuals and groups are excluded from taking part in the social exchanges, from the component practices and rights of social integration' (European Commission 1992, cited in Atkinson and Marlier 2010: 18).

Although the social inclusion approach was (and often still is) widely described as 'relative', this depends upon the evaluative space. Amartya Sen wrote, '[t]he characteristic feature of "absoluteness" is neither constancy over time, nor invariance between different societies, nor concentration merely on food and nutrition. It is an approach of judging a person's deprivation in absolute terms (in the case of poverty study, in terms of certain specified minimum absolute levels), rather than in purely *relative* terms *vis-à-vis* the levels enjoyed by others in the society' (1985: 673).

---

[8] Johansson (1973) had already raised the need for measures to employ indicators having dichotomous and ordinal scales; cf. section 2.3, section 3.6, and Chapter 5.

[9] For example, in 1989 the European Commission proposed a 'Community Charter of Fundamental Social Rights', which was adopted by eleven of the twelve then-member states. See discussions in Room (1995), Silver (1995), and Nolan and Whelan (1996, 2011).

[10] In order to define the 'minimally acceptable way of life' for empirical measurement, different processes were explored including the socially perceived necessities approach commented on later.

A landmark moment in the mainstreaming of social inclusion into European Union (EU) policies occurred at the Lisbon Summit of March 2000, where 'EU Heads of State and Government decided that the Union should adopt the strategic goal for the next decade of becoming "the most competitive and dynamic knowledge-based economy ... with more and better jobs and greater social cohesion". Importantly, the phrase "social cohesion" appeared in the same sentence as "most competitive economy"' (Atkinson et al. 2002: 17). Another inflection point in Europe was the very explicit political processes for engaging member states in the 'open method of coordination' for social measures and policies. 'The open method of coordination, which is designed to help member states progressively to develop their own policies, involves fixing guidelines for the Union, establishing quantitative and qualitative indicators to be applied in each member state, and periodic monitoring' (Atkinson et al. 2002: 1–5).

A third influential conceptual framework for developing counting-based poverty measures has been Amartya Sen's capability approach, outlined in section 1.1. It gained increasing recognition as providing an appropriate space for evaluating poverty: the space of capabilities and functionings rather than the space of resources upon which basic needs programmes had come to concentrate.[11] Applications of counting approaches intending to operationalize the capability approach sought to look at failures in such things as the ability to meet nutritional requirements, be clothed and sheltered, enjoy functional literacy and numeracy, or the power to participate in the social life of the community, which are some of the basic functionings mentioned by Sen from the very start (1980: 218). Yet even in work inspired by the capability framework, the indicators considered in counting approaches are data-constrained, hence often include resource-based indicators that are linked to key functionings, much as in the basic needs approach.

This chapter briefly reviews key empirical implementations of counting approaches to identifying the poor that are motivated by any of the aforementioned conceptual approaches.[12] Before proceeding to the salient applications of the counting approach, let us clarify that their emphasis is on *identifying* the poor. Most measurement applications of the counting approach have used the proportion of people identified as poor—the so-called headcount ratio defined in equation (3.23) in section 3.6—for the third fundamental step of poverty measurement: aggregation. By using only the headcount ratio, the poverty measure is not able to discriminate according to the number or extent of deprivations among the poor, what we call **intensity**.[13] The focus of this chapter is on

---

[11] Sen's capability approach built upon the basic needs approach: 'The focus on basic capabilities can be seen as a natural extension of Rawls's concern with primary goods, shifting attention from goods to what goods do to human beings' (Sen 1980: 218–19).

[12] See Nolan and Whelan (1996, 2011) for a more thorough review of counting approaches to identify the poor as well as for a review of empirical evidence of the mismatches between income poverty and non-monetary deprivations.

[13] As we shall see, some implementations of counting approaches use multiple poverty cutoffs (i.e. required alternative numbers of deprivations to identify the poor). While informative, this stops short of incorporating

the identification step; Chapters 3 and 5 address forms of aggregation that provide more informative poverty measures than the multidimensional headcount ratio.

4.2 Measures of Deprivation in Europe and their Influence

Townsend (1979) conducted an early seminal study using a counting approach to poverty in the United Kingdom, analysing a 1968–9 survey covering about 2000 households in Britain. To assess the magnitude of 'relative deprivation', Townsend defined sixty indicators covering twelve dimensions: diet, clothing, fuel and light, home amenities, housing conditions and facilities, the immediate environment of the home, conditions at work, family support, recreation, education, health, and social relations. Each indicator was equally weighted, although the number of indicators within each dimension varied greatly. For 'illustrative purposes', he then focused on a shorter list of twelve items covering major aspects of dietary, household, familial, recreational, and social deprivation. Townsend used a minimum score of five (out of the twelve) 'as suggestive of deprivation' (p. 252). In other words, a poverty cutoff of five out of twelve was chosen to identify the poor.[14] He did not use a union criterion because he recognized the potential problems: 'No single item by itself, or pair of items by themselves, can be regarded as symptomatic of general deprivation. People are idiosyncratic and will indulge in certain luxuries and apply certain prohibitions for religious, moral, educational or other reasons, whether they are rich or poor' (p. 252).[15] However, he actually did not use this counting approach to analyse poverty. Rather, he explored the correlation between deprivation scores and household income (adjusted for household size) in order to derive an income threshold below which people are 'disproportionately deprived' (p. 255). In other words, he used a *direct* approach to 'validate' the poverty line to be used in the indirect income poverty measure.

Townsend's study inspired much subsequent work on poverty and social exclusion in Europe and, in particular, another benchmark study on poverty: Mack and Lansley's *Poor Britain* (1985). This study was also influenced by Sen's writings on the direct approach to poverty measurement (Sen 1981). A novelty of this study was that the list of items considered as necessities was, for the first time, constructed using a survey of the public's perceptions of minimum needs (PSE 1983) known as Breadline Britain survey. That is why their method has been called the 'consensual or perceived deprivation approach to measuring poverty'. Of the original thirty-five items, they retained the twenty-six that were considered necessities by strictly more than 50% of the population. The survey

---

intensity into one summary measure, which, like the Adjusted Headcount Ratio (M_0), can be broken down by dimension.

[14] Townsend used the terms 'deprived' and 'poor' interchangeably, whereas we define these terms differently.

[15] Note however that he did not use the term 'union' to refer to this criterion.

usefully distinguished people who lacked an item because they could not afford it from those for whom it was a voluntary choice.[16] The authors identified as poor those who could not afford three or more of the equally weighted items (p. 178).[17] This poverty cutoff was selected after analysing the association between the number of deprivations, income levels, and spending patterns. Mack and Lansley proposed that a lack of three or more necessities was a matter of force rather than choice.[18] 'Very few of the better-off lack this level of necessities. And nearly all those who lack this level of necessities cut back on non-necessities, a majority cutting back substantially' (p. 176). In addition to their benchmark cutoff, the authors reported degrees of deprivation using two additional poverty cutoffs: 'Broadly speaking, those who cannot afford five or more necessities are sinking deeper into poverty; and those who cannot afford seven or more necessities are in intense poverty' (p. 184). British authors continue working along these lines, with new surveys in 1990, 1999, and 2012. Breadline-Britain-type surveys were also replicated elsewhere in Europe.[19] It also inspired the structure of two much-used datasets: the European Community Household Panel survey (ECHP) and the European Union Statistics on Income and Living Conditions (EU-SILC).[20]

Gordon et al. (2000) compare the 1983, 1990, and 1999 Breadline Britain surveys in terms of the items considered as necessities and assess the evolution in poverty levels. Using an updated list of thirty-five items to evaluate poverty, they identified a household as poor if they could not afford two or more items and, additionally, had relatively low incomes.[21] The report also constructed a measure of child poverty using a list of twenty-seven socially perceived necessities for children. They used a poverty cutoff of one or more and another cutoff of two or more. In both cases the poverty cutoff was set using discriminant function analysis.[22] Note that the poverty cutoff selected using discriminant analysis, which is a data-driven approach, may provide different conclusions when

---

[16] This pioneering study analysed patterns of what people considered necessary, correlations with income, and the free choice of voluntary deprivations. It includes vivid testimonies from interviews and a fascinating discussion of contemporary policies.

[17] The authors acknowledged that they could have discerned the 'seriousness' of deprivations in different indicators by assigning more weight to items considered by more people as a necessity (i.e. by the rank order of the necessities). However, they dismissed this possibility by arguing that people in poverty with an equal number but different combinations of indicators should, by definition, face an equally 'serious' situation.

[18] 'Two criteria have been applied: first, those who lack this level of necessities [three out of twenty-two] should have low incomes, falling in the bottom half of the income range; second, their overall spending patterns should reflect financial difficulty rather than high spending on other goods' (Mack and Lansley 1985: 175–6).

[19] Gordon et al. (2000: 72, appendix 1) lists other studies using the Breadline Britain survey.

[20] These surveys do not collect information on socially perceived necessities, but do ascertain whether the lack of an item is voluntary.

[21] The thirty-five items selected in 1999 were such that 50% of people or more considered them as necessities.

[22] A discriminant function analysis (DFA) divides the population into poor and non-poor by predicting whether each person belongs to one group or the other based on a set of characteristics of the unit of analysis, taken as 'explanatory variables'. In these studies, alternative numbers of deprivations (poverty cutoffs) were tested, and the explanatory variables included family income, the employment status of the household head, the number of children, ethnicity, and region of residence, among many others.

applied to different datasets, making comparison across time difficult (section 3.4.4). Because the poverty cutoff is not normatively considered or justified, in contrast to other measures reviewed, there is no link to ethical assessments of poverty.

Building upon the work of Mack and Lansley (1985) and Ringen (1987, 1988), Callan, Nolan, and Whelan (1993) also proposed to identify the poor by combining both resource *and* deprivation measures.[23] They used data from a household survey conducted in Ireland by the Economic and Social Research Institute (ESRI) in 1987, which used Mack and Lansley's (1985) format. Starting from a list of twenty-four items, the authors used factor analysis to observe possible indicator clusterings and accordingly used three dimensions: (1) basic lifestyle (eight items such as food and clothes), (2) housing and durables (seven items related to housing quality and facilities), and (3) 'other' aspects of lifestyle (nine items such as social participation, leisure activities, and having a car or telephone). People's perceptions regarding the necessity of indicators restricted their material deprivation index to the eight-item basic lifestyle dimension.[24] They identified as poor anyone who both lacked one or more of the eight items *and* fell below the relative income poverty line, set at 60% of the average equivalent disposable income in the sample.[25] This work sparked a series of surveys and studies to monitor poverty in Ireland using variations on this combined method of resources and material deprivation. These were used to build a 'consistent measure of poverty'[26] which identifies a person as poor if she is both income poor and deprived in some minimum set of deprivations.

Muffels et al. (1992) built upon Muffels and Vriens (1991) and designed an index of relative and subjective deprivation using a Dutch socioeconomic panel survey inspired by Mack and Lansley (1985). Their innovation was to use household weights and poverty cutoffs. They first constructed an (objective) deprivation score for every head of household as the weighted sum of deprivation in each of a large set of items related to living conditions. The weight for each item varied across households and represented the respondent's perceived importance of the item, compared to the perceived importance of the item by the reference group of the household head (p. 195). They selected a subjective poverty cutoff, termed the 'subjective deprivation poverty line', using an econometric model. In the model, the dependent variable was the respondent's subjective assessment of whether he/she was poor or not on a scale of one to ten. The explanatory variables were their deprivation score plus control variables such as income, age of the household

---

[23] Ringen (1987) stated, 'we need to establish not only that people live as if they were poor but that they do so because they do not have the means to avoid it' (p. 162, cited in Callan, Nolan, and Whelan 1993).

[24] The eight items are going into arrears/debt to meet ordinary living expenses such as food and rent, not having a substantial meal all day, having to go without heating because of lack of money, involuntary lack of new clothes, lack of two pairs of shoes, not being able to afford a roast or equivalent once a week, not being able to afford a meal with meat or fish every second day, and not being able to afford a warm coat.

[25] Those fulfilling both conditions were identified as experiencing 'generalised deprivation' due to a lack of resources (Callan, Nolan, and Whelan 1993; Nolan and Whelan 1996). They also identified subgroups who were income poor but not materially deprived and vice versa.

[26] Callan et al. (1999), Whelan et al. (2001a), Layte et al. (2000), and Whelan, Nolan, and Maître (2006), among others.

head, family status, and financial stress factors. Using the estimated coefficients, the 'subjective deprivation poverty line' was calculated for each household separately as the deprivation score that would produce a subjective assessment score of 5.5.[27] Then they explored the degree of overlap between those identified as poor using the subjective deprivation poverty line and those identified as 'insecure' using three alternative income poverty lines (a subjective line, equal to the minimum income reported by households as 'the minimum income they need to acquire a certain minimum standard of welfare'; a 'national social minimum income standard'; and a 'European statistical minimum income standard'). They examined the relationship between both measures in terms of bivariate distributions using contingency tables and regression analysis and found significant mismatches. They concluded that a multi-method approach combining income and (direct) deprivation measures was needed to assess poverty.

Halleröd (1994, 1995) used data from the Swedish standard of living survey in 1992, which also followed Mack and Lansley (1985). A key difference was that they retained all thirty-six originally included items but *weighted* them by the proportion of the population that regarded each as necessary. Weights were adjusted by certain groups to reflect significant differences in preferences.[28] The index was labelled the Proportional Deprivation Index (PDI). The author selected a poverty cutoff that produced the same headcount ratio as the Consensual Poverty Line (CPL). The CPL was an interpersonally comparable income level at which, on average, respondents in different circumstances would subjectively indicate that their current income was just sufficient for them to make ends meet. While both methods identified nearly 21.3% of the population as poor, only 8.8% of the population were identified as poor by both. Acknowledging that both the income and direct methods may be subject to substantial measurement problems, the author advocated the use of a combination of both methods and defined those 8.8% of the population who were poor by both CPL and PDI as the 'truly poor'. Subsequently, Halleröd et al. (2006) used a variant of the PDI to compare poverty levels in Britain, Finland, and Sweden.

Using ECHP data, Layte et al. (2001) constructed a material deprivation index from thirteen items to assess the relationship between (relative) income poverty and material deprivation. For each country, they weighted each item by the proportion of households possessing that item, and they defined the poverty cutoff of the deprivation index endogenously as the threshold which generated a headcount ratio equal to that of the (relative) income poverty line of the country. They performed this exercise for different relative poverty lines: at 40%, 50%, and 60% of the median income in each country. Their results showed that the overlap between the two poverty measures was very limited and thus supported a method that combines both measures. Whelan, Layte, and Maître

---

[27] The reason for using the subjective assessment score of 5.5 is that in the Netherlands schooling system, a score of 5.5 on a 1–10 scale is considered to be a dividing line between a 'satisfactory' and an 'unsatisfactory' score.

[28] The groups were men, women, age groups, household types, and geographic regions.

(2004), using the ECHP to identify persistently poor persons, found a similar mismatch, as mentioned in section 1.2.1.

Eurostat (2002) constructed an index of non-monetary poverty (*pauvreté d'existence*) for European countries. Following the analysis of Whelan et al. (2001) of the first ECHP survey, a list of twenty-four dichotomous items ('having'/'not having') available in that survey were grouped into five dimensions using factor analysis.[29] For each individual, a deprivation score per dimension was obtained as the weighted sum of deprivations in the indicators of that dimension, where the weight attached to an indicator was inversely related to the deprivation rate in that indicator in the corresponding country. Then, the dimensional deprivation scores were also aggregated by taking a weighted sum, where the dimensional weight attached to a dimension was proportional to the weighted average of the coefficients of variation among that dimension's indicators (pp. 155–6). People with a deprivation score of 60% or more were considered poor.[30]

Additional implementations of the counting approach to identifying the poor in Europe included studies of poverty in Sweden (Erikson 1993), the reports on poverty in Belgium by Vranken and other authors (Vranken 2002), and recent work on the search for a relative deprivation index for Europe (Guio 2005, 2009; Guio and Maquet 2006; Decanq et al. 2013). In 2011, the European Commission implemented an 'EU-2020' multidimensional poverty measure using union identification across three indicators: relative income poverty, severe material deprivation, and quasi-joblessness. This landmark measure identified those 'at risk of poverty and social exclusion' in order to set and monitor a poverty reduction target for 2020. It represents the most high-profile policy application to date—hence, perhaps, the most closely scrutinized.

Nolan and Whelan's book *Poverty and Deprivation in Europe* offers a systematic conceptual and empirical study of 'why and how non-monetary indicators of deprivation can play a significant role in complementing (not replacing) income in order to capture the reality of poverty in Europe' (2011: 1). It is thus relevant to this book at many points, as they too survey research on mismatches in identification between different indicators of poverty, by social group in one period and across time; scrutinize indicator design; apply robustness tests; consider the poverty cutoff; and propose ways of strengthening the EU-2020 Poverty Target. Maître, Nolan, and Whelan (2013) offer a critical evaluation of the EU-2020 Target, and Whelan, Nolan, and Maître (2014) explore the use of the AF method for the case of the European Union using EU-SILC data; they advocate the replacement of the current approach by the AF approach as it is more structured, less ad hoc, and more transparent, as well as being flexible in terms of the poverty cutoff and the axiomatic properties of its measures (see section 2.5 and Chapter 5). Alkire, Apablaza, and Jung (2014a) also apply an AF measure to EU-SILC data 2006–12 and explore the inclusion of social indicators.

---

[29] Boarini and d'Ercole (2006: 33) and Eurostat (2002: 25) present these.

[30] This threshold was selected so that the average rate of non-monetary poverty across the fifteen countries equalled the average income poverty rate.

Townsend (1979) and Mack and Lansley (1985) also influenced work outside Europe. For example, Mayer and Jencks (1989) severely criticized the income approach to poverty measurement in the United States based on a survey in Chicago on material hardship. They collected information on ten indicators covering dimensions of food, housing, and medical care. The number of hardships (equally weighted) were analysed alongside income and subjective satisfaction with living standard. They found that the family's income-to-needs ratio explained less than a quarter of the variation in the total number of hardships that families report.[31]

The consensual approach or socially perceived necessities to poverty measurement initiated by Mack and Lansley (1985) and its survey structure were replicated elsewhere. In particular, it served as a model for a Basic Necessities Survey (BNS) (Davies 1997; Davies and Smith 1998). The BNS method weights each item by the proportion of people who said it is a basic necessity. It suggests defining a poverty cutoff across the BSN score such that it identifies as poor the same proportion of people as those who have subjectively identified themselves as poor. Davies' BNS method was implemented in Vietnam and Mali (Nteziyaremye and MkNelly 2001), Bangladesh (Ahmed 2007), Ireland (Nolan and Whelan 1996), Japan (Abe 2006), Europe (Eurobarometer 2007), and South Africa (Wright 2008), among other countries.

4.3 Measures of Unsatisfied Basic Needs in Latin America and Beyond

Latin America is the other region where a counting approach to identifying the poor has been widely implemented. Rather than a focus on social exclusion or 'relative deprivation' as in Europe, in Latin America it was operationalized under the unsatisfied basic needs (UBN) approach. The first implementation was in Chile in 1975 when the first 'Map of Extreme Poverty' was produced (Kast and Molina 1975). However, the method became known and widespread in the region with a seminal study conducted by the Institute of Statistics and Census of Argentina (INDEC) and the United Nations Economic Commission for Latin America and the Caribbean (ECLAC or Comisión Económica para América Latina y el Caribe/CEPAL in Spanish) (INDEC 1984). INDEC recognized the multidimensionality of poverty and sought to assess disadvantage across a wide set of basic needs or—alternatively—with information on income (p. 10). Thus, initially the UBN method was presented as an imperfect proxy for income poverty measurement.

The selection of census indicators was first performed by ECLAC with an empirical study using data from the 1980 census of Argentina. The study acknowledges that the census did not provide data on income or consumption nor on key health variables

---

[31] Bauman (1998, 1999) critically evaluated their work and instead advocated the use of measures of hardship to complement, not substitute for, income poverty measures.

such as nutrition. However, the census provided data from all areas in the country and, importantly, with a useful level of disaggregation at smaller geographical entities. Within these constraints, three criteria guided the selection of indicators (INDEC 1984: 11):

1. the indicators represented the degree of failure to satisfy some specific group of basic needs;
2. these indicators were significantly associated with [income] poverty;
3. they were comparable across regions of the country so that poverty maps could be constructed.

In order to fulfil the second criterion, as part of the project, ECLAC undertook an empirical study using data from a 1980 survey of two urban areas of Argentina: the Greater Buenos Aires area and Goya (taken as representative of other urban areas).[32] The aim was 'to select the characteristics that not only represented some intrinsically important deprivation but were also sufficiently associated with situations of [income] poverty so as to represent the other [unmeasured] deprivations that constitute such situations' (INDEC 1984: 500). Both absolute and relative poverty lines were used; the former followed Altimir (1979) and the latter was set at half of the mean private per capita consumption according to national accounts. Census indicators were selected if they were empirically assessed to be strong predictors of income poverty in regression analysis—thus not using normative criteria. Step two, thus, in practice, dominated the three criteria mentioned above as well as the three-step selection of (a) the basic need, (b) the specific indicator, and (c) the deprivation cutoff (Feres and Mancero 2001). The census indicators chosen by INDEC and CEPAL were:

1. households with more than three people per room (overcrowding);
2. households with precarious housing;
3. households with no kind of toilet;
4. households with children of school age (6–12 years old) not attending school;
5. households with four or more dependents per occupied member (high dependency ratio) and whose household head's education was at most second grade of primary education.

The union criterion was used: all members of any household with at least one unsatisfied basic need were considered poor. The intuition was that because very low deprivation cutoffs were used for each indicator, one sole deprivation seemed sufficient to signal poverty (Rio Group 2006: 110). However, the information was reported in different ways and using different cutoffs: (1) the proportion of households and people experiencing

---

[32] The Encuesta Permanente de Hogares was already being conducted regularly by INDEC, but it was restricted to the Greater Buenos Aires area.

each UBN; (2) the proportion of households and people with one or more UBN; and also (3) the proportion of people with two or more and three or more UBNs.

The set of census indicators outlined by INDEC and CEPAL for Argentina was replicated by official statistical institutes in many Latin American countries: Bolivia, Chile, Colombia, Ecuador, Guatemala, Honduras, Nicaragua, Paraguay, Peru, Uruguay, and Venezuela. While there was some variation in indicators, the dimensions considered remained essentially the same, as they were limited by the information contained in the countries' censuses. Feres and Mancero (2001: 67) noted that they belonged to four broad categories:

1. access to housing that met minimum housing standards;
2. access to basic services that guarantee minimum sanitary conditions;
3. access to basic education;
4. economic capacity to achieve minimum consumption levels.

In all these countries, the UBN methodology was used to construct detailed and disaggregated poverty maps using census data. Poverty maps became a valuable tool for policy design (Kaztman 1996: 24). Coady, Grosh, and Hoddinott (2004) observe that poverty mapping has been widely used for geographical targeting purposes—and not only in Latin America. 'Much of the history of poverty mapping has used a "basic needs" approach with poverty defined in terms of access to basic services. The simplest form of geographic targeting involves the use of a single variable such as nutritional status. ... the choice of variables is largely guided by a combination of philosophy and data availability' (Coady, Grosh, and Hoddinott 2004: 63). In other cases, such as in Argentina or Chile, maps were constructed using the proportion of people with different numbers of UBNs. Poverty maps have guided investments in infrastructure, implementation of public works programmes and social funds, subsidized services, and the allocation of conditional cash transfer (CCT) programmes (usually alongside a complementary targeting method).[33] While some countries have built consumption-based poverty maps (Elbers, Lanjouw, and Lanjouw 2002), these have been less common than the basic needs maps, and their policy interpretation is more challenging.[34]

Beyond the policy impact that basic needs poverty maps have, it is worth noting that, while in Europe the direct method of measuring poverty was implemented alongside an effort to collect new data that would (a) reveal socially perceived necessities and (b) distinguish whether the lack of items was enforced or by choice, in Latin America the direct method was restricted to the data available at the time (census data). Thus, the

---

[33] Progresa (later renamed Oportunidades) in Mexico and Bolsa de Familia in Brazil started in 1997 and were pioneer programmes in Latin America and in the world (Fiszbein and Schady 2009).

[34] The construction of income poverty maps typically matches a census with household survey information to predict income poverty, which is not directly measured in the census. Tarozzi and Deaton (2009) criticize such methods as they require a degree of spatial homogeneity, which is not guaranteed by the matching methods. See also Elbers et al. (2007) and Bedi et al. (2007).

Table 4.1 The UBN poor and the income poor

	UBN poor	UBN non-poor
Income Poor	Chronically Poor	Recently Poor
Income Non-Poor	With Structural Deprivations	Socially Integrated

range of indicators that could be included was severely constrained. The direct method in Latin America did not seek to reflect people's views of their own necessities, and it did not deliberately permit 'choice'. Relatedly, it must also be noted that in Latin America the definition of the UBN indicators was done from an absolute poverty perspective, whereas in Europe it was justified with respect to a relative or perceptual concept of poverty. Despite these differences, a strong common feature emerged: the interest in crossing the direct method with the indirect one. This gave rise in Latin America to the 'integrated method' to measure poverty proposed by Beccaria and Minujin (1985) and Kaztman (1989). The indirect or income method was applied using data from household surveys, which started to be progressively implemented in the late 1980s and 1990s in the region. An absolute income poverty line approach was applied using the cost of basic needs method (Altimir 1979). The idea of the integrated method was to identify four sets of people: (1) the income and UBN poor, (2) the UBN poor but income non-poor, (3) the income poor but UBN non-poor, and (4) the non-poor by any method, as expressed in Table 4.1. This could be done using data from household surveys, which collected information on the UBN indicators as well as on income.

Kaztman (1989) terms the first group 'chronically poor', not because of information on poverty over time but because he assumes that insufficient income coupled with at least one UBN (most had more than one) would reproduce poverty over time. This group would be equivalent to the 'consistently poor' in the European literature. Other names belie other assumptions, but in any case empirical mismatches proved widespread.[35]

As Boltvinik (1991) argued, these studies showed that the two methods, income poverty and UBN poverty, were (unintentionally) complementary, identifying to a great extent different slices of the population. Evidence from Montevideo (Uruguay) in 1984 and from Greater Buenos Aires (Argentina) in 1976 suggested that 10–15% of the households were in the 'recently poor' category, 4–9% of the households were in the 'with inertial deprivations' category, and only 7% were poor by both methods, i.e. in the chronically poor category. In Peru nearly 40% of the population were identified as both income and UBN poor (chronically poor). Yet 30% of the population were identified as either income poor or UBN poor but not both, which shows the 'mismatches' between the two methods, covering nearly the entire population.

Boltvinik (1992) proposed an 'Improved Integrated Method to Measure Poverty', which involved changes in each method separately, as well as in their combination. His method was applied in Mexico (Boltvinik 1995, 1996). He proposed first that UBN indicators

---

[35] See Kaztman (1989: 130) and Stewart et al. (2007).

be those associated with public investment, which could not be purchased individually, and dimensions that could be purchased using private resources should be considered in the income component.[36] Second, a higher poverty line based on a more comprehensive basket of goods and services was generated. Third, he incorporated gaps in the measurement of income poverty and also of UBN. Thus, rather than dichotomizing achievements in each of the UBN indicators, he proposed (controversially) computing normalized deprivation gaps for each indicator as if they had cardinal data. Fourth, he allowed deprivation gaps to take negative values (reflecting achievements above the deprivation cutoff) thus permitting substitutability across deprived and non-deprived items. Finally he normalized the gaps to vary between minus one and one. Boltvinik's proposal entails *cardinalizing* ordinal variables, which imposes multiple value judgements for which there is no clear agreement (see section 2.3 for a detailed explanation of the problems involved). The problem is that measures thus constructed are very unlikely to be robust to different value judgements used in their construction.[37]

To identify the poor, Boltvinik suggested using three alternative poverty cutoffs. Boltvinik also discussed alternative methods for weighting the UBN indicators: (a) equal weights, (b) the complement of indicators' deprivation rates (Desai and Shah 1988), and (c) a combination of monetary and time valuations[38] of each need. As in the case of the UBN index, negative gaps were allowed for income. These were normalized to range between minus one and one by dividing them by (the absolute value of) a normative maximum negative gap and replacing them by minus one whenever the absolute value of the negative gap was higher than the maximum normative gap. On the other hand, each person would have an individual UBN score which would be the weighted sum of the normalized deprivation gaps (ranging from minus one to one). In the combined method, each UBN indicator would be weighted by the proportion of the total cost required to fulfil each set of needs, and an individual's UBN score would be *added* to her income poverty score.

Boltvinik's revised integrated method to measure poverty was altogether different from the integrated method outlined in Table 4.1 and is no longer a counting measure. It ceased to consider mismatches between the UBN poor and the income poor. His identification method is not a counting approach but relied on a score obtained as the weighted sum of the aggregated gaps of cardinalized ordinal data (permitting substitutability). The reasons for the 'Improved Integrated Method to Measure Poverty' not acquiring popularity seem to be (a) that it required a number of controversial estimations, such as those related

---

[36] Boltvinik (1992, 2012) proposed that the UBN indicators should be as follows: sanitation, electricity, and services (such as phone and garbage collection), housing and overcrowding, education, furniture and appliances, access to health care and social security. He considered the following items to be covered by income poverty: food, petrol, personal and household hygiene, clothing, footwear and personal care, transport, basic communications, recreation and culture, basic services expenditure in health care and education, and other expenditures.

[37] Boltvinik (1992) also proposes independent and revised UBN and income poverty measures.

[38] Boltvinik (1992: 360–1) has a detailed description of how this alternative was implemented.

to time use and monetary valuations of UBN indicators, (b) that it attached a cardinal meaning to categories of response in ordinal variables and thus the intensity in the UBN index was dependent on the particular cardinalization used (which again could be contested), and (c) some steps such as the cardinalization of ordinal data and the consideration of negative gaps prevented the resulting measure from satisfying many desirable axiomatic properties outlined in section 2.5.[39] Overall, in trying to accomplish too much, the method lost the public intuition and policy relevance that characterizes the counting approach and direct method of poverty measurement. That being said, many important distinctions were considered in this development, including the importance of time poverty.

The UBN approach has also been used in other parts of the world. In the Arab Region, Lebanon pioneered the UBN approach in 1997, using eleven indicators in four dimensions from the 1994–5 population and household survey (a mini census covering 10% of the population). The document *Mapping Living Conditions in Lebanon* was published in 1998 by the Lebanese Ministry of Social Affairs (MoSA) and UNDP, and was used to define poverty after the civil war in the absence of other data. This report, which mapped Lebanon's six governorates and twenty-six districts, was updated using 2004 survey data (UNDP and MoSA 2007), and an expanded index was published together with monetary poverty measures from the same survey in 2009. Iraq's Ministry of Planning together with UNDP also completed a significant three-volume study *Mapping of Deprivation and Living Conditions in Iraq* using 2003 data (UNDP and MPDC 2006). The study was used for budget allocation and policy priorities. In 2011 the same partners published a second study using 2007 data. A seven-country study was also produced using data from the Pan Arab Family and Health (PAPFAM) Surveys, which covered seventeen indicators grouped into five dimensions: education, health, housing, home necessities, and economic conditions (League of Arab States et al. 2009). Jordan published a similar two-volume study using 2010 data (first volume) and 2002–10 data (second volume). Other studies (ESCWA-AUDI) have covered particular topics such as an urban deprivation index in Tripoli, Lebanon (Nehmeh 2013).

The counting approach to identifying the poor has also been used in a new generation of poverty measures with renewed interest being shown in the direct method that uses solid aggregation methodologies based on axiomatic frameworks analogous to those which gave rise to the advances in income poverty measurement in the 1970s and 1980s (Alkire and Santos 2014). The following sections review some of these.

4.3.1 COUNTING APPROACHES IN MEASURES OF CHILD POVERTY

A counting approach to identifying the poor is a natural approach for various policy-oriented measures of child poverty. Understanding child poverty is widely agreed

---

[39] Boltvinik's aggregation method resembles the aggregate achievement approach described in sections 2.2.2 and 3.6.2.

to require a multidimensional approach in both European and developing contexts (Trani, Biggeri, and Mauro 2013; Boyden and Bourdillon 2012; Minujin and Nandy 2012; Gardiner and Evans 2011). A pioneering and internationally comparable measure of child poverty in developing countries was computed in 2003 (Gordon et al. 2001, 2003; UNICEF 2004), whose indicators and cutoffs reflect the Convention of the Rights of the Child. A number of studies have more recently measured and analysed child poverty using the AF method, including Alkire and Roche (2012), Apablaza and Yalonetzky (2011), Roche (2013), Trani et al. (2013), de Neubourg et al. (2012), and Dickerson and Popli (2013). In particular, it is worth highlighting that de Neubourg et al. (2012) is a step-by-step guide to implementing the Multiple Overlapping Deprivation Analysis (MODA) tool, developed at UNICEF's Research Office for global child comparisons adapting the M_0 measure of the AF method.[40]

4.4 Counting Approaches in Targeting

The implementations of the counting approach observed in Europe, the US, Latin America, and elsewhere were originally developed mostly within universities, and later became a tool for policy design and even targeting, although usually complemented by some other methodology. However, other implementations of the counting approach have stemmed directly from a much more pragmatic motivation: targeting beneficiaries in programmes run by the national or regional governments and non-governmental organizations.

One good illustration is the case of India, where a series of different methodologies have been used to identify rural households as 'below the poverty line' (BPL). BPL households are eligible for certain benefits, such as subsidized food or electricity, and programmes to construct housing and encourage self-employment. Poverty measurement in India has largely been based on consumption and expenditure poverty. Since 1992, the Indian government's census-based targeting methods have gradually evolved towards a counting approach (GOI 2009; Alkire and Seth 2013c). For example, in 2002, the BPL census collected information on thirteen dimensions covering topics such as food, housing, work, land ownership, assets, and education, and an aggregate achievement approach was implemented. This methodology was criticized on a number of grounds, including the cardinalization of ordinal variables and the substitutability of achievements among others.[41] Alkire and Seth (2008) compare the 2002 BPL method with a method based on a counting approach and show the possible mismatches that may occur between the two methods.

---

[40] <http://www.unicef-irc.org/MODA/>, accessed 24 November 2014.
[41] For a list of criticisms, see Sundaram (2003), Hirway (2003), Jain (2004), Mukherjee (2005), Jalan and Murgai (2007), Alkire and Seth (2008), GOI (2009), Thomas et al. (2009), Drèze and Khera (2010), and Roy (2011).

In 2008, the Indian government appointed an Expert Group Committee, under the chairmanship of N. C. Saxena, to provide a critical review of the 2002 BPL methodology and data contents, and to propose a new method for identification.[42] Their three-stage proposal implicitly used a counting method with a union approach in the first two stages leading to a counting-based identification in the third. It sparked informative empirical studies and ongoing methodological debates (Drèze and Khera 2010; Roy 2011; Sharan 2011; Alkire and Seth 2013).

Other subnational initiatives in South Asia use counting approaches for targeting. Two cases might illustrate this. The first concerns the Indian state of Kerala, an emblematic case of development and poverty reduction, whose government has been using a counting approach for targeting poor households since the late 1990s. The method was originally developed by non-governmental organizations (NGOs) and subsequently used for a women-based participatory poverty eradication programme named 'Kudumbashree' (Thomas et al. 2009). Kudumbashree uses nine equally weighted indicators related to housing, water, sanitation, literacy, income sources, food, presence of infants, presence of mentally or physically challenged or chronically ill persons, and caste/tribe. If the household presents deprivations in four or more indicators, it is considered poor; if it presents eight or nine, it is destitute. The identification of poor households is verified by neighbourhood groups comprising households that live in proximity. The identified households are eligible for a number of programmes, including microcredit.[43]

In our second case, a counting approach to celebrating 'graduation from poverty' is used by two acclaimed Bangladeshi NGOs, the Grameen Bank and the Bangladesh Rural Advancement Committee (BRAC). The Grameen Bank, the 'bank for the poor', was founded by Muhammad Yunus in 1976 in Bangladesh, originally as a local microcredit project. The project evolved into a nationwide bank with over eight million borrowers, of whom 96% were women, and has spread elsewhere. Grameen uses a set of ten indicators to identify participants. When a household has zero deprivations (intersection approach), it is considered to have 'graduated' from poverty. A counting approach to identifying the poor is also implicitly used by BRAC, another prominent microfinance NGO, initiated by Fazle Hasan Abed in 1972 in Bangladesh, which has spread widely. The BRAC programme, 'Target the Ultra-Poor Programme' (TUP), uses a counting-based method to target asset grants, skills training, community support, and healthcare services.

Moving further east, in Indonesia poverty is primarily measured using the indirect income approach. However, multidimensional perspectives using counting approaches are emerging (CBS 2008). A 'family welfare approach' was initially proposed by the Family Planning Coordination Board in 1999 (CBS 2008: 10). This approach identified a family

---

[42] Alkire and Seth (2013c) provide further details.
[43] The Kolkata-based NGO Bandhan also uses a counting approach to identify participants and 'graduates' from poverty.

as poor if it was deprived in one of five indicators (a union approach): religious freedom, meals per day, clothing, size of house, and access to modern medicine. The approach was not implemented, however, because the five indicators were not relevant to all families. The Central Bureau of Statistics (CBS) then proposed a 'poverty criteria approach', which identified people as poor if they were deprived in five out of eight indicators. The eight indicators were floor area; type of floor; water access; type of water; asset ownership; income per month; expenditure spent on food; and consumption of meat, fish, eggs, and chicken. A census instrument conducted in three provinces—South Kalimantan, DKI Jakarta, and East Java—in the years 1999, 2000, and 2011, respectively (CBS 2008: 18), used this method to determine whether households had the right to receive basic necessity subsidies (CBS 2008: 19).[44]

A distinct yet related methodology for identifying the poor is the **poverty scorecard** developed by Mark Schreiner (Schreiner 2002, 2006, 2010). Schreiner proposed the method both for measuring poverty as well as for targeting beneficiaries. The poverty scorecard uses an individual or household card, and grades five to ten achievements to produce a score. Indicators are sought that are strongly correlated with income poverty and have the following characteristics: ease of acceptance, inexpensive to observe and verify, already commonly collected, objective, liable to change over time as poverty status changes, variety vis-à-vis other selected indicators, and applicable across countries and across regions within a country. The indicators proposed for poverty scorecards for seven countries include housing quality; drinking water and toilet facilities; cooking arrangements; school attendance; ownership of land; and ownership of televisions, radios, or telephones (Schreiner 2010).

The indicators are fielded in nationally representative household surveys that also collect information on income or expenditure. Indicator weights are set through a logit regression as follows. The individuals are categorized into two groups: income poor and income non-poor, and this categorization is used as the dependent variable in the regression, with the selected indicators as explanatory variables. The logit weights are transformed such that all weights are non-negative integers and the minimum score is 0 and the maximum is 100.[45] For example, in his proposed scorecard for Pakistan (Schreiner 2010), if the household does not have a flush toilet (most deprived), it receives a score of 0; if it has a flush toilet to pit (less deprived), it receives fourteen points; and if it has a flush toilet to public sewer (not deprived at all), it receives nineteen points. The total poverty score for each household is obtained as the sum of the household's scores obtained in all indicators. A person is identified as poor if that person's poverty score lies below a poverty threshold which, as Schreiner indicates, can be determined according to the aim and scope of the particular programme.

---

[44] For other proposals for multidimensional non-counting approaches to poverty measurement, see Pradhan et al. (2000) and Gönner et al. (2007).

[45] Schreiner (2010) divides the sample into components for 'construction' (50%), 'calibration' (25%), and 'validation'.

As in the case of Boltvinik's method, Schreiner's poverty scorecard method departs from a counting approach. Furthermore, it cardinalizes ordinal data, based on logit regressions, which does not seem legitimate, as section 2.3 argued. Scores are then standardized and aggregated to obtain an overall score, which is compared to an overall threshold. This step, like the aggregate achievement approach (section 2.2.2), allows substitutability between non-deprived and deprived achievements. If all the variables had been cardinal, the score would be the (weighted) sum of achievements. But given that usually most variables are ordinal, such a score actually has no direct interpretation. This procedure has been followed in the UBN Index in Lebanon, Iraq, and other Arab states.[46] With a particular normalization of the variables, it has also been the method used by the Scottish Area Deprivation Index (Kearns et al. 2000), as well as by the Multidimensional Poverty Assessment Tool (MPAT) (Cohen 2010; Saisana and Saltelli 2010), among others.

With the method described above, Schreiner developed poverty scorecards for various microfinance institutions and also developed adaptations such as the Progress out of Poverty Index (PPI).[47] A related method was used by the Benazir Income Support Programme in Pakistan, which targets benefit recipients using a scorecard of twelve observable indicators, each of which receives a weight based on an Ordinary Least Squares (OLS) model of household expenditure per adult equivalent regressed on various sets of predictors (proxy-means test) (Khan and Qutub 2010).[48] The approach has thus spread widely yet without clarifying fundamental methodological concerns.

In the area of targeting, the AF methodology is also spreading both via academic studies and in policy programmes. For example, Robano and Smith (2014) examine the TUP programme of BRAC, developing M_0 measures for the existing targeting methods as well as for a proposed alternative, and present and implement an impact evaluation methodology using M_0 rather than any single outcome as the dependent variable. Azevedo and Robles (2013) propose an M_0 multidimensional targeting approach to identifying beneficiaries that explicitly takes into consideration the multiple objectives of conditional cash transfer programmes and the multiple deprivations of the poor household. Using data from Mexico's prominent Oportunidades programme, they find M_0 multidimensional targeting to be significantly better than either the current targeting method or an alternative income proxy-means test at identifying households with deprivations that matter for the programme objectives. An *ex ante* evaluation suggests that programme transfers could have a greater impact if potential beneficiaries were selected by the AF method. Alkire and Seth (2013c) set out the powerful benefits of linking multidimensional targeting methods to national multidimensional poverty measures, such as policy coherence, monitoring and evaluation synergies, and the ability to update the targeting methodology and the targeting census instrument consistently

---

[46] UNDP and MoSA (1998, 2007); UNDP and MDPC (2006); League of Arab States (2009); Nehmeh (2013).

[47] <http://www.progressoutofpoverty.org/ppi-construction>, accessed April 2013.

[48] <http://www.bisp.gov.pk/poverty_survey.aspx>, accessed April 2013.

across time. They suggest how an M_0 targeting method can be developed, justified, and linked with a national multidimensional poverty measure. This kind of approach is being implemented with increasing frequency: for example, Angulo et al. (2013) describe the geographical targeting that is used in Colombia.

In sum, the necessity of defining a target population for poverty reduction programmes has motivated the use of counting methods with a variety of specificities and prompted the development of related new identification methods. However, the measurement properties and features of the alternative targeting instruments are rarely discussed (or, one suspects, clearly communicated), which makes it difficult for policymakers to make an informed decision.

4.5 **Final Comments on Counting Approaches**

Counting approaches emerged as a natural procedure for identifying the poor with the basic needs and the social exclusion approaches, giving form to various direct methods to measure poverty. Counting the number of observable deprivations in core indicators has an intuitive appeal and simplicity that has attracted not only academics but also policymakers and practitioners. Over time, counting methods have been implemented in a variety of useful formats in terms of poverty measurement—namely, the European Measures of Relative Deprivation, the Consensual Approach to Poverty Measurement, the Consistent Poverty Approach, the Latin American Basic Needs Approach—and they have been incorporated into solid axiomatic poverty measures in the academic literature. Moreover, the counting approach has also been used to measure child poverty and to construct targeting tools for poverty reduction programmes. The counting approach has motivated the collection of new data in some cases, and the construction of powerful policy tools such as poverty maps, in others.

It is also worth observing that some prominent approaches look similar to the counting approach yet differ in fundamental ways—such as assigning (by a normative or a statistical procedure) cardinal values to categories of ordinal variables, or using an aggregate line approach—and thus, in the end, are altogether different. This is the case in Boltvinik's improved integrated method and Schreiner's poverty scorecard method, among others.

The AF methodology uses a counting approach to identify the poor, and, as a consequence, it inherits its simplicity and intuition and stands on the shoulders of this venerable tradition in both academic and policy circles. Additionally, it introduces axiomatic rigour by (a) scrutinizing the counting approach as an identification method of the multidimensionally poor in a formal framework and (b) combining it with aggregation methodologies, also within a formal axiomatic framework. Chapter 5 will present the AF methodology in depth.

5 The Alkire–Foster Counting Methodology

This chapter provides a systematic overview of the multidimensional measurement methodology of Alkire and Foster (2007, 2011a), with an emphasis on the first measure of that class: the Adjusted Headcount Ratio or M_0. It builds on previous chapters, which demonstrated the importance of adopting a multidimensional approach (Chapter 1), introduced the general framework (Chapter 2), and reviewed the alternative methods for multidimensional measurement and analysis (Chapter 3). Chapter 3 also highlighted the advantages of certain axiomatic measures that consider the joint distribution of deprivations and exhibit a transparent and predictable behaviour with respect to different types of transformations. The fourth chapter reviewed counting methods to identify the poor (Chapter 4), which are frequently used in axiomatic measures.

Why focus on the AF methodology and on M_0 in particular? As argued in section 1.3, we focus on this AF methodology for a number of technical and practical reasons. From a technical perspective, being an axiomatic family of measures, the AF measures satisfy a number of desirable properties introduced in section 2.5, detailed in this chapter. From a practical perspective, the AF family of measures uses the intuitive counting approach to identify the poor, and explicitly considers the joint distribution of deprivations. Among the AF measures, the M_0 measure is particularly applicable due to its ability to use ordinal or binary data rigorously and because the measure and its consistent sub-indices are intuitive. The technical and practical advantages of M_0 make it a particularly attractive option to inform policy.

It is worth noting from the beginning that the AF methodology is a *general framework* for measuring multidimensional poverty, although it is also suitable for measuring other phenomena (Alkire and Santos 2014). With the AF method, many key decisions are left to the user. These include the selection of the measure's purpose, space, unit of analysis, dimensions, deprivation cutoffs (to determine when a person is deprived in a dimension), weights or values (to indicate the relative importance of the different deprivations), and poverty cutoff (to determine when a person has enough deprivations to be considered poor). This flexibility enables the methodology to have many diverse applications. The design of particular measures—which entails value judgements—is the subject of Chapter 6.

As described in section 2.2.2, the methodology for measuring multidimensional poverty consists of an identification and an aggregation method (Sen 1976). This chapter first describes how the AF methodology identifies people as poor using a 'dual-cutoff' counting method, standing on the shoulders of a long tradition of counting approaches that have been used in policymaking (Chapter 4). The aggregation method builds on the unidimensional axiomatic poverty measures and directly extends the Foster–Greer–Thorbecke (FGT) class of poverty measures introduced in section 2.1. The main focus of this chapter is the Adjusted Headcount Ratio (M_0), which reflects the incidence of poverty and the intensity of poverty, and captures the joint distribution of deprivations. The chapter shows how to 'drill down' into M_0 in order to unfold the distinctive partial indices that reveal the intuition and layers of information embedded in the summary measure, such as poverty at subgroup levels and its composition by dimension. Examples illustrate the methodology and also present standard tables and graphics that are used to convey results.

This chapter proceeds as follows. Section 5.1 presents the overview and practicality of the AF class of poverty measures, focusing especially on the Adjusted Headcount Ratio. Section 5.2 sets out the identification of who is poor using the dual-cutoff approach. Section 5.3 outlines the aggregation method used to construct the Adjusted Headcount Ratio. Section 5.4 presents the main distinctive characteristics of the Adjusted Headcount Ratio, and section 5.5 presents its useful partial indices—the incidence and intensity in section 5.5.1, and consistent sub-indices in sections 5.5.2 and 5.5.3. We present a case study of the Adjusted Headcount Ratio using the global Multidimensional Poverty Index in section 5.6. Section 5.7 presents the members of the AF class of measures that can be constructed in the less common situations where data are cardinal, along with their properties and partial indices. Finally, section 5.8 reviews some empirical applications of the AF methodology.

5.1 The AF Class of Poverty Measures: Overview and Practicality

The AF methodology of multidimensional poverty measurement creates a class of measures that both draws on the counting approach and extends the FGT class of measures in natural ways. Before proceeding with a more formal description of the AF methodology, we first provide a stepwise synthetic and intuitive presentation of how to obtain the Adjusted Headcount Ratio (M_0), which is our focal measure. We use the person as the unit of identification in this overview. We also introduce the Adjusted Poverty Gap (M_1) and the Adjusted Squared Poverty Gap (or FGT) Measure (M_2). For clarity, we distinguish the steps that belong to the **identification** step and those that belong to the **aggregation** step.

Constructing these M_α measures entails the following components:

Identification

1. Defining the set of indicators which will be considered in the multidimensional measure. Data for all indicators need to be available for the same person.
2. Setting the deprivation cutoffs for each indicator, namely the level of achievement considered sufficient (normatively) in order to be non-deprived in each indicator.

3. Applying the cutoffs to ascertain whether each person is deprived or not in each indicator.

4. Selecting the relative weight or value that each indicator has, such that these sum to one.[1]

5. Creating the weighted sum of deprivations for each person, which can be called his or her 'deprivation score'.

6. Determining (normatively) the poverty cutoff, namely, the proportion of weighted deprivations a person needs to experience in order to be considered multidimensionally poor, and identifying each person as multidimensionally poor or not according to the selected poverty cutoff.

Aggregation

7. Censoring deprivations of the non-poor and computing the proportion of people who have been identified as multidimensionally poor in the population. This is the **headcount ratio** of multidimensional poverty H, also called the **incidence** of multidimensional poverty.

8. Computing the average share of weighted indicators in which poor people are deprived. This entails adding up the deprivation scores of the poor and dividing them by the total number of poor people. This is the average **intensity** of multidimensional poverty (A), also sometimes called the **breadth** of poverty.

9. Computing the M_0 measure as the product of the two previous partial indices: $M_0 = H \times A$. Analogously, M_0 can be obtained as the mean of the vector of censored deprivation scores, which is also the sum of the weighted deprivations that poor people experience, divided by the total population.

When all indicators are ratio scale, computing M_1 and M_2 entails the following components:

10. Computing the average poverty gap across all instances in which poor persons are deprived, or G. This entails computing the normalized (deprivation) gap as defined in equation (2.2): $g_{ij} = \frac{z_j - \tilde{x}_{ij}}{z_j}$, where $\tilde{x}_{ij}$ is censored at z_j for each person and indicator. In words, for a person who is deprived in a given indicator, the normalized gap is the difference between the deprivation cutoff and the person's achievement for the indicator, divided by is deprivation cutoff; if the person's achievement does not fall short of the deprivation cutoff, the normalized gap is zero. The average poverty gap is the mean of poor people's weighted normalized deprivation gaps in those dimensions in which poor people are deprived and is one of the partial indices. This **depth** of multidimensional poverty is denoted by G.

11. Computing the M_1 measure as the product of three partial indices: $M_1 = H \times A \times G$. Analogously, M_1 can be obtained as the sum of the weighted deprivation gaps that poor people experience, divided by the total population.

---

[1] We are following the 'normalized' notation here; for other notations see section 5.2.2 and Box 5.7.

12. Computing the average severity of deprivation across all instances in which poor persons are deprived, or S. This entails computing the squared (deprivation) gap, that is, squaring each normalized gap computed in step 10. The average severity of deprivation is the mean of poor people's weighted squared gaps in those dimensions in which they are deprived. The **severity** of multidimensional poverty is denoted by S.

13. Computing the M_2 measure as the product of the following partial indices: $M_2 = H \times A \times S$. Analogously, M_2 can be obtained as the sum of the weighted squared deprivation gaps that poor people experience, divided by the total population.

Note that in all three cases (M_0, M_1, and M_2) the deprivations experienced by people who have not been identified as poor (i.e. those whose deprivation score is below the poverty cutoff) are censored, hence not included; this censoring of the deprivations of the non-poor is consistent with the property of 'poverty focus' which—analogous to the unidimensional case—requires a poverty measure to be independent of the achievements of the non-poor. For further discussion see Alkire and Foster (2011a).

These three measures of the AF family, as well as any other member, satisfy many of the desirable properties introduced in section 2.5. Several properties are key for policy. The first is decomposability, which allows the index to be broken down by population subgroup (such as region or ethnicity) to show the characteristics of multidimensional poverty for each group. All AF measures satisfy population **subgroup decomposability**. So the poverty level of a society—as measured by any M_α—is equivalent to the population-weighted sum of subgroup poverty levels, where subgroups are mutually exclusive and collectively exhaustive of the population.

All AF measures can also be unpacked to reveal the dimensional deprivations contributing the most to poverty for any given group. This second key property—post-identification **dimensional breakdown** (section 2.2.4)—is not available with the standard headcount ratio and is particularly useful for policy.

The AF measures also satisfy **dimensional monotonicity**, meaning that whenever a poor person ceases to be deprived in a dimension, poverty decreases. The headcount ratio does not satisfy this. Dimensional monotonicity and breakdown are possible because all AF measures directly include the partial index of intensity.

A few comments on the AF class before we turn to the final key property for policy. All AF measures also have intuitive interpretations. The Adjusted Headcount Ratio (M_0) reflects the proportion of weighted deprivations the poor experience in a society out of the total number of deprivations this society could experience if all people were poor and were deprived in all dimensions. The Adjusted Poverty Gap (M_1) reflects the average weighted deprivation gap experienced by the poor out of the total number of deprivations this society could experience (which is the maximum possible value of the average weighted deprivation gap when H and A and G are all 100%). The Adjusted Squared Poverty Gap Measure (M_2) reflects the average weighted squared gap or poverty severity experienced by the poor out of the total deprivations this society could experience. In all cases, the term 'adjusted' refers to the fact that all measures incorporate the intensity of multidimensional poverty—which is key to their properties.

Additionally, while each of the AF measures offers a summary statistic of multidimensional poverty, they are related to a set of consistent and intuitive partial indices, namely, poverty incidence (H), intensity (A), and a set of subgroup poverty estimates and dimensional deprivation indices (which in the case of the M_0 measure are called **censored headcount ratios**) and their corresponding percent contributions. Each M_α measure can be unfolded into an array of informative indices.

Among the AF class of measures, the M_0 measure is particularly important because it can be implemented with ordinal data. This is critical for real-world applications. It is relevant when poverty is viewed from the capability perspective, for example, since many key functionings are commonly measured using ordinal variables. The M_0 measure satisfies the **ordinality** property introduced in section 2.5.1. This means that for any monotonic transformation of the ordinal variable and associated cutoff, overall poverty as estimated by M_0 will not change. Moreover, M_0 has a natural interpretation as a measure of 'unfreedom' and generates a partial ordering that lies between first- and second-order dominance (Chapter 6). Because of its properties and practicality, this book mainly focuses on M_0.

The remaining sections present the AF method more precisely yet, we hope, intuitively.

5.2 Identification of the Poor: The Dual-Cutoff Approach

Poverty measurement requires an identification function, which determines whether each person is to be considered poor. The unidimensional form of identification, discussed in section 2.1.1, entails a host of assumptions that restrict its applicability in practice and its desirability in principle.[2] From the perspective of the capability approach, a key conceptual drawback of viewing multidimensional poverty through a unidimensional lens is the loss of information on dimension-specific shortfalls; indeed, aggregation before identification converts dimensional achievements into one another without regard to dimension-specific cutoffs. In situations where dimensions are intrinsically valued and dimensional deprivations are inherently undesirable, there are good reasons to look beyond a unidimensional approach to identification methods that focus on dimensional shortfalls.

In the multidimensional measurement setting, where there are multiple variables, identification is a substantially more challenging exercise. As explained in section 2.2.2,

---

[2] One common assumption is that prices exist and are adequate normative weights for the dimensions; however, as noted by Tsui (2002), this assumption is questionable. Prices may be adjusted to reflect externalities, but exchange values do not and 'indeed cannot give … *interpersonal comparisons* of welfare or advantage' (Sen 1997: 208). Subjective poverty lines cannot replace prices for all attributes, and markets may be missing or imperfect (Bourguignon and Chakravarty 2003; Tsui 2002). In practice, income may or may not be used to expand key capabilities (Ruggeri Laderchi, Saith, and Stewart 2003; Sen 1980). Finally, aggregating across dimensions entails strong assumptions regarding cardinality and comparability, which are impractical when data are ordinal (Sen 1997).

a variety of methods can be used for identification in multidimensional poverty measurement. Here we follow a **censored achievement approach**. This approach first requires determining who is deprived in each dimension by comparing the person's achievement against the corresponding deprivation cutoff and thus considering only deprived achievements (and ignoring—or censoring—achievements above the deprivation cutoff) for the identification of the poor. One prominent method used within the censored achievement approach is the **counting approach**, which is precisely the identification approach followed in the AF methodology, among others (Chapter 4).

As we have seen, a counting approach first identifies whether a person is deprived or not in each dimension and then identifies a person as poor according to the number (count) of deprivations she experiences. Note that 'number' here has a broad meaning as dimensions may be weighted differently. As reviewed in Chapter 4, the use of a counting approach to identification in multidimensional poverty measurement is not new. However, the value added of the AF methodology is threefold. In the first place, the AF methodology has formalized the counting approach to identification into a **dual-cutoff approach**, clarifying the requirement of two distinct sets of thresholds to define poverty in the multidimensional context. One is the set of **deprivation cutoffs**, which identify whether a person is deprived with respect to each dimension. Then, a (single) **poverty cutoff** delineates how widely deprived a person must be in order to be considered poor.

Second, as a consequence of using a dual-cutoff approach, the AF methodology considers the **joint distribution of deprivations at the identification step** and not just at the aggregation step, as previous methodologies did (almost all non-counting methodologies used the union criterion). Third, the AF methodology has integrated the counting approach to identification with an aggregation methodology that extends the unidimensional FGT measures, overcoming the **limitations of the headcount ratio** (which most counting methods used) yet allowing intuitive interpretations.[3]

Thus the AF methodology draws together the counting traditions—well-known for their practicality and policy appeal—and the widely used FGT class of axiomatic measures in order to assess multidimensional poverty, and stands on the shoulders of both traditions.

5.2.1 THE DEPRIVATION CUTOFFS: IDENTIFYING DEPRIVATIONS AND OBTAINING DEPRIVATION SCORES

Bourguignon and Chakravarty (2003) contend that 'a multidimensional approach to poverty defines poverty as a shortfall from a threshold on each dimension of an individual's wellbeing.'[4] Following them and the plethora of counting methods reviewed

---

[3] The use of the word methodology when referring to AF indicates that it comprises both an identification and an aggregation method.
[4] See also Chakravarty et al. (1998) and Tsui (2002) on this point.

in Chapter 4, the AF measures use a deprivation cutoff for each dimension, defined and applied as described in this section.

As introduced in section 2.2, the base information in multidimensional poverty measurement is typically represented by an $n \times d$ dimensional achievement matrix X, where x_{ij} is the achievement of person i in dimension j. For simplicity, as done in section 2.2, it is assumed that achievements can be represented by non-negative real numbers (i.e. $x_{ij} \in \mathbb{R}_+$) and that higher achievements are preferred to lower ones.

For each dimension j, a threshold z_j is defined as the minimum achievement required in order to be non-deprived. This threshold is called a deprivation cutoff. Deprivation cutoffs are collected in the d-dimensional vector $z = (z_1, \ldots, z_d)$. Given each person's achievement in each dimension x_{ij}, if the ith person's achievement level in a given dimension j falls short of the respective deprivation cutoff z_j, the person is said to be deprived in that dimension (that is, if $x_{ij} < z_j$). If the person's level is at least as great as the deprivation cutoff, the person is not deprived in that dimension.

As Chapter 2 introduced, from the achievement matrix X and the vector of deprivation cutoffs z, one can obtain a deprivation matrix g^0 such that $g^0_{ij} = 1$ whenever $x_{ij} < z_j$ and $g^0_{ij} = 0$, otherwise, for all $j = 1, \ldots, d$ and for all $i = 1, \ldots, n$. In other words, if person i is deprived in dimension j, then the person is assigned a **deprivation status** of 1, and 0 otherwise. The matrix g^0 summarizes the deprivation status of all people in all dimensions of matrix X. The vector $g^0_{i \cdot}$ summarizes the deprivation statuses of person i in all dimensions, and the vector $g^0_{\cdot j}$ summarizes the deprivation statuses of all persons in dimension j.

The deprivation in each of the d dimensions may not have the same relative importance. Thus, a vector $w = (w_1, \ldots, w_d)$ of **weights** or **deprivation values** is used to indicate the relative importance of a deprivation in each dimension. The deprivation value attached to dimension j is denoted by $w_j > 0$. If each deprivation is viewed as having equal importance, then this is a benchmark 'counting' case. If deprivations are viewed as having different degrees of importance, general weights are applied using a weighting vector whose entries vary, with higher weights indicating greater relative value.

Intricate weighting systems create challenges in interpretation, so it can be useful to choose the dimensions such that the natural weights among them are roughly equal or else to group dimensions into categories that have roughly equal weights (Atkinson 2003). The deprivation values affect identification because they determine the minimum combinations of deprivations that will identify a person as being poor. They also affect aggregation by altering the relative contributions of deprivations to overall poverty (for more on weights see Chapter 6). Yet, importantly, the deprivation values do not function as weights that govern trade-offs between dimensions for every possible combination of ratio-scale achievement levels, as they do in a traditional composite index. Because each deprivation status takes binary value, the role of deprivation values differs from the role of weights in traditional composite indices.

Based on the deprivation profile, each person is assigned a deprivation score that reflects the breadth of each person's deprivations across all dimensions. The deprivation score of each person is the sum of her weighted deprivations. Formally, the deprivation score is given by $c_i = \sum_{j=1}^{d} w_j g_{ij}^0 = \sum_{j=1}^{d} \bar{g}_{ij}^0$. The score increases as the number of deprivations a person experiences increases, and reaches its maximum when the person is deprived in all dimensions. A person who is not deprived in any dimension has a deprivation score equal to 0. We denote the deprivation score of person i by c_i and the vector of deprivation scores for all persons by $c = (c_1, \ldots, c_n)$.

5.2.2 ALTERNATIVE NOTATION AND PRESENTATION

Distinct notational presentations can be employed for the weights, deprivation scores, deprivation score vector, poverty cutoff, poverty measures, and partial indices. Substantively, alternative presentations are identical in that they each identify precisely the same persons as poor and generate the same poverty measure value and identical partial indices. What differ are the numerical values of weights, deprivation scores, and poverty cutoff. For didactic purposes we explain the main options so as to avoid confusion among researchers using different notational conventions.

Alternative notations arise from two decisions. The first decision is whether to define weights that sum to one, i.e. $\sum_j w_j = 1$, or whether weights sum to the number of dimensions under consideration, $\sum_j w_j = d$. We refer to the first as **normalized weights** and to the second as **non-normalized or numbered weights**. The normalized weight of a dimension reflects the share (or percentage) of total weight given to a particular dimension. The deprivation score then shows the percentage of weighted dimensions in which a person is deprived and lies between 0 and 1. In the numbered case, deprivation scores range between 0 and d. If person i is deprived in all dimensions, then $c_i = d$. Depending on the weighting structure, one of these options may be more intuitive than the other. For example, if dimensions are equally weighted, the deprivation count vector shows the number of dimensions in which each person is deprived. Thus, while in the normalized case one may state that a person is deprived in 43% of the weighted dimensions, in the non-normalized case one states that a person is deprived in three out of seven dimensions, which is more intuitive. However, if dimensions are not equally weighted, normalized weights may be more intuitive. Suppose there are seven dimensions and a person is deprived in two dimensions having weights of 25% and 10%, respectively. Their numbered deprivation score would be $2.45 = (0.25^*7 + 0.10^*7)$. This same situation could be communicated more intuitively by saying that this person is deprived in 35% of the weighted dimensions.

The second decision is whether to express the formulas using the deprivation matrix g^0 and the weighting vector w in an explicitly separate way, or whether to express them in terms of a **weighted deprivation matrix** denoted by $\bar{g}^0$ such that $\bar{g}_{ij}^0 = w_j$ if $g_{ij}^0 = 1$ and $\bar{g}_{ij}^0 = 0$ if $g_{ij}^0 = 0$. These two decisions lead to four possible—but totally equivalent—notations, as detailed in Box 5.7. This chapter, and most of this book, uses normalized weights and expresses formulas using the deprivation matrix and the weight vector. We refer to this as Method I. Method II uses normalized weights with the weighted deprivation matrix. Method III uses non-normalized weights and expresses formulas using the deprivation matrix and the weight vector. Methods II and III are not further discussed in this chapter, but all the formulas are stated in Box 5.7. Finally, Method IV uses non-normalized weights and expresses the formulas using the weighted deprivation matrix, aligned with the notation used in Alkire and Foster (2011a), which is presented in Box 5.3, Box 5.6, and Box 5.7. What is particularly elegant about Method IV is that the AF measures can be expressed as the mean of the relevant censored deprivation matrix, as we shall elaborate subsequently.

5.2.3 THE SECOND CUTOFF: IDENTIFYING THE POOR

In addition to the deprivation cutoffs z_j, the AF methodology uses a second cutoff or threshold to identify the multidimensionally poor. This is called the **poverty cutoff** and is denoted by k. The poverty cutoff is the minimum deprivation score a person needs to exhibit in order to be identified as poor. This poverty cutoff is implemented using an **identification function** ρ_k, which depends upon each person's achievement vector $x_{i\cdot}$, the deprivation cutoff vector z, the weight vector w, and the poverty cutoff k. If the person is poor, the identification function takes on a value of 1; if the person is not poor, the identification function has a value of 0. Notationally, the identification function is defined as $\rho_k(x_{i\cdot};z) = 1$ if $c_i \geq k$ and $\rho_k(x_{i\cdot};z) = 0$ otherwise. In other words, ρ_k identifies person i as poor when his or her deprivation score is at least k; if the deprivation score falls below the cutoff k, then person i is not poor according to ρ_k. Since ρ_k is dependent on both the set of *within-dimension* deprivation cutoffs z and the *across-dimension* cutoff k, ρ_k is referred to as the dual-cutoff method of identification, or sometimes as the 'intermediary' method.

Within the counting approach to identification, the most commonly used multidimensional identification strategy is the **union criterion**.[5] Most of the poverty indices discussed in Chapter 3 use the union criterion, by which a person i is identified as multidimensionally poor if she is deprived in at least one dimension ($c_i > 0$). At the other extreme, another identification criterion is the **intersection criterion**, which identifies person i as being poor only if she is deprived in all dimensions ($c_i = 1$). Both these approaches have the advantage of identifying the same persons as being poor regardless of the relative weights set on the dimensions. But the identification of who is poor in each case is exceedingly sensitive to the choice of dimensions. Also these strategies can be too imprecise for policy: in many applications, a union identification identifies a very large proportion of the population as poor, whereas an intersection approach identifies a vanishingly small number of people as poor. A natural middle-ground alternative is to use an intermediate cutoff level for c_i that lies somewhere between the two extremes of union and intersection.

---

[5] Atkinson (2003) applied the terms 'union' and 'intersection' in the context of multidimensional poverty.

The AF dual-cutoff identification strategy provides an overarching framework that includes the two extremes of union and intersection criteria and also the range of intermediate possibilities.[6] Notice that ρ_k includes the union and intersection methods as special cases. In the case of union, the poverty cutoff is less than or equal to the dimension with the lowest weight: $0 < k \leq \min\{w_1, \ldots, w_d\}$. Whereas in the case of intersection, the poverty cutoff takes its highest possible value of $k = 1$. In Box 5.1, we present different identification strategies using an example.

BOX 5.1 DIFFERENT IDENTIFICATION STRATEGIES: UNION, INTERSECTION, AND INTERMEDIATE CUTOFF

Suppose there is a hypothetical society containing four persons and multidimensional poverty is analysed using four dimensions: standard of living as measured by income, level of knowledge as measured by years of education, nutritional status, and access to public services as measured by access to improved sanitation. The 4×4 matrix X contains the achievements of four persons in four dimensions; for simplicity 0–1 indicators are written as yes or no.

	Income	Years of Schooling Completed	Malnourished	Has Access to Improved Sanitation	
	700	14	No	Yes	Person1
$X =$	300	13	No	No	Person2
	400	3	Yes	No	Person3
	800	1	No	Yes	Person4

For example, the income of Person 3 is 400 Units; whereas Person 4's is 800 Units. Person 1 has completed fourteen years of schooling; whereas Person 2 has completed thirteen years of schooling. Person 3 is the only person who is malnourished of all four persons. Two persons in our example have access to improved sanitation. Thus, each row of matrix X contains the achievements of each person in four dimensions, whereas each column of the matrix contains the achievements of four persons in each of the four dimensions. All dimensions are equally weighted and thus the weight vector is $w = (0.25, 0.25, 0.25, 0.25)$. The deprivation cutoff vector is denoted by $z = (500, 5, \text{Not malnourished}, \text{Has access to improved sanitation})$, which is used to identify who is deprived in each dimension. The achievement matrix X has three persons who are deprived (see the underlined entries) in one or more dimensions. Person 1 has no deprivation at all.

Based on the deprivation status, we construct the deprivation matrix g^0, where a deprivation status of 1 is assigned if a person is deprived in a dimension and a deprivation status of 0 is given otherwise.

$$g^0 = \begin{bmatrix} 0 & 0 & 0 & 0 \\ 1 & 0 & 0 & 1 \\ 1 & 1 & 1 & 1 \\ 0 & 1 & 0 & 0 \end{bmatrix} \qquad \begin{array}{c} \text{Deprivation Score Vector (c)} \\ 0 \\ 0.5 \\ 1 \\ 0.25 \end{array}$$

$$w = \begin{bmatrix} 0.25 & 0.25 & 0.25 & 0.25 \end{bmatrix}$$

(column headers: Dimensions)

The weighted sum of dimensional deprivation statuses is the deprivation score (c_i) of each person. For example, the first person has no deprivation and so the deprivation score is 0, whereas the third person is deprived in all

---

[6] See Chapter 6 on the choice of k (and z).

> **BOX 5.1** (cont.)
>
> dimensions and thus has the highest deprivation score of 1. Similarly, the deprivation score of the second person is 0.5 (= 0.25 + 0.25). The union identification strategy identifies a person as poor if the person is identified as deprived in any of the four dimensions. In that case, three of the four persons are identified as poor. On the other hand, an intersection identification strategy requires that a person is identified as poor if the person is deprived in all dimensions. In that case, only one of the four persons is identified as poor. An intermediate approach sets a cutoff between union and intersection, say, $k = 0.5$, which is equivalent to being deprived in two of four equally weighted dimensions. This strategy identifies a person as poor if the person is deprived in half or more of weighted dimensions, which in this case means that two of the four persons are identified as poor.

The dual-cutoff identification function has a number of characteristics that deserve mention. First, it is 'poverty focused' in that an increase in an achievement level x_{ij} of a non-poor person leaves its value unchanged. Second, it is 'deprivation focused' in that an increase in any non-deprived achievement $x_{ij} \geq z_j$ leaves the value of the identification function unchanged; in other words, a person's poverty status is not affected by changes in the levels of non-deprived achievements. This latter property separates ρ_k from the 'aggregate achievement' approach which allows a higher level of achievement to compensate for lower levels of achievement in other dimensions. Finally, the dual-cutoff identification method can be meaningfully used with ordinal data, since a person's poverty status is unchanged when an admissible transformation is applied to an achievement level and its associated cutoff.

5.2.4 DUAL-CUTOFF APPROACH AND CENSORING

The transition between the identification step and the aggregation step is most easily understood by examining a progression of matrices. Identification entails two kinds of censoring, each of which follows the application of the two kinds of cutoffs: deprivation and poverty. By applying the deprivation cutoffs to the achievement matrix X, we constructed the deprivation matrix g^0 replacing each entry in X that is below its respective deprivation cutoff z_j with 1 and each entry that is not below its deprivation cutoff with 0. This is the first censoring, because any level of achievement beyond its deprivation cutoff is effectively being ignored. The deprivation matrix provides a snapshot of who is deprived in which dimension.

Next, the poor are identified by applying the poverty cutoff k and thus a new matrix can be obtained from the deprivation matrix: the censored deprivation matrix, which is denoted by $g^0(k)$. Each element in $g^0(k)$ is obtained by multiplying the corresponding element in g^0 by the identification function $(x_{i\cdot}; z)$. Formally, $g^0_{ij}(k) = g^0_{ij} \times \rho_k(x_{i\cdot}; z)$ for all i and for all j. What does this mean? If person i is poor and thus $\rho_k(x_{i\cdot}; z) = 1$, then the person's deprivation status in every dimension remains unchanged and so does the row containing the deprivation information of the person. If person i is not poor and thus $\rho_k(x_i;z) = 0$, then their deprivation status in every dimension becomes 0, which is equivalent to censoring the deprivations of persons who are not poor. This second censoring step is key to the AF methodology. As we will see in subsequent sections, the censored deprivation matrices embody the identification step and are the basic constructs used in the aggregation step.

A censored deprivation score vector can be obtained from the original deprivation score vector by multiplying each entry by the identification function. Alternatively, it can be derived directly from the censored deprivation matrix. The censored deprivation score of person i is denoted by $c_i(k)$, and can be obtained as $c_i(k) = \sum_{j=1}^{d} w_j g_{ij}^0(k)$. The censored deprivation score vector is denoted by $c(k)$.

Note that by definition, $c(k)$ has been censored of all deprivations that are less than the value of k. Thus, when $c_i \geq k$, then $c_i(k) = c_i$ (deprivation score of the person), but if $c_i < k$, then $c_i(k) = 0.$[7] There is one case where the second censoring is not relevant: when the poverty cutoff k corresponds to the union approach, then any person who is deprived in any dimension is considered poor and the censored and original matrices are identical, as are the scores.

Although the censored matrices are used to construct multidimensional poverty measures, the original deprivation matrix still provides useful information, as we shall see later in constructing 'raw' or uncensored deprivation headcount ratios by dimension and analysing their changes over time.

Before moving on to the aggregation step to create the Adjusted Headcount Ratio, let us provide an example of how to obtain the censored deprivation score vector from an achievement matrix in Box 5.2.

BOX 5.2 OBTAINING THE CENSORED DEPRIVATION SCORE VECTOR FROM AN ACHIEVEMENT MATRIX

Consider the 4 × 4 achievement matrix X and the deprivation cutoff vector z in Box 5.1. As earlier, each of the four dimensions receives a weight equal to 0.25 and weights sum to 1. Assume in this case that a person is identified as poor if deprived in half or more of the four equally weighted dimensions, i.e. $k = 0.5$.

The achievement matrix X has three persons who are deprived in one or more dimensions. Based on the deprivation status, a deprivation matrix g^0 is constructed in which a deprivation status of 1 is assigned if a person is deprived in a dimension and a status of 0 is given otherwise. The weighted sum of these status values yields the deprivation score of each person c_i.

Note that two persons (second and third) have deprivation scores that are greater than or equal to 0.5. They are considered to be poor ($c_i \geq k$), and hence their entries in the censored deprivation matrix are the same as in the deprivation matrix. However, the fourth person has a single deprivation and hence is not poor. This single deprivation is censored in the censored deprivation matrix, which only displays the deprivations of the

---

[7] In the case of deprivation scores, the poverty cutoff fixes a minimum level of deprivations that identify poverty. This is in contrast to the unidimensional context, where a person is identified as poor if her achievement is *below* the poverty line.

BOX 5.2 *(cont.)*

poor, as depicted below.[8]

	Dimensions	**Censored Deprivation Score** $(c(k))$

$$g^0(k) = \begin{bmatrix} 0 & 0 & 0 & 0 \\ 1 & 0 & 0 & 1 \\ 1 & 1 & 1 & 1 \\ 0 & 0 & 0 & 0 \end{bmatrix} \qquad \begin{matrix} 0 \\ \underline{0.5} \\ \underline{1} \\ 0 \end{matrix}$$

$$w = \begin{bmatrix} 0.25 & 0.25 & 0.25 & 0.25 \end{bmatrix}$$

5.3 **Aggregation: The Adjusted Headcount Ratio**

The aggregation step of our methodology builds upon the FGT class of unidimensional poverty measures and likewise generates a parametric class of measures. This section elaborates the Adjusted Headcount Ratio; the other measures in the AF class are presented in section 5.7. Just as each FGT measure can be viewed as the mean of an appropriate vector built from the original data and censored using the poverty line, the Adjusted Headcount Ratio, denoted as $M_0(X;z)$, is the mean of the censored deprivation score vector:

$$M_0 = \mu\,(c\,(k)) = \frac{1}{n} \times \sum_{i=1}^{n} c_i(k). \tag{5.1}$$

A second way of viewing M_0 is in terms of partial indices—measures that provide basic information on a single aspect of poverty. The Adjusted Headcount Ratio, can also be written as the product of two partial indices. The first partial index H is the percentage of the population that is poor or the **multidimensional headcount ratio** or the **incidence** of poverty. The second index A is the **intensity** of poverty, then:

$$M_0 = H \times A. \tag{5.2}$$

The headcount ratio or poverty incidence $H = H(X;z)$ is defined as $H = q/n$, where q is number of persons identified as poor using the dual-cutoff approach.[9]

---

[8] This example has an identical relative weight across dimensions; the general case admits a wide variety of identification approaches. For example, if one dimension had overriding importance and its relative weight was set above or equal to k, then any person deprived in that dimension would be considered poor.

[9] While informative, this measure is insufficient as a stand-alone index for two reasons. First, if a poor person becomes deprived in a new dimension, H remains unchanged, violating the property of dimensional monotonicity. Second, H cannot be further broken down to show how much each dimension contributes to poverty.

In turn, poverty intensity (A) is the **average deprivation score** across the poor. Notice that the censored deprivation score $c_i(k)$ represents the share of possible deprivations experienced by a poor person i. So the average deprivation score across the poor is given by $A = \sum_{i=1}^{q} c_i(k)/q$. Like the poverty gap information in income poverty, this partial index conveys relevant information about the intensity of multidimensional poverty, in that poor persons who experience simultaneous deprivations in a higher fraction of dimensions have a higher intensity of poverty and hence are poorer than others having a lower intensity. In sum, then

$$M_0(X;z) = \mu(c(k)) = H \times A = \frac{q}{n} \times \frac{1}{q} \sum_{i=1}^{q} c_i(k) = \frac{1}{n} \sum_{i=1}^{n} c_i(k)$$

$$= \frac{1}{n} \sum_{i=1}^{n} \sum_{j=1}^{d} w_j g_{ij}^0(k). \tag{5.3}$$

As a simple product of the two partial indices H and A, the measure M_0 is sensitive to the incidence and the intensity of multidimensional poverty. It clearly satisfies dimensional monotonicity, since if a poor person becomes deprived in an additional dimension, then A rises and so does M_0. Another interpretation of M_0 is that it provides the share of weighted deprivations experienced by the poor divided by the maximum possible deprivations that could be experienced if all people were poor and were deprived in all dimensions.

Let us provide an example using the same censored deprivation matrix and the censored deprivation score vector as in Box 5.2.

$$g^0(k) = \begin{array}{c} \textbf{Dimension} \qquad c(k) \\ \begin{bmatrix} 0 & 0 & 0 & 0 \\ 1 & 0 & 0 & 1 \\ 1 & 1 & 1 & 1 \\ 0 & 0 & 0 & 0 \end{bmatrix} \begin{array}{c} 0 \\ 0.5 \\ \underline{1} \\ 0 \end{array} \end{array}$$

The headcount ratio (H) is the proportion of people who are poor, which is two out of four persons in the above matrix. The intensity (A) is the average deprivation share among the poor, which in this example is the average of 0.5 and 1, i.e. equal to 0.75. It is easy to calculate the Adjusted Headcount Ratio using $M_0 = H \times A$. In this example $H = 0.5$ and $A = 0.75$, so $M_0 = 0.375$. It can also be calculated as the average of all elements in the censored deprivation score vector $c(k)$, i.e. $M_0 = (0 + 0.5 + 1 + 0)/4 = 0.375$. In addition, M_0 can be computed as the weighted sum of deprivation statuses of the poor divided by the total number of people: $M_0 = (0.25 \times 2 + 0.25 \times 1 + 0.25 \times 1 + 0.25 \times 2)/4 = 0.375$.

BOX 5.3 AN ALTERNATIVE PRESENTATION OF THE ADJUSTED HEADCOUNT RATIO USING NON-NORMALIZED WEIGHTS

Here we show an alternative approach for computing the Adjusted Headcount Ratio when the weights are non-normalized such that $w_j > 0$ and $\sum_{j=1}^{d} w_j = d$, i.e. adding to the total number of dimensions, following the notation presented in Alkire and Foster (2011a); for alternative notations see Box 5.7. In order to do so, we need to introduce the **weighted deprivation matrix**. From the deprivation matrix, a weighted deprivation matrix can be constructed by replacing the deprivation status of a deprived person with the value or weight assigned to the corresponding dimension. Formally, we denote the weighted deprivation matrix by $\bar{g}^0$ such that $\bar{g}_{ij}^0 = w_j$ if $g_{ij}^0 = 1$ and $\bar{g}_{ij}^0 = 0$ if $g_{ij}^0 = 0$. Like the censored deprivation matrix, the censored weighted deprivation matrix $\bar{g}^0(k)$ can be constructed such that $\bar{g}_{ij}^0(k) = \bar{g}_{ij}^0 \times \rho_k(x_{i\cdot}; z)$ for all i and all j. From the weighted deprivation matrix $\bar{g}^0(k)$, the **Adjusted Headcount Ratio** can be defined as

$$M_0 = \mu(\bar{g}^0(k)). \tag{5.4}$$

That is, M_0 is the mean of the weighted censored deprivation matrix. Thus, the Adjusted Headcount Ratio is the sum of the weighted censored deprivation statuses of the poor or $\sum_{i=1}^{q} \sum_{j=1}^{d} \bar{g}_{ij}^0(k)$ divided by the highest possible sum, or $n \times d$.

Let us provide an example and show how the Adjusted Headcount Ratio is computed using this approach. Recall the deprivation matrix in Box 5.1. In this example, suppose the dimensions are unequally weighted and the weight vector is denoted by $w = (1.5, 1, 1, 0.5)$. Note that the weights sum to the number of dimensions. The weighted deprivation matrix $\bar{g}^0$ for this example can be denoted as follows:

$$\bar{g}^0 = \begin{bmatrix} 0 & 0 & 0 & 0 \\ 1.5 & 0 & 0 & 0.5 \\ 1.5 & 1 & 1 & 0.5 \\ 0 & 1 & 0 & 0 \end{bmatrix} \quad \begin{matrix} \text{Deprivation Score } (c) \\ 0 \\ \underline{2} \\ \underline{4} \\ 1 \end{matrix}$$

The deprivation score of each person is obtained by summing the weighted deprivations. For example, the third person is deprived in all dimensions and so receives a deprivation score equal to four. Similarly, the fourth person is deprived only in the second dimension, which is assigned a weight of 1 and so her deprivation score is 1. If the poverty cutoff is $k = 2$, then only two persons are identified as poor. The censored weighted deprivation matrix can be obtained from the censored deprivation matrix as shown below.

$$\bar{g}^0(k) = \begin{bmatrix} 0 & 0 & 0 & 0 \\ 1.5 & 0 & 0 & 0.5 \\ 1.5 & 1 & 1 & 0.5 \\ 0 & 0 & 0 & 0 \end{bmatrix} \quad \begin{matrix} \text{Censored Deprivation} \\ \text{Score } (c(k)) \\ 0 \\ \underline{2} \\ \underline{4} \\ 0 \end{matrix}$$

The sum of the weighted deprivation statuses of the poor is 6. The highest possible sum of weighted deprivation statuses is $4 \times 4 = 16$. Thus, $M_0 = 6/16 = 0.375$.

BOX 5.4 AN ALTERNATIVE NOTATION FOR THE IDENTIFICATION FUNCTION

To relate better to statistics, the identification function can be equivalently expressed as $I(c_i \geq k)$ where $\mathbb{I}[\cdot]$ is an **identification function** that takes a value of 1 if the indicated condition $(c_i \geq k)$ is true for the ith person, and 0 otherwise.

In this notation, the identification function for the ith person is multiplied by the weighted deprivation score c_i of the ith person. This censors (replaces by 0) the deprivations of the non-poor. The sum of deprivation scores thus censored by the identification function, divided by $n \times d$, provides the alternative definition:

$$M_0(X;z) = \frac{1}{nd} \sum_{i=1}^{n} \left[\mathbb{I}(c_i \geq k) \sum_{j=1}^{d} w_j g_{ij}^0(x_{ij}) \right] \qquad (5.5)$$

The headcount ratio or incidence of multidimensional poverty (H) can also be expressed using this alternative notation as

$$H(X;w) = \frac{\sum_{i=1}^{n} \mathbb{I}[c_i \geq k]}{n}. \qquad (5.6)$$

And the other partial indices such as intensity or the censored headcount ratios h_j introduced in section 5.5.3 can also be expressed using this notation.

5.4 Distinctive Characteristics of the Adjusted Headcount Ratio

The M_0 measure described in section 5.3 has several characteristics that merit special attention. First, it can be implemented with indicators of ordinal scale that commonly arise in multidimensional settings. In formal terms, M_0 satisfies the ordinality property introduced in section 2.5. The ordinality property states that whenever variables (and thus their corresponding deprivation cutoffs) are modified in such a way that their scale is preserved—what has been defined in section 2.3 as an admissible transformation—the poverty value should not change.[10]

The satisfaction of this property is a consequence of the combination of the identification method and the aggregation method. Because identification is performed with the counting approach, which dichotomizes achievements into deprived and non-deprived, equivalent transformations of the scales of the variables will not affect the set of people who are identified as poor. Note that the weights attached to deprivations are independent of the indicators' scale and implemented after the deprivation status has been determined.

---

[10] The set of the poor and the measured value of poverty are therefore meaningful in the sense of Roberts (1979). Note that M_0 can also be applied to categorical variables (which do not necessarily admit a unique ordering across categories), so long as achievements can be separated into deprived and non-deprived sets.

This is clearly relevant for consistent targeting within policies or programmes using ordinal indicators. In turn, aggregation to obtain the M_0 measure is performed using the censored deprivation matrix, which represents the deprivation status of each poor person in every dimension and also uses the 0–1 dichotomy. In the aggregation procedure, the deprivations of the poor are weighted, but, again, the weights are independent of the indicators' scale and implemented after the deprivation status of the poor has been determined. Thus, equivalent transformations of the scales of the variables will not affect the aggregation of the poor and thus will not affect the overall poverty value.

The fact that M_0 satisfies the ordinality property is especially relevant when poverty is viewed from the capability perspective, since many key functionings are commonly measured using ordinal (or ordered categorical) variables. Virtually every other multidimensional methodology defined in the literature (including M_1, M_2, and, in general, the M_α measures with $\alpha > 0$, which are defined in section 5.7) do not satisfy the ordinality property. In the case of the M_α measures with $\alpha > 0$, while the set of people identified as poor does not change under equivalent representations of the variables, the aggregation procedure will be affected as it is no longer based on the censored deprivation matrix but on a matrix that considers the depth of deprivation in each dimension. In other measures, the violation of ordinality occurs at the identification step. Moreover, for most measures, the underlying ordering is not even preserved, i.e. an increase in poverty may become a decrease just by changing representations. Special care must be taken not to use measures whose poverty judgements are meaningless (i.e. reversible under equivalent representations) when variables are ordinal.

Consider a methodology that combines the identification method used in the AF measures ρ_k with the headcount ratio as the aggregate measure: $\mathcal{M}(\rho_k, H)$. This methodology which was used in previous counting measures surveyed in Chapter 4, satisfies the ordinality property. But it does so at the cost of violating dimensional monotonicity, among other properties. In contrast, the methodology that combines a counting approach to identification and M_0 as the aggregate measure, $\mathcal{M}(\rho_k, M_0)$, provides both meaningful comparisons and favourable axiomatic properties and is arguably a better choice when data are ordinal.

Second, while other measures have aggregate values whose meaning can only be found relative to other values, M_0 conveys tangible information on the deprivations of the poor in a transparent way. As stated in section 5.3, it can either be interpreted as the incidence of poverty 'adjusted' by poverty intensity or as the aggregate deprivations experienced by the poor as a share of the maximum possible range of deprivations that would occur if all members of society were deprived in all dimensions. As we shall see in section 5.5.3, the additive structure of the M_0 measure permits it to be broken down across dimensions and across population subgroups to obtain additional valuable information, especially for policy purposes.

Third, the adjusted headcount methodology is fundamentally related to the axiomatic literature on freedom. In a key paper, Pattanaik and Xu (1990) explore a counting approach to measuring freedom that ranks opportunity sets according to the number of (equally weighted) options they contain. Let us suppose that the achievement matrix X has been normatively constructed so that each dimension represents an equally valued functioning. Then deprivation in a given dimension is suggestive of capability deprivation, and since M_0 counts these deprivations, it can be viewed as a measure of 'unfreedom' analogous to Pattanaik and Xu. Indeed, the link between $\mathcal{M}(\rho_k, M_0)$ and unfreedom can be made precise, yielding a result that simultaneously characterizes ρ_k and M_0 using axioms adapted from Pattanaik and Xu.[11] This general approach also has an appealing practicality: as suggested by Anand and Sen (1997), it may be more feasible to monitor a small set of deprivations than a large set of attainments.

5.5 The Set of Partial and Consistent Sub-Indices of the Adjusted Headcount Ratio

The Adjusted Headcount Ratio condenses a lot of information. It can be unpacked to compare not only the levels of poverty but also the dimensional composition of poverty across countries, for example, as well as within countries by ethnic group, urban and rural location, and other key household and community characteristics. This is why we sometimes describe M_0 as a high-resolution lens on poverty: it can be used as an analytical tool to identify precisely who is poor and how they are poor. This section presents the partial indices and consistent sub-indices that serve to elucidate multidimensional poverty for policy purposes.

5.5.1 INCIDENCE AND INTENSITY OF POVERTY

We have already shown in section 5.3 that the M_0 measure is the product of two very informative partial indices: the multidimensional headcount ratio—or **incidence** of poverty (H)—and the average deprivation share across the poor—or the average **intensity** of poverty (A). Both are relevant and informative, and it is useful to present them both when reporting M_0. In Box 5.5, we present an example to show that two societies may have the same Adjusted Headcount Ratios but very different levels of incidence and intensity.

BOX 5.5 SAME M_0 BUT DIFFERENT COMPOSITION OF INCIDENCE AND INTENSITY

Suppose there are four persons in both societies X (as in Box 5.1) and X' and multidimensional poverty is analysed using four dimensions, which are weighted equally. A person is identified as poor if deprived in more than half of all weighted indicators ($k = 0.5$). The 4×4 achievement matrices of two societies are

---

[11] For a fuller discussion see Alkire and Foster (2007).

BOX 5.5 *(cont.)*

	Dimensions					Dimensions		
700	14	No	Yes		700	14	No	Yes
300	13	No	No		300	13	No	No
400	3	Yes	No		400	3	No	Yes
800	1	No	Yes		800	1	Yes	Yes

$$X = \begin{bmatrix} 700 & 14 & No & Yes \\ \underline{300} & \underline{13} & No & \underline{No} \\ \underline{400} & \underline{3} & \underline{Yes} & \underline{No} \\ 800 & 1 & No & Yes \end{bmatrix} \quad X' = \begin{bmatrix} 700 & 14 & No & Yes \\ \underline{300} & \underline{13} & No & \underline{No} \\ \underline{400} & \underline{3} & No & Yes \\ \underline{800} & \underline{1} & \underline{Yes} & Yes \end{bmatrix}$$

and the deprivation cutoff vector $z = (500, 5,$ Not malnourished, Has access to improved sanitation). The corresponding deprivation matrices are denoted as follows.

$$g^0 = \begin{bmatrix} 0 & 0 & 0 & 0 \\ 1 & 0 & 0 & 1 \\ 1 & 1 & 1 & 1 \\ 0 & 1 & 0 & 0 \end{bmatrix} \quad g^{0'} = \begin{bmatrix} 0 & 0 & 0 & 0 \\ 1 & 0 & 0 & 1 \\ 1 & 1 & 0 & 0 \\ 0 & 1 & 1 & 0 \end{bmatrix}$$

$$w = \begin{bmatrix} 0.25 & 0.25 & 0.25 & 0.25 \end{bmatrix} \quad w = \begin{bmatrix} 0.25 & 0.25 & 0.25 & 0.25 \end{bmatrix}$$

The deprivation score column vectors (not shown) are $c = (0, 0.5, 1, 0.25)$ and $c' = (0, 0.5, 0.5, 0.5)$, respectively. Clearly, the second and the third person are identified as poor in X and the second, third, and fourth persons are identified as poor in X'. The corresponding censored deprivation matrices are as follows.

$$g^0(k) = \begin{bmatrix} 0 & 0 & 0 & 0 \\ 1 & 0 & 0 & 1 \\ 1 & 1 & 1 & 1 \\ 0 & 0 & 0 & 0 \end{bmatrix} \quad g^{0'}(k) = \begin{bmatrix} 0 & 0 & 0 & 0 \\ 1 & 0 & 0 & 1 \\ 1 & 1 & 0 & 0 \\ 0 & 1 & 1 & 0 \end{bmatrix}$$

$$w = \begin{bmatrix} 0.25 & 0.25 & 0.25 & 0.25 \end{bmatrix} \quad w = \begin{bmatrix} 0.25 & 0.25 & 0.25 & 0.25 \end{bmatrix}$$

Then, using the formulation of $M_0 = \frac{1}{n} \sum_{i=1}^{n} \sum_{j=1}^{d} w_j g_{ij}^0(k)$, we obtain $M_0(X; z) = M_0(X'; z) = 3/8$. The two societies have the same level of Adjusted Headcount Ratio. However, if we break down M_0 into incidence and intensity, we find that $H = 1/2$ and $H' = 3/4$, whereas $A = 3/4$ and $A' = 1/2$. Clearly, X has a lower headcount ratio but the poor suffer larger deprivations on average.

The breakdown of M_0 into H and A can provide useful policy insights. A policymaker who is interested in reducing overall poverty when poverty is assessed by the Adjusted Headcount Ratio may do so in different ways. If M_0 is reduced by focusing on the poor who have a lower intensity of poverty, then there will be a large reduction in H. But there may not be a large reduction in the average intensity (A). On the other hand, if the policies are directed towards the poorest of the poor, then an overall reduction in M_0 may be accomplished by a larger reduction in A instead of H. Thus, while monitoring poverty reduction, it is possible to see how overall poverty has been reduced.

It should be noted that H and A are also partial indices of the other M_α measures. Additionally, these other measures, such as M_1 and M_2, also have other informative partial indices, discussed in section 5.1.

5.5.2 SUBGROUP DECOMPOSITION

In developing multidimensional methods, we would not want to lose the useful properties that the unidimensional methods have successfully employed over the years. Prime among them is **population subgroup decomposability**, which, as stated in section 2.5.3, posits that overall poverty is a population-share weighted sum of subgroup poverty levels. This property has proved to be of great use in analysing poverty by regions, by ethnic groups, and by other subgroups defined in a variety of ways.[12] The M_0 measure, as well as the other M_α measures, satisfies the population subgroup decomposability property, a property that is directly inherited from the FGT class of indices (Foster, Greer, and Thorbecke 1984).

Population subgroup decomposability allows us to understand and monitor the subgroup M_0 levels and compare them with the aggregate M_0. The population share and the achievement matrix of subgroup ℓ are denoted by $v^\ell = n^\ell / n$ and X^ℓ, respectively. We express the overall M_0 as:

$$M_0(X) = \sum_{\ell=1}^{m} v^\ell M_0(X^\ell).$$ (5.7)

Given the additive form of equation (5.7), it is also possible to compute the contribution of each subgroup to overall poverty. Let us denote the contribution of subgroup ℓ to overall poverty by $\mathbb{D}_\ell^0$, which is formulated as

$$\mathbb{D}_\ell^0 = v^\ell \frac{M_0(X^\ell)}{M_0(X)}.$$ (5.8)

Note that the contribution of subgroup ℓ to overall poverty depends both on the level of poverty in subgroup ℓ and on the population share of the subgroup. Whenever the contribution to poverty of a region or some other group greatly exceeds its population share, this suggests that there is a seriously unequal distribution of poverty in the country, with some regions or groups bearing a disproportionate share of poverty. Clearly, the sum of the contributions of all groups needs to be 100%.[13]

5.5.2.1 Subgroup Decompositions of the Adjusted Headcount Ratio (M_0)

Let us consider the example of the hypothetical society presented in Box 5.1 and show how the contribution of subgroups to the overall Adjusted Headcount Ratio is computed. For this example, let us assume a certain weighting structure and a certain poverty cutoff to identify who among these four persons is poor. We assume that a 40% weight is

---

[12] Population subgroup decomposable measures satisfy subgroup consistency, but the converse does not hold. See section 2.5 for further details on these and other properties.
[13] Note that other measures in the AF class discussed in section 5.7 satisfy the population subgroup decomposability property as well, and expressions (5.7) and (5.8) are equally applicable to these measures.

Table 5.1 Achievement matrices of subgroups in the hypothetical society

	Income	Years of schooling completed	Malnourished (1=no)	Has access to improved sanitation (1=yes)	
$X^1 =$	700	14	1	1	Person 1
	300	13	1	0	Person 2
	800	1	0	1	Person 4
$X^2 =$	400	3	0	0	Person 3
$z =$	500	5	1	1	

Table 5.2 (Censored) deprivation matrices of the subgroups

	Income	Years of schooling completed	Malnourished	Has access to improved sanitation		Deprivation score (c)
$g^{0,1} =$	0	0	0	0	Person 1	0
	1	0	0	1	Person2	0.50
	0	1	1	0	Person 4	0.50
$g^{0,2} =$	1	1	1	1	Person 3	1
$w =$	0.40	0.25	0.25	0.10		

attached to income, a 25% weight is attached to years of education, a 25% weight is attached to undernourishment, and the remaining 10% weight is attached to the access to improved sanitation. Thus, the weight vector is $w = (0.40, 0.25, 0.25, 0.10)$. We identify a person as poor if the person is deprived in 40% or more of weighted indicators, that is, $k = 0.40$.

For subgroup decomposition, we divide the entire population in X into two subgroups. Subgroup 1 consists of three persons, whereas Subgroup 2 consists of only one person as presented in Table 5.1. Note that the person in Subgroup 2 is deprived in all dimensions. We denote the achievement matrix of Subgroup 1 by X^1 and that of Subgroup 2 by X^2.

The deprivation matrices and deprivation scores of the two subgroups are presented in Table 5.2. Person 1 is not deprived in any dimension and so has a deprivation score of 0. Person 2 is deprived in two dimensions: income and access to improved sanitation, and so the deprivation score is 0.5. Similarly, the deprivation score of Person 4 is 0.5 and Person 3's is 1. Now, for $k = 0.4$, Person 2 and Person 4 are poor in Subgroup 1 and Person 3 is poor in Subgroup 2. In both subgroups, those who are deprived are identified as poor, and so there is no scope for censoring. The censored deprivation matrices for both groups are, in this particular case, the corresponding deprivation matrices.

Thus, $M_0(X^1) = (0 + 0.50 + 0.50)/3 = 0.33$ and $M_0(X^2) = 1$. The overall Adjusted Headcount Ratio is $M_0(X) = (0 + 0.50 + 0.50 + 1)/4 = 0.5$. It is straightforward to verify that the population-weighted sum of the subgroup-Adjusted Headcount Ratios is equal to the overall Adjusted Headcount Ratio. The population share of Subgroup 1 is $v^1 = 3/4$ and that of Subgroup 2 is $v^2 = 1/4$. Therefore, $v^1 M_0\left(X^1\right) + v^2 M_0\left(X^2\right) = 3/4 \times 0.33 + 1/4 \times 1 = 0.5 = M_0\left(X\right)$.

Note that the Adjusted Headcount Ratio in Subgroup 2 is more than three times larger than the Adjusted Headcount Ratio of Subgroup 1. Does this mean that the contribution of Subgroup 2 is also more than three times as large as the contribution of Subgroup 1? No it does not. Recall that the contribution of a subgroup to overall poverty depends on the population share of that subgroup as well. For our example, the contribution of Subgroup 1 to the overall Adjusted Headcount Ratio is $\mathbb{D}_\ell^0 = (3/4 \times 0.33)/0.5 = 0.5$ or 50%. The contribution of Subgroup 2 to the overall headcount ratio is $\mathbb{D}_\ell^0 = (1/4 \times 1)/0.50 = 0.5$ or 50%. It is worth noting that, in this case, the population Subgroup 2 does bear a disproportionate load of poverty since, despite being only 25% of the total population, it contributes 50% of overall poverty. Because population shares affect interpretation, tables showing subgroup decompositions can benefit from including population shares for each subgroup, as well as poverty figures.

5.5.3 DIMENSIONAL BREAKDOWN

As discussed in section 2.5, a multidimensional poverty measure that satisfies the dimensional breakdown property can be expressed as a weighted sum of the dimensional deprivations after identification. The M_0 satisfies the dimensional breakdown property and thus can also be expressed as a weighted sum of post-identification dimensional deprivations, which in the particular case of M_0 we refer to as the **censored headcount ratios**.

Why is this property useful? This property allows one to analyse the composition of multidimensional poverty. For example, Alkire and Foster (2011a), after decomposing overall poverty in the United States by ethnic group, break the poverty within those groups down by dimensions and examine how different ethnic groups have different dimensional deprivations, i.e. different poverty compositions.

The **censored headcount ratio** of a dimension is defined as the percentage of the population who are multidimensionally poor *and* simultaneously deprived in that dimension. Formally, we denote the jth column of the censored deprivation matrix $g^0(k)$ as $g_{.j}^0(k)$ and mean of the column for that chosen dimension as $h_j(k) = \frac{1}{n}\sum_{i=1}^n g_{ij}^0(k)$. Then $h_j(k)$ is simply the censored headcount ratio of dimension j. What is the interpretation of $h_j(k)$? The censored headcount ratio $h_j(k)$ is the proportion of the population that are identified as poor ($c_i \geq k$) and are deprived in dimension j.

The additive structure of the M_0 measure allows it to be expressed as a weighted sum of the censored headcount ratios, where the weight on dimension j is w_j, the relative weight assigned to that dimension. We have already seen in expression (5.3) that

$M_0 = \frac{1}{n} \sum_{i=1}^{n} \sum_{j=1}^{d} w_j g_{ij}^0(k)$. This expression can be reformulated as

$$M_0 = \frac{1}{n} \sum_{i=1}^{n} \sum_{j=1}^{d} w_j g_{ij}^0(k) = \sum_{j=1}^{d} w_j \left[\frac{1}{n} \sum_{i=1}^{n} g_{ij}^0(k) \right] = \sum_{j=1}^{d} w_j h_j(k). \qquad (5.9)$$

Analyses based on the censored headcount ratios can be complemented in an interesting way by considering the **percentage contribution** of each dimension to overall poverty. The censored headcount ratio shows the extent of deprivations among the poor but not the relative value of the dimensions. Two dimensions may have the same censored headcount ratios but very different contributions to overall poverty. This is because the contribution not only depends on the censored headcount ratio but also on the weight or value assigned to each dimension. Let us denote the contribution of dimension j to M_0 by ϕ_j^0, where

$$\phi_j^0(k) = w_j \frac{h_j(k)}{M_0}, \qquad (5.10)$$

for each $j = 1, \ldots, d$. Whenever the contribution to poverty of a certain indicator greatly exceeds its weight, there is a relatively high censored headcount ratio for this indicator. The poor are more likely to be deprived in this indicator than in others. Clearly, the sum of the contributions of all indicators is 100%.[14] The censored headcount ratios and the percentage contributions have policy relevance for understanding the composition of poverty in different regions. Chapter 9 describes how they may be used to analyse intertemporal changes in multidimensional poverty and percentage contributions.

The **uncensored (raw) headcount ratio** of a dimension is defined as the proportion of the population that are deprived in that dimension. It aggregates deprivations of the poor (censored headcount) with deprivations of the non-poor. The uncensored headcount ratio of dimension j is computed from the (uncensored) deprivation matrix g^0 as the mean of the jth column vector $g_{\cdot j}^0$. Therefore $h_j = \frac{1}{n} \sum_{i=1}^{n} g_{ij}^0$ is the uncensored (raw) headcount ratio of dimension j.

The censored headcount ratio generally differs from the uncensored headcount ratio except when the identification criterion used is *union*. In this case, a person is identified as poor if the person is deprived in any dimension, so no deprivations are censored. Thus, the censored and uncensored headcount ratios are identical.

---

[14] Note that if poverty as measured by M_0 is very low, the censored headcount ratios are also low, and contributions require care in interpretation. One indicator can have an 80% contribution, not because there is a massive deprivation in that indicator but because it is one of the few indicators that have a non-zero censored headcount, explaining most of the (very low) poverty.

Table 5.3 Deprivation matrix of the hypothetical society

	Income	Years of schooling completed	Malnourished	Has access to improved sanitation	Deprivation score (c)
$g^0 =$	0	0	0	0	0
	1	0	0	1	0.50
	1	1	1	1	1
	0	1	0	0	0.25
$w =$	0.40	0.25	0.25	0.10	
$h =$	0.50	0.50	0.25	0.50	

5.5.3.1 The Censored and Uncensored Headcount Ratios and Percentage Contributions

Using a hypothetical illustration, we now show how the uncensored headcount ratios and the censored headcount ratios are computed and then calculate the contribution of each dimension to the Adjusted Headcount Ratio. Let us consider the same achievement matrix and weight vector as was in the previous subsection, which consists of four persons and four dimensions.

First, we show how to compute the **uncensored headcount ratio**. The achievement matrix X and the deprivation cutoff vector z are used to obtain the deprivation matrix g^0, presented in Table 5.3. The uncensored headcount ratio of any dimension j is $h_j = \frac{1}{n}\sum_{i=1}^{n} g_{ij}^0$. The uncensored headcount ratio of the income dimension is $(0 + 1 + 1 + 0)/4 = 0.5$. In other words, 50% of the population is deprived in the income dimension. Similarly, the uncensored headcount ratio of the schooling dimension is 50%, of the nutritional status dimension is 25%, and of access to improved sanitation is 50%. The uncensored headcount ratios (summarized by vector h) are reported in the bottom row of the table.

Next, we show how to compute the **censored headcount ratio**. We identify a person as poor if the person is deprived in 40% of weighted indicators, i.e. $k = 0.4$. Using the identification function we construct the censored deprivation matrix, presented in Table 5.4. Note that we censor the deprivations of Person 4 and replace them by 0 even though Person 4 is deprived in the education dimension. Why do we do this? We do so because the deprivation score of Person 4 is only 0.25, which is less than the poverty cutoff of $k = 0.4$, and hence Person 4 is not poor. It can be easily verified that the M_0 measure is 0.375.

Let us finish this example by showing how to compute the contribution of a dimension to the Adjusted Headcount Ratio. We already know that the Adjusted Headcount Ratio is 0.350 and that the percentage contribution is $\phi_j^0(k) = w_j h_j(k)/M_0$. Let us consider the income dimension, which has a censored headcount ratio of 0.50 and a weight of

Table 5.4 Censored deprivation matrix of the hypothetical society

	Income	Years of schooling completed	Malnourished	Has access to improved sanitation	Deprivation score (c)
$g^0(k) =$	0	0	0	0	0
	1	0	0	1	0.50
	1	1	1	1	1
	0	0	0	0	0
$w =$	0.40	0.25	0.25	0.10	
$h(k) =$	0.50	0.25	0.25	0.50	$M_0 = 0.375$
$\phi^0(k) =$	53.3%	16.7%	16.7%	13.3%	

0.40. Then the contribution of the dimension to the Adjusted Headcount Ratio is $0.40 \times 0.50/0.375 = 0.533$ or 53.3%. Similarly, the contribution of the education dimension is $0.25 \times 0.25/0.375 = 0.167$ or 16.7%. An interesting aspect to note is that the censored headcount ratio of the access to sanitation dimension is the same as that of the income dimension, but its contribution to the Adjusted Headcount Ratio is only 13.3%, which is one-fourth the contribution of the income dimension. The reason is that the weight attached to the income dimension is four times the weight of the access to sanitation dimension.

5.6 A Case Study: The Global Multidimensional Poverty Index (MPI)

Now that we have learned how to compute the Adjusted Headcount Ratio and its partial indices, we provide an example showing one prominent implementation of the M_0 measure: the global Multidimensional Poverty Index (MPI). The global MPI was developed by Alkire and Santos (2010) with UNDP's Human Development Report Office and has been reported annually in the *Human Development Report* since 2010.[15] The index consists of ten indicators grouped into three dimensions, as outlined in Table 5.5.

Note that the index uses nested weights. The weights are distributed such that each dimension reported in the first column receives an equal weight of 1/3 and the weight is equally divided among indicators within each dimension (note the distinction in terms here between indicator and dimension). Thus, each education and health indicator

---

[15] See also Alkire and Santos (2014), where the MPI is presented and scrutinized with a host of robustness tests.

Table 5.5 Dimensions, indicators, deprivation cutoffs, and weights of the global MPI

Dimension	Indicator	Weight (w)	Deprivation cutoff (z)
Education	Schooling (Sc)	1/6	No household member has completed five years of schooling.
	Attendance (At)	1/6	Any school-aged child in the household is not attending school up to class 8.*
Health	Nutrition (N)	1/6	Any adult or child in the household with nutritional information is undernourished.**
	Mortality (M)	1/6	Any child has passed away in the household.***
Standard of Living	Electricity (E)	1/18	The household has no electricity.
	Sanitation (S)	1/18	The household's sanitation facility is not improved or it is shared with other households.
	Water (W)	1/18	The household does not have access to safe drinking water or safe water is more than a 30-minute walk (round trip).
	Floor (F)	1/18	The household has a dirt, sand, or dung floor.
	Cooking fuel (C)	1/18	The household cooks with dung, wood, or charcoal.
	Assets (A)	1/18	The household owns at most one of the following: radio, telephone, TV, bike, motorbike, or refrigerator; and does not own a car or truck.

Source: Alkire and Santos (2010, 2014); cf. Alkire, Roche, Santos, and Seth (2011) and Alkire, Conconi, and Roche (2013)

* If a household has no school-aged children, the household is treated as non-deprived.
** An adult with a Body Mass Index below 18.5 m/kg^2 is considered undernourished. A child is considered undernourished if his or her body weight, adjusted for age, is more than two standard deviations below the median of the reference population.
*** If no person in a household has been asked this information, the household is treated as non-deprived.

receives larger weights than the standard of living indicators. The weights for each indicator are reported in the third column. The deprivation cutoffs are outlined in the final column. Any person living in a household who fails to meet the deprivation cutoff is identified as deprived in that indicator. An abbreviation has been assigned to each indicator in the second column that will be useful for the presentations in the next table.

Table 5.6 presents a hypothetical example of people living in four households, which will help explain how the MPI is constructed. The first two households live in urban areas and the third and the fourth households live in rural areas. In this illustration, the households are not of equal size. The household sizes are reported in the third column of the table. The deprivation matrix (g^0) is presented in columns 4 through 13. Following the standard notation, a 1 indicates that a household is deprived in the corresponding indicator and 0 indicates that the household is not deprived in that indicator. For example, the first household is only deprived in mortality (M) and cooking fuel (C), whereas the fourth household is deprived in five indicators: schooling (Sc), mortality (M), electricity (E), cooking fuel (C), and asset ownership (A).

Let us first show how the deprivation score (c_i) of each person is computed. Note that in this example, all persons within a household are assigned the same deprivation score, which is the weighted sum of deprivations that the household faces. For example, the

Table 5.6 The deprivation matrix and the identification of the poor

1	2	3	4	5	6	7	8	9	10	11	12	13	14	15	16
			Education		Health		Standard of living								
Region	HH no.	HH size	Sc	At	N	M	E	S	W	F	C	A	c	Poor	c(k)
Urban	1	4	0	0	0	1	0	0	0	0	1	0	0.22	No	0
	2	7	1	1	0	1	1	0	1	0	1	1	0.72	Yes	0.72
Rural	3	5	0	0	1	0	1	1	1	0	1	0	0.39	Yes	0.39
	4	4	1	0	0	1	1	0	0	0	1	1	0.50	Yes	0.5
Weight (w)			1/6	1/6	1/6	1/6	1/18	1/18	1/18	1/18	1/18	1/18			
Uncensored Headcount Ratio			0.55	0.35	0.25	0.75	0.80	0.25	0.60	0.00	1.00	0.55			
Censored Headcount Ratio			0.55	0.35	0.25	0.55	0.80	0.25	0.60	0.00	0.80	0.55			
Percentage Contribution (in %)			20	13	9	20	10	3	7	0	10	7			

deprivation score of each person in the first household is

$$c_1 = \left(1 \times \frac{1}{6}\right) + \left(1 \times \frac{1}{18}\right) = 0.22.$$

The deprivation scores are reported in column 14. The deprivation scores of the second, third, and fourth households are 0.72, 0.39, and 0.50, respectively. Thus, the second household has the largest deprivation score and the first household has the lowest deprivation score.

In the computation of the global MPI, a person is identified as poor if the person's deprivation score is equal to 1/3 or higher. It is evident from column 14 that the first household's deprivation score is less than 1/3, whereas the three other households' deprivation scores are larger than 1/3. Thus, all persons in the first household are identified as non-poor, whereas all other persons in the last three households are identified as multidimensionally poor. Column 15 classifies the households as multidimensionally poor or not. The multidimensional headcount ratio or the incidence of poverty (H) is (hint: use the household size)

$$H = \frac{q}{n} = \left(\frac{7+5+4}{4+7+5+4}\right) = 0.80.$$

So 80% of the population are poor. Note that we have already discussed that the multidimensional headcount ratio (H) does not satisfy the dimensional monotonicity property, and so it does not change if any of the three poor households become deprived in an additional dimension. This limitation is overcome by the Adjusted Headcount Ratio (M_0), which is called the MPI in this example. The censored deprivation scores are reported in column 16, where the deprivation score of the non-poor household has been censored by replacing the score by 0. The MPI is the mean of the censored deprivation score vector and can be computed using expression (5.3) as (hint: use the household size)

$$MPI = \frac{1}{n}\sum_{i=1}^{n} c_i(k) = \frac{(4 \times 0) + (7 \times 0.72) + (5 \times 0.39) + (4 \times 0.50)}{4+7+5+4} = 0.450.$$

One may be also interested in knowing how poor the poor people are, or the intensity of multidimensional poverty. The intensity of poverty can be computed as

$$A = \frac{1}{q}\sum_{i=1}^{q} c_i(k) = \frac{(0.72 \times 7) + (0.39 \times 5) + (0.50 \times 4)}{(7+5+4)} = 0.563.$$

So, on average, poor people are deprived in 56.3% of the weighted indicators. It can be easily verified that the MPI is the product of the incidence of poverty and the intensity of poverty, i.e. $MPI = H \times A = 0.8 \times 0.563 = 0.450$.

Let us now show how the subgroup decomposition property may be used to understand the contribution of subgroups to overall multidimensional poverty. Using the same process as above, the MPI, H, and A can be computed for each population subgroup. The MPI of the two urban households is 0.46, which can be obtained either by summing the censored deprivation scores weighted by the population share of each household or as a product of $H = 0.64$ and $A = 0.72$. The MPI of the two rural households is 0.44, while $H = 1$ and $A = 0.44$. Indeed, the incidence of poverty in the rural households is higher because all persons are identified as multidimensionally poor, while in the urban households this is not the case. However, when comparing the MPIs, we find the urban households have higher poverty because the intensity is higher. The urban households contribute 55% of the total population, and the rural ones contribute 45%. Thus, following the decomposition formula in equation (5.7), it can be verified that the overall MPI is $0.55 \times 0.46 + 0.45 \times 0.44 = 0.45$. Again, using equation (5.8), it can be verified that the urban contribution to the overall MPI is 56%, whereas the rural contribution to the overall MPI is only 44%.

Next, using the last rows of Table 5.6, we show how the dimensional breakdown property is used. We have seen in equation (5.9) that the overall M_0 can be expressed as a weighted average of censored headcount ratios. How are the censored headcount ratios in Table 5.6 computed? The censored headcount ratio for the years of education indicator is equal to $(7+4)/20 = 55\%$. Similarly, the censored headcount ratio of the cooking fuel indicator is equal to $(7+5+4)/20 = 80\%$. Note that the first household is not identified as poor and thus is censored. This is why the censored headcount ratios are different from the uncensored headcount ratios reported in the row above. Looking at the censored figures, we can see that the poor in this society exhibit the highest deprivation levels in access to electricity and cooking fuel, followed (though with much lower headcount ratios) by sanitation, years of education, mortality, and assets. The percentage contributions of the indicators, which are computed using expression (5.10), are reported in the final column of the table. It is evident that neither electricity nor sanitation nor assets have the highest contribution to the overall MPI. Why? Because the weights assigned to these indicators are lower than those assigned to schooling and mortality.

We now provide the following example to show how the censored headcount ratio and the percentage contribution of dimensions are used in practice. Borrowing from Alkire, Roche, and Seth (2011), the example provides information on two subnational regions for a cross-country implementation of the MPI. These two regions have roughly the same M_0 levels reported in the final row of Table 5.7. Breaking M_0 down by dimension reveals how the underlying structure of deprivations differs across the two countries for the ten indicators.[16] In Ziguinchor (a region in Senegal), mortality deprivations contribute the most to multidimensional poverty, whereas in Barisal (a division in Bangladesh), the relative contribution of nutritional deprivations is much larger than, say, deprivations in school attendance. Although the overall poverty levels as measured by M_0 are very

---

[16] Data are drawn from the Demographic and Health Surveys (DHS) for Bangladesh (2007) and Senegal (2005), which are nationally representative household surveys.

Table 5.7 Same MPIs but different compositions in two subnational regions

Dimension	Indicators	Ziguinchor (Senegal)		Barisal (Bangladesh)	
		Censored headcount ratio	Percentage contribution	Censored headcount ratio	Percentage contribution
Education	Years of Education	0.165	8.6%	0.214	11.2%
	Child School Attendance	0.180	9.4%	0.095	5.0%
Health	Mortality	0.429	22.4%	0.242	12.7%
	Nutrition	0.103	5.4%	0.427	22.4%
Living Standards	Electricity	0.563	9.8%	0.532	9.3%
	Sanitation	0.597	10.4%	0.458	8.0%
	Water	0.534	9.3%	0.023	0.4%
	Floor	0.448	7.8%	0.612	10.7%
	Cooking Fuel	0.643	11.2%	0.630	11.0%
	Assets	0.333	5.8%	0.538	9.4%
MPI		**0.319**		**0.318**	
H		**62.7%**		**65.1%**	
A		**50.7%**		**48.9%**	

Source: Alkire, Roche, and Seth (2011)

similar, dimensional breakdown reveals a very different underlying structure of poverty, which in turn could suggest different policy responses.

5.7 **AF Class Measures Used with Cardinal Variables**

In this chapter, our discussion has focused on the Adjusted Headcount Ratio as many poverty indicators in practice are of ordinal scale. However, if all indicators are cardinal, we can go beyond the Adjusted Headcount Ratio to measures that additionally reflect the depth of deprivations poor people experience below the deprivation cutoff in each dimension. The identification step proceeds in exactly the same way as with M_0. The difference is in the aggregation step. This section introduces the normalized gap matrix, which is used for the aggregation step for all the M_α class of measures with $\alpha > 0$. The section also presents the two most common members of the M_α class with $\alpha > 0$: M_1 and M_2.

5.7.1 THE NORMALIZED GAP MATRIX

The basic matrix for measures drawing upon cardinal data is the **normalized gap matrix**, which, like the deprivation matrix, is constructed from the achievement matrix and the vector of deprivation cutoffs. The entries in the normalized gap matrix are the shortfall or gap in deprived people's achievements, expressed as a proportion of the respective deprivation cutoff.

In the **normalized gap matrix** g^1 the typical element is defined by $g_{ij}^1 = g_{ij}^0 \times (z_j - x_{ij})/z_j$. In other words, the normalized gap matrix replaces each deprived entry in X with the respective normalized gap and replaces each entry that is not below its deprivation cutoff with 0. The normalized gap matrix provides a snapshot of the depth of deprivation of each person in each dimension. The **squared gap matrix** g^2 replaces each deprived entry in X with the square of the normalized gap and replaces each entry that is not below its deprivation cutoff with 0. Thus the typical element of the squared gap matrix is $g_{ij}^2 = g_{ij}^0 \left[(z_j - x_{ij})/z_j \right]^2$. Squaring the normalized gaps puts relatively more emphasis on larger deprivations. Generalizing the above, we may define the **normalized gap matrix of order $\alpha > 0$** by raising the normalized gaps to the power α and denote this by g^α, whose typical element is $g_{ij}^\alpha = g_{ij}^0 \left[(z_j - x_{ij})/z_j \right]^\alpha$. Clearly, the squared gap and normalized gap matrices correspond to $\alpha = 2$ and $\alpha = 1$, respectively, while the deprivation matrix g^0 is obtained in the limit as α tends to zero.

From the normalized gap matrices, we apply the same identification function ρ_k to obtain the censored normalized gap matrix of order α as $g^\alpha(k)$ such that $g_{ij}^\alpha(k) = g_{ij}^\alpha \times \rho_k(x_i; z)$. Recall that the identification function ρ_k is based on the vector of weighted deprivation counts c (generated, as before, from the g^0 matrix and the vector of weights) and the poverty cutoff k. The identification function replaces all deprived entries of the non-poor with 0 and leaves the deprived entries of the poor unchanged. We define $g^1(k)$ as the censored normalized gap matrix and $g^2(k)$ as the censored squared gap matrix.

5.7.2 THE ADJUSTED POVERTY GAP, ADJUSTED FGT, AND M_α MEASURES

The Adjusted Poverty Gap measure $M_1(X; z)$ can be defined as

$$M_1 = \frac{1}{n} \sum_{i=1}^{n} \sum_{j=1}^{d} w_j g_{ij}^1(k). \tag{5.11}$$

In other words, the Adjusted Poverty Gap is the sum of the weighted normalized gaps of the poor or $\sum_{i=1}^{n} \sum_{j=1}^{d} w_j g_{ij}^1(k)$, divided by the population (n). Another way of viewing M_1 is in terms of partial indices: M_1 is the product of H (incidence) and A (intensity) (which in turn is M_0) *and* the average deprivation gap among the poor G. That is,

$$M_1 = \frac{1}{n} \sum_{i=1}^{n} \sum_{j=1}^{d} w_j g_{ij}^1(k) = \frac{q}{n} \times \frac{\sum_{i=1}^{q} \sum_{j=1}^{d} w_j g_{ij}^0(k)}{q} \times \frac{\sum_{i=1}^{q} \sum_{j=1}^{d} w_j g_{ij}^1(k)}{\sum_{i=1}^{q} \sum_{j=1}^{d} w_j g_{ij}^0(k)} = H \times A \times G.$$

$$\tag{5.12}$$

In words, G is the average value of the normalized gap among all instances in which any poor person is deprived (and hence where the censored normalized gap is positive). Thus, G provides information on the average depth of deprivations across all poor and deprived states.

As in the case of M_0, the partial indices greatly aid in comparing multidimensional poverty across time and space. Suppose for example that M_1 is higher in one region than in another. It could be useful to examine the extent to which the difference is due to a higher H, or to higher values of A or G. It is also possible to examine the average gaps for each dimension to identify the dimensions in which normalized gaps tend to be higher.

Under methodology (ρ_k, M_1), if the deprivation of a poor person deepens in any dimension, then the respective $g_{ij}^1(k)$ will rise and hence so will M_1. Consequently, (ρ_k, M_1) satisfies the property of monotonicity.

To incorporate sensitivity to one form of inequality among the poor, as embodied by the transfer property defined in section 2.5, we turn to the censored matrix $g^2(k)$ of squared normalized shortfalls. The **Adjusted Squared Gap** measure or **Adjusted FGT Measure** $M_2(X; z)$ can be defined as

$$M_2 = \frac{1}{n} \sum_{i=1}^{n} \sum_{j=1}^{d} w_j g_{ij}^2(k). \tag{5.13}$$

The adjusted squared gap is the sum of the weighted normalized squared gaps of the poor, or $\sum_{i=1}^{n} \sum_{j=1}^{d} w_j g_{ij}^2(k)$, divided by the population (n). M_2 can also be expressed in terms of partial indices as the product of H (incidence) and A (intensity) *and* the average severity S. That is

$$M_2 = \frac{1}{n} \sum_{i=1}^{n} \sum_{j=1}^{d} w_j g_{ij}^2(k) = \frac{q}{n} \times \frac{\sum_{i=1}^{q} \sum_{j=1}^{d} w_j g_{ij}^0(k)}{q} \times \frac{\sum_{i=1}^{q} \sum_{j=1}^{d} w_j g_{ij}^2(k)}{\sum_{i=1}^{q} \sum_{j=1}^{d} w_j g_{ij}^0(k)} = H \times A \times S. \tag{5.14}$$

S is the average squared gap (or severity) among all instances where a poor person is deprived (and hence where the censored squared gap is positive). By taking the square of the normalized gaps, S places relatively greater emphasis on the larger gaps. Therefore, under (ρ_k, M_2), a given-sized increase in a deprivation of a poor person will have a greater impact the larger the initial level of deprivation. Consequently, the methodology satisfies the weak transfer property and is sensitive to the inequality with which deprivations are distributed among the poor.

We generalize M_0, M_1, and M_2 to the class $M_\alpha(x, z)$ of multidimensional poverty measures associated with the unidimensional FGT class. The adjusted FGT class of multidimensional poverty measures can be defined as

$$M_\alpha = \frac{1}{n} \sum_{i=1}^{n} \sum_{j=1}^{d} w_j g_{ij}^\alpha(k); \quad \alpha \geq 0. \tag{5.15}$$

In other words, M_α is the weighted sum of the entries in the $g_\alpha(k)$ matrix, or $\sum_{i=1}^{n}\sum_{j=1}^{d} w_j g_{ij}^\alpha(k)$, divided by the population (n). In the notation (Method IV in Box 5.7 for M_0) used in Alkire and Foster (2011a), and described below in Box 5.6, the index M_α is the mean of the censored weighted matrix $g_\alpha(k)$.

The general methodology employing the dual-cutoff function ρ_k and an adjusted FGT measure M_α is denoted by $\mathcal{M}_{k\alpha} = (\rho_k, M_\alpha)$. It is important to define the AF methodology fully, both the dual-cutoff identification strategy and the poverty measures, because it is this combined methodology which assures that the resulting measures satisfy the principles here specified.

As stated in section 3.6.1 and as a way to wrap up this chapter, it is worth recalling that all measures in the AF family satisfy symmetry, replication invariance, scale invariance, poverty focus, deprivation focus, normalisation, non-triviality, weak and dimensional monotonicity, population subgroup decomposability, weak deprivation rearrangement, and dimensional breakdown. For $\alpha = 0$, the measure satisfies the ordinality property, making it suitable for implementation when at least some of the indicators used are of ordinal scale. For $\alpha > 0$, the measures require all indicators to be cardinal. When $\alpha > 0$, the measures satisfy monotonicity. When $\alpha \geq 1$, the measures satisfy weak transfer. When the union criterion is used for identification and $\alpha > 0$, the measures satisfy continuity.

BOX 5.6 AN ALTERNATIVE PRESENTATION OF M_α MEASURES USING NON-NORMALIZED WEIGHTS

In this chapter we have stated the formulas in terms of normalized weights (Method I in Box 5.7 for M_0), but they can also be expressed using non-normalized weights such that $w_j > 0$ for all j and $\sum_{j=1}^{d} w_j = d$, so that they add to the total number of dimensions (Method IV in Box 5.7). In order to do so, we introduce the weighted normalized gap matrices. Like the weighted deprivation matrix $\bar{g}^0$ that we defined earlier in Box 5.3, we may also define the *weighted* normalized gap matrix of order α as $\bar{g}^\alpha$ such that $\bar{g}_{ij}^\alpha = w_j g_{ij}^\alpha$. In other words, in weighted normalized gap matrices, each deprived entry in X is replaced with its respective normalized gap of order α multiplied by its relative weight and each entry that is not below its deprivation cutoff is replaced with 0. For $\alpha = 1$, $\bar{g}^1$ is the weighted normalized gap matrix with the typical element being $\bar{g}_{ij}^1 = w_j g_{ij}^1$. Similarly, for $\alpha = 2$, $\bar{g}^2$ is the weighted squared gap matrix with $\bar{g}_{ij}^2 = w_j g_{ij}^2$.

The censored weighted normalized gap matrix of order α can be obtained as $\bar{g}^\alpha(k)$ such that $\bar{g}_{ij}^\alpha(k) = \bar{g}_{ij}^\alpha \times \rho_k(x_i.; z)$. Thus, $\bar{g}^1(k)$ is the censored weighted normalized gap matrix and $\bar{g}^2(k)$ is the censored weighted normalized squared gap matrix. As with any censored matrix, these matrices are obtained by multiplying the entries of the weighted deprivation matrix by the identification function ρ_k.

The adjusted FGT class of multidimensional poverty measures can be defined as

$$M_\alpha = \mu\left(\bar{g}^\alpha(k)\right); \; \alpha \geq 0. \qquad (5.16)$$

In this case, M_α is the sum of the entries of the censored weighted matrix $\sum_{i=1}^{n}\sum_{j=1}^{d} \bar{g}_{ij}^\alpha(k)$ divided by the highest possible value for this sum, or $n \times d$.

Based on expression (5.16), the Adjusted Poverty Gap measure $M_1(X; z)$ is the mean of the censored weighted normalized gap matrix and can be defined as

$$M_1 = \mu\left(\bar{g}^1(k)\right). \qquad (5.17)$$

BOX 5.6 (*cont.*)

Thus, the Adjusted Poverty Gap is the sum of the weighted normalized gaps of the poor, or $\sum_{i=1}^{n} \sum_{j=1}^{d} \bar{g}_{ij}^1(k)$ divided by the highest possible sum of weighted normalized gaps, or $n \times d$.

Similarly, the Adjusted Squared Gap or the Adjusted FGT Measure is given by

$$M_2 = \mu\left(\bar{g}^2(k)\right). \tag{5.18}$$

Thus, M_2 is the sum of the weighted squared normalized gaps of the poor, or $\sum_{i=1}^{n} \sum_{j=1}^{d} \bar{g}_{ij}^2(k)$, divided by the highest possible sum of the weighted squared normalized gaps, or $n \times d$.

5.8 **Some Implementations of the AF Methodology**

As mentioned in Chapter 1, since its development, the Alkire-Foster approach to multidimensional poverty has generated practical interest. Examples include the global MPI, estimated for over 100 developing countries,[17] as well as official national multidimensional poverty measures in Mexico, Colombia, Bhutan, Chile, and the Philippines, with many other regional, national, and subnational measures in progress.[18] Adaptations of the methodology include the Gross National Happiness Index of the Royal Government of Bhutan (Ura et al. 2012) and the Women's Empowerment in Agriculture Index (Alkire, Meinzen-Dick, et al. 2013). Several academic studies have implemented the AF approach for different poverty measurement purposes and in different parts of the world. These are summarized in Table 5.8.

Other papers do not directly implement the AF methodology but engage with it in various ways. These include Ferreira (2011), Ravallion (2011b) and others in the *Journal of Economic Inequality*, vol. 9 (2011), Ferreira and Lugo (2013), Foster et al. (2010), Betti et al. (2012), Cardenas and Carpenter (2013), Larochelle (2014), Berenger et al. (2013), Siminski and Yerokhin (2012), and Smith (2012).

Chapter 6, which follows, explains the normative decisions required to apply the AF framework of multidimensional poverty measurement empirically. It identifies the different decisions required, delineates their normative content and key considerations, and presents alternative courses of action.

---

[17] UNDP (2010a); Alkire and Santos (2010, 2014); Alkire, Roche, Santos, and Seth (2011); Alkire, Conconi, and Roche (2013); Alkire, Conconi, and Seth (2014a).

[18] These experiences are documented on the often-updated site <www.mppn.org>.

Table 5.8 Summary of research studies that have implemented the AF methodology

Authors	Year	Paper title	Implements AF method to...	Country or region of the world for which it was implemented
Alkire, Apablaza, and Jung	2014b	Multidimensional Poverty Measurement for EU-SILC Countries	Construct trial measures using EU-SILC data 2006–12 and analyse by country, gender, age, and dimensional composition	Europe
Alkire and Seth	2013a	Identifying BPL Households: A Comparison of Methods	Compare a simple targeting-based method to some of the proposed methods for targeting the poor for the BPL (Below the Poverty Line) programme in India	India
Alkire and Seth	2013b	Multidimensional Poverty Reduction in India between 1999 and 2006: Where and How?	Monitor and study multidimensional poverty reduction in India	India
Alkire and Seth	2013c	Selecting a Targeting Method to Identify BPL Households in India	Propose a counting-based targeting methodology for the BPL programme in India	India
Arndt et al.	2012	Ordinal Welfare Comparisons with Multiple Discrete Indicators: A First-Order Dominance Approach and Application to Child Poverty	Perform child poverty comparison over time and between regions	Vietnam, Mozambique
Azevedo and Robles	2013	Multidimensional Targeting: Identifying Beneficiaries of Conditional Cash Transfer Programmes	Propose a targeting method	Latin America

Batana	2013	Multidimensional Measurement of Poverty Among Women in Sub-Saharan Africa	Measure multidimensional poverty among women in fourteen sub-Saharan African countries	Sub-Saharan Africa
Battiston et al.	2013	Income and Beyond: Multidimensional Poverty in Six Latin American Countries	Measure multidimensional poverty in six Latin American countries and track its reduction between 1992–2006	Latin America
Beja and Yap	2013	Counting Happiness from the Individual Level to the Group Level	Use the counting measure to assess group-level happiness	Philippines
Castro, Baca, Ocampo	2012	(Re)counting the Poor in Peru: A Multidimensional Approach	Compare headcount ratios of monetary poverty and multidimensional poverty between 2004 and 2008 in regions of Peru.	Peru, Latin America
Gradín	2013	Race, Poverty and Deprivation in South Africa	Measure poverty and material deprivation and the racial gap among South Africans after apartheid	South Africa
Mitra	2013	Towards a Multidimensional Measure of Governance	Develop a governance index for sub-Saharan African countries	Sub-Saharan Africa
Mitra, Posarac, and Vick	2013	Disability and Poverty in Developing Countries: A Multidimensional Study	Obtain the economic profile of persons (aged 18–65) with disabilities. Multidimensional poverty analysis is performed for persons with and without disability	Burkina Faso, Ghana, Kenya, Malawi, Mauritius, Zambia, and Zimbabwe; Bangladesh, Lao PDR, Pakistan, and the Philippines; Brazil, Dominican Republic, Mexico, and Paraguay

Table 5.8 (cont.)

Authors	Year	Paper title	Implements AF method to...	Region of the world for which it was implemented
Mitra, Jones, et al.	2013	Implementing a Multidimensional Poverty Measure Using Mixed Methods and a Participatory Framework	Measure multidimensional poverty among people with psychiatric diagnoses	USA
Nicholas and Ray	2011	Duration and Persistence in Multidimensional Deprivation: Methodology and Australian Application	Construct dynamic deprivation measures and assess the duration of deprivation across multiple dimensions	Australia
Notten and Roelen	2012	A New Tool for Monitoring (Child) Poverty: Measures of Cumulative Deprivation	Measure material deprivation, cumulative deprivation, and child poverty	UK, Germany, France, the Netherlands
Nussbaumer et al.	2012	Measuring Energy Poverty: Focusing on What Matters	Derive the Multidimensional Energy Poverty Index (MEPI)	Angola, Benin, Burkina Faso, Cameroon, Congo Brazzaville, Congo Democratic Republic, Egypt, Ethiopia, Ghana, Guinea, Kenya, Lesotho, Liberia, Madagascar, Malawi, Mali, Morocco, Mozambique, Namibia, Niger, Nigeria, Rwanda, Senegal, Sierra Leone, Swaziland, Tanzania, Uganda, Zambia, Zimbabwe
Peichl and Pestel	2013a	Multidimensional Affluence: Theory and Applications to Germany and the US	Construct an index of affluence instead of poverty to study affluence in Germany and the US	Germany, USA
Peichl and Pestel	2013b	Multidimensional Well-Being at the Top: Evidence for Germany	Construct an index of well-being to study well-being in Germany	Germany
Roche	2013	Monitoring Progress in Child Poverty Reduction: Methodological Insights and Illustration to the Case Study of Bangladesh	Measure multidimensional poverty among children in Bangladesh and analyse the patterns of poverty reduction	Bangladesh, South Asia
Santos	2013	Tracking Poverty Reduction in Bhutan: Income Deprivation Alongside Deprivation in Other Sources of Happiness	Measure multidimensional poverty in Bhutan and track its trend between 2003 and 2007	Bhutan, South Asia

Author	Year	Title	Country/Region
Siegel and Waidler	2012	Migration and Multidimensional Poverty in Moldovan Communities	Examine multidimensional poverty in 180 Moldovian communities in 2011	Moldova, Eastern Europe
Siani Tchouametieu	2013	Has Poverty Decreased in Cameroon between 2001 and 2007? An Analysis Based on Multidimensional Poverty Measures	Analyse changes in multidimensional poverty in Cameroon between 2001 and 2007	Cameroon, sub-Saharan Africa
Tonmoy	2014	An Exercise to Evaluate an Anti-Poverty Program with Multiple Outcomes Using Program Evaluation	Evaluate a programme using multidimensional poverty measures with difference-in-difference matching estimators	Bangladesh
Trani and Cannings	2013	Child Poverty in an Emergency and Conflict Context: A Multidimensional Profile and an Identification of the Poorest Children in Western Darfur	Measure child poverty	Darfur, Sudan
Trani, Biggeri, and Mauro	2013	The Multidimensionality of Child Poverty: Evidence from Afghanistan	Measure poverty among children in Afghanistan	Afghanistan
Yu	2013	Multidimensional Poverty in China: Findings Based on the CHNS	Measure multidimensional poverty in China and tracks its progress between 2000 and 2009	China
Wagle	2014	The Counting-Based Measurement of Multidimensional Poverty: The Focus on Economic Resources, Inner Capabilities, and Relational Resources in the United States	Compare a two-step process of the dimensional approach to AF method	USA

BOX 5.7 ALTERNATIVE NOTATIONS FOR THE AF METHOD

Methods	Normalized Weighting Structure $w_j > 0$ and $\sum_{j=1}^{d} w_j = 1$.		Non-normalized Weighting Structure $w_j > 0$ and $\sum_{j=1}^{d} w_j = d$.	
	Method I	**Method II**	**Method III**	**Method IV (AF 2011a)**
Relative values or weights				
The deprivation status	$g_{ij}^0 = \begin{cases} 1 & \text{if deprived} \\ 0 & \text{otherwise} \end{cases}$	$\bar{g}_{ij}^0 = \begin{cases} w_j & \text{if deprived} \\ 0 & \text{otherwise} \end{cases}$	$g_{ij}^0 = \begin{cases} 1 & \text{if deprived} \\ 0 & \text{otherwise} \end{cases}$	$\bar{g}_{ij}^0 = \begin{cases} w_j & \text{if deprived} \\ 0 & \text{otherwise} \end{cases}$
Deprivation score for person i	$c_i = \sum_{j=1}^{d} w_j g_{ij}^0; 0 \leq c_i \leq 1$	$c_i = \sum_{j=1}^{d} \bar{g}_{ij}^0; 0 \leq c_i \leq 1$	$c_i = \sum_{j=1}^{d} w_j g_{ij}^0; 0 \leq c_i \leq d$	$c_i = \sum_{j=1}^{d} \bar{g}_{ij}^0; 0 \leq c_i \leq d$
Poverty cutoff	$0 < k \leq 1$	$0 < k \leq 1$	$0 < k \leq d$	$0 < k \leq d$
Censored deprivation score entry for person i	$0 \leq c_i(k) \leq 1$	$0 \leq c_i(k) \leq 1$	$0 \leq c_i(k) \leq d$	$0 \leq c_i(k) \leq d$
Headcount ratio	$H = q/n,$	$H = q/n,$	$H = q/n,$	$H = q/n,$
Intensity	$A = \frac{1}{q} \sum_{i=1}^{n} c_i(k)$	$A = \frac{1}{q} \sum_{i=1}^{n} c_i(k)$	$A = \frac{1}{q} \sum_{i=1}^{n} c_i(k)/d$	$A = \frac{1}{q} \sum_{i=1}^{n} \mu(\bar{G}_{i\cdot}^0(k))$
M_0 as the product of incidence and intensity	$M_0 = H \times A$	$M_0 = H \times A$	$M_0 = H \times A$	$M_0 = H \times A$
M_0 in terms of the censored deprivation matrix	$M_0 = \sum_{i=1}^{n} \sum_{j=1}^{d} w_j g_{ij}^0(k)$	$M_0 = \mu(\bar{g}^0(k)) \times d = \frac{1}{n} \sum_{i=1}^{n} \sum_{j=1}^{d} \bar{g}_{ij}^0(k)$	$M_0 = \frac{1}{nd} \sum_{i=1}^{n} \sum_{j=1}^{d} w_j g_{ij}^0(k)$	$M_0 = \mu(\bar{g}^0(k)) = \frac{1}{nd} \sum_{i=1}^{n} \sum_{j=1}^{d} \bar{g}_{ij}^0(k)$
M_0 in terms of censored deprivation scores	$M_0 = \frac{1}{n} \sum_{i=1}^{n} c_i(k)$	$M_0 = \frac{1}{n} \sum_{i=1}^{n} c_i(k)$	$M_0 = \frac{1}{n} \sum_{i=1}^{n} \frac{c_i(k)}{d}$	$M_0 = \frac{1}{n} \sum_{i=1}^{n} \frac{c_i(k)}{d}$
M_0 as the mean of each person's deprivation score	$M_0 = \frac{1}{n} \sum_{i=1}^{n} \left[\sum_{j=1}^{d} w_j g_{ij}^0(k) \right]$	$M_0 = \frac{1}{n} \sum_{i=1}^{n} \sum_{j=1}^{d} \bar{g}_{ij}^0(k)$	$M_0 = \frac{1}{n} \sum_{i=1}^{n} \left[\frac{1}{d} \sum_{j=1}^{d} w_j g_{ij}^0(k) \right]$	$M_0 = \frac{1}{n} \sum_{i=1}^{n} \mu(\bar{G}_{i\cdot}^0(k))$

BOX 5.7 (cont.)

Methods	Normalized Weighting Structure		Non-normalized Weighting Structure	
Relative values or weights	$w_j > 0$ and $\sum_{j=1}^{d} w_j = 1$.		$w_j > 0$ and $\sum_{j=1}^{d} w_j = d$.	
	Method I	**Method II**	**Method III**	**Method IV (AF 2011a)**
Censored Headcount Ratio of dimension j	$h_j(k) = \mu(G_j^0(k))$	$h_j(k) = \frac{\mu(G_j^0(k))}{w_j}$	$h_j(k) = \mu(G_j^0(k))$	$h_j(k) = \frac{\mu(G_j^0(k))}{w_j}$
M_0 as the weighted sum of censored headcount ratios	$M_0 = \sum_{j=1}^{d} w_j h_j(k) = \sum_{j=1}^{d} w_j \mu(G_j^0(k))$	$M_0 = \sum_{j=1}^{d} \frac{w_j}{d} h_j(k) = \sum_{j=1}^{d} \mu(G_j^0(k))$	$M_0 = \sum_{j=1}^{d} \frac{w_j}{d} h_j(k) = \sum_{j=1}^{d} \frac{w_j}{d} \mu(G_j^0(k))$	$M_0 = \sum_{j=1}^{d} \frac{w_j}{d} h_j(k) = \frac{1}{d} \sum_{j=1}^{d} \mu(G_j^0(k))$
Percentage contribution of dimension j to M_0	$w_j \times \frac{\mu(G_j^0(k))}{M_0}$	$\frac{\mu(G_j^0(k))}{M_0}$	$\frac{w_j}{d} \times \frac{\mu(G_j^0(k))}{M_0}$	$\frac{\mu(G_j^0(k))}{d \times M_0}$

Note: Method I is the one mainly used throughout this chapter. Method IV is described in Box 5.3 and Box 5.6 and follows the notation used in Alkire and Foster (2011a). Method II is a variant of Method I, equivalent to Method IV in that weights are incorporated into the entries of the matrix, creating the weighted deprivation matrix, and thus do not explicitly appear in formulas. Method III is a minor variant of Method IV, equivalent to Method I in the sense that weights are kept outside the deprivation matrix and thus explicitly appear in formulas.

Appendix

Adjusted Headcount Ratio (M_0)—Interpretation
The proportion of deprivations that poor people in a society experience, as a share of the deprivations that would be experienced if all persons were poor and deprived in all dimensions of poverty. It is the product of two intuitive partial indices, the Incidence and Intensity of Poverty ($H \times A$).

Alkire–Foster methodology
The AF methodology uses dual cutoffs to identify who is poor according to the weighted sum of 'joint' deprivations a person experiences, and measures poverty using an extension of the FGT measures. AF measures are consistent with subindices that show the incidence and intensity and dimensional composition of poverty and, for cardinal variables, the depth and severity of deprivations in each dimension. The AF methodology can be used with different indicators, weights, and cutoffs to create measures for different societies and situations.

Censored headcount ratio
The proportion of people who are multidimensionally poor *and* deprived in a given indicator.

Censoring
This is the process of removing from consideration deprivations (achievements) belonging to people who do not reach the poverty (deprivation) cutoff and focusing on those who are multidimensionally poor (deprived).

Decomposition
The process of breaking down the poverty measures to show the poverty of different groups. Groups might include countries, regions, ethnic groups, urban versus rural location, gender, age, or occupational categories, or other groups.

Deprivation cutoffs (z_j)
The achievement levels for a given dimension below which a person is considered to be deprived in a dimension or indicator.

Deprived
A person is deprived if their achievement is strictly less than the deprivation cutoff in any dimension.

Functionings
Functionings are 'the various things a person may value doing or being' (Sen 1999: 75). In other words, functionings are valuable activities and states that make up people's

well-being—such as being healthy and well nourished, being safe, being educated, having a good job, and being able to visit loved ones. They are related to resources and income but describe what a person is able to do or be with these, given their particular ability to convert those resources into functionings.

Incidence (H)

The proportion of people (within a given population) who experience multidimensional poverty. This is also called the 'multidimensional headcount ratio' or simply the 'headcount ratio'. Sometimes it is called the 'rate' or 'incidence' of poverty. It is the number of poor people q over the total population n.

Intensity (A)

The average proportion of deprivations experienced by poor people (within a given population) or the average deprivation score among the poor. The intensity is the sum of the deprivation scores, divided by the number of poor people.

Percentage contribution of each indicator

The extent to which each weighted indicator contributes to overall poverty.

Poor

A person is identified as poor if their deprivation score (the sum of their weighted deprivations) is at least as high as the poverty cutoff.

Poverty cutoff (k)

This is the cutoff or cross-dimensional threshold used to identify the multidimensionally poor. It reflects the proportion of weighted dimensions a person must be deprived in to be considered poor. Because having more deprivations (a higher deprivation score) signifies worse poverty, the deprivation score of all poor people meets or exceeds the poverty cutoff.

Uncensored or raw headcount ratios

The deprivation rates in each indicator, which include all people who are deprived, regardless of whether they are multidimensionally poor or not.

6 Normative Choices in Measurement Design

The modern field of inequality measurement grew out of the intelligent application of quantitative methods to imperfect data in the hope of illuminating important social issues. The important social issues remain, and it is interesting to see the ways in which modern analytical techniques can throw some light on what it is possible to say about them.

(Cowell 2000: 133)

Human beings are diverse in many and important ways: they vary in age, gender, ethnicity, nationality, location, religion, relationships, abilities, personalities, occupations, leisure activities, interests, and values. Poverty measures seek to identify legitimate, accurate, and policy-relevant comparisons across people, whilst fully respecting their basal diversity. Further, they seek to do so using data that are affected by several kinds of errors and limitations. This is no straightforward task.

After a measurement methodology has been chosen, the design of poverty measures—whether unidimensional or multidimensional—also requires a series of choices. We turn to these now. The choices relate to the space of the measure, its purpose, unit of identification and analysis, dimensions, indicators, deprivation cutoffs, weights, and poverty line. Of these, 'purpose' is particularly influential in shaping the measure. As Ravallion states succinctly, 'One wants the method of measurement to be consistent with the purpose of measurement' (1998: 1). This chapter describes each of these normative choices in the context of multidimensional poverty measurement design and outlines alternative ways that these choices might be understood, made, and justified. Many normative theories or approaches might be used to inform measurement design, including human needs, objective lists, subjective well-being, human rights, and preference-based approaches, as well as many other less formally defined approaches.[1] Whichever are used, the normative contribution is not simply philosophical; it has a practical aim: to motivate poverty reduction.

Taken together, normative choices link the data and measurement design back to poor people's lives and values and forward to the policies that, informed by poverty analysis, will seek to improve these. For example, dimensions which contribute disproportionately

---

[1] See the following and the references therein: Chang (1997), Finnis (1997), Griffin (1986, 1996), Raz (1986), Brighouse and Robeyns (2010), Rawls (1971, 1993, 1999b), Roemer (1996), Dworkin (1986, 2000), Galtung (1994), Nussbaum (2000), Reader (2006), Stewart (1985), Streeten et al. (1981), Wiggins (1998), Cohen (1989), Adler (2011), Fleurbaey and Maniquet (2011), Fleurbaey and Blanchet (2013), Parfit (1984), Wolff and De-Shalit (2007), and Deneulin (2014).

to poverty might become policy 'priorities'. Do these reflect poor people's values? Regions showing high poverty levels may be targeted geographically. Do these accord with poor communities', taxpayers', and experts' understandings of who is poor? Programmes such as cash transfers may target households. Do the poorest households benefit? The headlines (and political leaders) celebrate when multidimensional poverty falls. Is this situation also applauded by those they seem to have assisted? It goes without saying that if the measure of poverty is unhinged from people's voices and values, poverty policies are unlikely to hit the mark.

The normative choices inherent in monetary and multidimensional poverty design appear to cause consternation, particularly if measurement conventions have not yet been established.[2] In a section of *The Idea of Justice* named 'The fear of non-commensurability', Sen describes 'non-commensurability' as 'a much-used philosophical concept that seems to arouse anxiety and panic' (2009: 240). Yet setting priorities is no weakness. As Sen points out, 'the need for selection and discrimination is neither an embarrassment, nor a unique difficulty, for the conceptualization of functionings and capabilities' (1992: 46 and 44).

Building on Sen in their extremely relevant work *Disadvantage*, Wolff and De-Shalit elaborate additional conceptual insights that are relevant to addressing the 'indexing problem' in measurement. Defining poverty as clustered disadvantage, their policy goal is 'a society in which disadvantages do not cluster, a society where there is no clear answer to the question of who is the worst off. To achieve this, governments need to give special attention to the way patterns of disadvantage form and persist, and to take steps to break up such clusters' (2007: 10). They argue that because disadvantages are interconnected and must be solved by policies that break up such clusters, and also because key policy decisions such as budget allocation require 'some sort of overall assessment of disadvantage', then 'an overall index of disadvantage seems inescapable' (95, 89). They then proceed to address how such an index could be legitimately constructed, and we will return to their work in following sections.

Given that multidimensional poverty measurement remains a relatively new field of endeavour, a clear overview of the judgements and comparisons that normative choices draw upon, using the capability approach as a springboard, may prove useful.[3] To motivate the discussion we begin by sharing a birds-eye view of how the Adjusted

---

[2] Rawls (1971: 93) rather unfortunately referred to 'weighting primary goods for the least advantaged, for those with the least authority and least income' as the 'index problem'—a problem which critics allege that Rawlsians failed to 'solve'. The title 'index problem' wrongly implied that value judgements are a 'problem' rather than an inherent component of measurement design.

[3] A clear and substantive part of Sen's writing, which is not here reflected, is his criticism of prices as an alternative. For example, he writes, 'While market prices certainly do exist for commodities, and do not for human functionings, the evaluative significance of the market prices has to be established. It is not obvious how, in making an evaluative judgement about progress, valuational decisions are to be avoided by simply "reading off" the market prices and the metric of exchange value. For one thing, the problems of externalities, missing markets, and other concerns will suggest that market prices be "adjusted", and we have to decide whether such adjustments should be made, and if so, how this should be done' (1997: 30).

Headcount Ratio (M_0) can—if a set of assumptions about the normative choices are fulfilled—reflect capability poverty. [4,5]

6.1 The Adjusted Headcount Ratio: A Measure of Capability Poverty?

Suppose that there are a set of dimensions, each of which represent functionings or capabilities that a person might or might not have—things like being well nourished, being able to read and write, being able to drink clean water, and not being the victim of violence. The deprivation profile for each person shows which functionings they have attained and in which they are deprived, and weights are applied to these dimensions that reflect the relative value of each among the set of dimensions. Suppose that there is considerable agreement regarding the value of achieving the deprivation cutoff level of these functionings, such that most people would achieve at least that level if they could. Furthermore, suppose that we can anticipate what percentage of people would refrain from such achievements in certain functionings—those who might be fasting to the point of malnutrition at any given time, for example. It is convenient but not necessary to assume that these indicators are equally weighted.[6] And let us assume that in identifying who is poor, the calibration of poverty cutoff k reflects these predictions of voluntary abstinence, as well as anticipated data inaccuracies, while recognizing that a sufficient battery of deprivations probably signifies poverty. Setting the cutoff in this way permits a degree of freedom for people to opt out if they so choose while seeking, insofar as is possible, to identify as poor people for whom the deprivations are unchosen. Applying such a poverty cutoff reduces errors in identification—for example, by permitting people who would voluntarily abstain not to be identified as poor and avoiding identifying people as poor because of data inaccuracies. Among the poor, the more deprivations they experience, the poorer they are. Having identified who is poor, we construct the Adjusted Headcount Ratio (M_0).

How might such an M_0 reflect capability poverty? The key insight is this: in such a measure, a higher value of M_0 represents more unfreedom, and a lower value, less. Given that the set of indicators will be unlikely to represent *everything* that constitutes poverty, if each element *is* widely valued, and if people who are poor and are deprived in a dimension

---

[4] Section 6.1 and Box 6.1 draw upon Alkire and Foster (2007).

[5] We are especially conscious in this chapter of being unable to cite or engage all the many scholars who have creative insights on measures of well-being and poverty that draw on the capability approach. Their work deserves its own in-depth constructive survey, building on other such surveys that already exist, including Chiappero-Martinetti and Roche (2009), Clark (2008), and Robeyns (2006), as well as references in recent applied work such as Arndt and Volkert (2011) and Van Ootegem and Verhofstadt (2012). We would refer interested readers to the Human Development and Capability Association (HDCA) and the bibliographies on capabilities published annually in the *Journal of Human Development and Capabilities*.

[6] This assumption can be relaxed to obtain more general results if required.

would value being non-deprived in it, then we anticipate that deprivations among the poor could be interpreted as showing that poor people do not have the capability to achieve the associated functionings. Thus M_0 would be a (partial) measure of unfreedom, or capability poverty.

As noted above, such an interpretation of M_0 relies on assumptions regarding the parameters:

(a) indicators measure or proxy functionings or capabilities;
(b) people generally value attaining the deprivation cutoff level of each indicator;
(c) the weights reflect a defensible set or range of relative values on the deprivations;
(d) the cross-dimensional poverty cutoff reflects 'who is capability poor'.

Such an interpretation implicitly also relies upon assumptions about data quality and accuracy, and empirical techniques (that measures are implemented accurately). It has quite a restricted and uniform approach to values: for example, using a non-union poverty cutoff to permit 'some' abstinence from functionings.[7] But it might at least signal an avenue worth pondering.

In fact, as Box 6.1 elaborates more formally, under these conditions, our identification strategy and Adjusted Headcount Ratio can be related to Pattanaik and Xu's signature work (1990), except that we now focus on unfreedoms rather than on freedoms. In their lucid and illuminating paper, Pattanaik and Xu elaborate on Sen's claim that freedom has intrinsic value, thus that the extent of freedom in an opportunity set matters—independently of its relationship to preferences and utility. In developing this claim axiomatically they propose that the ranking of two opportunity sets in terms of freedom should depend only on the number of options present in each set.[8]

Sen, responding to Pattanaik and Xu (1990), observed that not every additional option (singleton) would contribute to an expansion of freedom—only those options that a person values and has reason to value. 'The evaluation of the freedom I enjoy from a certain menu must depend to a crucial extent on how I value the elements included in that menu'. For example, 'if a set is enlarged by including an alternative which no one would choose in relevant circumstances (e.g., being beheaded at dawn), the *addition* of that alternative may not necessarily be seen as a strict enhancement of freedom ...'

---

[7] Of course, if direct information were available on coercion, this might also be either combined with functionings or as a separate indicator of agency deprivation. Sen writes, 'Offering the opportunity to all to lead a minimally decent life need not be combined with an insistence that everyone makes use of all the opportunities that the state offers; for instance, making everyone entitled to an adequate amount of food does not have to be combined with a state ban on fasting' (2009: 288). In the event that one had information on a ban on fasting that affected certain locations (or similar procedural unfreedoms), this might be used as an indicator alongside nutritional outcomes—with weights on each appropriately considered.

[8] Pattanaik and Xu subsequently extended their approach to reflect the quality of the option. A significant literature has further explored this theme, including Pattanaik and Xu (1990, 1998, 2000), Bavetta and Seta (2001), Fleurbaey (2002), Gekker (2001), Gravel (1994, 1998), and Klemisch-Ahlert (1993).

(Sen 1991: 21 and 25). Nor would a deprivation in that negatively valued alternative be seen as impoverishing.

Our assumptions regarding the choice of parameters avoid Sen's critique if each dimension of poverty reflects something that people value and have reason to value. Further, we follow Anand and Sen (1997), who argued that it may be easier to obtain agreement on the value of a small set of unfreedoms than an ample set of freedoms.[9] As Sen points out, 'in the context of some types of welfare analysis, e.g. in dealing with extreme poverty in developing economies, we may be able to go a fairly long distance in terms of a relatively small number of centrally important functionings (and corresponding basic capabilities, e.g. the ability to be well nourished and well sheltered, the capability of escaping preventable morbidity and premature mortality, and so forth)' (1992: 44–5; cf. 1985).

Note that this capability interpretation of M_0 does not directly represent 'unchosen' sets of capabilities in a counterfactual sense (Foster 2010). Nor does it necessarily incorporate agency (Alkire 2007). Rather, in a manner parallel to Pattanaik and Xu, it *interprets* the deprivations in at least a minimum set of widely valued, achieved functionings as unfreedom, or capability poverty (Box 6.1).

Naturally, capability poverty measures that have different specifications and reflect different purposes could be constructed for the same society. There might be a child poverty measure or a capability poverty measure reflecting the values of a specific cultural group such as nomadic populations, or there might be a national capability poverty measure that reflects important deprivations about which there is widespread agreement across social groups. Thus the decision to measure capability poverty does not generate one unique measure; decisions as to the scope and purpose of the measure and the data sources guide measurement design even if the choice of space has been settled.

We also hasten to point out that many legitimate and tremendously useful measures could be constructed using M_0 but located in a different space or in a mixture of spaces. These would not be measures of capability poverty but could be powerful tools for reducing capability poverty. For example, the dimensions might be resources such as service delivery (hopefully identifying whether marginalized groups have real access and clarifying the quality of the services). The point is that our measurement framework can be used for different purposes including those unrelated to capabilities. So it is vitally important (and not terribly difficult) to articulate and explain the purpose of each application and to justify the choices and calibration of parameters.

---

[9] Sen writes, 'it can be argued that if we concentrate on certain basic general functionings and the corresponding capabilities, there may be much more agreement on their importance than there would be if we concentrated on particular commodity bundles and particular ways of achieving these functionings. For example, there is likely to be more intercultural—and also interpersonal—agreement on the importance of having the capability to avoid acute hunger or severe undernourishment than on the significance of having an adequate supply of particular food items (e.g. some specific types of meat or fish or grains or pulses) to serve those functionings' (1992: 108–9). Such agreements may be incompletely theorized (Alkire 2002b; Ruger 2007; Sunstein 1996).

BOX 6.1 UNFREEDOMS AND M_0

Let $\mathcal{M}$ be a poverty methodology satisfying decomposability, weak monotonicity, non-triviality, and ordinality. The first three properties are satisfied by all members of **methodology** $\mathcal{M}$; however, $\mathcal{M}_0 = (\rho_k, M_0)$ is the only adjusted Foster–Greer–Thorbecke (FGT) measure that satisfies ordinality, and it is this property that ensures that its poverty levels and comparisons are meaningful when the dimensional variables are ordinal.

By decomposability, the structure of $\mathcal{M}$ depends entirely on the way that $\mathcal{M}$ measures poverty over singleton subgroups; and by dichotomization, this individual poverty measure can be expressed as a function $p(v)$ of the individual's **deprivation vector** v (which is any row g_i. of deprivation matrix g^0). In the case of (ρ_k, M_0), we have $p(v) = \mu(v(k))$, where $v(k)$ is the censored distribution defined as $v(k) = v$ if $\sum_{j=1}^{d} v_j \geq k$ and $v(k) = 0$ if $\sum_{j=1}^{d} v_j < k$. We will now explore the possible forms that p can take for dichotomized measures. Note that while the definition of M_0 is based in part on the dimensional cutoff k, we have not specified the identification method employed by the general index M. Hence a second question of interest is what forms of identification might be consistent with various properties satisfied by M_0.

The individual poverty function p for M_0 has two additional properties of interest. First, it satisfies *anonymity* or the requirement that $p(v) = p(v\Pi)$, where Π is any $d \times d$ permutation matrix. This property implies that all dimensions are treated symmetrically by the poverty measure. Second, it satisfies *semi-independence*, which states that if $v_j = v'_j = 1$, and $p(v) \geq p(v')$, then $p(v - e_j) \geq p(v' - e_j)$.[10] Under this assumption, removing the same dimensional deprivation from two deprivation vectors should preserve the (weak) ordering of the two. We have the following result:

> Let p be the individual poverty function associated with a dichotomized poverty measure. p satisfies anonymity and semi-independence if and only if there exists some $k = 1, \ldots, d$ such that for any deprivation vectors v and v' we have: $p(v') \geq p(v)$ if and only if $\mu(v'(k)) \geq \mu(v(k))$.

In other words, p ranks individual deprivation vectors in precisely the same way that (ρ_k, M_0) does for some $k = 1, \ldots, d$. This result is especially powerful since it simultaneously determines both the individual poverty index (p) associated with the Adjusted Headcount Ratio (M_0) and the identification method (based on a dimensional cutoff k) consistent with the assumed properties. To establish the result we extend the generalization of Pattanaik and Xu given in Foster (2010). In particular, if full *independence* were required, so that the conditional in semi-independence were converted to full equivalence, then a direct analogue of the Pattanaik and Xu result would obtain, namely, $p(v') \geq p(v)$ if and only if $\mu(v') \geq \mu(v)$. In this specification, p would make comparisons of individual poverty the same way that the union-identified M_0 does—by counting all deprivations.

While our result uniquely identifies the individual poverty ranking, it leaves open a multitude of possibilities for the overall index P—one for each specific functional form taken by p. For example, the individual poverty function $p(v) = \left[\mu(v(k))\right]^2$, when averaged across the entire population to obtain P, would place greater emphasis on persons with many deprivations. It would be interesting to explore alternative forms for p and the properties of the associated index P. Note that because of dichotomization, each of these measures would provide a way of evaluating multidimensional poverty when the underlying variables are ordinal.

Given the arguments in Foster (2010), it is straightforward to establish the above result. In particular, let $\mathcal{C} = [v \in \mathbb{R}^d : v_j = 0 \text{ or } v_j = 1]$ for all j be the set of all individual deprivation vectors, and let $p : \mathcal{C} \to \mathbb{R}$ be an individual poverty function associated with a standard dichotomized poverty measure such that p satisfies

---

[10] The symbol e_j refers to the jth usual d-dimensional basis vector whose j^{th} entry is equal to 1 and the rest of the elements are equal to 0. Note that semi-independence is a weakening of the property of 'independence' found in Pattanaik and Xu (1990).

BOX 6.1 *(cont.)*

anonymity and semi-independence. By anonymity, all vectors $v, v' \in \mathcal{C}$ with $\sum_{j=1}^{d} v_j = \sum_{j=1}^{d} v'_j$ must satisfy $p(v) = p(v')$. In other words, the value of $p(v)$ depends entirely on the number of deprivations in v. Weak monotonicity implies that $p(v) \leq p(v')$ for $\sum_{j=1}^{d} v_j \leq \sum_{j=1}^{d} v'_j$, and so the value of $p(v)$ is weakly increasing in the number of deprivations in v. By non-triviality and decomposability, it follows that $p(v) > p(0)$ for $\sum_{j=1}^{d} v_j = d$.[11] Let k be the lowest deprivation count for which $p(v)$ is strictly above $p(0)$; in other words, $p(v) = p(0)$ for $\sum_{j=1}^{d} v_j < k$, and $p(v) > p(0)$ for $\sum_{j=1}^{d} v_j \geq k$. Semi-independence ensures that p must be increasing in the deprivation count above k. For suppose that $p(v) = p(v')$ for $v, v' \in \mathcal{C}$ with $k \leq \sum_{j=1}^{d} v_j < \sum_{j=1}^{d} v'_j$. Then by repeated application of anonymity and semi-independence, we would have $p(v) = p(v')$ for some $v, v' \in \mathcal{C}$ with $\sum_{j=1}^{d} v_j \leq k < \sum_{j=1}^{d} v'_j$, a contradiction. It follows, then, that $F(v)$ is constant in $\sum_{j=1}^{d} v_j$ for $\sum_{j=1}^{d} v_j < k$ and increasing in $\sum_{j=1}^{d} v_j$ for $k \leq \sum_{j=1}^{d} v_j$. Clearly, this is precisely the pattern exhibited by the function $\mu(v(k))$.

This section set out the circumstances in which M_0 may measure capability poverty. The assumptions regarding values and data that must be fulfilled to do so were transparently stated. Under this interpretation, M_0 embodies a rather rudimentary kind of freedom; there could be many interesting extensions—for example, incorporating agency and process freedoms. Also, M_0 measures that do not reflect capability poverty will fulfil some purposes splendidly. Still, if the assumptions articulated here are fulfilled, we can indeed offer M_0 as a measure of capability poverty. For what is needed in this context is not a quixotic search for the perfect measure but rather methodologies that may be *sufficient* to advance critical ethical objectives. Most empirical outworkings of the capability approach have used drastic simplifications, and these can often be cheered as true advances, even while their limitations are borne in mind. 'In all these exercises, clarity of theory has to be combined with the practical need to make do with whatever information we can feasibly obtain for our actual empirical analyses. The Scylla of empirical overambitiousness threatens us as much as the Charybdis of misdirected theory' (Sen 1985: 49). In this sense, our methodology may be a step forward in operationalizing the measurement of capabilities.

6.2 **Normative Choices**

It may be asked whether choices underlying measurement design are normative and, if so, in what sense? If data are constrained and exactly one educational variable exists, in what sense is its selection normative? Similarly, if an indicator is redundant or invalid according to statistical assessments, how is its deselection normative? And if nutritional experts judge that an indicator of stunting is more accurate than wasting, in what way is a choice in its favour normative?

Normative considerations operate at different levels. Releasing a measure rather than not doing so may reflect a high-level normative judgement that releasing the measure

---

[11] Symbol 0 refers to a d-dimensional vector of zeros.

is more likely to improve welfare than not releasing it.[12] This assessment may be made after consideration of what Sen (2009) terms a 'comprehensive' description of the situation. At a lower level, in each part of measurement design, value judgements are used to justify particular choices—like dimensions, weights, and poverty cutoffs. The value judgements may pertain to the content directly, or they may address the methodologies or processes by which to justify design choices, as later sections will illustrate.

At this higher meta-level, the comprehensive description and its normative assessment will draw upon different kinds of analyses—statistical, axiomatic, deliberative, practical, and policy-oriented, for example—to authorize the use of measures that fulfil a set of plural purposes reasonably well.

These higher-level reasoned judgements that draw on a comprehensive description of the options often include the following types of assessments:

Expert (including qualitative) assessments of indicator accuracy—for example, in showing the level and changes of a key functioning like nutrition (Svedberg 2000) or the quality and legitimacy of a participatory process.

Empirical assessments, which could include analyses of measurement error, data quality, redundancy, robustness, statistical validity and reliability, or triangulation with other analyses and data sources.

Deliberative insights on people's values from participatory discussions, social movements, consultations, and from documentation of similar recent processes.

Theoretical assessments, which could consider properties and principles, sets of dimensions, standards or conventions on indicators, or legal and policy frameworks.

Practical constraints such as constraints of data, time, human resources, authority, political will, and political feasibility given the processes and authorities involved.

Policy relevance—for example, how the timing and content of the measure could dovetail with resource allocation decisions or how a measure might support and monitor a set of planned interventions as set out in a national plan or a current campaign.

This section introduces this meta-coordination role of normative reasoning; later sections describe how particular kinds of assessment mentioned already may inform particular design choices.

The higher normative function is inextricably linked to the purpose(s) of the measure, which are often multiple and normally motivate policy and public action. As Foster and

---

[12] It must be acknowledged that the possibility (and desirability) that a poverty measure would reflect reasoned normative assessments across plural criteria does not mean that it will do so. Both income and multidimensional poverty measures can be manipulated or carelessly implemented, and as a result, be inaccurate. No measure is strategy proof. An advantage of the direct M_0 measure is that its construction is easy to communicate, and uses explicit weights and cutoffs, so an informed public and technical advisors can more readily identify and criticize serious shortcomings.

Sen put it, 'The general conclusion that seems irresistible is that the choice of a poverty measure must, to a great extent, depend on the nature of the problem at hand' (1997: 187).

A relevant example is Mexico's move towards a multidimensional poverty measure. In his book *Numbers that Move the World,* Miguel Székely points out that:

Just like there are ideas that move the world, so too there are numbers and statistics that move the world. A number can awaken consciences; it can mobilize the reluctant, it can ignite action, it can generate debate; it can even, in the best of circumstances, lay to rest a pressing problem (2005: 13).[13]

In describing Mexico's steps towards new options of poverty measurement, Székely describes how a committee was formed whose mandate was 'to propose to the Secretary of Social Development a methodology that could be officially adopted as an instrument of the Mexican government to measure the magnitude of poverty, its intensity, and its characteristics' (Székely 2005: 17). In 2001, the committee invited three international experts, including James Foster who together with John Iceland and Robert Michael, identified the following *desiderata* that the proposed measurement methodology should fulfil—criteria that the committee adopted in its subsequent work:

- It must be understandable and easy to describe.
- It must reflect 'common-sense' notions of poverty.
- It must fit the purpose for which it is being developed.
- It must be technically solid.
- It must be operationally viable—e.g. in terms of data requirements.
- It must be easily replicable (Székely 2005: 10 and 19).[14]

As these criteria suggest, there are usually plural *desiderata* for a measure, and these must be taken into account within a coordinating normative framework.[15] Consider the first purpose: a measure should be simple and easy to communicate. Earlier we observed that the widely used headcount ratio of income poverty lacks some very desirable properties. Indeed, because the headcount ratio 'ignores the "depth" as well as the "distribution"

---

[13] Author's translation.

[14] Many related sets of principles have been proposed, some of which include voice or processes. For example, there is the Australian National Development Index (ANDI), which is described as: 'Informed by experts but defined by Australians'. It has the following principles: inclusive (everybody has a right to a say), independent (an apolitical index), accessible (easily understood information about well-being), trustworthy (best scientific practices in measurement and analysis), and balance (promotes broad and integrated definitions of well-being).

[15] Naturally each of these may have subcomponents. For example, the need to be 'technically solid' may entail combining several component principles. 'The possibility of combining is particularly important when some of the principles have a very narrow domain but are very persuasive over these domains. They may rank rather low in the context of ordering a much wider domain included in X, because of being silent on a great many comparisons. But since they are likely to be compatible with other principles with a narrow scope dealing with other types of comparisons, combining them may be both feasible as well as effective in generating highly valued rankings of X' (Sen 1980: 126–7).

of poverty', Foster and Sen found it 'remarkable that most empirical studies of poverty tend, still, to stop at the head-count ratio' (1997: 168 and 169). On the other hand, when formulated as a criterion, it becomes evident that this characteristic—that a measure not only be axiomatically sound and empirically solid, but also easy to understand—is actually essential if the measure is to inform and engage public debate and policy.

Returning to the income poverty headcount ratio, it seems that the desirability of certain properties is balanced against ease of communication. For measures whose purpose is to incite public action, the choice to favour communication is comprehensible. Indeed, the development of the Human Development Index, as Sen describes it, was largely driven by this need of communicability. Sen recounts how Mahbub ul Haq, the director of the then newly created Human Development Report Office of the United Nations Development Programme, called for an index 'of the same level of vulgarity as the GNP—just one number—but a measure that is not as blind to social aspects of human lives as the GNP is' (Sen 1999b). Properties vs communicability is not the only trade-off: at times statistical accuracy and non-sampling measurement error may need to be balanced with 'common sense', or an ideal measure tempered by the need to use existing data.

The 'higher' or coordinating normative reasoning creates a 'comprehensive' description of possible measures according to the criteria, rules out options that are strictly worse than others, and identifies their relative strengths and challenges.[16] Even if, as is likely, the final parameters used for a multidimensional poverty measure are but one subset of multiple plausible measures, each of which is defensible and cannot be further ranked, the criteria will still have worked to eliminate measures that may have been less comprehensible and violated more key properties—or had higher measurement error, lower robustness, and less policy salience than the ones that remain. They will also have identified the strengths and challenges of each candidate, and so the selection among them is essentially also a selection of which criteria to prioritize—a choice that will have been simplified by a clear analysis. For example, a society may wish to prioritize a measure that has legitimacy because it transparently draws on public consultations, which are important because recent history had discredited poverty statistics (so prioritizing criteria 2), or a measure that will incentivize policies because it is closely tied to a popular national plan (criteria 3), and so on.

In sum, multidimensional poverty measurement can seem rather bewildering at first because its justification may draw on axiomatic, statistical, ethical, data-related, deliberative/participatory, policy-oriented, political, and historical features. But in practice, poverty measurement is considerably more concrete (Anand and Sen 1997; Alkire 2002a). The available resources and actual constraints—from timing to data to funding to political demand—for a given exercise often provide considerable structure and limit the degrees of freedom considerably. Thus, although normative engagement is required, 'there is no general impossibility here of making reasoned choices over combinations of diverse objects' (Sen 2009: 241).

---

[16] This use of plural principles to identify that set of options 'than which nothing is better' is described in Sen (1985, 1997b, 2009) and Alkire (2002a: ch. 3.4).

6.3 **Elements of Measurement Design**

The Alkire–Foster (AF) methodology is a general framework for measuring multidimensional poverty—an open-source technology that can be freely altered by the user to best match the measure's context and evaluative purpose. As with most measurement exercises, it will be the designers who will have to make and defend the specific decisions underlying the implementation, limited and guided by the purpose of the exercise and other concrete constraints.

Traditional unidimensional measures require a set of parallel decisions with normative content.[17] For example, should the variable be expenditure or income? What indicators should comprise the consumption aggregate? How should 'missing' prices be set? What should the poverty line(s) be? If it reflects a food basket, how many calories should it total, and should it exclude cheap unhealthy foods? Choices to create comparability can likewise be important for final results, such as the construction of Purchasing Power Parity values or urban–rural adjustments, or adjustments for inflation. Robustness standards are crucial for all poverty measures, as they ensure that the results obtained are not unduly dependent upon the calibration choices (whether these are normatively based or not).[18]

The flexibility in AF measurement design means that measures at the country or subnational level can be designed to embody reasoned priorities or norms of what it means to be poor. For example, if dimensions, weights, and cutoffs are specified in a legal document such as the Constitution, the identification function might be developed using an axiomatic approach, as was done in Mexico.[19] Qualitative and participatory work can significantly enrich and substantively complement other analyses.[20] The weights can also be developed by a range of processes: expert opinion or coherence with a consensus document such as a national plan, focus groups, survey data, or human rights. And the poverty cutoff, which is analogous to poverty lines in unidimensional space, could be chosen so as to reflect poor people's assessments of who is poor, as well as wider social assessments.

This section introduces the purpose of a poverty measure and the normative choices that inhere in measurement design.[21] We cover eight design elements. The first five

---

[17] The literature is vast. For perceptive overviews of different aspects, see Foster, Seth, et al. (2013), Haughton and Khandker (2009), Chen and Ravallion (2010), Jenkins and Micklewright (2007), Grusky and Kanbur (2006), Hentschel and Lanjouw (2000), Klugman (2002), Banerjee and Duflo (2011), UNDESA (2010), World Bank (2000), Deaton (1992, 1997), Deaton and Grosh (2000), Ravallion (1992, 1996, 1998), and Anand (1983).

[18] See Chapter 8. For example, variable poverty line robustness methods such as those found in Foster and Shorrocks (1988b) helped make the fundamentally arbitrary $1.25-a-day poverty line more palatable.

[19] See Alkire and Foster (2009).

[20] Shaffer (2013) provides an excellent review of issues pertinent to multidimensional poverty measurement design in this extensive literature; cf. Addison, Hulme, and Kanbur (2009). Leavy and Howard et al. (2013) is an examplary synthesis of participatory studies; cf. Narayan et al. (2000); Narayan and Petesch (2007).

[21] Many examples were already covered in Chapter 3 and Chapter 4. Additional relevant assessments discuss these issues for other measurement approaches, like Michalos et al. (2011), Japan Commission on Measuring Well-Being (2011), Gunewardena (2004), and Wagle (2008: ch. 3).

serve to structure a poverty measure; the last three calibrate key parameters (cutoffs and weights).

1. **Purpose(s) of the measure:** The purpose(s) of a measure may include its policy applications, the reference population, dimensions, and time horizon.
2. **The choice of space:** The choice of space determines whether poverty is measured in the space of resources, inputs and access to services, outputs, or functionings and capabilities.
3. **The unit(s) of identification and analysis:** These are unit(s) for which the AF method reflects the joint distribution of disadvantages, identifies who is poor, and analyses poverty.
4. **Dimensions:** Dimensions are conceptual categories into which indicators may be arranged (and possibly weighted) for intuition and ease of communication.
5. **Indicators:** Indicators are the building blocks of a measure; they bring into view relevant facets of poverty and constitute the columns of the achievement and deprivation matrices.
6. **Deprivation cutoffs:** The deprivation cutoff for an indicator shows the minimum achievement level or category required to be considered non-deprived in that indicator.
7. **Weights:** The weight or deprivation value affixed to each indicator reflects the value that a deprivation in that indicator has for poverty, relative to deprivations in the other indicators.
8. **Poverty cutoff:** The poverty cutoff shows what combined share of weighted deprivations is sufficient to identify a person as poor.

In practice, these design choices are not made in a linear fashion but rather iteratively, and in combination with consultations and empirical work. Thus, discussing them sequentially may seem rather tedious. Just as it is far more pleasant to hear a horse whinny than to transcribe its whinny painstakingly onto a musical staff to learn how it is done, so too, considering these choices one by one makes the task seem rather dull. One can only hope the transcription is a one-time task, whereas the skill of whinnying lasts a while.

6.3.1 PURPOSE(S) OF A MEASURE

The purpose(s) of a measure clarify the way(s) in which the measure will be used to describe and understand situations, to make comparisons across groups or across time, and to guide policy or monitor progress. The purpose shapes the choice of space and many of the calibration decisions that will follow and so should be explicitly formulated and stated. The Stiglitz–Sen–Fitoussi Commission drew attention, in the case of quality of life measures, to the fundamental importance of the purpose of the measure to the identification of dimensions and indicators. 'The range of objective features to be considered in any assessment …will depend on the purpose of the exercise …the question of which elements should belong to a list of objective features inevitably depends on value judgements …' (2009).

The purpose may also identify constraints and shape processes. For example, if the purpose includes legitimacy to the wider public, then public consultations may be essential; if it is performance monitoring, involvement with the concerned agencies and institutions may be useful. While a measure may have a single purpose, it is more common for measures to seek to fulfil multiple purposes.

For example, a **national poverty measure** might aim to assess the population-wide levels and trends in capability poverty across regions and population groups in ways that are regarded as legitimate and accurate by the citizenry. Note that this statement of purpose has **scope** (population-wide), **space** (capability), **relevant comparisons** (across population groups and time trends), and popular **legitimacy** (which affects procedures). A study may design a **youth poverty measure** in order to understand, profile, and draw attention to youth capabilities at a given point in time. A **targeting measure** may use census data to identify and target the poorest of the poor in terms of social rights for certain services. A **performance monitoring measure** may track changes over time across a set of indicators reflecting the goals of a programmatic intervention, such as improvement in the quality of education or women's empowerment across various domains. A **local community development** measure may monitor a village development plan in ways that community members have proposed and understand. Measures might be designed to inform the private sector and civil society about the state of poverty in their country and so encourage **public debate** and action. They might also clarify what value-added proposed measure(s) have in **comparison with alternative poverty** measures.

The purpose of the measure will often also include political economy and institutional issues and constraints that are pertinent to the measure fulfilling its purpose, such as timescale, data, budgetary resources, political and legal procedures, updating procedures, and so on.[22] For example, will a given dataset be used or will a new survey be designed and implemented and if so what is its budget and frequency? Are particular committees, commissions, or institutional processes to be involved in measurement design and what is their authority? If a measure will be updated over time, what is its legal or institutional basis, which institution(s) or person(s) have the authority to update the measure, and when and how is occasional methodological updating to take place? Clarity on such issues during measurement design can greatly streamline design procedures.

6.3.2 CHOICE OF SPACE

As mentioned in section 6.1 another preliminary choice is the space in which measurement is to proceed. Will it be in the space of income, of resources and access to resources,

---

[22] Sen's argument that it could be useful to describe who is poor according to widespread judgements, even if resources do not suffice to address it (1980, 1997), supplements but does not rule out this option.

of functionings and capabilities, or of subjective utility? There are well-known arguments in favour of each space, and purposes for which each space might be appropriate. Conceptually, it is vital to be clear about the choice of space *prior* to the selection of indicators. This is because the same indicators—such as years of schooling—may be used in empirical measures of both types, but the interpretation and, at times, the treatment of the data may vary.

Following Sen, we may take the space that is of central interest to be the space of **functionings and capabilities** (they are the same space). Functionings are the beings and doings that people value and have reason to value, and capabilities are the freedoms to achieve valuable functionings. This implies that measurement should focus on valuable activities and states of being that people can actually achieve, given their values and their varying abilities to convert resources into functionings. The choice of space may have implications for the interpretation of variables' scales of measurement. In some cases, for example, capability measures use indicators that reflect achievements in other spaces (or subjective and self-reported states), if these can be justified empirically as proxies of functionings or capabilities.

An essential step at this stage is to revisit the scales of measurement introduced in section 2.3. To summarize, any achievement matrix may contain data having categorical, ordinal, or cardinal scales (which may be binary, interval, or ratio scale). In measures requiring cardinal data, the indicator's scale of measurement has to be reassessed *after* the space of measurement has been chosen. For example, years of schooling may seem to be a ratio-scale variable. But in terms of human functionings, is it? Or do the earlier years of education confer marginally more capabilities than later years, or the completion of the twelfth year (with a diploma) more than the eleventh year (without a diploma)? In using M_0, we dichotomize variables at a deprivation cutoff. This obviates the need to rescale indicators to construct an appropriate normalized gap in different spaces, but still requires that the deprivation cutoffs (discussed in section 6.3.6) reflect deprivations in the chosen space.

Not all measures focus on the capability space—or need to. They might reflect social rights, social exclusion, access to services, social protection, or the quality of services. And most poverty reduction requires, as intermediary steps, institutions that effectively deliver resources and services to people and communities. Thus, even if the goal is capability expansion, this might be stimulated or monitored in part by a multidimensional poverty measure that is framed in an intermediary space of inputs or outputs. The choice of space specifies how a given measure will advance the purpose.

6.3.3 UNITS OF IDENTIFICATION AND ANALYSIS

The unit(s) of identification or of analysis[23] may be a person, a household, a geographic area, or an institution (such as a school or firm or clinic). A common unit of *identification*

---

[23] Section 7.2.1 defines the unit of identification as the entity that is identified as poor or non-poor—usually the individual or the household.

for a poverty measure is a person (any adult, a child, a worker, a woman, an elderly person). This permits a poverty measure to be decomposed by variables like gender, age, ethnicity, occupation, and other relevant individual characteristics. It may also permit analysis of intra-household patterns of poverty or of group-specific poverty (indigenous groups, youth unemployed, urban slums). Alternatively, household members' information may be considered together, which has advantages in terms of supporting intra-household sharing and getting an overview of households. In this case, household members' combined achievements are used as a unit of identification for a population-wide measure, and all household members receive the same deprivation score.

The unit of *analysis*—meaning how the results are reported and analysed—may still reflect each person. That is, even if the unit of *identification* is the household, one can report the percentage of people who are identified as poor (by using individual sampling weights), rather than the percentage of households that are identified as poor (which is used if the household is the unit of analysis).

Where data are not available at the household level or where the measure focuses on topics such as infrastructure, poverty can be computed for data zones or geographic areas, so long as there is a justification for overlooking within-region inequality. Other measures may use a particular institution such as a school or clinic or firm as a unit of identification and/or analysis.

What is essential is that data for all variables must be available for (or transformed to represent) each unit of identification (see also Chapter 7), that the definition of applicable populations be transparent and complete, and that the unit of analysis be explicitly and clearly stated and justified.

There are ethical considerations in choosing and justifying a unit of analysis. For example, using the person as the unit of identification coheres with human rights policies, can show gendered or age disparities, and may permit intra-household analysis (Alkire, Meinzen-Dick, et al. 2013). Yet using the household as a unit of identification acknowledges intra-household caring and sharing—for example, educated household members reading for each other and multiple household members being affected by someone's severe health conditions. Policies targeting or addressing the household may also strengthen or at least not weaken the household unit. Normative and policy assessments may be supplemented by participatory insights regarding the appropriate unit of identification and the ensuing focus of policy interventions.

The justification of a unit of identification may include empirical assessments of bias and comparability. For example, if the unit of identification is the household, then indicators that draw on individual-level achievements may be checked for biases according to household size and composition (Alkire and Santos 2014). If the unit of identification is the person, then the comparability of indicators across diverse groups requires analysis—as in the case of education and health indicators for people of different ages (infants and toddlers, school-aged children, adults, and the elderly). The scale of errors that could be introduced if household-level variables are presumed to be equally shared by all household members is a further fruitful topic of empirical scrutiny.

For some policy purposes it could be useful to construct a set of measures, in which each measure takes a nested unit of identification that includes or is included by related measures: for example, the person, the household, the village or neighbourhood, and the district. The nested measures permit further analysis of the interactions between deprivations at different levels. For example, the individual-level data may have health and educational functionings, household data may have living standard and housing-related functionings, and village-level data may have environmental, infrastructure, and service delivery information. Analyses may explore the extent to which health- and education-deprived people live in living-standard-deprived households, for example, and whether these live in services-deprived villages. Alternatively one may study which poor children live in poor households. Analyses using nested measures can be compared to analyses of a multidimensional poverty index at the individual level that applies relevant household- and village-level deprivations to each individual.

In sum, although often data constraints will require that the household be the unit of identification, when other options are feasible, then this choice can be considered, made, and justified using different kinds of reasoning to assess the 'fit' between the proposed measure and its purpose.

6.3.4 DIMENSIONS

When these structural choices have been established, poverty measures require the selection and valuation of deprivations. Sen introduces the task as follows: 'In an evaluative exercise, two distinct questions have to be clearly distinguished: (1) What are the objects of value? (2) How valuable are the respective objects?' (Sen 1992: 42). These two tasks of *selecting* focal deprivations (using dimensions, indicators, and cutoffs), and setting relative *values* for them, recur in poverty measurement.

The term 'dimensions' in this chapter refers to conceptual categorizations of indicators for ease of communication and interpretation of results. By 'indicators' we mean the d variables that appear in columns of the achievement and deprivation matrices and are used to construct the deprivation scores and to measure poverty.

A multidimensional poverty measure is constructed using indicators. In some cases, these indicators may each represent distinct facets of poverty. In other cases, it may be useful to talk about several indicators as forming a 'dimension' of poverty. Why use dimensions? Dimensions may reflect the categories defined by some deliberative or synthetic processes. For example, a dimension might be children's education; indicators might include a child's years of completed schooling and their achievement scores last period. In this case the indicators may be the best possible approximation of those dimensions from an existing dataset. It may also arise from a theory or policy source. Noll (2002) develops a systematic conceptual framework for social indicators in Europe by reviewing concepts of welfare and common policy goals, then identifying fourteen dimensions that fit the measurement's purposes. Grouping indicators into dimensions may facilitate the communication of results because there are likely to be fewer dimensions than indicators and they are likely to be intuitive and accessible to non-experts.

Grusky and Kanbur argue that the selection of dimensions merits active attention because 'economists have not reached consensus on the dimensions that matter, nor even on how they might decide what matters' (2006: 12). Yet the extensive and historic discussions about the post-2015 development agenda have been tremendously useful in illuminating areas of agreement across different interest groups with respect to widely varying national and international considerations.

Unusually, the selection of dimensions does not necessarily rely on empirical or technical analysis. Naturally, sometimes analysts explore or confirm the extent to which dimensional grouping of indicators is corroborated statistically. Such statistical explorations should not *determine* the selection of dimensions or grouping of indicators; they may, however, contribute to their justification and expose interesting relationships that should be considered.

In addition to the inevitable consideration of data constraints, there are at least three overlapping kinds of information that may inform the selection of dimensions: deliberation and public reasoning, legitimate consensus, and theoretical arguments (Alkire 2008a).

The first approach is a repeated **deliberative or participatory exercise**, which engages a representative group of participants as reflective agents in making the value judgements to select focal capabilities. Deliberation may involve online assessments as well as face-to-face focus groups; it may also consolidate the body of recent and similar participatory work that has been undertaken for other purposes. In a supportive, well-informed, and equitable environment, participatory processes seem to be ideal for choosing dimensions, but not, however, if deliberation is dominated by conflict or inequality or misinformation, or coloured by the absence or dominance of certain groups. Furthermore, the process of aggregating the values of a diverse assembly of groups and people, whose deliberative processes may vary in quality, is neither elementary nor void of controversy (indeed it is an appropriate topic for further research). Even if a new set of deliberative exercises is not possible, it may be possible to consider documentation of previous such processes, be it from a previous measurement consultation, participatory exercises, a widely debated national plan, high-profile legal documents, the media, or a respectable set of life histories of disadvantaged people and communities (Leavy and Howard et al. 2013; Narayan et al. 2000). So it may be rare for a set of dimensions to be justified without *any* reference to participatory studies and public debates.

In writing on the selection of capabilities—which relate to dimensions and indicators[24]—Sen calls for deliberative engagement rather than using a pre-ordained list. 'I have

---

[24] The selection dimensions and/or indicators could reflect capabilities and functionings, with dimensions being broader (being educated) and indicators being more specific (finishing primary school). So the discussion on capabilities that follows should be considered as applying to both the present and the following

nothing against the listing of capabilities,' Sen writes, 'but must stand up against a grand mausoleum to one fixed and final list of capabilities' (2004: 80). A central reason against promulgating a fixed list is that to be relevant, the dimensions (and indicators) should reflect the purpose of the measure. 'What we focus on cannot be independent of what we are doing and why' (Sen 2004: 79). The deprivations in international measures will rightly differ from a national measure or a measure of child poverty or of an indigenous community, for example. A further motivation for not fixing a list of capabilities even for a given purpose—including poverty measurement—is that a fixed list would crowd out debate and public reasoning, which can play an educational and motivational role. It also would not catalyse constructive debate that may influence people's values. 'To insist on a fixed forever list of capabilities would …go against the productive role of public discussion, social agitation, and open debates' (Sen 2004: 80). Also, as technology advances and social values change, the list might become outdated (Sen 2004: 78). For example, recent approaches to poverty often incorporate environmental and energy considerations that were lacking previously.

A second approach to the selection of dimensions is the use of an authoritative document or list that has attracted a kind of **enduring consensus** and associated legitimacy. Examples include a constitution, a national development plan, a declaration of human rights, or some time-bound international agreements such as the MDGs. Most official multidimensional poverty measures have some transparent link to such a policy process or document. The use of a set of dimensions that already have a kind of visibility and legitimacy is useful for international or global measures (where public deliberation is difficult), as well as for those that are clearly designed to monitor policy processes. It also naturally connects measurement to policy management.

A third potential source of dimensions is a conceptual framework or **particular theory**—which may range from Maslow's hierarchy of human needs to a religious framework such as the Maqasid A-Sharia, to lists like Martha Nussbaum's set of central human capabilities. These approaches are particularly relevant for communities where the theory enjoys widespread approval and/or is consistent with lists generated by alternative theories or processes (Alkire 2008a).

Comparing the lists that groups generate by these and additional processes, one finds a striking degree of commonality between them. Table 6.1 lists dimensions generated by these processes that pertain to multidimensional poverty measurement. Indeed there are a plethora of similar resources for the selection of deprivations, which may contribute towards standards supporting multidimensional poverty measurement design. And whilst the particular names and grouping of indicators differ, the universe of options is not too great, and this fact itself may be of no little comfort to those designing multidimensional poverty measures.

sections. See Alkire (2002a, 2002b), Nussbaum (2003), Robeyns (2003, 2005), Sen (2004), Burchardt (2013), and Burchardt and Vizard (2007, 2011).

Table 6.1 Dimensions of poverty

Participatory—poor	Participatory—all	Measurement	Political	Philosophical
Voices of the poor (Dimensions of ill-being)*	**MyWorld Survey****	**Synthesis of AF and other MD poverty measures**	**17 proposed Sustainable Development Goals**	**Wolff and De-Shalit's six 'core' disadvantages**
1. The Body: hungry, exhausted, sick, and poor in appearance	1. Hunger, food security, and nutrition 2. Health 3. Population dynamics	1. Food and nutrition 2. Health	1. Hunger, food security and nutrition 2. Healthy lives and well-being	1. Life 2. Bodily health
2. Livelihoods and Assets: precarious, seasonal, and inadequate	4. Growth and employment	3. Employment, income, and labour	3. End poverty in all its forms everywhere 4. Growth, employment and decent work 5. Infrastructure & industrialization	
3. Skills and Abilities: lack of information, education, skills, and confidence	5. Education: quantity and quality	4. Education	6. Inclusive and equitable quality education	3. Sense/imagination/thought
4. Places: isolated, risky, unserviced, and stigmatized	6. Water 7. Energy	5. Utilities, services, and sanitation 6. Shelter/housing	7. Water and sanitation 8. Energy	
5. Security: lack of protection and peace of mind	8. Conflict, violence, and disaster	7. Security	9. Peaceful and inclusive societies	4. Bodily integrity
6. Organizations of the Poor: weak and disconnected		8. Empowerment		5. Control over environment
7. Behaviours: disregard and abuse by the more powerful				

8. Gender Relations: troubled and unequal		9. Child conditions	10. Gender equality and women's empowerment
9. Social Relations: discriminating and isolating	9. Inequalities	10. Social cohesion and connectedness	11. Reduce inequality
10. Institutions: disempowering and excluding	10. Governance	11. Governance	12. Global partnerships and means of implementation
	11. Environment and sustainability	12. Environmental conditions	13. Sustainable cities and human settlements
			14. Sustainable consumption and production
			15. Combat climate change
			16. Marine resources, oceans, and seas
			17. Ecosystems and biodiversity
			6. Affiliation

* Narayan et al. (2000)
** United Nations Development Group (UNDG) (2013)

It should be borne in mind that the selection of dimensions and indicators affects the selection of weights. In a book supporting the development of national poverty plans in Europe, Tony Atkinson and colleagues point out the convenience of keeping weights in mind when selecting dimensions and indicators. In particular, they commend choosing indicators (or, possibly, dimensions) such that their weights are roughly equal to facilitate policy interpretations: 'the interpretation of the set of indicators is greatly eased where the individual components have degrees of importance that, while not necessarily exactly equal, are not grossly different' (Atkinson et al. 2002). Sen also emphasizes the interconnection between these choices: 'There is no escape from the problem of evaluation in selecting a class of functionings in the description and appraisal of capabilities, and this selection problem is, in fact, one part of the general task of the choice of *weights* in making normative evaluation' (Sen 2008). Elsewhere we observed that this linkage holds not only for dimensions that are selected but also for those that are omitted: 'choosing one out of several possible variables is tantamount to assigning that dimension full weight and the remaining dimensions zero weight' (Alkire and Foster 2011b). And it is to the selection of indicators that we now turn.

6.3.5 INDICATORS

Indicators are the backbone of measurement. Their quality, accuracy, and reach determine the informational content of a poverty measure. Given data constraints, the process through which these are selected may include participatory and deliberative exercises, legal or political documents, statistical explorations, robustness tests, or theoretical guidelines.

While a considerable amount of attention, discussion, and practice has focused on the normative selection of dimensions of poverty and well-being, there is a paucity of comparable normative literature on the selection of indicators. The literature on indicator selection is, however, richly arrayed with a plethora of empirical considerations, which must be considered alongside normative and policy issues. Some of these will be raised in Chapter 7. These include:

- statistical techniques to assess aspects such as the reliability, validity, robustness, and standard errors of economic and social indicators;[25]
- indicators' comparability across time and for different population subgroups;

---

[25] The field is large and thriving. For a recent overview, see Land, Michalos, and Sirgy (2012) and Land, Ferriss, et al. (2012); see also Chapters 3, 4, and 7 of this book and journals such as *Social Indicators Research*. Tests are applied to single and composite indicators. Hagerty (2001) was a pioneering assessment using fourteen criteria; cf. Sirgy et al. (2006), Nardo et al. (2008), Zumbo (1998), and Andrews (1986). For recent applications, see Guio, Fusco, and Marlier (2009), Guio, Gordon, and Marlier (2012), Whelan and Maître (2010), and Fusco, Guio, and Marlier (2011).

- dataset-specific issues such as data quality, sample design, seasonality, and missing values;
- the justification of indicators as proxies for a hard-to-measure variable of interest.

Such analysis of each component indicator is fundamentally important for building rigorous measures, and, while these are not covered here, we presume readers will learn relevant techniques and consider how best to apply them.

Alongside these, numerous guidelines seek to match indicator selection with policy purposes (IISD 2009; Maggino and Zumbo 2012). For example, Atkinson and Marlier (2010: 8–14) provide an insightful overview of the purposes for which appropriate indicators should be stock or flow, subjective or objective, relative or absolute, static or dynamic, input or output or outcome, and so on. When statistics are used by the public, issues such as ease of interpretation also affect the choice. Still, as we saw in Chapter 4, the literatures on existing practices of addressing these technical, policy, and practical concerns are dispersed.

Naturally, the cost of data collection, cleaning, and preparing an indicator are also likely to influence indicator selection, especially when new surveys are fielded or regular updates are anticipated. This is a very important and underdocumented consideration, given the need both for better and more frequent data, and for timely, thorough analysis of new data (Alkire 2014).

The selection of indicators should be transparently justified—as many counting measures are. The criteria for selection will vary, however. For example, Atkinson and Marlier (2010: 45) outline five criteria for internationally comparable indicators of deprivation in social inclusion:

1. An indicator should identify the essence of the problem and have an agreed normative interpretation.
2. An indicator should be robust and statistically validated.
3. An indicator should be interpretable in an international context.
4. An indicator should reflect the direction of change and be susceptible to revision as improved methods become available.
5. The measurement of an indicator should not impose too large a burden on countries, on enterprises, or on citizens.

As the field of multidimensional poverty advances, we anticipate that conventions and standards will be further developed to facilitate the selection of indicators and the calibration of parameters described in the following sections, much as has been done for monetary poverty.[26] These will reduce although not eliminate the value judgements

---

[26] Foster, Seth, et al. (2013), Haughton and Khandker (2009), and Ravallion (1992). Naturally, standards too provoke debates. For a thoughtful exchange on global income poverty figures, see Anand, Segal, and Stiglitz (2010).

in measurement design. In the case of monetary poverty, conventions did not make the creation of a consumption aggregate mechanical, imputation of housing costs easy, or the comparison of rural and urban monetary poverty lines uncontroversial. There remain animated debates, such as whether to include popular sugary drinks in the food poverty basket or elite goods in the consumer price index. Yet conventions still serve to streamline and legitimize key choices during the design process and reflect an ongoing and evolving technical consensus (or partial consensus) regarding sound measurement principles.

6.3.6 DEPRIVATION CUTOFFS

Deprivation cutoffs are fundamentally normative standards. They define a minimum level of achievement, below which a person is deprived in each indicator or subindex.[27] As we saw in Chapter 2, the deprivation cutoffs, together with the deprivation values, create cardinal comparability across indicators for M_0 measures and may be interpreted as creating a 'natural zero'. Deprivation cutoffs for each indicator are a distinguishing feature of multidimensional poverty measures that reflect the joint distribution of deprivations (Bourguignon and Chakravarty 2003). This is because, by the property of deprivation focus, having more than the deprivation cutoff achievement level in one dimension—for example, clean water—does not 'erase' the deprivation in another dimension (like malnutrition). This coheres with a human rights approach, among others.

Deprivation cutoffs may be justified with reference to international or national standards.[28] They may be set to reflect 'basic minima' or 'aspirations' that have arisen in participatory, consultative, or deliberative exercises. They might reflect the 'targets' of national development plans or of some international agreement or legal guidelines—for example, on compulsory schooling and social protection—or a social contract or, in some cases, medical standards (e.g. for anaemia, micronutrients, stunting, wasting, and so on).

Note that in indicators that use the household as the unit of identification, deprivation cutoffs must be defined such that they combine individual-level data when it is available for multiple household members. For example, if the household is the unit of identification, a deprivation cutoff for an educational variable may consider data for some or all household members. This can be done in many ways. Alternative deprivation cutoffs for the variable 'years of schooling among adults aged 15 and above' could be: if any household member has *achieved* a certain level, if any adult *lacks* a given level, if the *women* of the household reach a certain level, if a certain *proportion* of adults

---

[27] Applications of the AF methodology use the same deprivation cutoffs for all units in a poverty measure. It could be an interesting research exercise to vary the cutoffs according to locally defined standards, although doing so would change certain properties of the measure.

[28] See Alkire and Santos (2010, 2014) for a description of how the global MPI cutoffs reflect international standards. For examples of cutoffs based on legal standards, see CONEVAL (2009); on cutoffs reflecting a national development plan, see Angulo et al. (2013).

achieve that level, if (all or some) household members have levels that were appropriate when they were of school-going age, or if the educational achievements for at least one male and at least one female (or some other combination) each meet a certain standard. Empirical implementation and analysis of several definitions can be useful to understand the patterns of educational deprivations within households—and their accuracy, for example, given the gender composition of households.

In other cases, deprivation cutoffs are set across subindices, such as defining housing deprivations if a person has substandard housing construction in terms of any two of: roof, flooring, walls. Again each subindex design requires independent and careful validation, which this chapter does not cover.

Having fixed one set of deprivation cutoffs, a second vector of cutoffs may be constructed in which at least one indicator reflects more (less) extreme deprivation. This second vector can be implemented across the same indicators, weights, and poverty cutoff as previously to identify a subset of the poor who are in more (less) extreme poverty according to these more (less) exacting standards.[29]

In practice, it is common in multidimensional poverty design to construct indicators and candidate multidimensional poverty measures using various cutoff vectors, in order to assess the sensitivity of measures to a change in deprivation cutoffs, and also, in the case of uncertainty about which cutoff to choose, to clarify the implications of a choice to policy users. For example, Alkire and Santos (2010, 2014) implemented cutoffs such as 'stunting', 'piped water into the dwelling', or 'flush toilet' to understand whether country rankings changed dramatically if these standards were used instead of the chosen MDG cutoffs.

The selection of deprivation cutoffs enables the computation of uncensored headcount ratios for all indicators. Reasoned consideration of these ratios is quite important for cross-checking indicator selection and for weighting. For example, if the uncensored headcount ratio for an indicator is much lower than other indicators, that indicator will be unlikely to influence the measure; however, if changes in this indicator would be quite precise and if its normative importance is high, a large weight can be attributed to it, returning it to prominence. Also, suppose the indicators have been selected, following Atkinson et al. (2002), such that their importance and hence weights are 'roughly equal'. If deprivation rates across indicators are exceedingly variable, then equal weights across indicators will produce a measure that is dominated by the indicators having the highest censored headcount ratios. We might do well to remind readers of the need to consider design issues iteratively rather than sequentially in practice.

---

[29] For example, Alkire, Conconi, and Seth (2014b) implement a measure of destitution for many countries in which eight of the global MPI cutoffs are lowered and the same weights and poverty cutoff of 33% is used. CONEVAL's definition of extreme poverty changes the cutoff of income poverty from the basic needs poverty line to the food basket poverty line and simultaneously raises the k cutoff from strictly greater than 50% to 75% (using a higher poverty cutoff still creates a strict subset of the extreme poor).

6.3.7 VALUES AND WEIGHTS

Another key component of normative choices is the relative weight placed on dimensional deprivations. In multidimensional poverty measures, weights could be applied (i) *to* each indicator (thus determining the relative importance of each indicator to the other as interpreted from the ratio of the weights); (ii) *within* an indicator (if a subindex such as an asset index or housing index is constructed); and (iii) *among* people in the distribution, for example to give greater priority to the most disadvantaged. This section focuses solely on the first of these.

As people are diverse and our values differ both from each other and from ourselves at different points in time, the relative values that people place on different indicators of disadvantage vary.[30] This is no catastrophe. Sen observes, 'It can, of course, be the case that the agreement that emerges on the weights to be used may be far from total', but continues, 'we shall then have some good reason to use ranges of weights on which we may find some agreement. This need not fatally disrupt evaluation of injustice or the making of public policy ... A broad range of not fully congruent weights could yield rather similar principal guidelines' (2009: 243). Thus, as Chapter 8 suggests, robustness tests should be undertaken to assess whether the main policy prescriptions are robust to a range of weights or to show their sensitivity to alternative weighting structures.

The weights applied in the M_0 measure differ radically from weights in 'composite' indicators and are, for that reason, easier to set and to assess normatively. Critics of M_0 at times overlook the dramatic simplicity of M_0 weights in comparison with composite measures or multidimensional poverty measures that require cardinal data, so we begin by clarifying this important distinction.

Weights in composite measures are applied to quantities (achievement levels), and the marginal rates of substitution across indicators are usually assumed to be meaningful at all achievement levels.[31] We elsewhere clarified that, unlike M_0, composite indices, including the Human Development Index (HDI), require 'strong implicit assumptions on the cardinality and commensurability of the three dimensions of human development. The key implication is that after appropriate transformations, all variables are measured using a ratio scale in such a way that levels are comparable across dimensions' (Alkire and Foster 2010). This is rather stringent. To take a very straightforward case, in the original arithmetic HDI the weights govern the effect that an improvement in one dimension has on the overall HDI. The weights must accurately reflect the value of such

---

[30] It is empirically possible with AF measures, and would be of research interest, to apply individual or group-based weighting vectors to each deprivation vector or set of vectors, rather than applying the same weighting vector to all. Doing so will change the properties of the measure, as well as its interpretation and that of consistent indices. It could also imply that each individual had fixed, consistent preferences regarding that indicator, which is a strong assumption. Yet such research could be of interest to those probing individual and group preferences (Adler 2011; Fleurbaey and Maniquet 2012; Decancq 2012).

[31] Decancq and Lugo (2012) clearly and thoroughly explain the role of what we call 'precision' weights and discuss eight approaches to setting these, which are grouped into data-driven, normative, or hybrid weight categories; see Decancq, Van Ootegem, and Verhofstadt (2011) and Ravallion (2011b).

a change, whether the increment occurs at the highest or the lowest level of achievement in that dimension. That is, changes from each starting level must be able to be justified separately and independently. Weights also govern trade-offs across all variables for every increment of each variable. That is, the trade-off between an increment in variable A from any starting achievement level and corresponding increments in variables B and C would need to be justified—whatever the starting level those variables take (Ravallion 2012). Weights are thus used to compare changes in the same indicator at any level of achievement and trade-offs across variables. We might refer to them as 'precision weights'.

Precision weights are also used in multidimensional poverty methodologies that require cardinal (normally ratio-scale) data, such as those proposed by Chakravarty, Mukherjee, and Ranade (1998), Tsui (2002), Bourguignon and Chakravarty (2003), Maasoumi and Lugo (2008), and Chakravarty and D'Ambrosio (2013), among others. Ratio-scale data are also required for M_α measures when $\alpha > 0$. In M_α measures when $\alpha > 0$, the deprivation cutoff creates a 'natural zero' and the normalized gaps for each indicator are understood to be cardinally meaningful. In this situation, in a manner similar to composite indices, the weights govern the impact that each increment or decrement in a deprived indicator has on poverty. Also similar to composite indices, weights govern trade-offs across all variables at all deprived levels of every variable.

In M_0 and other dichotomous counting approaches, weights are almost completely different. We may refer to them as deprivation values to mark this difference verbally. They are applied to the 0–1 deprivation status entry. Their function is to reflect the relative impact that the presence or absence of a deprivation has on the person's deprivation score and thus on identification and, for poor people, on poverty. Correspondingly, the weights affect how much impact the removal of a particular deprivation has on M_0. Thus, they create comparability across dichotomized indicators (see section 2.4). But because deprivation values are applied to dichotomous 0–1 variables, they need not calibrate different *levels* of deprivations in a single variable. Further, because all indicators are dichotomous, the only possible trade-offs across deprivations (presence or absence) take the value of the relative weights. Put differently, because M_0 uses dichotomized deprivations rather than normalized gaps, deprivation values are not required to govern trade-offs across different levels of achievement in different variables as they are in the measures requiring precision weights. They only reflect the presence or absence of a deprivation. This greatly simplifies their selection and justification, and is worth noting clearly as the distinction between precision weights and deprivation values is often overlooked.

Due to an appreciation of democratic debate, and to permit values to evolve, as in the selection of capabilities, Sen does not commend any fixed-and-forever vector of weights: 'The connection between public reasoning and the choice and weighting of capabilities in social assessment …also points to the absurdity of the argument that is sometimes presented, which claims that the capability approach would be usable—and "operational"—only if it comes with a set of "given" weights on the distinct functionings in some fixed list of relevant capabilities'. In contrast, Sen advocates occasional public discussion for similar reasons to those given in the selection of dimensions: 'The search for given, pre-determined weights is not only conceptually ungrounded, but it also overlooks the fact that the valuations and weights to be used may reasonably be influenced by our own continued scrutiny and by the reach of public discussion. It would be hard to accommodate this understanding with inflexible use of some pre-determined weights in a non-contingent form' (2009: 242–3). In practice, for measures used to compute changes over time, it can be useful to fix the weights and other parameters for a given time period, such as a decade, and update them thereafter.

The selection of deprivation values also reflects the purpose of the exercise. For example, if the purpose is to evaluate changes in poverty, weights might reflect the fundamental *importance* people place on each indicator, whereas if the purpose is to monitor progress in the short or medium term, the relative weights might partly depict the relative *priority* of reductions in indicator deprivations. For example, if a region has very high levels of educational achievements but deeply rutted roads, then a long-term poverty measure may give a higher weight to education because of its importance and value. But a measure used for participatory planning may give higher priority weights to roads because of the pressing need for progress in this area.

The potential value of public discussion does not mean that weights must be *created* by participatory processes—although Sen would suggest that they be made transparent in order to catalyse such discussion. Weights may also be corroborated or justified using expert opinion; analyses of survey data, such as perceived necessities (see Chapter 4); subjective evaluations; or the input of policymakers and relevant authorities. They may reflect values implicit in a legal document or national plan, or use some socially accepted value structure that has been applied in poverty measurement or similar exercises previously.

The justification of weights is explored extensively both theoretically and practically by Wolff and De-Shalit, who reach the conclusion that, '…even though disadvantage is plural, indexing disadvantages is possible, despite various theoretical and practical problems …' (2007: 181). Their proposal is to use multiple methods and create measures whose key policy proposals are robust to them. Let us unpack this. In terms of setting weights, for example, they (like Sen) point out the need for a democratic procedure, but also recognize 'that individual valuations might be liable to distortion, false consciousness, or the result of limited experience and thus ignorance of the real nature of various alternatives'. Hence they justify including additional inputs. 'Keeping both sides in play is sensitive to the fact that legitimacy in a democracy builds out of people's voices' while at the same time recognizing potential weaknesses of participatory processes (2007: 99).

In the end, Wolff and De-Shalit commend the creation of orderings that are robust to a range of plausible weights: 'A social ordering is weighting sensitive to the degree that it changes with different weighting assignments to different categories. A social ordering, therefore, is weighting insensitive—*robust*—to the degree it does not change with different weighting assignments to the different categories' (2007: 101–2).

So, first of all, the deprivation values that are used to create 'relative weights' across 0–1 deprivations are fundamentally straightforward, which simplifies matters. But there are plural ways to make and justify weights, which seems to reconstitute complexity. Happily, in fact, the plurality of potentially justifiable weights means that weights can be justified and cross-checked against different sources. Technically, given the legitimate pluralism in values, it would be desirable to implement a poverty measure with a range of weighting vectors and to release measures whose relevant policy implications were robust (Chapter 8 and Alkire and Santos 2014).

6.3.8 POVERTY CUTOFF k

The cross-dimensional poverty cutoff k identifies each person as poor or non-poor according to the extent of deprivations they experience, which are summarized in their deprivation score. It establishes the minimum eligibility criteria for poverty in terms of the breadth of deprivation. Normatively it reflects a judgement regarding the maximally acceptable set of deprivations a person may experience and not be considered poor. Thus the value of k can only be justified after fully articulating the parameters described previously.

Like the income poverty line, the final choice of k in most cases should be a normative one, with k describing the minimum deprivation score associated with people who are considered poor and consider themselves to be poor (Sen 1980). For multidimensional measures the normative content could come from participatory processes in which poor people articulate the conditions and combinations of deprivations that constitute poverty. They may be informed by subjective poverty assessments and qualitative studies.[32] As noted by Tsui, 'In the final analysis, how reasonable the identification rule is depends, *inter alia*, on the attributes included and how imperative these attributes are to leading a meaningful life' (2002: 74). If, for example, deprivation in each dimension meant a terrible human rights abuse and data were highly reliable, then k could be set at the minimal union level to reflect the fact that human rights are each essential, have equal status, and cannot be positioned in a hierarchical order.

In some circumstances, the value of k could be chosen to reflect priorities and policy goals.[33] For example, if a subset of dimensions were essential while the rest may be

---

[32] Ravallion presents the rationale for income poverty lines in terms of 'subjective' poverty lines which, it seems, reflect people's values and views on poverty: 'Arguably then, what one is doing in setting an objective poverty line in a given country is attempting to estimate the country's underlying "subjective poverty line". A close correspondence between subjective and objective poverty lines can then be expected, though arguably it is the subjective poverty line which can then claim to be the more fundamental concept for poverty analysis' (1998: 30). Given the potential for manipulation and adaptation (Clark 2012), as well as issues of comparability due to different aspirations (Narayan and Petesch 2007), purely subjective assessments of poverty should be combined with qualitative and participatory insights.

[33] Care must be taken in this case: Sen argued early on that 'the non-availability of public resources to help eliminate severe deprivations should not make us redefine poverty itself' (1992: 108; see also 1980).

replaced with one another, the weights and k could be set accordingly. For example, suppose $d = 4$, and $w_1 = 2$, and $w_2...w_4 = 2/3$. A cutoff of $k = 2$ would then identify as poor anyone who is either deprived in dimension 1 or in all the remaining dimensions, while a slightly higher value of k would *require* deprivation in the first dimension and in one other.[34] Alternatively, one could select a k cutoff whose resulting headcount identified the poorest segment of the population that the budgetary resources could address. Thus, the weights and poverty cutoff allow for a range of identification constellations.

To justify and communicate the poverty cutoff, the relative values of deprivations (or possibly dimensions) should be explicitly considered. While technically the poverty cutoff can be set at any level, in practice a range of poverty cutoff values may identify the same group as poor. For example, if there are five equally weighted indicators, then a poverty cutoff of 21% will identify the same set of persons to be poor as a cutoff of 25%, 33%, or 40%. Given these weights, any person who has at least two deprivations will be identified as poor by any poverty cutoff taking the value $20 < k \leq 40\%$. Yet if communication is a priority, then a poverty cutoff value of 40% might be chosen, as it most intuitively conveys the fact that poor people are deprived in at least two out of the five (2/5) deprivations. When deprivations take different weights, of course, the distribution may be smoother, but communicating the poverty cutoff in terms of indicators or dimensions may remain relevant.

No matter which technique is finally employed in selecting the parameter k, as in the case of income poverty lines, it should be routine to construct the poverty measure for a range of poverty cutoffs, to publish robustness results for alternative poverty cutoffs, and/or to explore dominance tests across relevant values of k. Techniques for doing so are set out in Chapter 8.

6.4 **Concluding Reflections**

Previous chapters drew readers' attention to normative issues in poverty measurement by explaining and applying various axioms and properties. This chapter moved on to clarify the wider normative choices inherent in measurement design—after a methodology has been selected. These choices affect every step of measurement design. At a higher level, normative choices assess measures according to plural desiderata, and draw on empirical, political, and procedural considerations, among others. More specific considerations can be drawn on, alongside empirical insights, to justify each of the design choices.

Value judgements are not a one-shot game. In the interest of facilitating repeated and ongoing self-critical consideration, we have argued that the design choices of multidimensional poverty measures should consider using deliberative processes, and that the normative issues and processes should be explicitly articulated in the public

---

[34] Such a weighting structure is used in Mexico (CONEVAL 2010); cf. Nolan and Whelan (1996).

domain, in order that the public might both understand the existing parameters and be able to debate or improve upon them. To counterbalance and inform this flexibility, we suggest the use of empirical and statistical techniques, for example, to explore redundancy and to show whether key points of comparison are robust to a range of plausible parameter choices.[35] Clearly, the initial choice of parameters would be more difficult if important comparisons were sensitive to small adjustments in them. By applying robustness tests, this sensitivity can be explored transparently. Before getting to robustness techniques in Chapter 8, Chapter 7 addresses practical data considerations and relationships among indicators that are pertinent to multidimensional poverty measurement design and implementation, and suggests some specific methods to address these, even if imperfectly.

[35] For example, see Alkire and Foster (2011a) and Lasso de la Vega (2010); see also Alkire and Santos (2010, 2014) and Alkire, Santos, Seth, and Yalonetzky (2010). A stringent and full set of dominance conditions that ensure the robustness of comparisons to widely varying weights, deprivation cutoffs, and poverty cutoffs has been derived in Yalonetzky (2012). Statistical tests for these conditions are available in Yalonetzky (2014) for discrete variables and in Anderson (2008) for continuous variables. Bennett and Mitra (2013) propose a test for multiple hypotheses that allows the researcher to check the robustness of the cutoffs and compare two groups.

7 Data and Analysis

Chapter 6 transitioned from considerations about selecting a measurement methodology (Chapters 3–5) to issues met in implementing real-world measures that undergird and reinforce policies to fight poverty. It mentioned in passing the *desiderata* criteria that indicators be 'technically solid'—a criterion that entails rigorous consideration of properties and also of empirical techniques. To take this forward, we now switch focus to emphasize the *practice* of empirical poverty measurement. In particular, this chapter introduces empirical issues that are distinctive to counting-based multidimensional poverty methodologies. Novel issues include the requirement that indicators accurately reflect deprivations at the individual level—not just on average—and that all indicators be transformed to reflect deprivations in the chosen unit of identification (person, household).

This chapter is not exhaustive. It presumes readers have a sound understanding of household survey data and their quantitative analysis, and also of various assessments of indicator validity. It supplements a presumed solid foundation with new elements that pertain to multidimensional poverty measurement design and analysis in particular.[1] A more extensive and detailed version is available at www.multidimensionalpoverty.org.

Section 7.1 introduces very briefly the different types of data sources available, namely, censuses, administrative records, and household surveys. Section 7.2 discusses issues to be considered when selecting the indicators to include in a multidimensional poverty measure. Finally, Section 7.3 presents some basic descriptive analytical tools that can prove helpful in exploring the relationships between different indicators and informing the process of the measure design. Box 7.1 discusses the different fronts on which data collection should be improved in the near future in order to permit the design of better poverty measures.

7.1 Data for Multidimensional Poverty Measurement

As stated in Chapter 1, the initial step in poverty measurement, even prior to identification, is to select the space of analysis (resources, capabilities, utility) and the purpose of the measure to be constructed. The choice of space, as well as the feasible options for measurement design, will necessarily be shaped by data availability. We briefly review the main types of data used for multidimensional measurement and considerations of when to use each.

---

[1] Deaton (1997) remains in our view an unsurpassed and essential guide for all analysts.

Multidimensional poverty is measured using *micro* data. By *micro* data we mean the unit-level data containing responses that each unit of analysis (such as person or household) provided. This contrasts with *macro* data, or aggregate indicators or marginal measures such as the mortality rate, literacy rate, mean household income, or the enrolment ratio, which summarize the achievements of a society. The three most common micro data sources are **censuses, household surveys**, and **administrative records**—also called register data. New relevant data sources such as mobile telephony and satellite imagery are rising sharply and will deeply enrich future multidimensional poverty analyses.

A **census** is an enumeration of all households in a well-defined territory at a given point in time (Mather 2007). National censuses are typically conducted every five to ten years and contain information on a strictly limited number of variables: demographic variables such as nationality, age, gender, marital status, place of birth, location, ethnicity or religion, and language; social variables such as literacy, educational attainment, and housing conditions; and economic variables such as activity condition and employment (UN 2008: 112–13, table 1). Special censuses may be implemented for targeting and monitoring certain programmes, again using a few simple variables.

Censuses provide information with negligible sampling error (the whole population is considered) at highly disaggregated levels (municipalities–neighbourhoods). Census variables are used in the construction of multidimensional poverty maps using M_0 (and were previously used in the unsatisfied basic needs tradition, for example, by the governments of Colombia, Mexico, and South Africa). And census data is essential for multidimensional measures that target individuals or households. The disadvantages of censuses are that (a) they have low frequency, (b) they offer information on a small set of indicators, and (c) micro data may not be available to researchers.

Administrative data refers to information typically collected by a government department or agency primarily for administrative purposes (birth registration, customs, administration of a social benefit, etc.). One prominent example is population registers constructed through a civil registration system (UN 2001). Population registers consist of an inventory of each member of the resident population of a country augmented continuously by information on vital events (births, deaths, adoptions, marriages, divorces, among others) (UN 2001). Other examples are tax, education, police, and health records.

Some advantages of using administrative datasets are that (a) they typically cover virtually 100% of the population of interest in a continuous form, (b) there are no added data collection costs, (c) there is data for individuals who might not normally respond to surveys, and (d) when linked to other unit-level data sources, administrative data can produce a powerful resource for multidimensional poverty. However, there are also some disadvantages: (a) the information collected in administrative records is limited and may not match the research purpose, (b) any changes in data collection procedures or definitions may prevent comparability over time, (c) serious data quality issues may compromise accuracy, (d) metadata is usually not available,[2] (e) access to

---

[2] Metadata refers to comprehensive information about the dataset (population on which the data was collected, definition of the variables, etc.).

BOX 7.1 THE MILE AHEAD IN DATA COLLECTION

As Chapter 1 mentioned, enormous progress has been made in data collection worldwide since the 1940s. International institutions, universities, national institutes of statistics, and census bureaus have played a crucial role in this progress. Now virtually every country in the world has a periodic census, administrative data, and at least one multi-topic household survey being conducted periodically, usually more. However, there is still a long way to go. Data remain limited in terms of frequency, population coverage, dimensional coverage, representation of vulnerable subgroups, international comparability, interconnectedness, and the unit of analysis.

In terms of **frequency**, poverty data continues to lag behind most other economic information. The lack of frequent data makes it impossible to inform policies responding to the impact of certain events such as financial crises and natural disasters on the poor.

In terms of **population coverage**, household surveys typically exclude certain groups such as nomadic people, recent or illegal migrants or refugees, and the homeless—as well as institutionalized groups such as prisoners, those hospitalized or in nursing homes, the military, and members of religious orders. They may also overlook the elderly within households. Some excluded groups may be particularly marginalized, thus should be considered in poverty measures.

A different though related problem consists of the falling **response rates** in household surveys over subsequent rounds, even when they are not panel surveys. Such a problem is being observed in some—usually developed—countries, such as the UK, particularly with respect to indicators such as wealth or assets. While such a problem can be partially overcome by reweighting the sample, this is not ideal, and creative ways to deal with falling response rates will need to be devised.

Dimensional coverage is limited, often in ways that would be relatively easy to address. Common missing dimensions that may be relevant for poverty studies include health functionings, safety from violence, the quality of work, empowerment, social connectivity, and potentially time use. Limited dimensional coverage hampers studies of **interconnectedness**, in the sense that it does not allow researchers to analyse the joint distribution of violence and other dimensions of poverty, and identify high-impact policy sequences and causal links across these.

Many surveys seek to define household-level achievements, but do not elucidate **intra-household** inequalities, gender inequalities, and age inequalities, nor do they cover overlooked topics such as the care economy and household duties.

The **nature of the indicators** that are collected is another area of potential improvement. Paraphrasing the *Report by the Commission on the Measurement of Economic Performance and Social Progress* (Stiglitz, Sen, and Fitoussi 2009), the time is ripe to move from the space of *resources* to the space of *functionings*. Functionings, as argued in Sen's capability approach, seem to be central to poverty reduction and are of intrinsic importance. Yet even such a central dimension as health functioning is absent from most good surveys that collect income or consumption data.

Last, but not least, given that the aim remains to reduce poverty, not to measure it, improved channels of **complementarity** are required between censuses, administrative records, household surveys, and other information such as from satellites and cell phones, in order to advance towards an integrated programme of data collection and compilation. Merging GIS data on environmental conditions with household surveys, for example, greatly strengthens poverty measurement and the monitoring and impact evaluation of sustainable poverty reduction programmes. In sum, despite incredible progress in data collection, there is still a way to go so that poverty reduction can be informed by a sufficient depth and frequency of data such as are available for societies' other priorities.

administrative (micro) data varies by country, and (f) linking data sources is rarely straightforward.

Household surveys are the most commonly used data source to study poverty. These are collected from a sample or subset of the population. The sample may be representative of the population of interest, which can be the total population of a country or of a particular region, or children under 15, or some other group.

The respondents for the survey are selected from what is called a 'frame' or list, which is usually obtained from the most recent census and is typically a list of households. Different sampling methods such as simple random sampling and complex multistage sampling are used in order for the sample to be representative of the population. Deaton (1997) offers a valuable introduction to each method.[3]

Household surveys were collected as early as the eighteenth century in England (Stigler 1954). After World War II, household surveys expanded internationally with India being a pioneer. Since the 1970s, several international programmes have promoted and supported the collection of household survey data in developing countries. These include the World Fertility Surveys, which were introduced in the 1970s and became the Demographic and Health Surveys (DHS) in 1984, and the World Bank Living Standards Measurement Study (LSMS) survey programme, ongoing since 1980 (Grosh and Glewwe 2000: 6). In 1995, the United Nations Children's Fund (UNICEF) began its Multiple Indicators Cluster Surveys (MICS), and in 2000 the World Bank launched the Core Welfare Indicator Questionnaire (CWIQ). The World Bank has also intensively supported the development and widespread fielding of household budget surveys and income and expenditure surveys that are used for income and consumption poverty measures and may contain other topics. Multidimensional poverty measures typically rely on multi-topic household surveys, which collect information with one survey instrument using a sample frame that has been defined to capture a diverse set of topics.[4]

7.2 Issues in Indicator Design

All data sources, however rich, impose constraints on a poverty measurement and analysis exercise. These are navigated via a number of important decisions that are made when designing a multidimensional poverty measure and choosing its component indicators. The following subsections address the 'new' empirical considerations that

---

[3] Whenever the sampling procedure departs from simple random sampling, survey weights must be used for estimations to be representative of the population under analysis. Metadata should be consulted in order to thoroughly understand the survey structure and the weights to be used.

[4] The substantial growth in the collection of household surveys towards the end of the twentieth century has been part of what Ravallion (2011b) called the 'Second Poverty Enlightenment' (the 'First Poverty Enlightenment' occurred near the end of the eighteenth century).

are relevant both in designing new surveys for multidimensional poverty and in implementing M_o measures using existing data.

7.2.1 UNIT-LEVEL INDICATOR ACCURACY

A first essential and distinctive criterion for counting-based multidimensional poverty measures is that each indicator must be a relatively accurate reflection of the achievements enjoyed by *each* unit of identification across the relevant period and not simply the achievements enjoyed 'on average' by some group, as we will clarify in this section.

The **unit of identification** refers to the entity who is identified as poor or non-poor (determination of the poverty status)—usually the individual or the household. In the literature of poverty measurement, this is typically referred to as the unit of analysis. However, the term unit of identification is more accurate because the identification may take place at a more aggregated level, but the analysis can still be performed at a more disaggregated level. For example, if the unit of identification is the household, analyses can still generate the percentage of the population who are poor.

Household surveys are usually designed to create indicators that are representative of the achievements and/or distributions of some population subgroups, such as states or ethnic groups, at the time of the survey. For example, there are indicators typically collected which have short reference periods in order to increase indicator precision and are judged to be accurate 'on average' (Deaton and Kozel 2005). Prominent examples include consumption in the last seven days, illness in the last two weeks, and time use in the past twenty-four hours. The assumption is that people with unusually high consumption/health problems in the reference period will balance others with unusually low values, with the average (and in some cases, the distribution) being assumed to be accurate across the representative unit at the level of the single indicator. However achievements may not be accurate at the *individual* level. For example, if the last seven days' consumption included a family wedding, if the respondent had a rare and brief bout of the flu in the past fortnight, or if the last twenty-four hours was a major public holiday, then a person's response will not provide a good indication of his or her average consumption, morbidity, or time use over the past year. In contrast, indicators used for targeting people or households are *always* required to be accurate at the individual level.

Multidimensional measures require the *joint distribution of deprivations* to be accurate on average. This is straightforward to achieve if, as in the case of targeting, each indicator accurately identifies each person's deprivations, and so the deprivation scores, which reflect *joint deprivations* and will determine whether or not the person is identified as poor, are similarly accurate at the individual level. Selected indicators ideally balance indicator precision and unit-level accuracy in order to justify the assumption that responses reflect individual or household achievement or deprivation status during the relevant period. A related requirement, which occurs when multidimensional poverty measures (and, incidentally, other measures) are used to track trends in poverty over time, is that the indicators should ideally reflect individual achievement levels across the relevant period so that the comparisons are not unduly distorted by seasonal effects or short-term shocks.

Many indicators are relatively unproblematic in this regard. Indicators such as child vaccination, completed years of schooling, child mortality, housing materials, chronic disability, or long-term unemployment, for example, are likely to reflect individual or household achievements accurately. Moreover, a non-union identification strategy in the poverty cutoff can partially, as we discussed in Chapter 6, 'clean' data of errors.

That being said, in the case of other indicators, particularly those with short reference periods, the ideal may be more difficult to obtain. In practice, when collecting primary data, the unit-level accuracy issue should be considered when creating the questionnaire. When using secondary data, unit-level accuracy may guide the choice between different indicators, when such an option exists.

7.2.2 INDICATOR TRANSFORMATION TO MATCH UNIT OF IDENTIFICATION

Alkire–Foster multidimensional poverty measures reflect the joint distribution of deprivations for a given unit of identification. While the advantages of this and related approaches have been much discussed in Chapter 3, its empirical implementation actually requires novel techniques. In particular, relevant data may be available for individuals, for the household, and, perhaps, also at the community level. But it is necessary to transform all indicators such that they reflect deprivations of just one (the chosen) unit of identification. Consideration of the unit-level profile of joint deprivations leads to its identification as poor or non-poor (based on the poverty cutoff and deprivation score) and hence to the inclusion or censoring of its deprivations in the resultant multidimensional poverty measure.

To begin with an elementary case, consider a child poverty measure covering children aged 6–12. Suppose that there are data on children's education, health, and nutrition; household-level data on income and housing; and village-level data on the quality of primary school facilities. In the $n \times d$ achievement matrix, each child will naturally have their own achievement levels in health, education, and nutrition. All children from the same household may take the household's achievements in income and housing. And all school-going children in the same village may have the same achievements in quality of school facilities. The proposed transformations of household- and community-level data imply the assumption that the household- and community-level variables affect each child in the same way—which may require justification. The deprivation cutoffs for each indicator will be applied to this matrix, and each child will be identified as deprived or non-deprived in each indicator and, subsequently, as poor or non-poor, based on their weighted deprivation score. Thus each child's deprivation profile will draw on data from individual-, household-, and community-level sources. In this way, household- and community-level indicators can be appropriately 'transformed' so they inform the deprivation profile of each child. But many cases are not so simple. The next section will set out how to proceed in those cases.

7.2.3 THE UNIT OF IDENTIFICATION AND APPLICABLE POPULATION

We begin with an important definition. The **applicable population** of a certain achievement refers to the group of people for which such an achievement is relevant; namely, it *can be* measured and *has been effectively* measured, in this case, to inform poverty measurement. Note that *both* conditions need to hold for the population group to be applicable.[5] In some cases, the achievement is conceptually applicable to the whole population (with appropriate adjustments in the levels considered adequate by age group or gender), but, despite this, data is typically not collected at the individual level. An example of this is the case of anthropometric indicators (nutritional indicators). While there are anthropometric indicators for all age groups and genders, these are often collected only for children under 5 years of age and for women of reproductive age. Thus for those anthropometric indicators, the remaining population groups are non-applicable because of data constraints. In other cases, the achievement is conceptually inapplicable to certain groups of the population, as in the case of income earned by infants. In either of the two cases, the existence of non-applicable populations poses a problem to be resolved when constructing a poverty measure, if that measure is to reflect their poverty also.

The choice of the unit of identification and the treatment of non-applicable populations are often constrained by data availability. In many cases, the ideal unit of identification would be the individual; another commonly used unit is the household. In this case, the household is judged to be poor or not, and all its members are then identified as poor. 'The standard apparatus of welfare economics and welfare measurement concerns the wellbeing of individuals. Nevertheless, a good deal of data have to be gathered from households ...' (Deaton 1997: 23). Both units have advantages, as discussed in Chapter 6.

If the unit of identification of the poor is the individual, then all the considered achievements need to be available at the individual level, and thus all the achievements need to be applicable to the whole population for which the poverty measure is defined. If the unit of identification is the household, then one data point on common achievements like housing and heating may be applied to all household members. But not all the considered achievements are equally applicable to the whole population—income being a case in point (see below, this section). In these cases, certain (explicit) assumptions need to be made regarding the sharing and impact of the achievements of certain household

---

[5] Note that 'applicable population' differs from 'eligible population', a term frequently used in the metadata of household surveys to refer to the population that has been defined as eligible to collect information on a specific indicator (say, nutrition) in a particular survey instrument.

members with respect to the others. Other achievements are individual—like health status or educational level—although they may affect household members also.

Strictly speaking, few household-level indicators are applicable to each household member. Most vary by age and some by gender. Housing conditions are an example of indicators that satisfy the 'universality' of applicable population. Any person, regardless of age or gender, needs a clean source of drinking water; adequate flooring, walls, and roof; clean cooking fuel; and adequate sanitation, for example. Such dwelling conditions are jointly consumed by the household. Household surveys collect information on the dwelling conditions, and for poverty analysis it is then assumed that all members equally share them—although this may or may not be accurate.

Another universally relevant and applicable indicator for all people, now at the individual level, is nutritional status. In this case, one will need to combine at least two indicators: one for the nutritional status of children under 5 years of age (which can be weight-for-age, weight-for-height, or height-for-weight) and another for the nutritional status of adults, typically the Body Mass Index (BMI).[6]

Food consumption is another universal indicator. Although nutritional requirements vary significantly by age and gender, it may be possible to define the relevant consumption range for each type of individual.[7] However, data availability usually poses a limitation: 'Household surveys nearly always collect data on household consumption (or purchases), not on individual consumption, and so cannot give us direct information about who gets what' (Deaton 1997: 205). Thus, even though conceptually food is a private consumption good, applicable to each member of the population, in practice, it is often assumed that total consumption is distributed within the household in proportion to the nutritional requirements of each member. This assumption may or may not be accurate.

Income is not a universal indicator, as it is inapplicable to people who lack income from non-labour sources like financial assets and do not earn an income (for example, babies and children, housewives, non-working students, and some elderly members) or are unemployed. Standard income poverty measures aggregate all forms of household members' income (labour or capital) and divide by the total household size (including the members who do not earn an income) to obtain the household per capita income. Equivalence scales may be applied to obtain the household adult equivalent income. The per capita or adult equivalent income is compared to the poverty line, and the household is identified as poor or not and thus all its members. Here, as in the case of consumption, assumptions regarding equal or proportional sharing have been made.

Some other relevant indicators for poverty measurement which are inapplicable for certain groups include child vaccination (adults and children older than the relevant age

---

[6] The nutritional status of older children and adolescents (children 5–19 years old) can be measured with height-for-age or BMI-for-age.

[7] The differences in nutritional requirements are the basis for the construction of adult equivalence scales on which there is a broad literature, including Deaton and Muellbauer (1980), OECD (1982), Morales (1988), Browning (1992), Nelson (1993), Hagenaars et al. (1994), Lanjouw and Ravallion (1995), Ravallion (1996), and Deaton (1997).

group do not qualify), child mortality (people who have not had children do not qualify), and employment status. Even education as measured, for example, by years of schooling is not universally applicable, as children below the official mandatory age for starting school do not qualify.

Given that some achievements relevant for poverty measurement are either conceptually or empirically applicable only for certain population groups, the selection and definitions of indicators may take one of the following three options, depending on the purpose of the measure. They may also work as complement measures. The options are:[8]

(a) to restrict consideration to universally applicable achievements;
(b) to construct group-specific poverty measures;
(c) to combine achievements that are not universally applicable and test assumptions regarding intra-household distribution and/or impact.

(a) Universal measures

One option is to include only 'universal' achievements, that is, achievements which are applicable to the whole population. This approach narrows the set of possible indicators, although it will include housing, consumption, nutrition, and access to services, if data permit.

(b) Group-specific measures

A second option is to construct different poverty measures for each relevant group, such as child poverty measures or measures of female or elder poverty. This is an attractive option and suited to group-based policies, such as for children or women or elders.

However, three issues need to be considered. First, discriminating by groups may lessen but not eliminate applicability issues. For example, the relevant nutritional indicators change at the age of 5, whereas schooling becomes mandatory typically at the age of 6 or 7, and vaccination ages vary. Thus, no group is perfectly homogeneous and indicators may need to be adjusted within population subgroups. Second, it may be critically important to have detailed poverty analyses by population subgroups and these may inform group-based policies profoundly. Yet 'general' measures may *also* be required to track national poverty or to target households. Finally, using unlinked poverty measures for different population subgroups may miss the overlaps of disadvantaged groups and fail to fully exploit possible synergies in policy design.

(c) Combined measures

The third option is to use achievements drawn from a subset of household members (or other unit of identification) and make explicit assumptions about the distribution of such achievements and potential positive or negative intra-household externalities.

---

[8] As multidimensional poverty measurement is a field that is rapidly expanding, researchers may devise other innovative options in the near future.

This has been the route taken when constructing the global Multidimensional Poverty Index (MPI) (Alkire and Santos 2010, 2014). Assume, for example, that one wants to include nutrition but information was only collected for children under 5 and women of reproductive age. Given these data constraints, a household nutrition deprivation indicator might be defined as 'having at least one child or woman undernourished'. Hence, any household member is considered deprived in nutrition if—despite being well nourished herself—any child or woman is undernourished in her household. Similarly, if one wants to include an indicator of child mortality in the poverty measure, one way to proceed is to consider all household members as deprived if even one child in the household has died. Analogously, one can consider all household members as deprived if there is at least a child of school age who is not attending school. In all of the three examples above there is an obvious assumption of a negative intra-household externality produced by the presence of an undernourished person, the experience of a child's death, or a child being out of school. Indicators based on the assumption of a positive intra-household externality are also possible. For example, in the global MPI all household members are considered non-deprived if at least one person has five years of schooling, assuming that there is interaction and mutual sharing of cognitive skills within the household as suggested by Basu and Foster (1998).

Two practical situations must be addressed in order to compute combined measures. First, there are households where not even one person qualifies for the achievement under consideration. For example, a household may not have any children in the relevant age bracket. What indicator is used to define deprivation in these households? There is no perfect procedure. Dropping these households from the sample would bias the estimates, as the inapplicability of a certain achievement to a particular population subgroup is not a random issue and households without that population subgroup would be systematically excluded.[9] Dropping any indicator for which no applicable person is present in a household and *reweighting* the remaining indicators would violate dimensional breakdown and compromise comparability across people. A viable option is to consider all households lacking the relevant data as non-deprived (or deprived) in that particular indicator, then scrutinize this assumption. For example, a household with no children of school age cannot be deprived in child school attendance, so they could be considered non-deprived in this indicator.

A second situation occurs when the survey has not collected information from all applicable members. The example of nutrition above illustrated this case. Nutrition is applicable to all household members, yet some surveys only collect information on children and women of reproductive age, for example. So households that do not have children or women of reproductive age lack data altogether. As above, all such households may be considered as non-deprived (or deprived) in that indicator. Clearly,

[9] Precisely because a group of households with the same characteristics (for example, absence of children) is excluded, reweighting the sample would not compensate for the problem. The measure becomes a form of group-specific poverty measure.

considering them as non-deprived is a heroic assumption, as we simply do not know because information is not available. But it could be seen as a 'conservative' approach (in the same spirit of the 'presumption of innocence' principle in legal arenas), and it will lead to a 'lower bound' poverty estimate. That is, it will offer the minimum possible estimate of the proportion of people in households with an undernourished member, which could be improved later.

Naturally the assumptions used in measurement design should be examined empirically as well as debated normatively. Special studies of omitted populations (such as the elderly), including qualitative studies, should be considered to enrich measurement design and analysis, and results should be compared with group-based results to cross-check conclusions.

7.2.4 ASSESSING COMBINED MEASURES

Most multidimensional poverty measures are **combined measures,** hence some assumptions are made to permit analysis. This section describes how to assess key assumptions. Two particular kinds of analysis may be especially relevant. The first is related to the household composition effect; the second is related to the prevalence of the indicators.

First, by including indicators referring to achievements that are specific to certain groups (such as school attendance), the composition of the household will affect the probability that the household will be identified as poor. Taken to the extreme, if *all* the indicators in the poverty measure refer to a deprivation that can *only* occur among children, then clearly households without children would never be identified as poor. Obviously, a balance regarding the relevant populations for the considered achievements is required. The potential effect of household composition need not prevent the inclusion of an indicator if its importance is normatively clear. For example, it may be the case that there is a national concern about child nutrition. Inclusion of such indicators can be made, provided (a) not all of the indicators in the poverty measure refer only to a particular specific group (if so, then a group-specific poverty measure is a better alternative); (b) the specific group for which the achievement is relevant is big enough so that a known and significant proportion of households have at least one member for whom the achievement is relevant; and (c) an empirical assessment of the impact of household composition is performed to test the sensitivity of the measure to its specification.

For example, Alkire and Santos (2014) present two assessments of the influence of household composition on the probability of being poor. The first are hypothesis tests of differences in means. In each country they test whether MPI-poor households have a significantly different average size, average number of children under 5, number of females, number of members 50 years and older, prevalence of female-headed households, and proportion of school-aged children, compared to non-poor households. The second analysis decomposes each country's MPI by age and gender and compares the rankings, correlations, and the proportion of robust pairwise country comparisons across subgroup MPIs.

Regarding requirement (b), some deprivations are intrinsically important yet are either rare events or pertain to population subgroups that are very small, and thus the presence of a household member for whom the deprivation is relevant is quite unlikely. Under such circumstances, it is best to keep this indicator separate from the multidimensional poverty measure. Examples of such indicators vary by context but might include prevalence of a rare condition that affects pregnant women.

7.2.5 HANDLING MISSING VALUES

The construction of household variables, for example, from data pertaining to a subset of household members described above is completely separate from the need to address missing values, to which we now turn.

Missing values are particular cases for which a variable that is collected by the survey is not available. For example, if there is a woman of reproductive age for whom the information on BMI should have been collected, given the survey design, but for whom this information is incidentally not available, that is a case of a missing value. Missing values require attention in all poverty measures; multidimensional poverty measures have the advantage of using fewer variables than many monetary measures, but the treatment of missing values also differs slightly.

There are essentially two ways of dealing with missing values. One is to drop that observation from the entire sample. That is, if the unit of identification is the household, households with a missing value in *any* indicator for a multidimensional measure are dropped from the sample.

The other option is to create a rule that may assign a value for the missing data, particularly in a combined measure in which, for example, data are missing only for some individuals for whom the indicator is applicable. For example, in the case of the global MPI, if at least one member has five or more years of education (although other members have missing values), the household was classified as non-deprived. If there was information on at least two-thirds of household members, each having less than five years of education, the household was classified as deprived; otherwise it was dropped from the sample (Alkire and Santos 2014).

If the observations with missing values systematically differ from those with observed values, the reduction in the sample leads to biased estimates. To assess whether the sample reduction creates biased estimates, the group with missing values is compared to the rest, using the indicators for which values are present for both groups. If the two groups are not (statistically) significantly different, then one may proceed with an estimation using the reduced sample. If they are (statistically) significantly different, then one may still use the reduced sample but should explicitly signal whether the poverty estimate is likely to be a 'lower' or an 'upper' bound, based on the results of the bias analysis (Alkire and Santos 2014).[10]

One might consider whether to use imputation to assign the observation with a missing value an *estimated* value of the indicator under consideration. This is commonly done in income poverty measurement, but further research is required before it is applied multidimensionally. Imputation techniques entail using the observations for which there is information to estimate a model with the achievement under consideration as the dependent variable against a set of explanatory variables. The estimated parameters are then used to predict the achievement for the cases with missing values, given their values in the explanatory variables. However, imputation techniques are not problem-free. First, the estimated model needs to be accurate. Second, in the case of multidimensional poverty measurement, the issue of missing values is multiplied because what is of interest is *each person's joint distribution of deprivations*. This poses a significant challenge for imputation. One could specify a different model for *each* indicator. However, when that option is taken, it is likely to incur endogeneity problems. Moreover, this option is blind to varying profiles of joint deprivations. The more accurate route to take would be to specify a model that could predict a vector of deprivations. This imputation would also have to be performed such that it was accurate for each unit of identification, not merely on average. But this has not been done yet. Third, and connected to the previous section, it is also worth noting that imputation techniques cannot solve the problem of non-applicable populations as there are no observations that can be used to estimate a model. For example, one cannot impute the BMI of elderly people using a survey that collects BMI information only for women of reproductive age. As the field of multidimensional poverty measurement progresses, appropriate imputation techniques may be developed for this context.

7.3 **Relationships among Indicators**

Before implementing any measure empirically, it is helpful to understand the variables that may be entered into the measure by looking at univariate and bivariate statistics such as measures of central tendency, dispersion, and association. In the presence of multiple dimensions it is helpful to view their joint distribution, in order to scrutinize the associations across dimensions, and explore similarities or redundancies that may exist.[11] Such analysis may lead one to drop or reweight an indicator, to combine some set of indicators into a subindex, or to adjust the categorization of indicators into dimensions. It can also inform the selection of indicators and their robustness checks, the setting of deprivation values, and the interpretation of results.

---

[10] Naturally, retained sample sizes should be reported and issues of representativeness and sampling weights reassessed.

[11] See Alkire and Ballon (2012) for a fuller discussion, on which this section draws.

Statistical approaches are relevant for multidimensional poverty measures, but as Chapter 6 argued, value judgements also constitute a fundamental prior element. Thus, information on relationships between indicators is used to improve rather than determine measurement design. For example, if indicators are very highly associated in a particular dataset, that is not sufficient grounds to mechanically drop either indicator; both may be retained for other reasons—for example, if the sequence of their reduction over time differs or if both are important in policy terms. So the normative decision may be to retain both indicators, with or without adjustments to their weights, but the analysis of redundancy will have clarified their justification and treatment.

The techniques commonly used to assess relationships between indicators include many of those already presented in section 3.4—that is, principle component analysis (PCA), multiple correspondence analysis (MCA), factor analysis (FA), cluster analysis, and confirmatory structural equation models, as well as cross-tabulations and correlations. This section is confined to explaining the limitations of correlation analysis between deprivations and introducing a distinctive indicator of redundancy. Both of these draw on contingency tables presented in section 2.2.3. It is further limited in that we restrict information to the dichotomized deprivation matrix, using only uncensored or censored headcount ratios for each indicator.

7.3.1 CROSS-TABULATIONS

As was mentioned earlier, cross-tabulations or contingency tables are a basic way to view the joint distribution between two dichotomous variables—which could be the uncensored or censored headcounts. We return to these to consider matters of correlation and redundancy. A two-way contingency table (Table 7.1) provides information on two kinds of matches:

$p_{00}^{jj'}$: The percentage of people simultaneously *not* deprived in any two indicators j and j',

$p_{11}^{jj'}$: The percentage of people simultaneously deprived in any two indicators j and j'.

It also shows two kinds of mismatches:

$p_{10}^{jj'}$: The percentage of people deprived in indicator j but not in indicator j',

$p_{01}^{jj'}$: The percentage of people deprived in indicator j' but not in indicator j.

Finally, it shows the marginal distributions as $p_{+1}^{j'}$ and so on. Note that two of these marginals will correspond to the uncensored or censored headcount ratios of the two indicators.

Table 7.1 A contingency table for deprivations in two indicators

		Dimension j'		
		Non-deprived	Deprived	Total
Dimension j	**Non-deprived**	$\mathbb{p}_{00}^{jj'}$	$\mathbb{p}_{01}^{jj'}$	$\mathbb{p}_{0+}^{j}$
	Deprived	$\mathbb{p}_{10}^{jj'}$	$\mathbb{p}_{11}^{jj'}$	$\mathbb{p}_{1+}^{j}$
	Total	$\mathbb{p}_{+0}^{j'}$	$\mathbb{p}_{+1}^{j'}$	1

We show this familiar building block to remind readers that correlations between dichotomous variables—which generate the same coefficient as the Cramer's V—draw on all elements of the cross-tab: the matches, the mismatches, and the marginal entries. In words, the correlation is the product of the matches minus the product of the mismatches, divided by the square root of the product of the marginals.

$$\text{Cramer's V} = \frac{\left(\mathbb{p}_{00}^{jj'} \times \mathbb{p}_{11}^{jj'}\right) - \left(\mathbb{p}_{10}^{jj'} \times \mathbb{p}_{01}^{jj'}\right)}{[\mathbb{p}_{+1}^{j'} \times \mathbb{p}_{1+}^{j} \times \mathbb{p}_{+0}^{j'} \times \mathbb{p}_{0+}^{j}]^{1/2}}. \tag{7.1}$$

What is important to notice is that while the correlation is affected by the extent to which deprivations between variables match (which is key for redundancy), it is *also* affected by values of the headcount ratios and their difference. This, as we will show, somewhat dilutes the insights that correlations offer for redundancy—so that the correlation coefficients are best interpreted alongside the contingency table for each indicator pair. Similarly, PCA, MCA, and FA also use all elements of the cross-tab.

Instead of using the correlation (Cramer's V) alone, we propose another measure of association, which has some attractive characteristics for a direct assessment of redundancy.[12] This measure shows the matches between deprivations as a proportion of the minimum of the marginal deprivation rates. If two deprivation measures are not independent, and if at least one of the headcount ratios is different from zero, then the measure of redundancy or overlap R^o is defined as

$$R^o = \mathbb{p}_{11}^{jj'}/\min(\mathbb{p}_{+1}^{j'}, \mathbb{p}_{1+}^{j}), \quad 0 \leq R^o \leq 1. \tag{7.2}$$

That is, the measure of redundancy displays the number of observations which have the same deprivation status in both variables, which reflects the joint distribution, as a proportion of the minimum of the two uncensored or censored headcount ratios. By using the minimum of the uncensored or censored headcounts in the denominator we ensure that the maximum value of R^o is 100%.

---

[12] For a constructive review of measures of both association and similarity see Alkire and Ballon (2012). This particular measure was first proposed by Simpson (1943).

Table 7.2 Contingency tables for Mozambique and Bangladesh

Panel I: Mozambique		Attendance		
		Non-deprived= 0	Deprived=1	Total
Schooling	Non-deprived=0	47.15%	14.52%	61.68%
	Deprived= 1	22.05%	**16.27%**	38.32%
	Total	69.20%	30.80%	100.00%
Panel II: Bangladesh		Attendance		
		Non-deprived= 0	Deprived=1	Total
Schooling	Non-deprived=0	71.07%	9.43%	80.49%
	Deprived= 1	13.76%	**5.75%**	19.51%
	Total	84.82%	15.18%	100.00%

If R^o takes the value of 80%, this shows that 80% of the people who are deprived in the indicator having the lower marginal headcount ratio are also deprived in the other indicator. Thus a high level of R^o is a more direct signal that a further assessment of redundancy is required than a correlation measure might be.

An example will clarify and close this section.

Consider the Contingency Tables in Panel I and II of Table 7.2, which draw on 2011 DHS surveys for each country. In Mozambique, 38% of the population are deprived in years of schooling and 31% in school attendance. Only 16% are deprived in both indicators. For Bangladesh, 20% and 15% are deprived in years of schooling and school attendance respectively, and 6% are deprived in both. How do we assess the association between these indicators? Consider first the correlation or Cramer's V coefficients, computed using equation (7.1). Using the values in Table 7.2 it can be easily verified that the Cramer's V between attendance and schooling is 0.199 for Mozambique and 0.196 for Bangladesh. They are quite similar. But when we compute the R^o measure using equation (7.2), we find that 52.8% of possible matched deprivations overlap for Mozambique, but only 37.9% match for Bangladesh. R^o focuses on the precise relationship of interest.

Table 7.3 gives the Cramer's Vs (correlation coefficients) and the measures of overlap/redundancy for three pairs of indicators for Mozambique. The highest redundancy values correspond to those between cooking fuel and other indicators. These are exceedingly high and might suggest that cooking fuel is redundant in these datasets, unless it is retained for other normative reasons (sequencing, policy). Yet the Cramer's Vs between cooking fuel and other dimensions are not particularly high and would not show this—indeed the correlation between water and schooling is much higher. As explained above, the divergence between these two values reflects the different components of the cross-tab that they draw upon. Although correlations are often used, we consider the

Table 7.3 Correlation matrix and overlap measure for Mozambique

	Cramer's V		
	Schooling	Attendance	Water
Attendance	0.199	1.000	
Water	0.330	0.188	1.000
Cooking Fuel	0.139	0.111	0.201
	Overlap/Redundancy measure		
	Schooling	Attendance	Water
Attendance	0.529		
Water	0.776	0.708	
Cooking Fuel	0.999	0.997	0.999

measure of overlap to provide clear and precise information that should be considered alongside other kinds of information in evaluating indicator redundancy.

Chapter 8 addresses robustness analysis and statistical inference, which are required to draw conclusions or guide policies based on estimated poverty measures.

8 Robustness Analysis and Statistical Inference

Chapter 5 presented the methodology for the Adjusted Headcount Ratio poverty index (M_0) and its different partial and consistent sub-indices; Chapter 6 discussed how to design multidimensional poverty measures using this methodology in order to advance poverty reduction; and Chapter 7 explained novel empirical techniques required during implementation. Throughout, we have discussed how the index and its partial indices may be used for policy analysis and decision-making. For example, a central government may want to allocate resources to reduce poverty across its subnational regions or may want to claim credit for strong improvement in the situation of poor people using an implementation of the Adjusted Headcount Ratio. One is, however, entitled to question how conclusive any particular poverty comparisons are for two different reasons.

One reason is that the design of a poverty measure involves the selection of a set of parameters, and one may ask how sensitive policy prescriptions are to these parameter choices. Any comparison or ranking based on a particular poverty measure may alter when a different set of parameters, such as the poverty cutoff, deprivation cutoffs, or weights is used. We define an ordering as robust with respect to a particular parameter when the order is maintained despite a change in that parameter.[1] The ordering can refer to the poverty ordering of two aggregate entities, say two countries or other geographical entities, which is a *pairwise* comparison, but it can also refer to the order of more than two entities, what we refer to as a ranking. Clearly, the robustness of a ranking (of several entities) depends on the robustness of all possible pairwise comparisons. Thus, the robustness of poverty comparisons should be assessed for different, but reasonable, specifications of parameters. In many circumstances, the policy-relevant comparisons should be robust to a range of plausible parameter specifications. This process is referred to as **robustness analysis**. There are different ways in which the robustness of an ordering can be assessed. This chapter presents the most widely implemented analyses; new procedures and tests may be developed in the near future.

The second reason for questioning claimed poverty comparisons is that poverty figures in most cases are estimated from sample surveys for drawing inferences about a population. Thus, it is crucial that inferential errors are also estimated and reported. This process of drawing conclusions about the population from the data that are subject to random variation is referred to as **statistical inference**. Inferential errors affect the degree

---

[1] This chapter is confined to assessing the robustness of rank ordering across groups. Naturally it is essential also to assess the sensitivity of key values (such as the values of M_0 and dimensional contributions) to parameter changes in situations in which policies use these cardinal values.

of certainty with which two or more entities may be compared in terms of poverty for a particular set of parameters' values. Essentially, the difference in poverty levels between two entities—states for example—may or may not be statistically significant. Statistical inference affects not only the poverty comparisons for a particular set of parameter values but also the *robustness* of such comparisons for a *range* of parameters' values.

In general, assessments of robustness should cohere with a measure's policy use. If the policy depends on levels of M_0, then the robustness of the respective levels (or ranks) of poverty should be the subject of robustness tests presented here. If the policy uses information on the dimensional composition of poverty, robustness tests should assess these—which lie beyond the scope of this chapter, but see Ura et al. (2012). Recall also from Chapter 6 people's values may generate plausible ranges of parameters. Robustness tests clarify the extent to which the same policies would be supported across that relevant range of parameters. In this way, robustness tests can be used for building consensus or for clarifying which points of dissensus have important policy implications.

This chapter is divided into three sections. Section 8.1 presents a number of useful tools for conducting different types of robustness analysis; section 8.2 presents various techniques for drawing statistical inferences; and section 8.3 presents some ways in which the two types of techniques can be brought together.

8.1 **Robustness Analysis**

In monetary poverty measures, the parameters include (a) the set of indicators (components of income or consumption); (b) the price vectors used to construct the aggregate as well as any adjustments such as for inflation or urban/rural price differentials; (c) the poverty line; and (d) equivalence scales (if applied). The parameters that influence the multidimensional poverty estimates and poverty comparisons based on the Adjusted Headcount Ratio are (i) the set of indicators (denoted by subscript $j = 1, \ldots, d$); (ii) the set of deprivation cutoffs (denoted by vector z); (iii) the set of weights or deprivation values (denoted by vector w); and (iv) the poverty cutoff (denoted by k). A change in these parameters may affect the overall poverty estimate or comparisons across regions or countries.

This section introduces tools that can be used to test the robustness of pairwise comparisons as well as the robustness of overall rankings with respect to the initial choice of the parameters. We first introduce a tool to test the robustness of pairwise comparisons with respect to the choice of the poverty cutoff. This tool tests an extreme form of robustness, borrowing from the concept of stochastic dominance in the single-dimensional context (section 3.3.1).[2] When dominance conditions are satisfied,

---

[2] There is a well-developed literature on robustness and sensitivity analyses for composite indices rankings with respect to relative weights, normalization methods, aggregation methods, and measurement errors. See Saisana et al. (2005), Cherchye et al. (2007), Cherchye et al. (2008), Foster, McGillivray, and Seth (2009, 2013), Permanyer (2011, 2012), Wolff et al. (2011), and Høyland et al. (2012). These techniques may require adaptation to apply to normative, counting-based measures using ordinal data.

the strongest possible results are obtained. However, as dominance conditions are highly stringent and dominance tests may not hold for a large number of the pairwise comparisons, we present additional tools for assessing the robustness of country rankings using the correlation between different rankings. This second set of tools can be used with changes in any of the other parameters too, namely, weights, indicators, and deprivation cutoffs.

8.1.1 DOMINANCE ANALYSIS FOR CHANGES IN THE POVERTY CUTOFF

Although measurement design begins with the selection of indicators, weights, and deprivation cutoffs, we begin our robustness analysis by assessing dominance with respect to changes in the poverty cutoff, which is applied to the weighted deprivation scores constructed using other parameters. We do this because as in the unidimensional context, it is the poverty cutoff that finally identifies who is poor, thereby defining the 'headcount ratio' and effectively setting the level of poverty. It is arguably most visibly debated.[3] We have introduced the concept of stochastic dominance in the uni- and multidimensional context in section 3.3.1. This part of the chapter builds on that concept and technique, focusing primarily on **first-order stochastic dominance (FSD)** and showing how it can be applied to identify any unambiguous comparisons with respect to the poverty cutoff for our two most widely used poverty measures—Adjusted Headcount Ratio (M_0) and Multidimensional Headcount Ratio (H). Recall from section 3.3.1 the notation of two univariate distributions of achievements x and y with **cumulative distribution functions (CDF)** F_x and F_y, where $F_x(b)$ and $F_y(b)$ are the shares of population in distributions x and y with achievement level less than $b \in \mathbb{R}_+$. Distribution x first-order stochastically dominates distribution y (or x FSD y) if and only if $F_x(b) \leq F_y(b)$ for all b and $F_x(b) < F_y(b)$ for some b. Strict FSD requires that $F_x(b) < F_y(b)$ for all b.[4] Interestingly, if distribution x FSD y, then y has no lower headcount ratio than x for all poverty lines.

Let us now explain how we can apply this concept for unanimous pairwise comparisons using M_0 and H between any two distributions of deprivation scores across the population. For a given deprivation cutoff vector z and a given weighting vector w, the FSD tool can be used to evaluate the sensitivity of any pairwise comparison to varying poverty cutoff k. Following the notation introduced in Chapter 2, we denote the (uncensored) deprivation score vector by c. Note that an element of c denotes the deprivation score and a larger deprivation score implies a lower level of well-being.

The FSD tool can be applied in two different ways: one is to convert deprivations into attainments by transforming the deprivation score vector c into an attainment score

---

[3] More elaborate dominance analysis can be conducted with respect to the deprivation cutoffs and weights. For multivariate stochastic dominance analysis using ordinal variables, see Yalonetzky (2014).

[4] In empirical applications, some statistical tests cannot discern between weak and strong dominance and thus assume x *first-order stochastically dominates* distribution y, if $F_x(b) < F_y(b)$ for all b. See, for example, Davidson and Duclos (2012: 88–9).

vector $1 - c$, and the other option is to use the tool directly on the deprivation score vector c. The first approach has been pursued in Alkire and Foster (2011a) and Lasso de la Vega (2010). In this section, because it is more direct, we present the results using the deprivation score vector and thus avoid any transformation. A person is identified as poor if the deprivation score is larger than or equal to the poverty cutoff k, unlike in the attainment space where a person is identified as poor if the person's attainment falls below a certain poverty cutoff. To do that, however, we need to introduce the **complementary cumulative distribution function (CCDF)**—the complement of a CDF.[5] For any distribution y with CDF F_y, the CCDF of the distribution is $\bar{F}_y = 1 - F_y$, which means that for any value b, the CCDF $\bar{F}_y$ is the proportion of the population that has values larger than or equal to b. Naturally, CCDFs are downward sloping. The first-order stochastic dominance condition in terms of the CCDFs can be stated as follows. Any distribution y first-order stochastically dominates distribution y' if and only if $\bar{F}_y(b) \geq \bar{F}_{y'}(b)$ for all b and $\bar{F}_y(b) > \bar{F}_{y'}(b)$ for some b. For strict FSD, the strict inequality must hold for all b.

Now, suppose there are two distributions of deprivation scores, c and c', with CCDFs $\bar{F}_c$ and $\bar{F}_{c'}$. For poverty cutoff k, if $\bar{F}_c(k) \geq \bar{F}_{c'}(k)$, then distribution c has no lower multidimensional headcount ratio H than distribution c' at k. When is it possible to say that distribution c has no lower H than distribution c' for all poverty cutoffs? The answer is when distribution c first-order stochastically dominates distribution c'. Let us provide an example in terms of two four-person vectors of deprivation scores: $c = (0, 0.25, 0.5, 1)$ and $c' = (0.5, 0.5, 1, 1)$. The corresponding CCDFs $\bar{F}_c$ and $\bar{F}_{c'}$ are denoted by a black dotted line and a solid black line, respectively, in Figure 8.1. No part of $\bar{F}_c$ lies above that of $\bar{F}_{c'}$ and so $\bar{F}_{c'}$ first-order stochastically dominates $\bar{F}_c$ and we can conclude that c has unambiguously lower poverty than c' in terms of the multidimensional headcount ratio.

Let us now try to understand dominance in terms of M_0. In order to do so, first note that the area underneath a CCDF of a deprivation score vector is the average of its deprivation scores. Consider distribution c with CCDF $\bar{F}_c$ as in Figure 8.1. The area underneath $\bar{F}_c$ is the sum of areas I, II, III, and IV. Area IV is equal to $0.25 \times 1/4$, Area III is $0.5 \times 1/4$, and Areas I+II is $1 \times 1/4$, so essentially each area is a score times its frequency in the population. The sum of the four areas, $(0.25 + 0.5 + 1)/4 = \sum_{i=1}^{4} c_i/4$, is simply the average of all elements in c and it coincides with the M_0 measure for a **union** approach. When an **intermediate** or **intersection** approach to identification is used, then the M_0 is the average of the censored deprivation score vector $c(k)$. In other words, the deprivation scores of those who are not identified as poor are set to 0. For example, for a poverty cutoff $k = 0.6$, the censored deprivation score vector corresponding to c is $c(k) = (0, 0, 0, 1)$. Obtaining the average of censored deprivation scores is equivalent to ignoring areas III and IV in Figure 8.1 or it is the area below the CCDF (censored) of $c(k) = (0, 0, 0, 1)$. The M_0 of c for $k = 0.6$ is the sum of the remaining area I, II which is $1 \times 1/4 = 0.25$.[6]

---

[5] This is also variously known as survival function or reliability function in other branches of studies.

[6] Technically, M_0 for poverty cutoff k can be expressed as $M_0 = \int_k^1 \bar{F}_c(x)dx + k\bar{F}_c(k)$. In our example, Area I is computed as $\int_k^1 \bar{F}_c(x)dx$ and Area II as $k\bar{F}_c(k)$.

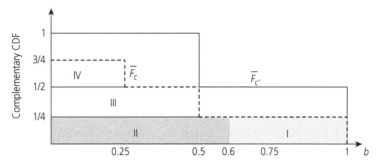

Figure 8.1. Complementary CDFs and poverty dominance

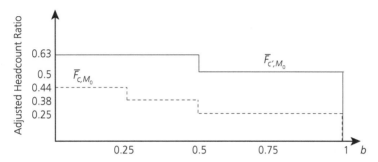

Figure 8.2. The Adjusted Headcount Ratio dominance curves

We now compute the area underneath the censored CCDF for every $k \in (0, 1]$ and plot the area on the vertical axis for each k on the horizontal axis and refer to it as an M_0 curve, depicted in Figure 8.2. We denote the M_0 curves of distributions c and c' by $\bar{F}_{c,M_0}$ and $\bar{F}_{c',M_0}$, respectively. Given that the M_0 curves are obtained by computing the areas underneath the CCDFs, the dominance of M_0 curves is referred to as second-order stochastic dominance. Given that first-order stochastic dominance implies second-order dominance, if first-order dominance holds between two distributions, then M_0 dominance will also hold between them. However, the converse is not necessarily true, that is, even when there is M_0 dominance there may not be H dominance. Therefore, when the CCDFs of two distributions cross—i.e. there is not first-order (H) dominance—it is worth testing M_0 dominance between pairs of distributions, which we refer to as pairwise comparisons from now on, using the M_0 curves. Batana (2013) has used the M_0 curves for the purpose of robustness analysis while comparing multidimensional poverty among women in fourteen African countries.

The dominance requirement for all possible poverty cutoffs may be an excessively stringent requirement. Practically, one may seek to verify the unambiguity of comparison with respect to a limited variation in the poverty cutoff, which can be referred to as **restricted dominance analysis**. For example, when making international comparisons in terms of the MPI, Alkire and Santos (2010, 2014) tested the robustness of pairwise comparisons for all poverty cutoffs $k \in [0.2, 0.4]$, in addition to the poverty cutoff of

$k = 1/3$. In this case, if the *restricted* FSD holds between any two distributions, then dominance holds for the relevant range of poverty cutoffs for both H and M_0.

8.1.2 RANK ROBUSTNESS ANALYSIS

In situations where dominance tests are too stringent, we may explore a milder form of robustness. It assesses the extent to which a ranking, that is, an ordering of more than two entities obtained under a specific set of parameters' values, is preserved when the value of some parameter is modified. How should we assess the robustness of a ranking? One first intuitive measure is to compute the percentage of pairwise comparisons that are robust to changes in parameters—that is, the proportion of pairwise comparisons that have the *same* ordering. As we shall see in section 8.3, whenever poverty computations are performed using a survey, the statistical inference tools need to be incorporated into the robustness analysis.

Another useful way to assess the robustness of a ranking is by computing a rank correlation coefficient between the original ranking of entities and the alternative rankings (i.e. those obtained with alternative parameters' values). There are various choices for a rank correlation coefficient. The two most commonly used rank correlation coefficients are the Spearman rank correlation coefficient (R^ρ) and the Kendall rank correlation coefficient (R^τ).[7]

Suppose, for a particular parametric specification, the set of ranks across m population subgroups is denoted by $r = (r_1, r_2, \ldots, r_m)$, where r_ℓ is the rank attributed to subgroup ℓ. The subgroups may be ranked by their level of multidimensional headcount ratio, the Adjusted Headcount Ratio, or any other partial and consistent sub-indices. We present the rank correlation measures using population subgroups, but they apply to ranking across countries as well. We denote the set of ranks for an alternative specification of parameters by r', where r'_ℓ is the rank attributed to subgroup ℓ. The alternative specification may be a different poverty cutoff, a different set of deprivation cutoffs, a different set of weights, or a combination of all three. If the initial and the alternative specification yield exactly the same set of rankings across subgroups, then $r_\ell = r'_\ell$ for all $\ell = 1, \ldots, m$. In this case, we state that the two sets of rankings are **perfectly positively** associated and the association is highest across the two specifications. In terms of the previous approach, 100% of the pairwise comparisons are robust to changes in one or more parameters' values. On the other hand, if the two specifications yield completely opposite sets of rankings, then $r_\ell = r'_{m-\ell+1}$ for all $\ell = 1, \ldots, m$. In this case, we state that the two sets of rankings are **perfectly negatively** associated and the association is

---

[7] In this book, we only focus on bivariate rank correlation coefficients, but there are various methods to measure multivariate rank concordance that we do not cover. For such examples, see Boland and Proschan (1988), Joe (1990), and Kendall and Gibbons (1990). For an application of some of the multivariate concordance methods to examine multivariate concordance of MPI rankings, see Alkire et al. (2010).

lowest across the two specifications. In terms of the previous approach, 0% of the pairwise comparisons are robust to changes in one or more parameters' values.

The Spearman rank correlation coefficient can be expressed as

$$R^\rho = 1 - \frac{6\sum_{\ell=1}^{m}\left(r_\ell - r_\ell'\right)^2}{m(m^2 - 1)}. \tag{8.1}$$

Intuitively, for the Spearman rank correlation coefficient, the square of the difference in the two ranks for each subgroup is computed and an average is taken across all subgroups. The R^ρ is bounded between -1 and $+1$. The lowest value of -1 is obtained when two rankings are perfectly negatively associated with each other, whereas the largest value of $+1$ is obtained when two rankings are perfectly positively associated with each other.

The Kendall rank correlation coefficient is based on the number of concordant pairs and discordant pairs. A pair (ℓ, ℓ') is concordant if the comparisons between two objects are the same in both the initial and alternative specification, i.e. $r_\ell > r_{\ell'}$ and $r_\ell' > r_{\ell'}'$. In terms of the previously used terms, a concordant pair is equivalent to a robust pairwise comparison. A pair, on the other hand, is discordant if the comparisons between two objects are altered between the initial and the alternative specification such that $r_\ell > r_{\ell'}$ but $r_\ell' < r_{\ell'}'$. In terms of the previously used terms, a discordant pair is equivalent to a non-robust pairwise comparison. The R^τ is the difference in the number of concordant and discordant pairs divided by the total number of pairwise comparisons. The Kendall rank correlation coefficient can be expressed as

$$R^\tau = \frac{\#\text{Concordant Pairs} - \#\text{Discordant Pairs}}{m(m-1)/2}. \tag{8.2}$$

Like R^ρ, R^τ also lies between -1 and $+1$. The lowest value of -1 is obtained when two rankings are perfectly negatively associated with each other, whereas the largest value of $+1$ is obtained when two rankings are perfectly positively associated with each other. Although both R^ρ and R^τ are used to assess rank robustness, the Kendall rank correlation coefficient has an intuitive interpretation. Suppose the Kendall Tau correlation coefficient is 0.90, from equation (8.2), it can be deduced that this means that 95% of the pairwise comparisons are concordant (i.e. robust) and only 5% are discordant. Equations (8.1) and (8.2) are based on the assumption that there are no ties in the rankings. In other words, both expressions are applicable when no two entities have equal values. When there are ties, Kendall (1970) offers two adjustments in the denominator of both rank correlation coefficients (R^ρ and R^τ) to correct for tied ranks; these adjusted Kendall coefficients are commonly known as tau-b and tau-c.

Let us present one empirical illustration showing how rank robustness tools may be used in practice. The first illustration presents the correlation between 2011 MPI rankings across 109 countries and the rankings for three alternative weighting vectors (Alkire et al. 2011). The MPI attaches equal weights across three dimensions: health, education, and standard of living. However, it is hard to argue with perfect confidence that the

Table 8.1 Correlation among country ranks for different weights

		Equal weights
Alternative Weights 1	Spearman	0.979
	Kendall	0.893
Alternative Weights 2	Spearman	0.987
	Kendall	0.918
Alternative Weights 3	Spearman	0.985
	Kendall	0.904

Note: The computations of the Spearman and Kendall coefficients in the table have been adjusted for ties. For the exact formulation of tie-adjusted coefficients, see Kendall and Gibbons (1990).

initial weight is the correct choice. Therefore, three alternative weighting schemes were considered. The first alternative assigns a 50% weight to the health dimension and then a 25% weight to each of the other two dimensions. Similarly, the second alternative assigns a 50% weight to the education dimension and then distributes the rest of the weight equally across the other two dimensions. The third alternative specification attaches a 50% weight to the standard of living dimension and then 25% weights to each of the other two dimensions. Thus, we now have four different rankings of 109 countries, each involving 5,356 pairwise comparisons. Table 8.1 presents the rank correlation coefficient R^ρ and R^τ between the initial ranking and the ranking for each alternative specification. It can be seen that the Spearman coefficient is around 0.98 for all three alternatives. The Kendall coefficient is around 0.9 for each of the three cases, implying that around 80% of the comparisons are concordant in each case.

The same type of analysis has been done to changes in other parameters' values, such as the indicators used and deprivation cutoffs (Alkire and Santos 2014).

8.2 **Statistical Inference**

The last section showed how the robustness of claims made using the Adjusted Head-count Ratio and its partial and consistent sub-indices may be assessed. Such assessments apply to changes in a country's performance over time, comparisons between different countries, and comparisons of different population subgroups within a country. Most frequently, the indices are estimated from sample surveys with the objective of estimating the unknown population parameters as accurately as possible. A sample survey, unlike a census that covers the entire population, consists of a representative fraction of the population.[8] Different sample surveys, even when conducted at the same time and despite having the same design, would most likely provide a different set of estimates for the

---

[8] Various sampling methods, such as simple random sampling, systematic sampling, stratified sampling, and proportional sampling, are used to conduct a sampling survey.

same population parameters. Thus, it is crucial to compute a measure of confidence or reliability for each estimate from a sample survey. This is done by computing the standard deviation of an estimate. The standard deviation of an estimate is referred to as its **standard error**. The lower the magnitude of a standard error, the larger the reliability of the corresponding estimate. Standard errors are key for hypothesis testing and for the construction of confidence intervals, both of which are very helpful for robustness analysis and more generally for drawing policy conclusions. In what follows we briefly explain each of these statistical terms.

8.2.1 STANDARD ERRORS

There are different approaches to estimating standard errors. Two approaches are commonly followed:

- **Analytical Approach**: Formulas that provide either the exact or the asymptotic approximation of the standard error and thus confidence intervals.[9]
- **Resampling Approach**: Standard errors and the confidence intervals may be computed through the bootstrap or similar techniques (as performed for the global MPI in Alkire and Santos 2014).

The Appendix to this chapter presents the formulas for computing standard errors with the analytical approach depending on the survey design.

The analytical approach is based on two assumptions. Such assumptions are based on the premise that the sample surveys used for estimating the population parameters are significantly smaller in size compared to the population size under consideration.[10] For example, the sample size of the Demographic and Health Survey of India in 2006 was only 0.04% of the Indian population. The first assumption is that the samples are drawn from a population that is infinitely large, so that *even* the finite population under study *is a sample* of an infinitely large superpopulation. This philosophical assumption is based on the **superpopulation approach**, which is different from the **finite population approach** (for further discussion see Deaton 1997). A finite population approach requires that a finite population correction factor should be used to deflate the standard error if the sample size is large relative to the population. However, if the sample size is significantly smaller than the finite population size, the finite population correction factor is approximately equal to one. In this case, the standard errors based on both approaches are almost the same.

---

[9] Yalonetzky (2010).
[10] If the particular condition under study does not justify the assumptions made here, then these assumptions need to be relaxed and the standard error formulations are adjusted accordingly.

The second assumption is that we treat each sample as drawn from the population *with replacement.* The practical motivation behind the assumption is the size of the sample survey compared to the population. The sample surveys are commonly conducted without replacement because, once a household is visited and interviewed, the same household is not visited again on purpose. When samples are drawn with replacement, the observations are independent of each other. However, if the samples are drawn without replacement, then the samples are not independent of each other. It can be shown that in the absence of multistage sampling, a sampling without replacements needs a Finite Population Correction (FPC) factor for computing the sampling variance. The FPC factor is of the order $1 - m/n$, where m is the sample size and n is the size of the population. The use of an FPC factor allows us to get a better estimate of the true population variance. However, when the sample size is small with respect to the population, i.e. $m/n \to 0$, the use of an FPC factor will not make much difference to the estimation of the sampling variance as the FPC factor is closer to one (Duclos and Araar 2006: 276). These assumptions would be required in order to justify our assumption that each sample is independently and identically distributed.

We now illustrate relevant methods using the Adjusted Headcount Ratio (M_0) denoting its sample estimate by $\hat{M}_0$ and standard error of the estimate by $se_{\hat{M}_0}$. However, the methods are equally applicable to inferences for the multidimensional headcount ratio, the intensity, and the censored headcount ratios as long the standard errors are appropriately computed, as outlined in the Appendix of this chapter.

8.2.2 CONFIDENCE INTERVALS

A confidence interval is a type of interval estimate of a parameter. The probability that a confidence interval contains the parameter is called the confidence level. A significance level that is used is the complement of the confidence level. Let us denote the significance level[11] by ω, which by definition ranges between 0 and 100%. The level of confidence is $(1 - \omega)$ percent. Thus, for a given estimate, if one wants to be 95% confident about the range within which the true population parameter lies, then the significance level is 5%. Similarly, if one wants to be 99% confident, then the significance level is 1%.

By the central limit theorem, we can say that the difference between the population parameter and the corresponding sample average divided by the standard error approximates the standard normal distribution (i.e. the normal distribution with a mean of 0 and a standard deviation of 1). Using the standard normal distribution, one can determine the *critical* value associated with that significance level, which is given by the **inverse of**

---

[11] The significance level is also referred to as the Type I error, which is the probability of rejecting the null hypothesis when it is true. See section 8.2.3 for the notion of null hypothesis. By statistical convention, the significance level is denoted with α. However, to avoid confusion with the use of this symbol for other purposes in this book, we denote it by ω.

Table 8.2 Confidence intervals for $\hat{M}_0, \hat{H}$, and $\hat{A}$

		India 2005–6		
Estimate	Value	Standard error	Confidence interval (95%)	Confidence interval (99%)
$\hat{M}_0$	0.251	0.0026	(0.245, 0.256)	(0.244, 0.258)
$\hat{H}$	48.5%	0.41%	(47.7%, 49.3%)	(47.4%, 49.6%)
$\hat{A}$	51.7%	0.20%	(51.3%, 52.1%)	(51.2%, 52.2%)

Source: Alkire and Seth (2013b, 2015)

the standard normal distribution at $\omega/2$. In other words, the critical value is the value at which the probability that the statistic is higher than that is precisely $\omega/2$.[12] The critical values to be used when one is interested in computing a 95% confidence interval are $|\mathfrak{z}_{\omega/2}| = 1.96$. If instead one is interested in computing a 99% or a 90% confidence interval, the corresponding critical values are $|\mathfrak{z}_{\omega/2}| = 2.58$ and $|\mathfrak{z}_{\omega/2}| = 1.645$, respectively.

For example, Table 8.2 presents the sample estimate of the Adjusted Headcount Ratio ($\hat{M}_0$), the multidimensional headcount ratio ($\hat{H}$), and the average deprivation share among the poor ($\hat{A}$) from the Demographic and Health Survey of 2005–6. India's sample estimate of the population Adjusted Headcount Ratio is $\hat{M}_0$, with a standard error $se_{\hat{M}_0} = 0.0026$. The 95% confidence interval is then $(\hat{M}_0 - \mathfrak{z}_{\omega/2} \times se_{\hat{M}_0}, \hat{M}_0 + \mathfrak{z}_{\omega/2} \times se_{\hat{M}_0}) = (0.245, 0.256)$. This means that with 95% confidence, the true population M_0 lies between 0.245 and 0.256. Similarly, the 99% confidence interval of India's $\hat{M}_0$ is $(0.244, 0.257)$.

Similar to $\hat{M}_0$, the confidence interval for $\hat{A}$ is $(\hat{A} - \mathfrak{z}_{\omega/2} \times se_{\hat{A}}, \hat{A} + \mathfrak{z}_{\omega/2} \times se_{\hat{A}})$, for $\hat{H}$ is $(\hat{H} - \mathfrak{z}_{\omega/2} \times se_{\hat{H}}, \hat{H} + \mathfrak{z}_{\omega/2} \times se_{\hat{H}})$, and for $\hat{h}_j$ is $(\hat{h}_j - \mathfrak{z}_{\omega/2} \times se_{\hat{h}_j}, \hat{h}_j + \mathfrak{z}_{\omega/2} \times se_{\hat{h}_j})$ for all $j = 1, \ldots, d$. It can be seen from the table that the standard error of $\hat{H}$ is 0.41%, whereas that of $\hat{A}$ is 0.20%.

8.2.3 HYPOTHESIS TESTS

Confidence intervals are useful for judging the statistical reliability of a point estimate when the population parameter is unknown. However, suppose that, somehow, we have a hypothesis about what the population parameter is. For example, suppose the government hypothesizes that the Adjusted Headcount Ratio in India is 0.26. Thus, the null hypothesis is $\mathcal{H}_0 : M_0 = 0.26$. This has to be tested against any of the three alternatives $\mathcal{H}_1 : M_0 \neq 0.26$ or $\mathcal{H}_1 : M_0 > 0.26$ or $\mathcal{H}_1 : M_0 < 0.26$.[13] This is a **one-sample test**. Note that the first alternative requires a so-called two-tailed test, and each of the

---

[12] The critical values will follow a Student-t distribution if the population standard deviation is estimated or if the sample size is small.

[13] We present the tests for country-level estimates but they are equally applicable to other population subgroups. Also, we only present the tests in terms of the M_0 measure, but again they are also applicable to A, H, and h_j for all j, and so we have chosen not to repeat the results.

other two alternatives requires a so-called one-tailed test. Now, suppose a sample (either simple random or multistage stratified) $\hat{X}$ of size n is collected. We denote the estimated Adjusted Headcount Ratio by $\hat{M}_0$. By the law of large numbers and by the central limit theorem, as $n \to \infty$, $(\hat{M}_0 - M_0) \overset{d}{\to} \text{Normal}(0, \sigma_0^2/n)$, where $\sigma_0^2 = E[\hat{c}_i(k) - M_0]^2$ is the population variance of M_0. The standard error $se_{\hat{M}_0}$ of $\hat{M}_0$ can be estimated using either equation (8.11) or (8.30) in the Appendix, whichever is applicable.

In a two-tail test, the null hypothesis can be rejected against the alternative $\mathcal{H}_1 : M_0 \neq 0.26$ with a $(1-\omega)$ confidence level if $|(\hat{M}_0 - 0.26)/se_{\hat{M}_0}| > |\mathfrak{z}_{\omega/2}|$; in words, if the absolute value of the statistic is greater than the absolute value of the critical value. An equivalent procedure to reject or not the null hypothesis entails, rather than comparing the test statistic against the critical value, comparing the significance level against the so-called p-value. The p-value is defined as the actual probability that the test statistic assumes a value greater than the value observed, i.e. it is the probability of rejecting the null hypothesis when it is true.

Let us consider the example of India's Adjusted Headcount Ratio reported in Table 8.2, where $\hat{M}_0 = 0.251$ and $se_{\hat{M}_0} = 0.0026$. Now, $|(\hat{M}_0 - 0.26)/se_{\hat{M}_0}| = 3.46 > 2.58 = \mathfrak{z}_{0.5\%}$. Thus, with 99% confidence, the null hypothesis can be rejected with respect to the alternative $M_0 \neq 0.26$ and the corresponding p-value is $2(1 - \Phi[(\hat{M}_0 - 0.26)/se_{\hat{M}_0}])$, where Φ stands for the cumulative standard normal distribution. Similarly, in a one-tail test to the right, the null hypothesis can be rejected against the alternative $\mathcal{H}_1 : M_0 > 0.26$ with a $(1-\omega)$ confidence level if $(\hat{M}_0 - 0.26)/se_{\hat{M}_0} > \mathfrak{z}_{1-\omega}$. The corresponding p-value is $[1 - \Phi((\hat{M}_0 - 0.26)/se_{\hat{M}_0})]$. Finally, in a one-tail test to the left, the null hypothesis can be rejected against the alternative $\mathcal{H}_1 : M_0 < 0.26$ with a $(1-\omega)$ confidence level, if $(\hat{M}_0 - 0.26)/se_{\hat{M}_0} < \mathfrak{z}_\omega$, where the relevant p-value is $\Phi((\hat{M}_0 - 0.26)/se_{\hat{M}_0})$.[14]

Note that the conclusions based on the confidence intervals and the one-sample tests are identical. If the value at the null hypothesis lies outside of the confidence interval, then the test will also show that the null hypothesis is rejected. On the other hand, if the value at the null hypothesis lies inside the confidence interval, then the test cannot reject the null hypothesis.

Formal tests are also required in order to understand whether a change in the estimate over time—or a difference between the estimates of two countries—has been statistically significant. The difference is that this is a **two-sample test**. We assume that the two estimates whose difference is of interest are estimated from two independent samples.[15] For example, when we are interested in testing the difference in M_0 across two countries, across rural and urban areas, or across population subgroups, it is safe to assume that the samples are drawn independently. A somewhat different situation may arise with a change over time. It is possible that the samples are drawn independently of each other

[14] See Bennett and Mitra (2013) for an exposition of hypothesis testing of M_0 and other AF partial sub-indices using a minimum p-value approach.

[15] See chapters 14 and 16 of Duclos and Araar (2006) for further discussion of non-independent samples for panel data analysis.

or that the samples are drawn from the same population in order to track changes over time, as, for example, in panel datasets. This section restricts its attention to assessments in which we can assume independent samples.

Suppose there are two countries, Country I and Country II. The population achievement matrices are denoted by X^I and X^{II}, respectively, and the population-adjusted headcount ratios are denoted by $M_{0,I}$ and $M_{0,II}$, respectively. We seek to test the null hypothesis $\mathcal{H}_0 : M_{0,I} - M_{0,II} = 0$, which implies that poverty in country I is not significantly different from poverty in country II, with regards to any of the three alternatives: (a) $\mathcal{H}_1 : M_{0,I} - M_{0,II} \neq 0$, which means that one of the two countries is significantly poorer than the other; or (b) $\mathcal{H}_1 : M_{0,I} - M_{0,II} > 0$, which means that country I is significantly poorer than country II; or (c) $\mathcal{H}_1 : M_{0,I} - M_{0,II} < 0$, which means the opposite. For the first alternative, we need to conduct a two-tailed test, and for the other two alternatives, we need to conduct a one-tailed test.

Now, suppose a sample (either simple, random, or multistage stratified) $\hat{X}^I$ of size n^I is collected from X^I and a sample $\hat{X}^{II}$ of size n^{II} is collected from X^{II}, where samples in $\hat{X}^I$ and $\hat{X}^{II}$ are assumed to have been drawn independently of each other. We denote the estimated Adjusted Headcount Ratios from the samples by $\hat{M}_{0,I}$ and $\hat{M}_{0,II}$, respectively. By the law of large numbers and the central limit theorem, $(\hat{M}_{0,I} - M_{0,I}) \xrightarrow{d}$ Normal $(0, \sigma_{0,I}^2/\mathrm{n}^I)$ and $(\hat{M}_{0,II} - M_{0,II}) \xrightarrow{d}$ Normal $(0, \sigma_{0,II}^2/\mathrm{n}^{II})$. The difference of two normal distributions is a normal distribution as well. Thus,

$$\left(\left(\hat{M}_{0,I} - \hat{M}_{0,II} \right) - (M_{0,I} - M_{0,II}) \right) \xrightarrow{d} \text{Normal}(0, \sigma_{0,I-II}^2), \tag{8.3}$$

where $\sigma_{0,I-II}^2 = \frac{\sigma_{0,I}^2}{\mathrm{n}^I} + \frac{\sigma_{0,II}^2}{\mathrm{n}^{II}}$. Note that, as we have assumed independent samples, the covariance between the two Adjusted Headcount Ratios is zero. Hence, the standard error of $\hat{M}_{0,I} - \hat{M}_{0,II}$, denoted by $se_{\hat{M}_0,I-II}$, may be estimated using Equations (8.11) or (8.30) in the Appendix, whichever is applicable, as:

$$se_{\hat{M}_0,I-II} = \sqrt{se_{\hat{M}_0,I}^2 + se_{\hat{M}_0,II}^2}, \tag{8.4}$$

where $se_{\hat{M}_0,I}^2$ is the variance of $\hat{M}_{0,I}$ and $se_{\hat{M}_0,II}^2$ is the variance of $\hat{M}_{0,II}$. Like the one-sample test discussed above, in the two-tail test, the null hypothesis can be rejected against the alternative $\mathcal{H}_1 : M_{0,I} - M_{0,II} \neq 0$ with a $(1-\omega)$ confidence level, if $|[(\hat{M}_{0,I} - \hat{M}_{0,II}) - (M_{0,I} - M_{0,II})]/se_{\hat{M}_0,I-II}| > |\mathfrak{z}_{\omega/2}|$. Similarly, in order to reject the null hypothesis against $\mathcal{H}_1 : M_{0,I} - M_{0,II} > 0$, we require $(\hat{M}_{0,I} - \hat{M}_{0,II})/se_{\hat{M}_0,I-II} > \mathfrak{z}_{1-\omega}$ and against $\mathcal{H}_1 : M_{0,I} - M_{0,II} < 0$, we require $(\hat{M}_{0,I} - \hat{M}_{0,II})/se_{\hat{M}_0,I-II} < \mathfrak{z}_{\omega}$. The corresponding p-values can be computed as discussed in the one-sample test.

Table 8.3 presents an example of an estimation of MPI (an adaptation of M_0) in four Indian states: Goa, Punjab, Andhra Pradesh, and Tripura, with their corresponding

Table 8.3 Comparison of Indian states using standard errors

States	MPI	Standard error	95% Confidence interval		Difference	
			Lower bound	Upper bound	MPI	Statistically significant
Goa	0.057	0.0062	0.045	0.069	0.031	Yes
Punjab	0.088	0.0078	0.073	0.103		
Andhra Pradesh	0.194	0.0093	0.176	0.212	0.032	No
Tripura	0.226	0.0162	0.195	0.258		

Source: Alkire and Seth (2013b)

standard errors, confidence intervals, and hypothesis tests.[16] These results are computed from the Demographic and Health Survey of India for the years 2005–6. In the table we can see that the MPI point estimate for Goa is 0.057, and with 95% confidence, we can say that the MPI estimate of Goa lies somewhere between 0.045 and 0.069. Similarly, we can say with 95% confidence that Punjab's MPI is not larger than 0.103 and no less than 0.073, although the point estimate of MPI is 0.088. We can also state, after doing the corresponding hypothesis test, that Punjab is significantly poorer than Goa. However, we cannot draw the same kind of conclusion for the comparison between Andhra Pradesh and Tripura, although the difference between the MPI estimates of these two states (0.032) is similar to the difference between Goa and Punjab.

It is vital to understand that in two sample tests, conclusions about the statistical significance obtained with confidence intervals do not necessarily coincide with conclusions obtained using hypothesis testing. Let us formally examine the situation. Suppose, $\hat{M}_{0,I} > \hat{M}_{0,II}$. If the confidence intervals do not overlap, then the lower bound of $\hat{M}_{0,I}$ is above the upper bound of $\hat{M}_{0,II}$, i.e. $\hat{M}_{0,I} - \mathfrak{z}_{\omega/2} \times se_{\hat{M}_{0,I}} > \hat{M}_{0,II} + \mathfrak{z}_{\omega/2} \times se_{\hat{M}_{0,II}}$ or $[\hat{M}_{0,I} - \hat{M}_{0,II}]/[se_{\hat{M}_{0,I}} + se_{\hat{M}_{0,II}}] > \mathfrak{z}_{\omega/2}$. Given that for two independent samples, $se_{\hat{M}_{0,I}} + se_{\hat{M}_{0,II}} > se_{\hat{M}_{0,I-II}}$, if the confidence intervals do not cross, a statistically significant comparison can be made. However, if the confidence intervals overlap, it does not necessarily mean that the comparison is *not* statistically significant at the same level of significance. It is thus essential to conduct statistical tests on *differences* when the confidence intervals overlap.

8.3 **Robustness Analysis with Statistical Inference**

In practice, the robustness analyses discussed in section 8.1 are typically performed with estimates from sample surveys. In at least two cases, it is necessary to *combine* the robustness analyses with the statistical inference tools just described. This section describes how to do so in practice.

---

[16] Alkire and Seth (2013b, 2015) use an MPI harmonized for strict comparability of indicator definitions across time.

The dominance analysis presented in section 8.1.1 assesses dominance between two CCDFs or two M_0 curves in order to conclude whether a pairwise ordering is robust to the choice of all poverty cutoffs. But it is also crucial to examine if the pairwise dominance of the CCDFs or M_0 curves are statistically significant. For two entities in a pairwise ordering, one should perform one-tailed hypothesis tests of the difference in the two M_0 estimates for *each* possible k value, as described in section 8.2.3. This will determine whether the two countries' poverty estimates are not significantly different or whether one is significantly poorer than the other *regardless* of the poverty cutoff.[17] One may also construct confidence interval curves around each CCDF curve (or M_0 curve) and examine whether two corresponding confidence interval curves overlap or not, in order to conclude dominance. More specifically, if the lower confidence interval curve of a unit does not overlap with the upper confidence interval curve of another unit, then one may conclude that statistically significant dominance holds between two entities. However, as explained at the end of section 8.2.3, no conclusion on statistical significance can be made when the confidence intervals overlap. Thus a hypothesis test for dominance should be preferred.[18]

This method also applies to the other type of robustness analysis presented in section 8.1.2, in the sense that one can implement this analysis to a ranking of entities and report the proportion of robust pairwise comparisons across the different k values. Moreover, the analysis described in section 8.2.3 (hypothesis testing or comparison of confidence intervals by pairs of entities) can be implemented not only with respect to the poverty cutoff but also with respect to changes in the other parameters, such as weights, deprivation cutoffs, or alternative indicators.

As Alkire and Santos observe (2014: 260), the number of robust pairwise comparisons may be expressed in two ways. One may report the *proportion of the total* possible pairwise comparisons that are robust. A somewhat more precise option is to express it as a *proportion of the number of significant pairwise comparisons in the baseline measure*, because a pairwise comparison that was not significant in the baseline M_0 cannot, by definition, be a *robust* pairwise comparison.

To interpret results meaningfully, it can be helpful to observe that the proportion of robust pairwise comparisons of alternative M_0 specifications is influenced by the number of possible pairwise comparisons, the number of significant pairwise comparisons in the baseline distribution, and the number of alternative parameter specifications. Interpretation of the percentage of robust pairwise comparisons in light of these three factors illuminates the degree to which the poverty estimates and the policy recommendations they generate are valid across alternative plausible design specifications.

Alkire and Santos (2014) perform both types of robustness analysis with the global MPI (2010 estimates) for every possible pair of countries with respect to (a) a restricted range of k values, namely, 20% to 40%; (b) four alternative sets of plausible weights; and

[17] For formal tests on stochastic dominance in unidimensional poverty and welfare analysis, see Anderson (1996), Davidson and Duclos (2000), and Barrett and Donald (2003).
[18] Other new ways of testing robustness may be developed in the near future.

(c) subgroup-level MPI values.[19] The country rankings seem highly robust to alternative parameters' specifications.[20]

Chapter 9 further develops the techniques of multidimensional poverty measurement and analysis. Specifically, we present techniques for analysing poverty over time (with and without panel data) and for exploring distributional issues such as inequality among the poor.

Appendix: Methods for Computing Standard Errors

This appendix provides a technical outline of how standard errors may be computed. We first present the analytical approach and then the bootstrap method using the notation in Method I, presented in Box 5.7. For the multidimensional and censored headcount ratios, we use the notation in Box 5.4. The M_0 and its partial and consistent sub-indices are written as

$$M_0(X; z, w, k) = \frac{\sum_{i=1}^{n} c_i(k)}{n} \qquad (8.5)$$

$$A(X; z, w, k) = \frac{\sum_{i=1}^{q} c_i(k)}{q} \qquad (8.6)$$

$$H(X; z, w, k) = \frac{\sum_{i=1}^{n} \mathbb{I}[c_i \geq k]}{n} \qquad (8.7)$$

$$h_j(X; z, w, k) = \frac{\sum_{i=1}^{n} \mathbb{I}\left[(c_i \geq k) \wedge \left(g_{ij}^0 = 1\right)\right]}{n} \qquad (8.8)$$

Note that $\wedge$ is the logical 'and' operator. The standard errors of the subgroups' M_0s and partial and consistent sub-indices may be computed in the same way and so we only outline the standard errors of equations (8.5)–(8.8).

Simple Random Sampling with Analytical Approach

Suppose n samples have been collected through simple random sampling from the population. We denote the dataset by $\hat{X}$ and its ij^{th} element by $\hat{x}_{ij}$ for all $i = 1, \ldots, n$ and $j = 1, \ldots, d$. We denote the deprivation status score for $\hat{x}_{ij}$ by $\hat{g}_{ij}^0$. For statistical inferences, our analysis focuses on the censored deprivation scores. The score, defined at the population level, becomes a random variable while performing statistical inference. We assume that a random sample (of size n) of censored deprivation scores $\{c_1(k), \ldots, c_n(k)\}$ is a sequence of independently and identically distributed random variables with an

---

[19] They compute the MPI for four population subgroups: children 0–14 years of age, women 15–49 years of age, women aged 50 years and older, and men 15 years and older, and test the rankings of subgroup MPIs across countries.

[20] Further methodological work is needed to propose overall robustness standards for measures that will be used for policy.

expected value $E(c_i(k)) = M_0$ and $\text{Var}(c_i(k)) = \sigma_0^2$. Then as n approaches infinity, the random variable $\sqrt{n}\left(\hat{M}_0 - M_0\right)$ converges in distribution to $\text{Normal}\left(0, \sigma_0^2\right)$, where $\hat{M}_0 = \left(\sum_{i=1}^n c_i(k)\right)/n$. That is

$$\sqrt{n}\left(\hat{M}_0 - M_0\right) \xrightarrow{d} \text{Normal}\left(0, \sigma_0^2\right). \tag{8.9}$$

The unbiased sample estimate of σ_0^2 is

$$\hat{\sigma}_0^2 = \frac{1}{n-1}\sum_{i=1}^n \left[c_i(k) - \hat{M}_0\right]^2, \tag{8.10}$$

and the standard error of the Adjusted Headcount Ratio is

$$se_{\hat{M}_0} = \frac{\hat{\sigma}_0}{\sqrt{n-1}} = \frac{1}{n-1}\sqrt{\sum_{i=1}^n \left[c_i(k) - \hat{M}_0\right]^2}. \tag{8.11}$$

The analytical approach based on the central limit theorem (CLT) also applies to the calculation of the standard errors of H, which leads to

$$\sqrt{n}\left(\hat{H} - H\right) \xrightarrow{d} \text{Normal}\left(0, \sigma_H^2\right), \tag{8.12}$$

where $\hat{H} = \left[\sum_{i=1}^n \mathbb{I}[c_i \geq k]\right]/n$ and $\sigma_H^2 = E\left[\mathbb{I}[\hat{c}_i \geq k] - H\right]^2$. Note that unlike M_0, H is an average across 0's and 1's, i.e. the mean is a proportion and σ_H^2 is estimated as

$$\hat{\sigma}_H^2 = \hat{H}\left(1 - \hat{H}\right), \tag{8.13}$$

and so the unbiased standard error is

$$se_{\hat{H}} = \frac{\hat{\sigma}_H}{\sqrt{n-1}} = \sqrt{\frac{\hat{H}\left(1 - \hat{H}\right)}{n-1}}. \tag{8.14}$$

With the same logic, the standard error for h_j, can be estimated as

$$se_{\hat{h}_j} = \frac{\hat{\sigma}_{h_j}}{\sqrt{n-1}} = \sqrt{\frac{\hat{h}_j\left(1 - \hat{h}_j\right)}{n-1}}, \tag{8.15}$$

where, $\hat{h}_j = \left[\sum_{i=1}^n \mathbb{I}[c_i \geq k \wedge (\hat{g}_{ij}^0 = 1)]\right]/n$.

The formulation of A is analogous to the formulation of M_0, and so the standard error of A is computed as

$$se_{\hat{A}} = \frac{\hat{\sigma}_A}{\sqrt{q-1}} = \frac{1}{q-1}\sqrt{\sum_{i=1}^q \left[c_i(k) - \hat{A}\right]^2}, \tag{8.16}$$

where $\hat{A} = \left(\sum_{i=1}^q c_i(k)\right)/q$ and q is the number multidimensionally poor in the sample.

Note that if the number of multidimensionally poor is extremely low, the sample size for estimating $se_{\hat{A}}$ may not be large enough. This may affect the precision of $se_{\hat{A}}$ using (8.16). It may then be accurate to treat A as a ratio of M_0 and H for computing $se_{\hat{A}}$. By the Taylor series expansion (see the discussion in Casella and Berger 1990, 240–245), $\hat{A}$ can be approximated as $\hat{A} \approx \hat{M}_0/\hat{H}$ and σ_A^2 can be estimated as

$$\hat{\sigma}_A^2 \approx \left(\frac{\hat{M}_0}{\hat{H}}\right)^2 \left[\frac{\hat{\sigma}_H^2}{\hat{H}^2} + \frac{\hat{\sigma}_0^2}{\hat{M}_0^2} - \frac{2\hat{\sigma}_{0,H}^2}{\hat{H}\hat{M}_0}\right], \tag{8.17}$$

where $\hat{\sigma}_0^2$ and $\hat{\sigma}_H^2$ are based on (8.10) and (8.13), respectively, and $\hat{\sigma}_{0,H}^2$ can be estimated as

$$\hat{\sigma}_{0,H}^2 = \frac{1}{\text{n}-1} \sum_{i=1}^{\text{n}} \left[\mathbb{I}\left[c_i \geq k\right] - \hat{H}\right]\left[c_i(k) - \hat{M}_0\right] = \hat{M}_0(1 - \hat{H}). \tag{8.18}$$

By combining (8.17) and (8.18), the alternative formulation becomes

$$se_{\hat{A}} = \frac{\hat{\sigma}_A}{\sqrt{\text{n}-1}} \approx \sqrt{\frac{1}{\text{n}-1}\left(\frac{\hat{M}_0}{\hat{H}}\right)^2 \left[\frac{\hat{\sigma}_H^2}{\hat{H}^2} + \frac{\hat{\sigma}_0^2}{\hat{M}_0^2} - \frac{2(1-\hat{H})}{\hat{H}}\right]}. \tag{8.19}$$

Stratified Sampling with an Analytical Approach

We next discuss the estimation of standard errors when samples are collected through two-stage stratification.[21] Using information on the population characteristics, the population is partitioned into several strata. The first stage, from each stratum, draws a sample of Primary Sample Units (PSUs) with or without replacement. The second stage draws samples, either with or without replacement, from each PSU.

We suppose that the population is partitioned into $\mathcal{S} > 1$ strata and there are $\mathcal{P}_s$ PSUs in the sth stratum for all $s = 1, \ldots, \mathcal{S}$. The population size of the jth PSU in the sth stratum is n_{js} so that $n = \sum_{s=1}^{\mathcal{S}} \sum_{j=1}^{\mathcal{P}_s} n_{js}$. We denote the total number of poor by q and the number of poor in the jth PSU in the sth stratum by q_{js}. The population M_0 measure and its partial and consistent sub-indices are presented in (8.20)–(8.23) with the same notation for the identity function as in (8.5)–(8.8).

$$M_0(X; z, w, k) = \frac{1}{n} \sum_{s=1}^{\mathcal{S}} \sum_{j=1}^{\mathcal{P}_s} \sum_{i=1}^{n_{js}} c_{ijs}(k) \tag{8.20}$$

$$A(X; z, w, k) = \frac{1}{q} \sum_{s=1}^{\mathcal{S}} \sum_{j=1}^{\mathcal{P}_s} \sum_{i=1}^{q_{js}} c_{ijs}(k) \tag{8.21}$$

$$H(X; z, w, k) = \frac{1}{n} \sum_{s=1}^{\mathcal{S}} \sum_{j=1}^{\mathcal{P}_s} \sum_{i=1}^{n_{js}} \mathbb{I}\left[c_{ijs} \geq k\right] \tag{8.22}$$

[21] Appendix D of Seth (2013) gives an example of standard error estimation for one-stage sample stratification in the multidimensional welfare framework; for consumption/expenditure see Deaton (1997).

$$h_j(X;z,w,k) = \frac{1}{n}\sum_{s=1}^{S}\sum_{j=1}^{\mathcal{P}_s}\sum_{i=1}^{n_{js}}\mathbb{I}\left[(c_{ijs} \geq k)\wedge(g_{ijs,j}^0 = 1)\right] \qquad (8.23)$$

Note that $g_{ijs,j}^0 = 1$ if the ith person from the jth PSU in the sth stratum is deprived in the jth dimension and $g_{ijs,j}^0 = 0$, otherwise; and c_{ijs} and $c_{ijs}(k)$ are the deprivation score and the censored deprivation score of the ith person from the jth PSU in the sth stratum, respectively. Thus, $c_{ijs} = \sum_{j=1}^{d}w_j g_{ijs,j}^0$; and $c_{ijs}(k) = c_{ijs}$ if $c_{ijs}\geq k$ and $c_{ijs}(k) = 0$, otherwise.

Now, suppose a sample of size n is collected through a two-stage stratified sampling. The first stage selects $\wp_s$ PSUs from the sth stratum for all s. The second stage selects n_{js} samples from the jth PSU in stratum s. So, $n = \sum_{s=1}^{S}\sum_{j=1}^{\mathcal{P}_s}n_{sj}$. Each sample i in the jth PSU in the sth stratum is assigned a sampling weight W_{ijs}, which are summarized by an n-dimensional vector W. The achievements are summarized by matrix $\hat{X}$, which is a typical sample dataset.

In order to estimate the measure from the sample, first, the total population and the total number of poor should be estimated from the sample. We denote the estimates of the population n by $\mathcal{N}$ and the estimate of the poor population q by $\mathcal{Q}$. Then,

$$\mathcal{N} = \sum_{s=1}^{S}\sum_{j=1}^{\mathcal{P}_s}\sum_{i=1}^{n_{js}}W_{ijs} \qquad (8.24)$$

and

$$\mathcal{Q} = \sum_{s=1}^{S}\sum_{j=1}^{\mathcal{P}_s}\sum_{i=1}^{q_{js}}W_{ijs} \qquad (8.25)$$

The sample estimates of the population averages in (8.20)–(8.23) are presented in (8.26)–(8.29).

$$\hat{M}_0 = \frac{1}{\mathcal{N}}\left[\sum_{s=1}^{S}\sum_{j=1}^{\mathcal{P}_s}\sum_{i=1}^{n_{js}}W_{ijs}c_{ijs}(k)\right] \qquad (8.26)$$

$$\hat{A} = \frac{1}{\mathcal{Q}}\left[\sum_{s=1}^{S}\sum_{j=1}^{\mathcal{P}_s}\sum_{i=1}^{q_{js}}W_{ijs}c_{ijs}(k)\right] \qquad (8.27)$$

$$\hat{H} = \frac{1}{\mathcal{N}}\left[\sum_{s=1}^{S}\sum_{j=1}^{\mathcal{P}_s}\sum_{i=1}^{n_{js}}W_{ijs}\mathbb{I}[c_{ijs}\geq k]\right] \qquad (8.28)$$

$$\hat{h}_j = \frac{1}{\mathcal{N}}\left[\sum_{s=1}^{S}\sum_{j=1}^{\mathcal{P}_s}\sum_{i=1}^{n_{js}}W_{ijs}\mathbb{I}\left[(c_{ijs}\geq k)\wedge\left(g_{ijs,j}^0 = 1\right)\right]\right] \qquad (8.29)$$

As each sample estimate is a ratio of two estimators, their standard errors are approximated using (8.17) and using equations (1.31) and (1.63) in Deaton (1997). The standard error for $\hat{M}_0$ in (8.26) is

$$se_{\hat{M}_0} = \frac{1}{\mathcal{N}}\sqrt{\sum_{s=1}^{S}\sum_{j=1}^{\mathcal{P}_s}\left[\left(\sum_{i=1}^{n_{js}}W_{ijs}c_{ijs}(k) - \hat{M}_0^s\right) - \left(W^{js} - \bar{W}^s\right)\hat{M}_0\right]^2}, \qquad (8.30)$$

where $\hat{M}_0^s = \left[\sum_{j=1}^{p_s}\sum_{i=1}^{n_{js}} W_{ijs}c_{ijs}\,(k)\right]\Big/\left[\sum_{j=1}^{p_s}\sum_{i=1}^{n_{js}} W_{ijs}\right]$, $\bar{W}^s = \left[\sum_{j=1}^{p_s}\sum_{i=1}^{n_{js}} W_{ijs}\right]\Big/$
$\left[\sum_{j=1}^{p_s} n_{js}\right]$ and $W^{js} = \sum_{i=1}^{n_{js}} W_{ijs}$.

The standard errors of $\hat{H}$ and $\hat{h}_j$ are

$$se_{\hat{H}} = \frac{1}{N}\sqrt{\sum_{s=1}^{S}\sum_{j=1}^{p_s}\left[\left(\sum_{i=1}^{n_{js}} W_{ijs}\mathbb{I}\,[c_{ijs} \geq k] - \hat{H}^s\right) - \left(W^{js} - \bar{W}^s\right)\hat{H}\right]^2} \quad (8.31)$$

$$se_{\hat{h}_j} = \frac{1}{N}\sqrt{\sum_{s=1}^{S}\sum_{j=1}^{p_s}\left[\left(\sum_{i=1}^{n_{js}} W_{ijs}\mathbb{I}\left[\left(c_{ijs} \geq k\right) \wedge \left(g_{ijs,j}^0 = 1\right)\right] - \hat{h}_j^s\right) - \left(W^{js} - \bar{W}^s\right)\hat{h}_j\right]^2}, \tag{8.32}$$

where $\hat{H}^s = \left[\sum_{j=1}^{p_s}\sum_{i=1}^{n_{js}} W_{ijs}\mathbb{I}\,[c_{ijs} \geq k]\right]\Big/\left[\sum_{j=1}^{p_s}\sum_{i=1}^{n_{js}} W_{ijs}\right]$ and $\hat{h}_j^s = \left[\sum_{j=1}^{p_s}\sum_{i=1}^{n_{js}}\right.$
$\left.W_{ijs}\mathbb{I}\left[\left(c_{ijs} \geq k\right) \wedge \left(g_{ijs,j}^0 = 1\right)\right]\right]\Big/\left[\sum_{j=1}^{p_s}\sum_{i=1}^{n_{js}} W_{ijs}\right]$. Terms $\bar{W}^s$ and W^{js} are the same as in (8.30).

Finally, we present the standard error for $\hat{A}$ in (8.27), where the denominator is Q instead of N as

$$se_{\hat{A}} = \frac{1}{Q}\sqrt{\sum_{s=1}^{S}\sum_{j=1}^{p_s}\left[\left(\sum_{i=1}^{q_{js}} W_{ijs}c_i\,(k) - \hat{A}^s\right) - \left(W^{js} - \bar{W}^s\right)\hat{A}\right]^2}, \tag{8.33}$$

where $\hat{A}^s = \left[\sum_{j=1}^{p_s}\sum_{i=1}^{q_{js}} W_{ijs}c_{ijs}\,(k)\right]\Big/\left[\sum_{j=1}^{p_s}\sum_{i=1}^{q_{js}} W_{ijs}\right]$, $\bar{W}^s = \left[\sum_{j=1}^{p_s}\sum_{i=1}^{q_{js}} W_{ijs}\right]\Big/$
$\left[\sum_{j=1}^{p_s} q_{js}\right]$ and $W^{js} = \sum_{i=1}^{q_{js}} W_{ijs}$. Intuitively, $\hat{A}^s$ is the estimated average intensity for stratum s, $\bar{W}^s$ is the average of sampling weights in stratum s across the poor, and W^{js} is the sum of all sampling weights in PSU j of stratum s also across the poor.

As a reasonably smaller sample size may affect the precision of the standard error of A, the variance var_A can be approximated as in (8.17), but using (8.30) and (8.31) as

$$\widehat{var}_A \approx \left(\frac{\hat{M}_0}{\hat{H}}\right)^2\left[\frac{se_{\hat{H}}^2}{\hat{H}^2} + \frac{se_{\hat{M}_0}^2}{\hat{M}_0^2} - \frac{2\hat{\sigma}_{0,H}^2}{\hat{H}\hat{M}_0}\right], \tag{8.34}$$

where

$$\hat{\sigma}_{0,H}^2 = \frac{1}{N^2}\sum_{s=1}^{S}\sum_{j=1}^{p_s}\left[\left(\sum_{i=1}^{n_{js}} W_{ijs}c_{ijs}\,(k) - \hat{M}_0^s\right) - \left(W^{js} - \bar{W}^s\right)\hat{M}_0\right]$$
$$\times \left[\left(\sum_{i=1}^{n_{js}} W_{ijs}\mathbb{I}\,[c_{ijs} \geq k] - \hat{H}^s\right) - \left(W^{js} - \bar{W}^s\right)\hat{H}\right]. \tag{8.35}$$

Hence, combining (8.34) and (8.35), we have

$$se_{\hat{A}} = \sqrt{\widehat{var}_A}. \tag{8.36}$$

Note that the analytical standard errors and confidence intervals may not serve too well when the sample sizes are small or when the estimates are too close to the natural upper or lower bounds.[22] In these cases, resampling methods, such as bootstrap, may be more suitable for computing standard errors and confidence intervals.

The Bootstrap Method

An alternative approach for statistical inference is the 'bootstrap', which is a data-based simulation method for assessing statistical accuracy. Introduced in 1979, it provides an estimate of the sampling distribution of a given statistic θ, such as the standard error, by resampling from the original sample (cf. Efron 1979; Efron and Tibshirani 1993). It has certain advantages over the analytical approach. First, the inference on summary statistics does not rely on the CLT as the analytical approach. In particular, for a reasonably small sample size, standard errors/confidence intervals computed through the CLT-based asymptotic approximation may be inaccurate. Second, the bootstrap can automatically take into account the natural bounds of the measure. Confidence intervals using the analytical approach can lie outside natural bounds, which can be prevented when the bootstrap resampling distribution of the statistic is directly used.

Third, the computation of standard errors may become complex when the estimator and its standard error have a complicated form or have a no-closed expression. These types of complexities are common both in the context of statistical inference of inequality or poverty measurement and in tests where comparisons of group inequality or poverty (across gender or region) are of particular interest (Biewen 2002). Although the delta-method can handle these analytical standard errors from stochastic dependencies, when the number of time periods or groups increases, computing the standard errors analytically can easily become cumbersome (cf. Cowell 1989; Nygård and Sandström 1989). In practice, Monte Carlo evidence suggests that bootstrap methods are preferred for these analyses and shows that the simplest bootstrap procedure achieves the same accuracy as the delta-method (Biewen 2002; Davidson and Flachaire 2007). In development economics, the bootstrap has been used to draw statistical inferences for poverty and inequality measurement (Mills and Zandvakili 1997; Biewen 2002).

Here we briefly illustrate the use of the bootstrap for computing standard errors. Readers interested in using the bootstrap for confidence interval estimation and hypothesis testing can refer to Efron and Tibshirani (1993), chapters 12 and 16, respectively.

The bootstrap algorithm can be described as a resampling technique, which is conducted $\mathbb{B}$ number of times by generating a random artificial sample each time, with

---

[22] When the estimate is too close to the natural upper and lower bounds (0 and 1), the confidence intervals using analytical standard error may fall outside these bounds. Different methods for adjustments are available. For a discussion of such methods, see Newcombe (1998).

replacement from the original sample, which in our case is the dataset $\hat{X}$. The $\mathbb{b}^{\text{th}}$ resample produces an estimate $\hat{\theta}^{*\mathbb{b}}$ for all $\mathbb{b} = 1, \ldots, \mathbb{B}$. Thus, we have a set of $\mathbb{B}$ resample estimates of $\hat{\theta}$: $\hat{\theta}^{*1}, \ldots, \hat{\theta}^{*\mathbb{B}}$. If the artificial samples are independent and identically distributed (*i.i.d.*), the bootstrap standard error estimator of $\hat{\theta}$, denoted $se_{\mathbb{b},\hat{\theta}}$, is defined as

$$se_{\mathbb{b},\hat{\theta}} = \left[\sum_{\mathbb{b}=1}^{\mathbb{B}} \frac{\left[\hat{\theta}^{*\mathbb{b}} - \hat{\theta}^* \right]^2}{\mathbb{B} - 1} \right]^{1/2}, \tag{8.37}$$

where $\hat{\theta}^*$ stands for the arithmetic mean over the artificial samples. Even if the artificial sample is drawn from a more complex but known sampling framework, the bootstrap standard error can be easily estimated from standard formulas (c.f. Efron 1979, Efron and Tibshirani 1993). If the resampling is conducted on an empirical distribution of a given dataset $\hat{X}$, then it is referred to as a non-parametric bootstrap. In this case, each observation is sampled (with replacement) from the empirical distribution, with probability inversely proportional to the original sample size. However, the resampling can also be selected from a known distribution chosen on an empirical or theoretical basis. In this case, it is referred to as a parametric bootstrap.

BOX 8.1 BOOTSTRAP STANDARD ERRORS OF THE ADJUSTED HEADCOUNT RATIO AND ITS COMPONENTS

	Step 1: Bootstrap Samples	Step 2: Bootstrap Replications of Estimates
Empirical Distribution (Original Sample)	Resample 1 ⟶	$\left[\hat{M}_0^{*1}, \hat{H}^{*1}, \hat{A}^{*1}, \hat{h}_j^{*1} \right]$
	Resample 2 ⟶	$\left[\hat{M}_0^{*2}, \hat{H}^{*2}, \hat{A}^{*2}, \hat{h}_j^{*2} \right]$
	⋮	⋮
	Resample $\mathbb{B}$ ⟶	$\left[\hat{M}_0^{*\mathbb{B}}, \hat{H}^{*\mathbb{B}}, \hat{A}^{*\mathbb{B}}, \hat{h}_j^{*\mathbb{B}} \right]$

Step 3: Standard Errors

$$se_{\mathbb{b},\hat{M}_0} = \left[\frac{1}{\mathbb{B}-1} \sum_{\mathbb{b}=1}^{\mathbb{B}} \left[\hat{M}_0^{*\mathbb{b}} - \hat{M}_0^* \right]^2 \right]^{1/2}, \quad \hat{M}_0^* = \frac{1}{\mathbb{B}} \sum_{\mathbb{b}=1}^{\mathbb{B}} \hat{M}_0^{*\mathbb{b}}$$

$$se_{\mathbb{b},\hat{H}} = \left[\frac{1}{\mathbb{B}-1} \sum_{\mathbb{b}=1}^{\mathbb{B}} \left[\hat{H}^{*\mathbb{b}} - \hat{H}^* \right]^2 \right]^{1/2}, \quad \hat{H}^* = \frac{1}{\mathbb{B}} \sum_{\mathbb{b}=1}^{\mathbb{B}} \hat{H}^{*\mathbb{b}}$$

$$se_{\mathbb{b},\hat{A}} = \left[\frac{1}{\mathbb{B}-1} \sum_{\mathbb{b}=1}^{\mathbb{B}} \left[\hat{A}^{*\mathbb{b}} - \hat{A}^* \right]^2 \right]^{1/2}, \quad \hat{A}^* = \frac{1}{\mathbb{B}} \sum_{\mathbb{b}=1}^{\mathbb{B}} \hat{A}^{*\mathbb{b}}$$

$$se_{\mathbb{b},\hat{h}_j} = \left[\frac{1}{\mathbb{B}-1} \sum_{\mathbb{b}=1}^{\mathbb{B}} \left[\hat{h}_j^{*\mathbb{b}} - \hat{h}_j^* \right]^2 \right]^{1/2}, \quad \hat{h}_j^* = \frac{1}{\mathbb{B}} \sum_{\mathbb{b}=1}^{\mathbb{B}} \hat{h}_j^{*\mathbb{b}}$$

Box 8.1 illustrates the use of the bootstrap for computing standard errors for M_0 and its partial and consistent sub-indices. In this case, the statistic θ comprises M_0, H, A, and h_j.

Thus, the estimate $\hat{\theta}$ includes $\hat{M}_0$, $\hat{H}$, $\hat{A}$, or $\hat{h}_j$. To obtain the bootstrap standard errors, we need to pursue the following steps.

1. Draw $\mathbb{B}$ bootstrap resamples from the empirical distribution function.
2. Compute the set of $\mathbb{B}$ relevant bootstrap estimates of $\hat{M}_0^{*b}$, $\hat{H}^{*b}$, $\hat{A}^{*b}$, or $\hat{h}_j^{*b}$ from each bootstrap sample $\mathbb{b}$.
3. Estimate the standard errors by the sampling standard deviation of the $\mathbb{B}$ replications: $se_{\mathbb{b},\hat{M}_0}$, $se_{\mathbb{b},\hat{H}}$, $se_{\mathbb{b},\hat{A}}$, or $se_{\mathbb{b},\hat{h}_j}$. (cf. Efron and Tibshirani 1993, 47)

We have already discussed that the bootstrap approach has certain advantages—especially that it does not rely on the central limit theorem. Although the non-parametric bootstrap approach does not depend on any parametric assumptions, it does involve certain choices. The first is the number of replications. Indeed a larger number of replications increases the precision of the estimates, but is costly in terms of time. There are different approaches for selecting the appropriate number of replications (see Poi 2004 for example). The second involves the choice of the bootstrap sample size being selected from the original sample. The third involves the choice of the resampling method. The bootstrap sample size in Efron's traditional bootstrap is equal to the number of observations in the original sample, but the use of smaller sample sizes has also been studied (for further theoretical discussions; see Swanepoel (1986) and Chung and Lee (2001)).

9 Distribution and Dynamics

This chapter provides techniques required to measure and analyse inequality among the poor (section 9.1), to describe changes over time using repeated cross-sectional data (section 9.2), to understand changes across dynamic subgroups (section 9.3), and to measure chronic multidimensional poverty (section 9.4). Each of these sections extends the M_0 methodological toolkit beyond the consistent sub-indices presented in Chapter 5, to address common empirical problems such as poverty comparisons and illustrates these with examples. We build upon and do not repeat material presented in earlier chapters, and, as in other chapters, confine our attention to issues that are distinctive in multidimensional poverty measures.

9.1 Inequality among the Poor

Given the long-standing interest in inequality among the poor, we first enquire whether M_0 can be extended to reflect inequality among the poor. To make a long story short, it can easily do so. But the problem is that the resulting measure loses the property of dimensional breakdown that provides critical information for policy. So, taking a step back, we consider key properties a measure should have in order to reflect inequality among the poor and be analysed in tandem with M_0. Our chosen measure uses the distribution of censored deprivation scores to compute a form of variance across the multidimensionally poor. We also illustrate interesting related applications of this measure: for example, assessing horizontal disparities across groups.

Chapter 5 showed that the Adjusted Headcount Ratio (M_0) can be expressed as a product of the incidence of poverty (H) and the intensity of poverty (A) among the poor. Thus, M_0 captures two very important components of poverty—incidence and intensity. But it remains silent on a third important component: inequality across the poor. Now, the ultimate objective is to eradicate poverty—not merely reduce inequality among the poor. However, the consideration of inequality is important because the same average intensity can hide widely varying levels of inequality among the poor. For this reason, following the seminal article by Sen (1976), numerous efforts were made to incorporate inequality into unidimensional and latterly multidimensional poverty measures.[1]

---

[1] For inequality-adjusted poverty measures in the unidimensional context, see Thon (1979), Clark, Hemming, and Ulph (1981), Chakravarty (1983b), Foster, Greer, and Thorbecke (1984), and Shorrocks (1995). For inequality-adjusted multidimensional poverty measures, i.e., those that satisfy transfer and/or strict rearrangement properties, see section 3.6.

This section explores how inequality among the poor can be examined when poverty analyses are conducted using the M_0 measure (Alkire and Foster 2013; Seth and Alkire 2014a).[2]

9.1.1 INTEGRATING INEQUALITY INTO POVERTY MEASURES

Section 5.7.2 already presented one way of bringing inequality into multidimensional poverty measures. This was achieved by using M_2 or some other gap measure applied to cardinal data, where the exponent on the normalized gap is strictly greater than one. Such an approach is linked to Kolm (1977) and generalizes the notion of a progressive transfer (or more broadly a Lorenz comparison) to the multidimensional setting by applying the same bistochastic matrix to every variable to smooth out the distribution of each variable (the powered normalized gap) while preserving its mean.[3] Poverty measures that are sensitive to inequality fall (or at least do not rise) in this case.

A second form of multidimensional inequality is linked to the work of Atkinson and Bourguignon (1982) and relies on patterns of achievements *across* dimensions. Imagine a case where one poor person initially has more of everything than another poor person and the two persons switch achievements for a single dimension in which both are deprived. This can be interpreted as a progressive transfer that preserves the marginal distribution of each variable and lowers inequality by relaxing the positive association across variables under the assumption that the dimensions are substitutes. The resulting transfer principle specifies conditions under which this alternative form of progressive transfer among the poor should lower poverty, or at least not raise it. The transfer properties are motivated by the idea that poverty should be sensitive to the level of inequality among the poor, with greater inequality being associated with a higher (or at least not lower) level of poverty.[4] Alkire and Foster (2011a) observe that the AF class of measures can be easily adjusted to respect the strict version of the second kind of transfer (the strong deprivation rearrangement property as discussed in section 2.5.2), involving a change in association between dimensions by replacing the deprivation count or score $M_\alpha(x_i; z)$ with a related individual poverty function $[M_\alpha(x_i; z)]^\beta$ for some $\beta > 0$, and averaging across persons.[5]

Many multidimensional poverty measures that employ cardinal data, including M_α, satisfy one or both of these transfer principles.[6] Alkire and Foster (2013) formulate

---

[2] This section summarizes these two papers.

[3] In order to say that one multidimensional distribution is more equal than another, each must be smoothed using the *same* bistochastic matrix.

[4] See Sen (1976) and Foster and Sen (1997).

[5] Bourguignon and Chakravarty (2003) and Datt (2013) also propose a similar class of indices but using a union identification criterion.

[6] We have already shown that our multidimensional measure M_α satisfies weak transfer, the first type of transfer property, for $\alpha \geq 1$, and the second type of transfer property, weak rearrangement, for $\alpha \geq 0$. See also Chakravarty, Mukherjee, and Ranade (1998), Tsui (2002), Bourguignon and Chakravarty (2003),

a strict version of distribution sensitivity—dimensional transfer (defined in section 2.5.2)—which is applicable to poverty measures such as M_0 that use ordinal data. This property follows the Atkinson–Bourguignon type of distribution sensitivity, in which greater inequality among the poor strictly raises poverty. Alkire and Foster (2013) also prove a general result establishing that 'the highly desirable and practical properties of subgroup decomposability, dimensional breakdown, and symmetry prevent a poverty measure from satisfying the dimensional transfer property'. In other words, M_0 does not reflect inequality among the poor, and, furthermore, no measure that satisfies dimensional breakdown and symmetry will be found that *does* satisfy dimensional transfer.

Given that it is necessary to choose between measures that satisfy dimensional transfer and those that can be broken down by dimension, and given that both properties are arguably important, how should empirical studies proceed? The first option is to employ measures that respect dimensional breakdown and to supplement these with associated inequality measures. The second is to employ poverty measures that are inequality-sensitive but cannot be broken down by dimension, and to supplement them with separate dimensional analyses.

9.1.2 ANALYSING INEQUALITY SEPARATELY: A DESCRIPTIVE TOOL

While both should be explored, this book favours the first route in applied work for several reasons. Dimensional breakdown enriches the informational content of poverty measures for policy, enabling them to be used to tailor policies to the composition of poverty, to monitor changes by dimension, and to make comparisons across time and space. Poverty reduction in measures respecting dimensional breakdown can be accounted for in terms of changes in deprivations among the poor and analysed by region and dimension. This creates positive feedback loops that reward effective policies. Also, the inequality-adjusted poverty measures may lack the intuitive appeal of the M_0 measure. Some of the inequality-adjusted measures (Chakravarty and D'Ambrosio 2006; Rippin 2012) are broken down into different components separately capturing incidence, intensity, and inequality, but without clarifying the relative weights attached to these components.

Whether or not an inequality measure is computed, M_0 measures can be supplemented by direct descriptions of inequality among the poor. A first descriptive but powerfully informative tool is to report subsets of poor people which have mutually exclusive and collectively exhaustive graded bands of deprivation scores. This is possible by effectively ordering all q poor persons according to the value of their deprivation score $c_i(k)$ and dividing them into groups. If the poverty cutoff is 30%, the analysis might then report the percentage of poor people whose deprivation scores fall in the band of 30–39.9% of deprivations, 40–49.9%, and so on to 100%. The percentage of people who experience

Chakravarty and D'Ambrosio (2006), Maasoumi and Lugo (2008), Aaberge and Peluso (2012), Bossert, Chakravarty, and D'Ambrosio (2013), and Silber and Yalonetzky (2014).

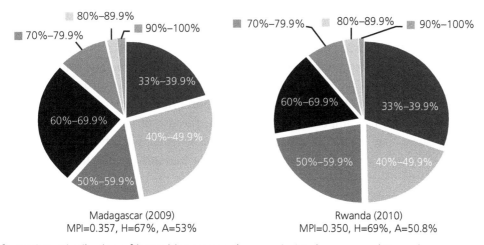

Figure 9.1. Distribution of intensities among the poor in Madagascar and Rwanda

Source: Country briefings, MPI 2013, <http://www.ophi.org.uk/multidimensional-poverty-index/mpi-data-bank/mpi-country-briefings>

different intensity gradients of poverty across regions and time can be compared to see how inequality among the poor is evolving.[7] Figure 9.1 presents an example of two countries—Madagascar and Rwanda—which have similar multidimensional headcount ratios (H) and global MPIs. However, the distributions of intensities across the poor are quite different. Also, data permitting, these intensity groups can be decomposed by population subgroups such as region or ethnicity. The comparisons can be enriched by applying a dimensional breakdown to examine the dimensional composition of poverty experienced by those having different ranges of deprivation scores.

9.1.3 USING A SEPARATE INEQUALITY MEASURE

Another option is to supplement M_0 with a measure of inequality among the poor. Using the distribution of (censored) deprivation scores across the poor or some transformation of these, it is actually elementary to create an inequality measure, much in the same way that traditional inequality measures such as Atkinson, Theil, or Gini are constructed. Such measures will offer a window onto one type of multidimensional inequality—one that is oriented to the breadth of deprivations people experience. This approach is quite different from other constructions of multidimensional inequality, but it is useful, particularly when data are ordinal. Building on Chakravarty (2001), Seth and Alkire (2014a) propose such an inequality measure that is founded on certain properties. Note that these are properties of *inequality* measures and are defined differently from those presented in Chapter 2 (despite similar names), but introduced intuitively in section 9.1.3.1. Let us briefly discuss these properties before introducing the measure.

---

[7] For empirical examples, see Alkire, Roche, and Seth (2013), who compare countries across four gradients of poverty.

9.1.3.1 Properties

The first property, **translation invariance**, requires inequality not to change if the deprivation score of every poor person increases by the same amount. Implicitly, we assume that the measure reflects *absolute* inequality. Seth and Alkire (2014a) argue that measures reflecting absolute inequality are more appropriate when each deprivation is judged to be of intrinsic importance. In addition, the use of the absolute inequality measure ensures that inequality remains the same whether poverty is measured by counting the number of deprivations or by counting the number of attainments. The use of the relative inequality measure is more common in the case of income inequality, where it is often assumed that as long as people's *relative* incomes remain unchanged, inequality should not change. However, it is difficult to argue that inequality between two poor persons who are deprived in one and two dimensions respectively is the same as the inequality between two poor persons who are deprived in five and ten dimensions, respectively, if these deprivations referred to, for example, serious human rights violations. Any relative inequality measure, such as the Generalized Entropy measures (which include the Squared Coefficient of Variation associated with the FGT2 index) or Gini Coefficient, would evaluate these two situations as having identical inequality across the poor. Moreover, a relative inequality measure may provide a counterintuitive conclusion while assessing inequality within a counting approach framework. In fact, no non-constant inequality measure exists that is simultaneously invariant to absolute as well as relative changes in a distribution.

The second property requires that the inequality measure should be **additively decomposable** so that overall inequality in any society can be broken down into within-group and between-group components. This can be quite useful for policy (Stewart 2010). We have shown in Chapter 5 that the additive structure of the indices in the AF class allows the overall poverty figure to be decomposed across various population subgroups. A country or a region with the same level of overall poverty may have very different poverty levels across different subgroups, or a country may have the same level of poverty across two time periods, but the distribution of poverty across different subgroups may change over time. Furthermore, within each population subgroup, there may be different distributions of deprivation scores across poor persons, thus various levels of within-group inequality can be compared with poverty levels.

The third property, **within-group mean independence**, requires that overall within-group inequality should be expressed as a weighted average of the subgroup inequalities, where the weight attached to a subgroup is equal to the population share of that subgroup. This assumption makes the interpretation and analysis of the inequality measure more intuitive.

Four additional properties are commonly satisfied when constructing any inequality measure. The **anonymity** property requires that a permutation of deprivation scores should not alter inequality. According to the **replication invariance** property, a mere replication of population leaves the inequality measure unaltered. The **normalization** property requires that the inequality measure should be equal to zero when the deprivation scores are equal for all. The **transfer** property requires that a progressive dimensional rearrangement among the poor should decrease inequality.

9.1.3.2 A Decomposable Measure

The proposed inequality measure, which is the only one to satisfy those properties, takes the general form

$$I\left(y; t, \tilde{\beta}\right) = \frac{\tilde{\beta}}{t} \sum_{i=1}^{t} [y_i - \mu\left(y\right)]^2, \qquad (9.1)$$

where $y = (y_1, \ldots, y_t)$ is a vector with t elements. Relevant applications using our familiar notation are provided in equations (9.6) and (9.7) below, but we first present the general form and notation. As we show below, in relevant applications an element y_i, may be the deprivation score of a person c_i or $c_i(k)$ or the average poverty level of a region. The size of the vector y for an entire population would be $t = n$ and for the poor it would be $t = q$.[8] The functional form in equation (9.1) is a positive multiple $(\tilde{\beta})$ of the variance. The measure reflects the average squared difference between person i's deprivation score and the mean of the deprivation scores in y. The value of parameter $\tilde{\beta}$ can be chosen in such a way that it normalizes the inequality measure to lie between 0 and 1.

The overall inequality in y may be decomposed into two components: total within-group inequality and between-group inequality. Following the notation in Chapter 2, suppose there are $m \geq 2$ population subgroups. The deprivation score vector of subgroup ℓ is denoted by y^ℓ with t^ℓ elements. The decomposition expression is given as follows:

$$I\left(y\right) = \underbrace{\sum_{\ell=1}^{m} \frac{t^\ell}{t} I\left(y^\ell; t^\ell, \tilde{\beta}\right)}_{\text{Total Within-group}} + \underbrace{I\left(\mu\left(y^1\right), \ldots, \mu\left(y^m\right); \frac{t^1}{t}, \ldots, \frac{t^m}{t}, \tilde{\beta}\right)}_{\text{Total Between-group}}, \qquad (9.2)$$

where $\frac{t^\ell}{t}$ is the population share of subgroup ℓ in the overall population and $\mu\left(y^\ell\right)$ is the mean of all elements in y^ℓ for all $\ell = 1, \ldots, m$.

The **between-group inequality** component $I(\mu\left(y^1\right), \ldots, \mu\left(y^m\right); \frac{t^1}{t}, \ldots, \frac{t^m}{t} \tilde{\beta})$ in (9.2) can be computed as

$$I\left(\mu\left(y^1\right), \ldots, \mu\left(y^m\right); \frac{t^1}{t}, \ldots, \frac{t^m}{t}, \tilde{\beta}\right) = \tilde{\beta} \sum_{\ell=1}^{m} \frac{t^\ell}{t} \left(\mu\left(y^\ell\right) - \mu\left(y\right)\right)^2, \qquad (9.3)$$

where $\mu\left(y\right)$ is the mean of all elements in y.

---

[8] There are many variations. For example, if data are relatively accurate one might consider inequality using the uncensored deprivation score vector c and alternatively if one only wishes to capture inequality within some subgroup ℓ, then $y = c^\ell$ and $t = n^\ell$.

The **within-group inequality** component of subgroup ℓ can be computed using (9.1) as

$$I\left(y^\ell;t^\ell,\tilde{\beta}\right) = \frac{\tilde{\beta}}{t^\ell}\sum_{i=1}^{t^\ell}\left[y_i^\ell - \mu\left(y^\ell\right)\right]^2;\tag{9.4}$$

and thus the **total within-group inequality** component in (9.2) can be computed as

$$\sum_{\ell=1}^{m}\frac{t^\ell}{t}I\left(y^\ell;t^\ell,\tilde{\beta}\right) = \frac{\tilde{\beta}}{t}\sum_{\ell=1}^{m}\sum_{i=1}^{t^\ell}\left[y_i^\ell - \mu\left(y^\ell\right)\right]^2.\tag{9.5}$$

9.1.3.3 Two Important Applications

There are different relevant applications of this inequality framework to multidimensional poverty analyses based on M_0. The first central case is to assess inequality among the poor. To do so we suppose that the deprivation scores are ordered in a descending order and the first q persons are identified as poor. The elements are taken from the censored deprivation score vector, $y = \left(c_1(k),\ldots,c_q(k)\right)$. We choose vector y such that it contains only the deprivation scores of the poor ($t = q$). The average of all elements in y then is the intensity of poverty which for q persons is $\mu(y) = A$. We can then denote the inequality measure that reflects inequality in multiple deprivations only among the poor by I^q, which can be expressed as

$$I^q = \frac{\tilde{\beta}}{q}\sum_{i=1}^{q}[c_i(k) - A]^2.{}^9\tag{9.6}$$

The I^q measure effectively summarizes the information underlying Figure 9.1. It goes well beyond that figure because each individual deprivation score is used, which effectively creates a much finer gradation of intensity than that figure portrays. Furthermore, it can be decomposed by subgroup to permit comparisons of within-subgroup inequalities among the poor. It can also be used over time to show how inequality among the poor changed.

Our second central case considers inequalities in poverty levels across population subgroups. It is motivated by studies of horizontal inequalities that find group-based inequalities to predict tension and in some cases conflict (Stewart 2010). Essentially, the measure reflects population-weighted disparities in poverty levels across population subgroups.

---

[9] If one is interested in decomposing (9.6) into within- and between-group components, then the total within-group inequality term can be computed as $\frac{\tilde{\beta}}{q}\sum_{\ell=1}^{m}\sum_{i=1}^{q^\ell}[c_i^\ell(k) - A^\ell]^2$ and the total between-group inequality term can be computed as $\tilde{\beta}\sum_{\ell=1}^{m}\frac{q^\ell}{q}(A^\ell - A)^2$, where A^ℓ is the intensity of each subgroup ℓ such that $A^\ell = \mu(y^\ell)$ and q^ℓ/q is the share of all poor in subgroup ℓ.

Suppose the censored deprivation score vector of subgroup ℓ is denoted by $c^\ell(k)$ with n^ℓ elements. If instead of only considering the deprivation scores of the poor, we now sum across the whole population so ($t = n$), then we realize that $\mu(c^\ell(k))$ or the average of *all* elements in $c^\ell(k)$ is actually the M_0 of subgroup ℓ, which for simplicity we denote by M_0^ℓ. The between-group component of $I^n(c(k))$ shows the disparity in the national Adjusted Headcount Ratio (M_0) across subgroups and is written using (9.3) as

$$I^n\left(M_0^1, \ldots, M_0^m; \frac{n^1}{n}, \ldots, \frac{n^m}{n}, \tilde{\beta}\right) = \tilde{\beta} \sum_{\ell=1}^{m} \frac{n^\ell}{n}\left(M_0^\ell - M_0\right)^2. \tag{9.7}$$

Thus, equation (9.7) captures the disparity in M_0s across m population subgroups, which can be used to detect patterns in horizontal disparities over time. Naturally, the number and population share of the subgroups must be considered in such comparisons.

While studying disparity in MPIs across subnational regions, Alkire, Roche, and Seth (2011) found that the national MPIs masked a large amount of subnational disparity within countries, and Alkire and Seth (2013b, 2015) and Alkire, Roche, and Vaz (2014) found considerable disparity in poverty trends across subnational groups. In some countries, the overall situation of the poor improved, but not all subgroups shared the equal fruit of success in poverty reduction and indeed poverty levels may have stagnated or risen in some groups. Therefore, it is also important to look at inequality or disparity in poverty across population subgroups. This separate inequality measure, elaborated in Seth and Alkire (2014a), provides such framework.

9.1.3.4 An Illustration

Table 9.1 presents two pairwise comparisons. For the inequality measure, we choose $\tilde{\beta} = 4$ because the deprivation scores are bounded between 0 and 1; hence the maximum possible variance is 0.25. $\tilde{\beta} = 4$ ensures that the inequality measure lies between 0 and 1. The first pair of countries, India and Yemen, have exactly the same levels of MPI. The multidimensional headcount ratios and the intensities of poverty are also similar. However, the inequality among the poor—computed using equation (9.6)—is much higher in Yemen than in India. We also measure disparity across subnational regions. Yemen has twenty-one subnational regions, whereas India has twenty-nine subnational regions. We find that, like the national MPIs, the disparities across subnational MPIs—computed using equation (9.7)—are similar. This means that the inequality in Yemen is not primarily due to regional disparities in poverty levels, but may be affected by non-geographic divides such as cultural or rural–urban.

A contrasting finding for regional disparity is obtained across Togo and Bangladesh. As before, the MPIs, headcount ratios, and intensities are quite similar across the two countries—but with two differences. The inequality among the poor is very similar, but

Table 9.1 Countries with similar levels of MPI but different levels of inequality among the poor and different levels of disparity across regional MPIs

Country	Year	M_0	A	H	Inequality among the poor	Disparity between MPIs	Number of regions
Yemen	2006	0.283	53.9%	52.5%	0.122	0.052	21
India	2005	0.283	52.7%	53.7%	0.104	0.050	29
Togo	2010	0.250	50.3%	49.8%	0.086	0.042	6
Bangladesh	2011	0.253	49.5%	51.2%	0.084	0.005	7

Source: Seth and Alkire (2014a)

the regional disparities are stark. Even though both countries have a similar number of subnational regions, the level of subnational disparity is much higher in Togo than that in Bangladesh.

9.2 **Descriptive Analysis of Changes over Time**

A strong motivation for computing multidimensional poverty is to track and analyse changes over time. Most data available to study changes over time are repeated cross-sectional data, which compare the characteristics of representative samples drawn at different periods with sampling errors, but do not track specific individuals across time. This section describes how to compare M_0 and its associated sub-indices over time with repeated cross-sectional data. It offers a standard methodology of computing such changes, and an array of small examples. This section does not treat the data issues underlying poverty comparisons, and readers are expected to know standard techniques that are required for such rigorous empirical comparisons. For example, the definition of indicators, cutoffs, weights, etc. must be strictly harmonized for meaningful comparisons across time, which always requires close verification of survey questions and response structures, and may require amending or dropping indicators. The sample designs of the surveys must be such that they can be meaningfully compared, and basic issues like the representativeness and structure of the data must be thoroughly understood and respected. We presume this background in what follows. This section focuses on changes across two time periods; naturally the comparisons can be easily extended across more than two time periods.

9.2.1 CHANGES IN M_0, H, AND A ACROSS TWO TIME PERIODS

The basic component of poverty comparisons is the absolute pace of change across periods.[10] The absolute rate of change is the difference in levels between two periods.

---

[10] This section draws on Alkire, Roche, and Vaz (2014).

Changes (increases or decreases) in poverty across two time periods can also be reported as a relative rate. The relative rate of change is the difference in levels across two periods as a percentage of the initial period.

For example, if the M_0 has gone down from 0.5 to 0.4 between two consecutive years, then the absolute rate of change is $(0.5 - 0.4) = 0.1$. It tells us how much the level of poverty (M_0) has changed: 10% of the total possible set of deprivations that poor people in that society could have experienced has been eradicated; 40% remains. The relative rate of change is $(0.5 - 0.4)/0.5 = 20\%$, which tells us that M_0 has gone down by 20% with respect to the initial level. While absolute changes are fundamentally important and easy to understand and compare, both absolute and relative rates may be important to report and analyse. The value-added of the relative changes is evident in relatively low-poverty regions. A region or country with a high initial level of poverty may be able to reduce poverty in absolute terms much more than one having a low initial level of poverty. It is, however, possible that although a region or country with low initial poverty levels did not show a large absolute reduction, the reduction was large *relative* to its initial level and thus it should not be discounted for its slower absolute reduction.[11] The analysis of both absolute and relative changes gives a clear sense of overall progress.

In expressing changes across two periods, we denote the initial period by t^1 and the final period by t^2. This section mostly presents the expressions for M_0, but they are equally applicable to its associated indices: incidence (H), intensity (A), censored headcount ratios ($h_j(k)$), and uncensored headcount ratios (h_j). The achievement matrices for period t^1 and t^2 are denoted by X_{t^1} and X_{t^2}, respectively. As presented in Chapter 5, M_0 and its partial and consistent sub-indices depend on a set of parameters: deprivation cutoff vector z, weight vector w, and poverty cutoff k. For simplicity of notation though, we present M_0 and its partial and sub-indices only as a function of the achievement matrix. For strict intertemporal comparability, it is important that the same set of parameters be used across two periods.

The **absolute rate of change** (Δ) is simply the difference in Adjusted Headcount Ratios between two periods and is computed as

$$\Delta M_0 = M_0(X_{t^2}) - M_0(X_{t^1}). \tag{9.8}$$

Similarly, for H and A:

$$\Delta H = H(X_{t^2}) - H(X_{t^1}), \tag{9.9}$$

$$\Delta A = A(X_{t^2}) - A(X_{t^1}) \tag{9.10}$$

The **relative rate of change** (δ) is the difference in Adjusted Headcount Ratios as a percentage of the initial poverty level and is computed for M_0, H, and A (only M_0

---

[11] Tables of the absolute levels and absolute rates of change make this feature visible; reporting the relative rate of change underscores this more precisely.

shown) as

$$\delta M_0 = \frac{M_0(X_{t^2}) - M_0(X_{t^1})}{M_0(X_{t^1})} \times 100. \tag{9.11}$$

If one is interested in comparing changes over time for the same reference period, the expressions (9.8) and (9.11) are appropriate. However, in cross-country exercises, one may often be interested in comparing the rates of poverty reduction across countries that have different periods of reference. For example the reference period of one country may be five years, whereas the reference period for another country is three years. It is evident in Table 9.2 that the reference period of Nepal is five years (2006–11), whereas that of Peru is only three years (2005–8). In such cases, it is essential to annualize the change in order to preserve strict comparison.

The **annualized absolute rate of change** ($\bar{\Delta}$) is the difference in Adjusted Headcount Ratios between two periods divided by the difference in the two time periods ($t^2 - t^1$) and is computed for M_0 as

$$\bar{\Delta} M_0 = \frac{M_0(X_{t^2}) - M_0(X_{t^1})}{t^2 - t^1}. \tag{9.12}$$

The **annualized relative rate of change** ($\bar{\delta}$) is the compound rate of reduction in M_0 per year between the initial and the final periods, and is computed for M_0 as

$$\bar{\delta} M_0 = \left[\left(\frac{M_0(X_{t^2})}{M_0(X_{t^1})} \right)^{\frac{1}{t^2 - t^1}} - 1 \right] \times 100. \tag{9.13}$$

As formula (9.8) has been used to compute the changes in H and A using formulae (9.9) and (9.10), formulae (9.11) to (9.13) can be used to compute and report annualized changes in the other partial and consistent sub-indices, namely H, A, $h_j(k)$, or h_j.

9.2.2 AN EXAMPLE: CHANGES IN THE GLOBAL MPI

Table 9.2 presents both the annualized absolute and annualized relative rates of change in global MPI, as outlined in Chapter 5, and its two partial indices—H and A—for four countries: Nepal, Peru, Rwanda, and Senegal, drawing from Alkire, Roche, and Vaz (2014). Taking the survey design into account, we also present the standard errors (in parentheses) and the levels of statistical significance of the rates of reduction, as described in the Appendix of Chapter 8. The figures in the first four columns present the values and standard errors for M_0, H, and A in both time periods. The results show that Peru had the lowest MPI with 0.085 in the initial year, while Rwanda had the highest with 0.460.

Table 9.2 Reduction in MPI, *H*, and *A* in Nepal, Peru, Rwanda, and Senegal

	Year 1		Year 2		Statistical significance of the change	Annualized change	
						Absolute	Relative
Panel I: Multidimensional Poverty Index (MPI)							
Nepal 2006–2011	0.35	−(0.013)	0.217	−(0.012)	***	−0.027	−9.1%
Peru 2005–2008	0.085	−(0.007)	0.066	−(0.004)	*	−0.006	−8.0%
Rwanda 2005–2010	0.46	−(0.005)	0.33	−(0.006)	***	−0.026	−6.4%
Senegal 2005–2010/11	0.44	−(0.019)	0.423	−(0.010)		−0.003	−0.7%
Panel II: Multidimensional Headcount Ratio							
Nepal 2006–2011	64.70%	−(2.0)	44.20%	−(2.0)	***	−4.1	−7.4%
Peru 2005–2008	19.50%	−(1.5)	15.70%	−(0.8)	*	−1.3	−6.9%
Rwanda 2005–2010	82.90%	−(0.8)	66.10%	−(1.0)	***	−3.4	−4.4%
Senegal 2005–2010/11	71.30%	−(2.4)	70.80%	−(1.5)		−0.1	−0.1%
Panel III: Intensity of Poverty (A)							
Nepal 2006–2011	54.00%	−(0.6)	49.00%	−(0.7)	***	−1	−1.9%
Peru 2005–2008	43.60%	−(0.5)	42.20%	−(0.4)	**	−0.5	−1.1%
Rwanda 2005–2010	55.50%	−(0.3)	49.90%	−(0.3)	***	−1.1	−2.1%
Senegal 2005–2010/11	61.70%	−(1.0)	59.70%	−(0.7)	*	−0.4	−0.6%

Notes: *** statistically significant at $\omega = 0.01$, ** statistically significant at $\omega = 0.05$, * statistically significant at $\omega = 0.10$. These figures have been computed so as to be strictly comparable with harmonized indicator definitions, and therefore do not match the MPI values released in UNDP reports.
Source: Alkire, Roche, and Vaz (2014)

Under the heading 'Annualized Change', Table 9.2 provides the annualized absolute and annualized relative reduction for M_0, *H*, and *A*, which are computed using equations (9.12) and (9.13). It shows, for example, that Nepal, with a much lower initial poverty level than Rwanda, has experienced a greater absolute annualized poverty reduction of −0.027. In relative terms, Nepal outperformed Rwanda. Peru had a low initial poverty level, and reduced it in absolute terms by only −0.006 per year, which means that the share of all possible deprivations among poor people that were removed was less than one-fourth that of Nepal or Rwanda. But relative to its initial level of poverty, its progress was second only to Nepal. It is thus important to report both absolute and relative changes and to understand their interpretation. The same results for *H* and *A* are provided in Panels II and III of the table. We see that Nepal reduced the percentage of people who were poor by 4.1 percentage points per year—for example, if the first year 64.7% of people were poor, the next year it would be 60.6%. Peru cut the poverty incidence by 1.3 percentage points per year. Relative to their starting levels, they had similar relative rates of reduction of the headcount ratio. Note that when estimates are reported in percentages, the absolute changes are reported in 'percentage points' and *not* in 'percentages'. Thus, Nepal's reduction in *H* from 64.7% to 44.2% is equivalent to an annualized absolute reduction of 4.1 percentage points and an annualized relative reduction of 6.3%.

Table 9.3 Changes in the number of poor accounting for population growth

	Population			Total MPI poor		
	Year 1	Year 2	Annual growth in population	Year 1	Year 2	Absolute reduction
	(in thousands)			(in thousands)		
Nepal 2006–2011	25,634	27,156	1.20%	16,585	12,003	−4,582
Peru 2005–2008	27,723	28,626	0.60%	5,406	4,494	−912
Rwanda 2005–2010	9,429	10,837	2.80%	7,817	7,163	−654
Senegal 2005–2010/11	11,271	13,141	3.10%	8,036	9,304	1,267

Note: Population figures correspond to United Nations, Department of Economic and Social Affairs, Population Division (2013), *World Population Prospects: The 2012 Revision*, DVD Edition. Figures for Senegal 2010/11 correspond to the average between both years.
Source: Authors' presentation, based on Alkire, Roche, and Vaz (2014)

The third column provides the results for the hypothesis tests which assess if the reduction between both years is statistically significant.[12] The reductions in M_0 in Nepal and Rwanda are significant at $\omega = 0.01$, but the same in Peru is only significant at $\omega = 0.10$. Interestingly, the reduction in intensity of poverty in Peru is significant at $\omega = 0.05$. The case of Senegal is different in that the small reduction in M_0 is not even significantly different at $\omega = 0.10$, preventing the null hypothesis that the poverty level in both years remained unchanged from being rejected.

9.2.3 POPULATION GROWTH AND CHANGE IN THE NUMBER OF MULTIDIMENSIONALLY POOR

Besides comparing the rate of reduction in M_0, H, and A as in Table 9.2, one should also examine whether the number of poor people is decreasing over time. It may be possible that the population growth is large enough to offset the rate of poverty reduction. Table 9.3 uses the same four countries as Table 9.2 but adds demographic information. Nepal had an annual population growth of 1.2% between 2006 and 2011, moving from 25.6 to 27.2 million people, and reduced the headcount ratio from 64.7% to 44.2%. This means that Nepal reduced the absolute number of poor by 4.6 million between 2006 and 2011.

In order to reduce the absolute number of poor people, the rate of reduction in the headcount ratio needs to be faster than the population growth. The largest reduction in the number of multidimensionally poor has taken place in Nepal. A moderate reduction in the number of poor has taken place in Peru and Rwanda. In contrast, there has been an increase in the total number of multidimensionally poor in Senegal, from 8 million to over 9 million between 2005 and 2011.

[12] For small samples, one needs to conduct hypothesis tests using the Student-t distribution which are very similar to the hypothesis tests described in Chapter 8 that use the Standard Normal distribution.

9.2.4 DIMENSIONAL CHANGES (UNCENSORED AND CENSORED HEADCOUNT RATIOS)

The reductions in M_0, H, or A can be broken down to reveal which dimensions have been responsible for the change in poverty. This can be seen by looking at changes in the uncensored headcount ratios (h_j) and censored headcount ratios ($h_j(k)$) described in section 5.5.3. We present the uncensored and censored headcount ratios of MPI indicators for Nepal in Table 9.4 for years 2006 and 2011 and analyse their changes over time. For definitions of indicators and their deprivation cutoffs, see section 5.6. Panel I gives levels and changes in uncensored headcount ratios, i.e. the percentage of people that are deprived in each indicator irrespective of deprivations in other indicators. Panel II provides levels and changes in the censored headcount ratios, i.e. the percentage of people who are multidimensionally poor and simultaneously deprived in each indicator. By definition, the uncensored headcount ratio of an indicator is equal to or higher than the censored headcount of that indicator. The standard errors are reported in parentheses.

As we can see in the table, Nepal made statistically significant reductions in all indicators in terms of both uncensored and censored headcount ratios. The larger reductions in censored headcount are observed in electricity, assets, cooking fuel, flooring, and sanitation; all censored headcount ratios have decreased by more than 3 percentage points. Nutrition, mortality, schooling, and attendance follow with annual reductions of 3, 2.3, 1.8, and 1.5 percentage points, respectively.

The changes in censored headcount ratios depict changes in deprivations among the poor. Recall that the overall M_0 is the weighted sum of censored headcount ratios of the indicators as presented in equation (5.9) and the contribution of each indicator to the M_0 can be computed by equation (5.10). Because of this relationship, the **absolute rate of reduction** in M_0 in equation (9.8) and the **annualized absolute rate of reduction** in M_0 in equation (9.12) can be expressed as weighted averages of the **absolute rate of reductions** in censored headcount ratios and **annualized absolute rate of reductions** in censored headcount ratios, respectively. When different indicators are assigned different weights, the effects of their changes on the change in M_0 reflect these weights.[13] For example, in the MPI, the nutrition indicator is assigned three times more weight than electricity. This implies that a one percentage point reduction in nutrition *ceteris paribus* would lead to an absolute reduction in M_0 that is three times larger than a one percentage point reduction in the electricity indicator.

Recall that it is straightforward to compute the contribution of each indicator to M_0 using its weighted censored headcount ratio as given in equation (5.10). Note that interpreting the real on-the-ground contribution of each indicator to the *change* in M_0 is not so mechanical. Why? A reduction in the censored headcount ratio of an indicator is not independent of the changes in other indicators. It is possible that the reduction in the censored headcount ratio of a certain indicator j occurred because a poor person

---

[13] Normative issues in assigning weights were discussed in details in Chapter 6.

Table 9.4 Uncensored and censored headcount ratios of the global MPI, Nepal 2006–11

	2006		2011		Statistical significance of the change	Annualized reduction	
						Absolute	Relative
Panel I: Uncensored Headcount Ratio							
Schooling	30.30%	−(3.3)	22.20%	−(2.6)	***	−1.6	−6.0%
Attendance	16.10%	−(3.1)	8.40%	−(1.9)	***	−1.5	−12.1%
Mortality	32.60%	−(3.5)	22.60%	−(1.9)	***	−2	−7.1%
Nutrition	44.00%	−(3.5)	32.10%	−(2.9)	***	−2.4	−6.1%
Electricity	50.70%	−(5.6)	24.40%	−(4.5)	***	−5.3	−13.6%
Sanitation	75.60%	−(3.0)	60.30%	−(4.0)	***	−3.1	−4.4%
Water	17.10%	−(3.3)	12.90%	−(2.9)	*	−0.8	−5.5%
Flooring	76.70%	−(4.1)	70.00%	−(4.0)	**	−1.3	−1.8%
Cooking fuel	86.80%	−(2.8)	79.30%	−(3.2)	***	−1.5	−1.8%
Assets	59.20%	−(0)	28.50%	−(2.7)	***	−6.2	−13.6%
Panel II: Censored Headcount Ratio							
Schooling	29.20%	−(3.3)	20.30%	−(2.7)	***	−1.8	−7.0%
Attendance	15.60%	−(3.2)	8.10%	−(1.9)	***	−1.5	−12.3%
Mortality	30.00%	−(3.8)	18.60%	−(2.0)	***	−2.3	−9.2%
Nutrition	40.30%	−(3.9)	25.30%	−(2.9)	***	−3	−8.9%
Electricity	43.40%	−(5.0)	20.10%	−(4.0)	***	−4.7	−14.3%
Sanitation	56.30%	−(4.2)	38.00%	−(4.3)	***	−3.7	−7.6%
Water	14.40%	−(3.0)	8.80%	−(2.4)	***	−1.1	−9.5%
Flooring	60.10%	−(4.5)	41.80%	−(4.1)	***	−3.7	−7.0%
Cooking fuel	63.40%	−(3.9)	43.00%	−(4.1)	***	−4.1	−7.5%
Assets	46.70%	−(0)	21.70%	−(2.7)	***	−5	−14.2%

Panel III: Dimensional Contribution to MPI

	2006	2011
Schooling	13.90%	15.60%
Attendance	7.40%	6.20%
Mortality	14.30%	14.30%
Nutrition	19.20%	19.40%
Electricity	6.90%	5.20%
Sanitation	8.90%	9.70%
Water	2.30%	2.20%
Flooring	9.50%	10.70%
Cooking fuel	10.10%	11.00%
Assets	7.40%	5.60%

Note: *** statistically significant at $\omega = 0.01$, ** statistically significant at $\omega = 0.05$, * statistically significant at $\omega = 0.10$
Source: Alkire, Roche, and Vaz (2014)

became non-deprived in indicator j. But it is also possible that the reduction occurred because a person who had been deprived in j became non-poor due to reductions in other indicators, even though they remain deprived in j. In the second period, their deprivation in j is now censored because they are non-poor (their deprivation score does not exceed k). The comparison between the uncensored and censored headcount distinguishes these situations. For example, we can see from Panel I of Table 9.4 that the reductions in the uncensored headcount ratios of flooring and cooking fuel are lower than the annualized reductions of the censored headcount ratios of the these two indicators. Thus some non-poor people are deprived in these indicators. In intertemporal analysis it is useful to compare the corresponding censored and uncensored headcount ratios to analyse the relation between the dimensional changes among the poor and the society-wide changes in deprivations. Of course in repeated cross-sectional data, this comparison will also be affected by migration and demographic shifts as well as changes in the deprivation profiles of the non-poor.

Panel III of Table 9.5 presents the contribution of the indicators to the M_0 for Nepal in 2006 and in 2011. The contributions of assets, electricity, and attendance have gone down, whereas the contributions of flooring, cooking fuel, sanitation, and schooling have gone up. The contributions of water, nutrition and mortality have not shown large changes. Dimensional analyses are vital and motivating because any real reduction in a dimensional deprivation of the poor will *certainly* reduce M_0. Real reductions are normally those which are visible both in raw and censored headcounts.[14]

9.2.5 SUBGROUP DECOMPOSITION OF CHANGE IN POVERTY

One important property that the adjusted-FGT measures satisfy is population subgroup decomposability, so that the overall M_0 can be expressed as: $M_0 = \sum_{\ell=1}^{m} v^\ell M_0(X^\ell)$, where $M_0(X^\ell)$ denotes the Adjusted Headcount Ratio and $v^\ell = n^\ell/n$ the population share of subgroup ℓ, as in equation (5.7). It is extremely useful to analyse poverty changes by population subgroups, to see if the poorest subgroups reduced poverty faster than less poor subgroups and to see the dimensional composition of reduction across subgroups (Alkire and Seth 2013b, 2015; Alkire and Roche 2013; Alkire, Roche, and Vaz 2014). Population shares for each time period must be analysed alongside subgroup trends. For example, let us decompose the Indian population into four caste categories: Scheduled Castes (SC), Scheduled Tribes (ST), Other Backward Classes (OBC), and the General category. As Table 9.5 shows, M_0 as well as H have gone down statistically significantly at the national level and across all four subgroups, which is good news. However, the reduction was slowest among STs who were the poorest as a group in 1999, and their intensity showed no significant decrease. Thus, the poorest subgroup registered the slowest progress in terms of reducing poverty.

To supplement the above analysis it is useful to explore the contribution of population subgroups to the overall reduction in poverty, which not only depends on the changes in subgroups' poverty but also on changes in the population composition. This can be seen by presenting the overall change in M_0 between two periods (t^1, t^2) as

$$\Delta M_0 = \sum_{\ell=1}^{m} \left(v^{\ell,t^2} M_0(X_{t2}^\ell) - v^{\ell,t^1} M_0(X_{t1}^\ell) \right). \tag{9.14}$$

[14] Comparisons of reductions in both raw and censored headcounts may be supplemented by information on migration, demographic shifts, or exogenous shocks, for example.

Table 9.5 Decomposition of M_0, H, and A across castes in India

	1999				2006				Change		
	Pop. share	M_0	H	A	Pop. share	M_0	H	A	M_0	H	A
SC	18.3%	0.378	68.8%	55.0%	19.1%	0.307	58.3%	52.6%	−0.071***	−10.5%***	−2.3%***
ST	8.9%	0.458	80.3%	57.0%	8.5%	0.417	74.0%	56.3%	−0.041***	−6.3%***	−0.7%
OBC	32.6%	0.301	57.9%	52.1%	40.2%	0.258	50.8%	50.8%	−0.043***	−7.1%***	−1.3%***
General	40.1%	0.229	45.2%	50.6%	32.2%	0.164	33.0%	49.7%	−0.065***	−12.2%***	−0.9%**
India	**100%**	**0.300**	**56.8%**	**52.9%**	**100%**	**0.251**	**48.5%**	**51.7%**	**−0.050*****	**−8.3%***	**−1.2%***

Note: *** statistically significant at $\omega = 0.01$, ** statistically significant at $\omega = 0.05$, * statistically significant at $\omega = 0.10$

Source: Alkire and Seth (2013b, 2015)

Note that the overall change depends both on the changes in subgroup M_0's and the changes in population shares of the subgroups.

9.3 **Changes over Time by Dynamic Subgroups**

The overall changes in M_0, H, and A discussed thus far could have been generated in many ways. It might be desirable for policy purposes to monitor how poverty changed. In particular, one may wish to pinpoint the extent to which poverty reduction occurred due to people leaving poverty vs a reduction of intensity among those who remained poor, and also to know the precise dimensional changes which drove each.

For example, a decrease in the headcount ratio by 10% could have been generated by an exit of 10% of the population who had been poor in the first period. Alternatively, it could have been generated by a 20% decrease in the population who had been poor, accompanied by an influx of 10% of the population who became newly poor. Furthermore, the people who exited poverty could have had high deprivation scores in the first period—that is, been among the poorest—or they could have been only barely poor. The deprivation scores of those entering and leaving poverty will affect the overall change in intensity (ΔA) as will changes among those who stay poor. In addition, these entries into and exits from poverty could have been precipitated by different possible increases or decreases in the dimensional deprivations people experienced in the first period, which will then be reflected in the changes in uncensored and censored headcount ratios.

This section introduces more precisely these dynamics of change. We first show what can be captured with panel data, then show empirical strategies to address this situation with repeated cross-sectional data. Finally we present two approaches related to Shapley decompositions which appear to decompose changes precisely, but rely on some crucial assumptions so their empirical accuracy is questionable.

9.3.1 EXITS, ENTRIES, AND THE ONGOING POOR: A TWO-PERIOD PANEL

Let us consider a fixed set of population of size n across two periods, t^1 and t^2. The achievement matrices of these periods are denoted by X_{t^1} and X_{t^2}. The population can be mutually exclusively and collectively exhaustively categorized into four groups that we refer to as **dynamic subgroups**, as follows:

Subgroup N Contains n^N people who are non-poor in both periods t^1 and t^2

Subgroup O Contains n^O people who are poor in both periods t^1 and t^2 (*ongoing poor*)

Subgroup E^- Contains n^{E^-} people who are poor in period t^1 but *exit poverty* in period t^2

Subgroup E^+ Contains n^{E^+} people who are not poor in period t^1 but *enter poverty* in period t^2

We denote the achievement matrices of these four subgroups in period t by X_t^N, X_t^O, $X_t^{E^-}$, and $X_t^{E^+}$ for all $t = t^1, t^2$. The proportion of the multidimensionally poor population in period t^1 is $H(X_{t^1}) = (n^O + n^{E^-})/n$ and in period t^2 is $H(X_{t^2}) = (n^O + n^{E^+})/n$. The change in the proportion of poor people between these two periods is $\Delta H = H(X_{t^2}) - H(X_{t^1}) = (n^{E^+} - n^{E^-})/n = H(X_{t^2}^{E^+}) - H(X_{t^1}^{E^-})$. In other words, the change in the overall multidimensional headcount ratio is the difference between the proportion of the population who are entering and exiting poverty. Note that, by construction, no person is poor in $X_{t^1}^N$, $X_{t^2}^N$, $X_{t^2}^{E^-}$, and $X_{t^1}^{E^+}$ and thus $H(X_{t^1}^N) = H(X_{t^2}^N) = H(X_{t^2}^{E^-}) = H(X_{t^1}^{E^+}) = 0$. This also implies, $M_0(X_{t^1}^N) = M_0(X_{t^2}^N) = M_0(X_{t^2}^{E^-}) = M_0(X_{t^1}^{E^+}) = 0$. On the other hand, all persons in $X_{t^1}^{E^-}$, $X_{t^2}^{E^+}$, $X_{t^1}^O$, and $X_{t^2}^O$ are poor and thus $H(X_{t^1}^O) = H(X_{t^2}^O) = H(X_{t^1}^{E^-}) = H(X_{t^2}^{E^+}) = 1$. Therefore, the M_0 of each of these four subgroups is equal to its intensity of poverty.

In a fixed population, the overall population and the population share of each dynamic group remains unchanged across two time periods.[15] The change in the overall M_0 can be decomposed using equation (9.14) as

$$\Delta M_0 = \frac{n^O}{n}\left(M_0\left(X_{t^2}^O\right) - M_0\left(X_{t^1}^O\right)\right) - \frac{n^{E^-}}{n}M_0\left(X_{t^1}^{E^-}\right) + \frac{n^{E^+}}{n}M_0\left(X_{t^2}^{E^+}\right). \qquad (9.15)$$

Thus, the right-hand side of equation (9.15) has three components. The first component $\Delta M_0^O = \frac{n^O}{n}\left(M_0\left(X_{t^2}^O\right) - M_0\left(X_{t^1}^O\right)\right)$ is due to the change in the intensity of those who remain poor in both periods—the ongoing poor—weighted by the size of this dynamic subgroup. The second component $\Delta M_0^{E^-} = \frac{n^{E^-}}{n}M_0\left(X_{t^1}^{E^-}\right)$ is due to the change in the intensity of those who exit poverty (weighted by the size of this subgroup) and the third component $\Delta M_0^{E^+} = \frac{n^{E^+}}{n}M_0\left(X_{t^2}^{E^+}\right)$ is due to the population-weighted change in the intensity of those who enter poverty. Together $\Delta M_0 = \Delta M_0^O - \Delta M_0^{E^-} + \Delta M_0^{E^+}$.

From this point there are many interesting possible avenues for analyses. Each group can be studied separately or in different combinations. For policy, it could be interesting to know who exited poverty and their intensity in the previous period, to see if the poorest of the poor moved out of poverty. The intensity of those who entered poverty shows whether they dipped into the barely poor group or catapulted into high-intensity poverty, perhaps due to some shock or crisis or (if the population is not fixed) migration. Intensity changes among the ongoing poor show whether their deprivations are declining, even though they have not yet exited poverty. Dimensional analyses of changes for each dynamic subgroup, which are not covered in this book but are straightforward extensions of this material, are also both illuminating and policy relevant.

In the case of panel data with a fixed population we are able to estimate these precisely. We can thus monitor the extent to which the change in M_0 is due to movement into

---

[15] Suitable adjustments can be made for demographic shifts when the population is not fixed across two periods.

and out of poverty, and the extent to which it is due to a change in intensity among the ongoing poor population. The example in Box 9.1 may clarify.

BOX 9.1 DECOMPOSING THE CHANGE IN M_0 ACROSS DYNAMIC SUBGROUPS: AN ILLUSTRATION

Consider the following six-person, six-dimension g^0 matrices, in which people enter and exit poverty, and intensity among the poor also increases and decreases.

$$g^0 \text{ Period 1} \qquad\qquad g^0 \text{ Period 2}$$

$$
\begin{bmatrix}
1 & 1 & 1 & 1 & 1 & 1 \\
1 & 1 & 1 & 1 & 1 & 0 \\
1 & 1 & 1 & 1 & 0 & 0 \\
1 & 1 & 1 & 0 & 0 & 0 \\
1 & 1 & 0 & 0 & 0 & 0 \\
0 & 0 & 0 & 0 & 0 & 0
\end{bmatrix}
\qquad
\begin{bmatrix}
0 & 0 & 0 & 0 & 0 & 0 \\
0 & 0 & 0 & 0 & 0 & 0 \\
1 & 1 & 1 & 0 & 0 & 0 \\
1 & 1 & 0 & 0 & 0 & 0 \\
1 & 1 & 1 & 0 & 0 & 0 \\
1 & 1 & 1 & 0 & 0 & 0
\end{bmatrix}
$$

Let us use a poverty cutoff of 33% or two out of six dimensions. Increases and decreases are depicted in bold. Below we summarize M_0, H, and A in two periods and their changes across two periods.

	t^1	t^2	Δ (Change)
M_0	5/9	11/36	−1/4
H	5/6	2/3	−1/6
A	2/3	11/24	−5/24

So in period 2 there are four kinds of changes affecting the dynamic subgroups as follows:

(1) E^-: persons 1 and 2 become non-poor (move out of or exit poverty).

(2) E^+ : person 6 enters poverty.

(3) O : two kinds of changes occur:

    a. deprivations of ongoing poor persons 3 and 4 **reduce** by one deprivation each;

    b. deprivations of ongoing poor person 5 **increases** by one deprivation.

The descriptions and the decompositions of M_0 for the changes are in the following table.

Subgroup Decompositions	E^-	E^+	O	Δ
$n^{subgroup}/n$	2/6	1/6	3/6	$\Delta H = \left(-\dfrac{2}{6}\right) + \dfrac{1}{6} = -\dfrac{1}{6}$
ΔA	−11/12	3/6	−1/18	
ΔM_0	$-\dfrac{11}{36}$	$\dfrac{1}{12}$	$-\dfrac{1}{36}$	$\Delta M_0 = -\dfrac{11}{36} + \dfrac{3}{36} - \dfrac{1}{36} = -\dfrac{1}{4}$
		E	O	
		89%	11%	100%
	E^-	E^+	O	
ΔM_0 (%)	−122%	+33%	−11%	−100%

BOX 9.1 *(cont.)*

What is particularly interesting for policy is that we can notice that, in this example, 11% of the reduction in poverty was due to changes in intensity among the 50% of the population who stayed poor, that poverty was effectively increased 33% by the new entrant, but that this was more than compensated by those who exited poverty (−122%), because they initially had very high intensities. In this dramatic example, the poorest of the poor exited poverty, while the less poor experienced smaller reductions.

9.3.2 DECOMPOSITION BY INCIDENCE AND INTENSITY FOR CROSS-SECTIONAL DATA

The previous section explained the changes for a fixed population over time. To estimate that empirically requires *panel data* with data on the same persons in both periods which can be used to track their movement in and out of poverty. Yet analyses over time are often based on *repeated cross-sectional data*, having independent samples that are statistically representative of the population under study, but that do not to track each specific observation over time. This section examines the decomposition of changes in M_0 for cross-sectional data.

With cross-sectional data, we cannot distinguish between the three groups identified above, nor can we isolate the intensity of those who move into or out of poverty. Observed values are only available for: $H(X_{t1}), H(X_{t2}), \Delta H, A(X_{t1}), A(X_{t2}), \Delta A, M_0(X_{t1})$, $M_0(X_{t2})$, and ΔM_0. Using these, it is categorically impossible to decompose ΔM_0 with the empirical precision that panel data permits.

Nonetheless, if required one can move forward with some simplifications. Instead of three groups (E^-, E^+, and O) let us consider just two, which might be referred to (somewhat roughly) as 'movers' and 'stayers'. We define movers as the ΔH people who reflect the net change in poverty levels across the two periods. Stayers are ongoing poor plus the proportion of previously poor people who were replaced by 'new poor', and total those who are poor in period 2, $H(X_{t2})$. In considering only the 'net' change in headcount, one effectively permits the larger of E^- or E^+ to dominate: if poverty rose nationally, it is the group who entered poverty who dominate; if poverty fell nationally, it is the group who exited poverty. The subordinate third group is allocated among the ongoing poor and the dominant group. For the remainder of this section we presume that both M_0 and H decreased overall. In this case, $E^- > E^+$. So $\Delta H = (H^E - H^{E'})$, and $H(X_{t2}) = (H^O + H^{E^+})$. As is evident, this simplification is performed because empirical data exist in repeated cross-sections for ΔH and $H(X_{t2})$.

Example: Suppose that 37% of people are ongoing poor, 3% enter poverty, 13% exit poverty, and 47% remain non-poor. Suppose the overall headcount ratio decreased by 10 percentage points, and the headcount ratio in period 2 is 40%, whereas in period 1 it was 50% (37%+13%). We now primarily consider two numbers: the headcount ratio in period 2 of 40% (interpreted broadly as ongoing poverty) and the change in headcount ratio of 10% (interpreted broadly as moving into/out of poverty). In doing so we are effectively permitting the 'new poverty entrants' to be considered as among the group in ongoing poverty in period 2 (37% + 3% = 40%). To balance this, we effectively replace 3% of those who exited poverty (13% − 3% = 10% = ΔH), and consider this slightly reduced group to be those who moved out of poverty. If poverty had increased overall, the swaps would be in the other direction.

If poverty has reduced and there has not been a large influx of people into poverty, that is, if $H^{E^+} = n^{E^+}/n$ is presumed to be relatively small empirically, then this strategy would be likely to shed light on the relative intensity levels of those who moved out of poverty $H^{E^-} = n^{E^-}/n$, and the changes in intensity among those who remained poor $H^O = n^O/n$. If empirically H^{E^+} is expected (from other sources of information) to be large, or if their intensity is expected to differ greatly from the average, this strategy is not advised.[16]

Consider the intensity of the net population who exited poverty—under these simplifying assumptions reflected by the net change in headcount, denoted $A^{\hat{E}}$—and the intensity change of the net ongoing poor, whom we will presume to be $H(X_{t2})$, denoted $\Delta A^{\hat{O}}$. The ΔM_0 can be decomposed according to these two groups. These decompositions can be interpreted as showing the percentage of the change in M_0 that can be attributed to those who moved out of poverty, versus the percentage of change which was mainly caused by a decrease in intensity among those who stayed poor. We use the terms movers and stayers to refer to these less precise dynamic subgroups in cross-sectional data analysis.

$$\Delta M_0 = \underbrace{\Delta H \times A^{\hat{E}}}_{\substack{\text{Movers} \\ \text{effect}}} + \underbrace{H(X_{t2}) \times \Delta A^{\hat{O}}}_{\substack{\text{Stayers} \\ \text{effect}}}. \tag{9.16}$$

Cross-sectional data does not provide the intensity of either of those who stayed poor or of those who moved out of poverty. One way forward is to estimate these using existing data. First, identify the $\Delta H \times n$ poor persons having the lowest intensity in the dataset (sampling weights applied), and use the average of these scores for $A^{\hat{E}}$, then solve for $A^{\hat{O}}$.[17] Subsequently, identify the $\Delta H \times n$ poor persons having the highest intensity in that dataset, and repeat the procedure. This will generate upper and lower estimates for $A^{\hat{E}}$ and $A^{\hat{O}}$ in a given dataset, which will provide an idea of the degree of uncertainty that

---

[16] The corresponding considerations apply if poverty has increased and H^{E^-} is expected to be small.

[17] Naturally it is also possible to create estimates for $A^{\hat{O}}$ where the upper bound was the overall change in intensity, and the lower bound was zero, and solve for $A^{\hat{E}}$. However this would not permit an increase in intensity (which would happen if the barely poor left poverty and the others stayed the same, for example), nor for an even stronger reduction in intensity. For example, in the example in Table 9.2, Nepal's A reduced by five percentage points, whereas in our upper bound, intensity among the stayers increased by 4% and in the lower bound it decreased by 13%.

different assumptions introduce. To estimate stricter upper and lower bounds it could be assumed that those who moved out of poverty had an intensity score of the value of k (the theoretically minimum possible), and subsequently assume that their intensity was 100% (the theoretically maximum possible).[18]

Table 9.6 provides the empirical estimations for the upper and lower bounds for the same four countries discussed above plus Ethiopia. At the upper bound, those who moved out of poverty could have had average intensities ranging from 59% in Peru (the least poor country) to 99% in Ethiopia or 100% in Senegal, according to the datasets. This in itself is interesting, as it would suggest that Rwanda—the poorest country of the four—had movers with lower average deprivations than Ethiopia. Those who stayed poor would have had, in this case, small if any increases or decreases in intensity—less than four percentage points. At the lower bound, those who moved out of poverty could have had intensities from 33% in Peru and Senegal to 38% in Nepal, and intensity reductions among the ongoing poor could have ranged from 2% in Senegal to 13% in Nepal. At the upper bound (where we assume the poorest of the poor moved out of poverty), for Nepal, Rwanda, and Peru, over 100% of the poverty reduction was due to the movers, because intensity among the ongoing poor would have had to increase (to create the observed ΔM_0). At the lower bound, where the least poor people moved out of poverty, movers contributed 47–67% to ΔM_0. Senegal did not have a statistically significant reduction in poverty. Ethiopia provides a different example where the upper and lower bounds are closer together and reductions in intensity among the ongoing poor would have contributed 31% to 73%.

This empirical investigation shows that, when implemented with the mild assumptions that are required for cross-sectional data, the upper and lower bounds according to each country's dataset are very wide apart. In reality, the relative contribution of the movers and stayers to overall poverty reduction could vary anywhere in this range.

As the example shows, the empirical upper and lower bounds vary greatly across countries. In the case of Ethiopia, movers explain 27% to 69% of the changes in poverty, and stayers account for 31% to 73%. These boundaries do not permit us to assess whether the actual contribution from movers was greater than or less than that of stayers. In Nepal and Peru the movers probably contributed more than stayers to poverty reduction, as in all cases their lowest effect is above 50%. Given these wide-ranging upper and lower bounds, empirically we are unable to answer questions such as whether the intensity of the ongoing poor decreased, or whether it was the barely poor or the deeply poor who moved out of poverty. While this can seem disappointing, for policy purposes, as Sen stresses, it may be better to be 'vaguely right than precisely wrong', and repeated cross-sectional data simply do not permit us, at this time, to move ahead with precision.

---

[18] These bounds are theoretically possible lower and upper bounds. Further research using panel datasets is required to investigate the likelihood of these bounds.

Table 9.6 Decomposing the change in M_0 by dynamic subgroups

Panel A

Country	M_0			H		A		ΔH
	t^1	t^2	ΔM_0	t^1	t^2	t^1	t^2	
Ethiopia 2005–2011	0.605	0.523	−0.081	89.7	84.1	67.4	62.3	5.66
Nepal 2006–2011	0.350	0.217	−0.133	64.7	44.2	54.0	49.0	20.55
Peru 2005–2008	0.085	0.066	−0.019	19.5	15.7	43.6	42.2	3.78
Rwanda 2005–2010	0.460	0.330	−0.130	82.9	66.1	55.5	49.9	16.75
Senegal 2005–2010/11	0.440	0.423	−0.017	71.3	70.8	61.7	59.7	0.46

Panel B

Country	Upper bound				Lower bound				Shapley decomposition	
	A Movers	ΔA Stayers	Movers' effect	Stayers' effect	A Movers	ΔA Stayers	Movers' effect	Stayers' effect	Incidence effect H	Intensity effect A
Ethiopia 2005–2011	0.99	−0.03	68.7%	31.3%	0.38	−0.07	26.6%	73.4%	45%	55%
Nepal 2006–2011	0.74	0.04	113.4%	−13.4%	0.38	−0.13	58.2%	41.8%	79%	21%
Peru 2005–2008	0.59	0.02	119.5%	−19.5%	0.33	−0.04	67.1%	32.9%	86%	14%
Rwanda 2005–2010	0.78	0	101.4%	−1.4%	0.36	−0.1	47.1%	52.9%	68%	32%
Senegal 2005–2010/11	1	−0.02	26.8%	73.2%	0.33	−0.02	8.9%	91.1%	16%	84%

Source: Alkire, Roche, and Vaz (2014)

9.3.3 THEORETICAL INCIDENCE–INTENSITY DECOMPOSITIONS

Whereas monitoring and policy inputs must be based on empirical analyses, some research topics utilize theoretical analyses. This section introduces two theory-based approaches to decomposing changes in repeated cross-sectional data according to what we call 'incidence' and 'intensity'. In each approach assumptions are made regarding the intensity of those who exit or remain poor. As we have already noted, the task implies some challenges because the empirical accuracy of the underlying assumptions is completely unknown, and as Table 9.6 showed, the actual range may be quite large. These techniques are thus offered in the spirit of academic inquiry.

For simplicity of notation, in this subsection, we denote the M_0, H, and A for period t^1 by $M_0^{t^1}$, H^{t^1}, and A^{t^1}; and for period t^2 by $M_0^{t^2}$, H^{t^2}, and A^{t^2}. The first approach consists in the additive decomposition proposed by Apablaza and Yalonetzky (2013), which is illustrated in Panel A of Figure 9.2. Since $M_0 = H \times A$, they propose to decompose the change in M_0 by changes in its partial indices as follows:

$$\Delta M_0 = \underbrace{A^{t^2} \left(H^{t^2} - H^{t^1} \right)}_{\substack{\text{Poverty effect} \\ \text{from entry and exit}}} + \underbrace{H^{t^2} \left(A^{t^2} - A^{t^1} \right)}_{\substack{\text{Poverty effect} \\ \text{among ongoing poor}}} \qquad (9.17)$$

$$- \underbrace{\left(\left(H^{t^2} - H^{t^1} \right) \left(A^{t^2} - A^{t^1} \right) \right)}_{\text{Interaction effect}}$$

Note that the illustration in Figure 9.2 assumes reductions in M_0, H, and A over time, but the graph can be adjusted to incorporate situations where they do not necessarily fall. This approach involves two assumptions. First, the intensity among those who left poverty is assumed to be the same as the average intensity in period t^2. Second, the intensity change among the ongoing poor is assumed to equal the simple difference in intensities of the poor across the two periods. The decomposition is completed using an interaction term, as depicted in Panel A of Figure 9.2. This is indeed an additive decomposition of changes in the Adjusted Headcount Ratio (M_0). Apablaza and Yalonetzky interpret these changes as reflecting: (1) changes in the incidence of poverty (H), (2) changes in the intensity of poverty (A), and (3) a joint effect that is due to interaction between incidence and intensity ($\Delta H \times \Delta A$).

A second theoretical approach corresponds to a Shapley decomposition proposed by Roche (2013). This builds on Apablaza and Yalonetzky (2013) and performs a Shapley value decomposition following Shorrocks (1999).[19] It provides the marginal effect of

---

[19] The Shapley value decomposition was initially applied to decomposition of income inequality by Chantreuil and Trannoy (2011, 2013) and Morduch and Sinclair (1998). Shorrocks (1999) showed that it can be applied to any function under certain assumptions.

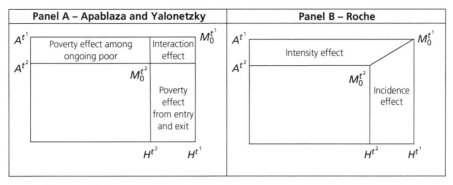

Figure 9.2. Theoretical decompositions

changes in incidence and intensity as follows:

$$\Delta M_0 = \underbrace{\frac{A^{t^2} + A^{t^1}}{2}\left(H^{t^2} - H^{t^1}\right)}_{\substack{\text{Incidence of} \\ \text{Poverty effect}}} + \underbrace{\frac{H^{t^2} + H^{t^1}}{2}\left(A^{t^2} - A^{t^1}\right)}_{\substack{\text{Intensity of} \\ \text{Poverty effect}}}. \tag{9.18}$$

Panel B of Figure 9.2 illustrates Roche's application of Shapley decompositions, which focuses on the marginal effect without the interaction effect. Roche's proposal assumes that the intensity of those who exited poverty (our terms) is the average intensity of the two periods $\frac{A^{t^2} + A^{t^1}}{2}\left(H^{t^2} - H^{t^1}\right)$, and calls this the 'incidence effect'. He takes the other group as comprising the average headcount ratio between the two periods, and their change in intensity as the simple difference in intensities across the periods $\frac{H^{t^2} + H^{t^1}}{2}\left(A^{t^2} - A^{t^1}\right)$, and describes this as the 'intensity effect'.

Roche's masterly presentation systematically applies Shapley decompositions to each step of dynamic analysis using the AF method. For example, if the underlying assumptions are transparently stated and accepted, the theoretically derived marginal contribution of changes in incidence and marginal contribution of changes in intensity can be expressed as a percentage of the overall change in M_0 so they both add to 100% and can be written as follows:

$$\Phi_H^0 = \frac{\left(\frac{A^{t^2} + A^{t^1}}{2}\left(H^{t^2} - H^{t^1}\right)\right) \times 100}{\Delta M_0}, \tag{9.19}$$

and

$$\Phi_A^0 = \frac{\left(\frac{H^{t^2} + H^{t^1}}{2}\left(A^{t^2} - A^{t^1}\right)\right) \times 100}{\Delta M_0}. \tag{9.20}$$

To address demographic shifts, Roche follows a similar decomposition of change as that used in FGT unidimensional poverty measures (Ravallion and Huppi 1991) and Shapley decompositions (Duclos and Araar 2006; Shorrocks 1999). This approach, presented in equation (9.21), attributes demographic effects to the average population shares and subgroup M_0s across time. Roche argues that if the underlying assumptions are accepted, the overall change in poverty level can be broken down in two components: (1) changes due to intra-sectoral or within-group poverty effect, and (2) changes due to demographic or inter-sectoral effects. So the overall change in the adjusted headcount between two periods, respectively (t^2, t^1), could be expressed as follows:

$$\Delta M_0 = \underbrace{\sum_{\ell=1}^{m} \left(\frac{v^{\ell, t^2} + v^{\ell, t^1}}{2} \right) \left(M_0^{\ell, t^2} - M_0^{\ell, t^1} \right)}_{\text{Within-group}} \tag{9.21}$$

$$+ \underbrace{\sum_{\ell=1}^{m} \left(\frac{M_0^{\ell, t^2} + M_0^{\ell, t^1}}{2} \right) \left(v^{\ell, t^2} - v^{\ell, t^1} \right).}_{\substack{\text{Demographic or} \\ \text{sectoral effect}}}$$

It is common to express the contribution of each factor as a proportion of the overall change, in which case equation (9.21) is divided throughout by ΔM_0.

The last columns of Table 9.6 Panel B provide Shapley decompositions for the same five countries. We see that in all cases the Shapley decompositions lie, as anticipated, between the upper and lower bounds. The Shapley decompositions have the broad appeal of presenting point estimates that pinpoint the exact contribution of each partial index to changes in poverty, according to their underlying assumptions, and thus may be used in analyses when empirical accuracy is not required or the assumptions are independently verified. A full illustration of the Shapley decomposition methods using data on multidimensional child poverty in Bangladesh is given in Roche (2013).[20]

9.4 **Chronic Multidimensional Poverty**

Panel datasets provide information on precisely the same individual or household at different periods of time. Good-quality panel datasets are particularly rich and useful for analysing multidimensional poverty because their analysis provides policy-relevant insights that extend what time series data provide. For example, using panel data we can

---

[20] The multidimensional poverty index implemented in Roche (2013) focuses on children under 5. The choice of dimensions and indicators are similar to Gordon et al. (2003).

distinguish the deprivations experienced by the chronically poor from those experienced by the transitory poor and thus identify the combination of deprivations that trap people in long-term multidimensional poverty. Also, we can analyse the duration over which a person was deprived in each indicator—and the sequences by which their deprivation profile evolved. As section 9.3.1 showed, we can identify precisely the contributions to poverty reduction that were generated by changes in entries and exits from poverty and by the ongoing poor.

The following section very briefly presents a counting-based class of chronic multi-dimensional poverty measures that use a triple-cutoff method of identifying who is poor. We give prominence here to the measure that can be estimated using ordinal data. The consistent sub-indices associated with the chronic multidimensional poverty methodology include the headcount ratio and intensity, as well as new indices related to the duration of poverty and dimensional deprivation. We also present a linked measure of transient poverty. As in other sections, we presume that interested readers will master standard empirical and statistical techniques that are appropriate for studies using panel data, and apply these in the analyses of poverty transitions and chronic poverty here described.

The closing section on poverty transitions informally sketches revealing analyses that can be undertaken without generating a chronic poverty measure. People are identified as multidimensionally poor or non-poor in each period, then population subgroups are identified that have differing sequences of multidimensional poverty. For example, one group might include non-poor people who 'fell' into multidimensional poverty, a second might include multidimensionally poor people who 'rose' out of poverty, a third might contain those who were poor in all periods, and a fourth might contain those who 'churned' in and out of poverty across periods. Naturally the number of 'dynamic subgroups' depends upon the sample design, the number of waves of data, and the precise definition of each group.

9.4.1 CHRONIC POVERTY MEASUREMENT USING PANEL DATA

Multiple approaches to measuring chronic poverty in one dimension exist, many of which have implications for the measurement of chronic multidimensional poverty.[21] Alongside important qualitative work, multiple methodologies for measuring chronic multidimensional poverty have also been proposed.[22] This section combines the

---

[21] This section draws upon Alkire, Apablaza, Chakravarty, and Yalonetzky (2014). See also McKay and Lawson (2003), Dercon and Shapiro (2007), Foster (2009), Foster and Santos (2013), Jalan and Ravallion (1998), Calvo and Dercon (2013), Hoy and Zheng (2011), Gradín, Del Rio, and Canto (2012), and Bossert, Chakravarty, and D'Ambrosio (2012).

[22] Hulme and Shepherd (2003), Chakravarty and D'Ambrosio (2006), Calvo (2008), Addison, Hulme, and Kanbur (2009), Baluch and Masset (2003), Bossert, Ceriani, Chakravarty, and D'Ambrosio (2012), Nicholas and Ray (2012), Nicholas, Ray, and Sinha (2013), and Porter and Quinn (2013).

AF methodology with the counting-based approach to chronic poverty measurement proposed in Foster (2009), which has a dual-cutoff identification structure and aggregation method that are very similar to the AF method. Foster (2009) provides a methodology for measuring unidimensional chronic poverty in which each time period t is equally weighted for all at $t = 1, \ldots, T$. An $n \times T$ matrix is constructed in which each entry takes a value of one if person i is identified as poor in period t and a value of 0 otherwise. A n-dimensional 'count' vector is constructed in which each entry shows the number of periods in which person i was poor. A second time cutoff τ is applied such that each person is identified as chronically poor if he or she has been poor in τ or more periods. Associated FGT indices and partial indices are then constructed from the relevant censored matrices.

9.4.1.1 Order of Aggregation

This combined chronic multidimensional poverty measure applies three sets of cutoffs: deprivation cutoffs z_j, a multidimensional poverty cutoff k, and a duration cutoff τ. It is possible to analyse multidimensional poverty using panel data by combining the AF methodology and the Foster (2009) chronic poverty methods using either one of two different orders of aggregation, which we call **chronic deprivation** and **chronic poverty**. These alternatives effectively interchange the order in which the poverty and duration cutoffs are applied. In both cases, we first apply a fixed set of deprivation cutoffs to the achievement matrix in each period.

In the **chronic deprivation** option (τ before k), we first consider the duration of deprivation in each indicator for each person and then compute a multidimensional poverty measure which summarizes only those deprivations that have been experienced by the same person across τ or, more periods. This approach aggregates all 'chronic' deprivations into a multidimensional poverty index, regardless of the period in which those deprivations were experienced. This approach would provide complementary information that could enrich analyses of multidimensional poverty, but cannot be broken down by time period, nor does it show whether the deprivations were experienced simultaneously (Alkire, Apablaza, Chakravarty, and Yalonetzky 2014).

In the **chronic multidimensional poverty** option (k before τ), we first identify each person as multidimensionally poor or non-poor in each period using the poverty cutoff k. We then count the periods in which each person experienced multidimensional poverty. We identify as chronically multidimensionally poor those persons who have experienced multidimensional poverty in τ or more periods.

9.4.1.2 Deprivation matrices

We observe achievements across d dimensions for a set of n individuals at T different time points. Let x_{ij}^t stand for the achievement in attribute j of person i in period t, where $x_{ij}^t \geq 0 \ \forall i, j, t$. Let X_t denote an $n \times d$ matrix whose elements reflect the dimensional achievements of the population in period t. The deprivation cutoff vector z_j is fixed across periods. As before, a person is deprived with respect to deprivation j in periods t if $x_{ij}^t < z_j$ and non-deprived otherwise. By applying the deprivation cutoffs to the achievement matrix for each period, we can construct the period-specific deprivation matrices $g_{ij}^{0,t}$. For simplicity, this section uses the non-normalized or numbered weights notation across dimensions, such that $\sum_{j=1}^d w_j = d$. Time periods are equally weighted. When achievement data are cardinal we can also construct normalized gap matrices $g_{ij}^{1,t}$ and squared gap matrices $g_{ij}^{2,t}$ or, more generally, powered matrices of normalized deprivation gaps $g_{ij}^{\alpha,t}$ where $\alpha \geq 0$. In a similar manner as previously, we generate the n-dimensional c_i^t column vector, which reflects the weighted sum of deprivations person i experiences in periods t.

9.4.1.3 Identification

To identify who is chronically multidimensionally poor we first construct an identification matrix. The same matrix can be used to identify the transient poor in each period and to create subgroups of those who exhibit distinct patterns of multidimensional poverty (for analysis of poverty transitions).

Identification Matrix Let $Q(k)$ be an $n \times T$ identification matrix whose typical element $Q_{it}(k)$ is 1 if person i is identified as multidimensionally poor in period t using the AF methodology, that is, using a poverty cutoff k, which is fixed across periods, and 0 otherwise.

The typical column $Q_{\cdot t}(k)$ reflects the identification status $\rho_i^t(k)$ for the ith person in period t, whereas the typical row $Q_{i\cdot}(k)$ displays the periods in which person i has been identified as multidimensionally poor (signified by an entry of 1) or non-poor (0). Thus we might equivalently consider each column of $Q(k)$ to be an identification column vector for period t such that $\rho_i^t(k) = 1$, if and only if person i is multidimensionally poor in period t according to the deprivation cutoffs z_j, weights w_j, and poverty cutoff k; and $\rho_i^t(k) = 0$ otherwise.

Episodes of Poverty Count Vector e_i From the $Q(k)$ matrix we construct the n-dimensional column vector $e(k)$ whose i^{th} element $e_i(k) = \sum_{t=1}^T Q_{it}(k)$ sums the elements of the corresponding row vector of $Q(k)$ and provides the total number of periods in which person i is poor, or the total episodes of poverty, as identified by poverty cutoff k. Naturally, $0 \leq e_i(k) \leq T$, that is, each person may have from 0 episodes of poverty to T episodes, the latter indicating that a person was poor in each of the t periods.

Chronic Multidimensional Poverty: Identification and Censoring We apply the duration cutoff τ where $0 < \tau \leq T$ to the $e_i(k)$ vector in order identify the status of each person as chronically multidimensionally poor or not. We identify a person to be chronically multidimensionally poor if $e_i(k) \geq \tau$, that is, if they have experienced τ

or more periods in multidimensional poverty. A person is considered non-chronically poor if $0 \leq e_i(k) < \tau$. We doubly censor the $e_i(k)$ vector such that it takes the value of 0 (non-chronically poor) if $0 \leq e_i(k) < \tau$ and takes the value of $e_i(k)$ otherwise. The notation $e_i(k, \tau)$ indicates the censored vector of poverty episodes—just as the notation $c_i(k)$ indicated the censored deprivation count vector. Positive entries reflect the number of periods in which chronically poor people experienced poverty; entries of 0 mean that the person is not identified as chronically poor.

Among the non-chronically poor, we could (as we will elaborate) identify two subgroups: the non-poor and the transient poor. A person is considered transiently poor if $0 < e_i(k) < \tau$. And naturally a person for whom $e_i = 0$, that is, who is non-poor in all periods, is considered non-poor.

An alternative but useful notation for the identification of chronic multidimensional poverty uses the identification function: we apply the identification function $\rho(\tau)$ to censor the $Q(k)$ matrix and the $e_i(k)$vector. The doubly censored Q matrix reflects solely those periods in poverty that are experienced by the chronically poor (censoring all periods of transient poverty) and is denoted by $Q(k, \tau)$. After censoring, the typical element $e_i(k, \tau)$ is defined by $\rho_i(\tau) = \mathbb{I}(e_i(k) \geq \tau)$. The entry takes a value of $e_i(k)$ if person i is chronically multidimensionally poor and 0 otherwise.

Censored (k, τ) Deprivation Matrices and Count Vector To identify the censored headcount ratios, as well as the dimensional composition of poverty in each period, we censor the T sets of $n \times d$ deprivation matrices by applying the twin identification functions $\rho^t(k)$ and $\rho(\tau)$. We denote the censored matrices by $g^{0,t}(k, \tau)$ and the censored deprivation count vectors for each period by $c_i^t(k, \tau)$.

Deprivation Duration Matrix Finally, to summarize the overall dimensional deprivations of the poor, as well as the duration of these deprivations, it will be useful to create a duration matrix based on the censored deprivation matrices $g_0(k, \tau)$. Let L be an $n \times d$ matrix whose typical element L_{ij} provides the number of periods in which i is chronically poor and is deprived in dimension j. Note that $0 \leq L_{ij} \leq T$. We can use the duration matrix to obtain the deprivation-specific duration indices, which show the percentage of periods in which, on average, poor people were deprived in each indicator.

9.4.1.4 Aggregation

The measure of chronic multidimensional poverty when some data are ordinal may be written as follows:

$$M_0^C(X;z) = H^C \times A^C \times D^C = \frac{1}{ndT} \sum_{i=1}^{n} \sum_{j=1}^{d} \sum_{t=1}^{T} w_j g_{ij}^{0,t}(k, \tau). \tag{9.22}$$

Thus the Adjusted Headcount Ratio of chronic multidimensional poverty M_0^C is the mean of the set of T deprivation matrices $(g^{0,t}(k,\tau))$ that have been censored of all deprivations of persons who are not chronically multidimensionally poor. Alternative notation for this measure can be found in Alkire, Apablaza, Chakravarty, and Yalonetzky (2014).

When data are cardinal, the M_α^C class of measures are, like the AF class, the means of the respective powered matrices of normalized gaps.

$$M_\alpha^C(X;z) = \frac{1}{ndT} \sum_{i=1}^{n} \sum_{j=1}^{d} \sum_{t=1}^{T} w_j g_{ij}^\alpha(k,\tau) \tag{9.23}$$

9.4.2 PROPERTIES

For chronic multidimensional poverty, as for multidimensional poverty, the specification of axioms is, in some cases, a joint restriction on the (triple-cutoff) identification and aggregation strategies and, hence, on the overall poverty methodology. The properties are now defined with respect to the chronically multidimensionally poor population. The class of measures present respects the key properties that were highlighted as providing policy relevance and practicality to the AF measures, such as subgroup consistency and decomposability, dimensional monotonicity, dimensional breakdown, and ordinality. In addition, this class of measures satisfies a form of **time monotonicity** as highlighted in Foster (2009) in the unidimensional case. The intuition is that if a person who is chronically poor becomes poor in an additional period, poverty rises.

A full definition of the properties that this chronic multidimensional poverty measure fulfils is provided in Alkire, Apablaza, Chakravarty, and Yalonetzky (2014). The methodology of multidimensional chronic poverty measurement fulfils the appropriately stated properties of anonymity, time anonymity, population replication invariance, chronic poverty focus, time focus, chronic normalization, chronic dimensional monotonicity, chronic weak monotonicity, time monotonicity, chronic monotonicity in thresholds, monotonicity in multidimensional poverty identifier, chronic duration monotonicity, chronic weak transfer, non-increasing chronic poverty under association-decreasing switch, and additive subgroup decomposability for all $\alpha \geq 0$. The class of measures also satisfies chronic strong monotonicity for $\alpha > 0$ and chronic strong transfer when $\alpha \geq 1$.

9.4.3 CONSISTENT SUB-INDICES

Like M_0, the chronic multidimensional poverty measure (M_0^C) is the product of intuitive partial indices that convey meaningful information on different features of a society's experience of chronic multidimensional poverty. In particular, $M_0^C(X;z) = H^C \times A^C \times D^C$ where:

- H^C is the headcount ratio of chronic multidimensional poverty—the percentage of the population who are chronically multidimensionally poor according to k and τ.
- A^C is the average intensity of poverty among the chronically multidimensionally poor—the average share of weighted deprivations that chronically poor people experience in those periods in which they are multidimensionally poor.
- D^C reflects the average duration of poverty among the chronically poor—the average share of T periods in which they experience multidimensional poverty.

These partial indices can also be calculated directly. In particular,

$$H^C = \frac{1}{n} \sum_{i=1}^{n} \rho_i(k;\tau) = \frac{q^C}{n}. \tag{9.24}$$

That is, the headcount ratio of chronic multidimensional poverty is the number of people who have been identified as chronically multidimensionally poor divided by the total population. We denote the number of chronically multidimensionally poor people by q^C.

The intensity of chronic multidimensional poverty is the sum of the weighted deprivation scores of all poor people over all time periods, divided by the number of dimensions times the total number of people who are poor in each period summed across periods. Note that $\frac{k}{d} \leq A^C \leq 1$.

$$A^C = \frac{\sum_{i=1}^{n} \sum_{t=1}^{T} c_i^t(k,\tau)}{d \times \sum_{i=1}^{n} \sum_{t=1}^{T} Q(k,\tau)} \tag{9.25}$$

The average duration of chronic multidimensional poverty—the percentage of periods on average in which the chronically poor person was poor—can be easily assessed using the $e_i(k,\tau)$ vector.

$$D^C = \frac{\sum_{i=1}^{n} e_i(k,\tau)}{q^C \times T} \tag{9.26}$$

The duration is the sum of the total number of periods in which the chronically poor experience multidimensional poverty, divided by the number of periods and the number of chronically poor. Note that $\frac{\tau}{T} \leq D^C \leq 1$. Box 9.2 illustrates these with a simple example.

BOX 9.2 COMPUTING THE INCIDENCE AND DURATION OF CHRONIC POVERTY

Consider three people and four periods, with $\tau = 2$.

Person 1 is multidimensionally poor in period 1
Person 2 is multidimensionally poor in periods 2, 3, and 4
Person 3 is multidimensionally poor in periods 1, 2, 3, and 4

Two people are chronically poor because they experience multidimensional poverty in $\tau = 2$ or more periods. So the percentage of people identified as chronically poor H^C is 67%.

In this case, the vector $e = (0,3,4)$, $q^C = 2$, and our duration index is $\frac{(3+4)}{2 \times 4} = \frac{7}{8} = 87.5\%$. That is, on average, chronically poor persons are poor during 87.5% of the time periods.

9.4.3.1 **Dimensional Indices**

For chronic multidimensional poverty, it is possible and useful to generate the standard dimensional indicators for each period: the censored headcount ratio and percentage contribution. It is also possible and useful to generate the period-specific Adjusted Headcount Ratio (M_0), headcount ratio (H), and intensity (A) figures, which are different from, but can be consistently related to, the chronic poverty headcount and intensity values presented in section 9.4.3. Finally, and of tremendous use, it is possible to present the average duration of deprivation in each dimension and to relate this directly to the overall duration of chronic poverty. Box 9.3 presents the intuition of this set of consistent indices; for their precise definition see Alkire, Apablaza, Chakravarty, and Yalonetzky (2014).

BOX 9.3 SINGLE- AND CROSS-PERIOD INDICES OF CHRONIC POVERTY

Cross-period indices reflecting chronic poverty:

M_0^C: Adjusted Headcount Ratio of chronic multidimensional poverty

H^C: Headcount ratio, showing the percentage of the population who are chronically poor

A^C: Intensity, showing the average percentage of deprivations experienced by the chronically multidimensionally poor in those periods in which they are poor

D^C: Average duration of chronic poverty, expressed as a percentage of time periods

$h_j^C(k,\tau)$: Average censored headcount of dimension j among the chronically poor in all periods in which they are poor and are deprived in dimension j

D_j: Average duration of deprivation in dimension j among the chronically poor, expressed as a percentage of time periods

$\phi_j^C(k,\tau)$: Percentage contribution of dimension j to the deprivations of the chronically poor.

Single-period indices reflecting the profiles of the chronic poor in that particular period of poverty:

H^t: Headcount ratio, showing the percentage of the population who are chronically poor in period t

A^t: Intensity, showing the average percentage of deprivations experienced by the chronically multidimensionally poor in period t

$h_j^t(k,\tau)$: Censored headcount of dimension j among the chronically poor in period t

$\phi_j^t(k,\tau)$: Percentage contribution of dimension j to the deprivations of the chronically poor in period t.

Cross-period averages of the unidimensional indices can also be constructed, such as $\bar{H}, \bar{A}$ and $\bar{h}_j^t(k,\tau)$, and analysed in conjunction with the relevant duration measure.

9.4.3.2 Censored Headcount Ratios

The censored headcount ratios for each period t are constructed as the mean of the dimensional column vector for each period and represent the proportion of people who are chronically poor in time period t and are deprived in dimension j:

$$h_j^t(k, \tau) = \mu\left(g_j^{0,t}(k, \tau)\right). \tag{9.27}$$

We can also describe the average censored headcount ratios of chronic multidimensional poverty across T periods in each dimension as simply the mean of the censored headcount ratios in each period:

$$h_j^C(k, \tau) = \frac{1}{T} \sum_{t=1}^{T} h_j^t(k, \tau). \tag{9.28}$$

The Adjusted Headcount Ratio of chronic multidimensional poverty across all periods is simply the mean of the average weighted censored headcount ratios:

$$M_0^C = \frac{1}{d} \sum_{j=1}^{d} w_j h_j^C(k, \tau) = \frac{1}{Td} \sum_{j=1}^{d} \sum_{t=1}^{T} w_j h_j^t(k, \tau). \tag{9.29}$$

9.4.3.3 Percentage Contributions of Dimension

The percentage contributions show the (weighted) composition of chronic multidimensional poverty in each period and across periods.

We may seek an overview of the dimensional composition of poverty across all periods. The total percentage contribution of each dimension to chronic poverty across all periods is given by

$$\phi_j^C(k, \tau) = \frac{h_j^C(k, \tau)}{d \times M_0^C}. \tag{9.30}$$

We may also be interested in analysing the percentage contributions of each dimension across various periods and thus in comparing the percentage contributions of dimensions across periods. The total percentage contribution in period t is

$$\phi_j^t(k, \tau) = \frac{h_j^t(k, \tau)}{d \times M_0^t}. \tag{9.31}$$

9.4.3.4 Censored Dimensional Duration

We are also able to construct a new set of statistics that provide more detail regarding the duration of dimensional deprivations among the chronically poor. We use the $n \times d$

deprivation duration matrix L, constructed in section 9.4.1.3, in which each entry reflects the number of periods in which person i was chronically poor (by k and τ) and was deprived in dimension j. Recall that for the chronically poor, $0 \leq L_{ij} \leq T$ in each dimension. The value of L_{ij} is, naturally, 0 for non-poor persons in all dimensions. Thus the matrix will have a positive entry for q^C persons and an entry of 0 for all persons who were never chronically poor.

For each dimension we can then define a dimensional duration index for dimension j as follows:

$$D_j = \frac{1}{q^C \times T} \sum_{i=1}^{n} L_{ij}.$$ (9.32)

The value of D_j provides the percentage of periods in which the chronically poor were deprived in dimension j on average.

The relationship between the mean across all D_j and the chronic multidimensional poverty figure provided earlier is also elementary:

$$M_0^C = H^C \sum_{j=1}^{d} w_j D_j,$$ (9.33)

and

$$\sum_{j=1}^{d} w_j D_j = A^C \times D^C.$$ (9.34)

9.4.3.5 Period-Specific Partial and Consistent Sub-Indices

From the $n \times T$ censored identification matrix $Q(k, \tau)$, we can also compute the period-specific headcounts of chronic multidimensional poverty. The headcount H^t for period t is the mean of the column vector of $Q(k, \tau)$ for period t. The average headcount across all periods is $\bar{H} = (1/T) \sum_{t=1}^{T} H^t$. The average headcount across all periods and the chronic multidimensional poverty headcount are related by the average duration of poverty thus:

$$H^C = \frac{\bar{H}}{D^C}.$$ (9.35)

Similarly,

$$A^C = \frac{\bar{A}}{D^C},$$ (9.36)

and

$$h_j^C(k, \tau) = \frac{\bar{h}(k, \tau)}{D_j}.$$ (9.37)

Table 9.7 Cardinal illustration with relevant values of K and τ

	$k = 1/3$			$k = 2/3$			$k = 1$		
	$\tau = 1/3$	$\tau = 2/3$	$\tau = 1$	$\tau = 1/3$	$\tau = 2/3$	$\tau = 1$	$\tau = 1/3$	$\tau = 2/3$	$\tau = 1$
M_0^C	0.124	0.095	0.049	0.053	**0.028**	0.007	0.008	0.003	0.000
H^C	**0.49**	0.27	0.10	0.16	**0.05**	0.01	0.02%	0.005	0.0005
D^C	0.58	0.79	1.00	0.46	**0.72**	1.00	0.43	70.01%	1.00
A^C	0.43	0.45	0.48	0.70	**0.72**	0.75	1.00	1.00	1.00

9.4.3.6 Illustration using Chilean CASEN

We present an example in Table 9.7 using three variables: schooling, overcrowding, and income in Chile's CASEN (Encuesta de Caracterización Socioeconómica Nacional) dataset for three periods: 1996, 2001, and 2006. The table reports the Adjusted Headcount Ratio of chronic multidimensional poverty (M_0^C) and its three partial indices: the headcount ratio (H^C), the average chronic intensity (A^C), and the average duration (D^C) for three poverty cutoffs $k = 1/3, 2/3, 1$, and three different duration cutoffs $\tau = 1/3, 2/3, 1$. All dimensions and periods are equally weighted for both identification and aggregation. When $k = 1/3$ and $\tau = 1/3$, the identification follows a double union approach. In this case, 49% of people are identified as chronically multidimensionally poor. However, a double-union approach does not appear to capture people who are either chronically or multidimensionally poor in any meaningful sense.

We thus consider the cutoffs where $k = \tau = 2/3$. In this situation, 5% of people are chronically multidimensionally poor. The average chronic intensity is 72%, meaning that people experience deprivations in 72% of dimensions in the periods in which they are poor. The average chronic duration is 72% also, meaning that the average poor person is deprived in 72% of the three periods. The overall chronic Adjusted Headcount Ratio of 0.028 shows that Chile's population experiences only 2.8% of the deprivations it could possibly experience. All possible deprivations occur if all people are multidimensionally poor in all dimensions and in all periods.

9.4.4 POVERTY TRANSITIONS USING PANEL DATA

Using the identification matrix and the associated doubly censored deprivation matrices that have been constructed in section 9.4.1.3, it is also possible to analyse poverty transitions. Comparisons can be undertaken—for example, between subgroups experiencing different dynamic patterns of multidimensional poverty—to ascertain different policy sequences or entry points that might have greater efficacy in eradicating multidimensional poverty. This section very briefly describes the construction of dynamic subgroups and some of the descriptive analyses that can be undertaken.

9.4.4.1 Constructing Dynamic Subgroups

The chronic multidimensional poverty measures constructed previously respect the property of subgroup consistency and subgroup decomposability; thus, they can be decomposed by any population subgroup for which the data are arguably representative. In addition, it can be particularly useful to describe multidimensional poverty for what we earlier called 'dynamic subgroups'—the definition of which can be extended when panel data cover more than two periods.

By dynamic subgroups, we mean population subgroups that experience different patterns of multidimensional poverty over time. These include the groups mentioned in section 9.3.1 who exited poverty (1,0), entered poverty (0,1), or were in ongoing poverty (1,1). The possible patterns will vary according to the number of waves in the sample as well as the observed patterns in the dataset. With three waves, there are four basic groups: **falling**—people who were non-poor and became multidimensionally poor; **rising**—people who were multidimensionally poor and exited poverty; **churning**—people who both enter and exit multidimensional poverty in different periods; and **long-term**—people who remain multidimensionally poor continuously.[23]

The dynamic subgroups are formed by considering the $n \times T$ identification matrix $Q(k)$. Note that we use the matrix that is censored by the poverty cutoff k but we do not, in this section on poverty transitions, apply the duration cutoff. Consider a matrix of four persons and three periods in which each person experiences one of the four categories mentioned above. Recall that an entry of 1 indicates that person i is multidimensionally poor in period t and a 0 indicates they are non-poor.

Falling:	0 0 1	(and	0 1 1)
Rising:	1 0 0	(and	1 1 0)
Churning:	1 0 1	(and	0 1 0)
Long-term:	1 1 1		

For more than three periods, additional categories can be formed. Note that the categories can and must be mutually exhaustive. Each person who is multidimensionally poor in any period (whether chronically or transiently poor) can be categorized into one of these four groups.

9.4.4.2 Descriptive Analyses

Having decomposed the population into the non-poor and these (or additional) dynamic subgroups of the population, it can be useful to provide the standard partial indices for each subgroup, both per period and across all three periods:

[23] See Hulme, Moore, and Shepherd (2001), Hulme and Shepherd (2003), and Narayan and Petesch (2007).

- M_0, H, and A (and standard errors);
- percentage composition of poverty by dimension and censored headcount ratios;
- intensity profiles across the poor (or inequality among the poor—see section 9.1).

It can also be useful to provide details regarding the sequences of evolution. For example, from the $Q(k)$ matrix, isolate the subgroup of the poor who 'fell into' poverty between period 1 and period 2 (that is, whose entries are 0,1 for the respective periods t_1 and t_2). Compare their evolution with those who stayed poor (1,1) and those who stayed non-poor (0,0), in the following ways:

- at the individual level, compare the uncensored headcount ratio in period 1 with that in period 2.
- identify the dimensions in which deprivations were (a) experienced in both periods, (b) only experienced in period 1, and (c) only experienced in period 2.
- summarize the results, if relevant and legitimate, further decomposing the population into relevant subgroups whose compositional changes follow different patterns.
- repeat for each adjacent pair of periods. Analyse whether the patterns are stable or differ across different adjacent periods.

10 Some Regression Models for AF Measures

From a policy perspective, in addition to measuring poverty we must perform some vital analyses regarding the transmission mechanisms between policies and poverty measures. Issues we may wish to explore with a regression model include the determinants of poverty at the household level in the form of poverty profiles or the elasticity of poverty to economic growth, while controlling for other determinants. We may also be interested in understanding how macro variables such as average income, public expenditure, decentralization, information technology, and so on relate to multidimensional poverty levels across groups or regions—and across time. Through regression analysis, we can partially study these transmission mechanisms by looking at the determinants of multidimensional poverty. In a regression model, we can account for the effect or the 'size' of determinants of multidimensional poverty, which would not be possible with a purely descriptive analysis.

Such analyses are routinely performed for income poverty using what we will term 'micro' or 'macro' regressions. As is explained below, the term 'micro' refers to analyses in which the unit of analysis is a person or household; the term 'macro' refers to analyses in which the unit of analysis is a subgroup, such as a district, a state, a province, or a country. This section provides the reader with a general modelling framework for analysing the determinants of Alkire–Foster poverty measures, at both micro and macro levels of analyses.

In general, in micro regressions, the focal variable to be modelled may be a binary variable denoting a person's status as poor (or non-poor) or a variable denoting the deprivation score assigned to the poor. In macro regressions, the focal variable to model is a subgroup poverty measure like the poverty headcount ratio or any other Foster–Greer–Thorbecke (FGT) poverty measure. As with regressions that model the monetary headcount ratio or the poverty gap, macro regressions with M_0-dependent variables must respect their nature as cardinally meaningful values ranging from zero to one. In these cases, a classic linear regression is not the appropriate model. The common assumptions of the classic linear regression fall short because the range of the dependent variable is bounded and may not be continuous or follow a normal distribution that is often assumed in linear regression models.

Generalized linear models (GLMs), by contrast, are preferred as the data-analytic technique because they account for the bounded and discrete nature of the AF-type dependent variables. GLMs extend classic linear regression to a family of regression models where the dependent variable may be normally distributed or may follow a distribution within the exponential family—such as the gamma distribution, Bernoulli distribution, or binomial distribution. GLMs encompass models for quantitative and qualitative dependent variables, such as linear regression models, logit and probit models, and models for fractional data. Hence they offer a general framework for our analysis of functional relationships.[1]

This section presents the GLM as an overall framework in which to study micro and macro determinants of multidimensional poverty. Within this framework we are able to account for the bounded nature of the Adjusted Headcount Ratio M_0 and the incidence H while modelling their determinants. We are also able to model these determinants for the probability of being multidimensionally poor.

This chapter is structured as follows. We begin by differentiating micro and macro regression analyses. For this purpose, we review the M_0 measure of the AF class, its partial and consistent sub-indices, and the type of variables they represent in a regression framework. We then present the general structure and possible applications of the GLMs to AF measures. We begin with an exposition of linear regression models and how these extend to models for binary dependent variables—logit and probit—and fractional[2] data. We assume readers have some background in applied statistics and key elements of estimation and inference. Our exposition deals with cross-sectional data but could be easily extended to panel data.[3]

Before we begin, we should point out that the notation used in this chapter is self-contained. Some notation may duplicate that used in other sections or chapters for different purposes. When the notation is linked to discussions in other sections or chapters, it will be specified accordingly.

10.1 **Micro and Macro Regressions**

The AF measures can be used to analyse poverty determinants[4] for a household or person (henceforth we use the term 'household') and for a population subgroup. We could study determinants of household or subgroup poverty in a micro and a macro context. In what follows, the term 'micro' refers to regressions where the unit of analysis is the person or household. The term 'macro' refers to regressions where the unit of analysis is some spatial or social aggregate, such as a district, state, province, ethnic group, or country. Micro regressions are useful for describing the distinctive features of multidimensional poverty profiles across households (in a given country) or to understand their determinants of poverty. Macro regressions, on the other hand, are useful for studying the determinants

---

[1] Cf. Nelder and Wedderburn (1972) and McCullagh and Nelder (1989).
[2] Also referred to as models for proportions.
[3] Skrondal and Rabe-Hesketh (2004), Rabe-Hesketh and Skrondal (2012) address this extension.
[4] The term determinants shall be understood in a 'weak' sense and refers to 'proximate' causes of poverty as defined in Haughton and Khandker (2009: 147).

of poverty at the province, district, state, or country levels. Both types of regressions use specific components of the AF measures. In the case of micro regressions, the focal variable is the (household) censored deprivation score. From the exposition of Chapter 5, we know that if the deprivation score of a household c_i is equal to or greater than the multidimensional poverty cutoff (k), the household is identified as multidimensionally poor. This poverty status of a household is represented by a binary variable (indicator function) that takes the value of one if the household is identified as multidimensionally poor and zero otherwise.

A natural question that arises is how to analyse the 'causes' (in the sense of determinants) that underlie the (multidimensional) poverty status of a household. An intuitive way would be to model the probability of a household becoming multidimensionally poor or falling into multidimensional poverty. A crucial point should be noted here, which may be more particular to multidimensional notions of poverty than their unidimensional monetary counterparts: when modelling the probability of a household being in monetary poverty, various health- and education-related variables, which are not embedded in the monetary poverty measures, are used as exogenous variables.[5] In a multidimensional case, these exogenous variables may be used directly to construct the poverty measure and so the probability models at the household level, which include these as explanatory variables, are subject to a potential endogeneity issue. For example, if among the explanatory variables we include an asset variable like car ownership, and if that indicator was also included among the 'assets' indicator that appears in the multidimensional poverty measure, there will be an endogeneity issue in the model. A typical approach to deal with endogeneity is to use an instrumental variable, but often it is very difficult to find a valid instrument.[6] An alternative approach would be to restrain the set of explanatory variables of the household regression model to non-indicator measurement variables[7]—like certain demographic variables—or additional socioeconomic characteristics of the household. From such a perspective one would be interested in examining household poverty profiles. Sample research questions would be: are female-headed households more likely to be multidimensionally poor? Are larger households more prone to be multidimensionally poor? How does the probability of being multidimensionally poor vary by household size and composition, caste, or ethnicity?

In the case of cross-sectional macro regressions, the focal variables are the M_α measures at the province, district, state, or country levels, or some other population subgroup or aggregate which leads to a proper sample size.[8] If the focus is on the Adjusted Headcount

---

[5] Also called independent, exogenous, or explanatory variables. We prefer the terms 'exogenous' or 'explanatory' to refer to the right-hand-side variables of a regression. In this section we use both terms interchangeably.

[6] See, for example, Bound, Jaeger, and Baker (1995) and Stock, Wright, and Yogo (2002).

[7] These are variables with explanatory power that were not used when constructing the poverty measure. These variables are assumed to be uncorrelated with the error term of the model.

[8] Small-sample statistical techniques could be envisaged in the case of aggregates with very few categories.

Ratio M_0, the focal variables in a macro regression could comprise M_0 or the intensity A and incidence H of multidimensional poverty. However, from Chapter 5 we know that H and A are partial indices that do not enjoy the same properties as the M_0 measure. In this chapter we do not further consider regression models for A. Although H is also a partial index that violates dimensional monotonicity, we still discuss its analysis, given the prominence of existing studies using the unidimensional poverty headcount ratio.

As already noted, M_0 and H are bounded between zero and one. In statistical terms, M_0 and H are fractional (proportion) variables that lie in the unit interval. Their restricted range of variation limits the use of the linear regression model because these models assume continuous variables comprised between $-\infty$ and $+\infty$. A natural model to be considered is one that reflects the fractional nature of any of these two indices (see section 10.4).

10.2 Generalized Linear Models

Our exposition of GLMs draws on Nelder and Wedderburn (1972), McCullagh and Nelder (1989), and Firth (1991). We treat GLMs in an applied manner covering the basic structure of the models, estimation, and model fitting. We do not provide a detailed exposition of the method itself. Readers interested in a complete statistical treatment of GLMs can refer to McCullagh and Nelder (1989) or to Dobson (2001). The former presents an excellent and comprehensive statistical overview of GLMs, but assumes an advanced statistics background on the part of the reader. The latter presents a briefer and more synthetic exposition of GLMs at a moderate level of statistical complexity.

Generalized linear models are an extension of classic linear models. The linear regression model has found widespread application in the social sciences mainly due to its simple linear formulation, easy interpretation, and estimation. In monetary poverty analysis, linear regression analysis has been used to study the determinants of household consumption expenditures or to model the growth elasticity of per capita income or income poverty aggregates like the headcount ratio or the poverty gap index.[9] Linear regressions are also used to model changes in (i) the income share of the poorest quintile (Dollar and Kraay 2004); (ii) adjusted GDP incomes (Foster and Székely 2008); (iii) the poverty rate (Ravallion 2001); and (iv) the growth rates of real per capita GDP (Barro 2003).

10.2.1 CLASSIC LINEAR REGRESSION

We begin with a brief review of the classic linear regression model and its notation and build on this to present the more generic case of GLMs. The classic linear regression

---

[9] See, for example, De Janvry and Sadoulet (2010) and Roelen and Notten (2011).

model (LRM) assumes that the endogenous or dependent variable (y) (hitherto referred to as 'endogenous') is a linear function of a set of K exogenous[10] variables (x). The LRM assumes that the endogenous variable y is continuous and distributed with constant variance. In addition, the LRM may also assume that the endogenous variable is normally distributed. However, this assumption is not needed for estimating the model but only to obtain the exact distribution of the parameters in the model. In the case of large samples one may not need to assume normality in an LRM as inference on parameters is based on asymptotic theory (cf. Amemiya 1985). These assumptions may be inappropriate if the endogenous variable is discrete (binary or categorical)—or continuous but non-normal.[11] GLMs overcome these limitations. They extend classic linear regression to a family of models with non-normal endogenous variables. In what follows, random variables are denoted in upper-case and observations in lower-case; vectors are represented with lower-case bold and matrices with upper-case bold.

Consider a sample of n observations of a scalar dependent variable (y) and a set of K exogenous variables ($\mathbf{x}$). This data is specified as $(y_i, \mathbf{x}_i)_{i=1,2,...,n}$, where $\mathbf{x}_i$ is a $K \times 1$ column vector. Each observation y_i is assumed to be a realization of a random variable Y_i independently distributed with mean μ_{Y_i}. The classic regression model with additive errors for the ith observation can be written as

$$y_i = E[Y_i|\mathbf{x}_i] + \varepsilon_i, \tag{10.1}$$

where $E[Y_i|\mathbf{x}_i]$ denotes the conditional expectation[12] of the random variable Y_i, given $\mathbf{x}_i$, and ε_i is a disturbance or random error. From equation (10.1) we see that the dependent variable is decomposed into two components: a systematic or deterministic component given the exogenous variables and an error component. The deterministic component is the conditional expectation $E[Y_i|\mathbf{x}_i]$, while the error component, attributed to random variation, is ε_i.

Equation (10.1) is a general representation of regression analysis. It attempts to explain the variation in the dependent variable through the conditional expectation without imposing any functional form on it. If we specify a *linear* functional form of the conditional expectation $E[Y_i|\mathbf{x}_i]$, we obtain the classic linear regression model. Then, the systematic part of the model may be written

$$E[Y_i|\mathbf{x}_i] = \mu_{Y|\mathbf{x}_i} = \beta_0 + \sum_{j=1}^{K} \beta_j x_{ij}, \tag{10.2}$$

[10] In the statistical literature x is referred to as a 'regressor' or 'covariate' that is exogenous when the assumptions on the disturbance term are conditional on the covariates. In our exposition, all assumptions on the disturbance term or the dependent variable are conditional on the regressors so we use the term 'exogenous' instead of the generic term 'regressor'. By 'exogenous' we mean non-stochastic or conditionally stochastic right-hand-side variables.

[11] An example of a non-normal continuous variable is income (consumption expenditures). The distribution of income is skewed (to the right), takes on only positive values, and is often heteroscedastic.

[12] Or conditional mean. We use both terms interchangeably.

where x_{ij} is the value of the jth exogenous variable for observation i. To show the relation between a linear regression model and a generalized linear model it will become convenient to denote the right-hand side of equation (10.2) by η_i, referred to as the predictor in the generalized linear model. Thus we can write

$$\eta_i = \beta_0 + \sum_{j=1}^{K} \beta_j x_{ij}, \qquad (10.3)$$

and then the systematic part can be expressed as

$$E[Y_i|\mathbf{x}_i] = \mu_{Y_i|\mathbf{x}_i} = \eta_i. \qquad (10.4)$$

Equations (10.1) to (10.4) lead to the familiar linear regression model:

$$y_i = \beta_0 + \sum_{j=1}^{K} \beta_j x_{ij} + \varepsilon_i; \quad i = 1,\ldots,n, \qquad (10.5)$$

where β_0, β_1,..., β_K are parameters whose values are unknown and need to be estimated from the data.[13] Note that in the linear regression model of equation (10.6), the conditional expectation is equal to the linear predictor:

$$y_i = \eta_i + \varepsilon_i. \qquad (10.6)$$

The LRM additionally assumes that the errors (ε_i) are independent, with zero mean, constant variance (σ_ε^2), and follow a Gaussian or normal distribution.[14] Often the assumptions on ε_i are made conditional on the exogenous variables, as these are possibly stochastic or random. Then, the errors have zero mean and homoscedastic or identical variance, conditional on the exogenous variables, that is, $\varepsilon_i|\mathbf{x}_i \sim N(0,\sigma_\varepsilon^2)$. Due to the relationship between y and ε, the dependent variable is also normally distributed with constant variance. In other words, in an LRM, the distribution of the dependent variable is derived from the distribution of the disturbance. However, as explained in section 10.2.2, in a GLM the distribution of the dependent variable is specified directly.

---

[13] An equivalent expression of the LRM is a matrix representation of the form $\mathbf{y} = \mathbf{X}\boldsymbol{\beta} + \boldsymbol{\varepsilon}$, where $\mathbf{y} = \{y_1,\ldots,y_n\}^{\text{T}}$ is an $n \times 1$ vector of observations; $\boldsymbol{\varepsilon}$ is an $n \times 1$ vector of disturbances; $\mathbf{X}$ is a $n \times K$ matrix of explanatory variables, where each row refers to a different observation, each column to a different explanatory variable; and $\boldsymbol{\beta} = \{\beta_1,\ldots,\beta_K\}^{\text{T}}$ is a $K \times 1$ vector of parameters. However, for the expositional purposes of this chapter we do not use the matrix representation but rather the one specified in equation (10.5).

[14] To denote a random variable as normally distributed we follow the statistical convention and denote it as $N(\cdot)$.

10.2.2 THE GENERALIZATION

The GLM family of models involves predicting a *function* of the conditional mean of a dependent variable as a *linear combination* of a set of explanatory variables. Classic linear regression is a specific case of a GLM in which the conditional expectation of the dependent variable is modelled by the identity *function*. GLMs extend the domain of applicability of classic linear regression to contexts where the dependent variable is not continuous or normally distributed. GLMs also permit us to model continuous dependent variables that have positively skewed distributions.

Generalized linear models relax the assumption of additive error in equation (10.1). The random component is now attributed to the dependent variable itself. Thus, for GLMs we need to specify the conditional distribution of the dependent variable, given the values of the explanatory variables, denoted as $f_Y(\mathbf{y})$. These distributions often belong to the linear exponential family, such as the Gaussian, binomial, poisson, and gamma, among others, but have also been extended to non-exponential families (McCullagh and Nelder 1989).

A generalized linear model is one that takes the form:

$$g(\mu_{Y_i|\mathbf{x}_i}) = \eta_i = \beta_0 + \sum_{j=1}^{K} \beta_j x_{ij}, \tag{10.7}$$

where the systematic part or linear predictor (η_i) is now a function (g) of the conditional expectation of the dependent variable $\mu_{Y_i|\mathbf{x}_i}$; $g(\cdot)$ is a one-to-one differentiable function referred to as the link function; and η is referred to as the linear predictor. The link function transforms the conditional expectation of the dependent variable to the linear predictor, which is a linear function of the explanatory variables that could be of any nature. This allows the linear predictor to include continuous or categorical variables, a combination of both, or interactions—as well as transformations of continuous variables. Note that when the link function $g(\cdot)$ is the identity function, we have an LRM.

In most applications, as in the regression analysis with AF measures, the primary interest is the conditional mean $\mu_{Y_i|\mathbf{x}_i}$. This could be easily retrieved from equation (10.7) by inverting the link function; hence we can write

$$\mu_{Y_i|\mathbf{x}_i} = G(\eta_i) = G(\mathbf{x}_i\boldsymbol{\beta}), \tag{10.8}$$

where $G(\cdot)$ is the inverse link $g^{-1}(\cdot)$, also called the mean function. Equations (10.7) and (10.8) provide two alternative specifications for a GLM, either as a *linear* model for the *transformed* conditional expectation of the dependent variable—given by (10.7)—or as a *non-linear* model for the conditional mean—given by (10.8).

A GLM is thus composed of three components: (i) a random component resulting from the specification of the conditional distribution of the dependent variable, given the values of the explanatory variables (ii) a linear predictor η_i; and (iii) a link function $g(\cdot)$ (cf. Fox 2008: ch. 15).

Table 10.1 Generalized linear regression models with AF measures

Dependent variable AF measure: Y	Range of Y	Regression model	Level	Conditional distribution $p_Y(y)$	Link $g(\mu_i) = \eta_i$		Mean function $\mu_i = G(\eta_i)$
Binary ($c_i \geq k$)	0,1	Probability	Micro	Bernoulli	Logit	$\log_e \frac{\mu_i}{1-\mu_i}$	$\Lambda(\eta_i)$
M_0, H	[0,1]	Proportion	Macro	Binomial	Probit	$\Phi^{-1}(\mu_i)$	$\Phi(\eta_i)$

Note: $\Phi(\cdot)$ and $\Lambda(\cdot)$ are the cumulative distribution functions of the standard-normal and logistic distributions, respectively. For the binary model, the conditional mean μ_i is the conditional probability π_i.

The distribution of the dependent variable $f_Y(\mathbf{y})$ and the choice of the link function are intimately related and depend on the type of variable under study. The form of a proper link function is determined to some extent[15] by the range of variation of the dependent variable and consequently by the range of variation of its conditional mean.

In the case of AF poverty measures, we may consider two types of dependent variables with a different range of variation and distribution. The first type is a binary indicator identifying multidimensionally poor households. This variable takes the value of one if the household is identified as multidimensionally poor and zero otherwise. The Bernoulli distribution is suitable to describe this kind of variable. A typical model in this case is the probit or logit model. As we will see, in a GLM this is equivalent to choosing a logit link. The second type of dependent variable that we could study in the AF approach is a proportion. The Adjusted Headcount Ratio M_0 and the incidence H are fractions or proportions that take values in the unit interval. The binomial distribution may be suitable as a model for these proportions.

In each of these cases, the link function should map the range of variation of the dependent variable—$\{0, 1\}$ for the binary indicator and $[0, 1]$ for the proportion—to the whole real line $(-\infty, +\infty)$. The scale is chosen in such a way that the fitted values respect the range of variation of the dependent variable. Columns one to five in Table 10.1 present the two types of dependent variables with AF measures that we study in this section, along with their range of variation, type of model, level of analysis, and random variation described by the conditional distribution. The link and mean functions are explained in the examples in sections 10.3 and 10.4. Before presenting the examples, we briefly explain the estimation and goodness of fit of GLMs.

10.2.3 ESTIMATION AND GOODNESS OF FIT

Once we have selected the particular models of our study, we need to estimate the parameters and measure their precision. For this purpose we maximize the likelihood

---

[15] The range of variation of the dependent variable is a mild requirement for the choice of a proper link function. As noted by Firth (1991), this mild requirement is complemented by multiple criteria where the choice of a proper link function is made on the grounds of its fit to the data, the ease of interpretation of parameters in the linear predictor, and the existence of simple sufficient statistics.

or log likelihood[16] of the parameters of our data denoted by $l[y; \mu(\beta)]$.[17] The likelihood function of a parameter is the probability distribution of the parameter given $\mu(\beta)$.

To assess goodness of fit of the possible estimates, we use the scaled deviance. This statistic is formed from the logarithm of a ratio of likelihoods and measures the discrepancy, or goodness of fit, between the observed data and the fitted values generated by the model. To assess the discrepancy we use as a baseline the full or 'saturated' model. Given n observations, the full model has n parameters, one per observation. This model fits the data perfectly but is uninformative because it simply reproduces the data without any parsimony. Nonetheless it is useful for assessing discrepancy vis-à-vis a more parsimonious model that uses K parameters. Hence in the saturated model the estimated conditional mean $\hat{\mu} = y$ and the scaled deviance is zero. For intermediate models, say with K parameters, the scaled deviance is positive.

The scaled deviance statistic

$$D^*(y; \hat{\mu}) = 2l(y; y) - 2l(y; \hat{\mu}) \sim \chi^2_{n-K} \tag{10.9}$$

is twice the difference between $l(y; y)$, which is the maximum log likelihood of a saturated model or exact fit, and $l(y; \hat{\mu})$ the log likelihood of the current or reduced model.

The goodness of fit is assessed by a significance test of the null hypothesis that the current model holds against the alternative given by the saturated or full model. Under the null hypothesis, D^* is approximately distributed as a χ^2_{n-K} random variable where the number of degrees of freedom equals the difference in the number of regression parameters in the full and the reduced models. However, an appropriate assessment of the goodness of fit is based on the conditional distribution of $D^*(y; \hat{\mu})$ given $\hat{\beta}$. If D^* is not significant, it suggests that the additional parameters in the full model are unnecessary and that a more parsimonious model with lesser parameters may be sufficient.

The scaled deviance statistic is also useful for model selection. Due to its additive property, the discrepancy between nested sets of models can be compared if maximum likelihood estimates are used. Suppose we are interested in comparing two models, A and B, that represent two different choices of explanatory variables, X_A and X_B, that are nested. Intuitively this means that all explanatory variables included in model A are also present in model B, a more complex or less parsimonious model. The improvement in fit may be assessed by a significance test of the null hypothesis that model A holds against the alternative given by model B. If the value of the scaled deviance statistic is found to be significant, there is an improvement in the fit of model B vis-à-vis model A, although a general conclusion on model selection should also consider the added complexity of model B.

---

[16] The parameters in a GLM are estimated by a numerical algorithm, namely, iterative weighted least squares (IWLS). For models with the links considered in this section, the IWLS algorithm is equivalent to the Newton–Raphson method and also coincides with Fisher scoring (McCullagh and Nelder 1989).

[17] Note we drop the subscript i as the log likelihood depends on the full sample. For ease of exposition we also write $\mu_{Y|x}$ as μ.

10.3 **Micro Regression Models with AF Measures**

In the case of micro regression analysis, the focal variable is the (household) censored deprivation score c_i. This score reflects the joint deprivations characterizing a household identified as multidimensionally poor. From a policy perspective a natural question that arises consequently is how to understand the 'causes' that underlie the (multidimensional) poverty status of a household. The simplest model for this purpose is a probability model, which we illustrate in this section; although one could also consider modelling the c_i vector directly. We are thus interested in assessing the probability of a household being multidimensionally poor. Within the AF framework this is equivalent to comparing the deprivation score of a household c_i with the multidimensional poverty cutoff (k). If c_i is above the multidimensional poverty cutoff (k), the household is identified as multidimensionally poor. This is represented by a binary random variable (Y_i) that takes the value of one if the household is identified as multidimensionally poor and zero otherwise, as follows:

$$Y_i = \begin{cases} 1 & \text{if and only if } c_i \geq k \\ 0 & \text{otherwise} \end{cases}. \tag{10.10}$$

The outcomes of this binary variable occur with probability π_i, which is a conditional probability on the explanatory variables. For a (sampled) household i identified as multidimensionally poor, this is represented as

$$\pi_i \equiv \Pr(Y_i) \equiv \Pr(Y_i|\mathbf{x}_i) \tag{10.11}$$

and thus the conditional mean equals the probability as follows:

$$\mu_{Y_i|\mathbf{x}_i} = \pi_i \times 1 + (1 - \pi_i) \times 0 = \pi_i. \tag{10.12}$$

For a binary model, the conditional distribution of the dependent variable, or random component in a GLM, is given by a Bernoulli distribution (Table 10.1). Thus the probability function of Y_i is

$$p_Y(y_i) = \pi_i^{y_i}(1 - \pi_i)^{1-y_i}. \tag{10.13}$$

To ensure that the conditional mean given by the conditional probability stays between zero and one, a GLM commonly considers two alternative link functions (g). These are given by the quantile functions of the standard normal distribution function $\Phi^{-1}(\mu_i)$ and the logistic distribution function $\Lambda^{-1}(\mu_i)$.[18] The former is referred to as the **probit link function** and the latter as the **logit link function**. The probit link function does not

---

[18] Note $\Phi(\cdot)$ and $\Lambda(\cdot)$ are the cumulative distribution functions of the standard-normal and logistic distribution, respectively.

have a direct interpretation, while the logit is directly interpretable, as we will discuss in this section.[19]

The logit of π is the natural logarithm of the odds that the binary variable Y takes a value of one rather than zero. In our context, this gives the relative chances of being multidimensionally poor. If the odds are 'even'—that is, equal to one—the corresponding probability (π) of falling into either category, poor or non-poor, is 0.5, and the logit is zero. The logit model is a linear, additive model for the logarithm of odds as in equation (10.14), but it is also a multiplicative model for the odds as in equation (10.15):

$$\ln\frac{\pi_i}{1-\pi_i} = \eta_i = \beta_0 + \beta_1 x_{i1} + \cdots + \beta_K x_{iK} \tag{10.14}$$

$$\frac{\pi_i}{1-\pi_i} = e^{\eta_i} = e^{\beta_0}\left(e^{\beta_1}\right)^{x_{i1}}\ldots\left(e^{\beta_K}\right)^{x_{iK}}. \tag{10.15}$$

The conditional probability π_i is then

$$\pi_i = \frac{1}{1+e^{-\eta_i}} = \frac{1}{1+e^{-\sum_{j=0}^{K}\beta_j x_{ij}}}. \tag{10.16}$$

The partial regression coefficients (β_j) are interpreted as marginal changes of the logit, or as multiplicative effects on the odds. Thus, the coefficient β_j indicates the change in the logit due to a one-unit increase in x_j, and e^{β_j} is the multiplicative effect on the odds of increasing x_j by one, while holding constant the other explanatory variables. For example, if the first explanatory variable increases by one unit, the odds ratio in equation (10.15) associated with this increase is $e^{\eta_i'} = e^{\beta_0}\left(e^{\beta_1}\right)^{x_{i1}+1}\ldots\left(e^{\beta_K}\right)^{x_{iK}}$, and $e^{\eta_i'}/e^{\eta_i} = e^{\beta_1}$. For this reason, e^{β_j} is known as the odds ratio associated with a one-unit increase in x_j. To see the percentage change in the odds, we need to consider the sign of the estimated parameter. If β_j is negative, the change in x_j denotes a decrease in the odds; this decrease is obtained as $(1-e^{\beta_j})*100$. Likewise if β_j is positive, the change in x_j indicates an increase in the odds. In this case, the increase is obtained as $(e^{\beta_j}-1)*100$.

10.3.1 A MICRO REGRESSION EXAMPLE

To illustrate the type of micro regression models that have been discussed, we use a subsample of the Indonesian Family Life Survey (IFLS) dataset. This is a dataset analysed by Ballon and Apablaza (2012) to assess multidimensional poverty in Indonesia during the period 1993–2007. The IFLS is a large-scale longitudinal survey of the socioeconomic, demographic, and health conditions of individuals, households, families, and communities in Indonesia. The sample is representative of about 83% of the population and contains over 30,000 individuals living in thirteen of the twenty-seven

---

[19] Alternative link functions include the log-log and the complementary log-log links; however, these two are not symmetric around the median.

Table 10.2 Logistic regression model of multidimensional poverty in West Java

Variable	Parameter estimate	Robust std. err.	t ratio	Significance level	Odds ratio
Years of education of household head	−0.68	0.03	−19.65	**	0.51
Female household head	0.24	0.09	2.71	**	1.28
Household size	0.09	0.01	7.02	**	1.10
Living in urban areas	−0.85	0.07	−11.40	**	0.43
Being Muslim	−0.02	0.32	−0.07	n.s.	0.98

** denotes significance at 5% level; n.s. denotes non-significance.

provinces in the country. Ballon and Apablaza (2012) measure multidimensional poverty at the household level in five equally weighted dimensions: education, housing, basic services, health issues, and material resources. For this illustration, we retain a poverty cutoff of 33%. Thus a household is identified as multidimensionally poor if the sum of the weighted deprivations is greater than 33%. That is, Y_i takes the value of one if $c_i \geq 33\%$ and zero otherwise. Within the GLM framework this binary dependent variable is estimated by specifying a Bernoulli distribution and a logit link function. This is equivalent to a logit regression.

The household poverty profile that we specify regresses the log of the odds of being multidimensionally poor (using $k = 33\%$) on the demographic and socioeconomic characteristics of the household head. For this illustration we use data for West Java in 2007. West Java is a province of Indonesia located in the western part of the island of Java. It is the most populous and most densely populated of Indonesia's provinces, which is why we selected it. The explanatory variables included in this illustration are non-indicator measurement variables and comprise:

- education of the household head, defined as the number of years of education (not necessarily completed);
- the presence of a female household head, represented by a dummy variable taking a value of one if the household head is a female and zero if male;
- household size, defined by the number of household members;
- the area in which the household resides, represented by a dummy variable taking a value of one if the household resides in the urban areas of West Java and zero otherwise;
- Muslim religion, represented by a dummy variable taking a value of one if the household's main religion is Muslim and zero if not.

Table 10.2 reports the logistic regression results of this poverty profile for West Java in 2007. Columns two to five report the estimated regression parameters along with their standard errors, t ratios, and significance levels at 5%.[20] Apart from being Muslim, all

---

[20] Note we can also report marginal effects if the interest is to see the effect of an explanatory variable on the change of the probability.

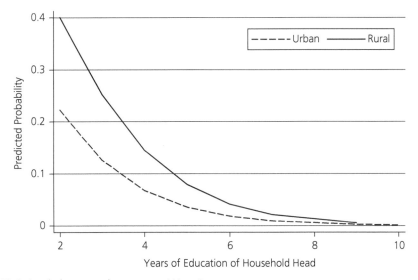

Figure 10.1. Logistic regression curve—West Java

other determinants are significant at the 5% level and show the expected signs. For a given household, the log of the odds of being multidimensionally poor decreases with the education of the household head and an urban location, and increases with the presence of a female household head and with household size. The odds ratio for years of education of the household head indicates that an increase of one year of education decreases the odds of being multidimensionally poor by 49%, *ceteris paribus*, whereas having a female household head increases the odds of being multidimensionally poor by 28%, *ceteris paribus*.[21] Similarly, the odds of a household of being multidimensionally poor decrease by 57% for households living in urban areas, *ceteris paribus*, and increase by 10% for each additional household member. Figure 10.1 shows the odds model for urban and rural areas as a function of the education of the household head, holding constant the gender status of the household head (female), assuming five household members (average), and being Muslim. The logistic curves show a decrease in the probability of a household being multidimensionally poor as the education of the household head improves. These probabilities are lower for households living in urban areas compared to rural ones.

As religion turns out to be statistically insignificant, we could consider an alternative poverty profile without religion as an explanatory variable (model B). To test whether this restrained model (without religion) is as good as the current model (model A), we compare the deviance statistics of both models.[22] Formally we test the following

---

[21] All estimated parameters exhibiting a negative sign denote a decrease in the odds; this is obtained as (1-odds ratio) × 100. Likewise, estimated parameters with a positive sign denote an increase in the odds; this is obtained as (odds ratio-1)×100. For the effect of education we have (1–0.51) × 100, and for the effect of gender we have (1.28–1) × 100%.

[22] The deviance statistic: $D^*(y;\hat{\mu}) = 2l(y;\hat{\mu}_B) - 2l(y;\hat{\mu}_A)$.

hypothesis:

$$H_0 : D^* = 0; \quad \text{model A is as good as model B.}$$

$$H_a : D^* > 0; \quad \text{model A fits better than model B.}$$

To reject the null hypothesis we compare D^* with the corresponding chi-square statistic χ^2_{df} with df degrees of freedom. These degrees of freedom correspond to the difference in the number of parameters in model A and model B. A non-rejection of the null hypothesis indicates that both models are statistically equivalent and thus the most parsimonious model, which has the smaller number of explanatory variables, should be chosen—which is B in this context. A rejection of the null hypothesis indicates a statistical justification for model A. In our case the comparison of the two nested models, A and B, gives a scaled deviance statistic D^* of 0.05. We compare this value with the corresponding chi-square statistic of one degree of freedom and a 5% type I error rate; this gives a value of 3.84. As D^* is smaller than 3.84, we cannot reject the null hypothesis; so we choose the more parsimonious model B and drop religion as an explanatory variable.

10.4 **Macro Regression Models for M_0 and H**

We now turn to the econometric modelling for the Adjusted Headcount Ratio M_0 and the incidence of multidimensional poverty H as endogenous or dependent variables. As M_0 and H are bounded between zero and one, an econometric model for these endogenous variables must account for the shape of their distribution. M_0 and H are fractional (proportional) variables bounded between zero and one with the possibility of observing values at the boundaries. This restricted range of variation also applies for the conditional mean, which is the focus of our analysis. Thus, specifying a linear model, which assumes that the endogenous variable and its mean take any value in the real line, and estimating it by ordinary least squares is not the right strategy, as this ignores the shape of the distribution of these dependent variables. Clearly if the interest of the research question is not in modelling the conditional mean of the proportion but rather in modelling the absolute change (between two time periods) of M_0 or H, which can take any value, standard linear regression models may apply. In what follows we describe the statistical strategy for modelling the conditional mean of M_0 or H as a function of a set of explanatory variables.

Various approaches have been used in the literature to model a fraction or proportion. We can differentiate between two types of approaches—often referred to as one-step or two-step approaches. These differ in the treatment of the boundary values of the fractional dependent variable. In a one-step approach, one considers a single model for the entire distribution of the values of the proportion, where both the limiting observations and those falling inside the unit interval are modelled together. In a two-step approach, the observations at the boundaries are modelled separately from those falling inside the unit interval. In other words, in a two-step approach one considers a two-part model where the boundary observations are modelled as a multinomial model and remaining observations as a fractional one-step regression model (Wagner 2001; Ramalho, Ramalho, and Murteira 2011). The decision whether a one- or a two-part model is appropriate is often based on theoretical economic arguments. Wagner (2001) illustrates this point. He models the export/sales ratio of a firm and argues that firms choose the profit-maximizing volume of exports, which can be zero, positive, or one. Thus the boundary values of zero or one may be interpreted as the result of a utility-maximizing mechanism. Following this theoretical economic argument he specifies a one-step fractional model for the exports/sales ratio. In the absence of an *a priori* criteria for the selection of either a one- or two-part model, Ramalho et al. (2011) propose a testing methodology that can be used for choosing between one-part and two-part models. In the case of M_0 or H we consider that non-poverty and full poverty, the boundary values, as well as the positive values, are characterized by the same theoretical mechanism. This is thus represented by a one-part model. For further references on alternative estimation approaches for one-part models, see Wagner (2001) and Ramalho et al. (2011).

10.4.1 MODELLING M_0 OR H

To model M_0 or H we follow the modelling approach proposed by Papke and Wooldridge (1996). For this purpose we denote the Adjusted Headcount Ratio or the incidence by y. For a given spatial aggregate, say a country, the Adjusted Headcount Ratio or the incidence is y_i. Papke and Wooldridge (PW hereafter) propose a particular quasi-likelihood method to estimate a proportion. The method follows Gourieroux, Monfort, and Trognon (1984) and McCullagh and Nelder (1989) and is based on the Bernoulli log-likelihood function which is given by

$$l_i(\boldsymbol{\beta}) \equiv y_i \log[G(\mathbf{x}_i\boldsymbol{\beta})] + (1 - y_i) \log[1 - G(\mathbf{x}_i\boldsymbol{\beta})], \qquad (10.17)$$

where $G(\mathbf{x}_i\boldsymbol{\beta})$ is a known non-linear function satisfying $0 \leq G(\cdot) \leq 1$. In the context of a GLM, $G(\cdot)$ is the mean function $\mu_{Y_i|\mathbf{x}_i}$ defined in equation (10.8) as the inverse link function. PW suggest as possible specifications for $G(\cdot)$ any cumulative distribution function, with the two most typical examples being the logistic function and the standard normal cumulative density function as described in Table 10.1.

The quasi-maximum likelihood estimator (QML) obtained from equation (10.17) is consistent and asymptotically normal, provided that the conditional mean $\mu_{Y_i|\mathbf{x}_i}$ is correctly specified. This follows the QML theory where consistency and asymptotic normality characterize all QML estimators belonging to the linear exponential family of distributions, which is the case of the Bernoulli distribution of equation (10.17).

10.4.2 ECONOMETRIC ISSUES FOR AN EMPIRICAL MODEL OF M_0 OR H

We would like to conclude with a few recommendations for performing a macro regression with M_0 or H as endogenous variables. First, we suggest testing for linearity before specifying a non-linear functional form. For this purpose one can apply the Ramsey RESET[23] test of functional misspecification. The test consists of evaluating the presence of non-linear patterns in the residuals that could be explained by higher-order polynomials of the dependent variable. Second, we recommend testing for possible endogeneity using a two-stage or instrumental variable (IV) estimation. In regressions of the type of the macro determinants of M_0 or H, it is very likely that there will be a correlation between one or more of the explanatory variables and the error term. Let us suppose we regress the Adjusted Headcount Ratio on the logarithm of the per capita gross national income in PPP of the same year for a group of countries. This is the GNI converted to international dollars using purchasing power parity rates. This gives a contemporaneous model for the semi-elasticity between growth and poverty. In this very simple model, it is highly likely that the GNI would be correlated with the disturbance of the equation, which consists of unobserved variables affecting the poverty rate. This violates a necessary condition for the consistency of standard linear estimators. To deal with endogeneity, often one uses an instrumental variable that is assumed to be correlated with the endogenous explanatory variable but uncorrelated with the error term.

Third, one is also very likely to find measurement errors among the explanatory variables in a model for M_0 or H. This issue can also be treated with the IV method by replacing the measured-with-error variable with a proxy. To minimize the loss of efficiency that may result from an IV estimation, one can in addition estimate the model using the Generalized Method of Moments. Lastly, we would like to point out that although this chapter has focused on the modelling of levels of poverty (rates of poverty: M_0, H), it is at once straightforward and necessary to analyse *changes* in poverty. It suffices to estimate the model in levels and then compute the marginal effects of the expected poverty rate with respect to the explanatory variables included in the model.

---

[23] RESET stands for Regression Equation Specification Error Test.

■ REFERENCES

Aaberge, R. and Peluso, E. (2012). 'A Counting Approach for Measuring Multidimensional Deprivation', Discussion Paper 700, Research Department, Statistics Norway.

Abe, A. (2006). 'Empirical Analysis of Relative Deprivation and Poverty in Japan', IPSS Discussion Paper Series 2005–07. Tokyo: National Institute of Population and Social Security Research.

Addison, T., Hulme, D., and Kanbur R. (2009). *Poverty Dynamics: Interdisciplinary Perspectives*. Oxford: Oxford University Press.

Adler, M. D. (2011). *Well-being and Fair Distribution beyond Cost-Benefit Analysis*. New York: Oxford University Press.

Ahmed, A. I. M. U. (2007). 'Consensual Poverty in Britain, Sweden and Bangladesh: A Comparative Study', *Bangladesh e-Journal of Sociology*, 4(2): 56–77.

Alkire, S. (2002a). *Valuing Freedoms: Sen's Capability Approach and Poverty Reduction*. Oxford: Oxford University Press.

Alkire, S. (2002b). 'Dimensions of Human Development', *World Development*, 30(2): 181–205.

Alkire, S. (2006). 'Needs and Capabilities', in S. Reader (ed.), *The Philosophy of Need*, Royal Institute of Philosophy Supplement 80. Cambridge: Cambridge University Press, 229–52.

Alkire, S. (2008a). 'Choosing Dimensions: The Capability Approach and Multidimensional Poverty', in N. Kakwani and J. Silber (eds), *The Many Dimensions of Poverty*. New York: Palgrave Macmillan, 89–119.

Alkire, S. (2008b). 'Using the Capability Approach: Prospective and Evaluative Analyses', in F. Comim, M. Qizilbash, and S. Alkire (eds), *The Capability Approach: Concepts, Measures and Applications*. Cambridge: Cambridge University Press, 26–49.

Alkire, S. (2011). 'Multidimensional Poverty and its Discontents', in Michel Aglietta et al. (eds), *Measure for Measure: How Well Do We Measure Development? Proceedings of the 8th AFD-EUDN Conference, 2010*. Paris: AFD, 55–90.

Alkire, S. (2013). The Overseas Development Institute (ODI) Blog, <http://www.odi.org.uk/sites/odi.org.uk/files/odi-assets/publications-opinion-files/8440.pdf>.

Alkire, S. (2014). 'Towards Frequent and Accurate Poverty Data', *OPHI Research in Progress* 43a, University of Oxford.

Alkire, S., Apablaza, M., Chakravarty, S., and Yalonetzky, G. (2014). 'Measuring Chronic Multidimensional Poverty: A Counting Approach', *OPHI Working Paper* 75, University of Oxford.

Alkire, S., Apablaza, M., and Jung, E. (2014a). 'Multidimensional Poverty Measurement for EU-SILC Countries', *OPHI Research in Progress* 36c, University of Oxford.

Alkire, S., Apablaza, M., and Jung, E. (2014b). 'Multidimensional Poverty Measurement for EU-SILC Countries', *OPHI Research in Progress* 36d, University of Oxford.

Alkire, S. and Ballon, P. (2012). 'Understanding Association across Deprivation Indicators in Multi-dimensional Poverty'. Paper presented at the Research Workshop on Dynamic Comparison between Multidimensional Poverty and Monetary Poverty, OPHI, University of Oxford.

Alkire, S., Conconi, A., and Roche, J. M. (2013). 'Multidimensional Poverty Index 2013: Brief Methodological Note and Results', *OPHI*, University of Oxford.

Alkire, S., Conconi, A., and Seth, S. (2014). 'Multidimensional Poverty Index 2014: Brief Methodological Note and Results', *OPHI*, University of Oxford.

Alkire, S. and Deneulin, S. (2009). 'A Normative Framework for Development' and 'The Human Development and Capability Approach', in S. Deneulin and L. Shahani (eds), *An Introduction to the Human Development and Capability Approach: Freedom and Agency*. London: Earthscan, chs 1–2.

Alkire, S. and Foster, J. (2007, rev. 2008). 'Counting and Multidimensional Poverty Measurement', *OPHI Working Paper* 7, University of Oxford.

Alkire, S. and Foster, J. (2009). 'An Axiomatic Approach to Identification and Measurement of Multidimensional Poverty', *OPHI Research in Progress* 21a, University of Oxford.

Alkire, S. and Foster, J. (2010). 'Designing the Inequality Adjusted Human Development Index (IHDI)', *OPHI Working Paper* 37, University of Oxford.

Alkire, S. and Foster, J. (2011a). 'Counting and Multidimensional Poverty Measurement', *Journal of Public Economics*, 95(7–8): 476–87.

Alkire, S. and Foster, J. (2011b). 'Understandings and Misunderstandings of Multidimensional Poverty Measurement', *Journal of Economic Inequality*, 9: 289–314.

Alkire, S. and Foster, J. (2013). 'Evaluating Dimensional and Distributional Contributions to Multidimensional Poverty'. Mimeo, *OPHI*, University of Oxford.

Alkire, S., Foster, J., and Santos, M. E. (2011). 'Where Did Identification Go?', *Journal of Economic Inequality*, 9(3): 501–5.

Alkire, S. and Klasen, S. (2013). 'The Multidimensional Poverty Index (MPI) and Monetary Poverty: Dynamic Comparisons from 12 Country Studies'. Mimeo.

Alkire, S., Meinzen-Dick, R., Peterman, A., Quisumbing, A. R., Seymour, G., and Vaz, A. (2013). 'The Women's Empowerment in Agriculture Index', *World Development*, 53: 71–91.

Alkire, S. and Roche, J. M. (2012). 'Beyond Headcount: Measures that Reflect the Breadth and Components of Child Poverty', in A. Minujin and S. Nandy (eds), *Global Child Poverty and Well-Being: Measurement, Concepts, Policy and Action*. Bristol: Policy Press, 103–34.

Alkire, S. and Roche, J. M. (2013). 'How Multidimensional Poverty Went Down: Dynamics and Comparisons?', *OPHI Briefing* 16, University of Oxford.

Alkire, S., Roche, J. M., and Seth S. (2011). 'Sub-national Disparities and Inter-temporal Evolution of Multidimensional Poverty across Developing Countries', *OPHI Research in Progress* 32a, University of Oxford.

Alkire, S., Roche, J. M., and Seth S. (2013). 'The Global Multidimensional Poverty Index 2013', *OPHI Briefing* 13, University of Oxford.

Alkire, S., Roche, J. M., Santos, M. E., and Seth, S. (2011). 'Multidimensional Poverty Index 2011: Brief Methodological Note', *OPHI Briefing* 07, University of Oxford.

Alkire, S., Roche, J. M., and Vaz, A. (2014). 'How Countries Reduce Multidimensional Poverty: A Disaggregated Analysis', *OPHI Working Paper* 76, University of Oxford.

Alkire, S. and Samman, E. (2014). 'Mobilising the Household Data Required to Progress toward the SDGs', *OPHI Working Paper* 72, University of Oxford.

Alkire, S. and Santos, M. E. (2009). 'Poverty and Inequality Measurement', in S. Deneulin and L. Shanai (eds), *An Introduction to the Human Development and Capability Approach*. Abingdon: Earthscan, ch. 6.

Alkire, S. and Santos, M. E. (2010). 'Acute Multidimensional Poverty: A New Index for Developing Countries', *OPHI Working Paper* 38, University of Oxford; also published as *Human Development Research Paper* 2010/11.

Alkire, S. and Santos, M. E. (2014). 'Measuring Acute Poverty in the Developing World: Robustness and Scope of the Multidimensional Poverty Index', *World Development*, 59: 251–74.

Alkire, S., Santos, M. E., Seth, S., and Yalonetzky, G. (2010). 'Is the Multidimensional Poverty Index Robust to Different Weights?', *OPHI Research in Progress* 22a, University of Oxford.

Alkire, S. and Sarwar, M. (2009). 'Multidimensional Measures of Poverty and Wellbeing', *OPHI Research in Progress* 6a, University of Oxford.

Alkire, S. and Seth, S. (2008). 'Determining BPL Status: Some Methodological Improvements', *Indian Journal of Human Development*, 2(2): 407–24.

Alkire, S. and Seth, S. (2013a). 'Identifying BPL Households', *Economic and Political Weekly*, 48(2): 49–67.

Alkire, S. and Seth, S. (2013b). 'Multidimensional Poverty Reduction in India between 1999 and 2006: Where and How?', *OPHI Working Paper* 60, University of Oxford.

Alkire, S. and Seth, S. (2013c). 'Selecting a Targeting Method to Identify BPL Households in India', *Social Indicators Research*, 112(2): 417–46.

Alkire, S. and Seth, S. (2015). 'Multidimensional Poverty Reduction in India between 1999–2006: Where and How?', *World Development*, 72: 93–108.

Alkire, S. and Stein, F. (2013). *The Data Deluge*. Mimeo.

Altimir, O. (1979). *La Dimensión de la Pobreza en América Latina*. Cuadernos de la Cepal No. 27, Naciones Unidas, Santiago de Chile.

Amarante, V., Arim, R., and Vigorito, A. (2010). 'Multidimensional Poverty among Children in Uruguay', in J. A. Bishop (ed.), *Studies in Applied Welfare Analysis: Papers from the Third ECINEQ Meeting*, Research on Economic Inequality 18. Bingley: Emerald Group Publishing, 31–53.

Amemiya, T. (1985). *Advanced Econometrics*. Cambridge, MA: Harvard University Press.

Anaka, M. and Kobus, M. (2012). 'Multidimensional Poverty Analysis in Polish Gminas', *Ekonomista*, 112(1): 101–17.

Anand, S. (1983). *Inequality and Poverty in Malaysia: Measurement and Decomposition*. New York: Oxford University Press.

Anand, S. (2008). 'Sen, Amartya', in S. N. Durlauf and L. E. Blume (eds), *The New Palgrave Dictionary of Economics*, 2nd edn. London: Palgrave Macmillan.

Anand, S. and Sen, A. (1994). 'Human Development Index: Methodology and Measurement', *Human Development Report Office Occasional Paper*, UNDP.

Anand, S. and Sen, A. (1997). 'Concepts of Human Development and Poverty: A Multidimensional Perspective', in *Human Development Papers 1997: Poverty and Human Development*, UNDP, 1–20.

Anand, S., Segal, P., and Stiglitz, J. E. (2010). *Debates on the Measurement of Global Poverty*, Initiative for Policy Dialogue Series. Oxford: Oxford University Press.

Anderson, G. (1996). 'Nonparametric Tests of Stochastic Dominance in Income Distributions', *Econometrica*, 64(5): 1183–93.

Anderson, G. (2008). 'The Empirical Assessment of Multidimensional Welfare, Inequality and Poverty: Sample Weighted Multivariate Generalizations of the Kolmogorov-Smirnov Two-Sample Test for Stochastic Dominance', *Journal of Economic Inequality*, 6(1): 73–87.

Andrews, F. M. (ed.) (1986). *Research on the Quality of Life*. Ann Arbor: Institute for Social Research.

Andrews, F. M., Klem, L., Davidson, T. N., O'Malley, P. M., and Rodgers, W. L. (1981). *A Guide for Selecting Statistical Techniques for Analyzing Social Science Data*. Ann Arbor, MI: University of Michigan, Institute for Social Research.

Angulo Salazar, R. C., Díaz, B.Y., and Pardo Pinzón, R. (2013). 'A Counting Multidimensional Poverty Index in Public Policy Context: The Case of Colombia', *OPHI Working Paper* 62, University of Oxford.

Apablaza, M. and Yalonetzky, G. (2011). 'Measuring the Dynamics of Multiple Deprivations among Children: The Cases of Andhra Pradesh, Ethiopia, Peru and Vietnam'. Mimeo, OPHI.

Apablaza, M. and Yalonetzky, G. (2013). 'Decomposing Multidimensional Poverty Dynamics', *Young Lives Working Paper* 101.

Arndt, C. and Volkert, J. (2011). 'The Capability Approach: A Framework for Official German Poverty and Wealth Reports', *Journal of Human Development and Capabilities*, 12(3): 311–37.

Arndt, C., Distante, R., Hussain, M. A., et al. (2012). 'Ordinal Welfare Comparisons with Multiple Discrete Indicators: A First-Order Dominance Approach and Application to Child Poverty', *World Development*, 40(11): 2290–301.

Asselin, L. M. (2009). *Analysis of Multidimensional Poverty: Theory and Case Studies*. Dordrecht: Springer.

Asselin, L. M. and Anh, V. T. (2008). 'Multidimensional Poverty and Multiple Correspondence Analysis', in N. Kakwani and J. Silber (eds), *Quantitative Approaches to Multidimensional Poverty Measurement*. New York: Palgrave Macmillan, 80–103.

Atkinson, A. B. (1970). 'On the Measurement of Inequality', *Journal of Economic Theory*, 2(3): 244–63.

Atkinson, A. B. (1987). 'On the Measurement of Poverty', *Econometrica*, 55(4): 749–64.

Atkinson, A. B. (1989). *Poverty and Social Security*. Hemel Hempstead: Harvester Wheatsheaf.

Atkinson, A. B. (1999). 'The Contributions of Amartya Sen to Welfare Economics', *Scandinavian Journal of Economics*, 101(2): 173–90.

Atkinson, A. B. (2003). 'Multidimensional Deprivation: Contrasting Social Welfare and Counting Approaches', *Journal of Economic Inequality*, 1(1): 51–65.

Atkinson, A. B. (2012). 'Public Economics after the Idea of Justice', *Journal of Human Development and Capabilities*, 13(4): 521–36.

Atkinson, A. B. and Bourguignon, F. (1982). 'The Comparison of Multi-dimensioned Distributions of Economic Status', *Review of Economic Studies*, 49(2): 183–201.

Atkinson, A. B. and Bourguignon, F. (1987). 'Income Distribution and Differences in Needs', in G. F. Feiwel (ed.), *Arrow and the Foundation of the Theory of Economic Policy*. London: Macmillan, 350–70.

Atkinson, A. B. and Marlier, E. (2010). *Analysing and Measuring Social Inclusion in a Global Context*. New York: United Nations Department of Economic and Social Affairs.

Atkinson, A. B., Cantillon, B., Marlier, E., and Nolan, B. (2002). *Social Indicators: The EU and Social Inclusion*. Oxford: Oxford University Press.

Atkinson, A. B., Cantillon, B., Marlier, E., and Nolan, B. (2005). *Taking Forward the EU Social Inclusion Process*. Luxembourg Presidency of the Council of the European Union.

Atkinson, A. B., Marlier, E., Monatigne, F., and Reinstadler, A. (2010). 'Income Poverty and Income Inequality', in A. B. Atkinson and E. Marlier (eds.), *Income and Living Conditions in Europe*. Eurostat Statistical Books. Luxembourg: Publications Office of the European Union, 101–32.

Azevedo, V. and Robles, M. (2013). 'Multidimensional Targeting: Identifying Beneficiaries of Conditional Cash Transfer Programs', *Social Indicators Research*, 112(2): 447–75.

Baliamoune-Lutz, M. and McGillivray, M. (2006). 'Fuzzy Well-Being Achievement in Pacific Asia', *Journal of the Asia Pacific Economy*, 11(2): 168–77.

Balisacan, A. M. (2011). 'What Has Really Happened to Poverty in the Philippines? New Measures, Evidence, and Policy Implications', *UP School of Economics Discussion Paper* 2011–14.

Ballon, P. (2011). 'A Structural Model of Female Empowerment', in *Model-Based Multidimensional Poverty Indices: Theoretical Construction and Statistical Properties*, doctoral dissertation, thesis no. 759, University of Geneva, ch. 3.

Ballon, P. and Apablaza, M. (2012). 'Multidimensional Poverty Dynamics in Indonesia'. Paper presented at the Research Workshop on Dynamic Comparison between Multidimensional Poverty and Monetary Poverty, OPHI, University of Oxford.

Ballon, P. and Duclos, J. Y. (2014). 'Multidimensional Poverty in North and South Sudan', African Development Bank Research Paper, forthcoming.

Ballon, P. and Krishnakumar, J. (2011). 'Measuring Capability Poverty: A Multidimensional Model-Based Index', in P. Ballon, *Model-based Multidimensional Poverty Indices: Theoretical Construction and Statistical Properties*, doctoral dissertation, thesis no. 759, University of Geneva, ch. 2.

Baluch, B. and Masset, E. (2003). 'Do Monetary and Non-monetary Indicators Tell the Same Story about Chronic Poverty? A Study of Vietnam in the 1990s', *World Development*, 31(3): 441–53.

Bandura, R. (2008). *A Survey of Composite Indices Measuring Country Performance: 2008 Update*. UNDP/ODS Working Paper. New York: United Nations Development Programme.

Banerjee, A. V. and Duflo, E. (2011). *Poor Economics: A Radical Rethinking of the Way to Fight Global Poverty*. New York: Public Affairs.

Barrett, G. and Donald, S. G. (2003). 'Consistent Tests for Stochastic Dominance', *Econometrica*, 71(1): 71–103.

Barrientos, A. (2010). 'Social Protection and Poverty', UNRISD Paper 42, United Nations Research Institute for Social Development.

Barrientos, A. (2013). *Social Assistance in Developing Countries*. Cambridge: Cambridge University Press.

Barro, R. J. (2003). 'Determinants of Economic Growth in a Panel of Countries', *Annals of Economics and Finance*, 4(2): 231–74.

Bartholomew, D. J., Steele, F., Moustaki, I., and Galbraith, J. I. (2008). *Analysis of Multivariate Social Science Data*. London: Chapman and Hall/CRC Press.

Bartholomew, D. J. and Tzamourani, P. (1999). 'The Goodness-of-Fit of Latent Trait Models in Attitude Measurement', *Sociological Methods and Research*, 27: 525–46.

Basilevsky, A. T. (1994). *Statistical Factor Analysis and Related Methods: Theory and Applications*. New York: John Wiley.

Basu, K. (1980). *Revealed Preference of Government*. Cambridge: Cambridge University Press.

Basu, K. and Foster, J. (1998). 'On Measuring Literacy', *Economic Journal*, 108(451): 1733–49.

Basu, K. and López-Calva, L. F. (2010). 'Functionings and Capabilities', in K. J. Arrow, A. Sen, and K. Suzumura (eds), *Handbook of Social Choice and Welfare*. Amsterdam: Elsevier, ii.153–88.

Batana, Y. M. (2013). 'Multidimensional Measurement of Poverty among Women in Sub-Saharan Africa', *Social Indicators Research*, 112(2): 337–62.

Batana, Y. M. and Duclos, J.-Y. (2008). 'Multidimensional Poverty Dominance: Statistical Inference and an Application to West Africa', *CIRPEE Working Paper* 08–08.

Batana, Y. M. and Duclos, J.-Y. (2010). 'Multidimensional Poverty among West African Children: Testing for Robust Poverty Comparisons', in J. Cockburn and J. Kabubo-Mariara (eds), *Child Welfare in Developing Countries*. New York: Springer, 95–122.

Batana, Y. M. and Duclos, J.-Y. (2011). 'Comparing Multidimensional Poverty with Qualitative Indicators of Well-Being', in J. Deutsch and J. Silber (eds), *The Measurement of Individual Well-Being and Group Inequalities: Essays in Memory of Z. M. Berrebi*. London: Routledge, ch. 13.

Battiston, D., Cruces, G., Lopez-Calva, L. F., Lugo, M. A., and Santos, M. E. (2013). 'Income and Beyond: Multidimensional Poverty in Six Latin American Countries', *Social Indicators Research*, 112(2): 291–314.

Bauman, K. (1998). 'Direct Measures of Poverty as Indicators for Economic Need: Evidence from the Survey of Income and Program Participation', *Population Division Technical Working Paper* 30, US census bureau.

Bauman, K. (1999). 'Extended Measures of Well-Being: Meeting Basic Needs', *Household Economic Studies*, US Department of Commerce.

Bavetta, S. and Del Seta, M. (2001). 'Constraints and the Measurement of Freedom of Choice', *Theory and Decision*, 50(3): 213–38.

Beccaria, L. and Minujin, A. (1985). 'Métodos alternativos para medir la evolución del tamaño de la pobreza', *INDEC Documento de Trabajo* 6, Buenos Aires.

Bedi, T., Coudouel, A., and Simle, K. (eds) (2007). *More Than a Pretty Picture: Using Poverty Maps to Design Better Policies and Interventions*. Washington, DC: World Bank.

Beja, E. L., Jr and Yap, D. B. (2013). 'Counting Happiness from the Individual Level to the Group Level', *Social Indicators Research*, 114(2): 621–37.

Belhadj, B. (2011). 'A New Fuzzy Poverty Index by Distinguishing Three Levels of Poverty', *Research in Economics*, 65(3): 221–31.

Belhadj, B. and Limam, M. (2012). 'Unidimensional and Multidimensional Fuzzy Poverty Measures: New Approach', *Economic Modelling*, 29(4): 995–1002.

Belhadj, B. and Matoussi, M. S. (2010). 'Poverty in Tunisia: A Fuzzy Measurement Approach', *Swiss Journal of Economic and Statistics*, 146(2): 431–50.

Bennett, C. J. and Mitra, S. (2013). 'Multidimensional Poverty: Measurement, Estimation, and Inference', *Econometric Reviews*, 32(1): 57–83.

Benzécri, J. P. and Bellier, L. (1973). *L'analyse de données: L'analyse des correspondances*. Paris: Dunod.

Berenger, V. and Verdier-Chouchane, A. (2007). 'Multidimensional Measures of Well-Being: Standard of Living and Quality of Life across Countries', *World Development*, 35(7): 1259–76.

Berenger, V., Deutsch, J., and Silber, J. (2013). 'Durable Goods, Access to Services and the Derivation of an Asset Index: Comparing Two Methodologies and Three Countries', *Economics Modeling*, 35: 881–91.

Betti, G., Cheli, B., Lemmi, A., and Verma, V. (2006). 'Multidimensional and Longitudinal Poverty: An Integrated Fuzzy Approach', in A. Lemmi and G. Betti (eds), *Fuzzy Set Approach to Multidimensional Poverty Measurement*. New York: Springer, 111–37.

Betti, G., Gagliardi, F., Lemmi, A., and Verma, V. (2012). 'Subnational Indicators of Poverty and Deprivation in Europe: Methodology and Applications', *Cambridge Journal of Regions Economy and Society*, 5(1): 129–47.

Betti, G. and Verma, V. (1999). 'Measuring the Degree of Poverty in a Dynamic and Comparative Context: A Multi-dimensional Approach Using Fuzzy Set Theory', in *Proceedings of the ICCS-VI*, Lahore, Pakistan, 27–31 August, xi.289–301.

Betti, G. and Verma, V. (2004). 'A Methodology for the Study of Multi-Dimensional and Longitudinal Aspects of Poverty and Deprivation', Working Paper 49, Dipartimento di Metodi Quantitativi, Università di Siena.

Betti, G. and Verma, V. (2008). 'Fuzzy Measures of the Incidence of Relative Poverty and Deprivation: A Multi-Dimensional Perspective', *Statistical Methods and Applications*, 17(2): 225–50.

Bibi, S., Duclos, J.-Y., and Verdier-Chouchane, A. (2012). 'Assessing Absolute and Relative Pro-poor Growth, with an Application to Selected African Countries', *Economics—The Open-Access Open-Assessment E-Journal*, 6: article no. 20127.

Biewen, M. (2002). 'Bootstrap Inference for Inequality, Mobility and Poverty Measurement', *Journal of Econometrics*, 108(2): 317–42.

Boarini, R. and d'Ercole, M. M. (2006). 'Measures of Material Deprivation in OECD Countries', *OECD Social, Employment and Migration Working Papers* 37.

Boland, P. J. and Proschan, F. (1988). 'Multivariate Arrangement Increasing Functions with Applications in Probability and Statistics', *Journal of Multivariate Analysis*, 25(2): 286–98.

Bollen K. A. (1989). *Structural Equations with Latent Variables*. New York: John Wiley.

Bollen, K. A., Glanville, J. L., and Stecklov, G. (2002). 'Economic Status Proxies in Studies of Fertility in Developing Countries: Does the Measure Matter?', *Population Studies*, 56(1): 81–96.

Boltvinik, J. (1991). 'La medición de la pobreza en América Latina', *Comercio Exterior*, 41(5): 423–28.

Boltvinik, J. (1992). 'El Metodo de Medicion Integrada de la Pobreza: Una propuesta para su desarrollo', *Comercio Exterior*, 42(4): 354–65.

Boltvinik, J. (1995). 'La Pobreza en México II. Magnitud', *Salud Pública México*, 37(4): 298–309.

Boltvinik, J. (1996). 'Evolución y Magnitud de la Pobreza en México', *Estudios Demograficos y Urbanos* 32.

Boltvinik, J. (2012). 'Medición multidimensional de la pobreza. América Latina, de precursora a rezagada. La experiencia contrastante de México: una guía para la región?'. Paper presented at the Seminario Internacional Multidimensionalidad de la pobreza, 'Alcances para su definición y evaluación en América Latina y el Caribe'. Universidad de Chile, 22–3 November.

Booth, C. (1894). *The Aged Poor: Condition*. London: Macmillan.

Booth, C. (1903). *Life and Labour of the People in London*. London: Macmillan.

Booysen, F., Servass Van Derberg, R., Von Maltitz, M., and Du Rand, G. (2008). 'Using an Asset Index to Assess Trends in Poverty in Seven Sub-Saharan African Countries', *World Development*, 36(6): 1113–30.

Bossert, W., Ceriani, L., Chakravarty, S. R., and D'Ambrosio, C. (2012). 'Intertemporal Material Deprivation', *CIREQ Cahier* 07-2012.

Bossert, W., Chakravarty, S. R., and D'Ambrosio, C. (2012). 'Poverty and Time', *Journal of Economic Inequality*, 10(2): 145–62.

Bossert, W., Chakravarty, S. R., and D'Ambrosio, C. (2013). 'Multidimensional Poverty and Material Deprivation with Discrete Data', *Review of Income and Wealth*, 59(1): 29–43.

Bound, J., Jaeger, D. A., and Baker, R. M. (1995). 'Problems with Instrumental Variables Estimation When the Correlation between the Instruments and the Endogenous Explanatory Variable Is Weak', *Journal of the American Statistical Association*, 90(430): 443–50.

Bourdieu, P. (1986). 'The Forms of Capital', in J. G. Richardson (ed.) and R. Nice (trans.), *Handbook of Theory and Research for the Sociology of Education*. New York: Greenwood.

Bourdieu, P. (1987). 'What Makes a Social Class? On the Theoretical and Practical Existence of Groups', *Berkeley Journal of Sociology*, 32: 1–17.

Bourguignon, F. (1989). 'Family Size and Social Utility: Income Distribution Dominance Criteria', *Journal of Econometrics*, 42(1): 67–80.

Bourguignon, F., Bénassy-Quéré, A., Dercon, S., Estache, A., Gunning, J. W., Kanbur, R., Klasen, S., Maxwell, S., Platteau, J.-P., and Spadaro, A. (2008). *Millennium Development Goals at Midpoint: Where Do We Stand?* European Report on Development, <http://ec.europa.eu/development/icenter/repository/mdg_paper_final_20080916_en.pdf>.

Bourguignon, F., Bénassy-Quéré, A., Dercon, S., Estache, A., Gunning, J. W., Kanbur, R., Klasen, S., Maxwell, S., Platteau, J.-P., and Spadaro, A. (2010). 'Millennium Development Goals: An Assessment', in R. Kanbur and M. Spencer (eds.), *Equity and Growth in a Globalizing World*. Washington, DC: World Bank, ch. 2.

Bourguignon, F. and Chakravarty, S. R. (2003). 'The Measurement of Multidimensional Poverty', *Journal of Economic Inequality*, 1(1): 25–49.

Bourguignon, F. and Chakravarty, S. R. (2009). 'Multidimensional Poverty Orderings: Theory and Applications', in K. Basu and R. Kanbur (eds), *Arguments for a Better World: Essays in Honor of Amartya Sen*, i: *Ethics, Welfare, and Measurement*. Oxford: Oxford University Press, ch. 18.

Bowley, A. L. and Burnett-Hurst, A. R. (1915). *Livelihood and Poverty: A Study in the Economic and Social Conditions of Working Class Households in Northampton, Warrington, Stanley, Reading (and Bolton)*. London: King.

Boyden, J. and Bourdillon, M. (2012). *Childhood Poverty: Multidisciplinary Approaches*. Basingstoke: Palgrave Macmillan.

Bradshaw, J. and Finch, N. (2003). 'Overlaps in Dimensions of Poverty', *Journal of Social Policy*, 32(4): 513–25.

Braybrooke, D. (1987). *Meeting Needs*. Princeton: Princeton University Press.

Brighouse, H. and Robeyns, I. (eds) (2010). *Measuring Justice: Primary Goods and Capabilities*. Cambridge: Cambridge University Press.

Brown, J. D. (2011). 'Questions and Answers about Language Testing Statistics: Likert Items and Scales of Measurement?', *SHIKEN: JALT Testing & Evaluation SIG Newsletter*, 15(1): 10–14.

Browne, M. W. and Arminger, G. (1995). 'Specification and Estimation of Mean-and-Covariance Structure Models', in G. Arminger, C. C. Clogg, and M. E. Sobel (eds), *Handbook of Statistical Modeling for the Social and Behavioral Sciences*. New York: Plenum Press, 311–59.

Browning, M. (1992). 'Children and Household Economic Behavior', *Journal of Economic Literature*, 30(3): 1434–75.

Burchardt, T. (2009). 'Agency Goals, Adaptation and Capability Sets', *Journal of Human Development and Capabilities*, 10(1): 3–19.

Burchardt, T. (2013). 'Deliberate Research as a Tool to Make Value Judgements', *CASE Paper* 159, LSE, <http://sticerd.lse.ac.uk/dps/case/cp/CASEpaper159.pdf>.

Burchardt, T. and Vizard, P. (2007). 'Developing a Capability List: Final Recommendations of the Equalities Review Steering Group on Measurement', *CASE Working Paper* 121.

Burchardt, T. and Vizard, P. (2011). 'Foundations for Equality and Human Rights Monitoring in 21st Century Britain', *Journal of Human Development and Capabilities*, 12(1): 91–119.

Burchi, F. and Passacantilli, A. (2013). 'Inequality in the Monetary and Functionings Space: The Case of Peru under the First Garcia Government (1985–1990)', *Journal of International Development*, 25(3): 340–61.

Callan, T., Layte, R., Nolan, B., Watson, D., Whelan, C. T., Williams, J., and Maître, B. (1999). *Monitoring Poverty Trends*. Dublin: ESRI.

Callan, T., Nolan, B., and Whelan, C. T. (1993). 'Resources, Deprivation and the Measurement of Poverty', *Journal of Social Policy*, 22(2): 141–72.

Callander, E. J., Schofield, D. J., and Shrestha, R. N. (2012a). 'Multiple Disadvantages among Older Citizens: What a Multidimensional Measure of Poverty Can Show', *Journal of Aging and Social Policy*, 24(4): 368–83.

Callander, E. J., Schofield, D. J., and Shrestha, R. N. (2012b). 'Capacity for Freedom: A New Way of Measuring Poverty Amongst Australian Children', *Child Indicators Research*, 5(1): 179–98.

Callander, E. J., Schofield, D. J., and Shrestha, R. N. (2012c). 'Towards a Holistic Understanding of Poverty: A New Multidimensional Measure of Poverty for Australia', *Health and Sociology Review*, 21(2): 141–55.

Callander, E. J., Schofield, D. J., and Shrestha, R. N. (2012d). 'Capacity for Freedom: Using a New Poverty Measure to Look at Regional Differences in Living Standards within Australia', *Geographical Research*, 50(4): 411–20.

Callander, E. J., Schofield, D. J., and Shrestha, R. N. (2013a). 'Chronic Health Conditions and Poverty: A Cross-Sectional Study Using a Multidimensional Poverty Measure', *British Medical Journal Open*, 3(11): article no. e003397.

Callander, E. J., Schofield, D. J., and Shrestha, R. N. (2013b). 'Freedom Poverty: A New Tool to Identify the Multiple Disadvantages Affecting Those with CVD', *International Journal of Cardiology*, 166(2): 321–6.

Calvo, C. (2008). 'Vulnerability to Multidimensional Poverty: Peru, 1998–2002', *World Development*, 36(6): 1011–20.

Calvo, C. and Dercon, S. (2013). 'Vulnerability to Individual and Aggregate Poverty', *Social Choice and Welfare*, 41(4): 721–40.

Cardenas, J. C. and Carpenter, J. (2013). 'Risk Attitudes and Economic Well-Being in Latin America', *Journal of Development Economics*, 103(C): 52–61.

Casella, G. and Berger, R. L. (1990). *Statistical Inference*, vol. 70. Belmont, CA: Duxbury Press.

Castro, J. F., Baca, J., and Ocampo, J. P. (2012). '(Re)counting the Poor in Peru: A Multidimensional Approach', *Latin American Journal of Economics* (formerly *Cuadernos de Economía*), 49(1): 37–65. Instituto de Economía, Pontificia Universidad Católica de Chile.

CBS (2008). *Analisis Dan Penghitungan Tingkat Kemiskinan 2008* [*Analysis and Measurement of Poverty Levels 2008*]. Jakarta: Central Bureau of Statistics Indonesia [Badan Pusat Statistick].

Cerioli, A. and Zani, S. (1990). 'A Fuzzy Approach to the Measurement of Poverty', in C. Dagum and M. Zenga (eds), *Income and Wealth Distribution, Inequality and Poverty*. Berlin: Springer, i.272–84.

CGD (2008). *The Growth Report: Strategies for Sustained Growth and Inclusive Development*. Commission on Growth and Development (CGD), World Bank, Washington, DC.

Chakravarty, S. R. (1983a). 'Ethically Flexible Measures of Poverty', *Canadian Journal of Economics*, 16(1): 74–85.

Chakravarty, S. R. (1983b). 'A New Index of Poverty', *Mathematical Social Sciences*, 6(3): 307–13.

Chakravarty, S. R. (2001). 'The Variance as a Subgroup Decomposable Measure of Inequality', *Social Indicators Research*, 53(1): 79–95.

Chakravarty, S. R. (2006). 'An Axiomatic Approach to Multidimensional Poverty Measurement via Fuzzy Sets', in A. Lemmi and G. Betti (eds), *Fuzzy Set Approach to Multidimensional Poverty Measurement*. New York: Springer, 49–72.

Chakravarty, S. R. (2009). *Inequality, Polarization and Poverty: Advances in Distributional Analysis*, Economic Studies in Inequality, Social Exclusion, and Well-Being 6. New York: Springer.

Chakravarty, S. R. and D'Ambrosio, C. (2006). 'The Measurement of Social Exclusion', *Review of Income and Wealth*, 52(3): 377–98.

Chakravarty, S. R. and D'Ambrosio, C. (2013). 'A Family of Unit Consistent Multidimensional Poverty Indices', in V. Bérenger and F. Bresson (eds.), *Poverty and Social Exclusion around the Mediterranean Sea*. New York: Springer, 75–88.

Chakravarty, S. R., Deutsch, J., and Silber, J. (2008). 'On the Watts Multidimensional Poverty Index and its Decomposition', *World Development* 36(6): 1067–77.

Chakravarty, S. R., Mukherjee, D., and Ranade, R. R. (1998). 'On the Family of Subgroup and Factor Decomposability Measures of Multidimensional Poverty', in D. J. Slottje (ed.), *Research on Economic Inequality*. London: JAI Press, viii.175–94.

Chakravarty, S. R. and Silber, J. (2008). 'Measuring Multidimensional Poverty: The Axiomatic Approach', in N. Kakwani and J. Silber (eds), *Quantitative Approaches to Multidimensional Poverty Measurement*. New York: Palgrave Macmillan, 192–209.

Chang, R. (ed.) (1997). *Incommensurability, Incomparability, and Practical Reason*. Cambridge, MA: Harvard University Press.

Chantreuil, F. and Trannoy, A. (2011). 'Inequality Decomposition Values', *Annals of Economics and Statistics*, 101–2: 13–36.

Chantreuil, F. and Trannoy, A. (2013). 'Inequality Decomposition Values: The Trade-Off between Marginality and Efficiency', *Journal of Economic Inequality*, 11(1): 83–98.

Cheli, B. and Betti, G. (1999). 'Totally Fuzzy and Relative Measures of Poverty Dynamics in an Italian Pseudo Panel, 1985–1994', *Metron*, 57(1–2): 83–104.

Cheli, B. and Lemmi, A. (1995). 'A "Totally" Fuzzy and Relative Approach to the Multidimensional Analysis of Poverty', *Economic Notes*, 24(1): 115–33.

Chen, S. and Ravallion, M. (2010). 'The Developing World is Poorer than We Thought, But No Less Successful in the Fight against Poverty', *The Quarterly Journal of Economics*, 125(4): 1577–625.

Chen, J., Sun, H., Wang, Z., et al. (2012). 'An Analysis of Income Components of Rural Households in Xinjiang, China', *Outlook on Agriculture*, 41(3): 163–9.

Cherchye, L., Moesen, W., Rogge, N., Puyenbroeck, T. V., Saisana, M., Saltelli, A., Liska, R., and Tarantola, S. (2007). 'Creating Composite Indicators with DEA and Robustness Analysis: The Case of the Technology Achievement Index', *Journal of the Operational Research Society*, 59(2): 239–51.

Cherchye, L., Ooghe, E., and Puyenbroeck, T. V. (2008). 'Robust Human Development Rankings', *Journal of Economic Inequality*, 6(4): 287–321.

Chiappero-Martinetti, E. (1994). 'A New Approach to Evaluation of Well-Being and Poverty by Fuzzy Set Theory', *Giornale degli Economisti e Annali di Economia*, 53(3): 367–88.

Chiappero-Martinetti, E. (1996). 'Standard of Living Evaluation Based on Sen's Approach: Some Methodological Suggestions', *Notizie di Politeia*, 12(43–4): 37–53.

Chiappero-Martinetti, E. (2000). 'A Multidimensional Assessment of Well-Being Based on Sen's Functioning Approach', *Rivista Internazionale di Scienze Sociali*, 108(2): 207–39.

Chiappero-Martinetti, E. (2008). 'Complexity and Vagueness in the Capability Approach: Strengths or Weaknesses?', in F. Comim, M. Qizilbash, and S. Alkire (eds), *The Capability Approach: Concepts, Applications and Measurement*. Cambridge: Cambridge University Press, 268–309.

Chiappero-Martinetti, E. and Roche, J. M. (2009). 'Operationalization of the Capability Approach, from Theory to Practice: A Review of Techniques and Empirical Applications', in E. Chiappero-Martinetti (ed.), *Debating Global Society: Reach and Limits of the Capability Approach*. Milan: Fondazione Feltrinelli, 157–203.

Chung, K. H. and Lee, S. (2001). 'Optimal Bootstrap Sample Size in Construction of Percentile Confidence Bounds', *Scandinavian Journal of Statistics*, 28(1): 225–39.

Clark, C. R., Hemming, R., and Ulph, D. (1981). 'On Indices for the Measurement of Poverty', *Economic Journal*, 91(362): 515–26.

Clark, D. A. (2008). 'The Capability Approach: Its Development, Critiques and Recent Advances', in R. Ghosh, K. R. Gupta, and P. Maiti (eds), *Development Studies*. New Delhi: Atlantic Books and Distributors, ii.105–27.

Clark, D. A. (2012). *Adaptation, Poverty and Development: The Dynamics of Subjective Well-Being*. Basingstoke: Palgrave Macmillan.

Clark, D. A. and Hulme, D. (2010). 'Poverty, Time and Vagueness: Integrating the Core Poverty and Chronic Poverty Frameworks', *Cambridge Journal of Economics*, 34(2): 347–66.

Clarke, M. (2013). 'Good Works and God's Work: A Case Study of Churches and Community Development in Vanuatu', *Asia Pacific Viewpoint*, 54(3): 340–51.

Coady, D., Grosh, M., and Hoddinott, J. (2004). *Targeting of Transfers in Developing Countries: Review of Lessons and Experience*. Washington, DC: World Bank.

Cohen, A. (2010). 'The Multidimensional Poverty Assessment Tool: A New Framework for Measuring Rural Poverty', *Development in Practice*, 20(7): 887–97.

Cohen, A. and Saisana, M. (2014). 'Quantifying the Qualitative: Eliciting Expert Input to Develop the Multidimensional Poverty Assessment Tool', *Journal of Development Studies*, 50(1): 35–50.

Cohen, G. A. (1989). 'On the Currency of Egalitarian Justice', *Ethics*, 99(4): 906–44.

Cohen, L., Manion, L., and Morrison, K. (2000). *Research Methods in Education*, 5th edn. London: Routledge Falmer.

CONEVAL (2009). 'Programa Anual de Evaluación para el Ejercicio Fiscal 2009 de los Programas Federales de la Administración Pública Federal'. Consejo Nacional de Evaluación de la Política de Desarrollo Social (CONEVAL), <http://www.coneval.gob.mx/rw/resource/coneval/eval_mon/2607.pdf>.

CONEVAL (2010). *Methodology for Multidimensional Poverty Measurement in Mexico*. Consejo Nacional de Evaluación de la Política de Desarrollo Social (CONEVAL).

Coste, J., Bouee, S., Ecosse, E., Leplege, A., and Pouchot, J. (2005). 'Methodological Issues in Determining the Dimensionality of Composite Health Measures Using Principal Component Analysis: Case Illustration and Suggestions for Practice', *Quality of Life Research*, 14: 641–54.

Cowell, F. A. (1980). 'Generalized Entropy and the Measurement of Distributional Change', *European Economic Review*, 13(1): 147–59.

Cowell, F. A. (1989). 'Sampling Variance and Decomposable Inequality Measures', *Journal of Econometrics*, 42(1): 27–41.

Cowell, F. A. (2000). 'Measurement of Inequality', in A. Atkinson and F. Bourguignon (eds), *Handbook of Income Distribution*. Amsterdam: Elsevier, i.87–166 .

Cowell, F. A. and Kuga, K. (1981). 'Additivity and the Entropy Concept: An Axiomatic Approach to Inequality Measurement', *Journal of Economic Theory*, 25(1): 131–43.

Crocker, D. (2009). *Ethics of Global Development: Agency, Capability, and Deliberative Democracy*. Cambridge: Cambridge University Press.

Curran, C. E. (2002). *Catholic Social Teaching, 1891–Present: A Historical, Theological, and Ethical Analysis*. Washington, DC: Georgetown University Press.

D'Ambrosio, C., Deutsch, J., and Silber, J. (2011). 'Multidimensional Approaches to Poverty Measurement: An Empirical Analysis of Poverty in Belgium, France, Germany, Italy and Spain, Based on the European Panel', *Applied Economics*, 43(8): 951–61.

Dag Hammarskjöld Foundation (1976). *What Now? Another Development. The 1975 Report on Development and International Cooperation*. Motala, Sweden: Motala Grafiska.

Dalton, H. (1920). 'The Measurement of the Inequality of Incomes', *The Economic Journal*, 31(121): 348–61.

Datt, G. (2013). 'Making Every Dimension Count: Multidimensional Poverty without the "Dual Cut-Off"', *Monash Economics Working Papers* 32–13.

Davidson, R. and Duclos, J.-Y. (2000). 'Statistical Inference for Stochastic Dominance and for the Measurement of Poverty and Inequality', *Econometrica*, 68: 1435–64.

Davidson, R. and Duclos, J.-Y. (2012). 'Testing for Restricted Stochastic Dominance', *Econometric Reviews*, 32(1): 84–125.

Davidson, R. and Flachaire, E. (2007). 'Asymptotic and Bootstrap Inference for Inequality and Poverty Measures', *Journal of Econometrics*, 141(1): 141–66.

Davies, R. (1997). 'Beyond Wealth Ranking: The Democratic Definition and Measurement of Poverty'. Briefing note prepared for the ODI Workshop 'Indicators of Poverty: Operational Significance' in London, October.

Davies, R. and Smith, W. (1998). *The Basic Necessities Survey (BNS): The Experience of ActionAid Vietnam*. Hanoi: ActionAid.

Deaton, A. (1992). *Understanding Consumption*. Oxford: Oxford University Press.

Deaton, A. (1997). *The Analysis of Household Surveys: A Microeconometric Approach to Development Policy*. Baltimore, MD: John Hopkins University Press.

Deaton, A. and Grosh, M. (2000). 'Consumption', in M. Grosh and P. Glewwe (eds), *Designing Household Survey Questionnaires for Developing Countries: Lessons from 15 Years of the Living Standards Measurement Study*. Washington, DC: World Bank, iii.91–133.

Deaton, A. and Kozel, V. (2005). 'Data and Dogma: The Great Indian Poverty Debate', *World Bank Research Observer*, 20(2): 177–99.

Deaton, A. and Muellbauer, J. (1980). *Economics and Consumer Behavior*. Cambridge: Cambridge University Press.

Decancq, K. (2012). 'Elementary Multivariate Rearrangements and Stochastic Dominance on a Fréchet Class', *Journal of Economic Theory*, 147(4): 1450–9.

Decancq, K. and Lugo, M. A. (2012). 'Weights in Multidimensional Indices of Well-Being: An Overview', *Econometric Reviews*, 32(1): 7–34.

Decancq, K. and Neumann, D. (2014). 'Inclusive and Multidimensional Methodologies for Measuring Well-Being: An Empirical Comparison', in M. D. Adler and M. Fleurbaey (eds), *Oxford Handbook on Well-Being and Public Policy* (forthcoming).

Decancq, K., Fleurbaey, M., and Maniquet, F. (2014). 'Multidimensional Poverty Measurement with Individual Preferences', *Princeton University William S. Dietrich II Economic Theory Center Research Paper* 058.

Decancq, K., Van Ootegem, L., and Verhofstadt, E. (2011). 'What if We Voted on the Weights of a Multidimensional Well-Being Index? An Illustration with Flemish Data', *Fiscal Studies*, 34(3): 315–32.

Delors, J. (1971). *Les indicateurs sociaux*. Paris: Futuribles.

Deneulin, S. (2014). *Wellbeing, Justice and Development Ethics*, Human Development and Capability Debates Series. London: Routledge.

Deneulin, S. and Shahani, L. (2009). *An Introduction to the Human Development and Capability Approach: Freedom and Agency*. London: Earthscan.

Dercon, S. and Shapiro, J. (2007). 'Moving On, Staying Behind, Getting Lost: Lessons on Poverty Mobility from Longitudinal Data', in D. Narayan and P. Petesch (eds), *Moving out of Poverty*. Washington, DC: World Bank, i.77–126.

Desai, M. and Shah, A. (1988). 'An Econometric Approach to the Measurement of Poverty', *Oxford Economic Papers*, 40(3): 505–22.

Deutsch, J. and Silber, J. (2005). 'Measuring Multidimensional Poverty: An Empirical Comparison of Various Approaches', *Review of Income and Wealth*, 51(1): 145–74.

Deutsch, J., Guio, A. C., Pomati, M., and Silber, J. (2014). 'Material Deprivation in Europe: Which Expenditures are Curtailed First?', *Social Indicators Research* (April), DOI 10.1007/s11205-014-0618-6.

Deutsch, J., Lazar, A., and Silber, J. (2013). 'Becoming Poor and the Cutback in the Demand for Health Services in Israel', *Israel Journal of Health Policy Research*, 2(1): 49–58.

Deutsch, J. and Silber, J. (2008). 'The Order of Acquisition of Durable Goods and the Measurement of Multidimensional Poverty', in N. Kakwani and J. Silber (eds), *Quantitative Approaches to Multidimensional Poverty Measurement*. New York: Palgrave Macmillan, 226–43.

Deutsch, J., Silber, J., and Verme, P. (2012). 'On Social Exclusion in Macedonia: Measurement and Determinants', in C. Ruggeri Laderchi and S. Savastano (eds), *Poverty and Exclusion in the Western Balkans: New Directions in Measurement and Policy*. New York: Springer, ch. 7.

DHS Bangladesh (2007): National Institute of Population Research and Training (NIPORT), Mitra and Associates, and Macro International (2009). *Bangladesh Demographic and Health Survey 2007*. Dhaka, Bangladesh, and Calverton, MD: NIPORT, Mitra and Associates, and Macro International.

DHS Senegal (2005): Ndiaye, Salif and Ayad, Mohamed (2006). *Enquête Démographique et de Santé au Sénégal 2005*. Calverton, MD: Centre de Recherche pour le Développement Humain (Senegal) and ORC Macro.

Dickerson, A. and Popli, G. (2013). 'The Many Dimensions for Child Poverty: Evidence from the UK Millennium'. Paper presented at the V ECINEQ Meeting, Bari, Italy.

Di Tommaso, M. (2007). 'Children Capabilities: A Structural Equation Model for India', *Journal of Socio-Economics*, 36(3): 436–50.

Dobson, A. J. (2001). *An Introduction to Generalized Linear Models*. Boca Raton, FL: Chapman & Hall/CRC Press.

Dollar, D. and Kraay, A. (2004). 'Trade, Growth, and Poverty', *The Economic Journal*, 114(493): F22–F49.

Drèze, J. and Khera, R. (2010). 'The BPL Census and a Possible Alternative', *Economic and Political Weekly*, 45(9): 54–63.

Drèze, J. and Sen, A. (2002). *India: Development and Participation*. Oxford: Oxford University Press.

Drèze, J. and Sen, A. (2013). *Uncertain Glory: India and its Contradictions*. London: Allen Lane.

Dryzek, J. (2010). *Foundations and Frontiers of Deliberative Governance*. Oxford: Oxford University Press.

Dubois, D. and Prade, H. (1980). *Fuzzy Sets and Systems: Theory and Applications*. New York: Academic Press.

Dubois, W. E. B. (1899, 1967). *The Philadelphia Negro*. Philadelphia: University of Philadelphia Press.

Duclos, J.-Y. and Araar, A. (2006). *Poverty and Equity: Measurement, Policy and Estimation with DAD*. Berlin and Ottawa: Springer.

Duclos, J. Y. and Échevin, D. (2011). 'Health and Income: A Robust Comparison of Canada and the US', *Journal of Health Economics*, 30(2): 293–302.

Duclos, J. Y., Sahn, D. E., and Younger, S. D. (2006a). 'Robust Multidimensional Poverty Comparisons', *The Economic Journal*, 116(514): 943–68.

Duclos, J. Y., Sahn, D. E., and Younger, S. D. (2006b). 'Robust Multidimensional Spatial Poverty Comparisons in Ghana, Madagascar, and Uganda', *World Bank Economic Review*, 20(1): 91–113.

Duclos, J. Y., Sahn, D. E., and Younger, S. D. (2011). 'Partial Multidimensional Inequality Orderings', *Journal of Public Economics*, 95(3–4): 225–38.

Duclos, J.-Y., Tiberti, L., and Araar, A. (2013). 'Multidimensional Poverty Targeting', *Cahiers de recherche* 1339, CIRPEE.

Dworkin, R. (1986). *Law's Empire*. Cambridge, MA: Harvard University Press.

Dworkin, R. (2000). *Equality and Capability*. Cambridge. MA: Harvard University Press.

Efron, B. (1979). 'Bootstrap Methods: Another Look at the Jackknife', *The Annals of Statistics*, 7(1): 1–26.

Efron, B. and Tibshirani, R. (1993). *An Introduction to the Bootstrap*. Boca Raton, FL: Chapman & Hall/CRC Press.

Elbers, C., Fujii, T., Lanjouw, P., Özler, B, and Yin, W. (2007). 'Poverty Alleviation through Geographic Targeting: How Much Does Disaggregation Help?', *Journal of Development Economics*, 83(1): 198–213.

Elbers, C., Lanjouw, J. O., and Lanjouw, P. (2002). 'Micro-level Estimation of Poverty and Inequality', *Econometrica*, 71(1): 355–64.

Erikson, R. (1993). 'Descriptions of Inequality: The Swedish Approach to Welfare Research', in M. Nussbaum and A. K. Sen (eds), *The Quality of Life*. Oxford: Oxford University Press, 67–83.

Eurobarometer (2007). *Special Eurobarometer 279/Wave 67.1: Poverty and Exclusion: Report*. European Commission.

Eurostat (2002). *Statistiques Sociales Européennes : Deuxième rapport sur le revenu, la pauvreté et l'exclusion sociale*. Luxembourg: Office des publications officielles des Communautés européennes.

Fattore, M., Maggino, F., and Colombo, E. (2012). 'From Composite Indicators to Partial Orders: Evaluating Socio-Economic Phenomena through Ordinal Data', in F. Maggino and G. Nuvolati (eds), *Quality of Life in Italy*, Social Indicators Research Series 48. Dordrecht: Springer, 41–68.

Fay, M., Leipziger, D., Wodon, Q., and Yepes, T. (2005). 'Achieving Child-Health-Related Millennium Development Goals: The Role of Infrastructure', *World Development*, 33(8): 1267–84.

Feres, J. C. and Mancero, X. (2001). 'El método de las necesidades básicas insatisfechas (NBI) y sus aplicaciones a América Latina', *Series Estudios Estadísticos y Prospectivos* 4. CEPAL, Naciones Unidas, Santiago de Chile.

Ferreira, F. H. G. (2011). 'Poverty Is Multidimensional. But What Are We Going To Do About It?', *Journal of Economic Inequality*, 9(3): 493–5.

Ferreira, F. H. G. and Lugo, M. A. (2013). 'Multidimensional Poverty Analysis: Looking for a Middle Ground', *World Bank Research Observer*, 28(2): 220–35.

Fields, G. S. (2001). *Distribution and Development: A New Look at the Developing World*. New York: Russell Sage Foundation and Cambridge, MA: MIT Press.

Filmer, D. and Pritchett, L. H. (1999). 'The Effect of Household Wealth on Educational Attainment: Evidence From 35 Countries', *Population and Development Review*, 25(1): 85–120.

Filmer, D. and Pritchett, L. H. (2001). 'Estimating Wealth Effects without Expenditure Data—or Tears: An Application to Educational Enrolments in States of India', *Demography*, 38(1): 115–32.

Finnis, J. (1997). 'Commensuration and Public Reason', in R. Chang (ed.), *Incommensurability, Incomparability, and Practical Reasoning*. Cambridge, MA: Harvard University Press, 215–33.

Finnis, J. (1998). *Aquinas: Moral, Political, and Legal Theory*. Oxford: Oxford University Press.

Firth, D. (1991). 'Generalized Linear Models', in D. V. Hinkley, N. Reid, and E. J. Snell (eds), *Statistical Theory and Modeling*. Boca Raton, FL: Chapman & Hall.

Fisher, R. A. (1940). 'The Precision of Discriminant Functions', *Annals of Eugenics*, 10: 422–9.

Fiszbein, A. and Schady, N. (2009). 'Conditional Cash Transfer: Reducing Present and Future Poverty', *World Bank Policy Research Report* 47603.

Fleurbaey, M. (2002). 'Development, Capabilities, and Freedom', *Studies in Comparative International Development*, 37(2): 71–7.

Fleurbaey, M. (2006a). 'Social Welfare, Priority to the Worst-Off and the Dimensions of Individual Well-Being', in F. Farina and E. Savaglio (eds), *Inequality and Economic Integration*. London: Routledge, 225–68.

Fleurbaey, M. (2006b). 'Capabilities, Functionings and Refined Functionings', *Journal of Human Development*, 7(3): 299–310.

Fleurbaey, M. and Blanchet, D. (2013). *Beyond GDP: Measuring Welfare and Assessing Sustainability*. Oxford: Oxford University Press.

Fleurbaey, M. and Maniquet, F. O. (2011). *A Theory of Fairness and Social Welfare*. Cambridge: Cambridge University Press.

Fleurbaey, M. and Maniquet, F. O. (2012). *Equality of Opportunity: The Economics of Responsibility*. Singapore: World Scientific Publishing.

Flórez, C. E., Sánchez, L. M., and Espinosa, F. (2008). *Diseño del Índice SISBEN en su tercera versión (Resumen Ejecutivo)*. Colombia: Departamento Nacional de Planeación.

Flórez, C. E., Sánchez, L. M., Espinosa, F., and Angulo, R. (2011). *The SISBEN III Index*. Paper presented at the HDCA Conference 2011, The Hague, 5–8 September.

Foster, J. E. (1985) 'Inequality Measurement', in H. Peyton Young (ed.), *Fair Allocation*. Providence, RI: American Mathematical Society, 31–68.

Foster, J. E. (2006). 'Poverty Indices', in A. de Janvry and R. Kanbur (eds), *Poverty, Inequality and Development: Essays in Honor to Erik Thorbecke*. New York: Springer, 41–66.

Foster, J. E. (2009). 'A Class of Chronic Poverty Measures', in T. Addison, D. Hulme, and R. Kanbur (eds), *Poverty Dynamics: Interdisciplinary Perspectives*. Oxford: Oxford University Press, 59–76.

Foster, J. E. (2010). 'Freedom, Opportunity and Wellbeing', in K. Arrow, A. Sen, and K. Suzumura (eds), *Handbook of Social Choice and Welfare*. Amsterdam: Elsevier, ii.687–728.

Foster, J. E. and Santos, M. E. (2013). 'Measuring Chronic Poverty', in G. Betti and A. Lemmi (eds), *Poverty and Social Exclusion: New Methods of Analysis*. London: Routledge, 143–65.

Foster, J. E. and Shorrocks, A. F. (1988a). 'Poverty Orderings and Welfare Dominance', *Social Choice and Welfare*, 5(2–3): 179–98.

Foster, J. E. and Shorrocks, A. F. (1988b). 'Poverty Orderings', *Econometrica*, 56(1): 173–7.

Foster, J. E. and Shorrocks, A. F. (1991). 'Subgroup Consistent Poverty Indices', *Econometrica*, 59(3): 687–709.

Foster, J. E. and Sen, A. K. (1997). 'On Economic Inequality after a Quarter Century', an annex to A. Sen, *On Economic Inequality*. Oxford: Oxford University Press, 107–220.

Foster, J. E. and Székely, M. (2008). 'Is Economic Growth Good for the Poor? Tracking Low Incomes Using General Means', *International Economic Review*, 49(4): 1143–72.

Foster, J. E., Seth, S., Lokshin, M., and Sajaia, Z. (2013). *A Unified Approach to Measuring Poverty and Inequality: Theory and Practice*. Washington, DC: World Bank.

Foster, J. E., Greer, J., and Thorbecke, E. (1984). 'A Class of Decomposable Poverty Measures', *Econometrica*, 52(3): 761–6.

Foster, J. E., Greer, J., and Thorbecke, E. (2010). 'The Foster–Greer–Thorbecke (FGT) Poverty Measures: 25 Years Later', *Journal of Economic Inequality*, 8(4): 491–524.

Foster, J. E., Horowitz, A. W., and Méndez, F. (2012). 'An Axiomatic Approach to the Measurement of Corruption: Theory and Applications', *World Bank Economic Review*, 26(2): 217–35.

Foster J. E., McGillivray, M., and Seth, S. (2009). 'Rank Robustness of Composite Indices', *OPHI Working Paper* 26, University of Oxford.

Foster, J. E., McGillivray, M., and Seth, S. (2012). 'Rank Robustness of Composite Indices: Dominance and Ambiguity', *OPHI Working Paper* 26b, University of Oxford.

Foster, J. E., McGillivray, M., and Seth, S. (2013). 'Composite Indices: Rank Robustness, Statistical Association and Redundancy', *Econometric Reviews*, 32(1): 35–56.

Fox, J. (2008). *Applied Regression Analysis and Generalized Linear Models*. Thousand Oaks, CA: Sage Publications.

Fukuda-Parr, S. and Kumar, A. K. S. (2003). *Readings in Human Development: Concepts, Measures, and Policies for a Development Paradigm*. Oxford: Oxford University Press.

Fusco, A., Guio, A.-C., and Marlier, E. (2011). 'Income Poverty and Material Deprivation in European Countries', *CEPS/INSTEAD Working Paper* 2011-04.

Gajdos, T. and Weymark, J. A. (2005). 'Multidimensional Generalized Gini Indices', *Economic Theory*, 26(3): 471–96.

Galtung, J. (1980). 'The Basic Needs Approach', in K. Lederer, D. Antal, and J. Galtung (eds), *Human Needs: A Contribution to the Current Debate*. Cambridge: Oelgeschlager, Gunn & Hain, 55–125.

Galtung, J. (1994). *Human Rights in Another Key*. Cambridge: Polity Press.

Garcia-Diaz, R. (2013). 'Poverty Orderings with Asymmetric Attributes', *The B. E. Journal of Theoretical Economics*, 13(1): 347–61.

Gardiner, K. and Evans, M. (2011). 'Exploring Poverty Gaps among Children in the UK', *Department for Work and Pensions Working Paper* 103.

Garnett, J. C. (1919). 'General Ability, Cleverness and Purpose', *British Journal of Psychology, 1904–1920*, 9(3–4): 345–66.

Gekker, R. (2001). 'On the Axiomatic Approach to Freedom as Opportunity: A General Characterization Result', *Mathematical Social Sciences*, 42(2): 169–77.

Gifi, A. (1990). *Nonlinear Multivariate Analysis*. New York: John Wiley.

Gillie, A. (1996). 'The Origin of the Poverty Line', *Economic History Review*, 49(4): 715–30.

GOI (2009). *Report of the Expert Group to Review the Methodology for Estimation of Poverty*. New Delhi: Government of India (GOI), Planning Commission.

Gönner, C., Cahyat, A., Haug, M., and Limberg, G. (2007). *Towards Wellbeing: Monitoring Poverty in Kutai Barat, Indonesia*. Bogor, Indonesia: Center for International Forestry Research (CIFOR).

Gordon, D. and Pantazis, C. (1997). *Breadline Britain in the 1990s*. Aldershot: Ashgate.

Gordon, D., Levitas, R., Pantazis, C., Patsios, D., Payne, S., and Townsend, P. (2000). *Poverty and Social Exclusion in Britain*. York: Joseph Rowntree Foundation.

Gordon, D., Pantazis, C., and Townsend, P. (2001). *Child Rights and Child Poverty in Developing Countries*. Bristol: Centre of International Poverty Research, University of Bristol.

Gordon, D., Nandy, S., Pantazis, C., Pemberton, S., and Townsend, P. (2003). *Child Poverty in the Developing World*. Bristol: Policy Press.

Gourieroux, C., Monfort, A., and Trognon, A. (1984). 'Pseudo Maximum Likelihood Methods: Theory', *Econometrica*, 52(3): 681–700.

Gräb, J. and Grimm, M. (2011). 'Robust Multiperiod Poverty Comparisons'. *Journal of Statistics: Advances in Theory and Applications*, 6(1–2): 19–54.

Gradín, C. (2013). 'Race, Poverty and Deprivation in South Africa', *Journal of African Economies*, 22(2): 187–238.

Gradín, C., del Rio, C., and Canto, O. (2012). 'Measuring Poverty Accounting for Time', *Review of Income and Wealth*, 58(2): 330–54

Gravel, N. (1994). 'Can a Ranking of Opportunity Sets Attach an Intrinsic Importance to Freedom of Choice', *American Economic Review*, 84(2): 454–8.

Gravel, N. (1998). 'Ranking Opportunity Sets on the Basis of their Freedom of Choice and their Ability to Satisfy Preferences: A Difficulty', *Social Choice and Welfare*, 15(3): 371–82.

Gravel, N. and Mukhopadhyay, A. (2010). 'Is India Better Off Today Than 15 Years Ago? A Robust Multidimensional Answer', *Journal of Economic Inequality*, 8(2): 173–95.

Greenacre, M. J. (1984). *Theory and Applications of Correspondence Analysis*. New York: Academic Press.

Greenacre, M. J. and Blasius, J. (eds) (2006). *Multiple Correspondence Analysis and Related Methods*. London: Chapman & Hall.

Griffin, J. (1986). *Well-Being: Its Meaning, Measurement, and Moral Importance*. Oxford: Clarendon Press.

Griffin, J. (1996). *Value Judgement: Improving our Ethical Beliefs*. Oxford: Clarendon Press.

Grosh, M. and Glewwe, P. (2000). *Designing Household Survey Questionnaires for Developing Countries: Lessons from 15 Years of the Living Standard Measurement Study*, i. Washington, DC: World Bank.

Grusky, D. B. and Kanbur, R. (eds) (2006). *Poverty and Inequality*. Stanford, CA: Stanford University Press.

Guio, A.-C. (2005). 'Material Deprivation in the EU'. *Statistics in Focus, Population and Social Conditions, Living Conditions and Welfare*, 21/2005.

Guio, A.-C. (2009). 'What Can Be Learned from Deprivation Indicators in Europe?' Paper presented at the Indicator Subgroup of the Social Protection Committee, 10 February.

Guio, A.-C., Fusco, A., and Marlier, E. (2009). 'A European Union Approach to Material Deprivation Using EU-SILC and Eurobarometer Data', *CEPS/INSTEAD, IRISS Working Paper* 2009-19.

Guio, A.-C., Gordon, D., and Marlier, E. (2012). 'Measuring Material Deprivation in the EU: Indicators for the Whole Population and Child-Specific Indicators'. Mimeo.

Guio, A.-C. and Maquet, I. E. (2006). '"Material Deprivation and Poor Housing": What Can Be Learned from the EU–SILC 2004 Data? How can EU–SILC Be Improved in this Matter?'. Draft paper for the conference 'Comparative EU Statistics on Income and Living Conditions: Issues and Challenges', Helsinki, November.

Gunewardena, D. (2004). *Poverty Measurement: Meanings, Methods and Requirements*. Colombo: Centre for Poverty Analysis.

Guttman, L. (1941). 'The Quantification of a Class of Attributes: A Theory and Method of Scale Construction', in P. Horst (ed.), *The Prediction of Personal Adjustment*. New York: Social Science Research Council, 321–48.

Guttman, L. (1977). 'What Is Not What in Statistics', *The Statistician*, 26(2): 81–107.

Gwatkin, D. R., Rutstein, S., Johnson, K., Pande, R., and Wagstaff, A. (2000). *Socio-Economic Differences in Health, Nutrition, and Population within Developing Countries*. HNP/Poverty Thematic Group. Washington, DC: World Bank.

Hagenaars, A., de Vos, K., and Zaidi, M. A. (1994). *Poverty Statistics in the Late 1980s: Research Based on Micro-Data*. Luxembourg: Office for Official Publications of the European Communities.

Hagerty, M. R., Cummins, R. A., Ferris, A. L., Land, K., Michalos, A. C., Peterson, M., Sharpe, A., Sirgy, J., and Vogel, J. (2001). 'Quality of Life Indexes for National Policy: Review and Agenda for Research', *Social Indicators Research*, 55(1): 1–96.

Halleröd, B. (1994). 'A New Approach to Direct Measurement of Consensual Poverty', *SPRC Discussion Paper* 50.

Halleröd, B. (1995). 'The Truly Poor: Direct and Indirect Consensual Measurement of Poverty in Sweden', *Journal of European Social Policy*, 5(2): 111–29.

Halleröd, B., Larsson, D., Gordon, D., and Ritakallio, V.-M. (2006). 'Relative Deprivation: A Comparative Analysis of Britain, Finland and Sweden', *Journal of European Social Policy*, 16: 328–45.

Hametner, M., Dimitrova, A., Endl, A., Fliedner, J., Schwab, S., Umpfenback, K., and Timeus Cerezo, K. (eds) (2013). 'Poverty and Social Exclusion', in I. Savova (ed.-in-chief), *Smarter, Greener, More Inclusive? Indicators to Support the Europe 2020 Strategy*. Luxembourg: Eurostat, European Commission, ch. 5.

Hamilton, L. (2003). *The Political Philosophy of Needs*. Cambridge: Cambridge University Press.

Hansen, J. P. (2003). 'CAN'T MISS—Conquer any Number Task by Making Important Statistics Simple. Part 1: Types of Variables, Mean, Median, Variance and Standard Deviation', *Journal for Healthcare Quality*, 25(4): 19–24.

Haughton, J. H. and Khandker, S. R. (2009). *Handbook on Poverty and Inequality*. Washington, DC: World Bank.

Hentschel, J. and Lanjouw, P. (2000). 'Household Welfare Measurement and the Pricing of Basic Services', *Journal of International Development*, 12(1): 13–27.

Herrera, A. O., Scolnik, H. D., Chichilnisky, G., Gallopin, G. C., et al. (1976). *Catastrophe or New Society? A Latin America World Model*, IDRC–064e. Ottawa: IDRC.

Hicks, N. and Streeten, P. (1979). 'Indicators of Development: The Search for a Basic Needs Yardstick', *World Development*, 7(6): 567–80.

Hidalgo-Capitán, A., Guillén, A., and Deleg, N. (2014). *Sumak Kawsay Yuyay: Antología del pensamiento indigenista ecuatoriano sobre Sumak Kawsay*, CIM-FIUCUHU-PYDLOS, Huelva y Cuenca.

High-Level Panel (2013). *A New Global Partnership: Eradicate Poverty and Transform Economics through Sustainable Development: The Report of the High-Level Panel of Eminent Persons on the Post-2015 Development Agenda*. New York: United Nations Publications.

Hirschfeld, H. O. (1935). 'A Connection between Correlation and Contingency', *Mathematical Proceedings of the Cambridge Philosophical Society*, 31(4): 520–4.

Hirway, I. (2003). 'Identification of BPL Households for Poverty Alleviation Programmes', *Economic and Political Weekly*, 38(45): 4803–38.

Hollen Lees, L. (1998). *The Solidarities of Strangers: The English Poor Laws and the People, 1700–1948.* Cambridge: Cambridge University Press.

Hotelling, H. (1933). 'Analysis of a Complex of Statistical Variables into Principal Components', *Journal of Educational Psychology*, 24(6): 417–41.

Hoy, M. and Zheng, B. (2011). 'Measuring Lifetime Poverty', *Journal of Economic Theory*, 146(6): 2544–62.

Høyland, B., Moene, K., and Willumsen, F. (2012). 'The Tyranny of International Index Rankings', *Journal of Development Economics*, 97(1): 1–14.

Hugo, V. (2007). *Hugo's Works: Les Misérables*, iii. Rockville: Wildside Press.

Hulme, D. and Shepherd, A. (2003). 'Conceptualizing Chronic Poverty', *World Development,* 31(3): 403–23.

Hulme, D., Moore, K., and Shepherd, A. (2001). 'Chronic Poverty: Meanings and Analytical Frameworks', *CPRC Working Paper* 2.

IISD (2009). *BellagioSTAMP: SusTainability Assessment and Measurement Principles.* International Institute for Sustainable Development (IISD), OECD.

ILO (1976). *Meeting Basic Needs: Strategies for Eradicating Mass Poverty and Unemployment: Conclusions of the World Employment Conference.* Geneva: International Labour Organization.

INDEC (1984). *La Pobreza en la Argentina, Indicadores de Necesidades Básicas Insatisfechas a partir de los datos del censo nacional de Población y Vivienda 1980.* Buenos Aires: Instituto Nacional de Estadísticas y Censos (INDEC), Presidencia de la Nación, Secretaría de planificación.

Jain, S. K. (2004). 'Identification of the Poor: Flaws in Government Surveys', *Economic and Political Weekly*, 39(46): 4981–4.

Jalan, J. and Murgai, R. (2007). *An Effective 'Targeting Shortcut'? An Assessment of the 2002 Below-Poverty Line Census Method.* Mimeo, World Bank.

Jalan, J. and Ravallion, M. (1998). 'Transient Poverty in Post-Reform Rural China', *Journal of Comparative Economics*, 26: 338–57.

Jamieson, S. (2004). 'Likert Scales: How to (Ab)use Them', *Medical Education*, 38(12): 1217–18.

Janvry, A. de and Sadoulet, E. (2010). 'Agricultural Growth and Poverty Reduction: Additional Evidence', *The World Bank Research Observer*, 25(1): 1–20.

Japan Commission on Measuring Well-Being (JCMW) (2011). *Measuring National Well-Being: Proposed Well-Being Indicators*, The Commission on Measuring Well-Being, Japan.

Jayaraj, D. and Subramanian, S. (2009). 'A Chakravarty–D'Ambrosio View of Multidimensional Deprivation: Some Estimates for India', *Economic and Political Weekly*, 45(6): 53–65.

Jenkins, S. P. and Lambert, P. J. (1998). 'Three "I"s of Poverty Curves and Poverty Dominance: Tips for Poverty Analysis', *Research on Economic Inequality*, 8: 39–56.

Jenkins, S. P. and Micklewright, J. (eds) (2007). *Inequality and Poverty Re-examined.* Oxford: Oxford University Press.

Joe, H. (1990). 'Multivariate Concordance', *Journal of Multivariate Analysis*, 35(1): 12–30.

Johansson, S. (1973). 'The Level of Living Survey: A Presentation', *Acta Sociologica*, 16(3): 211–19.

Jolliffe, I. T. (2002). *Principal Component Analysis*, 2nd edn. New York: Springer.

Joreskog, K. G. (1970). 'A General Method for Analysis of Covariance Structures', *Biometrika*, 57(2): 239–51.

Joreskog, K. G. and Moustaki, I. (2001). 'Factor Analysis or Ordinal Variables: A Comparison of Three Approaches', *Multivariate Behavioral Research*, 36(3): 347–87.

Joreskog, K. G. and Sorbom, D. (1979). *Advances in Factor Analysis and Structural Equation Models*. Cambridge, MA: Abt Books.

Joreskog, K. G. and Sorbom, D. (1999). *LISREL 8 User's Reference Guide*. Lincolnwood, IL: Scientific Software International.

Kahneman, D. and Krueger, A. (2006). 'Developments in the Measurement of Subjective Well-Being', *Journal of Economic Perspectives*, 20(1): 3–24.

Kakwani, N. and Silber, J. (eds) (2008). *Quantitative Approaches to Multidimensional Poverty Measurement*. New York: Palgrave Macmillan.

Kannai, Y. (1980). 'The ALEP Definition of Complementarity and Least Concave Utility Functions', *Journal of Economic Theory*, 22(1): 115–17.

Kast, M. and Molina, S. (1975). *Mapa de la extrema pobreza*. Santiago: Odeplan, Escuela de Economía Pontificia Universidad Católica de Chile.

Kaztman, R. (1989). 'La Heterogeneidad de la Pobreza. El Caso de Montevideo', *Revista de la Cepal*, 37: 141–52.

Kaztman, R. (1996). 'Virtudes y Limitaciones de los Mapas Censales de Carencias Críticas', *Revista de la Cepal*, 58: 23–32.

Kearns, A., Gibb, K., and Mackay, D. (2000). 'Area Deprivation in Scotland: A New Assessment', *Urban Studies*, 37(9): 1535–60.

Kendall, M. G. (1970). *Rank Correlation Methods*. London: Griffin.

Kendall, M. G. and Gibbons, J. D. (1990). *Rank Correlation Method*. London: Edward Arnold.

Khan, S. N. and Qutub, S. (2010). 'The Benazir Income Support Programme and the Zakat Programme: A Political Economy Analysis of Gender'. London: Overseas Development Institute (ODI).

Klasen, S. (2000). 'Measuring Poverty and Deprivation in South Africa', *Review of Income and Wealth*, 46(1): 33–58.

Klasen, S. (2008). 'Economic Growth and Poverty Reduction: Measurement Issues Using Income and Non-income Indicators', *World Development*, 36(3): 420–45.

Klemisch-Ahlert, M. (1993). 'Freedom of Choice: A Comparison of Different Rankings of Opportunity Sets', *Social Choice and Welfare*, 10(3): 189–207.

Klugman, J. (2002). *A Sourcebook for Poverty Reduction Strategies*. Washington, DC: World Bank.

Kolm, S. C. (1976a). 'Unequal Inequalities. I', *Journal of Economic Theory*, 12(3): 416–42.

Kolm, S. C. (1976b). 'Unequal Inequalities. II', *Journal of Economic Theory*, 13(1): 82–111.

Kolm, S. C. (1977). 'Multidimensional Egalitarianisms', *Quarterly Journal of Economics*, 91(1): 1–13.

Krishnakumar, J. and Ballon, P. (2008). 'Estimating Basic Capabilities: A Structural Equation Model Applied to Bolivia', *World Development*, 36(6): 992–1010.

Krishnakumar, J. and Nagar, A. (2008). 'On Exact Statistical Properties of Multidimensional Indices Based on Principal Components, Factor Analysis, MIMIC and Structural Equation Models', *Social Indicators Research*, 86(3): 481–96.

Kuklys, W. (2005). *Amartya Sen's Capability Approach: Theoretical Insights and Empirical Applications*. Berlin: Springer.

Kullback, S. and Leibler, R. A. (1951). 'On Information and Sufficiency', *Annals of Mathematical Statistics*, 22(1): 79–86.

Labar, K. and Bresson, F. (2011). 'A Multidimensional Analysis of Poverty in China from 1991 to 2006', *China Economic Review*, 22(4): 646–68.

Layard, R. (2005). *Happiness: Lessons from a New Science*. Harmondsworth: Penguin.

Land, K. C., Ferriss, A., Michalos, A. C., and Sirgy, M. J. (2012). 'Prologue: Social Indicators and Quality of Life', in K. C. Land, A. C. Michalos, and M. J. Sirgy (eds), *Handbook of Social Indicators and Quality of Life Research*. New York: Springer, 1–22.

Land, K. C., Michalos, A. C., and Sirgy, M. J. (2012). *Handbook of Social Indicators and Quality of Life Research*. New York: Springer.

Lanjouw, P. and Ravallion, M. (1995). 'Poverty and Household Size', *The Economic Journal*, 105(433): 1415–34.

Larochelle, C., Alwang, J., and Taruvinga, N. (2014). 'Inter-temporal Changes in Well-Being during Conditions of Hyperinflation: Evidence from Zimbabwe', *Journal of African Economics*, 23(2): 225–56.

Lasso de la Vega, M. C. (2010). 'Counting Poverty Orderings and Deprivation Curves', in J. A. Bishop (ed.), *Studies in Applied Welfare Analysis: Papers from the Third ECINEQ Meeting. Research on Economic Inequality* 18. Bingley: Emerald Group Publishing, 153–72 (ch. 7).

Lawley, D. N. and Maxwell, A. E. (1971). *Factor Analysis as a Statistical Method*, 2nd edn. London: Butterworth.

Layte, R., Maître, B., Nolan, B., Watson, D., Williams, J., and Casey, B. (2000). 'Monitoring Poverty Trends: Results from the 1998 Living in Ireland Survey', *ESRI Working Paper* 132.

Layte, R., Maître, B., Nolan, B., and Whelan, C. (2001). 'Persistent and Consistent Poverty in the 1994 and 1995 Waves of the European Community Household Panel Survey', *Review of Income and Wealth*, 47(4): 427–49.

League of Arab States, UNDP, PAPFAM (2009). 'Poverty and Deprivation in Arab States: A Comparative Study of Seven Countries Based on PAPFAM Surveys 2001–2004'.

Leavy, J. and Howard, J., et al. (2013). *What Matters Most? Evidence from 84 Participatory Studies with Those Living with Extreme Poverty and Marginalisation*. Participate, Brighton: IDS.

Lelli, S. (2001). 'Factor Analysis vs. Fuzzy Sets Theory: Assessing the Influence of Different Techniques on Sen's Functioning Approach', *Center of Economic Studies Discussion Paper*, 01.21.

Lemmi, A. and Betti, G. (2006). *Fuzzy Set Approach to Multidimensional Poverty Measurement*. New York: Springer.

Lenoir, R. (1974). *Les Exclus*. Paris: Seuil.

Lewis, C. I. (1918). *A Survey of Symbolic Logic*. Berkeley: University of California Press.

Likert, R. (1932). 'A Technique for the Measurement of Attitudes', *Archives of Psychology*, 140: 1–55.

Lin, W. and Wong, C. (2012). 'Are Beijing's Equalization Policies Reaching the Poor? An Analysis of Direct Subsidies under the "Three Rurals" (Sannong)', *China Journal*, 67: 23–45.

Lord, F. M. (1953). 'On the Statistical Treatment of Football Numbers', *American Psychologist*, 8: 750–1.

Luce, R. D. (1956). 'Semiorders and a Theory of Utility Discrimination', *Econometrica*, 24: 178–91.

Luce, R. D. (1959). 'On the Possible Psychophysical Laws', *Psychological Review*, 66(2): 81–95.

Maasoumi, E. (1986). 'The Measurement and Decomposition of Multi-Dimensional Inequality', *Econometrica*, 54(4): 991–7.

Maasoumi, E. (1993). 'A Compendium to Information Theory in Economics and Econometrics', *Econometric Reviews*, 12(2): 137–81.

Maasoumi, E. and Lugo, M. A. (2008). 'The Information Basis of Multivariate Poverty Assessments', in N. Kakwani and J. Silber. (eds), *Quantitative Approaches to Multidimensional Poverty Measurement*. New York: Palgrave Macmillan, 1–29.

Mack, J. and Lansley, S. (1985). *Poor Britain*. London: Allen and Unwin.

Maggino, F. (2009). 'Towards More Participative Methods in the Construction of Social Indicators: Survey Techniques Aimed at Determining Importance Weights'. Paper presented at 62nd Annual Conference of the World Association for Public Opinion Research, Lausanne, 11–13 September.

Maggino, F. and Zumbo, B. D. (2012). 'Measuring the Quality of Life and the Construction of Social Indicators', in K. C. Land, A. C. Michalos, and M. J. Sirgy (eds), *Handbook of Social Indicators and Quality of Life Research*. New York: Springer, 201–38.

Maître, B., Nolan, B., and Whelan, C. T. (2013). 'A Critical Evaluation of the EU 2020 Poverty and Social Exclusion Target: An Analysis of EU-SILC 2009', GINI Discussion Paper 79, August, <http://www.uva-aias.net/uploaded_files/publications/79-4-1-2.pdf>.

Makdissi, P., Sylla, D., and Yazbeck, M. (2013). 'Decomposing Health Achievement and Socioeconomic Health Inequalities in Presence of Multiple Categorical Information', *Economic Modelling*, 35: 964–8.

Makdissi, P. and Wodon, Q. (2004). 'Fuzzy Targeting Indices and Ordering', *Bulletin of Economic Research*, 56(1): 41–51.

Marcus-Roberts, H. and Roberts, F. S. (1987). 'Meaningless Statistics', *Journal of Educational Statistics*, 12(4): 383–94.

Mardia, K. V., Kent, J. T., and Bibby, J. M. (1979). *Multivariate Analysis: Probability and Mathematical Statistics*. New York: Academic Press.

Marshall, A. W. and Olkin, I. (1979). *Theory of Majorization and its Applications*. New York: Academic Press.

Mather, M. (2007). 'Demographic Data: Censuses, Registers, Surveys', in G. Ritzer (ed.), *Blackwell Encyclopedia of Sociology*, Blackwell Reference Online, accessed 22 August 2013.

Mayer, S. E. and Jencks, C. (1989). 'Poverty and the Distribution of Material Hardship', *Journal of Human Resources*, 24(1): 88–113.

McCullagh, P. and Nelder, J. A. (1989). *Generalized Linear Models*, 2nd edn. Boca Raton, FL: Chapman & Hall/CRC Press.

McGillivray, M. (1991). 'The Human Development Index: Yet Another Redundant Composite Development Indicator?', *World Development*, 19(10): 1461–8.

McGillivray, M. and White, H. (1993). 'Measuring Development? The UNDP's Human Development Index', *Journal of International Development*, 5(2): 1183–92.

McKay, A. and Lawson, D. (2003). 'Assessing the Extent and Nature of Chronic Poverty in Low Income Countries: Issues and Evidence', *World Development*, 31(3): 425–39.

McKenzie, D. (2005). 'Measuring Inequality with Asset Indicators', *Journal of Population Economics*, 18(2): 229–60.

Metz, T. and Gaie, J. B. R. (2010). 'The African Ethic of *Ubuntu/Botho*: Implications for Research on Morality', *Journal of Moral Education*, 39(3): 273–90.

Michalos, A. C., Smale, B., Labonté, R., Muharjarine, N., Scott, K., Moore, K., Swystun, L., Holden, B., Bernardin, H., Dunning, B., Graham, P., Guhn, M., Gadermann, A. M., Zumbo, B. D., Morgan, A., Brooker, A.-S., and Hyman, I. (2011). 'The Canadian Index of Wellbeing', Technical Report 1.0. Waterloo, ON: Canadian Index of Wellbeing and University of Waterloo.

Mills, A. M. and Zandvakili, S. (1997). 'Statistical Inference via Bootstrapping for Measures of Inequality', *Journal of Applied Econometrics*, 12(2): 133–50.

Minujin, A. and Nandy, S. (2012). *Global Child Poverty: Concepts, Policy and Action*. Bristol: Policy Press.

Minujin, A. and Shailen, N. (eds) (2012). *Global Child Poverty and Well-Being: Measurement, Concepts, Policy and Action*. Bristol: Policy Press.

Mishra, A. and Ray, R. (2013). 'Multi-Dimensional Deprivation in India During and After the Reforms: Do the Household Expenditure and the Family Health Surveys Present Consistent Evidence?', *Social Indicators Research*, 110(2): 791–818.

Mitra, S. (2013). 'Towards a Multidimensional Measure of Governance', *Social Indicators Research*, 112(2): 477–96.

Mitra, S., Posarac, A., and Vick, B. (2013). 'Disability and Poverty in Developing Countries: A Multidimensional Study', *World Development*, 41: 1–18.

Mitra, S., Jones, K., Vick, B., et al. (2013). 'Implementing a Multidimensional Poverty Measure Using Mixed Methods and a Participatory Framework', *Social Indicators Research*, 110(3): 1061–81.

Morales, E. (1988). 'Canasta Basica de alimentos: Gran Buenos Aires', *Documento de Trabajo* 3. INDEC/IPA.

Morduch, J. and Sinclair, T. (1998). *Rethinking Inequality Decomposition, with Evidence from Rural China*. Mimeo.

Morris, M. D. (1978). 'A Physical Quality of Life Index', *Urban Ecology*, 3(3): 225–40.

Muffels, R., Berghman, J., and Dirven, H.-J. (1992). 'A Multi-Method Approach to Monitor the Evolution of Poverty', *Journal of European Social Policy* 2(3): 193–213.

Muffels, R. and Vriens, M. (1991). 'The Elaboration of a Deprivation Scale and the Definition of a Subjective Deprivation Poverty Line'. Paper presented at the Annual Meeting of the European Society for Population Economics, Tilburg University, 6–8 June.

Mukherjee, N. (2005). *Political Corruption in India's Below the Poverty Line (BPL) Exercise: Grassroots Perspectives on BPL in Perpetuating Poverty and Social Exclusion*. New Delhi: Development Tracks in Research, Training and Consultancy.

Muthén, B. O. (1984). 'A General Structural Equation Model with Dichotomous, Ordered Categorical, and Continuous Latent Variable Indicators', *Psychometrika*, 49(1): 115–32.

Muthén, L. K. and Muthén, B. O. (1998–2012). *Mplus User's Guide*, 7th edn. Los Angeles, CA: Muthén & Muthén.

Naga, R. H. A. and Bolzani, E. (2006). 'Poverty and Permanent Income: A Methodology for Cross-Section Data', *Annales d'Economie et de Statistique*, 81: 195–223.

Narayan, D. and Petesch, P. (eds) (2007). *Moving out of Poverty*, i: *Cross-Disciplinary Perspectives on Mobility*. Washington, DC: World Bank.

Narayan, D., Chambers, R., Shah, M. K., and Petesch, P. (2000). *Voices of the Poor: Crying Out for Change*. Oxford: Oxford University Press.

Nardo, M., Saisana, M., Saltelli, A., Tarantola, S., Hoffman, A., and Giovannini, E. (2008). *Handbook on Constructing Composite Indicators: Methodology and User Guide* (No. 2008/3). Ispra, Italy: OECD Publishing.

National Statistics Bureau, Royal Government of Bhutan (2014). *Bhutan: Multidimensional Poverty Index 2012*. Thimphu, Bhutan: National Statistics Bureau.

Nehmeh, A. (2013). 'Urban Deprivation Index: The Methodology and Field Study Results in Tripoli, Lebanon' (forthcoming).

Nelder, J. A. and Wedderburn, R. W. M. (1972). 'Generalized Linear Models', *Journal of the Royal Statistical Society*, Series A, 135: 370–84.

Nelson, J. (1993). 'Household Equivalence Scales: Theory Versus Policy?', *Journal of Labor Economics*, 11: 471–93.

Neubourg, C. de, Chai, J., Milliano, M. de, Plavgo, I., and Wei, Z. (2012). 'Step-by-Step Guidelines to the Multiple Deprivation Analysis (MODA) for Children', *UNICEF Research Working Paper* WP-2012-10.

Newcombe, R. G. (1998). 'Two-Sided Confidence Intervals for the Single Proportion: Comparison of Seven Methods', *Statistics in Medicine*, 17(8): 857–72.

Nicholas, A. and Ray, R. (2012). 'Duration and Persistence in Multidimensional Deprivation: Methodology and Australian Application', *Economic Record*, 88(280): 106–26.

Nicholas, A., Ray, R., and Sinha, K. (2013). 'A Dynamic Multidimensional Measure of Poverty', Discussion Paper 25/13, Monash University, Melbourne.

Nolan, B. and Whelan, C. (1996). *Resources, Deprivation, and Poverty*. Oxford: Oxford University Press.

Nolan, B. and Whelan, C. (2011). *Poverty and Deprivation in Europe*. Oxford: Oxford University Press.

Noll, H.-H. (2002). 'Towards a European System of Social Indicators: Theoretical Framework and System Architecture', *Social Indicators Research*, 58(1–3): 47–87.

Norman, G. (2010). 'Likert Scales, Levels of Measurement and the "Laws" of Statistics', *Advances in Health Science Education*, 15(5): 625–32.

Notten, G. and Roelen, K. (2012). 'A New Tool for Monitoring (Child) Poverty: Measures of Cumulative Deprivation', *Child Indicators Research*, 5(2): 335–55.

Nteziyaremye, A. and MkNelly, B. (2001). 'Mali Poverty Outreach Study of the Kafo Jiginew and Nyèsigiso Credit and Savings with Education Programs', *Freedom from Hunger Research Paper* 7. Davis, CA: Freedom from Hunger.

Nussbaum, M. (2000). *Women and Human Development: The Capabilities Approach*. Cambridge: Cambridge University Press.

Nussbaum, M. (2003). 'Capabilities as Fundamental Entitlements: Sen and Social Justice', *Feminist Economics*, 9(2–3): 33–59.

Nussbaum, M. (2011). *Creating Capabilities: The Human Development Approach*. Cambridge, MA: Harvard University Press.

Nussbaum, M. and Sen, A. (eds) (1993). *The Quality of Life*. Oxford: Clarendon Press.

Nussbaumer, P., Bazilian, M., and Modi, V. (2012). 'Measuring Energy Poverty: Focusing on What Matters', *Renewable & Sustainable Energy Reviews*, 16(1): 231–43.

Nygård, F. and Sandström, A. (1989). 'Income Inequality Measures Based on Sample Surveys', *Journal of Econometrics*, 42(1): 81–95.

O'Donnell, O., Doorslaer, E. van, Wagstaff, A., and Lindelow, M. (2008). *Analyzing Health Equity Using Household Survey Data: A Guide to Techniques and their Implementation*. Washington, DC: World Bank.

OECD (1982). *The OECD List of Social Indicators*. Paris: OECD Publishing.

OECD (2013). *Development Co-operation Report 2013: Ending Poverty*. Paris: OECD Publishing.

Pagani, A. (1960). *La Linea Della Poverta*. Milan: ANEA.

Papke, L. E. and Wooldridge, J. M. (1996). 'Econometric Methods for Fractional Response Variables with an Application to 401(K) Plan Participation Rates', *Journal of Applied Econometrics*, 11(6): 619–32.

Parfit, D. (1984). *Reasons and Persons*. Oxford: Clarendon Press.

Pattanaik, P. K., Reddy, S., and Xu, Y. (2012). 'On Measuring Deprivation and Living Standards of Societies in a Multi-Attribute Framework', *Oxford Economic Papers*, 64: 43–56.

Pattanaik, P. K. and Xu, Y. (1990). 'On Ranking Opportunity Sets in Terms of Freedom of Choice', *Recherches Economiques de Louvain*, 56: 383–90.

Pattanaik, P. K. and Xu, Y. (1998). 'On Preference and Freedom', *Theory and Decision*, 44(2): 173–98.

Pattanaik, P. K. and Xu, Y. (2000). 'On Diversity and Freedom of Choice', *Mathematical Social Sciences*, 40(2): 123–30.

Pearson, K. (1901). 'On Lines and Planes of Closest Fit to Systems of Points in Space', *Philosophical Magazine*, 6(2): 559–72.

Peichl, A. and Pestel, N. (2013a). 'Multidimensional Affluence: Theory and Applications to Germany and the US', *Applied Economics*, 45(32): 4591–601.

Peichl, A. and Pestel, N. (2013b). 'Multidimensional Well-Being at the Top: Evidence for Germany', *Fiscal Studies*, 34(3): 355–71.

Pereira, G. (2013). *Elements of a Critical Theory of Justice*. Houndmills, Basingstoke: Palgrave Macmillan.

Permanyer, I. (2011). 'Assessing the Robustness of Composite Indices Rankings', *Review of Income and Wealth*, 57(2): 306–26.

Permanyer, I. (2012). 'Uncertainty and Robustness in Composite Indices Rankings', *Oxford Economic Papers*, 64(1): 57–79.

Permanyer, I. (2013). 'The Measurement of Success in Achieving the Millennium Development Goals', *Journal of Economic Inequality*, 11(3): 393–415.

Pett, M. A. (1997). *Non-parametric Statistics for Health Care Research*. London and Thousand Oaks, CA: Sage Publications.

Poi, B. P. (2004). 'From the Help Desk: Some Bootstrapping Techniques', *Stata Journal*, 4(3): 312–28.

Porter, C. and Quinn, N. (2013). 'Measuring Intertemporal Poverty: Policy Options for the Poverty Analyst', in G. Betti and A. Lemmi (eds), *Poverty and Social Exclusion: New Methods of Analysis*. London: Routledge, 166–93.

Pradhan, M., Suryahadi, A., Sumarto, S., and Pritchett, L. (2000). 'Measurements of Poverty in Indonesia—1996, 1999, and Beyond', *Policy Research Working Paper* 2438. Washington, DC: World Bank.

PSE (1983). *Breadline Britain 1983*. Poverty and Social Exclusion, <http://www.poverty.ac.uk/pse-research/past-uk-research/breadline-britain-1983>.

Qizilbash, M. (2006). 'Philosophical Accounts of Vagueness, Fuzzy Poverty Measures and Multidimensionality', in A. Lemmi and G. Betti (eds), *Fuzzy Set Approach to Multidimensional Poverty Measurement*. New York: Springer, 9–28.

Quigley, W. (1998). 'Backwards into the Future: How Welfare Changes in the Millennium Resemble English Poor Law of the Middle Ages', *Stanford Law & Policy Review*, 9(1): 101–13.

Rabe-Hesketh, S. and Skrondal, A. (2012). *Multilevel and Longitudinal Modeling Using Stata*, i: *Continuous Responses*, 3rd edn. College Station, TX: Stata Press.

Ragin, C. C. (2000). *Fuzzy-Set Social Science*. Chicago: University of Chicago Press.

Rahman, T., Mittelhammer, R. C., and Wandscheider, P. (2011). 'Measuring the Quality of Life Across Countries: A Multiple Indicators and Multiple Causes Approach', *Journal of Socio-Economics*, 40(1): 43–52.

Ramalho, E. A., Ramalho, J. J., and Murteira, J. M. (2011). 'Alternative Estimating and Testing Empirical Strategies for Fractional Regression Models', *Journal of Economic Surveys*, 25(1): 19–68.

Ranis, G., Samman, E., and Stewart, F. (2006). 'Human Development: Beyond the Human Development Index', *Journal of Human Development*, 7(3): 323–58.

Ravallion, M. (1992). 'Poverty Comparisons: A Guide to Concepts and Methods', *Living Standards Measurement Study, Working Paper* 88. Washington, DC: World Bank.

Ravallion, M. (1994). *Poverty Comparisons*, Fundamentals of Pure and Applied Economics 56. Chur, Switzerland: Harwood Academic Press.

Ravallion, M. (1996). 'Issues in Measuring and Modelling Poverty', *The Economic Journal*, 106(438): 1328–43.

Ravallion, M. (1998). *Poverty Lines in Theory and Practice*. Washington, DC: World Bank.

Ravallion, M. (2001). 'Growth, Inequality and Poverty: Looking beyond Averages', *World Development*, 29(11): 1803–15.

Ravallion, M. (2011a). 'The Two Poverty Enlightments: Historical Insights from Digitized Books Spanning Three Centuries', *Poverty & Public Policy*, 3(2): 1–46.

Ravallion, M. (2011b). 'On Multidimensional Indices of Poverty', *Journal of Economic Inequality*, 9(2): 235–48.

Ravallion, M. (2012). 'Troubling Tradeoffs in the Human Development Index', *Journal of Development Economics*, 99(2): 201–9.

Ravallion, M. (2013). *Poverty Comparisons*. London: Taylor & Francis.

Ravallion, M. and Huppi, M. (1991). 'Measuring Changes in Poverty: A Methodological Case Study of Indonesia during an Adjustment Period', *World Bank Economic Review*, 5(1): 57–82.

Rawls, J. (1971). *A Theory of Justice*. Cambridge, MA: Harvard University Press.

Rawls, J. (1993). *Political Liberalism*. New York: Columbia University Press.

Rawls, J. (1999a). *A Theory of Justice*, revised edn. Cambridge, MA: Harvard University Press.

Rawls, J. (1999b). *The Law of Peoples: with, The Idea of Public Reason Revisited*. Cambridge, MA: Harvard University Press.

Rawls, J. (2001). *Justice as Fairness*, ed. E. Kelly. Cambridge, MA: Harvard University Press.

Raz, J. (1986). *The Morality of Freedom*. Oxford: Oxford University Press.

Reader, S. (ed.) (2006). *The Philosophy of Need*, Royal Institute of Philosophy Supplement 80. Cambridge: Cambridge University Press.

Rencher, A. C. (2002). *Methods of Multivariate Analysis*, 2nd edn. New York: John Wiley.

Ringen, S. (1987). *The Possibility of Politics*. Oxford: Oxford University Press.

Ringen, S. (1988). 'Direct and Indirect Measures of Poverty', *Journal of Social Policy*, 17(3): 351–66.

Rio Group (2006). 'Compendium of Best Practices in Poverty Measurement', <http://www.eclac.cl/publicaciones/xml/3/26593/rio_group_compendium.pdf>, accessed January 2014.

Rippin, N. (2012). *Considerations of Efficiency and Distributive Justice in Multidimensional Poverty Measurement*, PhD dissertation, Georg-August-Universität Göttingen.

Robano, V. and Smith, S. C. (2014). 'Multidimensional Targeting and Evaluation: A General Framework with an Application to a Poverty Program in Bangladesh', *OPHI Working Paper* 65, University of Oxford.

Roberts, F. S. (1979). *Measurement Theory with Applications to Decisionmaking, Utility, and the Social Sciences*, Encyclopedia of Mathematics and its Applications 7. Reading, MA: Addison-Wesley.

Roberts, F. S. and Franke, C. H. (1976). 'On the Theory of Uniqueness in Measurement', *Journal of Mathematical Psychology*, 14(3): 211–18.

Robeyns, I. (2003). 'Sen's Capability Approach and Gender Inequality: Selecting Relevant Capabilities', *Feminist Economics*, 9(2): 61–92.

Robeyns, I. (2005). 'Selecting Capabilities for Quality of Life Measurement', *Social Indicators Research*, 74(1): 191–215.

Robeyns, I. (2006). 'The Capability Approach in Practice', *Journal of Political Philosophy*, 14(3): 351–76.

Robeyns, I. and Veen, R. J. van der (2007). 'Sustainable Quality of Life: Conceptual Analysis for a Policy-Relevant Empirical Specification', *MNP Report* 550031006/2007.

Roche, J. M. (2008). 'Monitoring Inequality among Social Groups: A Methodology Combining Fuzzy Set Theory and Principal Component Analysis', *Journal of Human Development and Capabilities*, 9(3): 427–52.

Roche, J. M. (2013). 'Monitoring Progress in Child Poverty Reduction: Methodological Insights and Illustration to the Case Study of Bangladesh', *Social Indicators Research* 112(2): 363–90.

Roelen, K. and Notten, G. (2011). 'The Breadth of Child Poverty in Europe: An Investigation into Overlap and Accumulation of Deprivations', *Innocenti Working Paper* 2011-04. Florence: UNICEF Innocenti Research Centre.

Roelen, K., Gassmann, F., and Neubourg, C. de (2009). 'The Importance of Choice and Definition for the Measurement of Child Poverty: The Case of Vietnam', *Child Indicators Research*, 2(3): 245–63.

Roemer, J. E. (1996). *Theories of Distributive Justice*. Cambridge, MA: Harvard University Press.

Room, G. (ed.) (1995). *Beyond the Threshold*. Bristol: Policy Press.

Rowntree, B. S. (1901). *Poverty: A Study of Town Life*. London: Macmillan.

Roy, I. (2011). '"New" List for "Old": (Re)constructing the Poor in the BPL Census', *Economic and Political Weekly*, 46(22): 82–91.

Ruger, J. P (2007). 'Health, Health Care, and Incompletely Theorized Agreements: A Normative Theory of Health Policy Decision-Making', *Journal of Health Politics, Policy, and Law*, 32(1): 51 –87.

Ruggeri Laderchi, C. (1997). 'Poverty and its Many Dimensions: The Role of Income as an Indicator', *Oxford Development Studies*, 25(3): 345–60.

Ruggeri Laderchi, C., Saith, R., and Stewart, F. (2003). 'Does It Matter that We Don't Agree on the Definition of Poverty? A Comparison of Four Approaches', *Oxford Development Studies*, 31(3): 243–74.

Sahn, D. E. and Stifel, D. (2000). 'Poverty Comparisons over Time and Across Countries in Africa', *World Development*, 28(12): 2123–55.

Sahn, D. E. and Stifel, D. (2003). 'Exploring Alternative Measures of Welfare in the Absence of Expenditure Data', *Review of Income and Wealth*, 49(4): 463–89.

Saisana, M. and Saltelli, A. (2010). 'The Multidimensional Poverty Assessment Tool (MPAT): Robustness Issues and Critical Assessment', *Scientific and Technical Reports* JRC56806 (EUR 24310 EN). Publications Office of the European Union.

Saisana, M., Saltelli, A., and Tarantola, S. (2005). 'Uncertainty and Sensitivity Analysis as Tools for the Quality Assessment of Composite Indicators', *Journal of the Royal Statistical Society: Ser. A (Statistics in Society)*, 168(2): 307–23.

Santos, M. E. (2013). 'Tracking Poverty Reduction in Bhutan: Income Deprivation Alongside Deprivation in Other Sources of Happiness', *Social Indicators Research*, 112(2): 259–90.

Santos, M. E. and Santos, G. (2013). 'Composite Indices of Development', in B. Currie-Alder, D. Malone, R. Y. Medhora, and R. Kanbur (eds), *International Development: Ideas, Experience and Prospects*. Oxford: Oxford University Press, ch. 5.

Sarle, W. S. (1995). 'Measurement Theory: Frequently Asked Questions', *Disseminations of the International Statistical Applications Institute*. Wichita: ACG Press, i.61–6, <ftp://ftp.sas.com/pub/neural/measurement.html>, accessed 2 August 2013.

Sastry, N. (2004). 'Trends in Socioeconomic Inequalities in Mortality in Developing Countries: The Case of Child Survival in São Paulo, Brazil', *Demography*, 41(3): 443–64.

Schellenberg, J. A., Victora, C. G., Mushi, A., Savigny, D. de, et al. (2003). 'Inequities Among the Very Poor: Health Care for Children in Rural Southern Tanzania', *The Lancet*, 361(9357): 561–6.

Schreiner, M. (2002). 'Scoring: The Next Breakthrough in Microfinance?' *Consultative Group to Assist the Poorest Occasional Paper* 7.

Schreiner, M. (2004). 'Benefits and Pitfalls of Statistical Credit Scoring for Microfinance', *Savings and Development*, 28(1): 63–86.

Schreiner, M. (2006). 'A Simple Poverty Scorecard for Bangladesh'. Report to Grameen Foundation.

Schreiner, M. (2010). 'Seven Extremely Simple Poverty Scorecards', *Enterprise Development and Microfinance*, 21(2): 118–36.

Scutella, R., Wilkins, R., and Kostenko, W. (2013). 'Intensity and Persistence of Individuals' Social Exclusion in Australia', *Australian Journal of Social Issues*, 48(3): 273–98.

Sen, A. K. (ed.) (1960). *Growth Economics*. Harmondsworth: Penguin.

Sen, A. K. (1970). *Collective Choice and Social Welfare*. Edinburgh: Oliver & Boyd.

Sen, A. K. (1973). *On Economic Inequality*. Oxford: Oxford University Press.

Sen, A. K. (1976). 'Poverty: An Ordinal Approach to Measurement', *Econometrica*, 44(2): 219–31.

Sen, A. K. (1980). 'Equality of What?', in S. McMurrin (ed.), *Tanner Lectures on Human Values*. Cambridge: Cambridge University Press, 197–220.

Sen, A. K. (1981). *Poverty and Famines: An Essay on Entitlement and Deprivation*. Oxford: Oxford University Press.

Sen, A. K. (1984). *Resources, Values and Development*. Cambridge, MA: Harvard University Press.

Sen, A. K. (1985). 'Well-Being, Agency and Freedom: The Dewey Lectures 1984', *Journal of Philosophy*, 82(4): 169–221.

Sen, A. K. (1987). 'The Standard of Living: Lectures I and II', in G. Hawthorn (ed.), *The Standard of Living: The Tanner Lectures*. Cambridge: Cambridge University Press, 1–38.

Sen, A. K. (1989). 'Food and Freedom', *World Development*, 17(6): 769–81.

Sen, A. K. (1991). 'Development as Capability Expansion', in K. Griffin and J. Knight (eds), *Human Development and the International Development Strategy for the 1990s*. London: MacMillan, 41–58.

Sen, A. K. (1992). *Inequality Re-examined*. Oxford: Oxford University Press.

Sen, A. K. (1993). 'Capability and Well-Being', in M. C. Nussbaum and A. Sen (eds), *The Quality of Life*. Oxford: Oxford University Press, 9–29.

Sen, A. K. (1996). 'On the Foundations of Welfare Economics: Utility, Capability and Practical Reason', in F. Farina, F. Hahn, and S. Vannucci (eds), *Ethics, Rationality and Economics*. Oxford: Oxford University Press, ch. 4.

Sen, A. K. (1997a). *On Economic Inequality*. Expanded edition with a substantial annex by James E. Foster and Amartya Sen. Oxford: Oxford University Press.

Sen, A. K. (1997b). 'Maximization and the Act of Choice', *Econometrica*, 65(4): 745–79.

Sen, A. K. (1999a). *Development as Freedom*. Oxford: Oxford University Press.

Sen, A. K. (1999b). 'Mahbub ul Haq: The Courage and Creativity of his Ideas', *Journal of Asian Economics*, 10(1): 1-6. Text of speech at the Memorial Meeting for Mahbub ul Haq at the United Nations, New York, 15 October 1998.

Sen, A. K. (2000). 'A Decade of Human Development', *Journal of Human Development and Capabilities*, 1(1): 17–23.

Sen, A. K. (2002). *Rationality and Freedom*. Cambridge, MA: Harvard University Press.

Sen, A. K. (2004). 'Capabilities, Lists, and Public Reason: Continuing the Conversation', *Feminist Economics*, 10(3): 77–80.

Sen, A. K. (2008). 'The Economics of Happiness and Capability', in L. Bruni, F. Comim, and M. Pugno (eds), *Capability and Happiness*. New York: Oxford University Press.

Sen, A. K. (2009). *The Idea of Justice*. Harmondsworth: Penguin.

Seth, S. (2009). 'Inequality, Interactions, and Human Development', *Journal of Human Development and Capabilities*, 10(3): 375–96.

Seth, S. (2010). *Essays in Multidimensional Measurement: Welfare, Poverty, and Robustness*, doctoral dissertation, Vanderbilt University.

Seth, S. (2013). 'A Class of Distribution- and Association-Sensitive Multidimensional Welfare Indices', *Journal of Economic Inequality*, 11(2): 133–62.

Seth, S. and Alkire, S. (2014a). 'Measuring and Decomposing Inequality Among the Multidimensionally Poor Using Ordinal Variables: A Counting Approach', *OPHI Working Paper* 68, University of Oxford.

Seth, S. and Alkire, S. (2014b). 'Did Poverty Reduction Reach the Poorest of the Poor? Assessment Methods in the Counting Approach', *OPHI Working Paper* 77, University of Oxford.

Shaffer, P. (2013). 'Ten Years of "Q-Squared": Implications for Understanding and Explaining Poverty', *World Development*, 45: 269–85.

Shannon, C. E. (1948). 'A Mathematical Theory of Communication', *The Bell System Technical Journal* 27(3): 379–423.

Sharan, M. R. (2011). 'Identifying BPL Households: A Comparison of Competing Approaches', *Economic and Political Weekly*, 46(26): 256–62.

Shorrocks, A. F. (1980). 'The Class of Additively Decomposable Inequality Measures', *Econometrica*, 48(3): 613–25.

Shorrocks, A. F. (1995). 'Revisiting the Sen Poverty Index', *Econometrica*, 63(5): 1225–30.

Shorrocks, A. F. (1999). 'Decomposition Procedures for Distributional Analysis: A Unified Framework Based on the Shapley Value', *Journal of Economic Inequality*, 11(1): 1–28.

Siani Tchouametieu, J. R. (2013). 'Has Poverty Decreased in Cameroon between 2001 and 2007? An Analysis Based on Multidimensional Poverty Measures', *Economics Bulletin*, 33(4): 3059–69.

Siegel, M. and Waidler, J. (2012). 'Migration and Multi-dimensional Poverty in Moldovan Communities', *Eastern Journal of European Studies*, 3: 105–19. Centre for European Studies, Alexandru Ioan Cuza University.

Silber, J. and Yalonetzky, G. (2014). 'Measuring Multidimensional Deprivation with Dichotomized and Ordinal Variables', in G. Betti and A. Lemmi (eds), *Poverty and Social Exclusion: New Methods of Analysis*. London: Routledge, ch. 2.

Silver, H. (1995). 'Reconceptualizing Social Disadvantage: Three Paradigms of Social Exclusion', in G. Rodgers, C. Gore, and J. Figueiredo (eds), *Social Exclusion: Rhetoric, Reality, Responses*. Geneva: International Labour Organization.

Siminski, P. and Yerokhin, O. (2012). 'Is the Age Gradient in Self-Reported Material Hardship Explained By Resources, Needs, Behaviors, or Reporting Bias?', *Review of Income and Wealth*, 58(4): 715–41.

Simpson, G. G. (1943). 'Mammals and the Nature of Continents', *American Journal of Science*, 241(1): 1–31.

Sirgy, M. J., Michalos, A. C., Ferriss, A. L., Easterlin, R., Patrick, P., and Pavot, W. (2006). 'The Quality-of-Life (QOL) Research Movement: Past, Present and Future', *Social Indicators Research*, 76(3): 343–466.

Skrondal, A. and Rabe-Hesketh, S. (2004). *Generalized Latent Variable Modeling: Multilevel, Longitudinal, and Structural Equation Models*. Boca Raton, FL: Chapman & Hall/CRC Press.

Smith, S. C. (2012). 'The Scope of NGOs and Development Programme Design: Application to Problems of Multidimensional Poverty', *Public Administration and Development*, 32(4–5): 357–70.

Smithson, M. and Verkuilen, J. (2006). *Fuzzy Set Theory: Applications in the Social Sciences*. London and Thousand Oaks, CA: Sage Publications.

Spearman, C. (1904). '"General Intelligence", Objectively Determined and Measured', *American Journal of Psychology*, 15(2): 201–93.

Stevens, S. S. (1946). 'On the Theory of Scales of Measurement', *Science*, NS 103(2684): 677–80.

Stevens, S. S. (1951). 'Mathematics, Measurement and Psychophysics', in S. S. Stevens (ed.), *Handbook of Experimental Psychology*. New York: John Wiley, 1–49.

Stevens, S. S. (1959). 'Measurement, Psychophysics, and Utility', in C. W. Churchman and P. Ratoosh (eds), *Measurement: Definitions and Theories*. New York: John Wiley, 18–63.

Stewart, F. (1985). *Basic Needs in Developing Countries*. Baltimore, MD: Johns Hopkins University Press.

Stewart, F. (2010). *Horizontal Inequalities and Conflict*. Basingstoke: Palgrave Macmillan.

Stewart, F., Saith, R., and Harriss-White, B. (2007). *Defining Poverty in Developing Countries*. Basingstoke: Palgrave Macmillan.

Stifel, D. and Christiaensen, L. (2007). 'Tracking Poverty over Time in the Absence of Comparable Consumption Data', *World Bank Economic Review*, 21(2): 317–41.

Stigler, G. J. (1954). 'The Early History of Empirical Studies of Consumer Behavior', *Journal of Political Economy*, 62(2): 95–113.

Stiglitz, J. E., Sen, A., and Fitoussi, J.-P. (2009). *Report by the Commission on the Measurement of Economic Performance and Social Progress*, <www.stiglitz-sen-fitoussi.fr>.

Stock, J. H., Wright, J. H., and Yogo, M. (2002). 'A Survey of Weak Instruments and Weak Identification in Generalized Method of Moments', *Journal of Business & Economic Statistics*, 20(4): 518–29.

Streeten, P., Burki, J. S., Haq, M. U., Hicks, N., and Stewart, F. (1981). *First Things First: Meeting Basic Human Needs in Developing Countries*. Oxford: Oxford University Press.

Sundaram, K. (2003). 'On Identification of Households Below Poverty Line in BPL Census 2002: Some Comments on Proposed Methodology', *Economic and Political Weekly*, 38(9): 896–901.

Sunstein, C. R. (1996). *Legal Reasoning and Political Conflict*. New York: Oxford University Press.

Svedberg, P. (2000). *Poverty and Undernutrition: Theory, Measurement, and Policy*. Oxford: Oxford University Press.

Swanepoel, J. W H. (1986). 'A Note on Proving that the (Modified) Bootstrap Works', *Communications in Statistics (Theory and Methods)*, 15(11): 3193–203.

Székely, M. (ed.) (2005). *Números que mueven al mundo: La medición de la pobreza en México*. Mexico City: Miguel Ángel Porrúa.

Tarozzi, A. and Deaton, A. (2009). 'Using Census and Survey Data to Estimate Poverty and Inequality for Small Areas', *Review of Economics and Statistics*, 91(4): 773–92.

Theil, H. (1967). *Economics and Information Theory*. Chicago: Rand McNally and Company.

Thomas, B. K., Muradian, R., Groot, G. de, and Ruijter, A. de (2009). 'Multidimensional Poverty and Identification of Poor Households: A Case from Kerala, India', *Journal of Human Development and Capabilities*, 10(2): 237–57.

Thon, D. (1979). 'On Measuring Poverty', *Review of Income and Wealth*, 25: 429–40.

Thurstone, L. L. (1931). 'Multiple Factor Analysis', *Psychological Review*, 38(5): 406–27.

Tonmoy Islam, T. M. (2014). 'An Exercise to Evaluate an Anti-Poverty Program with Multiple Outcomes Using Program Evaluation', *Economics Letters*, 122(2): 365–9.

Tout, H. (1938). *The Standard of Living in Bristol*. Bristol: Arrowsmith.

Townsend, J. (1786). *A Dissertation on the Poor Laws*. Republished online at <http://socserv2.socsci.mcmaster.ca/econ/ugcm/3ll3/townsend/poorlaw.html>.

Townsend, P. (1952). *Political and Economic Planning, Poverty: Ten Years after Beveridge*, Planning No. 344. London: Political and Economic Planning.

Townsend, P. (1954). 'Measuring Poverty', *British Journal of Sociology*, 5: 130–7.

Townsend, P. (1979). *Poverty in the United Kingdom: A Survey of Household Resources and Standards of Living*. London: Peregrine Books.

Trani, J.-F. and Cannings, T. I. (2013). 'Child Poverty in an Emergency and Conflict Context: A Multidimensional Profile and an Identification of the Poorest Children in Western Darfur', *World Development*, 48(C): 48–70.

Trani, J.-F., Biggeri, M., and Mauro, V. (2013), 'The Multidimensionality of Child Poverty: Evidence from Afghanistan', *Social Indicators Research*, 112(2): 391–416.

Tsui K.-Y. (1995). 'Multidimensional Generalizations of the Relative and Absolute Inequality Indices: The Atkinson–Kolm–Sen Approach', *Journal of Economic Theory*, 67(1): 251–65.

Tsui K.-Y. (1999). 'Multidimensional Inequality and Multidimensional Entropy Measures: An Axiomatic Derivation', *Social Choice and Welfare*, 16(1): 145–57.

Tsui, K.-Y. (2002). 'Multidimensional Poverty Indices', *Social Choice and Welfare*, 19(1): 69–93.

Tukey, J. W. (1961/1986). 'Data Analysis and Behavioral Science or Learning to Bear the Quantitative Man's Burden by Shunning Badmandments', in L. V. J. Belmont (ed.), *The Collected Works of John W. Tukey*. Belmont, CA: Wadsworth, iii.391–484.

UN (2001). 'Principles and Recommendations for a Vital Statistics System: Revision 2', ST/ESA/STAT/SERM/19/REV2. New York: United Nations Department of Economic and Social Affairs, Statistics Division.

UN (2008). 'Principles and Recommendations for Population and Housing Censuses: Revision 2', Statistical Papers Series M 67/Rev2. New York: United Nations Department of Economic and Social Affairs, Statistics Division.

UNDESA (2010). *Rethinking Poverty: Report on the World Social Situation 2010*. New York: United Nations Department of Economic and Social Affairs.

UNDESA (2011). *World Population Prospects: The 2010 Revision*, i-ii. New York: United Nations, Department of Economic and Social Affairs, Population Division, <http://esa.un.org/wpp/Excel-Data/population.htm>, accessed July 2011.

UNDESA (2013). *World Population Prospects: The 2012 Revision*. New York: United Nations Department of Economic and Social Affairs, Population Division, <http://esa.un.org/wpp/Excel-Data/population.htm>, accessed March 2014.

UNDG (2013). *A Million Voices: The World We Want: A Sustainable Future with Dignity for All*. United Nations Development Group (UNDG).

UNDP (1990). *Human Development Report 1990*. United Nations Development Programme. New York: Oxford University Press.

UNDP (1995). *Human Development Report 1995: Gender and Human Development*. New York: Oxford University Press.

UNDP (2010a). *The Real Wealth of Nations: Pathways to Human Development*. Human Development Report 2010. New York: United Nations Development Programme.

UNDP (2010b). *What Will it Take to Achieve the Millennium Development Goals?: An International Assessment*. New York: United Nations Development Programme.

UNDP (2013). *The Rise of the South: Human Progress in a Diverse World*. Human Development Report 2013. New York: United Nations Development Programme.

UNDP and MOSA (1998). *Mapping of the Living Conditions in Lebanon*. United Nations Development Programme (UNDP) and the Ministry of Social Affairs (MOSA) of the Republic of Lebanon.

UNDP and MOSA (2007). *Development of Mapping of Living Conditions in Lebanon, 1995–2004: A Comparison with the Results of 'Mapping of Living Conditions in Lebanon, 1998'*. United Nations Development Programme (UNDP) and the Ministry of Social Affairs (MOSA) of the Republic of Lebanon.

UNDP and MPDC (2006). *Unsatisfied Basic Needs Mapping and Living Standards in Iraq, Study in Three Volumes: Analytic Report*. United Nations Development Programme (UNDP) and the Central Organization for Statistics and Information Technology, Ministry of Planning and Development Cooperation (MPDC) of the Republic of Iraq.

UNEP/UNCTAD (1975). 'The Cocoyoc Declaration. Adopted by the Participants in the UNEP/UNCTAD Symposium on 'Patterns of Resource Use, Environment, and Development Strategies', *International Organization*, 29(3): 893–901.

UNICEF (2004). *The State of the World's Children 2005: Childhood Under Threat*. New York: UNICEF.

UNRISD (2010). *Combating Poverty and Inequality: Structural Change, Social Policy and Politics*. United Nations Research Institute for Social Development Flagship Report. Geneva: UNRISD/UN Publications, <http://www.unrisd.org/publications/cpi>.

Ura, K., Alkire, S., Zangmo, T., and Wangdi, K. (2012). *An Extensive Analysis of The Gross National Happiness Index*. Thimphu, Bhutan: Centre for Bhutan Studies.

Van Ootegem, L. and Verhofstadt, E. (2012). 'Using Capabilities as an Alternative Indicator for Well-Being', *Social Indicators Research*, 106(1): 133–52.

Velleman, P. F. and Wilkinson, L. (1993). 'Nominal, Ordinal, Interval, and Ratio Typologies are Misleading', *The American Statistician*, 47(1): 65–72.

Venn, J. (1880). 'On the Diagrammatic and Mechanical Representation of Propositions and Reasonings', *Philosophical Magazine and Journal of Science*, Series 5, 10(59): 1–18.

Verkuilen, J. (2005). 'Assigning Membership in a Fuzzy Set Analysis', *Sociological Methods and Research*, 33(4): 462–96.

Vero, J. (2006). 'A Comparison of Poverty According to Primary Goods, Capabilities and Outcomes: Evidence from French School Leavers' Survey', in A. Lemmi and G. Betti (eds), *Fuzzy Set Approach to Multidimensional Poverty Measurement*. New York: Springer, 211–32.

Vogel, J. (1997). 'The Future Direction of Social Indicators Research', *Social Indicators Research*, 42(2): 103–16.

Vranken, J. (2002). *Belgian Reports on Poverty*. Paper presented at the conference 'Reporting on Income Distribution and Poverty—Perspectives from a German and European Point of View', organized by Hans Böckler Stiftung, Berlin, February.

Wagle, U. R. (2008). *Multidimensional Poverty Measurement: Concepts and Applications*, Economic Studies in Inequality, Social Exclusion and Well-Being 4. New York: Springer.

Wagle, U. R. (2014). 'The Counting-Based Measurement of Multidimensional Poverty: The Focus on Economic Resources, Inner Capabilities, and Relational Resources in the United States', *Social Indicators Research*, 115(1): 223–40.

Wagner, J. (2001). 'A Note on the Firm Size–Export Relationship', *Small Business Economics*, 17(4): 229–37.

Walker, R., Kyomuhendo, G. B., Chase, E., et al. (2013). 'Poverty in Global Perspective: Is Shame a Common Denominator?', *Journal of Social Policy*, 42(2): 215–33.

Watts, H. W. (1968). 'An Economic Definition of Poverty', in D. P. Moynihan (ed.), *On Understanding Poverty*. New York: Basic Books, 316–29.

Whelan, C. T., Layte, R., and Maître, B. (2004). 'Understanding the Mismatch between Income Poverty and Deprivation: A Dynamic Comparative Analysis', *European Sociological Review*, 20(4): 287–302.

Whelan, C. T., Layte, R., Maître, B., Gannon, B., Nolan, B., Watson, D., and Williams, J. (2001a). *Monitoring Poverty Trends in Ireland: Results from the 2001 Living in Ireland Survey*, ESRI Policy Research Series 51. Dublin: Economic and Social Research Institute.

Whelan, C. T., Layte, R., Maître, B., and Nolan, B. (2001b). 'Income, Deprivation and Economic Strain: An Analysis of the European Community Household Panel', *European Sociological Review*, 17(4): 357–72.

Whelan, C. T. and Maître, B. (2010). 'Comparing Poverty Indicators in an Enlarged European Union', *European Sociological Review*, 26(6): 713–30.

Whelan, C. T., Nolan, B., and Maître, B. (2006). 'Measuring Consistent Poverty in Ireland with EU-SILC Data', *ESRI Working Paper* 165. Dublin: Economic and Social Research Institute.

Whelan, C. T., Nolan, B., and Maître, B. (2014). 'Multidimensional Poverty Measurement in Europe: An Application of the Adjusted Headcount Approach', *Journal of European Social Policy*, 24(2): 183–97.

WHO Programme of Nutrition (1997). *Global Database on Child Growth and Malnutrition*, compiled by M. de Onis and M. Blössner. Geneva: World Health Organization.

WHO Multicentre Growth Reference Study Group (2006). *WHO Child Growth Standards: Length/Height-for-Age, Weight-for-Age, Weight-for- Length, Weight-for-Height and Body Mass Index-for-Age: Methods and Development*. Geneva: World Health Organization.

Wiggins, D. (1998). *Needs, Values, Truth*, 3rd edn. Oxford: Clarendon Press.

Wolff, H., Chong, H., and Auffhammer, M. (2011). 'Classification, Detection and Consequences of Data Error: Evidence from the Human Development Index', *The Economic Journal*, 121(553): 843–70.

Wolff, J. and De-Shalit, A. (2007). *Disadvantage*. Oxford: Oxford University Press.

World Bank (1990). *World Development Report 1990: Poverty*. Washington, DC: World Bank.

World Bank (2000). *World Development Report 2000/2001*. Washington, DC: World Bank

World Bank (2013). *Global Monitoring Report 2013: Monitoring the MDGs*. Washington, DC: World Bank, <http://data.worldbank.org/mdgs/progress-status-across-groups-number-of-countries>, accessed 1 April 2014.

World Bank (2014). *World Development Indicators*. Washington, DC: World Bank, <http://data.worldbank.org/products/wdi>.

Wright, G. (2008). *Findings from the Indicators of Poverty and Social Exclusion Project: A Profile of Poverty Using the Socially Perceived Necessities Approach, Key Report 7*. Pretoria: Department of Social Development, Republic of South Africa.

Yalonetzky, G. (2009). 'Testing for Stochastic Dominance Among Additive, Multivariate Welfare Functions with Discrete Variables', *OPHI Research in Progress* 9a, University of Oxford.

Yalonetzky, G. (2011). 'A Note on the Standard Errors of the Members of the Alkire–Foster Family and its Components', *OPHI Research in Progress* 25a, University of Oxford.

Yalonetzky, G. (2012). 'Poverty Measurement with Ordinal Variables: A Generalization of a Recent Contribution', *ECINEQ Working Papers* 246, Society for the Study of Economic Inequality.

Yalonetzky, G. (2013). 'Stochastic Dominance with Ordinal Variables: Conditions and a Test', *Econometric Reviews*, 32(1): 126–63.

Yalonetzky, G. (2014). 'Conditions for the Most Robust Multidimensional Poverty Comparisons Using Counting Measures and Ordinal Variables', *Social Choice and Welfare*, 43(4): 773–807.

Yu, J. (2013). 'Multidimensional Poverty in China: Findings Based on the CHNS', *Social Indicators Research*, 112(2): 315–36.

Zadeh, L. A. (1965). 'Fuzzy Sets', *Information and Control*, 8(3): 338–53.

Zaidi, A. and Burchardt, T. (2005). 'Comparing Incomes When Needs Differ: Equivalization for the Extra Costs of Disability in the UK', *Review of Income and Wealth*, 51(1): 89–114.

Zavaleta, D., Samuel, K., and Mills, C. (2014). 'Social Isolation: A Conceptual and Measurement Proposal', *OPHI Working Paper* 67, University of Oxford.

Zheng, B. (1997). 'Aggregate Poverty Measures', *Journal of Economic Surveys*, 11(2): 123–62.

Zheng, B. (2007). 'Unit-Consistent Poverty Indices', *Economic Theory*, 31: 113–42.

Zumbo, B. D. (ed.) (1998). 'Validity Theory and the Methods Used in Validation: Perspectives from the Social and Behavioral Sciences', *Social Indicators Research*, 45(1): 1–509.

■ INDEX